Renaissance Genres

# Renaissance Genres

Essays on Theory, History,
and Interpretation

Edited by
Barbara Kiefer Lewalski

Harvard University Press
Cambridge, Massachusetts
and London, England
1986

This book is printed on acid-free paper, and its binding materials have been chosen for strength and durability.

*Library of Congress Cataloging-in-Publication Data*
Main entry under title:

Renaissance genres.

(Harvard English studies ; 14)
    1. English literature—Early modern, 1500–1700—
History and criticism—Addresses, essays, lectures.
2. Literary form—Addresses, essays, lectures.
3. Renaissance—England—Addresses, essays, lectures.
I. Lewalski, Barbara Kiefer.   II. Series.
PR418.L57R46 1986     820'.9'003     86–257
ISBN 0-674-76040-9 (alk. paper)
ISBN 0-674-76041-7 (pbk. : alk. paper)

# Contents

Renaissance Genres

BARBARA K. LEWALSKI

# Introduction:
# Issues and Approaches

Since issues of genre were so manifestly important to Renaissance critics and Renaissance authors, genre studies have always
been a staple of Renaissance literary scholarship. But however
historically grounded, such studies are inevitably affected by
contemporary literary theory and its assumptions about genre.
Not surprisingly, genre-based studies of old and new kinds are
now flourishing, as Crocean antagonism to the idea of genre
has given way to a very general recognition of its importance.
Also, more sophisticated conceptions of genre have made the
highly complex and flexible Renaissance uses of literary forms
more visible to us.

If we no longer assume, with Croce, that considerations of
genre violate the essential nature of the work of art as an in-
tuitive, unique, individual entity, neither are we now locked
into neoclassical or neoaristotelian conceptions of genres as fixed
and prescriptive categories by which literary works may be clas-

sified and evaluated.[1] To be sure, poststructuralist emphasis on
écriture as a single entity may dispense with genre considerations as readily as Croce did, though from the other side. And
the impulse to classification (though not to prescriptive evaluation) persists in the elaborate, all-inclusive, synchronic genre
systems devised by some structuralists, most impressively by
Northrop Frye and Paul Hernadi.[2]

The fact is, however, that the present proliferation and diversity of genre studies are nourished by many strands of contemporary theory. Most important perhaps is the structuralist
conception of genres as codes, as instruments of communication
rather than classification (whether or not they are originally
founded upon speech acts, as Tsvetan Todorov supposes).[3] Also
important are theories of reception: Hans Robert Jauss recognizes genre as a major frame of reference establishing the
"horizon of expectations" of a work's readers (and its author)
at the historical moment of its appearance and, in altered form,
conditioning later readers at subsequent historical moments.[4]
Recognition that generic codes change over time has engaged
modern genre critics with issues of history, politics, gender, and
audience expectation as well as with complex literary historical
issues of mixed genre and generic transformations.

Certain studies, evidencing a profound and intimate knowledge of Renaissance literature and criticism, have proved especially helpful to students of Renaissance genres. In *Literature
as System* Claudio Guillén treats genre from the standpoint of
the writer, as a problem-solving model for construction, an invitation to match experience to form in a specific yet dynamic
and undetermined way. Combining synchronic and diachronic

1. Benedetto Croce, *Aesthetic as Science of Expression and General Linguistic,* trans. Douglas Ainslie, 2nd ed. (London, 1922). For the neoaristote-
lians, see essays in *Critics and Criticism: Ancient and Modern,* ed. Ronald S.
Crane (Chicago, 1957).

2. Northrop Frye, *Anatomy of Criticism: Four Essays* (Princeton, 1957); Paul
Hernadi, *Beyond Genre: New Directions in Literary Classification* (Ithaca and
London, 1972).

3. See Tzvetan Todorov, "The Origin of Genres," *New Literary History,* 8
(1976–77), 159–170.

4. Hans Robert Jauss, "Literary History as a Challenge to Literary Theory,"
trans. Elizabeth Bensinger, *New Literary History,* 2 (1970–71), 7–37.

approaches, system and history, he explores generic evolution
and dialectical interaction—genres giving rise to countergenres.
He also highlights the important concept of mixed genre, insisting that any major work incorporates several kinds and must
be viewed from several generic coordinates.[5] In *The Resources
of Kind* Rosalie Colie approaches Renaissance genres as a set
of value-laden "frames or fixes" upon the world; that is, a literary genre often stands for a kind of subject matter, literary
and intellectual, and some generic allusions may function as
metaphors for the whole kind. She also emphasizes the generic
inclusionism and experimentation in Renaissance theory and
practice—the recognition of mixed and encyclopedic kinds, and
the elevation of new or subliterary forms into the canon.[6] And
in *The Light in Troy* Thomas Greene invites attention to genre
as a primary element of a work's *mundus significans*—the rhetorical and symbolic vocabulary shared by Renaissance writer
and reader.[7]

The recently translated work of Mikhail Bakhtin has reinforced these flexible, inclusivist, and symbolic approaches to
Renaissance literary kinds. Offering the important suggestion
that many genres in the Renaissance were undergoing "novelization"—penetration by certain features of the emerging Renaissance novel—Bakhtin looks especially to the works of Rabelais
and Cervantes to identify those features: multiple genres, including extraliterary kinds, that create multiple perspectives upon
the subject; the dialogic interaction of forms within the work;
the "polyglossia" of several generic languages within the work;
strong connectives linking the work to contemporary reality;
and the valorization of process.[8]

5. Claudio Guillén, *Literature as System: Essays toward the Theory of Literary
History* (Princeton, 1971).

6. Rosalie L. Colie, *The Resources of Kind: Genre-Theory in the Renaissance,*
ed. Barbara K. Lewalski (Berkeley, 1973).

7. Thomas M. Greene, *The Light in Troy: Imitation and Discovery in Renaissance Poetry* (New Haven and London, 1982), esp. pp. 20–27, 32–43.

8. M. M. Bakhtin, *The Dialogic Imagination: Four Essays,* ed. Michael
Holquist, trans. Caryl Emerson and Michael Holquist (Austin and London,
1981); *Problems of Dostoevsky's Poetics* (1929, 1963; Ann Arbor, 1973); *Rabelais and His World* (1965; Cambridge and London, 1968).

Alastair Fowler's *Kinds of Literature* synthesizes many such insights, proposing a comprehensive scheme that draws heavily upon Renaissance examples and is especially useful for that period.[9] Fowler makes clear and practical distinctions between different orders of literary kinds: radicals or strategies of presentation (narrative, dramatic, lyric); historical kinds, or genres (tragedy, comedy, sonnet, epigram, epic, eclogue, and the like); subgenres (specified by subject matter and motifs, such as the piscatory eclogue); modes (expressive kinds identified chiefly by subject matter, attitude, tonality, and *topoi,* such as satiric, heroic, elegiac); and constructional types (catalogue, anatomy). Focusing on the historical genres as codes or instruments of communication, he argues that they are best studied not as fixed forms but at some particular stage in their continuously changing development, since every work of literary significance necessarily alters generic possibilities. Particularly useful is Fowler's metaphor of "family resemblance" as the basis for identifying works in a given historical genre: such works share several but not always the same mix of characteristics or features drawn from a specific generic repertoire (formal structure, meter, size, scale, subject matter, values, mood, occasion, attitude, style, *topoi,* and more).

As the essays in this volume will indicate, critics agree readily on the necessity of distinguishing the various orders of literary kinds but do not agree on names and definitions. Terms and classifications such as genre, mode, and radical of presentation are nowhere to be found in Renaissance critical texts, though "the meaning not the name" seems to be implicit in many of them. That being so, it is worth recalling the schemes and the language we do find there. When it appears at all, the narrative-dramatic-lyric triad, regarded by some modern theorists as foundation genres, was most often understood in relation to Plato's and Aristotle's three kinds of imitation or representation: dramatic, in which the characters alone speak (tragedy and comedy); "narrative," in which the poet alone speaks (Plato instances the dithyramb); and mixed, combining the former two (Homer's

9. Alastair Fowler, *Kinds of Literature: An Introduction to the Theory of Genres and Modes* (Cambridge, Mass., 1982).

epics). But a few Renaissance theorists transformed the classical triad into something closer to the modern one: Minturno proposed epic, dramatic, and melic or lyric as the three general "parts" of poetry, and Milton invoked the same broad categories in his *Reason of Church Government*.[10]

More prominent is the very influential system of generic classes deriving from the Alexandrian *Canons,* Horace, Cicero, and Quintilian. In that system a few major classes of poetry and prose are identified by canonical lists of writers, on grounds of poetic meter (where relevant), structure, and purpose. Quintilian's classes are: epic (including didactic, historical, and pastoral poems written in hexameters), elegy, lyric, iambic, satire, tragedy, Old Comedy, New Comedy, history, philosophy, and oratory.[11] The most important Renaissance genre theorist, Julius-Caesar Scaliger, drew heavily upon this tradition, grouping within a few major classes literally hundreds of historical genres and subgenres, both poetic and rhetorical.[12] This system reinforces two basic elements of the Renaissance poetics of genre: the primary importance of model texts and authors in establishing the conception of the kinds, and the ready paralleling of prose and poetic kinds.

The Renaissance term for what Guillén and Fowler call historical genres is "kind," used to refer to the many literary forms identified in classical and Renaissance theory and poetic practice by specific formal and thematic elements, *topoi,* and conventions. Such kinds, or historical genres, include epic, tragedy, sonnet, ballad, funeral elegy, hymn, epigram, masque, eclogue, encomium, verse satire, deliberative oration, dialogue, debate, and more. Modes seem to have evolved from certain historical genres (heroic from epic, pastoral from idyl and eclogue) and may interpenetrate works or parts of works in several genres.

10. Antonio Sebastiano Minturno, *L'arte poetica* (Venice, 1563 [1564]), p. 3; Milton, *The Reason of Church-government Urg'd against Prelaty* (preface to bk. 2), *Complete Prose Works of John Milton,* ed. Don M. Wolfe et al., 8 vols. (New Haven, 1953–1982), I, 813–816.

11. For discussion of this system see James J. Donohue, *The Theory of Literary Kinds: Ancient Classifications of Literature* (Dubuque, 1943); *The Theory of Literary Kinds: The Ancient Classes of Poetry* (Dubuque, 1949).

12. Julius-Caesar Scaliger, *Poetices libri septem* (Geneva, 1561).

In the Renaissance, as in later literature, we find *pastoral* comedies and elegies and songs; *heroic* tragedies and romances and sonnets; *satiric* comedies and verse epistles and epigrams. Although he does not use the term "mode," Sidney anticipates the concept in his treatment of eight major "parts, kindes or species" of poetry: *"Heroick, Lyrick, Tragick, Comick, Satyrick, Iambick, Elegiack, Pastorall,* and certaine others."[13] While these classes derive from the Alexandrian tradition, Sidney does not describe them by meter or form but by modal qualities of tone, attitude, and effect: the lamenting *"Elegiack";* the "bitter but wholesome *Iambick"*; "the *Satirick,* who . . . sportingly . . . make[s] a man laugh at follie"; the *"Lyricke . . .* who with his tuned *Lyre* and well accorded voice, giveth praise."[14]

Something of the complexity of genre concepts in the Renaissance may be illustrated by the case of epic. Contemporary critics usually positioned epic at the apex of the genre system, as the noblest of the kinds, though a few Italian Aristotelians accorded that honor to tragedy, and a few others (on Christian or neoplatonic principles) accorded it to the hymn. In Renaissance critical statements "epic" refers in the first instance to the historical genre for which the poems of Homer and Virgil were normative; Tasso's *Gerusalemme liberata* was commonly recognized as the most influential contemporary epic, having a Virgilian subject and an Aristotelian epic structure. The modal term "heroic poetry" was also regularly used as a synonym for epic. But many works proclaimed as epic were not, or not very, heroic and departed widely in conception and structure from the paradigmatic poems of Homer, Virgil, and Tasso. Controversy raged throughout the Renaissance over the epic claims of romantic epics such as Ariosto's *Orlando furioso;* allegorical romantic epics such as Spenser's *Faerie Queene;* philosophical poems such as Lucretius' *De rerum natura;* historical poems such as Lucan's *De bello civili (Pharsalia);* allegorical dream-visions such as Dante's *Divine Comedy;* hexaemeral poems such as Du Bartas' *Divine Weekes and Workes;* and biblical poems on Old and New Testament topics such as Vida's *Christiad.*

13. Sir Philip Sidney, *The Defense of Poesie* (London, 1595), sig. C2v.
14. Ibid., sigs. E3v–F.

Sidney even included the prose romance, describing Xenophon's *Cyropaedia* as "an absolute heroicall Poeme"[15]—a designation he would probably extend to his own *Arcadia,* at least in its revised form. Moreover, works taken to be epics were often viewed as heterocosms or encyclopedias of subjects, literary genres, and styles, in accordance with the pervasive idea that Homer's epics were the source and origin of all the arts, sciences, and literary kinds.[16] On this basis epics might be seen to incorporate a wide variety of lyric, rhetorical, narrative, and dramatic kinds, and genre-conscious poets such as Milton or Spenser could deliberately conceive their epics on inclusivist principles.[17]

That similar complexities characterize other Renaissance genres is indicated by the essays in this volume, which register a continuing emphasis on the mixture of genres and the transformations of kinds. Three of the essays address themselves directly to genre theory, but all are concerned more or less explicitly with theoretical issues. Appropriately enough, perhaps, I have arranged them not by subject matter but by kind, so as to emphasize the diversity of approaches genre study in the Renaissance now sustains. Appropriately also, my classification by kind is only approximate and the examples are more often mixed than pure, indicating how issues pertaining to literary history, political and social history, feminism, audience reception, and literary interpretation impinge not singly but together on issues of genre. But for all their theoretical interest, most of the essays exemplify their approaches in relation to specific problems and works, yielding rich insights for Renaissance literature.

The essays on genre theory take quite different positions on

15. Ibid., sigs. 2v–3.

16. For example, George Chapman, "The Preface to the Reader," *Homer's Iliad,* in *Chapman's Homer,* ed. Allardyce Nicoll, 2 vols. (Princeton, 1967), I, 14; "To the Understander," *Achilles Shield* (1598), in *Chapman's Homer,* ed. Nicoll, 1, 549. Also, Torquato Tasso, *Discorso del poema eroico* (Naples, 1594); *Discourses on the Heroic Poem,* trans. Mariella Cavalchini and Irene Samuel (Oxford, 1973), pp. 76–78. See Colie, *Resources of Kind,* pp. 22–23.

17. For Milton, see Barbara K. Lewalski, *Paradise Lost and the Rhetoric of Literary Forms* (Princeton, 1985).

the status of the familiar triad, narrative-dramatic-lyric. Approaching Western genre theory from the special perspective of non-Western systems that privilege lyric (and prose history) rather than mimetic forms, Earl Miner takes these three to be the essential, foundation genres of all literature (though he does not insist on terming them genres). Miner proposes homology in function as the fundamental criterion for classifying literary works by kind and comparing them. Also, finding problems with Fowler's pragmatic conception of genre as family resemblance, he offers a complex but very useful synchronic scheme distinguishing several "kinds of kinds" that belong logically to different orders.[18]

Ann Imbrie's essay is offered as a prolegomenon to the study of Renaissance nonfiction prose genres (defense, sermon, dialogue, debate, essay, anatomy, and more)—an effort to establish their place in a genre system devised on Renaissance principles. Adopting Northrop Frye's notion of narrative-dramatic-lyric as "radicals of presentation" rather than foundation genres, she takes issue with Miner and Fowler in arguing that nonfiction prose constitutes a fourth such radical. She proposes to define specific genres (including the prose genres) as a coordination of specific subject matter, formal structure, and especially generic attitude or values (what Colie terms "frames or fixes" upon the world).

Claudio Guillén takes up several important issues of theory and method from a Western comparatist perspective, as he examines the Renaissance epistolary literature and theory in Latin and in several vernacular languages. Revising Frye, he proposes that narrative, dramatic, and lyric are only three of several historically determined channels of communication in particular societies—with epistolary writing prominent among them in Renaissance society, serving as the hinge between orality and

18. Miner's important trilogy on seventeenth-century literary history is based on what he terms "mode"—the relationship between self and world established in a literary work—a category he finds especially useful in tracing and accounting for the dominance of different genres over the course of the century. See *The Metaphysical Mode from Donne to Cowley, The Cavalier Mode from Jonson to Cotton, The Restoration Mode from Milton to Dryden* (Princeton, 1969, 1971, 1974).

writing. Guillén's detailed history of several epistolary genres—including verse letters, humanist imitations of classical epistles, vernacular familiar letters, and fictional letters (providing a bridge to the novel)—emphasizes their interaction, their relation to other kinds as countergenres, and the frequent *contaminatio* or mixture of kinds within them.

Another set of papers approaches genre in terms of literary history, engaging questions of the genesis, definition, development, and transformation of particular Renaissance genres, with primary reference to literary factors. Fowler's essay offers both a theoretical defense and an impressive demonstration of this approach, as he responds to sociological explanations for the supposed lateness of English georgic by making a crucial generic distinction between Augustan formal imitations of Virgil's *Georgics* and Renaissance georgic loosely modeled on Hesiod, Virgil, and Tusser. He then demonstrates the georgic essence of many Renaissance topographical and country-house poems, and the prominence of georgic topics and tonalities in several pastorals, romances, and odes.

In similar vein, Harry Levin's essay traces in brilliant detail the long association of comedies with cities (by supposed etymology, stage conventions and settings, bourgeois characters and attitudes). The implicit suggestion is that "city comedy" as a distinct Renaissance subgenre may be a tautology, but the essay precisely locates its various forms within the permutations traced by the central New Comedy tradition from ancient Greece to the prose fiction of Balzac and Dickens. Morton Bloomfield undertakes to make precise the important distinction between the funeral elegy as genre and the elegiac as mode, pressing that distinction to illuminate works of both kinds, from medieval to modern literature. Mary Crane refines the definition and traces the development of the sixteenth-century epigram in terms of its several subgenres and its two principal strains: one from Martial, of witty trifles; the other didactic, looking back to the medieval *Distichs of Cato*, which strongly influenced the epigrams of the humanists, the reformers, and Ben Jonson.

Other papers, yielding important theoretical and interpretative insights, explore the intersection of literary genre with sociological and political forces. Barbara Bono's stimulating essay

brings together feminist and genre theory to probe the question
of whether Shakespeare's *As You Like It* reinforces or in some
ways subverts the patriarchy of the era. Bono argues that both
Rosalind and Orlando resolve their crises of gender-identity
formation in ways consonant with Nancy Chodorow's model,[19]
though in terms of the conventional Renaissance generic vocabulary. Rosalind develops a "double-voiced" feminine discourse within a fictive romance mode, criticizing and challenging,
even as she finally accommodates herself to, Orlando's masculine heroic discourse and the patriarchal society to which it
pertains. Janel Mueller, arguing the limitations of genre inventorying to deal with issues of genesis and transformation in
genre, examines a mesh of formal, personal, and political factors
bearing upon Milton's politicizing of the sonnet in a group of
poems from 1642 to 1656. Her illustrative analysis of "Captain
or Colonel" yields fascinating parallels between the form of
Milton's political sonnets and the local rhetoric of passages in
his prose tracts, supporting the thesis that the two kinds are
analogues in their treatment of political power, with each sonnet
probing some specific personal crisis in political experience.

Impressive essays by Annabel Patterson and Steven Zwicker
explore how certain genres and their literary conventions function as sociopolitical codes. Focusing on the Stuart and Crom-
wellian periods, Patterson challenges interpretations of pastoral
and georgic as embodying Marxist class struggle or the Stuart
Court's neoplatonic illusions, by following a trail of quotations
from Virgil's *Eclogues* (especially Eclogue 1). Arguing that these
quotations carry with them the ambiguities and tensions inherent in Virgil's own juxtaposition of pastoral Arcadian motifs
with political criticism and with georgic, she shows how they
fostered a highly complex vision of political reality in seventeenth-century texts ranging from Sir John Davies' eclogues (1612)
to Milton's 1645 poems and Marvell's *Appleton House*. Steven
Zwicker explores the consequences for genre of the ubiquitous
Restoration concern to further civil stability through strategies
of deception in language and literature. Focusing especially on

19. Nancy Chodorow, *The Reproduction of Mothering: Psychoanalysis and
the Sociology of Gender* (Berkeley and Los Angeles, 1978).

Dryden's deliberate generic elusiveness in *Annus Mirabilis* and *Absalom and Achitophel* and on his use of genres that provide masks ("Advice to a Painter" fables, translations), Zwicker provides penetrating interpretative insights into the period as a whole.

Drama of course invites special attention to audience response, and that approach yields fascinating results in the essays of Marjorie Garber and Robert Watson. Garber's fine paper on Shakespeare's history plays probes the ways in which an audience's privileged knowledge of history, of the dramatic convention that prophecies are fulfilled, and of chronologically later plays in Shakespeare's two tetralogies affects its responses to the prophecies (both true and ironic) in the English (and Roman) history plays. Suggesting that a starting point for defining the genre of the history play may be its special way of assimilating the audience into history, she explores striking instances of audience discomfiture as prior knowledge leaves it powerless either to affect outcomes or to escape involvement in the dramatic and moral choices enacted before it. Watson's persuasive essay reads Ben Jonson's comedies as a direct challenge to the audience to approve his kind of realistic city comedy over other competing comic kinds, using *The Alchemist* as test case. Noting that Lovewit's house in Blackfriars is like a theater, and that Lovewit himself serves as surrogate for the audience, Watson shows how the several gull characters play out roles that properly belong in other kinds of contemporary plays, while Face (as Jonsonian playwright) exposes them all to ridicule.

The several essays in interpretation focus especially on the complex interplay or mixture of generic traditions and conventions in authors who especially invite such attention—Spenser, Shakespeare, Donne, Milton. John King reads Spenser's *Shepheardes Calender* as an inclusionist work in which imported continental elements are balanced by the native Protestant and biblical elements that dominate the five moral eclogues, making of them a new and complex kind of Protestant pastoral satire. Heather Dubrow studies Shakespeare's *Lucrece* as a "problem complaint," arguing that its attention to psychology, rhetoric, and moral complexity constitutes a deliberate critique of the platitudes common to the specific kind—a subgenre comprising (in addition to *Lucrece*) six other complaints by a heroine threatened by a ruler, all of them published in the years 1592–1594.[20]

Genre studies of Donne have not been numerous, but the two essays included here testify to the fruitfulness of the approach. John Klause finds in Donne's *Metempsychosis* the elements of many genres—epic, satire, theological commentary, metahistory, allegory—all of them deliberately undercut as the work establishes formal as well as thematic association with Montaigne's *Essais*. It does so by adopting a deliberate stance of skeptical uncertainty, extemporaneousness, and indecisiveness, while presenting the play of mind from moment to moment. James Baumlin's chief text is Donne's "Satyre 1," read as an imitation of Horace that is at the same time a critique of the Horatian persona. Baumlin's larger argument proposes that the Elizabethan satirists of the 1590s (Hall, Marston, and especially Donne) made dialectical, evaluative, and often revisionary use of the quite distinct satiric personae and methods associated with the classical satiric models Juvenal, Persius, and Horace.

*Paradise Lost* has long been studied in relation to various epic traditions, and more recently as a polygeneric work incorporating many kinds. In this vein Francis Blessington's essay focuses on the several hymns in *Paradise Lost*—ideal, mixed, and parodic. His scholarly account of the theory and history of classical and especially epic hymns culminates in the argument that Milton's epic hymns subsume and transcend that tradition, functioning as an ideal and antithetical generic alternative to epic narrative to evoke the timeless world of bliss. It is entirely appropriate that this volume end with a paper on Milton, the most genre-conscious of English poets and the poet who most fully exploited and most radically transformed the entire spectrum of Renaissance literary kinds.

20. Dubrow provides a useful historical survey of genre-theory in the Critical Idiom Series (*Genre* [London and New York, 1982]).

# I  Theory of Genre

EARL MINER

# Some Issues of Literary "Species, or Distinct Kind"

*What he* [Dryden] *has done in any one species, or
distinct kind, would have been sufficient to have
acquired him a great name.*

—Congreve, Preface, Dryden's *Dramatick Works*

There may be those who take comfort in the fact that multi-
various Dryden at least did not write novels, lest the issues of
genre become issues of Dryden. If there are those, they will not
be pleased to learn that Dryden did translate "novels." In a
letter to Pepys dated 14 July 1699, he informs his friend that
he is translating "Novills from Boccace," and in his preface to
*Fables* he uses the same term in ways showing that he thought
of the novel primarily as a romance in verse.[1] One obvious
problem is that words such as "genre" or "novel" are used in
differing ways. Another problem involves using the historical
evidence without bafflement. And yet a third, now no longer
obvious, entails freeing ourselves from a purely Western European mindset. But the most troublesome matter of all is that
we enmesh ourselves so thoroughly in debates over "tearms of

1. *The Poems of John Dryden,* ed. James Kinsley, 4 vols. (Oxford, 1958),
IV, 1446, 1456, 1459.

Art" that we find it most difficult to see beyond them to
"th'Argument."

> So when men argue, the great'st part
> O'th'Contest falls on tearms of Art,
> Until the fustian stuff be spent,
> And then they fall to th'Argument.[2]

Before defining terms or doing anything grander in "th'Contest,"
I would like to present a few parables.

### 1

Lima, Peru, May 11. Controversy increases over the remarkable Stone Age paintings revealed by the earthquake last April
29 in the Los Cruces mountains east of here.

Some have speculated that the pictures are religious. Others
find evidence of political purpose. A few anthropologists have
declared the pictures to be general portrayals of the lives of the
vanished people.

Only one young anthropologist, José-Maria Padilla, has maintained that the paintings are purely artistic.

### 2

She recalled that, during her childhood in the Yorkshire Dales,
there was a shepherd who admitted there were such things as
hounds and terriers. But he insisted that when you talked about
*dogs,* there was only one kind, a sheepdog. And he would point
to his Gyp. "Aye, Gyp?" he would ask, and the dog's tail would
wag rapidly.

### 3

[From a Chinese textbook] Animate reproduction. There are
three kinds: the divisive of the "parent" unit; the oviparous;
and the viviparous.

---

2. *Samuel Butler, Hudibras,* ed. John Wilders (Oxford, 1967), pt. 1, canto
3, pp. 1363–66. In the present context, is there more hope or less despair in
his famous saying, "For all a Rhetoricians Rules / Teach nothing but to name
his tools" (1.1.89–90)?

4

Borges never published his brief story, "The Tire," which parodies human efforts to categorize. A man needing a tire for his automobile goes from store to store. One does not have rubber things. The next does not sell single objects. Another does not deal with round things. Next door they will touch nothing with a hole in it. Another will have nothing to do with black things. Another has no automotive section. When at last he discovers a store with great stacks of tires, he is told that they are of no use until the company completes invention of the wheel.

Our situation today must seem to many rather like some bizarre counterpart of the Borges parable. Western classical classifications by prosody exist along with prose, verse, and alliterative verse romances in the Middle Ages. In the Renaissance an elegy might be a poem on someone's death or a love poem like those of Ovid, Tibullus, Catullus, and Propertius. For that matter, Donne's *Songs and Sonnets* has neither a Petrarchan nor an English sonnet in it, and nobody seems able to describe the genre of Dryden's *Absalom and Achitophel*. What is meant by the Romantic genre, if it is one, of "lyrical ballads"? And how do we distinguish some of those from Victorian "dramatic monologues"? Fielding defined the novel as an epic in prose mingling the serious and the comic, but liked to entitle his novels "histories." What is the difference between a "Victorian novel," the "classical realistic novel," and a *Bildungsroman* when *David Copperfield* is the example? Is the feminist novel a genre? Problems like these have led not a few people to consider the issues of genre to be a mare's nest, a Pandora's box, or a species of critical phlogiston.

The third parable is offered as something of a proleptic parody of some of my own ideas. An even clearer example of the "Omnia Gallia divisa est" mentality will be found in Thomas Hobbes's "Answer" to Davenant's preface to *Gondibert:*

As Philosophers [scientists] have divided the Universe, their subject, into three Regions, *Celestiall, Aëriall,* and *Terrestiall,* so the Poets . . .

have lodg'd themselves in the three Regions of mankinde, *Court, City,*
and *Country,* correspondent in some proportion to those three Regions of the World . . .

   From hence have proceeded three sorts of Poesy, *Heroique, Scommatique,* and *Pastorall.* Every one of these is distinguished again in
the manner of *Representation,* which sometimes is *Narrative,* wherein
the Poet himself relateth, and sometimes *Dramatique* . . . There is
therefor neither more nor less than six sorts of Poesy. For the Heroique
Poem narrative . . . is called an *Epique Poem.* The Heroique Poem
Dramatique is *Tragedy.* The Scommatique Narrative is *Satyre,* Dramatique is *Comedy.* The Pastorall narrative is called simply *Pastorall,*
anciently *Bucolique;* the same Dramatique, *Pastorall Comedy.*[3]

Hobbes goes on to dismiss lyric and other shorter kinds as "but
Essayes and parts of an entire Poem" (2.55–56). Perhaps Hobbes
did take up mathematics too late, as Dryden said. In any event,
this three-times-two approach to genre will surely seem less like
our own thoughts than does the pseudo-Borgesian parable.

   Let us therefore consider the first parable. (The order of the
four is a heuristic historical one.) Those Andean pictures represent a time when, as it were, the various departments of a
modern university did not exist. Thought and its expression are
undifferentiated in kind. Art—including literature—exists undifferentiated from religion, politics, history, and other "departments." That proposition is by no means the thesis of Claude
Lévi-Strauss in his *Pensée sauvage.* He is concerned to show
that "savage" counterparts of modern, sophisticated thought
exist in the primitive mind. But an attending reader will see that
those counterparts are undifferentiated.[4] What is only implicit
in *La Pensée sauvage* is made explicit and shown with evidence
in the first volume of Konishi Jin'ichi's *History of Japanese
Literature.*[5] In short, the historical study of genre must take into
account not only Hobbesian multiplication and modern expo-

   3. Hobbes, "Answer," in *Critical Essays of the Seventeenth Century,* ed.
J. E. Spingarn, 3 vols. (Bloomington, Ind., 1957), II, 54–55.
   4. Claude Lévi-Strauss, *The Savage Mind* (Chicago, 1966).
   5. Konishi Jin'ichi, *A History of Japanese Literature* (Princeton, 1984), I,
508 and esp. 81–110, which also offers evidence from study of modern primi-
tives. (Japanese names are given with surnames first and in Japanese order for
appellations not names.)

nential proliferation of terms but also a period of human history in which the concept did not exist.

More correctly, there is an early time in every developed culture when there was no distinct sense of literature, a stage from which some primitive cultures still have not evolved. This is to say that the first requisite for a concept of literary kinds is that there be a conception of literature as a way of thought differing from other ways. This is sufficiently obvious, but it has gone unremarked, as far as I am aware, and like much else that is obvious it is the better for being haled into view. That is, a conception of literature as a distinct cognitive entity is a conception prior to our subject of literary kinds, and conversely a conception of literary kinds requires as a kind of syllogistic major premise that there be a species, literature, of which the kinds are genera. It is not suggested here that we can arrange all the kinds into species, subspecies, genera, and subgenera. That way Hobbism lies. But the logic is inescapable.

The second parable, of the shepherd and his dog, allegorizes that period in the development of a culture when literature is an integral cognitive entity and when more than one kind is recognized, but when normative considerations are also introduced. For the Yorkshire shepherd, we may read Aristotle. He was aware that lyric poetry existed, as well as the narratives of Homer and Hesiod. But in defining the properties of literature, drama was his sheepdog, with lyric and narrative being mere hounds and terriers. More than that, we observe that Aristotle's moment in the Academy involved the distinction of numerous kinds of thought, as if he were the inventor of a modern university. It almost seems as if a poetics was necessary to him in his treatment of the various kinds of knowledge. Literature was one of the practical kinds of knowledge, a *technē,* along with other arts, rhetoric, politics, and ethics. In addition there were for him the more theoretical kinds of knowledge, preeminently logic. Of course he did not rest with these individual kinds named but considered astronomy, zoology, and other kinds of knowledge. The instinctive epistemological urgency in his grand intellectual effort bears some resemblance to Hobbesian arithmetic, but anyone is likely to find it a serious rather than parodic version. His effort has great importance to a consideration of

literary kinds, both as significant versions of the second and
third parables and as a counsel of hope to those of us who are
inclined to Borgesian pessimism.

If Memory is the mother of the Muses and confusion the
necessary precursor of order, both she and confusion have ample
material in the evidence provided under the heads of various
national literatures as represented by *The Princeton Encyclopedia of Poetry and Poetics*.[6] An examination of the entry "Persian Poetry" is instructive. There is mention of "epic" and "idyll"
(or shorter epic?) along with lyric. Nothing is said of drama.
Reading more closely, we discover that the defining distinctions
appear to be those of (quantitative) prosody and of stanza forms
like the rhymed couplet *(mathnavī)* and rhymed quatrain *(rubāʿi)*.
Persian definitions seem almost like classical Western distinctions according to prosody—hexameter, iambic, elegiac distich,
and lyric or melic prosodies. (The nature of the prosody of
biblical Hebrew poetry is still uncertain.) In the absence of
drama, the question therefore turns on what the equivalent
of Aristotle's dramatic sheepdog might be. That is an issue to
return to.

China offers us the oldest continuous and distinguished literature. The word usually translated as "literature," *wen,* includes kinds of lyric with certain kinds of historical writing in
prose. (With some differences, the same holds for early stages
of Japanese and Korean literature.) In its long history Chinese
literature also came to include, by modern reckoning, prose
fictional narrative and drama—the so-called Peking opera, although there are several versions, and although the "Peking"
opera originally came from another area. Yet until some date
on which total agreement does not exist, neither prose narrative
nor dramatic literature was accounted anything other than hounds
and terriers. The twin sheepdogs were lyric and a range of
historical prose narrative. The problem for the Western assumptions is sorting those two together, since history has come
to seem distinct from literature—so far so that we may come

---

6. *Encyclopedia,* ed. Alex Preminger et al. enl. ed. (Princeton, 1974). Prose
kinds and practice are omitted by definition.

to think of certain sometime histories as literature, although examples of the reverse are very difficult to discover.

It will be evident that cognitive classes are not the same the world round. Chinese literature includes some posers that trouble easy Western distinctions between prose and verse. One species is that found in ornate parallel prose in lines or units of four- and six-character syllables, with occasional odd units for variety. Above all, there is the *fu,* "rhymeprose" or "rhapsody." Even more ornate than ornate prose, this is a virtuoso kind of writing. If a given *fu* concerns trees or plants, the reader finds a bewildering number of characters with the left-hand element for "tree" or the upper element for "plant." In addition, the prose (if it is prose) is rhymed like Chinese verse (if the *fu* is verse), that is, by kinds of tone (level, deflected, entering) rather than by like sounds.

Japanese literature is unique in the early emergence of esteemed prose kinds, apart from the historical writing that had been valued from the outset with lyric. In addition to *monogatari* (usually translated as "tale," but meaning "relating of things" and also "person relating"), there are other kinds such as *nikki* (commonly translated as "diaries" or "memoirs") and *setsuwa* (shorter narratives, commonly religious in subject, for which no standard translation exists). In addition, in later periods the kinds of *monogatari* proliferated beyond those in existence from the tenth century. The later kinds are almost Borgesian in variety. Some take their names from the kinds of subjects treated or the atmosphere of the works so called (*ukiyozoshi, ninjobon,* and the like) and some from the color of their paper covers. For drama, *nō* was divided into two classes and five kinds. The pieces of the puppet theater, followed by the actors' theater, were at first distinguished into two groups, those on older times *(jidaimono)* and those on contemporary subjects *(sewamono).* But distinctions multiplied, giving such further and different distinctions as ghost or spectral pieces *(kaidanmono).*

These few examples will suffice to show that the most valiant attempts to regularize literary kinds along solely Western lines will lack true explanatory power. Of course, anything that will straighten out conceptually the Western parish is to be wel-

comed heartily. But inattention to non-Western practice is sure
to produce limited results. One problem that follows with urgency is this: should we dismiss the effort to distinguish kinds
of literature as a vain attempt or should we take a historical,
relativistic approach that will account for non-Western as well
as Western evidence? There is another possibility, which will
be attempted in what follows—with what success others must
judge—to offer distinctions that might go under various names.
The names that will be given are dispensable, since like Milton's
narrator in *Paradise Lost,* "The meaning, not the Name I call"
(7.5).

Literature is clearly not a scientific matter in the sense that
we can define it as the species and then classify its genera in
strictly logical fashion. After a certain point in the development
of a culture, however, it becomes evident that there is a need
to think not only of literature and not only of individual literary
examples but of intermediate cognitive abstractions, whether
tragedy, *rubā'i,* or *monogatari.* Literary history shows, and daily
experience confirms, that the cognitive act is necessary. The
need to think of kinds is apparent from consideration of the
alternatives. On the one hand, we would then have "the literature of the world" as a conceptual entity, and indeed it is
important that we bear that in mind. Yet it is most difficult to
appreciate or even make much sense of that true entity, and
the more comfortable conception, the *literatures* of the world,
already constitutes a cognitive step toward major distinction.
On the other hand, we also require a conception of an individual
work, for even the most ardent intertextualist or arguer for
general écriture must concede that "texts" cannot be related
nor writings become one unless they are individual in the first
instance. In fact, most of us go further and prize the individual
work as a radical more empirical and more valuable than the
largest radical, literature. The problem with this valuable radical
of the individual work is that conceptualizing it alone keeps us
from speaking about much else that interests us. As Donne put
it in "Aire and Angels" about a similar dilemma:

> Ev'ry thy haire for love to worke upon
> Is much too much, some fitter must be sought;

> For, nor in nothing, nor in things
> Extreme, and scatt'ring bright, can love inhere.
>                                         (ll. 19–22)

If we are considering "That time of year thou mayst in me behold," we shall wish to consider other poems of that kind, and we shall be able to make better sense of "That time of year" by awareness that it is a sonnet using certain conventions while manipulating them. An entity termed "Shakespeare's sonnets" will occur to us, along with groupings of them and connections by way of likeness to, or contrast with, sonnets by other writers. Again, we may find it useful to compare the sonnets with the songs in Shakespeare's plays. Or it may be more useful for some purpose to distinguish the sonnets from the narrative poems and the plays.

All this is obvious, but the implication of the obvious has not always been honored precisely because the obvious has not been faced. The implication is that thought about literature (and other subjects) requires conceptions enabling us to think about and discuss entities between the two prime radicals: literature and the individual work. We may regret the lack of a scientific taxonomy. We may find certain conceptions more useful to us than to others. We shall certainly discover that denizens of differing literary cultures find some conceptions more useful than do denizens of others. But we also discover that we cannot do without these so-to-speak midrange conceptions. Willy-nilly we are committed to think in terms of "species, or distinct kind."

What are the properties of a given conceptual kind? "The taxonomic problem seems intractable."[7] But since we *will* think

---

7. Alastair Fowler, *Kinds of Literature: An Introduction to the Theory of Genres and Modes* (Cambridge, Mass., 1982), p. 17. Anyone seriously interested in these problems will find this modestly titled "introduction" a greatly illuminating account, although restricted to Western evidence. Fowler's wide net seems not to have caught his most worthy predecessor, who still has much to teach, again about Western literature: I. Behrens, *Die Lehre von der Einteilung der Dichtkunst, Beihefte zur Zeitschrift für romanische Philologie,* 92 (1940). There are numerous other excellent studies. To restrict reference to a few of book length and in English, see Paul Hernadi, *Beyond Genre: New Directions in Literary Classification* (Ithaca, 1972); E. D. Hirsch, *Validity in Interpretation* (New Haven, 1967), chap. 3; and J. P. Strelka, *Theories of Literary Genre* (University Park, 1978). See also n. 13, below, on Northrop Frye.

and talk of kinds, it behooves us to know what we are up to.
Alastair Fowler has made excellent use of Ludwig Wittgenstein's
concept of family resemblance, following the example of some
predecessors. In his words, "Representatives of a genre may
then be regarded as making up a family whose sets and individual members are related in various ways, without necessarily
having any single feature shared in common by all."[8] Anyone
can see that the concept of family resemblance exchanges, for
purposes of definition, a sense of isomorphic for the aggre-
gate. Since all of us have our sheepdogs, and since everybody
but Number One seems to shop in Borgesian stores, none of
us is likely to be able to rest content with family resemblance
alone. The great virtue of the concept is its pragmatic nature.
A gestalt of likenesses is presumed, and some little difference
here or there does not matter. One can admit sonnets in sixteen
lines, in hexameter or trochees, and in an unusual rhyme pattern, providing there is enough in other respects to give us a
sense of a sonnet. Moreover, Fowler shows in his study that,
at least in his hands, the concept has considerable explanatory
power, both historically and synchronically.

The logical difficulty with the principle of family resemblance
is that it posits likeness for admissibility to a set and minimizes
difference to exclude from a set. In other words, how is one to
decide that family resemblance does *not* exist? Presumably we
must consider a largish number of families of kind. *Hamlet*
belongs to the family of tragedies. Does it belong to the family
of revenge tragedies? And if it is a revenge tragedy, on what
grounds do we dismiss from that family *Coriolanus* and *King
Lear*? Or *Julius Caesar*? Is it more important to belong to the
family of the Roman play or to the family of tragedy? That is,
which family has the greater explanatory power for defining
more of the characteristics of the play? In short, we need grounds
for postulating that a work's assignment to a given family is
more explanatory than its assignment to other families. Perhaps
we have not yet achieved the means of making these distinctions.
Perhaps we never shall. But family resemblance, useful as it is,
does not fill all our needs.

8. Fowler, *Kinds of Literature*, p. 41.

Of course the basic problem is that "family" is a metaphor. A distinction in kind by prosody (iambic—that is, satire), a distinction in kind by subject matter (a Roman play), and a distinction in kind by place and era (Southern Sung lyric) simply do not imply "family" in parallel senses. The many midrange conceptions we find useful posit likenesses. They also imply differences of Borgesian inconsistency. To dismiss these distinctions may seem the easiest and tidiest way out. But the need will soon be felt to posit them or replacements for them, and the problem is quickly reborn. Another approach is the permissive one of allowing for any term. The problem with that is that although the number of terms and the number of phenomena are considerable, the repertoire of choice terms is small and so usage is very inconsistent. Take the "genres" and "modes" of Fowler's subtitle. A lexicon, perhaps a dictionary, could be made of the various usages of these two terms, and they are common only to English and French.

It appears to me that we shall never agree that "genre" means thus-and-so. The meaning, not the name, is the important thing, although each of us finds it necessary to give a name to our meaning. We owe it to others to use care in defining terms; making clear does not always mean making right, but it enables others to judge whether the meaning is right or, more likely, whether it is useful to their ends. We may therefore turn to some issues of principle in these matters.

The first principle carries some hope: historically later conceptions may explain things that authors and readers had not until then explained. Homer and Hesiod were not aware that they were writing *narrative* poems. Our term comes from Roman rhetoricians, who coined it for that part of an oration in which what happened in the case discussed was related. But once having been conceptualized, a term like "narrative" comes to be useful and to seem just when used with some sensitivity. The second principle carries with it some warning: once a term is devised, it is used to explain more and other things than it was first designed for. "Tragedy" derives (it is uncertain why) from "goat song" (*tragos* or "male goat" and *ōidē* or "song"). Once it was coined as a literary term, the word began to set up house for a nonliterary family of its own. By our time, an issue of a daily newspaper can hardly do without at least one "tragic" and one "dramatic" account per issue, although neither usage deals with anything literary or performed on a stage. There is an even clearer example in "tragicomedy," the locus classicus of which is the prologue to Plautus' *Amphitruo*. In this story of Jupiter's disguising himself as Amphitryon in order to spend a night with Alcmena and sire Hercules, the presence of Jupiter and Mercury raised the level of awesomeness in the play beyond comedy. Yet the marvelous invention of Sosia, Amphitryon's servant, beaten out by a Mercury disguised as Sosia, keeps us within the comic sphere. Centuries later in England during the time of the Civil Wars, tragicomedy became identified with the royalist cause, both because the Stuart kings enjoyed drama and because it was hoped that the royalist cause would resemble that kind of tragicomedy in which a course of events tending toward disaster would end in restoration and happiness. In demonstrating this, Lois Potter has been able to show that there exists a work of the interregnum entitled "A True Tragicomedy." It is true simply in presentng the royalist argument. It is a political tract— not a play at all—and Plautus would never have been able to recognize in it any family resemblance whatsoever.[9]

We need not necessarily suspect, then, the application of later terms for earlier phenomena. But we must be on the watch for what happens to words in our use of them.

A third principle follows from the second. Our understanding will be improved by knowledge of the historical application of terms. To consider "tragedy" again, there are those who say that Christian tragedy is impossible because of a providentially disposed afterlife. Presumably Buddhist tragedy is impossible because of the two future possibilities of reincarnation or enlightenment. Such sticklers for purity do not much speak about the one Greek trilogy that survives whole, the *Oresteia,* with its triumphant last play, the *Eumenides.* Nor do the sticklers make much of some extraordinary plays by Euripides, or of Aristotle's remark that there are tragedies that end happily. The family resemblance among these kinds is, one would think,

9. Potter presented her findings in a panel on tragicomedy led by Nancy Maguire at the December 1983 meeting of the Modern Language Association.

strong or weak, depending on what we consider the fundamental principle. They are plays the Greeks thought to be tragedies and were performed as such at civic feasts. Yet the late Middle Ages produced a kind of tragedy usually termed *de casibus*, of which the first famous exemplars are in Boccaccio's *De casibus virorum illustrium*. As Chaucer's "Monk's Tale" shows, these tragedies might be in prose, and as his *Troilus and Criseyde* shows, they might be in verse. But the chief family resemblance shared by the Greek examples—theatrical performance—is missing.

The value of understanding historical usage is that knowledge of the usage enables one to sort out criteria that have been used previously. By sorting out the criteria, which are usually implicit, one may better understand the choices of elements that have been used to express a given meaning or set of meanings for a given term or set of terms: tragedy, comedy, and tragicomedy, for example.[10] The principle of the utility of knowledge of historical usage has a corollary in the utility of plentiful data, and those data can be extended many times over by looking beyond a single cultural tradition. Nobody can master all the data, but we could all know more than we do.

Yet data are not sufficient without evidence, that is, without means of using data probatively, convincingly. Let us consider the question of whether or not there is epic writing in China. What are the data? There are no very lengthy poems, and the Chinese cyclical treatment of empires violates the Western epic sense of the greatness that once was but is no longer. To that extent, the data are both less than kin—or family resemblance—and less than kind. But suppose we consider the evidentiary canon of function. If the function of epic includes explaining the human situation through great action in the past, if the function of an epic includes impressing us with the awesomeness that is not in our own lives, and if the function of an epic includes definition of what is important to a people, then some Chinese prose historical narrative is epic. This is not merely suppositious, as a reading of Ssu-ma Ch'ien's *Records of the Historian* would

10. Behrens is especially good on the historical meanings attached to such terms as drama and comedy. See n. 7.

show. A definition of epic that includes Virgil, Lucan, and Sir Richard Blackmore but leaves out Ssu-ma Ch'ien can have little to recommend it.

There is a reciprocal relation between the function of a literary kind and a validity determined by differing evidence. We may take it for granted that Homer, Virgil, and Milton establish an epic canon (along with writers in other languages as well as in theirs). Yet our taking for granted is solely a matter of custom. The proof that the epic category describes Homer's poems is that Homer's poems are epic: tautology. With no other evidence than that, we deal merely in arbitrary nomenclature. The continuance and development of an epic tradition in the West offers substantial corroboration of the validity of the epic kind. But to the extent that Chinese historiography confirms by function the same ends, we have evidence of a higher order: the (international) validity of the epic kind.

Chinese poetry has a variety of kinds that are usually termed "genres" by contemporary students writing in English. These include the *shih* (songs/poems) *lü-shih* (regulated poems), *yüeh-fu* (ballads), and so on. Because the *functions* of these kinds are very much the same—because there is only a general lyric counterpart in other literatures—the Chinese distinctions do not appear to have validity of a theoretical kind in comparative terms. Much the same holds for Western sonnets, sestinas, and epigrams.

The Japanese conception of *monogatari* is somewhat different. It applies to prose rather than verse. And as has been suggested, the term has a double meaning. To use the Japanese particles designating parts of speech, *monogatari* means both *mono [o] kataru,* or "to relate matters," and *mono [ga] kataru,* or "a person relates." In terms of function, this is obviously a counterpart to "narrative" and theoretically superior to that term in showing two quite different criteria. Yet comparative evidence also shows that the Japanese restriction of the application of *monogatari* to prose relation is without theoretical validity, and in that respect we must consider "narrative" the superior term.

The conception of function as a criterion in these matters depends on comparative evidence. Virtually no work has been done on canons of comparability, however. What are the grounds for making meaningful comparison?[11] In my view the basis is homology, which is a much more thoroughgoing degree of commonalty than analogy. The spine of a vertebrate and the case of a worm have some things in common but not enough. The spine of a vertebrate and the shell of a crustacean approach homology more nearly, and a human arm is definitely homologous with a bird's wing. Because literature does not approach zoology in taxonomic exactness, we are unable to reach a sufficient degree of homology merely by comparing like things. In my view literary comparison—and adequate homology—are fully possible only when we have a presumed identity among phenomena in different cultural traditions. To take examples apart from literary kinds, there is a presumed identity in the concepts of metaphor and allegory in various cultural traditions. Close examination would show, however, that in Chinese and Japanese literature there is no such radical distinction between "tenor" and "vehicle" or "signifier" and "signified" in the conception and working of metaphor as we find in Western literature. Similarly, allegory in those literatures is much closer to allegoresis—much more a matter of interpretation than of authorial intention or so-called textual fact.[12] We have grounds for *comparison,* because the presumed identity has enough difference to allow comparison. (We cannot compare what is fully identical.)

There is also a conflict between traditional Western concepts of figures and some recent semiotic concepts. Traditionally, figures include both tropes (including metaphor) involving "abuse" (or ab-use) of words and schemes (abuse of syntax). Most cur-

---

11. I have tried to deal with this question in an essay, "Comparative Poetics: Some Theoretical and Methodological Topics for Comparative Literature," which will appear eventually in *Poetics Today*. It has appeared twice in Chinese translation. The more accessible is the first issue of *Comparative Literature in China* (Chinese title in style preferred in Peking, *Zhongguo Bijiao Wenxue;* 1984), pp. 249–275.

12. For a discussion of Japanese metaphor, see Konishi Jin'ichi, *Image and Ambiguity: The Impact of Zen Buddhism on Japanese Literature* (Tokyo, 1973), pp. 14–16, 20–26. For Chinese, see Pauline Yu, "Metaphor in Chinese Poetry," *Chinese Literature, Essays, and Reviews,* 3 (1981), 205–224.

rent Western semiotic theory presumes that signs are arbitrary. If that is the case, metaphor, for example, is a less than arbitrary sign, because there is a resemblance not purely arbitrary. The metaphorical statement "The poor are the blacks of Europe" involves a signifier and a signified that have too much in common to be considered arbitrary in the sense now typically posited for signs.

In what immediately follows, and as a step toward a topology of some range, I should like to rephrase an earlier thesis about "genre" that utilizes these concepts, particularly of homological canons for comparability and therefore for validating a concept of "genre." The meaning, not the name, is involved with the quoted term. It is not necessary that others use the term "genre" for my triad of lyric, narrative, and drama. Some people have preferred to refer to those entities as "radicals of presentation." Other terms have been employed, and in the seventeenth century the epic or heroic poem was often the exemplar of narrative, as tragedy was for drama, so entering normative as well as descriptive distinctions. Some people, notably Northrop Frye, have wished to add "prose" as a fourth genre.[13] This is an issue I shall deal with subsequently. To some it may seem that these three genres, as I call them, have an a priori or axiomatic existence. To others it may seem that since few or no works of any length are purely lyric, narrative, or dramatic, the terms have little utility or basis in practice. I have obvious sympathy with the former group, and to the latter I must say that if a given work mixes narrative, drama, and lyric, the very mixture logically requires the existence of what is mixed. Again, these are cognitive entities of an order between a given literary work and the generalized total, literature. Saying this is but describing what any talk of kinds is about, and as for any other position, so for mine, proof is necessary. The grounds for proof of the existence of my triad's entities require a kind of evidence (not

13. Frye, *Anatomy of Criticism* (Princeton, 1957), pp. 243–337. Goethe's phrase was *Naturformen der Poesie* for the three kinds I term genres. For further discussion there is my "On the Genesis and Development of Literary Systems," *Critical Inquiry*, 5 (1979), 339–353, 553–568.

simply data) distinct from empiricism, which shows that we do make the distinctions.

My evidence involves history, homology, and therefore comparability. The historical evidence is surely secure. There is a time in a given literary culture before, and a time after, an account of the systematic nature of literature exists. Plato and Aristotle, especially the latter, provide us with the evidence of this major innovation. If this is true of the Western theoretical tradition, we may presume that it is true of other cultural conceptions of literature as well. In fact, the evidence can be supplied without difficulty. Here we have a presumed identity that turns out to be not identity but homology, since Aristotle used drama to define literature and, not surprisingly, produced a representational or mimetic theory of literature. From all the evidence I have been able to obtain, that definition of poetics out of drama is unique to Western literature, and all other literary cultures have defined literature and its principles, in one fashion or another (a fashion sometimes including certain kinds of narrative), out of lyric. Given this and other evidence, my thesis is that a critically systematic or theoretical understanding of literature emerges from the engagement of powerful critical minds with the culturally esteemed genre (in the sense mentioned). To repeat: the definition by Aristotle in terms of drama presumes mimesis, representation.[14] The other culturally systematic views of literature have used lyric as the defining basis for literature, so yielding not a mimetic but an affective-expressive theory. To those views—and it is the dominant conception of literature throughout the world—literature involves someone's being moved to expression and a reader's being moved by the expression, even to the point of further writing or expression.

14. Toward the beginning of chap. 9 of the *Poetics,* Aristotle posits that literature may deal with either the fictional or the historical. The historical possibility has gradually been lost from mimetic theory among students of vernacular literatures, although not among classicists. It seems that Renaissance drama, romance, and then the novel have distorted by exaggerating the importance of fiction. East Asian definitions go further than Aristotle, assuming that even lyric poetry need not be fictional.

This evidence does not deny that there may be other genres. Aristotle was evidently aware of Homeric and other varieties of narrative. Although he does not show as much, he was surely aware as well of lyric practice. Obviously normative definitions operated along with the descriptive. Similarly, non-Western systematic theories were devised by those who were well aware of narrative, as is shown by the inclusion of history with lyric in Chinese *wen* or Japanese conceptions of *bun* or *fumi* or *aya* (various readings of the same character). Neither Chinese nor Japanese considered drama sufficiently normative for it to enter into their initial definitions, a fact that accounts for the distinctly nonrepresentational nature of their theoretical systems of literature. The subsequent histories of those systematic views are another matter. Japanese criticism was enlarged far more quickly than Chinese by the accordance of normative status to literary (as opposed to literary-historical) narrative and to drama. For that matter, Horace redefined mimesis as *imitatio* (largely of the Greeks) and developed an affective-expressive theory out of his own practice in lyrics and satire.[15]

In other words, this historical, homological, and comparative evidence justifies a triadic conception of genre (or whatever other name one wishes to use) involving lyric, drama, and narrative. These three terms have conceptual, theoretical validity, at least if we imply concepts rather than the terms that are used in various cultural traditions.

In addition to the large category of genres (as defined here), there are other kinds. (It will have been clear long before this that I have been using "kinds" as the most general, neutral term in the spirit of Congreve's "species, or distinct kind.") I shall curtail discussion of these in various respects. Most of the discussion will emphasize poetic kinds and Western kinds, with the obvious caveat that this is a very great reduction of the literary range. Not everything can be discussed, however, in an essay of this length.

Let us first consider what will be termed the "affective kinds," including epic, tragedy, comedy, satire, panegyric, didactic, and

---

15. See, in his *Ars Poetica*, the famous *dulce et utile*, *audesse*, and *prodesse*, along with his numerous references to *verba* and related terms.

pastoral. These are affective in that their cognitive status is dominated by the kind of affective claim they are made to exert on us. It seems pointless to argue the existence of these kinds with proof, although it is necessary to repeat what was said earlier: the functions of these Western affective kinds may be fulfilled by different means in other cultures, just as the function of a Japanese *utamonogatari* (tales centered on poems) may be fulfilled by oral accounts of circumstances surrounding a given poem and featuring the poem. Or again, the function of Chinese drama (in which the main characters sing but others do not) may be fulfilled in the West by opera. In any event, the accumulated evidence of Western criticism testifies to the propriety of the meanings of these terms. Without them, criticism would be sorely impoverished.

The genres and the affective kinds share the possibility of being used attributively and in mingled or distorted versions. It seems almost inevitable that once affective cognition of one kind or another becomes familiar—for example, the comic—the richness of human experience will lead to many things being termed comic. In fact, a pure affective kind is scarcely to be found, and for the reason just given. The readiest example may be tragicomedy, which illustrates in the kinds designated by that name certain qualifications of simple affective kind. Tragicomedy may mean plays that seem headed for catastrophic outcome but that end happily. Again, the name designates plays with two plots, one tragic and the other comic. There are also tragicomedies in which the tragic and comic elements are finely mingled throughout.

To sort out such minglings, we can identify first the attributive versions of both genres and affective kinds. Attributive generic features are so common that it almost seems the pure variety is a hypothetical construct. Here are the beginning and the end of Herbert's lyric "The Collar."

> I struck the board, and cry'd, No more.
> I will abroad.
> What? shall I ever sigh and pine?
> My lines and life are free; free as the rode,
> Loose as the winde, as large as store.
> . . . . .

> But as I rav'd and grew more fierce and wilde
>            At every word,
> Me thoughts I heard one calling, *Child!*
>            And I reply'd, *My Lord.*
>                              (ll. 1–5, 33–36)

The opening of what everyone would term a lyric has a strong dramatic attributive element in the outburst. This is no literal performance, no drama, but the expostulation is rebellious, and the dramatic quality is clear. The narrative element is slight in the opening, although present in the quasi-narrative past tense of the first line. The narrative element becomes clearer in the close.

Attributive versions of affective kinds also abound. The *Eumenides,* the third and last play of the *Oresteia,* ends in a comically tragic triumph. In Ibsen or Chekhov, the tragic and comic are often so finely mingled as to make distinction nearly impossible. Satiric pastorals are as old as Theocritus' twenty-third idyll, dealing with an older man's despair over his younger male lover. Horace's second epode ("Ille beatus . . .") leads into a satiric ending, and Rochester's pastoral lyric "Fair Cloris in a pig-sty lay," obviously begins in a satiric fashion that coarsens into low sexuality.

As abundant evidence testifies, genres and affective kinds offer evidence of mingling. There are songs and narrative reports (such as the nuncius or messenger of offstage action) in many plays. English drama is richer than many in comic scenes or plots in tragedies. A play like Dryden's *Marriage A-la-mode* has what many would describe as a comic main plot and a "serious" (that is, tragicomic) underplot. As these examples suggest, attributive and mingled examples also exist. Donne's poem "The Indifferent" is a dramatic lyric in its first two stanzas: "I can love both faire and browne . . ." (l. 1); "Will no other vice content you? . . ." (l. 10). But there is a mingled narrative cast to the last stanza:

> *Venus* heard me sigh this song,
> And by Loves sweetest Part, Variety, she swore,
> She heard not this till now; and't should be so no more.
>    She went, examin'd, and return'd ere long,
>       And said, . . .   (ll. 19–23)

As these examples suggest, it is not a far step from them to distorted versions. Congreve's *Incognita* is a narrative ordered as if it were a five-act play. Davenant made the same claim for his incomplete *Gondibert,* and it has been argued that the ten-book version of *Paradise Lost* had the same conception. Neither of these has the clear status of Congreve's story, but "the lyrical novel" has numerous counterparts in Asian narrative.[16] Dryden's *Mac Flecknoe* distorts panegyric as satire and is mock heroic to boot. Pope's *Dunciad* adds (in its fourth book) tragic elements to Dryden's mix. The literature of the last several decades is characterized with some consistency by such distorted versions of genres and affective kinds. The echoes by T. S. Eliot in *The Waste Land* and the musical conception of his *Four Quartets* provide familiar evidence. Later writing uses distortions of genres and affective kinds increasingly often, and what may seem rare among the *Idylls* of Theocritus has come to seem standard fare, the modern soup du jour. But to glance at non-Western evidence, throughout Japanese literature the boundaries between distinctions are consistently blurred. *Nō,* for example, can only be termed dramatic, since it is performed by actors on a stage. Yet within that general dramatic condition, individual plays are dominated by narrative and lyric, and in former times performances involved five different varieties of plays (within the distinction of two types) with comic interludes *(kyōgen).* Similarly, the first great work of Chinese prose narrative, the *Hsi-yu Chi (The Journey to the West),* includes a large number of lyric poems and mingles a variety of affective kinds to such a radical degree that description does not come easily. Yet in what seems so striking in modern or current Western literature, or what seems so ordinary in classical non-Western writing, we are still able to distinguish the attributive, mingled, or distorted versions of genres and affective kinds. These complex versions are cognitive elements necessary to any discussion of important literary examples.

Other distinctions of kinds return us to difficult matters. Kinds

16. Ralph Freedman, *The Lyrical Novel* (Princeton, 1963). Murasaki Shikibu includes nearly eight hundred poems in her narrative, along with songs and allusions to numerous poems in Japanese and Chinese.

of presentation, whether these be recited-oral or written-visual, may well seem simple and today usually are. Historically, however, matters are a great deal more complex. It is evident that the Homeric epics are oral and therefore were originally recited, and it is equally obvious that what we know of them is visual in reception because they are read. The same holds for the Germanic heroic poetry, whether those in Middle High German or the *Beowulf*. And the earliest work of Japanese literature, the *Kojiki* (*The Record of Ancient Matters;* a kind of history) was set down from a reciter's memory. As nearly as can be understood at present, the reciter set forth both what she had heard delivered from oral sources and gained from written sources, possibly through reading but more likely from having had read aloud by others certain written works for her to put in her famously retentive memory. Japanese literature has later complexities of mixture. *Waka,* or lyrics of the court period, were often composed for immediate oral presentation, often requiring an immediate oral reply in kind. *Waka* later came to be thought of as a written kind, but the custom was to recite aloud from written texts. As we know, well into the Christian era oral reading of written works was the dominant practice in the West, and recitation continued to be a staple of teaching into this century. Japanese literature provides a kind of contrary instance. *Renga* (linked poetry) was usually composed by more than one person, as they alternated stanzas. Each poet in turn composed a stanza in the mind and then recited it for the others to hear so that the successor could have an idea of what to add. Yet there was also a scribe at hand to set down what was recited and to check it for the elaborate rules of the kind. Because those rules included such things as requirements that certain topics be continued for a number of stanzas, that certain words be suspended for given numbers of stanzas, and above all that each sheet of the paper used have one moon stanza per side and one flower stanza per sheet, the oral art was also a profoundly written one.

Presentation is obviously a complex matter. But the complexities are more those of evidence and description than of theoretical difficulty. Other matters of kind differ in that they seem very simple to common sense but pose considerable difficulties for any of us who seek to explain them theoretically and/or comparatively. Perhaps the most striking of these can be termed rhythmical kinds: verse and prose, along with verse-prose. If Molière's bourgeois gentleman (a paradox like Pope's "mob of gentlemen") discovered that he spoke prose, what do these distinctions mean?

It has been argued that prose is a genre to itself, like drama, lyric, and narrative.[17] Those who find the idea sympathetic seem to feel that there is to prose an ordinariness or a grasp of reality that no play, lyric, or narrative can achieve. Others seem to wish to have a category allowing for inclusion of the occasional treatise, essay, sermon, or other prose work. Yet the most humdrum subjects have been presented in verse and the most exalted in prose. In one culture or another one will find an example of something in verse found elsewhere in prose, and vice versa. Hesiod's *Works and Days,* Lucretius, Virgil's *Georgics,* Traherne's verse and prose meditations, Pope's essays in verse—not to mention nursery rhymes like "Thirty days hath September . . ."—all show verse in the cause of the "prosaic." Or once again, in East Asia the comparable term for literature (Chinese *wen,* Japanese *bun,* and so on) is defined by kinds of history as well as by lyric. The greatest work of Japanese literature, *The Tale of Genji,* is highly elevated, as is *The Tale of the Heike* (the *Heike monogatari*), and both are in prose.

Western medieval matter well illustrates that prose and verse are alternatives to each other rather than matters classifiable as genres. There are romances in verse and romances in prose. Some sagas are in one medium, some in the other. Arthurian stories may be in either, whether during the Middle Ages or subsequently. It is very strange that so little study has been made, for example, of resemblances and differences between narrative in verse and narrative in prose. It is strange, that is, until one searches for evidence sustaining, or even data for illustrating, one or another notion. Even notions are scarce. Yet if we cannot account for the difference, we are in the absurd

17. By Frye; see n. 13.

position of saying that although the verse-prose distinction matters for nonliterary use of language, it does not matter for literature.

By distinguishing the two as different *rhythms*, somewhat as Dryden suggested in "the other harmony of prose," I offer a basis of differentiation.[18] Good prose will have some rhythmical features, but they are not as recurrent as the rhythms of poetry, and the use of the intensifications of poetry (rhyme, lineation, concentrations of metaphors, and the like) makes prose seem either precious or comic. At the same time, it is possible to write interestingly in prosaic verse or poetic prose. Jonson's verse in *The Alchemist* has to be spoken carefully if on the stage it is not to sound like prose. And we all know prose poems. In fact, as with genres, so with rhythms, combinations are feasible. The two may be mingled, as in *The Tale of Genji* and *The Journey to the West*. But the mingling is yet more remarkable in certain Japanese Shinto liturgies in which lines of verse have units of prose interspersed with them. The prose poem shows how attributive features of one rhythm (verse) may be incorporated into another (prose).

This line of discussion offers us a description and examples fitting the description. It does not offer us a theoretical explanation. For that we must go to linguistics and the concept of markedness.[19] The marked form of something is the variant of the ordinary, normal, simple, or holistic. The normal features of an English verb are positive, present, and indicative. The negative, another tense, and the interrogative, another mood, are taken as variants requiring other inflection or words. In Western culture "man" is the ordinary form, and "woman" the marked; conventionally "man" includes the concept of "woman" but not the reverse. The opposite is true of most familiar animals: duck, goose, cow, chicken, and so on, with drake, gander, bull, and cock or rooster the marked versions. With less familiar

18. Dryden "Preface" to *Fables, Poems*, IV, 1446.
19. On markedness, see Joseph H. Greenberg, *Language Universals* (The Hague, 1966); and Michael Shapiro, *The Sense of Grammar* (Bloomington, Ind., 1983), index, s.v. "Markedness."

animals like the male lion, English has it the ordinary form and
the lioness the marked form. Markedness has many versions,
and they are taken to be one of the most important of linguistic
universals.

Since the rhythms of verse are additional to those of prose,
verse is the marked form of speech and writing. M. Jourdain's
discovery that he spoke prose is absurd, precisely because he
treats it as a marked form of language rather than as the ordinary. The linguistic concept must not be abused. Because the
Homeric poems are in verse does not mean that verse is the
ordinary or unmarked form of the epic. It may be the natural
or most useful form, especially for an oral literature, since verse
writing is easier to remember than prose writing. But the many
conversations throughout those two poems show how marked
is the conducting of conversation in verse. It must also be said
that we should not simply assume that we can define literature
as the marked form of verbal discourse. It is positively ordinary
by comparison with the artificial languages of physics, algebra,
and deductive logic. Literature is a kind of knowledge distinguished from other kinds at a certain stage in the development
of a culture. But it is not *the* marked form of verbal discourse.
Yet the marked form of linguistic rhythm, verse, is almost au-
tomatically taken to signal the literary, whereas the prosaic
rhythm requires other signals for us to assume a given example
to be literary.

With such a distinction in mind, the Shinto liturgies or, for
that matter, *nō* with its alternations of prose and verse, can be
interpreted in terms of ends being served by the ordinary or the
marked versions of verbal discourse. In East Asia, however,
distinctions that seem definite in the West are often less thought
of as *cordons sanitaires*. The *fu* may be recalled—"rhyme-prose"
being one translation for it. And there are other kinds of ornate
prose that approach in rhythm the recurrences of poetry.[20] Such
instances are of interest more for exemplifying the nonexclusive

20. For examples of Shinto liturgy using verse-prose and of ornate prose,
see Konishi, *History,* I, 295–297 (verse-prose), 72, 366–367, 390–391 (ornate
prose).

tendencies of East Asians than as marginal examples. After all, the distinction between prose and verse is clearly one of rhythm and is accountable for by the principle of markedness.

Two other distinctions can be drawn along the lines of kind. What I term "mode" involves the relation taken by a writer between self and world, including others in that world. And "attitude" involves the conception shared by the writer and the reader of the degree of awe in the world and in characters of a work. To the extent that the mode adopted by a writer involves valuing the individual against the common world, the mode is private. To the extent that the mode involves valuing what is shared rather than what is idiosyncratic, the mode is public. These are merely the extremes, with a social mode somewhere in the middle, the social being taken to represent the individual and the world in balance. Attitude is also a matter of emphasis, of a spectrum rather than exclusive alternatives, but once again we can posit three points. The attitude we hold toward the characters and their world may lead us to think them higher than, like, or lower than our own world and ourselves. Aristotle treats this matter more than once (for example, in *Poetics,* chap. 25), but he casts the matter almost solely in moral terms. Moral matters are indeed extremely important to literature, but they are not matters of kind. Yet attitude determines, as it were, the pitch or key of our response.

Like the other kinds, mode and attitude are extremely useful in accounting both for literary change and for individual works.[21] In seventeenth-century England the many social upheavals are variously shown in terms of politics, religion, and literature. All three are extremely unstable. Although Donne and Jonson revolutionize poetic language by bringing it far closer to actual speech, their characteristic lyric poetry differs in mode, Donne's being private and Jonson's social; both also write in a variety of modes including at times the public. Milton and Dryden differ drastically in the kinds of language employed. Milton invents an artistic language all his own, whereas Dryden brings language

21. See "On the Genesis and Development of Literary Systems." I also include style there as a historical differentia, but omit that here as not appropriate to a discussion of kinds.

far closer to actual speech. And yet they share the public mode and a higher attitude—Dryden going to great pains to do so even for the world of *Mac Flecknoe* and the implied politics of *Absalom and Achitophel,* not to mention his greatest work, *Fables.* But the major historical change came in the next century with a crucial shift in attitude and in narrative rhythm. The heroic and romance *attitudes* that dominate the later seventeenth century and that found best expression in verse alter in the eighteenth century, as the novel discovered a resource for prose in depiction of a lower world than that of the writer and the audience. It is quite striking how persistently novelists from Defoe to Austen and beyond were termed "low." It is equally striking that the lower world was so profoundly and fruitfully made to provide a new kind of knowledge of the human condition.

The two greatest poetic narratives of the seventeenth century, *Paradise Lost* and *Fables,* share in their differing ways a descent in attitude within the heroic as the works near their ends. From that point in book 9 when Adam and Eve are first said to separate their hands, they become more like ourselves, although never quite so. More accurately, Adam dwindles and Eve emerges as first a tragic and then a comic heroine in the Eviad of the last four books. In *Fables* the degree of fluctuation is enormous, but the heroic in Dryden's wide sense of it dominates until almost the end. The last four parts (of this narrative twice as long as *Paradise Lost*) begins with "Of the Pythagorean Philosophy. From Ovid's Metamorphoses Book XV," a heroic account of time and change. The next part, "The Character of A Good Parson; Imitated from Chaucer, And Inlarg'd," introduces a Christian example to correct the pagan Numa, but the poem is much lower in attitude, even if not as low as Chaucer's "character" of "a povre persoun of a towne." The decline in attitude continues into the next part, "The Monument of A Fair Maiden Lady," another Christian example curiously humbler than the pagan examples. The last part, "Cymon and Iphigenia," versifies one of the novelle by Boccaccio and is extremely complex, making matters of attitude as difficult as all else in this complex work.

The decline in awe is a feature common to the end of many

heroic writings throughout the world, since writing about the
heroic world seems either to require its being considered something past or to involve a more sophisticated but less awesome
poet and readership. This is as true of *The Tale of Genji* as of
*Beowulf* and other examples. It is in fact extremely rare to find
examples of works that rise in awe, much as it is rarer for a
great work to treat a simply good person than one whose moral
features are as mixed as our own. There is one notable example
of such a rise, however: *Don Quixote*. The Knight of the Sad
Countenance never becomes quite sane, but from about the
chapter on the lions (pt. 2, chap. 17) his folly seems more and
more a kind of wisdom for a sorry world. It would be better
for us if the world were as that dreamer supposed it than as it
is. For that matter, even Sancho rises. He is not really appointed
governor of an island, but in the mummery that deceives him
he governs more wisely than those who are born above him and
are better educated.

These are thumbnail sketches. But like those immediately
preceding them, they are offered to show that this account of
kinds has evidence that can be given and therefore some descriptive power. We understand literary history and individual
works by these concepts, even if we do not name them, even
if we are not aware of using them. As I have been proposing
from the outset, the kinds are cognitive in nature, concepts as
it were between the levels of literature and the individual work.
Since we think by these concepts, it seems desirable to give
them names, to attempt to define them and, where there is some
question, provide evidence for the validity of a given concept.
In pursuing this aim I have not accounted for every kind, especially for kinds associated with prose and drama; and for much
evidence from non-Western literatures, I have provided what
attention I could, as much as can be attempted from my limited
knowledge and in short compass.

In closing I wish to represent this discussion rather more
taxonomically and with a couple of what I hope are evident
additions.

*Presentation:* recited-oral and written-visual.
*Rhythm:* verse, prose, and verse-prose.

*Mode:* the relation taken by the writer between self and world (including others) on a spectrum from private to social to public.

*Attitude:* the conception by the writer and reader of the degree of awesomeness of the characters and world of a work on a spectrum from higher to like to lower.

*Genre:* lyric, narrative, and drama.

### Other kinds: mostly poetic and Western

*Affective kinds:* epic, tragedy, comedy, panegyric, satire, pastoral.

*Occasional kinds:* aubade, funeral verse, epithalamion, banquet poem, parting poem.

*Topical kinds:* poems on a season, love as a (set) topic, specified topics (snow at a mountain village).

*Formal* (including prosodic) *kinds:* elegy, sonnet, sestina, *shih, tz'u, chōka, tanka, hyangga, sijo.*

The genres and other kinds, especially the affective, can be construed attributively, be mingled, and be distorted.

*Genres and affective kinds can be construed attributively.*

As a dramatic lyric—the poem is lyric with attributive dramatic features.

As tragicomedy, satiric pastoral.

*Genres and other kinds can be mingled.*

As lyric (song) moments in a drama, narrative passages in a drama.

As verse and prose in combination.

*Genres and affective kinds can be distorted.*

As narration that dwells on the same thing or is otherwise made to work against normal continuity; mock heroic; affectionate satire; mock panegyric; cynical pastoral.

*Genres and affective kinds can be both adapted attributively and mingled.*

As a dramatic lyric that ends in narrative fashion; a satiric comedy that ends in pastoral.

To conclude without a peroration is to recall that there are many important cognitive features of literature not recognized here: beginning and ending, for example. And to speak of a peroration is to remind oneself again that a name such as "narrative" is derived from Roman rhetoricians. Lyric poetry in Greek was termed "melic" and was reductively related to prosody, musical accompaniments, and occasion. In non-Western literatures there are quite different topologies and many other

names. No doubt a universal account of the kinds lies beyond
our powers to conceive, although we must try as best we can
with the evidence known to us. Any irenic person will recognize
that there are many useful ways of construing the meaning of
kinds, will hope to clarify somewhat that meaning, and will
regret—while multiplying—the profusion of terms in critical
Babledom. The basic problem is perhaps insoluble, but we *must*
seek to understand how we know what we do know in literary
terms. Some lines by Pound have haunted my thoughts for many
years and apply once again:

> This is not vanity.
> Here error is all in the not done,
> all in the diffidence that faltered.[22]

22. Ezra Pound, *Cantos*, LXXXI, last three lines.

ANN E. IMBRIE

# Defining Nonfiction Genres

Milton, we know, wrote prose with his left hand. Shakespeare's rustics, clowns, peasants, and other corrupters of language speak prose; his heroes descend to it when, clouded in confusion or distracted by evil, they forego the high talk of poetry. Although we might discount Milton's remark as characteristically ironic and judge Hamlet's discourse a function of tragic eccentricity, we have tended to accept uncritically an apparent Renaissance prejudice against prose, using comments like Milton's to buttress our own prejudices against prose as a less immediately artful medium than poetry, drama, or fiction. Our own prejudice accounts in part for the tendency of modern genre theory to neglect nonfiction prose in particular. To this way of thinking, if generic choice represents a self-consciously literary option, then nonfiction prose, almost by definition nonliterary, seems outside—or beneath—the view of generic criticism.[1]

We must exercise caution, however, in attempting to locate

1. In recognizing that the lists of "canonical forms" and the definitions of genres themselves will change from generation to generation, Alastair Fowler's

this prejudice specifically in Renaissance literary theory. In fact, a reassessment of Renaissance attitudes toward prose will convince us of its value as a medium of intentioned literary expression. And for Renaissance writers, a literary intention is registered primarily in the choice of generic form. Thus a poetics of nonfiction prose must include a study of its generic forms. For such a study, however, we must reconstruct a definition of genre itself, consistent with Renaissance principles, that can accommodate nonfiction prose within the scope of literary art. Finally, then, we can identify some of the generic options available to nonfiction prose writers in the Renaissance.[2]

Recent scholarship has suggested that we can no longer accept the so-called puritan attack on art, represented in Stephen Gosson's *Schoole of Abuse* (1579), as the only stimulus for Sidney's eloquent defense of poetry. The early humanists, in fact, had so revered prose and so relegated poetry to the leisure hours

---

*Kinds of Literature* (Cambridge, Mass., 1984) encourages the reassessment I offer here of Renaissance attitudes toward prose. Fowler's book is more a broad survey of those shifts in literary values, and their significance for generic consideration within the literary system, than a reconstruction of the attitudes of any one period in literary history. To this extent Fowler incorporates this historical prejudice against prose kinds. Although he notes the granting of literary status to nonfictional and otherwise "extraliterary" forms in the Renaissance (p. 157), he asserts that "ambiguity of literary status is confined to a few genres" (p. 11)—all of them nonfictional—and the essay is the only nonfictional form he treats at any length. Where my definitions accord with, and differ from, Fowler's will be noted in the following pages.

2. Among studies of the Renaissance in particular, Rosalie Colie's work, both in *The Resources of Kind* (Berkeley, 1973) and in her studies of Shakespeare (Princeton, 1974) and Marvell (Princeton, 1970), has greatly enriched our understanding of Renaissance genres; my conclusions about the "idea" of genre are similar to hers. Although *The Resources of Kind* devotes considerable attention to prose forms, the relationship Colie establishes between generic theory and particular texts is more general than what I propose: to project from Renaissance notions of genre and attitudes toward prose not only a theoretically inclusive definition of genre itself (as Colie does) but also a set of practical generic options that, while not in themselves exclusive to prose forms, will nonetheless illuminate the special conditions under which they were produced and provide as well a literary vocabulary for generic analysis of these forms.

of life that by the 1580s—even without Stephen Gosson—poor poetry needed a good defense. Sidney's effort to reevaluate poetry, in other words, identifies as much a generational difference as a theological one.[3] But in seeking to correct an imbalance in the literary values of their fathers, the sons among Sidney's generation incorporated rather than repudiated those values, defending poetry without necessarily maligning prose. In the later Renaissance—between, say, Sidney and Dryden— when we do encounter distinctions between prose and poetry, the arguments develop carefully according to two principles that continue to recognize the potential literary value of prose discourse. First, the detractors of prose point less to the medium itself than to its abuses. In a period in which verse has its "wooden rythmours [swarming] in stacioners shops" and "doltish coystrels" writing "rude rythming and balducktoom ballads,"[4] so prose has its own hack representatives at the book fair, writers who demean the art by excessive ornamentation and affected learning, who "sette before us nought but a confused masse of wordes wihout matter, a Chaos of sentences without any profitable sence, resembling drummes, which beeing emptie within sound big without." Thus, even as Nash swaggers through this condemnation, he objects to those who "estimat[e] Artes by the insolence of Idiots" and values eloquent and restrained prose

3. Barbara K. Lewalski's *Protestant Poetics and the Seventeenth-Century Religious Lyric* (Princeton, 1979) and more recently John N. King's *English Reformation Literature* (Princeton, 1982) have discouraged the traditional view of English protestantism as "anti-art." Similarly, Margaret Ferguson (*Trials of Desire* [New Haven, 1983]) identifies a "radical protestant twist" in Sidney's *Defense of Poetry* (p. 145). In arguing that the *Defense* is in part an allegory in which the author focuses his attention on "trials in which young men who resemble their creators find themselves accused of a crime" (pp. 137–138), Ferguson suggests a psychological motive for the *Defense* in "generational conflict." I see the conflict as more narrowly historical: Sidney's literary fathers are those humanists who, like Vives, regarded prose eloquence more highly, relegating poetry "to the leisure hours of life." By emphasizing the persuasive powers of poetry, and suggesting curbs on that power, Sidney and his generation raise poetry to the status of oratory, co-opting the values of the previous generation. The shift in emphasis here is like the one we find in the redefinition of values that typically occurs between parents and children.

4. Richard Stanyhurst, "Preface to the Translation of the *Aeneid*" (1582) in *Elizabethan Critical Essays*, ed. G. Gregory Smith (Oxford, 1904), I, 141.

as "in highest reputation, without the which all [other arts] are naked, and she onely garnished."[5] Such attacks on prose writers, in fact, register respect for prose well used, the irritation rising in proportion to the abuse.

Second, English critics qualify their judgment that prose is less musical, less memorable, and generally less effective than poetry by making clear that they mean the prose of ordinary discourse rather than literary prose. According to Puttenham, for example, where prose falters, it does so because "it is dayly used, and by that occasion the eare is overglutted with it."[6] Here Puttenham, and others, draw the distinction between poetry and "daily talke," or "flatte prose," or sentences delivered "at random in prose."[7] Having made this distinction, English critics can maintain that prose eloquence is poetry's "sister art." Indeed, until the mid-sixteenth century we commonly find prose implicitly valued as the higher of the two, and vestiges of this attitude continue into the seventeenth century. Francis Meres's distinction between grand and lyric poets, for example, recalls the earlier humanists' descriptions of the grave eloquence of prose writers: in ancient Greece, he notes, writers who "handled in the audience of the people grave and necessary matters were called wise men or eloquent men, which they ment by Vates: so the rest, which sang of love matters, or other lighter devises alluring unto pleasure and delight, were called Poets or makers."[8] Poetry, he implies, when it handles "grave and necessary

5. Thomas Nash, *The Anatomie of Absurditie* (1589), in Smith, *Elizabethan Critical Essays*, I, 322, 334.

6. George Puttenham, *The Arte of English Poesie* (1589), ed. Gladys Willcock and Alice Walker (Cambridge, 1936), p. 8.

7. The phrases are Puttenham's, Samuel Daniel's, and Francis Meres's, cited in Smith, *Elizabethan Critical Essays*, II, 8, 364, 310, respectively. These typical qualifications suggest English versions of the phrase in Aristotle's *Poetics, logois psilois* ("naked words"), used to describe insufficiently literary diction. Although some Renaissance scholars translated the phrase "prose," and barred prose works from the literary canon because Aristotle seemed to do so, others, notably the influential Castelvetro and Vettori, translated it *parlari nudi* and *sermonibus nudis*. Such expressions, like their English counterparts, would imply a distinction between "bare" and "fashionably dressed" prose.

8. Francis Meres, *Palladis Tamia* (1598), in Smith, *Elizabethan Critical Essays*, II, 313.

matters," matches or assumes the eloquent office of prose. Similarly, Ben Jonson praises the comic poet who, in his capacity to move his audience and stir the affections, "comes neerest" the borders of oratory.[9]

As these comments suggest, the modern distinction between rhetoric and literature—that rhetoric is historically specific and situational while literature is universally applicable and only fictively situational—is rarely articulated so precisely in the Renaissance. English practice preserves this distinction only in the most limited way: throughout the Renaissance prose remains the favored medium for the public address of historically specific issues. But we should understand that this practice does not relegate rhetorical prose to subliterary status. Sidney, for example, defends poetry by distinguishing it from history and philosophy; and while he ironically asserts that he should be "pounded for straying from *Poetrie*, to *Oratory*," he insists that the two kinds "have such an affinitie" as to have clarified his argument by that very digression.[10] Even more interesting, although English critics feel compelled to defend poetry against Plato's ban, they do not respond specifically to Plato's diatribes against rhetoric, which, to the modern reader at least, seem stronger and more sweeping than his criticisms of poetry. The love of fine prose roots so deeply in the English imagination that I suspect English readers could not accommodate Plato's

9. Ben Jonson, *Discoveries* (1641; rpt. New York, 1923), p. 95.

10. Philip Sidney, *The Defense of Poesie,* in *The Prose Works,* ed. Albert Feuillerat (Cambridge, 1962), III, 43. The proximity of poetry and oratory remains the most distancing feature of Renaissance literary theory for those modern readers who either condescend to Renaissance writers for maintaining a "practical" definition of literature as opposed to a more purely aesthetic one, or simply misread Renaissance literature because they ignore the essential connection between literature and rhetoric that Sidney here identifies. As examples of the first difficulty, see Walter J. Ong, "The Province of Rhetoric and Poetic," in *The Province of Rhetoric,* ed. Joseph Schwartz and John A. Rycenga (New York, 1965), and O. B. Hardison, "The Orator and the Poet: The Dilemma of Humanist Literature," *Journal of Medieval and Renaissance Studies,* 1 (1971), 33–44. Stanley Fish's *Self-Consuming Artifacts* suggests the second difficulty: in applauding the "Platonic/dialectic" impulses of Renaissance writers, and condemning the "rhetorical" impulses, Fish fails to take this principle into account and so misreads such "rhetorical" writers as Browne.

judgments—in fact, that those judgments did not even register in their minds.

Renaissance critics, however, especially in England, do not limit their respect for prose to specific rhetorical forms but rather extend literary status to prose works well beyond the scope of classical oratory. This extension is nowhere more surprising than in Renaissance discussions of mimesis. We might least expect to find Aristotle's dictum—that poetry should fictively represent human action—urged in the defense of nonfiction works. The Renaissance understanding of mimesis, of course, may be less accurate than our own; certainly Aristotle himself would not have recognized as literature some of the very works Renaissance critics justify on "Aristotelian" grounds. But the misunderstanding itself instructs us in Renaissance literary values because it betrays an a priori affection and respect for certain texts and a desire to grant them literary status. If not a method, we find a motive in the shaping of Aristotle's dictum to the Renaissance image. Moderate critics like Sidney, who make mimesis the essential feature of literature, use this argument to include in the literary canon works that are neither fictional nor rhetorical—More's *Utopia,* for instance, and Boethius' *Consolation of Philosophy,* and certain forms of biography like the *Cyropaedia.* Such justifications occur so frequently that we err in ascribing them simply to muddle-headed misreadings of Aristotle. Rather, the broadening of the definition of mimesis to include such works results from the effort to reconcile classical authorities, even to wrench definitions where necessary to establish peace among them.

Among those classical authorities, of course, Aristotle was a relative newcomer, and it stands to reason that in conflicts among authorities, Aristotle's claims on English critical thinking might be more readily challenged, his literary principles accommodated and qualified. In one such conflict the Aristotelian doctrine of mimesis runs headlong into a community of values already established in England by the mid-sixteenth century. Among these values are the imitation of model texts, a staple of literary training since the early Renaissance; the shifting definition of decorum, already occurring in the 1580s; and the Horatian concept of the function of literature, carried into the Renaissance from the Middle Ages. Taken together, these ideas suggest the existence of a literary continuum that necessarily includes nonfictional and rhetorical prose.

The imitation of model texts as a basis of literary training reveals the considerable value Renaissance critics place on nonfiction prose. This educational enterprise, which we might call Ciceronian imitation to distinguish it from Aristotelian mimesis, encourages writers to see relationships rather than distinctions among the literary arts, allowing for cross references between mimetic literature and nonfiction prose. Vida, for example, urges the practicing poet to imitate the orations of Cicero and other great rhetoricians in preparing speeches assigned to characters in plays.[11] Likewise, Ascham outlines with missionary zeal a compendium of imitative models for the student, moving progressively from prose forms to poetic ones, and then back to prose again. Ascham proposes "A booke thus wholie filled with examples of Imitation, first out of Tullie, compared with Plato, Xenophon, Isocrates, Demosthenes, and Aristotle, than out of Virgil and Horace, with Homer and Pindar, next out of Seneca, with Sophocles and Euripides, lastlie out of Livie, with Thucydides, Polibius, and Halicarnassaeus"; he requires comparison within type (for example, Cicero with Demosthenes) but allows that prose and poetry alike provide appropriate models.[12] We should note too that prose histories figure perhaps even more emphatically than oratory among Ascham's examples for imitation.

Also, the relaxation of the demands of decorum both justifies and encourages literary experiments even as the principle of decorum fosters a strong connection between literature gener-

11. Marco Giralmo Vida, *De Arte Poetica* (1527), in *The Art of Poetry,* ed. Albert S. Cook (Boston, 1892); see esp. bk. 2, ll. 496–525. John Shawcross has suggested that this kind of direction provides a new approach to the rhetoric of seventeenth-century poetry by encouraging us to define rhetoric itself more broadly. See "The Poet as Orator: One Phase of his Judicial Pose," in *The Rhetoric of Renaissance Poetry from Wyatt to Milton,* ed. Thomas O. Sloan and Raymond B. Waddington (Berkeley, 1974), pp. 5–36. Certainly Milton's early training in oratory served him well in his construction of poetic orations in bk. 2 of *Paradise Lost.*

12. Roger Ascham, *The Schoolemaster* (1570), in Smith, *Elizabethan Critical Essays,* I, 20.

ally and rhetoric. When the principle of decorum governs simply
the appropriate matching of style and genre, it functions con-
servatively to protect a literary status quo. When, however, the
doctrine of decorum refers to the social world outside the literary system—that heroes should talk like heroes and fools act
like fools—it fosters literary innovation. In the late sixteenth
and early seventeenth centuries we find this social definition of
decorum increasingly urged to defend the use of prose in tragedies as well as comedies; prose speaks more directly to contemporary audiences, and its basis in ordinary usage makes it
a more accurate instrument for recreating human action on the
stage.[13] Ben Jonson's *Sejanus* might have fared better had he
curbed the artificial effulgence of his language to this new rule
of custom. Shakespeare left no critical record other than the
plays themselves; examination of his use of dramatic prose,
however, would dispel the critical shibboleth with which this
essay began. Certainly the stylistic transformations we witness
between the self-conscious artifice of *Richard II* and the more
naturalistic prose and poetry of the later tragedies and romances
indicate Shakespeare's incorporation of this principle.

A new definition of decorum, then, emerges in response to
such anticlassical techniques as the use of prose in drama, a
definition that clearly shows the influence of rhetorical theory
on poetic theory. In this version decorum establishes a social
contract between writer (or work) and reader: a decorous work
operates through the forms most readily accessible to the audience. Defining decorum and hence the communication of literary meaning as a function of "what without dishonor the place
and the time require" assigns the audience a determining position with regard to a literary work.[14] That the audience maintains such a position is, of course, a commonplace of rhetorical

13. Extended theoretical justifications of the use of prose in the drama, which
follow these principles, appear more frequently among the Italians, particularly
Paolo Beni (1600) and Agostino Michele (1592). See Bernard Weinberg, *The
History of Literary Criticism in the Italian Renaissance,* 2 vols. (Chicago, 1961),
II, 708, 678–679.

14. The phrase is quoted from Giraldi Cinthio's preface to *Orbecche* (1541),
in which he defends the nonclassical form of his play as that of a man "born
just now of a young father" who "can appear only as young." See Allan H.

theory. The orator must establish a contract of style and subject
with his audience if, as Sidney says, he is to "winne credit of
popular eares . . . the nearest steppe to perswasion, which perswasion, is the chiefe marke of Oratorie."[15] The application of
this rhetorical doctrine to all literary art makes of decorum a
means rather than an end and thus sanctions a good deal of
literary experiment—not only in the use of vernacular models
for the drama but more generally in the development of literary
styles less obviously artificial, more directly communicative. In
prose we see the fruits of this development in the movement
from Ciceronian to Senecan styles in the seventeenth century.
The Senecan style, precisely because it is less ornate, is capable
of a more flexible response to the demands of its audience.[16]

Both the educational program defined by the imitation of
model texts and the relaxed definition of decorum—important
as these are to maintaining a literary continuum that includes
nonfiction prose—develop as effects of a greater cause. Their
theoretical justification depends on the Horatian concept of the
functions of literature—that it should teach, delight, and move—
which continues throughout the Renaissance to locate the value
of literature in its moral and social force. The Aristotelian definition of literary works according to principles of artistic unity
took hold less firmly in England than in Italy, in part because
it lacks this social dimension. The English understanding of

Gilbert, *Literary Criticism: Plato to Dryden* (Detroit, 1962), pp. 243–244. The
redefinition of decorum as a social rather than purely aesthetic concept is most
fully articulated among English critics in Puttenham's *Arte of English Poesie,*
bk. 2, chaps. 23 and 24. Most of Puttenham's examples come from social
conversation rather than literature, and it is difficult to distinguish here an
aesthetic principle from the more general social concerns. In all instances,
because "the actions of man with their circumstances be infinite, and the world
likewise replenished with many judgements" (p. 263), Puttenham insists that
decorum must follow the rule of custom, and writers must be constantly attentive
to the demands of their audiences.

15. Sidney, *Defense of Poesie,* p. 43.

16. Francis Bacon's *Advancement of Learning* provides extensive evidence
of this principle, both in its style and in its directions for the dissemination of
learning. Essentially, in identifying the various ways in which learning can be
transmitted, Bacon consistently uses the psychological and intellectual needs of
the audience as a defining perspective.

literature emphasizes the practical effects of art, its capacity to persuade an audience and to commit human will to moral action. Sidney's "medicine of cherries" expresses this impulse in an apt metaphor. Thus, for Sidney, versifying does not make a poet in part because poetry imitates, but more importantly because verse is merely the instrument of the poet, a means to make the matter more memorable and delightful. The poetry, it seems, is in the pith.

Typically, then, Francis Meres's *Palladis Tamia* (1598), an English Renaissance effort in practical criticism, collects from great writers wise remarks about their art; and when Meres comments on the writers of his own day, he most frequently compliments their sententious qualities. The practical approval of *sententiae* diminishes the distinction between poetry and prose because, as Bernard Weinberg notes, gravity and truth are "equally appropriate to maxims found in orations, in histories, in philosophical writings, or anywhere else."[17] Given the location of literary merit in moral value, writers could give both philosophy and history literary shape, a possibility that complicates the easy assignment of relative value to prose or poetry. In organizing the relationship among the three Horatian functions of literature, critics line up on both sides, some arguing that literature moves best through its teaching function (for example, Jonson, Bacon), others through its delighting function (for example, Puttenham). But if there is a consistent movement on this issue into the seventeenth century, it is away from delightful ornament and toward utility, a shift in values that gives further impetus to the development of prose forms, always recognized as less necessarily ornamented than poetic ones.

Over and over again, then, Renaissance literary theory indicates and reinforces the value of nonfiction prose as one constituent of the literary continuum. This value exerts pressure against the notion of mimesis, encouraging a broadening of that definition sufficient to allow nonfiction prose into its scope. We recognize here the assertion of one set of literary values against another, so that mimesis loses the definitional force that con-

17. Weinberg, *Literary Criticism in the Italian Renaissance,* I, 199.

temporary mimetic theory attempts to give it.[18] But that loss in critical clarity in fact directs our attention to essential literary values in the Renaissance. As frequently as we cite the Renaissance argument that the imitation of reality "makes" literature, we cannot finally accept mimesis as the sine qua non of literary expression without significantly qualifying that term. In Sidney's memorable phrase, literature "creates a *golden* world where nature left a *brazen*," reproducing reality only in its most ideal forms that thereby discover the moral value of experience. For Renaissance writers, in short, literary imitation is essentially value centered. They respect mimesis for its recreation of ideal *truth* and value the moral force of that truth. The ideal truth can appear in prose forms as well as in poetic or dramatic ones, a point underscored in Renaissance discussions of rhetoric, in the educational program outlined by the imitation of model texts, and in the Horatian definitions of the function of literature that dominated English theory. To recover a concept of genre that can accommodate nonfiction prose—in short, to define genres as a Renaissance writer might—we must recognize the moral basis of literary form. It is to that definition I now turn.

The modern prejudice against nonfiction prose as a less artful medium than poetry derives from a conviction that literature is mimetic. Similarly, nonfiction prose has seemed inaccessible to generic analysis because our definition of genre itself has been too narrowly prescribed, excluding the Renaissance preoccupation with the relation of generic form to moral value. An analysis of Sidney's *Defense,* along with corroborative evidence from other Renaissance theorists, will recover a definition of genre that can correct this misperception and thus provide a reliable and interesting means for generic analysis of nonfiction prose.

The difficulty of using Sidney's *Defense* as a critical guide is that he shifts his definition of genre to accommodate both his

18. The fullest modern development of the mimetic theory of literature is offered in Bennison Gray's *The Phenomenon of Literature* (The Hague, 1975).

various purposes—sometimes descriptive, sometimes evaluative—and also to account for the variety of literary texts he examines. He does, however, incorporate the various definitions of genre that a Renaissance critic might bring to the examination of a particular text. At various points in his argument Sidney isolates three distinct bases for generic identification: the formal features of the text; its subject matter; and what I shall call "generic attitude," the set of values implied in a literary work through the attitude it takes toward its subject. It is important to notice in which instances Sidney applies each of these definitions if we are to develop from these applications a coherent set of generic principles.

Defining a literary kind according to its external features leads Sidney to deplore Spenser's stylistic innovations in *The Shepheardes Calender,* objecting that the formal character of those eclogues differs from the models in Theocritus, Virgil, and Sannazar which codify the rules for that form. Similarly, Sidney's accusation that contemporary tragedy "mingles clowns and kings" arises from a formal concept of the proper disposition of tragedy—that it must preserve a single, high style, present only certain types of characters, and so forth. Where Sidney's judgments are most conservative, he is relying on such external rules, preconceived notions of form that a writer must observe. He is, in short, adhering to a prescriptive theory of genre. A similar adherence to rules leads Jonson to charge Sidney himself with a breach of decorum in "making every one [of his characters] speak as well as himself," and to dismiss so abruptly contemporary epigrammatists for not fulfilling their formal generic responsibilities. Characteristically, Jonson's criticism is riddled with ambiguity as he sorts out the conflicting demands of "genius" and "the narrow limits of lawes" in a poet; but among English critics Jonson most consistently favors the poet's following rules prescribing the formal character of literature. His discussion of epic and tragedy in particular insists upon the formal regulation of these types.[19]

19. Jonson's remarks on Sidney and contemporary epigrammatists can be found in his *Conversations with William Drummond of Hawthorndon,* in the

A definition of genre according to subject matter, however, provides a more relaxed distinction among kinds and as such might more successfully encourage literary experiment. Significantly, we find the development of this definition most frequently among Renaissance "moderns" who defend literary experiments in form against various charges of unruliness. Sidney joins this company when he uses subject matter as the basis of generic identification, making more tolerant literary judgments than in those cases where he applies prescriptive rules. Among literary kinds distinguished by subject, Sidney allows that some have "mingled matters" like "Heroicall and Pastorall, but that commeth all to one in this question, for if severed they be good, the conjunction cannot be hurtfull."[20] A mingling of "matters heroical and pastoral" would in all likelihood bring together clowns and kings, a conjunction Sidney here allows but condemns when he discusses tragedy according to prescriptive rules.

The epic, of course, is by Renaissance definition a compendium of kinds, and Sidney's acceptance of "mingled matters" in heroic forms may simply register his recognition of their inclusive impulses. Of the English critics, however, Puttenham most thoroughly describes the various genres according to their subjects and in the process consistently minimizes their formal character. Whether the subjects are "profitable Artes and sciences," rejoicings, lamentations, or "bitter taunts and privy nips," every genre has an appropriate subject that dictates its form. The form develops, in a sense, from within and offers no more than the most convenient means of expressing what the writer has to say. The subject of love, for example, because it

---

edition of *Discoveries* cited earlier, pp. 3, 4, and 10 (separate pagination). His discussion of epic and tragedy emphasizes the demands of unity, proportion, and singleness of action; see *Discoveries,* pp. 101–105. Richard Helgerson's recent study of Jonson (in *Self-Creating Laureates: Spenser, Jonson, Milton and the Literary System,* Berkeley, 1983) sets Jonson's typical ambivalence about the "narrow limits of lawes" in literary art in the context of his lifelong quarrel with the previous generation of poets, and their respect for "inspiration." See esp. pp. 119–121.

20. Sidney, *Defense of Poesie,* p. 25.

is "of all other humane affections the most puissant and passionate, and most generall to all sortes and ages of men and
women," requires

a forme of Poesie variable, inconstant, affected, curious and most witty
of any others, whereof the joyes [are] to be uttered in one sorte, the
sorrowes in an other, and by the many formes of Poesie, the many
moodes and pangs of lovers, throughly to be discovered.[21]

Puttenham's method of defining the kinds is to see them as
various responses to the entire range of human experience;
encountering these responses in particular forms, then, the reader
may "discover" the variety of human life. Guided by such an
inclusive literary system, Puttenham's judgments are characteristically tolerant, allowing into the canon certain forms that
would be excluded by more rigorously formal definitions of
"poesie."

  Finally, Sidney suggests a third means of distinguishing one
genre from another in his descriptions of literary kinds. I quote
from his defense of the heroic:

Who if the saying of Plato and Tully bee true, that who could see
vertue, woulde bee woonderfullie ravished with the love of her bewtie.
This man [the epic poet] setteth her out to make her more lovely in
her holliday apparrell, to the eye of anie that will daine, not to disdaine
untill they understand. But if any thing be alreadie said in the defence
of sweete *Poetrie*, all concurreth to the mainteining the *Heroicall*, which
is not onelie a kinde, but the best and the most accomplished kindes
of Poetrie. For as the Image of each Action stirreth and instructeth
the minde, so the loftie Image of such woorthies, moste enflameth the
minde with desire to bee woorthie: and enformes with counsaile how
to bee woorthie.[22]

We recognize the heroic, then, by an attitude of elevation—
setting out Virtue in her holiday apparel; so also we recognize
comedy by an attitude of ridicule, satire by an attitude of correction, elegiacs by an attitude of compassion, and so forth.
This is the third feature of literary form to which Renaissance

  21. Puttenham, *Arte of English Poesie*, p. 45. Puttenham's division of the
kinds of poetry according to subject matter is found in bk. 1, chaps. 12–31.
  22. Sidney, *Defense of Poesie*, p. 22.

theorists have recourse, that feature which most clearly underscores their value-centered definition of literature itself. Not
incidentally, then, in defining the heroic by the values it maintains, Sidney reinforces the idea that the essence of literature
itself is in its expression of a moral interpretation of experience.
Similar definitions of literary "kindness" underlie much of
the criticism in the English tradition, so generally understood—
even assumed—that they need not be articulated precisely, as
they are in the Italian critical tradition.[23] Bacon, for example,
shares Sidney's definition of the heroic kind as having "a special
relation to human dignity," showing "that there is agreeable to
the spirit of man a more ample greatness, a more perfect order,
and a more beautiful variety than it can anywhere (since the
Fall) find in nature." Accordingly, of all literary kinds the epic
most conduces to "magnanimity and morality."[24] Similarly, Jonson rejects, somewhat defensively, the attitude typically assigned to comedy—that it ridicules or demeans—redefining the
form as a "corrective" genre closer in its values to satire.[25] Even
Puttenham's organization of the kinds suggests the interpretive
function of literary forms that, because they codify values, lead
us to "discover" the value in the experiences they define.

We can distinguish, then, three methods of generic classification at work in Sidney's *Defense* and also in other theorists
of the period: classification by formal properties to which prescriptive rules apply; classification by subject matter; and classification by generic attitude, the set of values a literary form
expresses, codifies, or preserves. We can now recast the varying

23. Italian theorists articulate a value-based definition of genre most frequently in their defense of literary experiments, particularly the romance. Vin-
cenzo Borghini, for example, argues that every literary form has an "idea" that
gives rise to its form; a modern epic may differ substantially from Homer's
because its "epicness" resides in a set of values rather than in forms. See *Prose
Fiorentine,* ed. Carlo Dati (Venice, 1740), pt. 4, pp. 283–284. Similarly, Mal-
atesta's elaborate defenses of Ariosto prefer the romance precisely because it
combines different perspectives on experience into a complete and varied view
of reality.

24. Francis Bacon, from *The Advancement of Learning,* bk. 2, chap. 13, in
*The Works of Francis Bacon,* ed. James Spedding, Robert Ellis, and D. D.
Heath (London, 1860), IV, 315–316.

25. Jonson, *Discoveries,* pp. 99–101.

constructions of genre offered in Renaissance literary theory into one synthetic definition that articulates the Renaissance commitment to a value-centered literature without deviating from the terms Renaissance writers themselves use. Such a definition would distinguish one genre from another by the way in which it expresses human experience (subject matter) through an identifiable form (formal character) that clarifies or discovers the values in or attitude toward that experience (generic attitude). This means of generic distinction accords proper weight to the third method of classification I have identified among Renaissance critics who, as Rosalie Colie has shown, view genre less as a codification of specific rules for composition than as a larger epistemological system, a way of seeing and interpreting the world, and expressing that interpretation in a coherent way.[26] In giving shape to human experience, genres represent the norms of human life through formal arrangements that, in turn, clarify those norms for writer and reader alike. In the broadest sense, genre is the moral form of literary art that distinguishes it from and connects it to human life.

This definition of literary form prevents generic identification from becoming purely taxonomic, making it contingent upon a critical reading of the text rather than an imposition upon it or an irrelevancy after the fact. Even as broad generic definitions in the Renaissance encourage writers to experiment with literary forms, recognizing genre as a cooperation of different kinds of generic features will liberate the critic into experimental readings. If we define a genre strictly in terms of its explicit and recognizable features, we are likely to push critical exploration no further than an effort to account for those features. If we see, however, that external features may proceed from subject matter or from a set of values, we have created a critical opportunity for examining the subtleties of literary texts.

26. Rosalie Colie, *The Resources of Kind* (Berkeley, 1973), esp. pp. 28–31. I accept Colie's argument that genres and genre systems in the Renaissance suggest this kind of epistemological perspective on experience; I argue here as well that those perspectives, which Colie discovers in the "idea" of genre or in the very pervasiveness of generic thinking in this period, are actually encoded into particular forms, that one form differs from another by virtue of the different perspective it allows or creates.

Similarly, if we restrict our definition of literary form to a description of external features, we are likely to overlook as intriguing generic forms those examples in which formal indicators are shadowy or diffuse. Even some poetic forms—the Renaissance epigram, for example—are difficult to categorize according to such an accounting of formal characteristics, and certainly many prose forms will not be forced into rigidly fixed molds. Where Renaissance critics emphasize one of these three elements at the expense of others, it seems an honest recognition that literary works fall into "kinds of kind": some genres have more rigidly organized external features while others are "informed" by subject matter or the set of values or attitudes they maintain. Without denying the necessary cooperation of these three elements, a principle of relative emphasis among them in our reading of texts will account more accurately for the real variety among literary works.[27]

Such a variety exists among nonfiction prose forms. Here, the range of possibilities extends from prose genres that have rigorously organized structures and highly codified external features to those whose forms are almost exclusively a function of attitude. If we recognize generic form, however, as a cooperation among qualitatively different kinds of generic indicators, we will encourage a more attentive critical reading of nonfiction prose, discovering generic attitudes in rigorously organized gen-

---

27. I share Alastair Fowler's conviction that "attempts to clarify literary genre founder in the confusion of treating all generic types as belonging to the same category" (*Kinds of Literature,* p. 54). In order to distinguish "kinds of kind," Fowler develops a "range of potential points of resemblance," which he calls the "generic repertoire" (see pp. 55–74). The "generic repertoire" I suggest here is far more limited than Fowler's, in part because this study is limited historically as Fowler's is not. Furthermore, Fowler uses his generic repertoire to group genres according to the features of the repertoire they share; although I have identified a more limited repertoire, I would argue that among Renaissance texts, those in the same genre will participate in the same points of resemblance, and that distinctions among kinds of genres develop out of varying relationships among these features. Such a system of relative emphasis seems particularly useful for describing nonfiction prose, genres that remain "marginal" in Fowler's system. Finally, I argue that these three features of the generic repertoire must exist in relationship to each other. In many cases the critical exercise comes from determining the nature of that relationship, how the three qualitatively different features cooperate to define the form itself.

res, and formal direction in those genres which more obviously
rely on or express attitudes. Recovering this broader definition
of genre can provide a means of generic analysis for certain
texts that have, under other generic systems, resisted that analysis. From this definition of genre, then, we can begin to identify
the conscious generic choices available to Renaissance prose
writers.

Toward defining those options, an anecdote in Puttenham's *Arte
of English Poesie* provides a place to start in its suggestion of
a theory of prose genres writ small. Puttenham tells the tale of
the knight of Yorkshire who, speaking before the queen and
the houses of Parliament, was ridiculed by a member of the
audience: " 'me thinks I heard not a better alehouse tale told
this seven yeares.' " Puttenham comments that this poor knight
did not make the proper distinction between an oration—suitably artful for the occasion—and "an ordinary tale to be told
at his table in the countrey."[28] In short, his choice of kind was
wrong. Like other theorists of the period, Puttenham implies
that literary art is a function of literary "kindness"; that generic
form is essentially social, establishing a connection between
writer and audience; and even that artful expression involves
creating a relationship among form, subject matter, and a set
of values. I now want to project the generic possibilities available to the conscious choice of the prose writers as the means
by which that relationship can be established. At the same time,
I want to suggest briefly the ways in which various generic features may cooperate to produce interesting and reliable generic
readings of these texts.

The recognition of an implicit theory of prose genres in Puttenham's remark is simplified by the fact that he refers to rhetorical performance—even more specifically to oratory, a literary
mode whose division into individual kinds developed in classical
schools of rhetoric. Given the literary status of rhetoric in the
Renaissance, the persistence of these rhetorical forms provides
one set of generic options for Renaissance writers. Many of the

28. Puttenham, *Arte of English Poesie*, p. 139.

prose works we continue to read as literature—Sidney's *Defense*
and Milton's *Areopagitica,* for example—represent Renaissance
instances of two classical genres of oratory (judicial and deliberative). Cicero had insisted that the various styles of oratory
distinguished the orator's purpose rather than his choice of kind—
that the low style advanced his teaching function, the middle
style his power to delight, and the high style his office to move
the audience—and this decorous mixture of styles remains true
of the formal character of texts we can identify as representing
oratory proper.[29] Written oratory in the Renaissance, then,
maintains the closest tie with the classical model and as such
has an easily recognized external form. Its subjects are the historically specific issues of the day; but in developing them, literary orations will commonly suggest attitudes toward those
subjects which reverberate for readers historically removed from
the immediate situation.

A generic theory which recognizes those values as an essential
feature of the form itself insures the specifically literary character of written oratory. In these instances it is not simply that
the work is literary if its style affords sufficient pleasure, or that
the work "becomes" literary only when it has outlived its practical usefulness, as Graham Hough would have us believe.[30]
Rather, the literary value inheres in the rhetorical form itself,
arising from the investment of form and subject with values that
make the work contiguous with human values as they have been
and continue to be experienced in the world.

The generic system represented in classical oratory creates
two other options for nonfiction prose writers: translation of
oratory proper into mock or ironic treatment, and the development of extended rhetorical forms. The first of these variations, as Alastair Fowler has suggested, indicates a natural
evolution for such forms.[31] The rigorous codification of oratory,
which allowed its incorporation into the ordinary lessons of the

29. Cicero's views are must fully developed in *De optimo genere oratorium*
and *Orator.*

30. Graham Hough, *An Essay on Criticism* (London, 1966), pp. 52–53.

31. Similar variations are treated under the topic "tertiary stages" in *Kinds
of Literature,* pp. 162–164. An earlier version of Fowler's description of typical
developments in the history of a genre, which identifies the mock or ironic form

Renaissance schoolchild, makes the form available for such ironic reduction—or expansion. Any number of mock encomia in the Renaissance indicate that mock rhetoric represents such a generic option. In these examples the subject matter is no longer a historically specific issue, but something more generalized. Using the rigid form of the oration for a satiric praise of beards, for example, a writer can ridicule the all-too-human tendency to follow unreasonably the dictates of whimsical fashion. Where the object of satire is the oratorical form itself, as is in part the case with Erasmus' *Praise of Folly,* mock rhetoric may satirize the foolish ease with which the human mind reduces the possibilities of choice to an either-or dilemma.

In addition to producing oratory proper or mock rhetoric, writers could modify or extend the generic system represented in classical oratory, adapting those forms to vernacular usage. What we might call extended rhetorical forms sort themselves out by stylistic character, developing a consistent style per kind. Rather than mix the three styles as Cicero had suggested, such forms isolate the particular level of oratorical style best suited to their purposes. Sixteenth-century sermons, for example, take over the patterns of organization developed in oratory proper but favor the plain style as best suited to their teaching function.[32] Similarly, the prose epistle develops from the genres of classical oratory, and epistolary manuals of the period translate the three oratorical kinds into specific epistolary kinds.[33] In these cases the derivation of extended rhetorical forms from oratory proper would insure the literary self-consciousness of their writers. Generally speaking, we can say that as such extended forms move away from the forms of oratory proper, they become increasingly less obvious in their external features and characterized more by the values they define.

---

in the "tertiary phase," appeared in *New Directions in Literary History,* ed. Ralph Cohen (Baltimore, 1974).

32. For an analysis of the preference of the plain style in sixteenth-century sermons, see John N. Wall, "The *Book of Homilies* (1547) and the Continuity of English Humanism in the Sixteenth Century," *Anglican Theological Review,* 58 (1976), 75–87.

33. See, for example, Angel Day, *The English Secretary,* ed. Robert O. Evans (Gainesville, 1976), pp. 1–11.

Recognizing a genre in the cooperation of form, subject, and generic attitude is particularly useful in creating access to the literary character of extended rhetorical forms. The familiar epistle, the most literary form of the letter, establishes a strong relationship among form, subject, and attitude. James Howell's *Epistolae Ho-Elianae* provides a ready example.[34] The formal character of these letters is essentially defined by Howell's experiments in the middle style, taken to be the most flexible for the range of the letters' subjects—not only philosophical speculation and intimate confession but also the discussion of those mundane details in which only his friends can be interested. From this cooperation of style and subject we can determine the generic attitude of these representative epistles: the celebration of friendship itself. In another kind, recourse to the definition of generic attitude will allow us to distinguish between the typical sixteenth-century sermon, like those included in the *Book of Homilies* (1547), and the seventeenth-century sermons of such writers as Donne and Andrewes.

Among the generic options for prose writers, then, we find oratory proper and the forms developing out of this generic system. Renaissance literary prose, however, extends well beyond those genres generated by rhetorical norms. In the broadened definition of mimesis we find direction for another kind of nonfiction genre, which—at the risk of some whimsy—we might call mimetic form. Minturno, whose influence on Sidney is well known, agrees with Aristotle that literature should imitate, but he finds the Aristotelian object of imitation, human action per se, too narrow and extends it to include "not only an imitation of life and manners, and an image of truth, and the semblance of all things both private and public; but also all kinds of knowledge, all the arts, all varieties of writings in abun-

34. Howell's letters, of course, were written self-consciously as literary letters; as such, they exhibit that peculiar combination of contrivance and intimacy—the contrivance, in fact, designed to imitate the values of intimacy—which has typified the form of the epistle since Cicero. Margaret Maurer's recent analysis of Donne's letters, however, which were written out of the ordinary circumstances of his life, would suggest a description of the form similar to the one I offer here. See Margaret Maurer, "The Poetic Familiarity of Donne's Letters," *Genre*, 15 (1982), 183–199.

dance."[35] If the definition of mimesis is broadened to include certain nonfictional forms, then the continued practice of those forms preserves—and further extends—that broadened definition. The clearest example of this dynamic exchange between theory and practice is the prose dialogue. Certain Renaissance definitions of mimesis defended Plato's *Dialogues* as literature; by extension those examples of the instructional dialogue which take Plato as their model (for example, Petrarch's *Secretum*, Walton's *The Compleat Angler*) share in that literary status. These "mimetic" prose texts exploit mimetic means—the creation of character, for example—for nonfictional purposes, to render what Minturno included in "all things both private and public" or "kinds of knowledge." Among Renaissance examples such prose kinds include the dialogue; the character; forms of biography and autobiography; the utopia; the travelogue; forms of satire that have as their basis the recreation of a social world or the mimetic realization of character; and the meditation, which usually begins in the imaging forth of a picture drawn from life.

In *The Compleat Angler* specifically, analysis of the relationship between the work's formal properties, governed by mimetic representation, and its explicit subject, knowledge of fishing, will reveal its generic attitude: a celebration of the civil life in which the exchange of ideas leads to the discovery of truth. According to Minturno's definition, even dialogues more explicitly instructional or didactic—colloquies, dialogues working out religious controversies—could be thought literary in intention by Renaissance standards. By the standards outlined here, however, such works will gain literary status only if we can demonstrate in them the cooperation of form and subject that generates an interpretation of experience and defines a generic attitude toward the norms of human life.

In terms of mimetic form, the Renaissance essay provides an

---

35. Antonius Minturno, *De Poeta* (1559), facsimile ed. (Munich, 1970), p. 9: "non modo vitae ac morum imitationem, & imaginem veritatis; rerumque omnium et privatorum, & publicarum simulcra; sed etiam omne genus doctrinae, omnes artes, omnes varitates locupletissime contineri."

interesting case. Both Montaigne and Bacon, the earliest practitioners of this form, recognized its inception in the epistle, a prose form whose ties to oratory are quite strong. But both Montaigne and Bacon, and most of the Renaissance writers who follow them, extend the essay beyond the limits of oratory, crossing this border into mimetic nonfiction. Oratory proper ends in a decision or a judgment; the orator typically urges his audience to accept a particular historical choice or a more general ethical position. These essays, however, either resist rhetorical decision altogether, as is the case with Montaigne, or submerge rhetorical choice, as Bacon tends to do, so as to distract our attention from it. In addition, the stylistic features typical of essays—their Senecan point, their usual method of conjunction (but, and, if), their aphoristic wit—and their inclusive content will suggest their connection to mimetic forms. A critical examination of these features will reveal that the Renaissance essay is essentially mimetic, taking as the object of imitation either the individual mind and the processes of its thought (Montaigne) or the "collective" mind and the value of its wisdom (Bacon). These two values are sufficiently similar to suggest that the differences between Bacon's and Montaigne's essays are not simply tonal—a function of the individual writer's attitude toward his subject.[36] Rather, an exploration of the object of imitation in each case will reveal differences in generic

36. We readily recognize the difference between "tone," the individual writer's attitude toward subject or audience, and generic attitude in those cases in which tone seems awkwardly adjusted to form. Certain passages in Chaucer's *Book of the Duchess,* for example, seem *tonally* inconsistent with the *attitude* we expect from an elegy. If genres viewed historically exhibit patterns of change, we can identify one such pattern in the ways in which an individual writer's tone is brought into generic attitude so as to be part of our definition of the form ever after. Where the writer's tone is particularly strong and well defined, especially if it expresses an attitude toward the form in which the writer works, that tone may alter our understanding of the form's generic attitude. Horace's affability, for example, and Juvenal's bitterness, two distinct tones, have been so subsumed into the generic attitude of satire, allowing us to distinguish two distinct subgenres of this larger type. Similarly, Milton's tone, his individual view of the subject and form of the epic itself, can be said to have been incorporated into the larger attitude of epic.

attitude, illustrating how examples of the same prose kind can vary the generic definition without obliterating the value of the category itself.

This account of the development of the essay, beginning in a rhetorical form but moving into a mimetic one, indicates a third option for nonfiction prose writers. Like poets and dramatists of the period, they have ample encouragement in both literary theory and practice to mix genres. In works of *genera mista*, combinations of genres will clarify and accomplish the writer's purpose. These combinations may be of various sorts: a simple combination of rhetorical kinds, a mixture of mimetic and rhetorical kinds, the infusing of one external form with the themes or values of another, the imbedding of two or more structures within a larger structure, the mixture of two or more sets of generic values, and so forth. In their new combinations, however, the genres must retain their articulated edges in order to provide direction for the reader as to the purpose that the writer's innovation attempts to serve. Again, only careful examination of texts will reveal such mixtures. At its most extreme, *genera mista* defines the great examples of encyclopedic works in the Renaissance—Burton's *Anatomy of Melancholy*, for instance, whose generic indeterminacy is a function of its comprehensive accumulation of generic forms and attitudes, some of them conflicting with each other. If I were to venture a statement of this work's generic attitude, it would be to celebrate—or satirize—the human and particularly Renaissance desire to say it all. But despite the apparent shapelessness of Burton's book, this attitude is nonetheless governed and chastened by his incorporation of generic forms.

Burton's *Anatomy*. Browne's *Religio Medici*. Sidney's *Defense*. Bacon's *Essays* or his *Advancement of Learning*. Walton's *Compleat Angler*. Milton's "left-handed" prose. Donne's sermons. These are all texts we value. Too often, however, they have been explored only for their historical interest; or, in particular cases, they have been studied for the access they provide to more obviously literary texts by the same authors. Milton's *Areopagitica*, for example, becomes a prose sketch for the pre-

sentation of free will in *Paradise Lost,* or Donne's *Death's Duel*
is seen to corroborate the high-strung intensity of the holy sonnets. Even when we feel these prose works to be essentially
literary, we cannot always articulate *why,* except through subjective identification of a "literary" style. But if a literary style
is in part the cause of literary excellence, it is also the effect of
a literary intention. And we recognize the beginnings of a literary intention most effectively in the author's choice of generic
form. Recovering a value-based definition of literature itself—
and defining genres in part through the values they codify or
express—can insure fuller readings of Renaissance prose, which
in turn will reveal its essentially literary character. What is more,
applying the definition of genre suggested here may also allow
us to discover the literary value in less well known texts of this
period. Freed of Puttenham's social prejudices, which would
expect outlandish behavior from a Yorkshireman, we might
even discover a literary motive—if not a literary talent—in that
misunderstood knight whose alehouse tale might have invested
country matters with values fit for the hearing of the queen.

CLAUDIO GUILLÉN

# Notes toward the Study
# of the Renaissance Letter

The reasonable thing to do, when writing a brief article, or even a book, is to limit the subject to a field that can be effectively surveyed or thoroughly researched. But there are moments when a crying need exists for the overview and the probing questions of general relevance, even though they may seem hasty or premature. The epistle, I think, is such a case. Its varied appearances during the Renaissance, in prose or in verse, as fictions or as samples of supposedly real correspondence, have led to a number of isolated investigations. It would be tempting to pursue a comparative study of the poetic epistle alone, which is itself underrated, in my opinion, and poses what may be interesting questions from the angle of genre theory. But its connection with other sorts of correspondence, and in general with that awareness of the letter that is so characteristic of the Renaissance, and of the processes that will elevate epistolary literature to new peaks in Europe during the sixteenth and seventeenth centuries, is a problem that cannot be much longer

70

avoided. I shall try and approach these broad developments here, if only in the form of notes.

The letter may be regarded as one of the classical genres that are cultivated again or resurrected during the Renaissance. I allude to that quality or phenomenon of regeneration—"reaching into the past," in René Wellek's words—that is a peculiar feature of the history of literature; Claus Uhlig calls it *Palingenese* in his *Theorie der Literarhistorie*. This seems true of the verse epistle, to which Garcilaso de la Vega, for example, returns in the 1530s, as he does to the elegy and the eclogue, just as Thomas Lodge, in England, cultivates the epistle, the eclogue, and satire in 1595: *A Fig for Momus*. But this observation does not apply to the familiar letter in prose, nor to the association of letter writing with rhetoric, which made possible the medieval *ars dictamini,* as well as some comparable manuals during the sixteenth century. What we see in such cases is a swelling tide, a continuing development, whose origins go back a great many centuries. The connections between these various kinds should doubtless be questioned. And it could be useful to recall what some of these kinds were in the first place. In the meantime, it will be helpful to keep in mind that our topic is heterogeneous enough, and that we are talking about the simultaneous progress of more than one temporal flow in the period under consideration.[1]

The field is huge, and it becomes necessary to distinguish among at least seven kinds of writing, each of which can be seen as following its own career and rhythm of development. (1) The neo-Latin prose letter, central in the history of Humanism (Erasmus). At the same time there is a revival of interest in the classical Latin epistolographers: Cicero, Pliny the Younger. Es-

---

1. See R. Wellek, "The Fall of Literary History," in R. Koselleck and W. D. Stempel, eds., *Ereignis und Erzählung* (Munich, 1973), p. 439; C. Uhlig, *Theorie der Literarhistorie* (Heidelberg, 1982), pp. 63–69.

pecially the *Epistolae ad diversos,* or *familiares,* of Cicero, re-
discovered by Petrarch, go through numerous editions following
the in-folio volumes in Rome, 1467, and those by Aldo in 1502,
1512, 1522, and so on, and the critical edition of 1540. (2) The
prose letter in the vulgar tongue: Pietro Aretino and Fray Antonio de Guevara. Here one might wish further to subdivide
the form into fictional and nonfictional epistles; but the distinction is problematic in practice and can be regarded at times
as irrelevant or superficial. Suffice it to recall now that volume
after volume of vernacular letters will first be published in Italy,
while the fictional uses of the form will emerge and flourish in
Spain. (3) Following Petrarch's *Epistolae metricae,* the neo-Latin
verse epistle: Janus Secundus, Petrus Lotichius, Kaspar Ursinus
Vellius, and many others in numerous European countries, from
Scotland to Croatia and Hungary. The verse letter is closely
allied and at times confused with the elegy, satire, and other
poetic genres. This *contaminatio* is essential to the career of the
genre during the Renaissance, as we shall see in a moment.
Horace is of course the principal model for the subgenre of the
"moral epistle," which is central and exemplary. But the paradigmatic role of the neo-Latin poems will also be significant
until the seventeenth century; for example, in Germany: Opitz.[2]
(4) The verse epistle in the vernacular tongues, which will have
an intermittent history. I allude mostly to a crucial wave in the
1530s: Luigi Alamanni (*Opere toscane,* 1532), Clément Marot
(*Suite de l'adolescence Clémentine,* 1533), Garcilaso de la Vega
("Epistola a Boscán," 1534), and Sir Thomas Wyatt too—if we
admit the *contaminatio* in some of the satires, to John Poins,
or to Francis Bryan—and a little later Sá de Miranda in Por-
tugal. England will have a second wave, from Lodge in 1595 to
Donne and Jonson (*The Forest,* 1616). In France, shortly after
Jean Bouchet's *Epistres morales et familières* (1545), Du Bellay
and the *Pléiade* will turn their backs to what they considered
an overly informal and playful genre—in other words, to Marot.
The next great poet writing epistles in French will be, on the
contrary, an admirer of Marot: La Fontaine. (5) The tradition

2. See M. R. Sperberg-McQueen, "Martin Opitz and the Tradition of the
Renaissance Poetic Epistle," *Daphnis,* 11 (1982), 519–546.

of the theory of the letter, which goes back to Artemon's lost preface to the letters of Aristotle and, among extant Greek treatises, to a highly interesting excursus in Demetrius' *De elocutione*. The passage from the *ars dictamini* of the Middle Ages to the Humanist treatises of the late fifteenth and sixteenth centuries—from Erasmus to Lipsius, to mention but two outstanding figures—has been thoroughly studied. A most valuable volume was printed in Basel in 1547, joining Erasmus' *De conscribendis epistolis* (first published in 1522) to three other treatises, similarly titled, by J. L. Vives, K. Celtis, and K. Hagendorf. It may well be that insufficient attention has been paid to the impact of this theoretical tradition, singularly rich during the sixteenth century, on literary practice and, in general, on the Renaissance awareness of the letter. (6) Practical manuals for letter writing, which may in some cases merge with the tradition I have just mentioned, though they normally seem as distinct from theory as a cookbook does from a meditation on the aesthetics of taste. Largely a commercial venture, this sort of volume was probably seen by editors as a way of reaching a growing literate class, particularly after the middle of the sixteenth century and the rise of the letter itself as publishable literature. I refer to the more than twenty *Segretari* published in Italy before 1600, following Francesco Sansovino's *Segretario* of 1564;[3] and Gabriel Chappuys' *Le Secrétaire, comprenant le stile et méthode d'escrire en tous genres de lettres missives* (1568); or Angel Day's *The English Secretorie, or plaine and direct Method, for the editing of all manner of Epistles, or Letters* (1586).[4] The Italian-type manual for the "Secretary" is not, however, the only kind of practical textbook, nor the earliest one: witness Gaspar de Texeda's important *Libro de cartas mensajeras en estilo cortesano* (Valladolid, 1549). (7) Letters inserted within other genres, providing us with further testimony of what I have been calling the Renaissance awareness of the letter, as

3. See K. T. Butler, *"The Gentlest Art" in Renaissance Italy: An Anthology of Italian Letters, 1459–1600* (Cambridge, 1954), p. 19.

4. I have seen the 1595 edition, *The English Secretorie: Or, plaine and direct Method, for the editing of all manner of Epistles or Letters, as well Familliar, as others . . . The like whereof hath neuer hetherto beene published* (London: by R. I. for C. Burbie).

in Gargantua's letter to Pantagruel, or Hamlet's to Ophelia
(read by a third person—I shall return to this characteristic
indiscretion), or Don Quixote's to Dulcinea, or the final correspondence in Lily's *Euphues.*

Subsidiary though they may seem, these uses confirm the
status of the letter as literature; and in the case of the pre-
novelistic Spanish narratives of the late fifteenth and sixteenth
centuries, there is a clear progression in the importance of these
epistolary insertions and in the room they occupy. These range
from the so-called sentimental novels of Diego de San Pedro
and Juan de Flores, first published during the 1490s and widely
translated in Europe (for example, San Pedro's *Arnalte y Lucenda,* 1491, which had ten editions in French from 1539 to
1560, as *L'Amant mal traicté de s'amye,* and several in English
after 1543 and in Italian from 1553), to the first purely epistolary
novel, where the letters of two lovers take over the whole story,
Juan de Segura's *Proceso de cartas de amores* (1548), and, finally, to the presenting or framing of an entire narrative in the
form of an epistle, as in *Lazarillo de Tormes* (1554). The confes-
sional device was to be found in Boccaccio's *Fiammetta;* and
the injection of letters into a long narrative, in the Byzantine
romances by Heliodorus and Achilles Tatius, as later in the
celebrated *Historia de duobus amantibus* (1444) of Aeneas Sylvius Piccolomini. What we observe, once more, is a groundswell
during the Renaissance. The interpolation of letters will become
a narrative convention: in the pastoral novels by Montemayor,
Alonso Pérez, and Cervantes, who includes ten letters in his
*Galatea;* in the stories of "Moorish" content, or *novela morisca,*
like the early *Abencerraje* (circa 1560), where letters delineate
character and further the plot in a decisive manner; and, for
that matter, in the romances of chivalry themselves, starting
with the Catalan *Tirant lo Blanch* (1490), where no less than
thirty letters also contribute to the main action. Doubtless we
shall have to reflect on the connections between the letter and
the rise of the modern novel.


These developments enjoyed the support—although at times it
could also have been a hindrance—of the underlying theory of

the letter. Let us say that whether a convergence of theory and practice actually takes place or not, an awareness of theoretical points is often noticeable in the writer, and to such an extent that this consciousness—as will later occur with the novel— appears to be characteristic of epistolary literature. Garcilaso's epistle to Boscán, the first verse epistle of the Spanish Renaissance, begins with these lines:

> Señor Boscán, quien tanto gusto tiene
> de daros cuenta de los pensamientos,
> hasta las cosas que no tienen nombre,
> no le podrá faltar con vos materia,
> ni será menester buscar estilo
> presto, distinto, de ornamento puro
> tal cual a culta epístola conviene.
> Entre muy grandes bienes que consigo
> el amistad perfeta nos concede
> es aqueste descuido suelto y puro,
> lejos de la curiosa pesadumbre . . .

> Señor Boscán, he who has such pleasure
> in giving you an account of his own thoughts,
> even of things that have no name at all,
> will not lack subjects in addressing you,
> nor will there be a need to seek a style
> swift, clear, pure of ornament
> as befits an epistle of the cultured kind.
> Among the very great benefits that with itself
> are granted by a perfect friendship
> there is this carefreeness, loose and pure,
> far from any diligent gravity . . .

The theoretical tradition that is alluded to here is so rich that it becomes impossible to point to any specific origin for Garcilaso's references to the choice of subject matter *(materia),* style, clarity, swiftness, and looseness *(descuido suelto),* or for the uses of friendship as a framework in which the topic and the style may conveniently fit. Pliny in practice limits each letter to one theme; and Sidonius Apollinaris recommends this limitation (6.18). Cicero's comments were common knowledge in Garcilaso's time, such as the distinction *(Fam.,* 4.2) between the various *genera epistolarum:* "unum familiare et iocosum,

alterum severum et grave." Erasmus and Vives open up the
question considerably, allowing any theme at all—"quas-
cumque res potest continere," states Vives[5]—as long as it is
appropriate to the addressee and the occasion. *Brevitas* and/or
*claritas,* or *perspicuitas,* are required by nearly all theorists,
from Demetrius (231) to Quintilian (3.3.8), Pliny (epists. 7, 9,
16), Gregory of Naziance (epist. 51), and especially the *Rhetoric*
of Julius Victor (fourth century), who writes: "in familiaribus
litteris primo brevitas observanda," and "lucem vero epistolis
praefulgere oportet . . . ut his, ad quos mittuntur, clarae per-
spicuaque sint."[6] E. R. Curtius makes much of the ideal of
brevity ("Kürze als Stilideal") in the medieval *ars dictamini,* for
example, of Albericus Casinensis.[7] Erasmus, ever inclined to
see both sides of an argument, weighed the virtues of *perspicuitas,* which he tended to favor, against those of *obscuritas,*
both terms being relative to the knowledge of the reader: "quod
huic obscurum est, illi dilucidum est."[8] After Garcilaso's day,
later in the sixteenth century, the terms will not change. Angel
Day, in Lodge's time, demands "brevity"; and John Hoskins
too (1599), who plundered Justus Lipsius' *Epistolica institutio*
(1590).[9] Ben Jonson will in turn appropriate Hoskins in his
*Discoveries,* including the "perspicuity" and "brevity"[10] that
Jonson the poet mentions, as Garcilaso had, at the start of an
epistle ("To Master John Selden"; 1614):

> I know to whom I write. Here, I am sure,
> Though I am short, I cannot be obscure.

5. J. L. Vives, *De conscribendis epistolis,* in *Opera omnia* (Valencia, 1782),
II, 269.
6. *C. Iulii Victoris ars rhetorica,* chap. 27, "De epistolis," in Carolus Halm,
*Rhetores Latini minores* (Lipsiae, 1863), p. 448.
7. "Post salutationem exordium inibis, post exordium narrationem promov-
ebis, que sic erit honesta, sic brevis fuerit et clara," in E. R. Curtius, *Europäische
Literatur und lateinisches Mittelalter* (Bern, 1948), p. 483.
8. Erasmus, *De conscribendis epistolis: Anleitung zum Briefschreiben,* ed. K.
Smolak (Darmstadt, 1980), p. 34.
9. See J. Hoskins, *Directions for Speech and Style,* ed. H. H. Hudson (Princeton, 1935), s.v. "For Penning of Letters," p. 4.
10. See B. Jonson, *Explorata: or Discoveries,* in *The Complete Poems,* ed.
G. Parfitt (Harmondsworth, 1975), p. 440.

As for the notion in Garcilaso of open-ended or loose structure, it goes back also to Demetrius (229), "The structure of a letter should be loose," and to Quintilian (9.4.20), who admits the convenience in a letter of an *oratio soluta.*

I shall add, in remembrance of this continuing theoretical tradition of a thousand years, some remarks on three points made by the Demetrius or pseudo-Demetrius who wrote *Peri hermēneías,* or *De elocutione* (second century B.C.?), often known in the Renaissance as "Demetrius Phalareus."

The first is a response to Artemon, who edited Aristotle's letters and proposed what became a frequent *topos* in epistolary theory: the idea that the letter is a halved dialogue, or part of a conversation with an absent friend. I shall return later to the themes of friendship and absence. What matters now is the conversation. In Erasmus' words, "epistola absentium amicorum quasi mutuus sermo."[11] Vives does without the *quasi:* "epistola est sermo absentium per litteras."[12] A letter, repeats Angel Day, is "the familiar and mutuall talke of one absent friend to another."[13]

In a recent study Alain Viala not only quotes but adopts the venerable commonplace by citing the definition of the letter by an author of a seventeenth-century manual, Vaumorière—"un écrit envoyé à une personne absente pour lui faire savoir ce que nous lui dirions si nous étions en état de lui parler"—and adding on his own as follows: "la lettre est donc un substitut de la parole, un *discours,* au sens défini par E. Benvéniste, c'est-à-dire un acte de communication privilégiant la manifestation du rapport entre celui qui s'exprime et le destinataire. Substitut de pratiques orales de la conversation et de l'éloquence, l'art épistolaire présente les mêmes subdivisions que celles-ci . . ."[14]

Benvéniste is scarcely needed here—Derrida would be more

11. Erasmus, *De conscribendis epistolis,* p. 44.
12. Vives, *De conscribendis epistolis,* p. 263.
13. Day, *English Secretorie,* p. 8.
14. A. Viala, "La Genèse des formes épistolaires en français et leurs sources latines et européennes: Essai de chronologie distinctive (XVIe–XVIIe s.)," *Revue de littérature comparée,* 55 (1981), 168.

to the point—in order to avoid the obvious trap, namely, thinking that the letter is a substitute for speech not through change
but in the analogical fashion of a replica. Writing, an activity
generating its own dynamics and irretrievable consequences,
obviously does not coincide with speech. This was precisely the
thrust of Demetrius' comment upon Artemon (in G. M. A.
Grube's version):

223.   . . . Artemon, who edited the letters of Aristotle, says that letters and dialogues should be written in the same way, for a letter is
like one side of a dialogue.

224.   There may be something in what he says, but it is not the whole
story. A letter should be written rather more carefully than a dialogue.
Dialogue imitates impromptu conversation, whereas a letter is a piece
of writing and is sent someone as a kind of gift.

Demetrius made the essential point. Today Genette indicates
in his analysis of narrative that the only place in a story where
mimesis does not replace narrated experience with language,
where words imitate words and not things, is dialogue. A letter
does not reproduce a dialogue either fully or in part, except
when it quotes one. In the history of our civilization letters have
signified a crucial passage from orality to writing itself—or a
practical interaction between the two. As écriture, it begins to
involve the writer in a silent, creative process of self-distancing
and self-modeling, leading perhaps, as in autobiography, to fresh
knowledge or even to fiction.

Demetrius in his excursus stresses also that the letter is a gift
and an exercise in friendship. Commentators suggest that he
may have been indebted, within the peripatetic tradition, to the
evaluation of friendship in the works of Theophrastus and of
Aristotle himself. There is no doubt but that the formal and
thematic functions of friendship have been, as a matter of fact,
fundamental in epistolary literature. During the Renaissance
the "moral epistle" in verse is really a footnote to the achievement of Horace. The framework of the epistle in Horace is the
friendly advice given by an older man to a younger man who

is not as advanced as he is in the long road to experience and wisdom. The enveloping feeling and practice of friendship make possible the epistolary persona—the formulation of counsel without didactic pride—and, above all, the attachment of existential and concrete features to what otherwise might be abstract moral philosophy.

In this tradition the relationship is normally masculine. Garcilaso writes to Boscán about the generosity of friendship among men—unmixed with "madness,"

> que no es locura este deleite mío—

while standing near the grave of Petrarch's Laura. The celebrated opening of an epistle by Donne is directed to a man, Sir Henry Wotton:

> Sir, more than kisses, letters mingle Soules;
> For, thus friends absent speake.

Women are not excluded as correspondents by Donne or Jonson. But when writing to them the letter swerves (with some exceptions, like Donne's "To the Countess of Bedford")[15] from the thematic breadth of the Horatian model and tends to concentrate on love or on the nature of woman. It becomes a letter to a woman rather than, more generally, to a friend, and it is certainly not about friendship itself, a favorite topic of the verse epistle, as in Ben Jonson's "An Epistle to a Friend"[16] or "To Master Arthur Squib":

> Then rest, and a friend's value understand:
> It is a richer purchase than of land;

or as in Garcilaso's epistle to Boscán, which is taken up mostly by a discourse on friendship, based on book 8 of the *Nicomachean Ethics*.

                    *        *        *

15. Beginning "T'Have written then, when you writ, seem'd to mee / Worst of spirituall vices, Simony . . ."
16. Beginning "Sir, I am thankful, first, to heaven, for you . . ."

D. J. Palmer is barking up, I think, the wrong tree when he states that the verse epistle calls for "the low, or familiar style."[17] It is most instructive once again to turn to Demetrius, who—having described earlier not three but four levels of style—makes the following prophetic comment:

235.   In general, the style of a letter should be a mixture of two styles, the elegant and the plain.

Let us reread Ben Jonson's "To Master John Selden" or Francisco de Aldana's "A Benito Arias Montano," and it will be clear that the informality of the letter permits considerable flexibility and, as in rhetorical discourse, the resources of eloquence, meditation, and wit. These ups and downs, from the concrete and rich vocabulary of satire to the lofty metaphors of religious feeling, are characteristic of the moral verse epistle. To perceive in it a single level of style is as limiting as it would be in the case of a novel like *Don Quixote*. The main point is that the Renaissance letter makes an important contribution to the dissolution of that strict division into styles *(Stiltrennung),* according to genre, on which Auerbach placed so much emphasis in his *Mimesis*. This is a sign of the tension existing between the letter—and other "new" genres of the Renaissance—and the orthodox institutions of literature.

The truly peculiar characteristic of the verse epistle, the original feature that allows us to begin to make sense of the large field that I surveyed at the start of these notes, is what it has in common with other letters: that it presents itself as writing. In that sense, it is not lyrical poetry. It is not language creating its own space and situation for the reader, or words sung—potentially—for an audience, or heard by the mind's ear, or attracting attention merely to themselves. It is writing proclaiming itself as writing in the process of correspondence.

It becomes helpful, in order to grasp this peculiarity, to recall an elementary dimension of genre theory: the distinction be-

17. D. J. Palmer, "The Verse Epistle," in *Metaphysical Poetry,* Stratford-upon-Avon Studies 11 (London, 1970), p. 73.

tween genre and radical of presentation. By radical of presentation (Northrop Frye's term) I have in mind Goethe's *Naturformen der Dichtung—Epos, Lyrik,* and *Drama*—which he differentiated from the historical list of more limited and precise *Dichtarten* or genres; except with two qualifications on my part: that the basic radicals of presentation, or of communication, are not necessarily natural or unchanging but are, rather, conventional and socially conditioned "long durations" (in Braudel's sense); and that there are more than three. There were more than three since legendary times: together with story-telling, rhythmic song, and dramatic stimulation, there was also monologic discourse. If the radical of presentation derives from a channel of communication in a particular society, the question becomes: which are, in a particular historical period, the real, viable, established, radical channels of communication? It could be said that historiography, philosophy, and scientific discourse were radicals of communication. Or journalism in our time. Suffice it to recall here a less arguable notion: that letter writing has been, from the beginnings of Mediterranean civilization, a radical of presentation. Hence its profoundly primitive quality—a quality that is reborn, so to speak, for every human being who practices and experiences it as the basic hinge between orality and writing. Hence also its highly conventional character, visible since antiquity in the worn and yet indispensable formulas of salutation, apology, recommendation, farewell, and the like, on which both the humble letter writer and the sophisticated poet depend.

During the sixteenth century we observe a notorious growth of both the social practice of correspondence and the printing of books incorporating that practice as a channel of communication, while also providing models that in turn enrich and stimulate actual letter writing. This is a persuasive instance, it seems to me, of the interplay between literature and social life during the Renaissance.

An item of poetry or of prose can be identified, then, as an epistle, or as approximating an epistle, insofar as it presents or declares itself or functions as writing and as correspondence. A poem dedicated to the Earl of Woosex, or addressed to the eyes of Amarillis, is not an epistle at all unless the mental relationship

with the person in question is indivisible from the conscious
process of writing. D. J. Palmer is puzzled by this and thinks
that Jonson's transforming through the verse letter of the conventions of the "complimentary poem" makes it impossible
henceforth to distinguish between complimentary verse and
epistle.[18] I share the puzzlement but not the conception of genre
as descriptive taxonomy on the part of the literary historian of
today. Let us think for a moment of the epistle as a conceptual
model belonging to the ideal spaces of poetics, and of the poem
as an activity taking into consideration that model, but in practice not coinciding with it fully, or only in some degree, and
not without reference to other paradigms, through either acceptance or rejection. A piece of writing can be a hybrid; and
to the question of its generic definition the answer need not be,
as in a law court, either yes or no. A poem can be more or less
of an epistle; and the degree of its epistolarity, as I have just
suggested, derives from its commitment to writing and to correspondence as the underlying radical of presentation. Thomas
Lodge is aware of this dimension as he willfully revitalizes the
verse epistle in English in *A Fig for Momus,* through rather
obvious devices. One example is the reply ("To Master W.
Bolton"):

> Bolton, amidst thy many other theames
> Thou dost desire me to discourse of dreames:
> Of which, what I would gather, reade, or find,
> I here set downe to satisfie thy mind.

Another is the reference, by means of learned circumlocution
(an epistolary convention), to the chronology of the correspondence ("To his deere friend H. L."):

> That verie day wherein the sunne began
> To visit Aries, by the Scot thy man
> I did receiue thy letters: and with thease
> Thy guifts which in this world no better please,
> Thy letters, I with letters doe reward.

When put to this test, only a fraction of Donne's verse letters
make tangible use of the epistolary radical of presentation—

18. Ibid., p. 75.

the sense of place and time, the ability to imagine the other, the willingness to let the words affect the words, process and improvisation as form—but I would venture saying that the best do; and one wonders why the pretense of the letter appears in other cases. In Spain the more illustrious verse epistles, Aldana's to Arias Montano and the "Epístola moral a Fabio," now attributed to Fernández de Andrada, are unequivocally epistolary. Thus the final quatrain of Aldana's poem, which rounds off the earlier *terza rima:*

> May our Lord sow in you his grace
> to gather the glory of his promise.
> From Madrid the seventh of September
> fifteen hundred and seventy-seven.
>
> Nuestro Señor en ti su gracia siembre
> para coger la gloria que promete.
> De Madrid a los siete de setiembre
> mil y quinientos y setenta y siete.

Could it really have been 7 September 1577? The inner rhymes and repetitions—*siete, setiembre, setenta y siete*—could not be more timely. The soberness of tone—following a long religious meditation and also a rich description of seascape—the precision of detail, the hard consonant rhyme and falling cadence, the lifting up to necessity of a completely contingent and trivial date and place are, I think, powerfully effective. It is the very proximity of the epistle to prose, its unwillingness to seduce, or its self-denial as lyric that can produce at times first-rate poetry. But the effect of these prosaic moments is relative to others of different tonality and elevation, within the flexibility of styles—beyond *Stiltrennung*—that I pointed out earlier.

I am emphasizing the letter as a sort of language in which a particular quality of written communication is palpable. Yet at times it cannot be denied that the position of the author vis-à-vis writing is equivocal and that certain features of orality are contained within the message, not as an imitation of a conversation but as the use of a literary resource, analogous to the exhibiting of a voice in a narrative. I mention this as a possible

explanation for the merging on so many occasions of epistolary
theory with rhetoric. This occurred not only in the medieval *ars
dictamini* or *dictandi*, developed by Alberico of Monte Cassino
(eleventh century) and later the school of Bologna (Guido Faba),
applying to the letter the five canonical parts of oratorical discourse,[19] but to some extent in texts of the sixteenth and seventeenth centuries. I say to some extent because, though the
rhetorical terms are retained by the Humanist theorists, from
Francesco Negri (*Ars epistolandi*, Venice, 1488) and Konrad
Celtis (*Tractatus de condendis epistolis*, Ingolstadt, 1492) to
Erasmus (1522) and Vives (1533), one should not underestimate
the ways in which the last two bend, adapt, and ultimately break
the monistic aims of rhetoric: to offer a single and universal art
of writing. Erasmus states that the language of a letter should
adapt itself to the addressee and the subject as a *Polypus* does
to a particular soil, or as Mercury could appear in any dress—
as long as the language is pure, educated, and reasonable.[20]
And Vives, who goes further in refining what has been called
the psychology of letter writing, its appropriateness to the social
class, profession, culture, sex, and character of the correspondent, abandons the notion of any fixed order of discourse: "ordo
in epistolae corpore nullus est certus."[21] Alain Viala takes up
the rhetorical categories that are maintained in seventeenth-
century authors like Vaumorière—the three *genera:* judiciary,
deliberative, and demonstrative.[22] But I would submit that this
is characteristic of what I included at the beginning of these
notes as a sixth class of publication: practical manuals of letter
writing. Mostly, this sort of applied theory remains rhetorical.
Such is the case with Angel Day's *English Secretorie* (1586).[23]
One might think that the alliance of rhetoric with epistolary
guidebooks is due to a common concern with the passage from
orality to writing, and all the more so when the intent is largely

19. See Charles Faulhaber's introduction to Juan Gil de Zamora, *Dictaminis
epithalamium* (Pisa, 1978).

20. See Erasmus, *De conscribendis epistolis*, p. 38.

21. Vives, *De conscribendis epistolis*, p. 291.

22. See Viala, "La Genèse des formes épistolaires," p. 169.

23. Day distinguishes, in chap. 7, between "demonstrative, deliberative,
judiciall, and familiar" letters (p. 20).

didactic. The epistolary skills are viewed then as a basic introduction to literacy.

The letter as literacy, as writing committed in fact, if not always
in theory, to its own potentialities and peculiarities as writing,
had tended, since at least classical times in Greece, toward
fictionality. This is the essential legacy that will evolve and fruc-
tify during the Renaissance.

Heiki Koskenniemi, in a splendid study of the Greek letter,
says that it is usually impossible or irrelevant in Greece to distinguish between the real and the literary letter.[24] The real letter
can be stiff, or pretentious, or artificial, or insincere. The literary
one may appear more spontaneous, or friendly, or even intimate. Adolf Deissmann's attempt to differentiate a natural *Brief*
from an artificial *Epistel*—an aftergrowth of the Romantic terms
*Naturpoesie* and *Kunstpoesie*—turns out to be dependent on
external evidence. Whether Seneca's concern for Lucilius is
feigned or authentic has no bearing on the experience of the
reader, who is not Lucilius and can only respond to the effectiveness of friendship and the epistolary form of presentation
as a device of communication. This device, of course, has been
used to convey a variety of moral, philosophical, and learned
messages, from Epicurus and Seneca to the Christian epistle
and the "philological letter" of Alexandria and the Renaissance
humanists.

The author of a real letter may be mirroring and shaping
through the written word a particular version of himself, a particular moment of an interpersonal relationship, a particular
aspect of his future—and of his correspondent's. This coefficient
of creativity and imagination is like an élan that the fictional
letter needs only to extend and multiply, as obviously Rousseau
and Richardson will in their epistolary novels. But, in order to
achieve this effect, the fictional letter pretends that it is not
fiction and thus imitates the conventions of ordinary correspondence.

24. See H. Koskenniemi, *Studien zur Idee und Phraseologie des griechischen
Briefes bis 400 n. Chr.* (Helsinki, 1946), p. 50.

This pretense and this imitation of the letter by the letter have been practiced for pedagogical, stylistic, and literary purposes since the beginnings of Mediterranean civilization. A. Falkenstein has analyzed a Sumerian letter addressed, before 1500 B.C., to Nonna, the moon goddess; and O. R. Gurney, an epistle found in Sultantepe and fictitiously attributed to the hero Gilgamesh. In 1925 Adolf Erman published, in his edition of *Papyrus Lansing*—Egyptian papyri of the twelfth century B.C. discovered in a tomb in Thebes from the twentieth dynasty—a collection of ten literary epistles that were school exercises. These exercises imply the existence of models, conventions, and themes—imagined situations like "I arrive in a great city and describe its beauty"—that were imitated time and again.[25]

In Athens fictional letters were composed in schools as rhetorical training since at least the end of the fourth century B.C., according to Franz Susemihl, though later scholars like Koskenniemi propose a later date—first century B.C.—for the exercises or *Progymnasmata* that Nicholas of Myra describes in his collection thus titled. The student would place himself in different situations, or write as if he were a well-known figure of the past, in order to try his hand at different styles.[26] It is not surprising that such training led during the Hellenistic period to the cultivation of the fictional letter as literature—by Alciphron, Aelian, or Philostratus, to mention the more illustrious authors—and to the only Greek novel in letters that is extant, *Chion of Heraclea* (first century A.D., according to I. Düring). Many of these letters—fictional, fictitious, or fraudulent—were edited by Marcus Masurus for the *editio Aldina* of 1499 in Venice. Other editions would follow, which witness to the growing interest of publishers and readers in various kinds of letters.[27] As the sixteenth century opens, the popularity of Ovid's fictional

25. See A. Falkenstein, "Ein Sumerischer Brief an den Mondgott," *Analecta Biblica*, 12 (1959), 69–77; O. R. Gurney, "The Sultantepe Tablets. VI. A Letter of Gilgamesh," *Anatolian Studies*, 7 (1957), 127–136; A. Erman, *Die ägyptischen Schulhandschriften* (Copenhagen, 1925), p. 14.

26. See Koskenniemi, *Studien*, p. 29.

27. See I. Düring, ed., *Chion of Heraclea: A Novel in Letters* (Göteborg, 1951); A. R. Benner and F. H. Fobes, eds., *The Letters of Alciphron, Aelian and Philostratus* (Cambridge and London, 1949).

verse epistles, the *Heroides,* was very considerable too—a fact that must be stressed as well if we are to grasp both the *contaminatio* among poetic genres and the movement of the letter toward fictionality during the Renaissance.

Epistles, elegies, and verse satires touch one another, intermingle or merge so often in sixteenth-century poetry that some critics have had trouble making sense of the apparent confusion. Jay Arnold Levine, writing more than twenty years ago on the English verse epistle before Pope, nearly threw in the towel:

Ranging as they do from chatty dinner invitations to full-blown critical and moral disquisitions, the Horatian epistles cannot be conveniently categorized by such simple criteria as theme and/or form, unlike pastoral or satire, which can be identified by subject matter (as well as by stylistic and structural elements), or the ode, elegy, and epigram, which must conform to certain formal requirements. As Trapp suggests, therefore, the verse epistle should probably be viewed not as a genre in its own right, but as a manner of writing adaptable to such fixed forms as the elegy and the satire.[28]

The phenomena of *contaminatio,* as I began saying in a previous note, cannot be grasped by a purely descriptive attitude toward genres, based on either/or assumptions and the hope that each poem can be assigned to a particular slot or box. Only a historical approach can do justice to the interplay *in illo tempore* between the paradigms of the poetics of the period and the practical choices of poets.

Early sixteenth-century poetics, to be sure, were in a state of flux, as its theoretical spaces were being reconstituted under the impact of Aristotle or of the rereading of Horace and Plato; and we have to wait, in the case of the verse letter, until Lodovico Dolce's brief "Discorso sopra le epistole" of 1559.[29] There

---

28. J. A. Levine, "The Status of the Verse Epistle before Pope," *Studies in Philology,* 59 (1962), 660.

29. This "Discorso" is a brief epilogue to Lodovico Dolce's translations, *I dilettevoli sermoni, altrimenti satire, e le morali epistole di Horatio* . . . (Venice, 1559), p. 316. Dolce distinguishes sharply between the satires and the epistles: "nelle Satire fu la sua intentione di levare i vitii dal petto de gli huomini, e in queste di piantarvi le virtù."

were signs, in this transitional period, of hesitation and disarray, as well as of discovery and innovation, which were certainly fruitful for the generation of Marot, Wyatt, and Garcilaso.

The theoretical space that the author of verse letters faced, one might say, was a triangle formed by three adjoining genres: the verse epistle, the elegy, and the verse satire. The elegy and the epistle could be regarded as having a premise in common: the need to confront or suppress an absence. Satire could be considered as cultivating the opposite: the need to deny or suppress a presence. But I do not have to think that these contacts are due to the structure of the human brain. Let us recall briefly some decisive historical developments.

The *contaminatio* of verse epistle and verse satire follows above all from the example of Horace. His epistles practice already the fusion of the two, as they relapse time and again into the thematics of satire. Latinists have had some difficulty in dealing with this simple fact,[30] for the same reasons that I have just indicated à propos of the English verse letter. As Horace opens a new collection of poems, in which the *sermo* uses the radical of presentation of the letter, he makes clear to Maecenas that his intent is to pursue the good and the true (1.1), "quid verum atque decens, curo et rogo et omnis in hoc sum," while leaving behind his previous occupations, in keeping with his change of age and mind: "Non eadem est aetas, non mens . . ." The older poet, in short, will write epistles and seek the positive guidance of moral philosophy. It is not enough to chastise and denounce vice and error. The epistolary poet is an ex-satirist. At least this is his declared purpose.

If the verse epistle becomes the countergenre of satire, what will occur in fact is that they imply and involve each other. In practice Horace's letters will make room frequently for the satirical posture. Innumerable generations of readers have noticed and appreciated the turns, jolts, antitheses, anticlimaxes, and sudden changes that are characteristic of these poems. Ideas, Guillaume Stégen shows, are arranged "par groupes de deux

30. A classical article was G. L. Hendrickson, "Are the Letters of Horace Satires?" *The American Journal of Philology,* 18 (1897), 313–324.

qui forment entre elles des contrastes, des oppositions."[31] If the
epistle is a typically Horatian chain of oppositions and polarities,
the main, all-embracing opposition confronts an "epistolary
principle," rooted in the pursuit of moral philosophy, with a
"satirical principle." The search for truth must refer to the
existence of error. It may be necessary, in order to attain the
moral good, to preserve the memory of falsehood and social
make-believe and to feel that minimum of anger without which
wisdom places itself too far from the world of human beings.
Thus the genre and the countergenre will mingle and even coincide, in the Horatian tradition of the Renaissance moral epistle.

The encounter of that tradition with an Ovidian model is the
condition for the *contaminatio* of verse epistle and elegy during
the sixteenth century. We should keep in mind, first of all, that
the *Heroides* themselves—fictitious letters written by women
who have been forsaken by their famous lovers: Dido to Aeneas,
Briseis to Achilles, and so on—are elegiac and, in some degree,
epistolary. Then, in Ovid's exile poetry the dynamics of the two
genres can be observed: the *Tristia* and *Epistulae ex Ponto* use
the elegiac meter; but the *ex Ponto* poems, where the exiled
poet yearns elegiacally for Rome, for his lost center and absent
culture, are mostly epistolary in form, while the *Tristia* elegies
only begin on a few occasions to function as letters—to traverse
space and return to Rome. The success of the *Heroides* at the
end of the fifteenth and beginning of the sixteenth centuries was
indeed considerable. More than forty editions were printed before 1500. In France Octovien de Saint-Gelais translates since
1496 the *XXI Epistres d'Ovide,* a book that was edited twenty
times between 1500 and 1550 and led, above all, to the "heroides" by Marot. The Latin love elegy (including Ovid's) had
inspired Marot, as Salmon Macrin and Luigi Alamanni also did.
But soon after the first version of *L'Adolescence Clémentine,*

31. G. Stégen, *Essai sur la composition de cinq epîtres d'Horace* (Namur,
1960), p. 6. As to the Odes, see Steele Commager's comment on *Carm.,* 1.5,
in his *The Odes of Horace* (Bloomington and London, 1967), p. 65: "the Ode
progresses through the antithetical similes and metaphors, and its logic lies in
terms of the various tensions it maintains."

Marot wrote "L'Epître de Maguelonne," which is a "heroid."[32]
The *Epistres morales et familières* of Jean Bouchet (1545) will
proceed to include both Horatian epistles and Ovidian fictional
letters. I mentioned earlier that the application of new Renaissance poetics to the various poetic genres or subgenres would
have to wait some decades. In France at the middle of the
century the fusion or confusion was remarkable. Thomas Sébillet writes in 1548: "pren donc l'élégie pour épistre amou-
reuse."[33] Between 1553 and 1560 Ronsard will compose numerous
elegies—like the splendid "Elégie sur le trépas d'Antoine Cha-
teignier, poète élégiaque"—and in the second edition of his
collected works, in 1568, the elegies are gathered in a separate
section. The following lines will appear in the posthumous edition of 1587:

> Les vers de l'Elégie au premier furent faits
> Pour y chanter des morts les gestes et les faicts,
> Joincts au son du cornet: maintenant on compose
> Divers sujets en elle, et reçoit toute chose.

In Spain Garcilaso himself wrote a brief poem recasting the
ending of the seventh *Heroid* ("Pues este nombre perdí, / Dido,
mujer de Siqueo . . ."), and there are numerous traces of the
Ovidian models in Hurtado de Mendoza, Francisco de Aldana,
and the poems in Cervantes' *Galatea* (the epistle "De Timbrio
a Nísida"). But what I find most interesting is the effect of the
Ovidian fictional letter on the long prose narrative. Juan Rod-
ríguez de la Cámara translated the *Heroides* and also wrote *El
siervo libre de amor*. The highly popular *Arnalte y Lucenda* by
Diego de San Pedro (1491) owes, in Keith Whinnom's expert
opinion, a great deal to Ovid.[34] So will, in a way, Juan de
Segura's epistolary novel (1548). An original sort of fictionality,
one might think, was perhaps latent in the letter. Could the

32. See, on this subject, V. L. Saulnier, *Les Elégies de Clément Marot* (Paris,
1952); and C. M. Scollen, *The Birth of the Elegy in France, 1500–1550* (Geneva,
1967).

33. T. Sébillet, *Art poétique françoys*, ed. F. Gaiffe (Paris, 1932), p. 155.

34. See K. Whinnom, *Diego de San Pedro* (New York, 1974), "The beginnings of the epistolary novel," pp. 68 ff.; and C. E. Kany, *The Beginnings of
the Epistolary Novel in France, Italy, and Spain* (Berkeley, 1937).

"heroid," in which the author and the reader identify with legendary or imaginary persons found in Homer or Virgil or other great poets, be viewed in a sense as prequixotic?

The geographical dimensions of our subject are variable enough, as we proceed from one century to another. At times the area within which the letter fulfills its function, as remote correspondents maintain their verbal network, is markedly international. On other occasions it is the focusing effect of a national language that is most effective. But the final outcome, when all is said and done, is the supranational existence, as a social and creative mode of communication, of the modern prose letter.

From Petrarch to the first third of the sixteenth century, the neo-Latin letter enjoys an exceptional development, which, like the learned communications in Greece of an Epicurus, and later the Christian epistle, reaches far-flung correspondents in distant lands. The models are Cicero, Pliny, Petrarch himself, later Poliziano, and others. An ideal of friendship—quite conscious in Guillaume Budé, who honors Cicero's *De amicitia*—and the pursuit of scholarship join these men, who share items of philological or philosophical knowledge, erudite commentaries, travel descriptions, the incidents of vanity, and fluctuations of fame. The results, relatively coherent, go on to reach new readers through the printing press and reach a peak, *grosso modo,* from 1510 to 1540, that is, the years during which the correspondence of Erasmus stands out and prevails. The Latin letter, of course, will be cultivated much longer—as the Humanist and philological letter will also, in other languages. But the scene has to be shared with ever more popular rivals. The dates I have just given contain a number of simultaneous evolutions. The first half of the sixteenth century, in fact, encompasses the continuing success or the rise of the reedited Greek and Latin epistles, the theoretical treatises, the Humanist letter, the Ovidian and Horatian paradigms, the verse epistle in sundry languages, the *lettere volgari* in Italy, the fictional epistle and novel in letters in Spain.

The process includes a spatial concentration, through the sharpened awareness of nationality and the uses of the national

languages. But this geographical restriction is more than coun-
terbalanced by the expansion of the reading public, by new
strata of readers whom the vernacular letter was able to attract.
Blasco de Garay, the author of a short collection of letters made
up of proverbs that was very popular in its day, *Cartas en refranes* (Toledo, 1541), asserts in his preface that he is appealing
not to the learned but to the readers of *La Celestina* and "similar
things"—probably meaning popular fiction: "no tanto a los muy
bien doctrinados, cuanto a los que no suelen leer sino Celestina
o cosas semejantes."[35] Initially this occurred in Italy and Spain.

There is little I can add to the general knowledge of the
triumphant rise of the vernacular prose letter in Italy, which
was swift, unstoppable, and quite extraordinary. The controversy regarding the *questione della lingua,* in which Pietro Bembo
played a central role, supported this sudden ascent during the
third decade of the century. The pioneer was Pietro Aretino,
whose first volume appeared in 1537. Five volumes of his letters
in Italian were published during his lifetime; and a sixth, post-
humously, in 1557. Aretino opened the floodgates of the genre,
as new writers and publishers profited from his example and his
success: from Claudio Tolomei (1547) and Bembo himself to
Anton Francesco Doni, Annibal Caro, Torquato Tasso (1558),
and innumerable others. The boldness and vivacity of Aretino
seemed to make available to the reader, without excessive artistic embellishments, the common and sometimes rough experiences that were normally confined to the *novella* or to comedy.
Will the wealth of detail, the self-exhibition, the pride in anecdote and adventure, the dramatic assertion of individuality
by these writers (and others elsewhere, like Fray Antonio de
Guevara) contribute decisively to the rise, soon to follow, of
the essay?[36] At any rate, Montaigne was familiar with them.
"Ce sont grands imprimeurs de lettres," he notes, "que les
Italiens. J'en ay, ce croy-je, plus de cent volumes."

35. J. del Val, ed., *Processo de cartas de amores . . . y Cartas en refranes de
Blasco de Garay . . .* (Madrid, 1956), p. 113.
36. There is a useful summary of the issue in Gerhard Haas, *Essay* (Stuttgart,
1969), pp. 7–8. Hugo Friedrich thought that the letter was the formal origin of
the essay, and dialogue that of its style of thought (p. 6).

These could indeed have been more than a hundred.[37] I am referring to a time when the commerce of books and the initiatives of publishers began to influence the career of literature. The starting point was clearly Venice, where Gabriele Giolito, who published the last volumes of Aretino's correspondence, edited also Tolomei's and, in 1554, an anthology entitled *Lettere di diversi eccellentissimi uomini,* whose success followed that of the often reedited collection of Paolo Manuzio, *Lettere volgari di diversi nobilissimi uomini e chiari ingegni* (1542) in three volumes. Giolito, profiting from the popularity of the genre, published in a single volume in Spanish the epistolary novel by Juan de Segura and the letters in proverbs by Blasco de Garay, *Processo de cartas de amores que entre dos amantes pasaron . . . Assimesmo hay en este libro otras excelentissimas cartas que allende de su dulce y pulido estilo, estan escriptas en reffranes traydos a proposito* (1553). The simultaneous interest of this alert Venetian editor in the Italian vernacular letter and the Spanish fictional epistle may seem representative of the convergent developments that I am discussing in these notes.

The vogue in France and England of these letters has been studied with care. One can observe, as in Italy, a double process of nationalization and expansion of the reading public. In France the verse epistle, Ovidian or Horatian (the *Grands rhétoriqueurs,* Marot), and the Humanist letter in Latin appear half a century at least before the vernacular letter in prose. The latter genre, according to Alain Viala, is born between 1550 and 1580,[38] in derivative fashion. It will not yield important results until another half-century: Guez de Balzac (1624). The first French manual is published in 1555 in Lyon, *Le Stille ou manière de composer, dicter et escrire toutes sortes d'épistres ou lettres missives;* and the first Italian letters to be translated are, in 1556, the *Lettres amoureuses* of Girolamo Parabosco, which will be followed by many others, such as an anthology by Girolamo Ruscelli, offered in 1572 as *Epistres des princes.* In the meantime a relatively original collection of prose letters had been written

37. See T. K. Butler, introduction to *Anthology of Italian Letters.*
38. Viala, "La Genèse des formes épistolaires," p. 182.

by Etienne du Tronchet, *Lettres missives et familières,* published
in 1569 and reprinted some thirty times between that date and
1623. Du Tronchet expresses in the preface his unbounded admiration for his Italian models. If today, he asserts, one can
approach a multiplicity of topics in French, if one can

> discourir de la guerre, des factions, d'une cavalerie, d'une infanterie,
> d'une écuyerie, des armes, voire de l'amour, et généralement de toutes
> choses graves et ordinaires, les plus beaux traits des plus disertes langues
> qui se veulent faire ouïr, sont en plupart épuisés dans les propres
> facultés de l'Italie.[39]

And I might add one more title, an instance, if I am not mistaken, of the *contaminatio* of the Italian and the Spanish influences on the French letter, *Les Épistres argentées* of Claudio
Tolomei (1572); for one of Guevara's versions had been called
*Les Épistres dorées,* as in England also the *Golden Epistles,* in
G. Fenton's translation, which had a great success. In England
the origins and the chronology are quite similar to those in
France, leading during the second half of the sixteenth century
to collections of translated, or original, or also fictional letters,
as in A. Fleming's *Panoplie of Epistles* (1576), an anthology of
Latin and neo-Latin examples (Cicero, Isocrates, Erasmus, P.
Manutius, K. Celtis, Vives).

In Spain the career of epistolarity was quite literary from the
start and amounted progressively, as I have already suggested,
to a powerful impulse in the direction of fiction, either in the
form of self-inventive epistles or of novels built on letters. Although Spanish Humanists, like Juan Luis Vives and Juan Ginés
de Sepúlveda (*Epistolarum libri septem,* Salamanca, 1557) cultivated the Humanist letter in Latin, with or against Erasmus,
whose *De componendis epistolis* was published in Alcalá in 1525
and 1529, letters in the vernacular tongue appeared earlier rather

39. *Lettres missives et familieres d'Estienne du Tronchet, secretaire de la royne
mere du roy* . . . (Paris, 1569), s.f., "Au lecteur de bonne volonté." See also
Janine Basso, "Les Traductions en français de la littérature épistolaire italienne
aux XVIe et XVIIe siècles," *Revue d'histoire littéraire de la France,* 78 (1978),
906–918.

than later. I do not allude to private letters of the sort that were collected many years after, but to the *Cartas* of Hernando del Pulgar (1485; reedited in 1498) and the *Epístolas y tratados* of Mosén Diego de Valera. These writings, closely allied to the annals and histories of the kingdoms of Enrique IV and Juan II, are testimonies and commentaries on public topics, most of all, by chroniclers and moralists—"memoriales, disertaciones y arengas políticas disfrazadas en forma epistolar,"[40] says Valbuena Prat of Valera. This is not as yet the pliant, variegated letter, improvised and open to many aspects of daily life. But the epistolary form is functional, I think, in Pulgar's delineation of exemplary models of behavior. A process of literarization has begun, parallel to the use of the epistle in the sentimental novel and other kinds of fiction. The letter in Spain will be an instrument, a springboard, a device for the liberation of the critical imagination, either in poetry or in prose. It will not be a real person, like Aretino, self-inventing in part, who asserts his individuality, but a fictional character pretending to be real, like Lazarillo de Tormes. Epistles will serve to criticize obliquely, or transcend, the limiting environment of social and personal life. Such is the process, quite unstoppable too, that one observes between 1520 and 1560.

I have spoken already of the love story called by Spanish literary historians *novela sentimental,* and of its appearance during the last decade of the fifteenth century: Diego de San Pedro's *Arnalte y Lucenda* (1491) and *Cárcel de amor* (1492), and Juan de Flores' *Grimalte y Grandissa* (1495) and *Grisel y Mirabella* (1495). During that same decade Saint-Gelais translates in France the *Heroides* and, in 1493, Aeneas Sylvius' very popular *Historia de duobus amantibus,* which contains ten letters. The role of letter writing in the furtive advancement of the affair of a closely guarded lady with her lover is prominent in the Spanish novels, like *Cárcel de amor,* translated as *La Prison d'amours* in Paris, 1526 (reedited in 1527, 1528, and 1533) and again in 1552 (reprinted in 1556, 1560, and 1567). As for Spain itself, Agustín Redondo points out, in his book on Fray Antonio de Guevara,

40. A. Valbuena Prat, *Historia de la literatura española* (Barcelona, 1957), I, 392.

that a second wave of popularity of the *novela sentimental* took place in the 1520s. The *Cárcel de amor* is reprinted in 1522, 1523, 1525, 1526, and so on—Redondo thinks as a consequence of the return of the emperor and the reanimation of courtly life. *Arnalte y Lucenda* appears in 1522 in Burgos, and also the *Cartas y coplas para requerir nuevos amores*. These "cartas de amores" prepared the way, in Redondo's opinion, for the exceptional success of Guevara's *Marco Aurelio,* parts of which circulated in manuscript form, before the first publication in 1528.[41] The epistles contained in the *Libro áureo de Marco Aurelio* are of moral and satirical character at first and only slowly build up, around the figure of the Roman emperor, something like an epistolary-historical novel, as Francisco Márquez Villanueva has shown.[42] Hernando del Pulgar's letters are reprinted that same year, 1528. And, curiously enough, Guevara proceeds from the apparently historical but fictional epistles of Marcus Aurelius to his supposedly real but largely rhetorical and self-creating *Epístolas familiares* (1539, 1541), which became immensely popular all over Europe. The reception of Guevara's various kinds of epistles—often rearranged and mixed freely by his translators—does not need to be retold here; and I shall only quote the words of eulogy with which Edward Hellows presents his translation in 1574—one of a great many editions—of *The Familiar Epistles of Sir Antony of Guevara,*

Containing rules so general for all estates, so furnished with Philosophy, uttered with so rare eloquence, with antiquities so aptly alleged, and with the perfect practise of strange histories so plentifully performed, that it seemeth no thing is omitted, or that any thing may be added.[43]

41. See A. Redondo, *Antonio de Guevara (1480?–1545) et l'Espagne de son temps* (Geneva, 1976), p. 494.

42. See F. Márquez Villanueva, "Marco Aurelio y Faustina," *Insula,* 28 (1972), 3–4.

43. *The Familiar Epistles of Sir Antony of Gueuara, Preacher, Chronicler, and Councellor, to the Emperour Charles the fifth, Translated out of the Spanish toung, by Edward Hellows, Groome of the Leash* . . . (London: Raufe Newberry, 1574), p. iii. The next year, 1575, the same Newberry prints, for Henry Middelton, Geffray Fenton's version of Guevara's *Golden Epistles* . . .

Hellows' comments remind us of the fact that, whatever our opinion may be today of Guevara, his writings, regarded as a kind of handbook of rhetorical forms, moral or historical *exempla,* and memorable tales, attracted and fascinated a large number of his contemporaries. Guevara reached a very vast public through the fresh, insolent, and innovative freedom— writes Francisco Márquez Villanueva—with which he deviated from medieval conventions and also from the restricting rectitude of the Humanists:

Porque Guevara era, antes que nada, un espíritu creador en plena libertad, un revolucionario práctico que rompía con la cultura literaria de la clerecía medieval en la misma medida en que se apartaba de las ideas oficiales del humanismo renacentista.[44]

The two best-selling genres of the period were, it seems to me, the long narrative—sentimental novel or romance of chivalry— and the prose letter. And there is every reason to think that Guevara reached this new and larger audience. I shall only make a critical comment about his letters: that what I have termed the epistolary radical of presentation is very much in evidence. Guevara, as Asunción Rallo has remarked, is constantly aware of the existence of his correspondents, who appear frequently by means of vocatives, appeals to their attention, gifts, and responses.[45] Above all, the familiar epistle tends to be a reply. "Escribísme, Señor, que os escriba . . ."(1.10); or "Escribisme que os escriba qué es lo que siento del embajador de Venecia . . ."(1.15); "Mandaisme que os escriba . . ."(1.16), and so on. Such formulas prepare for the communication of news, characteristic of the *carta noticiosa* or newsworthy letter that Cicero described (*Ad Quintum fratrem,* 1.1.13; *Ad fam.,* 2.4).

The first epistolary novel, Juan de Segura's *Proceso de cartas de amores* (1548), simply reduces a love story to the correspondence between the lovers, both of whom write letters. These are, then, replies, as when "Captivo," the young man, begins:

44. F. Márquez Villanueva, *Espiritualidad y literatura en el siglo XVI* (Madrid, 1968), p. 56.
45. See A. Rallo, *Antonio de Guevara en su contexto renacentista* (Madrid, 1979), pp. 264–268.

"Escribísme, mi señora, que no sois servida que más os escriba . . ." The conventional formula returns in *Lazarillo de Tormes* (1554), whose author goes quite a bit further. The entire narrative is a reply, demanded by a "Your Grace" or *Vuestra Merced,* who had first written the narrator asking him for news of his "case," as the famous words of the prologue make quite clear: "Y pues Vuestra Merced *escribe le escriba* y relate el caso muy por extenso, parecióme no tomarle por el medio, sino del principio, porque se tenga entera *noticia* de mi persona."

*Lazarillo de Tormes,* of course, is the proto-picaresque tale, to be followed by Alemán's *Guzmán de Alfarache,* which Cervantes in turn counters with his proto-novel, *El ingenioso hidalgo Don Quijote de la Mancha.* One could submit that *Lazarillo* is like a bridge spanning the distance between the Renaissance letter and the novel.

Students of English literature tend to think that the rise of the novel is an eighteenth-century phenomenon. Although they do not ignore Cervantes, *Don Quixote* does not fit their scheme and is rather vaguely assigned the status of predecessor. If these specialists can be made to realize that Cervantes' masterpiece is rooted in the rich humus of the previous century—the real or fictional letter, the sentimental tale, the epistolary novel, the romance of chivalry, the picaresque, and the like—these notes may serve a useful purpose.

With respect to the impact of the letter on subsequent developments, I would propose, in closing, two observations. First, obliged though we are by the conditions of analysis to limit ourselves in our study to a single topic, in this case an isolated literary kind, we could remember that a literary kind is structurally related to a constellation of models, constituting the options, differences, and choices of the literary system of the period. The vernacular letter in prose belongs to a group of what might be termed—arguably—minor genres of the Renaissance, the others being dialogue, autobiography, and the forms of nonfictional prose leading to the essay. What they may have had in common is not for me to ask now. The instituted classical "radicals of presentation"—epic, lyrical, dramatic—

were not sufficient for the writer willing to confront ample regions of human living and feeling: either the opulent New World recently discovered, beyond the Atlantic, or the humble and endlessly rich regions of inner, individual, daily experience. The Russian formalists thought of literary systems as zones of conflict and combat between established, canonical genres and those intent on dethroning them. This neo-Romantic conception, well adapted to the nineteenth century and the avant-garde prior to World War I, cannot be applied to the Renaissance without important qualifications. Both zones of the system, the instituted and the innovating, are prosperous and produce results of great value. But there is a significant tension between them, promoting the rise of such original genres as the novel and the essay, in contact with new classes and masses of readers.

We have observed, secondly, throughout these notes, the connection between the letter and the imminent ascent of the novel. I wish to stress that I do not have in mind a one-to-one influence or filiation, whereby a single genre in a historical system A is the source of another genre in a later system B or C. Most important in each situation is the function that the particular genre fulfills within the formal and thematic repertory of the system to which it belongs. I would much rather ask: what functions do we recognize in the Renaissance vernacular letter that would later adhere to the novel?

I suggest the following, of which several have already appeared in these notes. (1) The dissolution of the separation of styles according to genre *(Stiltrennung)*. (2) The theoretical self-questioning of the letter as an acceptable kind of writing—implying a critical attitude toward the established canons and institutions of literature. (3) The saturation of individuality and near-autobiographical impulse—not always leading to introspection and the intimacy of the self. Suffice it that noncomical prose should admit daily living, the singularity and interest of the simplest acts, the *relicta circunstantia* scorned by nobler genres, and a profusion of things. (4) The primacy of the moment in which what is seen, felt, or told occurs; that is, the fragmentation of time. Like the novel later—precisely the epistolary novel in particular—or the diary or the *reportage,* the letter provides us with the illusion of a vital present from the

angle of the present, and with that of an open and perhaps
unpredictable future. (5) The adequacy of ideas to the apprenticeship of an individual, who tests their relevance to day-to-
day living.

Finally, and (6), let us take note of what Aretino and Guevara
had in common: indiscretion. Gossip, rumors, and fresh news
abound about persons and events external to the relationship
between the correspondents. What is more important, the reader
is an accomplice. Will not the letter be read by numerous persons for whom the information was not intended? From Cicero
to Guevara—who protests, as convention requires, that he never
meant his epistles to be published: "confieso a nuestro Señor
que jamás escribí carta con pensamiento de que había de ser
publicada" (preface to the *Epístolas familiares*)—we notice what
I have observed elsewere, on the subject of dialogue: the double
intentionality of language.[46] The words of a dialogue are really
meant for three, at the very least (and those of a monologue
for two). The same may be said of the letter, though with a
difference, for dialogues presuppose usually a public space and
the directness and enveloping involvement of speech, while letters or epistles imply, more often than not, solitude, separation,
silence, privacy, or even secrecy. The question then comes up
of the relatively open and comprehensive character of letters,
of their topics and addressees, in the case of a Cicero, a Pulgar,
or Erasmus and Aretino and Guevara themselves, writing as
public figures to powerful men and women. The equivocal triangle, the latent voyeurism that I allude to here—the only innocent participant being the original addressee of the letter—
exists or increases in the exact degree in which the moral or
newsworthy epistle becomes so familiar and private as to be
lacking apparently in general interest and only be of concern
to immediate friends and near relatives. What was intended to
be read, in principle, is actually reread; and, most important,
reread by others. Literary letter reading has to be the rereading
of curious minds. Hence the proximity, when intimacy is shared,
not of dialogue but of autobiography and of the forerunners of

46. See C. Guillén, *Entre lo uno y lo diverso: Introducción a la literatura
comparada* (Barcelona, 1985), pp. 202–203.

the essay. When this individual discovery of the other is carried to the terrain of fiction, what is being obviously played is one of the roles of the future novel. Both genres are substitutes and supplements of personal experience. Ideas about human nature in general, no longer sufficient, are qualified by the anxious access to alterity. Writing, in Italy and Spain and then other nations, becomes the conveyor of this knowledge. First of all, I argue here, through letters and epistles. Such is the indiscreet charm of epistolography.

## II  Genre and Literary History

ALASTAIR FOWLER

# The Beginnings of
# English Georgic

Perhaps unfortunately for our understanding of Renaissance
literary history, English georgic has mostly been discussed by
critics of Augustan literature, from an eighteenth-century perspective. John Chalker is representative in ascribing the appeal
of georgic to the Augustan analogy of its post–Civil War occasion and in holding that "although the *Georgics* began to affect
English literature in important ways as early as Denham's *Cooper's Hill* (1642), the most significant phase of its influence did
not come until after the turn of the century."[1] According to the
received idea, georgic developed very late in England, the decisive stimulus coming from Dryden's 1697 translation of Virgil's
*Georgics*, which was published together with Addison's essay
on the genre. From its own standpoint this account is coherent
and sound—although unable, we should notice, to do more than
concede the awkwardly early date of *Cooper's Hill*, paradig-

1. John Chalker, *The English Georgic* (London, 1969), p. 17; cf. Dwight L.
Durling, *Georgic Tradition in English Poetry* (New York, 1935), pp. 5, 14.

matic as that work is. What literary historians have felt the need
to explain is English georgic's lateness. And a learned article
by Anthony Low has attributed that to aristocratic prejudice
against demeaning labor. He finds, in the later seventeenth
century, a gradual amelioration of this, reflected in agricultural
reform and in proposals for a college of husbandry.[2] This essay,
however, argues that the Augustan conception of georgic has
no standing in the earlier period, and that if we think in terms
of Renaissance generic conceptions, English georgic will seem
less belated.

Low is aware of Tusser's *Five hundreth points of good husbandry* (1573) but treats it as an exception to the rule of gentle-
manly disinclination. He reminds us that Christopher Johnson,
teaching his class at Winchester Virgil's *Georgics* in 1563,

felt obliged to warn them not to despise agricultural labor . . . In a
hierarchical society it was proper for a schoolboy or an agricultural
laborer to work hard, but not for a full-grown man of the educated
classes. "Goe chide / Late schoole boyes, and sowre prentices," Donne
tells his intrusive taskmaster, the sun; "Call countrey ants to harvest
offices."[3]

But Donne's sour prentice was quite likely to be the younger
son of a gentleman, like Quicksilver in *Eastward Ho* (1605),
while Johnson's warning was conventional in its high valuation
of industry.[4] It was in the later seventeenth century, in fact, that
the upper classes were tending to grow more remote, and superior to honest toil. Bacon urged his practical georgic vision
of empire as early as 1605, and Ralegh earlier still.[5] The gardening books of the Elizabethan and Jacobean periods communicate an impassioned prophecy of the whole earth as a
potential garden, cultivable through efforts of husbandry. Rich-

2. Anthony Low, "New Science and the Georgic Revolution in Seventeenth-
Century English Literature," *English Literary Renaissance,* 13 (1983), 231–259.
   3. Ibid., p. 233.
   4. See T. W. Baldwin, *William Shakspere's Small Latine and Lesse Greek*
(Urbana, 1944), I, 327, 331.
   5. See Low, "New Science and the Georgic Revolution," pp. 245, 251–253,
citing 1625 texts; also William A. Sessions, "Spenser's Georgics," *English Literary Renaissance,* 10 (1980), 236, citing *The Advancement of Learning.*

ard Surflet strikes a typical note: "there is never a precept of paynefull toyle and laborious husbandrie throughout the Whole Booke, but it soundeth an alarum and proclaimeth an open defiance against thee as a Sluggard."[6]

Throughout the first Protestant century, indeed, writers were revaluing practical work as a sphere for Christian obedience. Luther found it necessary to take up the question "whether we all ought to be farmers or at least work with our hands," opposing the fundamentalism of some readers of Genesis 3:19 and introducing the idea of mental labor.[7] Just as today (although for very different reasons), the work ethic was a matter of dispute. The Protestant reformers stood for work and the active life, as against what they saw as the mere observances of "idle Monkes." Thus Ascham speaks of the monastic ethos as an "ydle and blynde kinde of lyuynge," and Lyly of "Abbaie lubbers" who "laboured till they were colde, eat till they sweate, and lay in bed till their boanes aked."[8] England was committed, at least in theory, to an austere course of industrious labor. And enthusiasm for Virgil's *Georgics* was by no means lacking: Sir John Harington in 1591 thought it so well written "that I could find it in my hart to drive the plough."[9] Strange, then, that the values of work and active life should not have been embodied

6. Cited by Terry Comito, *The Idea of the Garden in the Renaissance* (New Brunswick, N.J., and Hassocks, Sussex, 1978), p. 197; see also pp. 16, 19, and esp. 20. Cf. John Prest, *The Garden of Eden: The Botanic Garden and the Re-Creation of Paradise* (New Haven and London, 1981); and see Paul H. Johnstone, "In Praise of Husbandry," *Agricultural History*, 11 (1937), 86: "agricultural literature flourished greatly in the latter third of the sixteenth century" but "tended generally to decline through the seventeenth"—except in England, where output continued.

7. Jaroslav Pelikan, ed., *Luther's Works*, trans. George V. Schick, vol. 1 (St. Louis, 1958), pp. 211, 212; cited by Sessions, "Spenser's Georgics," p. 236.

8. Roger Ascham, *English Works*, ed. W. A. Wright (Cambridge, 1904), p. 230; cf. Bacon, *The Advancement of Learning*, cited by Sessions, "Spenser's Georgics," p. 236. Ascham, *English Works*, p. xiv; cf. Thomas Nashe, *The Anatomie of Absurditie*, in *Works*, ed. R. B. McKerrow and F. P. Wilson (Oxford, 1966), I, 11: "the fantasticall dreames of those exiled Abbie-lubbers, from whose idle pens . . ." John Lyly, *The Complete Works*, ed. R. W. Bond (Oxford, 1902), I, 250.

9. "A Briefe Apologie of Poetrie," in *Elizabethan Critical Essays*, ed. G. Gregory Smith, 2 vols. (Oxford, 1904), II, 207.

in georgic poetry rather than pastoral, the genre of contemplation or ease. It seems that recourse to the historical context—
to real-life attitudes—makes the problem of georgic's lateness
more acute, not less so.

Perhaps a more internal approach may help, through genre
history itself. The fact to be explained, we recall, is the lateness
specifically of English formal georgic. Now, formal imitation
(that is, lexical imitation *in extenso* of a classical author or work)
itself constitutes a quasi-generic form, with its own so to say
intramural history. And it too is an Augustan form, beginning—
for all target genres but one—only in the mid-seventeenth century. For it necessarily depended on conscious focusing of individual words, which in turn came about only through the
general epigrammatic transformation earlier in the century.[10]
By a series of stages not to be abrogated, imitation of Martial
and other Latin satiric epigrammatists was first extended, by a
natural step, to satire; then this local imitation developed, in
Oldham and Rochester, into formal imitation of whole satires;
and finally formal imitation became generalized among other
kinds. The first parallel text of a formal imitation was not printed
until 1691.[11]

Augustan ideas of English georgic centered on imitation of a
single work. It was a specifically Virgilian tradition—and necessarily so, since it dealt in close imitation of familiar passages.
The only considerable exceptions are Diaper's and Somerville's
subsidiary use of the Oppians' *Halieuticon* ("On Fishing") and
*Cynegiticon* ("On Hunting").[12] As for Hesiod, he was much too
simple and homely for those taught by Addison to look for
"pomp" and elevation. (Addison could even disparage Hesiod's
seminal digression on winter: "Thus does the old gentleman
give himself up to a loose kind of tattle."[13] Modern critics have

10. See Alastair Fowler, *Kinds of Literature* (Cambridge, Mass., and Oxford,
1982), pp. 222 ff., and index, s.v. "Epigrammatic modulation."
11. I am grateful to Dr. M. C. Phillips for this information. See John Wilmot,
Earl of Rochester, *Poems . . . on Several Occasions . . .* (London, 1691), pp.
108–113, where Ovid's Elegy 9 is printed in parallel with an imitation of it.
12. See Chalker, *English Georgic,* index, s.v. "Oppian."
13. "An Essay on Virgil's *Georgics*" (1697), in *Eighteenth-Century Critical
Essays,* ed. Scott Elledge (Ithaca, 1961), I, 6.

understandably shared the same focus: they assume an English georgic to be a formal imitation of Virgil. By contrast, pre-Augustan critics seldom refer to a single georgic model. Meres compares Tusser with Hesiod, not Virgil; Webbe cites as georgic poets Hesiod and Virgil (and Heresbachius and Tusser); Sidney links Virgil's *Georgics* with Lucretius; and Puttenham groups Oppian with Lucretius, Aratus, Manilius, and Nicander.[14]

What then did the unfocused conception of georgic amount to? Such questions are among the critic's most elusive, since getting behind a more recent generic idea is like unlearning or unknowing. And here we meet an additional problem, that the Renaissance conception of georgic seems to have been distinctly—or indistinctly—loose. The medieval state of the genre partly continued, extended to so many subjects as to be in effect all didactic poetry. Sidney's categories, perhaps based on Campanella's, are illuminating.[15] His "second kinde" of poets offer "the sweet food of sweetly uttered knowledge" and "deal with matters philosophical, either moral . . . or natural, as Lucretius and Virgil's *Georgics;* or astronomical, as Manilius and Pontanus. . . ."[16] Such poets presented difficulties to theories based on fiction and were denied to be poets at all by Speroni and Castelvetro. Hence Sidney allows some doubt whether this second cadre "properly be Poets or no," in view of their being "wrapped within the fold of the proposed subject." The problem was not just that the subject art imposed its own organization, but that the things taught were not feigned. On the other hand, Hesiod witnessed authoritatively to the truth of poetry. Tasso cites the famous passage in the *Theogony,* where the Muses tell Hesiod "We know how to speak many false things as though they were true; but we know when we will, to utter true things [*alēthea gērusasthai*]."[17] This first description of a poet's visitation by the Muses was often to be repeated in defenses of

14. Smith, *Elizabethan Critical Essays,* II, 323; I, 265; I, 158; II, 46.
15. See Bernard Weinberg, *A History of Literary Criticism in the Italian Renaissance,* 2 vols. (Chicago, 1961), II, 794.
16. K. Duncan-Jones and J. van Dorsten, eds., *Miscellaneous Prose of Sir Philip Sidney* (Oxford, 1973), p. 80.
17. *Discourses on the Heroic Poem,* trans. Mariella Cavalchini and Irene Samuel (Oxford, 1973), p. 34; *Theogony,* pp. 27–29.

poetry.[18] Its valuable idea of the mixture of truth and fiction
was developed by Fracastoro in *Naugerius, sive de poetica dialogus* (1555), where he stresses the poet's power to go beyond
the mere system of instruction and "omit no beauty."[19]

Several writers dwelt on georgic's variety. So Sir Thomas
Elyot, recommending Virgil in 1531, exclaims with unmistakable pleasure:

In his *Georgics,* Lord, what pleasant variety there is; the divers grains,
herbs, and flowers that be there described, that, reading therein, it
seemeth to a man to be in a delectable garden or paradise. What
ploughman knoweth so much of husbandry as there is expressed? Who,
delighting in good horses, shall not be thereto more inflamed, reading
there of the breeding, choosing, and keeping of them? In the declaration whereof Virgil leaveth far behind him all breeders, hackneymen,
and skosers [dealers].[20]

And Chapman, in the rather more sophisticated preface to his
Hesiod translation, ends on the same note: "Here being no
dwelling on any one subject but of all human affairs instructively
concluded."[21] Elyot also praises Hesiod's variety of digressive
fiction: he is "more brief than Virgil . . . and doth not rise so
high in philosophy, but is fuller of fables: and therefore is more
illecebrous."[22] *Works and Days* contains, after all, precepts of
husbandry; mythological fables; a theology of labor; a theodicy
of ages of history; meditations on peace and justice; an imitation
of the happy herdsman's day; precepts on the good life; an idyll;

18. See Rudolf Pfeiffer, *History of Classical Scholarship from 1300 to 1850*
(Oxford, 1976), pp. 6–7.

19. Girolamo Fracastoro, *Naugerius,* trans. Ruth Kelso, ed. M. W. Bundy
(Urbana, 1924), p. 68, cited by Durling, *Georgic Tradition,* p. 11 (as "Frascatoro").

20. *The Boke Named the Governour* (1531), 1.10; ed. H. H. S. Croft (London, 1880), I, 61. L. P. Wilkinson, *The Georgics of Virgil* (Cambridge, 1969),
pp. 294–295, unaccountably questions Elyot's knowledge of Virgil ("Mere lip-service")—possibly because he forgets that "granges" meant barns.

21. "Of Hesiodus," in *Homer's Batrachomyomachia . . . Hesiod's "Works
and Days . . . ,"* trans. George Chapman, ed. Richard Hooper (rev. ed., London, 1888), p. 145.

22. *The Governour,* 1.10; cf. William Webbe, *A Discourse of English Poetrie,*
in *Elizabethan Critical Essays,* ed. Smith, I, 237.

a vivid description of winter; and an account of astronomical phenomena accompanying the cycle of times and seasons and occupations. And this pursuit of variety was taken up in various ways by other writers of georgic. In Oppian, it reached one logical conclusion in the claim to novelty.

Another main interest of georgic lay in description, especially of landscape. Sharp realizations of physical appearances of things abound in *Works and Days*. And Hesiod's winter scene might be said to approach landscape description more closely than does Virgil's famous praise of Italy (2.136–176), generalized as that is and muted by negation. This aspect of Hesiod's descriptions was not always attractive to Renaissance critics. In his discussion of poetic prudentiality J. C. Scaliger warns the poet of natural philosophy against giving too much factual detail. Scenes should be mentioned "briefly without elaboration": "you should not so much describe as mention, in case you deserve to be faulted with Hesiod, who seems to have known two or three winds, but not to have got their orientation right."[23] He could not have foreseen that factual truth and specificity would be precisely what attracted many poets in the seventeenth century.

Around 1600 the idea of georgic, we may suppose, was of a digressive poem containing precepts, instruction in an art, or meditation on the good life. It might touch on labor and the retired life of the country; comparison of historical periods; seasonal change; or landscape description. And it was spoken in the poet's own person, neither elevated like epic nor dramatized and deliberately unlearned like pastoral. Thinking in terms of this looser conception allows us to recognize many pre-Augustan appearances of georgic. Some are local modulations within other kinds, such as the opening of "The Black Lady," an anonymous poem in the Arundel Harington manuscript:

> In autume when mynerves men
>    with Sythe and Sickell had shorne
> Suche frute as Ceares yelded then
>    of everye kynde of corne

23. Julius Caesar Scaliger, *Poetices libri septem* (Lyons, 1561), 3.26.114b, col. 1.

> And when eache shock and sheafe was laide
> in carte and home ycarried . . .[24]

In other instances the modulation pervades a whole work, as with *The Faerie Queene,* which William Sessions has argued to be georgic throughout.[25] The plural labors of Spenser's heroes differ from romance adventures in being redemptive achievements in time, saving the land and its history from time's disorders. This is almost overt in book 1, where Contemplation reveals the hero to be Georgos, found by a ploughman "As he his toylesome teme that way did guyde," and brought up "in ploughmans state to byde"(1.10.66).[26] Sessions is right to think that Virgil's combative georgic ideal—*labor omnia vicit*—is close to the thematic center of *The Faerie Queene* (as it is to that of the *Aeneid*). But we miss something of Spenser's intention unless we see how he also uses georgic to humble the pretensions of epic, and, in book 6 particularly, to redefine pastoral. There, references to georgic activities accumulate, until at 6.8.35 it is the unpastoral ploughmen, not the shepherds, who are contrasted with the savages. These

>                       ne did give
> Them selves to any trade, as for to drive
> The painefull plough, or cattell for to breed,
> Or by adventrous marchandize to thrive . . .

The herdsmen and shepherds of book 6, symbolizing active life and contemplation, coexist in mutual support of one another. Spenser's fictive persona may be the shepherd Colin Clout; but in his own person he counts himself a farmer—"Now turne againe my teme thou jolly swayne, / Backe to the furrow which I lately left" (6.9.1). The poem as furrow was a conventional

24. Ruth Hughey, ed., *The Arundel Harington Manuscript of Tudor Poetry* (Columbus, 1960), I, 329. "Minerva's men" may reflect Hesiod, *Works and Days,* l. 430, where herdsmen are called "Athena's men."

25. Sessions, "Spenser's Georgics." See also *Variorum Spenser,* index, s.v. "Virgil: *Georgics.*" Wilkinson (*Georgics of Virgil,* p. 295) says that Spenser "took . . . hardly anything" from the *Georgics* compared with the *Eclogues* and the *Aeneid.* But the context shows that he refers to lexical echoes.

26. Upton noticed that *Georgos* means "husbandman."

topos (itself georgic, the *persona auctoris* genre); but Spenser gives it an unusually full development.[27] Hesiodic too are *The Faerie Queene*'s many genealogical passages, digressive variety, choice of myths (many from the *Theogony*),[28] and agricultural imagery.[29]

More striking are Spenser's modifications of pastoral eclogue itself, the very kind supposed to be in direct contrast with georgic. *The Shepheardes Calender* (1579) is undeniably pastoral; yet from the outset its realistically harsh weather and dialect-speaking shepherds indicate a generic modulation. These shepherds, it turns out, are "mortal men, that swincke and sweate."[30] "October," on poetic vocation, refers explicitly to Virgil's *Georgics,* the work in which he left pastoral "And laboured lands to yield the timely eare."[31] Throughout the poem, farmyard images— bulls, "cock on his dunghill"—abound in a distinctly antipastoral way. The imagery does not even exclude ploughing: the "frostie furrows" of "February" (l. 44) may be wittily anthropomorphized; but the "gasping furrowes thirst" quenched with rain at "April" (1.6) are more than half real. Above all, Spenser's eclogues do not keep up the expected pastoral stasis but instead have been made subject, by the addition of a calendar, to georgic seasonal variety.[32] As I have argued elsewhere, Shakespeare followed Spenser in mixing pastoral and georgic in *As You Like It.*[33] And a taste for such mixtures developed,

27. See, for example, 3.12.47; 5.3.40.

28. See *Variorum Spenser,* index, s.v. "Hesiod."

29. See, for example, 3.7.34; 3.9.35; 6.4.14; 6.8.12; 6.10.39.

30. "November," l. 154; cf. "July," l. 34, "September," l. 132, "Envoy," l. 10. On georgic's contrast with pastoral, see Thomas G. Rosenmeyer, *The Green Cabinet* (Berkeley and Los Angeles, 1969), index, s.v. "Hesiodic tradition."

31. "October," l. 58; see Sessions, "Spenser's Georgics," pp. 205, 217.

32. "A Discourse on Pastoral Poetry," in *The Prose Works of Alexander Pope, 1711–1720,* ed. Norman Ault (Oxford, 1936), p. 301. On the pastoral stasis, see Rosenmeyer, *Green Cabinet,* pp. 86–88; on time in *The Shepheardes Calender,* see Robert Allen Durr, "Spenser's Calendar of Christian Time," *ELH,* 24 (1957), 269–295, and Maren-Sofie Røstvig, "*The Shepheardes Calender*—a Structural Analysis," *Renaissance and Modern Studies,* 13 (1969), 49–75.

33. "Pastoral Instruction in *As You Like It,*" John Coffin Memorial Lecture, University of London, 1984.

which perhaps we can see at work when the anonymous 1588 translator of *Sixe idillia* of Theocritus selects the "impurely" pastoral *Idylls* 8 (Bucoliastae), 11 (Cyclops), and 21 (Neatherd).

In a different, more idealizing tonality Michael Drayton's airy "Sixth Nymphal" (1630) pits georgic against pastoral in a subtle *paragone* of forester, fisherman, and shepherd. Silvius describes the happy forester's day with a Hesiodic crispness of detail:

> My Doghooke at my Belt, to which my Lyam's tyde,
> My Sheafe of Arrowes by, my Woodknife at my Syde,
> My Crosse-bow in my Hand, my Gaffle or my Rack
> To bend it when I please, or it I list to slack,
> My Hound then in my Lyam, I by the Woodmans art
> Forecast, where I may lodge the goodly Hie-palm'd Hart . . .

Yet this representative of georgic makes light of his labor: with beauties of nature and delights of the chase, his life "in pleasure . . . continually is spent" (92). Halcio the fisherman replies in kind; and where we might expect him to dwell on fishing's contemplativeness, he insists instead on its laboriousness: "noe hower I idely spend, / But wearied with my worke I bring the day to end . . . Whilst Ropes of liquid Pearle still load my laboring Oares . . ."[34] Fishing offers an interface or mediating overlap, being susceptible to treatment either as piscatorial pastoral or as halieutic georgic. This ambiguity is also exploited by Izaak Walton in *The Compleat Angler* (1653), with its dialogue of Piscator, Venator, and Auceps. There, fishing both figures pastorally as a contemplative symbol of the spiritual life and receives preceptive georgic exposition as a practical art.[35]

The beginning of English georgic may be located in Gavin Douglas' great "Prologues" to his *Eneados* (completed in 1513). These bring to an end the late medieval phase of georgic, when Virgil's poem was not very well known and the genre itself was formally incoherent and diffuse. Douglas has long been credited with introducing the *Georgics* to the English poetic tradition,

34. "The Muses Elizium," 6.143, 147–148, 163, in *Works,* ed. J. William Hebel et al., 5 vols. (Oxford, 1931–1941), III, 297. Earlier, in "Nymphal," 3.118, Drayton refers to Hesiod ("th'Ascrean swaine").

35. For Walton's spiritual symbolism, see Jonquil Bevan's introduction to *The Compleat Angler* (Oxford, 1983), pp. 27–28.

in that he alluded to many particular passages, like the bird catalogue (Prologue 7) and the praise of spring (Prologue 12).[36] It is a more novel idea that the "Prologues" together in some sense compose a georgic poem. Yet what else does their range of topics suggest?—the combination of praise of labor, explanation of an art, portrayal of times and seasons, and description of landscape, with precepts sometimes drawn from Virgil ("O Lord, quhat writis myne author of thi forss / In hys Georgikis . . ." [Prologue 4.58–59]).

Externally Douglas adopts the prologue or "preambill" genre, a flexible medieval form easily hospitable to georgic's digressive method and use of the poet's own voice. But, besides the individual "Prologues" being relevant each to a book of the *Aeneid,* they have also a calendrical sequence.[37] And they are further unified by georgic topics: consistently Douglas explains his own or Virgil's art, or portrays seasonal or diurnal changes in nature. Especially in Prologues 7, 12, and 13, his landscape description manifests a precision and evocative power that have given it a permanent place in our literature. In Prologue 7 he departs from medieval custom (but returns to georgic tradition) in a brilliant winter scene with many details of a Hesiodic particularity: windlestraws wagging in the wind like "hirstis" (hinges), and exact colors—"Broune muris kythit [made known] thair wysnyt mossy hew" (7.56). And in Prologue 13 the conventional comparison of writing to ploughing becomes a whole genre scene, in which after an awesome dawn the grieve calls his herdsmen to their tasks, and the reluctant poet feels obliged to join in and begin his own. Yet Douglas is far from idealizing labor unreasonably, as his picture of herdsmen's miseries in winter shows:

> Puyr lauboraris and bissy husband men
> Went wait and wery draglit in the fen.
> The silly scheip and thar litil hyrd gromys

---

36. There are also some lexical allusions: see Wilfred P. Mustard, "Virgil's *Georgics* and the British Poets," *American Journal of Philology,* 29 (1908), 1–32; and Priscilla Bawcutt, *Gavin Douglas* (Edinburgh, 1976), chap. 7.

37. On relevance to books of the *Aeneid,* see Bawcutt, *Gavin Douglas,* pp. 172–175; on calendrical structure, Alastair Fowler, "Virgil for 'every gentil Scot,' " *Times Literary Supplement,* 22 July 1977, pp. 882–883.

> Lurkis vndre le of bankis, woddis and bromys . . .
>                                       (7.75–78)

There is not much formal georgic, in the sense of lexical imitation of Virgil; but then that was avoided in the early Renaissance and only become fashionable after Vida's *De arte poetica* (1520–1527).[38] Douglas evidently thought of his "Prologues" as imitating Virgil's *Georgics* formally; he even gave them approximately the same line total.[39] (Such numerical echoes were once common enough, perhaps the most notorious being that between the 9896-line totals of Virgil's *Aeneid* and Boccaccio's *Teseide*.)

Even allowing for the later Renaissance south of the border, England produced little original georgic in the sixteenth century, so that one might be tempted to turn to external explanations, such as Low's idea of the gentry's contempt for manual labor. But William Webbe, writing in 1586, gives a different explanation. The only verse imitation he knows of Hesiod or of Virgil's *Georgics* is Tusser's: "I thinke the cause why our Poets have not travayled in that behalfe is, especially, for that there have beene alwayes plenty of other wryters that have handled the same argument very largely."[40] "Other writers" presumably refers to the many English prose writers on gardening and husbandry, or perhaps to continental authorities like Gallo, Estienne and Liebault, and de Serres. He continues: "Among whom Master Barnabe Googe, in translating and enlarging the most profitable worke of Heresbachius, hath deserved much commendation . . ." There were many Italian and neo-Latin georgics, such as Poliziano's *Rusticus* (1483) and Alamanni's *La coltivazione* (1546);[41] and some of the earliest English activity was in editing or translation. First there were treatments of Virgil's *Georgics*—Fleming's translation (1589), Grimald's *Para-*

38. See Wilkinson, *Georgics of Virgil*, p. 291n.; also pp. 295–296, where he points out that the Winchester syllabus in the sixteenth century was incompatible with close attention to words.

39. That is, 2199 for the Virgilian "Prologues," as against 2189 for the *Georgics* in Ascensius' 1501 edition, which Douglas is known to have sometimes used (see Bawcutt, *Gavin Douglas*, p. 102 and chap. 5, passim).

40. Smith, *Elizabethan Critical Essays*, I, 265.

41. See Wilkinson, *Georgics of Virgil*, pp. 291–293.

*phrasis* (1591), and two editions of May's translation (1628). Then Thomas Moffat closely modeled his *Silkewormes and Their Flies* (1599) on M. G. Vida's *De bombycum cura et usu* (1527). And Googe's translation of Conrad Heresbach, *Foure Bookes of Husbandry* (1577), went through five editions before it was enlarged in 1614 by Googe himself, and again in 1631 by Gervase Markham, author of several prose treatises on husbandry.[42] Others took up the astronomical strand of ancient didactic poetry (Hesiod, Aratus, Virgil, Manilius): Christopher Middleton in *The Historie of Heaven* (1596); Sylvester in his translation of Du Bartas (that "Fourth Day of the First Week," which Spenser knew by heart); and, best of the group, Drayton, in *Endimion and Phoebe* (1595).

A turning point came with George Chapman's translation of *The Georgicks of Hesiod* (1618), dedicated to Bacon. By making accessible a second georgic (in the stricter sense of the term), Chapman did much to form a clearer idea of the kind. In a preface he mentions Hesiod's authority in "teaching good life and humanity" and in writing, before the philosophers, "of life, of manners, of God, of nature, of the stars, and general state of the universe." He notices a digressive tendency, more extreme than Virgil's: "Here being no dwelling on any one subject but of all human affairs instructively concluded."[43] Chapman was a good Grecian, able in translation to give some idea of Hesiod's sensuous epithets—"sweating heat," "swift-sharp-sighted sun," "still-roaring-noise-resounding seas."[44] He makes a fair attempt at the passage on Boreas' winter effects—noting Melanchthon's appreciation of it. Chapman's notes on key passages were calculated to foster an understanding of georgic's values. Thus he comments on mediocrity; on Prometheus (invoking Bacon's interpretation); on the Golden Age (seeing Hesiod's authoritativeness); on justice as the state's soul; on toil as virtue's body; and on the Happy Man as a lover of virtue.[45] His interpretations tend to interiorize: he allegorizes the Pandora

42. On Markham, see Low, "New Science and the Georgic Revolution," p. 246.
43. "Of Hesiodus," Hooper, *Homer's Batrachomyomachia* . . . , p. 145.
44. *The Georgicks of Hesiod,* 2.54, 55, 413.
45. Ibid., 1.77, 88, 183, 372, 455, 464.

myth, seeing an analogue of the Fall; and at 2.290 he introduces
from Melanchthon the idea of "labours of the soul," later important for Milton.[46] Several notes draw attention to justification
of economic activity—like the one at 1.46, citing Plutarch's
agreement with Hesiod (against Plato, Aristotle, and Galen) in
assigning the profit motive to virtuous contention rather than
harmful discord: "He shows artizans' emulation for *riches,* and
approves that kind of contention."

Chapman's Hesiod was prefaced by a verse epistle "To my
worthy friend Mr. George Chapman," by Michael Drayton.
Drayton's own *Poly-Olbion* (pt. 1, 1612; pt. 2, 1622) is itself a
massive georgic poem, although treated by Durling (p. 295)
merely as anticipating "many features of later local verse." True,
Drayton boasts that his "Chorographicall Description," "this
Essay of my poem," finds a "new clear way"; but this claim to
novelty in itself points to georgic.[47] Much of *Poly-Olbion* could
be regarded as an enormous *macrologia* of Virgil's *laus Italiae*
passage,[48] describing landscapes and towns and local products,
in its expansive Elizabethan way. A characteristically georgic
feature is the sustained historical element, considerable enough
in itself for George Wither to refer to the poem as "Topo-
chrono-graphicall,"[49] and receiving powerful amplification from
Selden's erudite commentary. This element was authorized not
only by the organized temporality of georgic labors but, more
specifically, by Virgil's prophecy of the farmer's finding relics
of war and giant bones. (Wither is aware of this when he speaks
of *Poly-Olbion*'s showing "the Workes of *Peace,* the Marks of
Civill-rages.")[50] But the historical descriptions had a more immediate impulse in the strong northern European passion for
complete description, about which we have recently learned
from Svetlana Alpers. Drayton's poem is geographical, and

46. Cf. 2.204, where Melanchthon is quoted on industry and the danger of
idleness.
47. Hebel et al., *Works,* IV, v* and 391. The claim to novelty, which occurs
in Oppian, would be familiar from Virgil, *Georgics,* 3.292.
48. *Georgics,* 2.136–176.
49. Hebel et al., Drayton, *Works,* IV, 394.
50. Ibid.; cf. Virgil, *Georgics,* 1.494–497.

geography was "the eye of history."[51] In this spirit he promises to show "the ancient people of this Ile delivered thee in their lively images."[52] Like certain other early georgics, Drayton's poem has to be understood in relation to antiquarian topographical research: it was the age of Leland, Camden, Norden, Selden, and William Burton.

Drayton's own interest in history is deeply felt and issues in some fine passages on ancient ruins:

> Even in the agedst face, where beautie
> once did dwell,
> And nature (in the least) but seemed to excell,
> Time cannot make such waste, but something
> will appeare,
> To shewe some little tract of delicacie there.
> Or some religious worke, in building manie
> a day,
> That this penurious age hath suffred to decay,
> Some lim or modell, dragd out of the ruinous
> mass,
> The richness will declare in glorie whilst
> it was . . .
>
> (1.194–201)

Behind such antiquities loom more distant mythological origins, in the manner of Hesiod or Virgil, or hints of a Golden Age contrasted with the inferior present.[53] Georgic comparison of ages sometimes takes an ecological turn in Drayton, as when he worries about improvident destruction of forests: "no man ever plants to our posteritie."[54] Other georgic notes include the exotic places: "*Chinas* wealthie Realms, and . . . The pearlie rich *Peru*" (2.417–418). And the praise of labor extends to his

---

51. Svetlana Alpers, *The Art of Describing: Dutch Art in the Seventeenth Century* (Chicago and London, 1983), pp. 159 et passim.

52. Drayton, in Hebel et al., *Works*, IV, v*.

53. For example, the mythologizing of mining at 1.104–108. Selden justifies the mythological personifications on the authority of "greek antiquities"; see Hebel et al., *Works,* IV, 43.

54. *Poly-Olbion*, 2.68; cf. (among many such passages) 2.141–148; 3.149–156.

own: his 1612 preface boldly asserts that if his poem defeats
the lazy, "the fault proceeds from thy idlenesse, not from any
want in my industrie."

In a revealing passage, Drayton promises (georgic) variety:
he will "sute [his] varying vaine" to that of nature—"Now, as
the Mountain hie; then, as the Valley lowe: / Heere, fruitful as
the Mead, there as the Heath be bare . . ."[55] Such effects of
imitative form were to become one of English georgic's most
usual features. But Drayton's content, too, ranges widely, from
animistic visions of metamorphosis to empirical description with
a distinctly scientific emphasis. Song 13 may illustrate. It contains Warwickshire topography; a bird catalogue (no mere re-
daction of *Georgics* 1, but a vivid account of British birds); "a
description of hunting the Hart" in the Virgil-Oppian tradition,
flavored with technical terms like "rechating"; a luscious "description of the afternoone"—the topos subsequently to be favored by Jago, Gay, and late Augustan georgic;[56] and an account
of a hermit, "king in his desire" (184). This recluse significantly
combines georgic retirement with scientific interest. A botanical
hermit, he "choicely sorts" herbal remedies from among "un-
numbered sorts of Simples," of which Drayton lists a few; but
even "skilful Gerard" could not set down all.

*Poly-Olbion* is an impressive transitional work—perhaps
old-fashioned in its style and ambitious scale, but forward-
looking in generic orientation and content. Durling supposes
that it was not taken up by succeeding poets. But this is to
leave out of account Denham's *Cooper's Hill* with its historical landscape, Cotton's *Wonders of the Peak* with its links
to *Poly-Olbion* 26, and Pope's *Windsor-Forest* with its verbal
imitations.

In the next phase, georgic shrank in scale to rural odes or
short poems on the Happy Man. New models were added, such
as Horace's second epode ("Beatus ille") and Casimire Sar-
biewski's Horatian odes. But as the tendency's historian, Maren-
Sofie Røstvig, makes clear, the central *locus classicus* remained
Virgil's praise of retirement and of the industrious husbandman

55. Ibid., 2.1–18.
56. See Chalker, *English Georgic,* pp. 142, 195.

in *Georgics* 2.458–540 ("O fortunatos . . .").[57] Nevertheless, among the many rural odes and poems of retirement not a few seem Hesiodic in mood, like Herrick's "The Hock-cart, or Harvest home," or his indirectly preceptive "The Country life, to the honoured Master Endimion Porter." It is notable that Herrick can advise that prominent courtier to get his hands dirty: "the best compost for the Lands / Is the wise Masters Feet, and Hands."[58] The georgic model for such poems is well recognized. Indeed, it is obvious; for they begin to introduce lexical imitation, as in Herrick's lines "O happy life! if that their good / The Husbandmen but understood!" But it appears not to have been considered whether, according to the generic conceptions of the time, they may actually have been English georgics.

Nor are their values quite appreciated. Perhaps this is partly because we have neglected Hesiodic georgic—a form less austere than Virgil's, more intimate and parochial and hospitable to idyll. So one critic complains that Jacobean poems of retirement relax from arduous georgic into pastoral—instancing William Browne's imitation of "Beatus ille," where the vision has "nothing of Vergil's constant and even terrifying toil."[59] Strange, to think of recommending country life by showing it to be disagreeable. Surely anachronistic ideals of social realism have intruded here. After all, considering the shortness of his poem Browne is rather specific: "His plough, his flock, his scythe, and rake, / Do physic, clothe, and nourish him." Similarly with Henry Vaughan's Guevara imitation, *The Praise and Happinesse of the Countrie-Life* (1651), which seems to Low "an idyll that turns its plowmen into pleasant fixtures of the landscape, making their discourses one with the singing of the birds" (p. 240). But when Vaughan speaks of "the pleasant discourses of the *Old Ploughmen*," he seems to me to show that he likes talking to them.[60] The view that landowners imagined their laborers merely as

57. *The Happy Man: Studies in the Metamorphoses of a Classical Ideal,* vol. I: *1600–1700,* 2 vols. (rev. ed., Oslo, 1962, 1971), chap. 1.
58. "The Country life," 11.23–24, in *The Poetical Works,* ed. L. C. Martin (Oxford, 1956), p. 230.
59. Low, "New Science and the Georgic Revolution," p. 236.
60. L. C. Martin, ed., *Works* (rev. ed., Oxford, 1957), p. 130. It is particularly inappropriate to represent Vaughan as a remote landowner, since his

property hardly does justice to the good relations that sometimes obtained between ranks (as they still were—not classes).
And to suppose that early Augustan georgic represented a great
revaluation of labor is naive progressivism. On the contrary:
lexical imitation of Virgil very easily went with a distanced eu-
phemizing and blurring of the details of work.

A closely related grouping is that of country-house or estate
poems. Sometimes, indeed, the estate poem overlaps the rural
ode, as in Jonson's influential emphasis on retirement in "To
Sir Robert Wroth." But these are modern, not Renaissance,
categories. From the present standpoint the estate poem may
be regarded as a subgenre of English georgic. Seasonal labors,
abundant fruits, renunciation of stately mansions, contented
retirement, allusions to the Golden Age: all these topics of the
estate poem are also familiar georgic topics.[61] Less obviously,
perhaps, conduct at public feasts was a topic of Hesiod's (715–
736), although in estate poems it is usually developed in lexical
imitation of Latin poets—Martial or Lucian or Juvenal.

Considering estate poems as georgics enables us to appreciate
the generic coherence of Marvell's *Upon Appleton House,* a
poem that has previously seemed out of scale and abrupt in its
transitions.[62] For digressive structure is itself a georgic feature—
the *ambages* that Virgil draws attention to in the *Georgics,* while
pretending to eschew.[63] Rosalie Colie has recognized many of
Marvell's Virgilian allusions and related them to their paradigms
in *Georgics* 2: the flood at harvest; the militarized garden (Virgil's heroic bees); the mock epic element; the rail's death, like
the baby nightingale's; the context of reconstruction after civil
war.[64] Others could be added, such as the prominent significant

---

"estate" was only a small farm, worked by men whom, as their "loved physi-
cian," he would have come to know well.

61. See, for example, Ian Donaldson's notes to "To Sir Thomas Wroth," in
Ben Jonson, *Poems* (London, 1975), pp. 91–94, for details of six distinct debts
to Virgil's *Georgics* alone.

62. See, for example, Rosalie L. Colie, *"My Ecchoing Song": Andrew Marvell's Poetry of Criticism* (Princeton, 1970), p. 181. Durling, significantly, ignores
the poem.

63. *Georgics,* 2.46.

64. See Colie, *"My Ecchoing Song,"* pp. 202, 240, 279, 241, 223–224.

birds; the poet's retirement and meditated vocation; the times of day used as an ordering principle; the recurrent bees; and the playful changes of scale—men like grasshoppers and fleas like constellations—which not only express the descriptive urge of the time but specifically imitate *Georgics* 4. And Marvell rewrites as well as embodies georgic myths. The harmless Nun Appleton flood comes after reaping, not before. The convent digression looks back not to an idle Golden Age but to a false *hortus conclusus*—"I know what fruit their gardens yield"— escaped through the deliverance of the Protestant new "Israalites." Marvell's reapers may labor under a certain weight of symbolism; still, they are visibly at work on agricultural reconstruction, "With whistling Sithe, and Elbow strong." The nuns' "work," by contrast, is ritual and "serves for *Altar's Ornaments*." A deeper georgic retrospect, however, to the "*Paradise* of four Seas" (stanza 41), recurs as a leitmotif.

A number of other familiar poems obviously belong to the same georgic grouping: Denham's *Cooper's Hill* with its stag hunt and symbolic Virgilian river; Waller's "On St James's Park"; Cotton's "Morning Quatrains," "Winter Quatrains," and the rest; and Cowley's imitations printed with his essays "Of Agriculture" and "The Garden." Milton's contribution is more debatable: Louis Martz argues *Paradise Regained* to be georgic, whereas Walter MacKellar roundly rejects this—while holding it to be "unquestionably . . . *didactic* . . . like *Works and Days*"! It may be best to think of *Paradise Regained* as brief epic with georgic modulation, as I have argued elsewhere.[65] But two other of Milton's poems that have been hard to identify generically prove to be almost unmixed georgic: *L'Allegro* and *Il Penseroso*. These have already been located in the Happy Man tradition. Anachronistic conceptions of georgic, however, have obscured

65. "*Paradise Regained:* Some Problems of Style," in *Medieval and Pseudo-Medieval Literature*, ed. P. Boitani and A. Torti, J. A. W. Bennett Memorial Lectures, 3rd series, Perugia 1982–83 (Tübingen and Cambridge, 1984), pp. 181–189. See Louis Martz, "*Paradise Regained:* The Meditative Combat," *ELH*, 27 (1960), 223–247, followed by A. Low in "Milton, *Paradise Regained* and Georgic," *PMLA*, 98 (1983), 152–169, and rebutted by W. MacKellar in *A Variorum Commentary on the Poems of John Milton*, 4 vols. (New York, 1975), IV, 15.

their generic identities. Yet *L'Allegro* abounds in images of physical work—plowing, reaping, mowing, milking—and although this is absent from *Il Penseroso,* it is replaced there by the poet's work of meditation, calling for "retired Leisure." (Even so, woodcutting comes in by negation, and the "flowery work" of the bee.) Each poem uses the idyllic day for its structuring pattern; and each has a version of the Orpheus myth from *Georgics* 4.[66] The implication of all this is not merely taxonomic—to lengthen the list of English georgics. It also helps us to appreciate formal coherence, by disclosing a basis of relevance, as with the opening mythological genealogies, derived from Hesiod. It attunes us to Milton's digressive variety. And it encourages us to notice descriptive precision. This in turn may take us back to the line of criticism linking the poems with Burton's prefatory ode, with the descriptive *Anatomy* itself, and with analysis of mental states.[67]

There seems to be no lack of English georgics in the seventeenth century—if the term refers to the older grouping of Hesiodic and loosely Virgilian inspiration. On this basis there is little need to explain English lateness. If on the other hand the term implies close lexical imitations of Virgil, English georgic does not begin until the eighteenth century. But then the late development is easily explained, as we saw, in terms of literary history, without introducing "external" explanations.

Nevertheless, we may reasonably suppose that georgic went through a development with both internal and external aspects. Close imitation of the classics was bound up with the Augustan ideal, and the Augustan ideal had a complex political etiology, as we are beginning to discover. Then, reconstruction after the Civil War, and later the agricultural revolution, played their parts. Another factor, so far neglected, was the impulse toward detailed description that animated intellectual life and art throughout the century. Among inhibiting factors (if we need to look for these), distance of rank no doubt operated in the late seventeenth century. Earlier, however, it was probably less important than a quite specific cause: namely, reluctance on the

66. *Georgics,* 4.454–558.
67. *Variorum Milton,* II, pt. 1, 231–233.

part of magnates (who were also potential patrons) to go in for large-scale demesne farming—through fear, it is said, of being cheated by officials.[68] The early Augustan Virgilian georgics represented little of an "advance" in attitudes toward labor. Compared with Jonson's and Drayton's, indeed, they made something more like a retreat, into remote artificializing and "ennoblement" of practicalities. It was only after the Enlightenment, in later Augustan literature—in Dyer's *The Fleece* (1757), for example—that particularity in the description of labor was recovered.

68. See Lawrence Stone, *The Crisis of the Aristocracy, 1558–1641* (Oxford, 1965), pp. 295–301.

HARRY LEVIN

# Notes toward a Definition
# of City Comedy

City comedy has never been accorded more than a very limited
recognition as a genre, or rather—to employ the more precise,
if hybrid, term adopted by Alastair Fowler—a subgenre.[1] Given
the long and consistent association of the generic with the thematic in this mode of expression—that is to say, of comedies
with cities—the compounded epithet might seem slightly re-
dundant. My present concern is less to see it recognized amidst
the terminology of criticism than to consider some aspects of
the relationship it brings out. The usage seems uniquely, if not
peculiarly, English, though it is not lacking in approximate counterparts elsewhere. Such adjectives as *bourgeois* or *bürgerlich*
carry more of a social connotation than our awkward substantive, whereas the imported cognate *burgher* might sound too
much like a comic opera. Our concept has been most pertinently
invoked within the context of Elizabethan drama, where the

1. Alastair Fowler, *Kinds of Literature: An Introduction to the Theory of
Genres and Modes* (Cambridge, Mass., 1982), passim.

continuous permutation of organic forms lends itself to a Polonian multiplication of formal categories, and where the redolence of local color needs to be sharply distinguished from the atmosphere of what Ben Jonson termed "some fustian countrie."[2] Since the distinction applies with fullest force to the voluminous and heterogeneous work of Thomas Middleton, it seems appropriate that Anthony Covatto has singled out his city comedies for monographic treatment.[3] Brian Gibbons' effort to broaden the ground actually clouds the definition by including the Italianate plays of John Marston.[4] Alexander Leggatt, opting for the designation of "Citizen Comedy," profitably centers upon the sociological purport of his subject matter.[5]

Drama—*pace* Calvin and Rousseau—has usually ranked high among the attractions of urban life. The first of Thomas Heywood's arguments on its behalf was that it constituted "an ornament to the Citty . . ."[6] His proud depiction of theatrical London could be paralleled by the Venetian painter Gabriele Bella, whose view of the Piazzetta San Marco is crowded with strangers from all nations, flocking to watch the rival troupes of mountebanks perform.[7] Epochs in the history of drama have been marked by cultural capitals: Sophocles' Athens, Shakespeare's London, Lope de Vega's Madrid. Courts, both royal and ducal, have also functioned as dramatic matrices; but, as Erich Auerbach has convincingly shown, the ideal public for Molière and the French classics was drawn conjointly from *"la cour et la ville,"* from the courtiers of Versailles and the *grande bourgeoisie* of Paris.[8] To be sure, no city has ever been more

2. C. H. Herford and Percy Simpson, eds., *Ben Jonson* (Oxford, 1932), IV, 36 (*Cynthia's Revels*, Induction, 43).

3. Anthony Covatto, *Thomas Middleton's City Comedies* (Lewisburg, 1973).

4. Brian Gibbons, *Jacobean City Comedy: A Study of Satiric Plays by Jonson, Marston, and Middleton* (Cambridge, Mass., 1968).

5. Alexander Leggatt, *Citizen Comedy in the Age of Shakespeare* (Toronto, 1973).

6. Thomas Heywood, *An Apology for Actors* (1613), ed. R. H. Perkinson, Scholars' Facsimiles and Reprints (New York, 1941), p. F3.

7. Reproduced in Allardyce Nicoll, *Masks, Mimes, and Miracles: Studies in the Popular Theatre* (New York, 1931), p. 223.

8. Erich Auerbach, *Scenes from the Drama of European Literature* (New York, 1959), pp. 133–179.

closely, or more seminally, identified with the development of
the theater than Athens. Old Comedy, while it lasted, was one
of its leading institutions; the civic scene itself in war and peace,
in morals and politics, in tragedy and philosophy, was the major
theme of Aristophanes' invectives and celebrations. These,
however, were traced back by the Athenians to a rural origin.
Scholars are no longer disposed to credit, as Aristotle evidently
did (*Poetics*, 3), the Doric claim that comedy—both the word
and the activity—originated in *kōmē*, "a village." It seems to
have been derived more directly from *kōmos*, "revelry," which
is etymologically related (originally signifying "village festival"). Such revelry is often reenacted in a culminating episode
of the play itself.

The conflated meaning, though Aristotle cautioned against
it, has exerted an influence over the critical tradition. Hence
*comoedia* was defined in 1500, by the glossary of Wynkyn de
Worde, as "a town song."[9] Town, of course, interposes a further
ambiguity: if it appeared to be countrified from the viewpoint
of a walled and fortified city, it could look relatively citified
when viewed from the open countryside. The comic stage, from
its metropolitan standpoint, has habitually tended to ridicule
the denizens of the small town; the zanies of the Commedia
dell'Arte started as provincials from Bergamo; and communities
along the Hudson River, with funny names like Hoboken or
Yonkers, gain easy laughs for Broadway comedians. Town and
country were brought into confrontation with one another in a
theory sketched by some of the late Greek scholiasts.[10] It was
their assumption that peasants from the outlying hamlets of
Attica, having been mistreated by certain townsmen, disguised
themselves and repaired to Athens at night; there, in streets
before the dwellings of their oppressors, they staged vocal dem-
onstrations of protest; and that practice, gradually evolving in
an Aristophanic direction, was turned over to municipal choruses, which aired common grievances and denounced aberrant
citizens. This speculation gets echoed in the poetics of Antonio

9. Quoted by Madeleine Doran, *Endeavors of Art: A Study of Form in
Elizabethan Drama* (Madison, 1954), p. 383.
10. See Arthur Pickard-Cambridge, *Dithyramb, Tragedy, and Comedy*, rev.
T. B. L. Webster (Oxford, 1962), p. 184.

Minturno and other Renaissance theorists, but it had little in the way of classical substantiation.[11] Whatever the genesis of comedy—and we have not progressed beyond conjecture—its regular audiences would be composed of city-dwellers, who expected it to mirror the circumstances of their lives.

It has been repeatedly and perfunctorily described in the Aristotelian terms of a polar opposition to tragedy: the style colloquial rather than heroic, the characterization vulgar rather than noble, the plot fictitious rather than legendary, the ending happy rather than sorrow-laden. The lapidary description attributed to Cicero—*"imitatio vitae, speculum consuetudinis, imago veritatis"*—has been handed down to us through the Latin commentators.[12] The first and last phrases of that tripartite formula simply reaffirm the notion of mimesis, and might do almost as well for tragedy. It is the middle phrase, the trope of the mirror, that signalizes the difference: what is to be reflected here is custom, typical behavior, quotidian existence. Medieval tragedies could also be envisaged as metaphorical mirrors for kings or magistrates, insofar as their storied protagonists serve as awful examples illustrating cautionary object-lessons. Similarly, Robert Greene and Thomas Lodge, through the choric voice of the prophet Jonah, could warn their compatriots against the fate of Nineveh in *A Looking-Glass for London and England*. Jonson's experiments in "Comical Satire" would add the metaphor of a scourge to that of the looking-glass, when his spokesman Asper fulminated:

> Well I will scourge those apes;
> And to these courteous eyes oppose a mirrour,
> As large as is the stage, whereon we act:
> Where they shall see the times deformitie
> Anatomiz'd in euery nerve and sinnew,
> With constant courage and contempt of fear.[13]

Anatomizing is still another metaphor (vivisection), anticipated by the threat "to strip the ragged follies of the time." And when

11. Antonio Minturno, *L'arte poetica,* ed. Bernhard Fabian, Poetiken des Cinquecento (Munich, 1970), pp. 111–112.

12. Georg Kaibel, ed., *Comicorum Graecorum fragmenta* (Berlin, 1958), p. 67.

13. Herford and Simpson, *Ben Jonson,* III, 432, 428 (*Every Man out of His Humour,* Induction, 117–122, 17).

the angry man goes on to speak of "pills to purge," the medical
catharsis is proposed as a satirical corrective. But Jonson protested too much when he cracked the whip of a moral activist
and social reformer, probably to counter the mounting Puritan
charges of histrionic immorality. He would be more successful
when he gave up his didactic asperity for a good-natured realism,
enjoying the reflection for its own sake, and contenting himself
with what naturalistic playwrights would call *"une tranche de
vie."*

Old Comedy faced the reality of public situations, often so
grossly caricatured and so heavily propagandized that it finally
lost its satiric license. Consequently New Comedy focused attention on private lives, shifting its milieu from the forensic
center to the domestic suburbs, shying away from recognizable
individuals and building up its roster of stock types. Its *agōnes*
were not political contests but struggles of will between the
generations, the sexes, and the classes (masters versus servants).
Its titles, like its nomenclature, were inclined to set forth psychological traits: *Dyskolos, Heauton timorumenos, Le Misanthrope,* or—more cheerfully—*The Good-Natured Man.* Where
tragedies are ordinarily titled after their main characters, comedies more frequently use place-names: *Romeo and Juliet* not
*The Lovers of Verona;* not *Valentine and Proteus* but *The Two
Gentlemen of Verona.* In the Latin adaptations, our principal
corpus for New Comedy, the location is always significant. Plautus and Terence both concentrated on *fabulae palliatae,* plays
in Greek dress rather than Roman *(togatae).* Most of these were
located in a conventional Athens. Some of them took place in
Hellenistic seaports, which could fitly provide accommodation
for merchants, shipwrecked lovers, and long-lost-recognition
scenes. It was assumed, by convention, that the stage exits led
at one side to the harbor and at the other to the forum. Thus
the prologue to the *Menaechmi* apologetically tells us that the
argument will be more or less Greekish, not truly Attic but
more likely Sicilian: *". . . hoc argumentum graecissat, tamen /
non atticissat verum sicilicissitat."*[14]

14. Paul Nixon, ed., *Plautus,* Loeb Classical Library (London, 1925), II,
366, 370 (*Menaechmi,* 11–12, 72–76).

But the actual locale, to which we are so circumstantially introduced, proves to be on the Illyrian seacoast:

> Haec urbs Epidamnus est, dum haec agitur fabula;
> quando alia agetur, aliet fiet oppidum.
> sicut familiae quoque solent mutarier:
> Modo hic habitat leno, modo adulescens, modo senex,
> pauper, mendicus, rex, parasitus, hariolus.

Epidamnus is where the damage will be incurred, to anticipate a subsequent pun on *damnum,* and we are likewise informed about the Syracusan prehistory, since what we shall witness, after all, is a tale of two cities. Plautus makes it clear that, on due occasion, the stage can be whatever town the stage-directions call for. This adjustability is compared with that of families who move from one house to another or, to be more specific, with that of their transient inhabitants—though a more exact analogy would be with changeable residences, not with changing residents. Nor does the concluding list announce the cast of characters, even though the play will involve a parasite, an old man, not one but two young men, a doctor if not a soothsayer, and a prostitute if not a procurer. The juxtaposition of a beggar and a king—no comic figure (Plautus apologizes for letting his incognito Jupiter stray into the *Amphitryon*)—seems to imply a cross section of society as a whole, rather than the standard dramatis personae. Performing a similar task some 1500 years afterward, Machiavelli's prologue to his *Mandragola* (first published in 1524) would jocosely allude to such shifts from one locality to another. Today the scene will be Florence, the Florentine audience is told, in the manner of an officious guide pointing out the well-known landmarks. And yet again tomorrow it could be Rome or Pisa, and that might prompt us to jawbreaking laughter, for better or for worse.

> Vedete l'apparato,
> Quale or vi si dimostra:
> Questa è Firenze vostra,
> Un'altra volta sarà Roma, o Pisa;
> Cosa da smascellarsi per le risa.[15]

15. Niccolò Machiavelli, *Il teatro e gli scritti letterari,* ed. Franco Gaeta (Milan, 1965), p. 56 (*Mandragola, Prologo,* 7–11).

New Comedy had been able to retain its Grecian *pallium*
when it was translated to ancient Rome. When it was revived
in the sixteenth century under princely patronage, it was trans-
posed to the Tuscan vernacular and localized into the town-
scapes of the Italian Renaissance. The lavish revivals of Plautus
in the great courtyard of the Duke's palace at Ferrara, beginning
with the *Menaechmi* in 1486, prepared the way for the *commedia
erudita.*[16] Ludovico Ariosto may have been present at that performance; he seems indeed to have acted in another production
of the same play seven years later. By the time his own first
comedy was produced there in 1508, the Estensi rulers had built
a pioneering theater, where perspective scenery could be tried
out, with Mantegna among the contributing painters. But that
preliminary endeavor, the *Cassaria,* happened to be set in Myt-
ilene (Taranto), far away and long ago. During the following
year it was the première of Ariosto's *Suppositi* that really in-
augurated a new trend by updating the action and transferring
it to where else but Ferrara? There was even a pun upon *"fè
rara* (rare faith)."[17] The play, in its initial prose version, would
be restaged ten years later before Leo X at the Vatican, where
the scene designer was Raphael. Yet we may wonder whether
this kind of comedy would ever have been so fully reanimated
if it had not been relocated in—and fostered by—a special
community. The mise-en-scène, both original and papal, had
attempted to recreate the Ferrarese topography; and, as dramatic spectacles multiplied among the rival city-states, they vied
with one another in festive reconstructions of themselves.

Artists and artisans joined their skills in putting together the
varied architectural vistas within a framing proscenium. The
mystery plays had utilized multiple settings, where the actors
moved on from *domus* to *domus;* now, by the art of perspective,
many mansions could be organized into a single illusionistic
prospect. This could consist of "house fronts, squares, porticoes,
streets embellished with arches, columns, statues of various

16. See W. L. Gundersheimer, *Ferrara: The Style of a Renaissance Despotism*
(Princeton, 1973), pp. 210–211.
17. Ludovico Ariosto, *Commedie,* ed. Angela Casella, Gabriella Ronchi,
and Elena Varosi, *Tutte le opere,* IV (Milan, 1974), pp. 239, 327 (*I suppositi,*
4.7.29–30 [prose], 1509–10 [verse]).

kinds," according to the Mantuan impresario Leone di Somi, "the models being taken from this city or that, ancient or modern, according to the demands of the script."[18] Such monumental appurtenances could hardly be duplicated on the makeshift platforms of strolling players. Yet we should take a second look, among Callot's engravings of the Italian comedians, at the absorbing triptych *Les Trois pantalons;* for, while each of these three figures—the Pantalone in person, the Capitano, and the Zanni—looms large over an unlocalized foreground, he is reduced to miniature in the background and presented onstage with other actors; and there the wings jut out to form a street scene framed by receding lines of houses on both sides.[19] Browsing through the repertory of the Commedia dell'Arte, in the standard collection of Flamineo Scala, we may note how the setting passes on from town to town: Rome, Venice, Naples, Milan, Bologna, Florence, Mantua, and Parma. Only the final ten of these fifty scenarios are set in exotic places like Fez, Egypt, Persia, Sparta, and Arcadia; and it is significantly uncharacteristic that, instead of being comedies like the rest, these are classified as operas, except for one tragedy and one pastoral.[20]

Summing the matter up in Aristotelian language, Francesco Robortello flatly affirmed: ". . . no comedy can be recited if the Music and Spectacle are not employed so that the play on the stage appears to be enacted in city or town."[21] The outdoor theater of the Romans had been constructed around a permanent *frons scaenae,* an imposing structure three stories high, symmetrically adorned with pedestals, pilasters, niches, and other components of classical architecture. Along with the entrances *"a foro"* on stage left and *"a peregre"* on stage right, five doors punctuated this ornate façade in the composite plan of Vitru-

18. Translated by Allardyce Nicoll in *The Development of the Theatre* (New York, 1946), p. 257.

19. Gerald Kahan, *Jacques Callot: Artist of the Theatre* (Athens, Ga., 1976), pp. 20–23.

20. See H. F. Salerno, trans., *Scenarios of the Commedia dell'Arte: Flamineo Scala's Il Favole Rappresentative* (New York, 1967).

21. Translated by M. T. Herrick in *Comic Theory in the Sixteenth Century* (Urbana, 1964), p. 231.

vius.[22] The central door was understood as belonging to a royal
palace in tragedy, where the two adjacent ones were assigned
to strangers and sojourners. In comedy the whole array might
conventionally be regarded as a row of habitations fronting on
a square. But the two outermost doorways were arranged to
present at least a stylized suggestion of painted scenery, with
revolving panels or *periaktoi* to designate which of the three
official genres held sway at the moment. The tragic décor *("or-
natus")* would feature pillars, pediments, statues, and other
royal things *("reliquisque regalibus rebus")*. A comic panel would
offer a reproduction of familiar buildings *("imitatione com-
munium aedificiorum")* with windows and balconies. And since
the ancients had realized from the outset that all of human
experience could not be subsumed within the tragic/comic di-
chotomy, they left room for a *tertium quid:* a glimpse of trees,
rocks, mountains, and other rustic features *("reliquisque agres-
tibus rebus")* of the satyric landscape.

Vitruvian principle could be put into practice much more
flexibly and realistically through the two new technical devices
of the Cinquecento, perspective painting and movable scenery.
Scene design was formulated and illustrated and widely influenced by the architectural treatises of Sebastiano Serlio, which
showed how raked stages, canvas side-wings, and *trompe l'oeil*
backcloths could approach the graphic effects of contemporary
painting. The houses in the Comic Scene should be those of
*"personaggi privati, come saria di cittadini, avocati, mercanti,
parasiti, & altre simili persone."*[23] The implication—that law-
yers, merchants, and other citizens are much like professional
parasites—is virtually Machiavellian. But above all *("Ma supra
il tutto")* a bawdy-house is specified (and part of the word *Ruf-
fiana* can be seen, in the illustration, next to the door of the
smallest and nearest house), together with a church, an inn,
and evidently shops. Further specifications indicate practical
windows and balconies, thereby facilitating many an amorous

22. Frank Granger, ed., *Vitruvius on Architecture,* Loeb Classical Library
(London, 1931), I, 288–289.

23. Sebastiano Serlio, *Tutte l'opere d'architettura e prospetiva* (Venice, 1519),
pp. 45–47.

dialogue. The contrasting Tragic Scene is graced by the statelier homes of *"grandi personaggi,"* since the high adventures and cruel deaths in ancient and modern tragedies always occur on the premises of *"Signori, Duchi, ò gran Prencipi, anzi de Rè."* As for the Satyric Scene, here Serlio follows Vitruvius in recommending trees, grass, flowers, rocks, hills, mountains, and fountains, and for good measure includes a rustic hut to house indigenous shepherds or fishermen. He goes somewhat farther by accepting, and attempting to rationalize, the old confusion between *satyr* and *satire.*

Assuming that the Satyr-Plays were vehicles for reproof and castigation, he argues that such chidings of misbehavior could be most appropriately voiced by the *"gente rustica,"* inasmuch as rude countrymen are no respecters of persons. But this bears more resemblance to Old Comedy than to what we know about Greek satyr-drama, a form more firmly linked with tragedy, to which it served as a sportive mythological afterpiece. Serlio's bosky instructions would have their real impact upon the scenography of the pastoral. Previously it would have been much easier to devise a stage-picture involving structures rather than landscapes. But panoramic views of nature, serried in gardens or untamed in forests, were better suited to courtly spectacles than to dramatic performances. The masque was, in some ways, an indoor version of the *fête champêtre.* It was unusual for Inigo Jones, brilliant architect though he was, to depict "a street scene in perspective of fair building,"[24] rather than plazas or groves. When he came to do so, for the antimasque of puppets and pantaloons in Jonson's *Vision of Delight,* he combined suggestions he had borrowed from Serlio's Tragic and Comic Scenes; and for a later masque by the Sieur de Racan, *Artenice,* he drew—with a blending eclecticism—upon the Satyric Scene as well as the other two. Proscenium staging could adapt itself handsomely to interiors, when they were palatial in scale and ornamentation, like the marbled halls and angled apartments of the Bibienas, most suitable for tragedy or opera. New Com-

---

24. Stephen Orgel and Roy Strong, eds., *Inigo Jones: The Theatre of the Stuart Court* (London, 1973), pp. 273–275, 383.

edy has frequented exteriors conceived as neighboring domi-
ciles, with much business in doorways and much speculation
about what might be going on inside.

The circumstance that finds lovers, enemies, or unacquainted
relatives living next door to each other may be one of those
coincidences that turn the sphere of comedy into such a small
world after all. Accordingly, the heroine of the *Miles gloriosus*
can conceal herself by sneaking into the adjacent house and
pretending to be her own twin sister, while the game of cuck-
oldry can rotate through three adjoining households in the scenario of *I tre becchi*.[25] When the comic action went indoors, it
was looking—so to speak—behind the scenes. The neoclassical
playhouse, shaped by aristocratic patronage, would be awkwardly and belatedly adjusted to more democratic needs and
means. Its proportions had become too cavernous, its tormen-
tors and traverses and flats too unrealistic, to be comfortably
domesticated. Comedy of manners was urbane, if no longer
altogether urban. In making up its mind, or regulating its conduct, the English Restoration still deferred to whatever it meant
by "the town"—an area consisting largely of lodgings and cof-
feehouses and parks convenient for rendezvous. The privacy of
the box set grew more and more confining as the middle class,
succeeding the gentry, in its turn was challenged by the working
class, and as the drawing rooms of Somerset Maugham and Noel
Coward were superseded by the kitchen sinks of John Osborne
and Harold Pinter. Yet comedy has never completely relaxed
its municipal ties:

Patched canvas drops of American street scenes hang in almost every
vaudeville and burlesque house in the country. They usually depict a
perspective view of a spotless street broken by car tracks, but unworn
by traffic. On one side a fire plug, on the other a piece of high park
wall showing signboards and paid ads of some of the town's most
enterprising firms; a few hybrid flowers; above the wall green trees;
overhead, a cerulean sky with summer clouds . . . From Tacoma all
the way to Tallahassee, they look like.

25. Reconstructed by Leon Katz in *The Classic Theatre,* ed. Eric Bentley
(New York, 1958), I, 79–144.

Several generations of comedy-teams had cracked their jokes on the "scene-in-one" (on the forestage), in front of those drop curtains which the late Donald Oenslager so nostalgically recollected.[26] And, even while he was writing, he could have pointed to recent and painstaking reproductions of New York City in its theaters: Elmer Rice's *Street Scene* (1929), where a squalid apartment house teemed with ethnic antagonisms, or Sidney Kingsley's *Dead End* (1935), where dripping street urchins emerged from an orchestra pit simulating the East River. Comedy was overshadowed by melodrama in both locations.

Yet comedy—ever since the Renaissance, and preeminently with Shakespeare—has capered increasingly on playgrounds nearer to nature. The satyr-play had prefigured, as it turned out, not so much the satirical as the pastoral drama: *favola boscareccia,* for which the primary example was Torquato Tasso's *Aminta.* The overelaborated imitation by Giambattista Guarini, *Il pastor fido,* which would be so widely imitated, was characterized as *tragicommedia boscareccia.* One of the polemical objections, in the controversy it met, was that city-dwelling playgoers would have little to learn from the mouths of simple-minded rustics—not a very serious argument against the conventions of Virgil and Theocritus. Precept and example for tragicomedy were relayed explicitly to England through John Fletcher's *Faithful Shepherdess;* closer to the vein of the court masque, it could claim no popular success. The romantic comedies of George Peele and Robert Greene, heralded at a more exclusive level by John Lyly, brought some alfresco touches into the public theater. But it was Shakespeare who imposed the pattern that would be summed up in the stage-direction of his editors, "*Another part of the wood* (or *forest*)," and suggestively explained by the paradigm of Northrop Frye: the restorative conception of a "green world."[27] The working-day world to which his characters are restored, after retreat and renewal in a wood near Athens, the Forest of Arden, or an enchanted

26. Donald Oenslager, *Scenery Then and Now* (New York, 1936), p. 77.
27. Northrop Frye, *Anatomy of Criticism: Four Essays* (Princeton, 1957), pp. 182–185.

island, is a ducal court. But in *The Merchant of Venice,* where
the place of refuge is a country villa, the arena of conflict remains
a comic metropolis, the bustling native city of Pantaloon himself.

Treading the Plautine maze in *The Comedy of Errors,* Shakespeare still managed to stay within the purlieus of a Greco-
Roman seaport, though he meaningfully substituted a mysterious Ephesus for a picaresque Epidamnus. His broadest and
darkest depiction of a city is the scandal-ridden Vienna of *Measure for Measure,* whose eavesdropping Duke admits shame-
facedly: ". . . I have seen corruption boil and bubble / Till it
o'errun the stew."[28] That the man of Stratford could be totally
at home in London, holding his own on the chosen ground of
Jonson and Middleton, is demonstrated by the convivial humors
of Eastcheap in both parts of *Henry IV.* Yet, when Falstaff was
suddenly lifted out of history to be anticlimactically set down
in comedy, he found himself rusticated to Windsor (apparently
for ceremonial reasons). "Under the greenwood tree" was the
characteristic site for Shakespearean comedy; and, if the stage
manager could contribute no more than a property-hedge to its
literal flowering, then the resources of speech and song were
ready to supply—as John Keats would observe—an impression
of verdure.[29] At the other extreme the Jonsonian ambience,
whether at Saint Paul's Walk or Saint Mark's Square, was in-
variably and traditionally urbanized. Englishmen, in their life-
style and outlook, have been prone to oscillate between country
and city. Shakespeare and Jonson, in their respective venues,
seem to confirm an inherent disparity between the romantic and
the satirical modes of comedy. But *romantic* is never a satisfactory label, least of all for a dramatic vehicle; C. L. Barber's
*festive* might catch the merry note more aptly, or even Mikhail
Bakhtin's *carnivalesque.*[30]

28. *The Riverside Shakespeare,* ed. G. B. Evans et al. (Boston, 1974), p. 583
(*Measure for Measure,* 5.1.318–319).

29. Ibid., p. 379 (*As You Like It,* 2.5.1); C. F. E. Spurgeon, *Keats's Shakespeare: A Descriptive Study Based on New Material* (Oxford, 1929), p. 52.

30. C. L. Barber, *Shakespeare's Festive Comedy: A Study of Dramatic Form
and Its Relation to Social Custom* (Princeton, 1959), pp. 3–15; Mikhail Bakhtin,
*Rabelais and His World,* trans. Helene Iswolsky (Cambridge, Mass., 1968), pp.
7–23.

The important matter, at all events, is the divergence between these two distinctive strains. M. C. Bradbrook recognizes this in *The Structure of Elizabethan Comedy,* where—taking a hint from Lear's Fool—she subdivides her material into "sweet" and "bitter."[31] The so-called bitter strain, it should be added, is the one that stretches back to the mainstream of New Comedy, whereas sweet comedy seems to have been something of a novelty with—and a specialty of—the Elizabethans. Antithetical parallels could be multiplied: wit and humor, derision or risibility, put-down versus up-beat. Comparably, in earlier Italian literature Francesco De Sanctis discerned the interplay of two opposing impulses: idyll *("ozio di villa")* and carnival *("ozio di città").*[32] The latter, in a different sense from Bakhtin's, was related to the *canti carnascialeschi,* the licensed buffoonery of the towns. The former connoted the secluded elegance of the villas; it fostered idealization as opposed to caricature. Antithesis is converted to paradox in an overstated essay by Vernon Lee, "The Italy of the Elizabethan Dramatists."[33] If, despite "the monstrous immorality of the Italian Renaissance," its writers could escape into an innocent pastoralism, she speculated, then it was left for dramatists like John Webster and Cyril Tourneur to recreate those sins and vices in England's "purer moral atmosphere." Italy was unquestionably ill-famed as a breeding-ground of poison, plot, popery, and Machiavellianism, especially corrupting for susceptible English travelers: *"Inglese italianato è diavolo incarnato."* But, more than any other land, it also provided a wholesome playground for Shakespearean comedy.

And Italy cannot be said to have exercised any monopoly over sinister motivation; France, to seek no farther, is the country of *The Massacre at Paris, Bussy d'Ambois,* and *The Atheist's Tragedy.* Nor was English life deficient in criminal deeds, so far as that goes, such as the case history dramatized in *Arden of*

31. M. C. Bradbrook, *The Structure of Elizabethan Comedy* (London, 1963), p. 13. See *The Riverside Shakespeare,* p. 1262 (*King Lear,* 1.4.144).

32. Francesco De Sanctis, *Storia della letteratura Italiana,* Opere, VIII (Turin, 1958), I, 464.

33. Vernon Lee (Violet Paget), *Euphorion: Being Studies of the Antique and the Mediaeval in the Renaissance* (Boston, 1884), I, 87.

*Feversham* and apocryphally fathered on Shakespeare. Sordid crimes befalling commoners might have been considered unworthy of dramatization by classical-minded critics. Some degree of hesitation is registered by the Induction to *A Warning for Fair Women,* where the tutelary spirit of Tragedy—after contending with personifications of History and Comedy for control of the stage—apologizes to the audience:

> My Sceane is London, natiue and your owne,
> I sigh to thinke, my subiect too well knowne . . .[34]

Her subject is the stuff of sensational broadsheet journalism rather than of grandiose historical chronicles. Take away the sensation of violence, leaving adultery and death, as Thomas Heywood did in *A Woman Killed with Kindness,* and you have a preview of domestic drama, its ethical departures emphasized by the paradoxical title and embodied in the personage of the sympathetic cuckold. Heywood strove to bring the middle class into the realm of chronicle history in *The Life and Death of Sir Thomas Gresham, with the Building of the Royal Exchange.* Most of these documentaries took an admonitory and moralistic tone, which recalls the occasional urban echoes in the moralities and interludes. The transition is evident in a hybrid play like *The Three Ladies of London* (1581) and its sequel, where the abstractions are secularized with cockney overtones. Jonson was to refine upon this process, but not wholly to transcend it, with *The Devil Is an Ass.* In the pseudo-Shakespearean morality, *The London Prodigal,* a harsh outline is again filled in with local coloring. The prodigal motif repeats itself not infrequently, since the scriptural parable was reinforced by the gap between errant sons and ultimately forgiving fathers in New Comedy.

Playwrights could be vague about foreign lands, and careless about shifting scenes from one territory—or period—to another. In the two plots of *Satiromastix,* under the stress of an altercation with Jonson—"the War of the Theaters"—Marston and Thomas Dekker spliced together Augustan Rome and Norman England. Patriotism and xenophobia, which gathered full

34. *A Warning for Fair Women,* ed. J. S. Farmer, Tudor Facsimile Texts (London, 1912), p. A3.

scope in the histories, animated lesser episodes like the international courtship in William Haughton's *An Englishman for
My Money*. Heywood truckled to such sentiments in his *Four
Prentices of London, with the Conquest of Jerusalem;* his heroes
had rehearsed for their crusading triumphs by selling groceries,
jewelry, haberdashery, and dry goods respectively. This attempt
to wrap commerce in the trappings of romance provoked an
upper-class response from Francis Beaumont's *Knight of the
Burning Pestle,* which burlesques a play-within-a-play entitled
*The London Merchant* and employs the antiromantic formula
of *Don Quixote* to demythologize an enchanted forest into Wal-
tham Green. With *The Shoemakers' Holiday* (1599) Dekker had
already glorified the middle-class workshop-household and established the genial tradesman as hero. Simon Eyre's success-
story was authenticated by the chronicles, and had figured in
Thomas Deloney's *Gentle Craft* along with two saints' legends
advertising the same trade. Touchstone, the master-goldsmith
of *Westward Ho,* is such another benevolently paternalistic em-
ployer, presiding over the Hogarthian fable of an idle and an
industrious apprentice, while the golden quest of the new-world
adventurer Sir Petronel Flash winds up at the Isle of Dogs, a
garbage-dump in the Thames.

*Eastward Ho* (1605), written in an unlikely collaboration between Jonson and Marston together with George Chapman,
was a successor to *Westward Ho* and a predecessor of *Northward
Ho* (both by Dekker collaborating with Webster), which dealt
with unattractive triangles of citizens' wives, cuckolded merchants, and gallants-about-town. Those centrifugal titles are not
as expansive as their transatlantic reverberations may seem to
modern ears; they were river-cries—if not street-cries—of London, when boatmen ferried passengers up and down and across
the Thames. This seamy-sided trilogy, all three within a year
or so of *Othello, Macbeth,* and *King Lear,* bears witness to the
many-leveled range of Jacobean drama. Even within the pre-
cincts of city comedy, two schools were now diverging. To the
more easygoing tendency, the sentimental cult of homespun
virtue, the reaction was a reversion, not less observant because
it was hard-boiled, combining—in its worldly wisdom and resourceful roguery—the oldest traditions of New Comedy with

the latest muckraking exposures of the Coney-Catching Pamphlets. The protean Middleton emerged as a frequent collaborator, working early with Dekker on the breezy topicalities of *The Roaring Girl*. He proceeded to put his own stamp upon a prolific sequence of vivid and fast-moving comedies before turning, with incisive effect, to Italianate (or, in the most notable instance, *The Changeling*, Hispanic) tragedy. Under Cavalier or Restoration auspices, the attitude toward the citizenry would be scornful or patronizing; with the gradual ascendancy of the bourgeoisie, it would once more be softened and sentimentalized.

Though he is adept at portraying the colorful vagrants of the underworld, Middleton's recurrent issue is the tension between the landed gentry and the money-grubbing shopkeepers. The rise and fall of Quomodo, the social-climbing usurer of *Michaelmas Term*, lodges a serious reservation against the Touchstones and Simon Eyres. Twenty-five years after *A Trick to Catch the Old One*, Philip Massinger reworked the situation in *A New Way to Pay Old Debts* (1633), casting it into the melodramatic shadow of the mortgage-brandishing Sir Giles Overreach. During that era of sharpened commercial pressures, from Elizabeth's last years through James's reign, drama became an implicit "critique of society," which has been thoughtfully elucidated by L. C. Knights.[35] Yet, as an underlying motive, "the acquisitive attitude" has been one of the comic universals. The axiom that everything has its price carried the corollary that men and women—some or all, depending on the playwright's cynicism—are reducible to rogues and whores. If they are unwilling to engage in the general chicanery, if they are not deceitful coney-catchers, then they are credulous gulls, for Jonson at any rate. And if they are more eager to cheat than most of the others, then it is the irony of ironies to behold the cheater cheated, the knave exposed as fool. The terse concluding statement in the Plautine acrostic that summarizes Volpone, *"all are sold,"* has a double meaning: all are bartered, all are fooled.[36]

35. L. C. Knights, *Drama and Society in the Age of Jonson* (London, 1951), pp. 175ff.

36. Herford and Simpson, *Ben Jonson*, V (1937), p. 23 (*Volpone*, Argument, 7).

This could not have happened anywhere else with such guile, such seduction, or such bedazzlement as in Venice, the most mercantile of cities, the delusive capital of Shylock and Iago.

Jonson, the congenital Londoner, had first made his mark with *Every Man in his Humor* (1598), but it had been situated in Florence by the original text, which would be naturalized in the Folio version (1616), where "Thorello" and "Musco" became "Kitely" and "Brainworm," while "Friary" and "Rialto" became "Tower" and "Exchange."[37] Though we cannot precisely date the metamorphosis, it may well have been Jonson's participation in *Eastward Ho* that determined him to anglicize his future work for the stage, just when he was beginning to envision remoter regions through the scenic possibilities of the masque. His first play set in London, *The Silent Woman* (1609), confined itself to the more fashionable quarters; fittingly, it was performed by child actors in one of the private theaters, and would be most highly rated by the generation of John Dryden and Samuel Pepys. His only other comedy in prose, *Bartholomew Fair* (1614), is his broadest and most atmospheric evocation of low-life in its sights and sounds and smells. At his most effective in *The Alchemist* (1610), he there repatriated and tightened up the structure and the strategy of *Volpone*. The house in Blackfriars where the coneys are gulled could have abutted on Jonson's personal residence. With the exception of one neighborly chorus gossiping outside, all of the action goes on within it, moving from room to room with the door-slamming acceleration of a Georges Feydeau. Jonson proclaims his dramaturgic homecoming in the prologue:

> Our Scene is London, 'cause we would make knowne,
>   No countries mirth is better than our owne.
> No clime breeds better matter, for your whore,
>   Bawd, squire, impostor, many persons more,
> Whose manners, now call'd humors, feed the stage.[38]

The idealistic endeavors of Renaissance humanism to emulate and outrival its classical precedents are turned upside down in

37. Ibid., I (1925), pp. 358ff.
38. Ibid., V, 294 (*The Alchemist*, Prologue, 5–9).

this declaration. Its first two lines read like an ironic repetition
of the couplet quoted above from *A Warning for Fair Women*
(1599). Jonson's fragmentary and posthumous pastoral, *The Sad
Shepherd*, would promise *"a Fleece / To match, or those of*
Sicily, *or* Greece," woven out of *"such wooll, / As from meere*
English *Flocks his* Muse *can pull."*[39] Here the mock-encomium
of the last three lines is the unpatriotic boast that England can
outdo all other nations when it comes to nurturing *mauvais
sujets.*

No more than four specific exemplars are mentioned: "im-
postor," broadly relevant to nearly every comedy; "whore" and
"bawd," momentarily applicable to Doll Common and Face;
and "squire," referring concretely but untypically to the minor
figure of Kastril. Yet Jonson must have had, at the back of his
mind, the roll call of classical archetypes that Terence rather
wearily enumerates in his prologues: *senex iratus, servus currens,
parasitus edax, miles gloriosus*, and the rest.[40] And Sir Philip
Sidney, in defending "the right use of *Comoedie*," had instanced
the eye-opening display "of a niggardly *Demea*, of a craftie
*Davus*, of a flattering *Gnato*, of a vain-glorious *Thraso*," all of
them Terentian prototypes—Demea from the *Adelphoe*, Davus
from the *Andria* or the *Phormio*, Gnatho and Thraso from the
*Eunuchus*.[41] Any repertory company, whether the Commedia
dell'Arte or Hamlet's players at Elsinore, must operate through
typecasting with such roles. When Shakespeare revivified the
*topos* of the world as stage, *theatrum mundi*, he allotted seven
parts to be successively experienced by one developing individual. Jonson's more collective outlook stressed the constants of
human nature, though he seems here to have reached the point
of reconciling humors with manners. Having left behind his
reforming zeal to put every man out of his humor, he was all
the happier in his delineation of humorous varieties and oddities, which could be sorted out and codified by the norms of
classical decorum. But psychology never freed itself from ty-

39. Ibid., VII (1941), p. 9 (*The Sad Shepherd*, 13–14, 9–10).

40. John Sargeant, ed., *Terence*, Loeb Classical Library (London, 1939), I,
120, 238 (*Heauton timorumenos*, 35–40; *Eunuchus*, 36–40).

41. Sir Philip Sidney, *The Defense of Poesie* . . . , ed. Albert Feuillerat,
*Complete Works*, III (Cambridge, 1929), p. 23.

pology. He would not, as a classicist, have questioned the conditions laid down by Ovid for poetic survival:

> Dum fallax servus, durus pater, inproba lena
> Vivent et meretrix blanda, Menandros erit.[42]

Jonson went out of his way to smooth Christopher Marlowe's nervous translation of this elegiac couplet from the *Amores:*

> Whil'st Slaves be false, Fathers hard, or Bauds be whorish,
> Whilst Harlots flatter, shall Menander florish.[43]

Immortality is uncertain, however, if it is contingent upon the persistence of unchanging models and customs. When slavery has been abolished, when parasitism is no longer acceptable as a profession, when women are released from the subordination and effacement that constrained Menander's heroines, some of the stereotypes get outmoded and the conventions need to be modified. Insofar as these advances are less than complete, New Comedy continues to revive—or, at all events, survive—in the realization that many of its *personae* are still with us, *mutatis mutandis. "Plus ça change, plus c'est la même chose"* is one of its stalest and most durable gags, true enough as far as it goes, but never very encouraging.

Introducing *Terence in English,* his Elizabethan translator wrote: "he will tell you the nature of the fraudulent flatterer, the grimme and greedie old Sire, the roysting ruffian, the minsing mynion, and the beastly baud; that in telling the truth by these figments, men might become wise to auoid such vices, and learne to practise vertue."[44] Stated with such generality, this comment allows for broader applications. Yet, when the roistering Thraso and the flattering Gnatho were exhumed in the academic guise of Ralph Roister Doister and Matthew Merrygreek, they were ineptly and incompletely reincarnated. Comedy, more than tragedy, is a creature of its times. Responding

---

42. Ovid, *Heroides* and *Amores,* ed. Grant Showerman, Loeb Classical Library (London, 1914), p. 376.

43. Christopher Marlowe, *Complete Works,* ed. Fredson Bowers (Cambridge, 1973), II, 340.

44. Richard Bernard, trans., *Terence in English: Fabulae Comici . . .* (London, 1598), p. A2v.

to the urbanization of the Renaissance, it was soon caught up
in that cultural process, and commenced to lose the distance
needed for maintaining a critical vantage-point. *La cour* could
laugh at *la ville* when the première of *Le Bourgeois Gentil-
homme* took place before Louis XIV at his Chateau de Cham-
bord. During the eighteenth century, satire was at its sharpest
in theatrical pieces like John Gay's *Beggar's Opera* or Alain-
René Lesage's *Turcaret;* but sentiment was taking over, with a
newer bourgeois audience which preferred its drama to dwell
upon family rather than business. It is not surprising, confronted
with so wide a diversity in ideological premises, that the nineteenth century should wonder whether or not it was a time
for comedy—a problem which I have discussed elsewhere.[45]
Since by then the novel had everywhere been confirmed as the
*genre par excellence* of its age, perhaps we might more positively
conclude that the heritage of city comedy is best sought in the
prose fiction of Balzac, Dickens, Gogol, and Joyce.

45. "Dramatic Auspices: The Playwright and His Audience," in Harry Levin,
*Shakespeare and the Revolution of the Times: Perspectives and Commentaries*
(New York, 1976), pp. 284–312.

MORTON W. BLOOMFIELD

# The Elegy and the Elegiac Mode: Praise and Alienation

Although by no means the same as the relation between tragedy and the tragic mode,[1] the relation of elegy to the elegiac mode bears similarities to the former distinction. Certain genres, not all, are accompanied in the history of literature by modal relations. Both tragedy and elegy belong to this class. It is important, moreover, to distinguish the two. Matthew Arnold's "Dover Beach" is written in the elegiac mode, whereas Shelley's "Adonais" and Auden's "Elegy on the Death of Yeats" are true elegies in the English manner of presenting this genre.[2] Like elegies, Shelley's and Auden's poems praise, lament, and console (the consolation often saved to the end). These three

1. On this distinction, see Clayton Koelb, " 'Tragedy' and 'The Tragic': The Shakespearean Connection," *Genre,* 13 (1980), 275–286.
2. "Tragedy," as Koelb points out, is a subdivision of the "tragic"; so also elegy is a subdivision of the elegiac mode. All tragedies are tragic and all elegies are elegiac (that is, they belong to the elegiac mode). Yet the tragic and the elegiac modes include a vast number of poems or works which are not tragedies or elegies. This distinction is a useful one.

purposes appear in different proportions in different poems. In the elegiac mode, however, we find alienated and/or sad poems which mix various moods and actions and are extremely personal. In English, the elegiac mode is largely, though not exclusively, the creation of the Romantic movement, and it has flourished from about 1750 to today, when it has perhaps become the predominant mode and mood of lyric poetry.

The mode is harder to define precisely than is the genre. It does not appear in English literature much before the 1740s. Coleridge, confusing the elegy with the elegiac mode, defines it as follows: "Elegy is the form of poetry natural to the reflective mind. It may treat of any subject [*sic*], but it must treat of no subject *for itself*, but always and exclusively with reference to the poet himself. As he will feel regret for the past or desire for the future, so sorrow and love become the principal themes of elegy."[3]

In other words, any personal poem could be called an elegy in the Romantic and later periods. That meaning did not, however, drive out the older sense of the word, which I shall try to define shortly. As is well known, elegy was considered in classical times a genre making use of a special meter and dealing with a variety of subjects. The elegiac mode is not a genre but a mode of approaching reality and was hardly named before the eighteenth century, although it is certainly to be found in earlier poetry. It will be helpful to make use of both these terms.

Turning first to "elegy," let us begin with Aristotle, as is proper. It is about time to take seriously Aristotle's dictum in the *Poetics* that all poetry arises in praise, blame, or hymns. I think we can ignore hymns, which are obviously a variety of praise poems, and reduce the categories to the remaining two. Whether Aristotle is totally correct in this statement one cannot be sure, but I am convinced that praise and blame are historically the final causes (as Aristotle would put it) of much early poetry. Although many scholars and thinkers have admitted the importance of praise and blame in the whole history of Western and indeed world poetry, especially before the nineteenth century, few have explored the implications of Aristotle's dictum.

3. *Table Talk,* 12 October 1833.

It is not my purpose here to pursue this matter, but I should like to discuss the notion of praise as applicable to the history of elegy. Many other genres (in the loose sense of the word) have strong links to praise. I have myself written that much narrative, especially of the epic, heroic, and romance variety, can be best explained by the original drive to praise, and I think the notion can be extended.

The word "elegy" has a long and complex history. Poems called elegies in English have been strongly influenced by the classical and, to a lesser extent, biblical traditions. The Bible includes an entire elegiac book in the Book of Lamentations, as well as David's poetic lamentations over the deaths of Saul, Absalom, and Abner. Other biblical examples are to be found, especially in the prophetic books.

To complicate matters, the word "elegy" has been used for a number of poems, some so far apart in purpose that it is hard to see how the same word could be used to describe them. Elegy first referred to a metrical form in Greek literature, a form which must have had a wide range of usage.[4] In Latin the elegiac couplet approximating the Greek form consisted of a distich (unrhymed of course), having a first line of six feet followed by one of what has been somewhat dubiously counted as five feet. The basic effect, which one can only guess at, must have been rather stately and formal. In Greek it was probably originally used in lamenting the death of a person or a people, or the destruction of a city or army.[5] Later it became for some surprising reason a popular form for love poetry. The only common element was the use of elegiac, a general metrical pattern which defined the form. The term until the end of the Renaissance was used to define any poem using this meter. Yet the use of the metrical form to express both love and lamentation per-

4. On this metrical form, see M. L. West, *Greek Metre* (Oxford, 1982), pp. 44–46.

5. See esp. Margaret Alexiou, *The Ritual Lament in Greek Tradition* (Cambridge, 1974), pp. 104–108 et passim. An introduction to ancient Greek elegies may be found in C. M. Bowra, *Early Greek Elegists* (Cambridge, Mass., 1935). An edition with commentary on the Greek elegies may be found in Jean Defradas, *Les élégiaques grecs: édition, introduction, et commentaire*, Erasme: Collection de textes grecs commentés (Paris, 1962).

sisted. Love has its ups and downs, and perhaps the term "lamentation" unifies funerals and love affairs. During the Renaissance, Latin elegies written in an artificial and reconstructed classical Latin flourished: in fact, one can say that in every century down to today, "classical" elegies continued to be written about death and sorrow or about love. In the Middle Ages there were few in comparison with classical poetic structures, but Latin elegies in rhythmic verse were common.

The word in English, however, tended to be used primarily to indicate lamentation or, later, various mood poems. It also moved over into music as well, to describe stately and serious works. By Coleridge's time the meaning of the word in English poetry was exceedingly vague. Any personal poem in any meter could be called an elegy; in English and possibly in other Western European languages the term referred to a self-oriented poem often but not always rather melancholic. Self-reflection was its characteristic feature. This meaning must have taken over in the last half of the eighteenth century—the age of Werther, of "The Elegy in a Country Churchyard," and of poems featuring death or its approach, or lamentation over the world or the self, or poems concentrating on *Sehnsucht*. Yet in the Romantic period we do have many elegies in the lamentation mode—Shelley's *Adonais* and Matthew Arnold's *Thyrsis* come to mind. German literature knows few lamentation elegies, although there are many in French. There we may recall the *oraisons funèbres* of Bossuet and others also in prose, not to speak of poems as well.

Inasmuch as lamentation was probably the original purpose of the elegy, the eighteenth-century and Romantic elegy was not so novel as it might seem, but the tone was novel with its emphasis on the author rather than on what is being lamented. The shift to the self made a difference; for the voice, unlike those of classical Greek elegies, does not represent the community but the self.

In the nineteenth century, also, as the difficulties of Anglo-Saxon or Old English were gradually being unfolded and explained, poems like "The Wanderer" and "The Seafarer," which were in some sense personal lamentations, were classified as elegies. That name for them has persisted, even though they were not poems like Milton's *Lycidas* or Shelley's *Adonais*. Possibly, the early nineteenth-century Old English scholar Conybeare gave them this name. These poems seemed to be personal and to some degree, although probably not heavily, autobiographical. No ready literary generic term springs to mind for them. It was natural to think of them as elegies, though I myself have always preferred to call them meditative poems, belonging to that large category of poetry, now generally thought little of, called wisdom literature. On the surface these poems seem to report the personal experience of a wanderer and a seafarer. Their tone is somewhat mournful it is true, but a mournful strain alone does not make an elegy. Furthermore, the speakers are representative, not individual. The lament of the last survivor and of the professional woman mourner at the death of Beowulf are true elegies, or perhaps more exactly, elegiac passages in that poem. But "The Wanderer" and "The Seafarer" are not, though lines 19–57 of "The Wanderer" constitute an elegiac section.

The Middle Ages produced elegies of the meditative kind in its whole length. Sometimes they are subdivisions of longer poems, usually narratives, and at other times they stand on their own. There is a long, continuous line of such poems or passages extending from the ancient Middle and Near East down to today. They flourish more in Asia and Africa than in Western Europe or North America, but even in these latter continents they have not entirely disappeared.

Elegies in the Middle English period tend to be incidental, with a lamentation on someone's death occupying a small part of a longer poem.[6] Chaucer's *Book of the Duchess* is, however, an elegy on the death of Blanche, wife of John of Gaunt. *The Pearl* is a notable English elegy. Sir Ector's lamentation on the death of his brother, Sir Lancelot, in Malory's *Morte* is powerful, moving, and beautiful. It echoes anaphorically a long list of virtues:

6. See V. Bourgeois Richmond, *Laments for the Dead in Medieval Narrative,* Duquesne Studies: Philological Series 8 (Pittsburgh, 1966), and her earlier thesis at the University of North Carolina, Chapel Hill, 1959, covering the English Renaissance period to Christopher Marlowe.

Thou were head of all Christian knights; . . .
Thou were never matched of earthly knight's hand; . . .
Thou were the courteoust knight that ever bore shield; . . .
Thou were the truest friend to thy lover that bestrode
    horse; . . .
Thou were the truest lover of sinful men that ever
    loved woman; . . .
Thou were the kindest man that ever struck with the
    sword; . . .
Thou were the goodliest person that ever came among
    press of knights; . . .
Thou were the meekest man and the gentlest that ever
    ate in hall among ladies; . . .
Thou were the sternest knight to thy mortal foe that
    ever put spear in the rest.[7]

With the Renaissance, however, elegy enjoyed an exuberant growth which has never been explained, except perhaps with general reference to the revival of the classics, especially Latin. But this hardly accounts for the English Renaissance emphasis on elegy as a lament for a death. While there were some love elegies in the English Renaissance, the subject of most elegies was lamentation rather than wooing. Spenser, Sidney, Jonson, Drummond, Giles Fletcher, and Donne, not to speak of less renowned Elizabethans or Jacobeans, all wrote mourning elegies.

The funeral elegy, as O. B. Hardison notes,[8] is composed of praise, lament, and consolation. We find these three elements in Donne's *Anniversaries* and many other poems. Curtius in his *European Literature and the Latin Middle Ages*[9] identifies the following topics in both classical and medieval praises: inexpressibility, outdoing (subject surpasses all those with whom he is compared), and universal renown, all of which were claimed for the dead man and his acts.

The elegy tradition of the early and mid-seventeenth century

7. Thomas Malory, *Le Morte d'Arthur,* Caxton ed., xxi, 13.

8. See his *Enduring Monument* (Chapel Hill, 1962) and also Barbara K. Lewalski, *Donne's Anniversaries and the Poetry of Praise: The Creation of a Symbolic Mode* (Princeton, 1973), esp. for Donne's elegies and praise.

9. Bollingen Series 36, trans. Willard R. Trask (New York, 1963), pp. 154–164.

culminated in Milton's great elegy *Lycidas*, and in the somewhat personal moodiness of *Il Penseroso*, close to the elegiac mode. The elegy in the Restoration and the eighteenth century proliferated greatly. Elegies are to be found almost everywhere, many of them badly written, but some passable and a few even good. Widely but not exclusively regarded as a mortuary or death poem of praise, lamentation, and/or consolation, eighteenth-century elegies were usually objective and not very personal. Those written for the deaths of royalty and persons of high rank were not personal at all, but they did perform a social function for those memorialized. In the so-called graveyard poetry of Parnell, Blair, and Gray we find a proto-romanticism which led ultimately to the personalization of the elegy in the nineteenth century. Gray's *Elegy* is, however, somewhat unique in that it celebrates the death of a representative group of humble, ordinary people, in a kind of early socialist or populist spirit.[10]

I have already referred to several nineteenth- and twentieth-century elegists; others are Matthew Arnold, Keats, Whitman, Hardy, Yeats, Lawrence, and Eliot. All of these drew upon the lamentative aspect of elegy and often wrote elegies in form.[11]

In spite of the various tones and subjects associated with the genre, I wish to concentrate on the lamentation. While German elegies are rarely, if ever, lamentations or dirges, the English have tended to emphasize what I consider the oldest and central aspect of the elegy: the lamentation.

Lamentation or threnody or dirge as it appears in early cultures strongly emphasizes praise of the deceased. It may also offer consolation and lamentation (in the narrow sense of the word), but praise is the major element. There are a number of tropes which pertain to the lamentation, with some deviation depending on the culture studied, but with surprising similarities. The Bantu lamentations in southern Africa seem to be directed at the ancestors of the deceased one. I believe the purpose is to call their descendants to the attention of these

10. On the eighteenth-century elegy, see John W. Draper, *The Funeral Elegy and the Rise of English Romanticism* (New York, 1929).

11. See also Abbie Findlay Potts, *The Elegiac Mode: Poetic Form in Wordsworth and Other Elegists* (Ithaca, 1967).

deceased spirits, who like to hear their living relatives praised. In ancient cultures such lamentations seem to be recited by the mourners (usually women who are regularly called upon to perform this office) to accompany the soul or spirit to the abode of its ancestors and to ensure a good reception for it. As the Bible puts it, they sleep with their fathers. Usually a special type of incantation as well as traditional gestures are used while the intonation goes on, and music is often performed. In some cultures, such as the Greek, the flute is played with a characteristic melody.

While the early elegy as preserved in Greece usually is not a funeral song, there is no doubt that music and lamentation did accompany burial or incineration. There are also later elegies, not always in elegiac meter.[12] Although obviously this cannot be proved, the actions and the words of modern Greek lamentations, and those of other cultures including China, are centered on praise of the dead one. The guardian spirits or, in Greek, the *telonia* of the heavens who block the passage of souls could thereby perhaps be influenced to be kind.

Praise is in this matter decisive. Praise still is the usual accompaniment of burials and incinerations throughout the world. It also is used to welcome and honor heroes or great men. It is still echoed today in toasts, in introductions, and even at sports stadiums. Blame still survives too, in spells, games, cursing, and other manifestations. We in the West no longer have professional praisers and blamers, but praise and blame occupy an important place in modern Western life and an extremely important place in other areas of the world.

The elegy as a mourning or funeral poem was surely the root of elegies. I cannot explain with any certainty why it came to be a favorite form for the Latin and, to some extent, Greek

12. For example, Theocritus' *Pastorals* 15 contains an elegy over Adonis, as does Bion's *Lament for Adonis*. Moschos has left us, inter alia, a *Lament over Bion*. These elegies may all be found in J. M. Edwards' edition of *The Greek Bucolic Poets,* Loeb Library (rpt. Cambridge, Mass. and London, 1950 [1912 original]), pp. 190–196 (Theocritus), pp. 386–395 (Bion), and pp. 443–455 (Moschos). See also Virgil's Eclogue 10, a lamentation by Gallus on his desertion by his lover, another type of elegy. It may be found in vol. 1 of the Loeb edition of Virgil's poetry, ed. Rushton Fairclough, rev. 1962.

love poems, but it seems to me that praise of one's beloved provided the transition. If elegiac distichs could praise the dead person on his journey to the next world, they could certainly be suitable for a love song, and even possibly for soldiers going into battle. In other words, "praise" is the crucial and unifying notion, which brings together spirited military and love poems with lamentations for the dead. It may even explain the use of Greek elegiac meter in poems written for public meetings, competitions, and banquets. Elegies reflect one of the basic psychological needs of humanity: praise, with consolation and lament given with less emphasis.

The nineteenth- and twentieth-century emphasis upon the elegiac mood rather than the elegy is a noteworthy change. In such poems sadness, depression, and grief rather than praise, lamentation, and consolation receive the chief emphasis. In recent years alienation has also found its place in the trilogy of sadness, depression, and grief. Alienation from this world, the goal of Stoicism, Platonism, and early Christianity alike, was often admired by humans as ennobling, but it has since become a deplorable emotion. Hegel is probably the father of the modern concept, which received a great boost from Marx, from romanticism, and from the loss of faith in religion. The modern Western poem in the elegiac mode is a lamentation on the loss of faith in the goodness and joy of this world and on self-despair, or *Sehnsucht*.

This new alienation is found in much modern poetry. Robert Lowell, Anne Sexton, and Sylvia Plath spring to mind, not to speak of others, like Ashbery, Stevens, Trakl, Mandelstam, and Celan. Suggestions of alienation may be found earlier, but it does not flourish until the nineteenth and twentieth centuries. These poems are only superficially similar to the long tradition of praise elegies, in spite of their name. Both the personal poems Coleridge speaks of and the alienation poems which have flourished in our century indicate the rise of a new kind of mood poem. This is not simply a new turn in the long history of the elegy, but a new kind of poem which has branched off from its parent line. The traditional elegy, however, is still to be found, although it is not as significant a genre as formerly. The elegiac mode is not a new type of traditional elegy, but rather a new type of poem bearing only a slight resemblance to its ancestor. It is more romantic, more personal, and more despairing. It is self-directed for the most part, rather than socially directed. It brings little or no comfort and is often mired in despair. By contrast, the traditional elegy is not personal nor despairing nor lost.

In a recent talk, the well-known American poet Maxine Kumin, who has been the Library of Congress Poet, spoke of the elegiac mode as the dominant mode of modern poetry. I am inclined to agree. Alienation, the loss of faith in religion and the liberal spirit, and the increase in violence and hate have all contributed to a deep mood of depression, if not despair, in the Western world.

The modern elegy which is a descendant of the traditional one is somewhat more personal than its ancestor, but it is basically in the same tradition. The elegiac poem, however, represents a mode, not a genre, and reflects a psychological state rather than a social or historical occasion. The purpose of the elegiac is the total expression of a personality, whereas the traditional elegy is rather an answer to a social and national need.

What we have is a long tradition, beginning with oral poetry of praise[13]—from praise of the living to praise of the dead, and then to praise of warriors and of feasts, banquets, festivals, public meetings, and competitions, and above all, praise of the beloved. The epideictic and memorial function no doubt was present from the beginning, but chance has preserved only a few such early poems. Then, in the Hellenistic Age a great flood of love elegies is found, although not so many as in the later Latin tradition. The elegy as praise of a dead person persisted, however, and began to flourish again in the late Classical period and early Middle Ages. This tradition continued down to at least the early twentieth century, but beginning in the eighteenth century the term "elegy," without losing its earlier meaning, came to be applied to poems of personal mood, especially congenial to the Romantic soul.

13. For a recent discussion of oral praise poems, see Paul Zumthor, *Introduction à la poésie orale* (Paris, 1983), p. 94.

The elegiac mode must be seen, if we look at the matter historically, as an offshoot of the older tradition of elegy. It is not a new genre but a new mode, satisfying the yearnings of the Romantic movement and reflecting the modern notion of alienation. The story is not over yet. The funeral elegy will certainly persist in some form, inasmuch as we can count on death being with us for a good while. What will happen to the elegiac poems is especially interesting if, as I think, the alienation they express is the forerunner of a new religiousness, which may manifest itself in traditional or nontraditional forms.

MARY THOMAS CRANE

*Intret Cato:*
Authority and the Epigram in
Sixteenth-Century England

The complex interrelationships between forms of authority and
forms of authorship in the sixteenth century have been the subject of a number of recent studies that explore the issue of
authority in various dramatic, epic, and lyric kinds.[1] Critics have
not, however, given much attention to the authoritative epigram, a genre that might seem initially to have no claim to
authority in the company of tragedy, epic, lyric, and masque.[2]
This essay will indicate the basis for such a claim, tracing through
the sixteenth century the development of several subgenres of

1. For example, Stephen Greenblatt, *Renaissance Self-Fashioning* (Chicago,
1980); and also a special issue of *Genre,* 15 (1982), ed. Greenblatt, called *The
Forms of Power and the Power of Forms in the Renaissance;* John Guillory,
*Poetic Authority* (New York, 1983); and Richard Helgerson, *Self-Crowned Laureates* (Berkeley, 1983).
2. The epigram is not a lyric kind, although it came to impinge upon the
lyric and other genres in the late sixteenth and early seventeenth centuries, for
which see Rosalie Colie, *The Resources of Kind,* ed. Barbara K. Lewalski
(Berkeley, 1973), pp. 67–75; and Alastair Fowler, *Kinds of Literature* (Cambridge, Mass., 1982), pp. 195–202.

epigram that sought to embody poetically the moral authority of humanists and reformers.

Richard Helgerson, examining the efforts of Ben Jonson to distinguish himself as a serious and authoritative "laureate" poet, finds Jonson's attempt to make the epigram a vehicle for laureate ambition both original and ultimately unsuccessful.[3] For Helgerson, the epigram is a youthful, "amateur" genre, finally unable to bear the weight of Jonson's efforts at laureate self-presentation.[4] Jonson's choice of the epigram, however, is best understood in relation to the subgenres of serious epigram established in the sixteenth century as the chief poetic outlet for humanist moral authority.[5] In fact, the development of the epigram in England in the course of the sixteenth century involved a struggle between rival forms of the genre—between the epigram in the tradition of Martial as a witty, youthful "trifle," and the epigram in the tradition of several classical and nonclassical sources as a serious didactic kind. The epigrams of the seventeenth century, particularly those of Jonson, Herbert, and Herrick, rest upon the experiments of sixteenth-century epigrammatists and upon the strong tradition of the authoritative moral epigram that some of them established.

Most critics divide the epigrams written in England in the sixteenth century into two groups: an early, quite disparate cluster, consisting of both neo-Latin and English poems, and the entirely separate series of satiric epigrams written in the 1590s.[6] Many writers follow T. K. Whipple in tracing a gradual

3. Helgerson, *Self-Crowned Laureates,* pp. 101–103. Helgerson defines "self-crowned laureates" as poets "whose ambition preceded and determined their work . . . who strove to achieve a major literary career and who said so" (p. 1). He focuses on the "gestures of self-presentation" by which these poets found a place for serious poetry within a "system of authorial roles" that seemed to allow only for frivolous amateurs or professional dramatists.

4. Ibid., pp. 108–109, 183–184.

5. Helgerson, ibid., pp. 26–28, contrasts the stance of Elizabethan "amateur" poets with the "Humanist" idea that poetry obstructed the educated man's ideal goal of service to the state. "Amateur" poets presented themselves as indulging in a youthful pastime that they would soon renounce to undertake a serious career.

6. T. K. Whipple, *Martial and the English Epigram from Sir Thomas Wyatt to Ben Jonson,* University of California Publications in Modern Philology, 10, no. 4 (Berkeley, 1925), p. 302.

progression toward the effective imitation of Martialian wit, culminating, of course, in Jonson's masterful return to "the old way, and the true."[7] Considered in this light, the efforts of the early writers are puzzling; they are blamed for their lack of interest in classical models, especially Martial, and for their inability to imitate his "point." The general feeling seems to be that these writers did not understand the genre, that they were not really writing epigrams.[8]

If, however, we try to judge these early English epigrammatists on their own terms and not in comparison with a single classical model, their versions of the epigram begin to make more sense. In the first place, theorists of the epigram in sixteenth-century England do not consider the "pointed" conclusion as a defining characteristic of the genre; the word "point" was not applied to the epigram in England until 1643.[9] Puttenham is the only English critic of the period to refer, even briefly, to the end of an epigram and to the rhetorical device "epiphonema," which is usually identified with "point."[10] And in the second place, a careful and sympathetic reading of the early epigrams themselves reveals that a number of nonclassical sources were as important as classical ones in defining the possibilities of the genre. Particularly important are the several classical and nonclassical models for the seriously moral or didactic epigram.

7. C. H. Herford and Percy and Evelyn Simpson, eds., *Ben Jonson,* 11 vols. (Oxford, 1947), VIII, 18, 2. See also Ira Clark, "Ben Jonson's Imitation," *Criticism,* 20 (1978), 107–127; and Jack D. Winner, "Ben Jonson and the Conventions of Formal Verse Satire," *Studies in English Literature,* 23 (1983), 61–76, for different accounts of Jonson's use of Martial.

8. Whipple, *Martial and the English Epigram,* p. 303, for example. Leicester Bradner, *Musae Anglicanae* (New York, 1940), pp. 77–78, notes that the term "epigram" in the sixteenth century "covered a wide variety of short poems, imitative of a wide variety of sources." But he calls Constable "dull" and "medieval" (p. 18). Hoyt Hopewell Hudson, *The Epigram in the English Renaissance* (1947; rpt. New York, 1966), chaps. 3–4, gives a more sympathetic account of what he calls the "scholarly" tradition of epigram, but he still considers the Martialian satiric epigram as the standard form of the genre from which the earlier writers diverge in various ways (p. 13).

9. The *OED* gives 1643 as the date of the first usage in this context.

10. George Puttenham, *The Arte of English Poesie,* ed. Gladys Willcock and Alice Walker (1936; rpt. Cambridge, 1970), pp. 216–217.

The classical epigram is not, for the most part, a serious or authoritative kind of poem. Although the *Greek Anthology* does contain gnomic and Christian elements, the greater part of those poems concern themselves with wine, women (or boys), and song.[11] And although some critics have tried to show that Martial's satire has a serious moral purpose, it seems fairly clear that this is not how he presents most of his poems.[12] He calls his epigrams *nugae* (trifles, 8.3), the collection a *liber iocorum* (book of jokes, 5.15), and he describes his style variously as *argutus* (1.1) and *lepidus* (3.20).[13] Furthermore, in the famous prefatory passage that Jonson would later reverse, Martial cautions that Cato, the embodiment of seriousness and moral authority, had better not read his poems: "non intret Cato theatrum meum" (praef. 1.15).

The satiric epigrammatists of the 1590s were no more seriously moral than was Martial, although their satiric persona is more complex.[14] Moreover, these are the writers whom Jonson claims to overlook and supersede in his return to the "old way" of writing epigrams. Several critics have wondered, therefore, where Jonson gets his concept of the epigram as a vehicle for serious moral judgment.[15] This use of the genre could, of course, be original to Jonson, and it seems clear that many aspects of his treatment of the form are original. I think it likely, however, that he was influenced by the serious epigrams of the early

11. Peter Jay, ed., *The Greek Anthology* (London, 1973), pp. 16–17, comments on the "presence of so much occasional and light verse" in the *Anthology.*

12. Clark, "Ben Jonson's Imitation," p. 117, points to Martial as a source for Jonson's seriously moral purpose in his *Epigrammes;* see also Bruce R. Smith, "Ben Jonson's *Epigrammes:* Portrait-Gallery, Theater, Commonwealth," *Studies in English Literature,* 14 (1974), 98.

13. Martial, *Epigrammata,* ed. W. M. Lindsay, 2nd ed. (1903; rpt. Oxford, 1969), *Argutus* and *lepor* might both be translated as "wit."

14. Alvin Kernan, *The Cankered Muse* (New Haven, 1959), pp. 247–252, on the complexities of the satiric persona. Whipple, *Martial and the English Epigram,* p. 365, notes that they have "little true moral fervor."

15. R. V. Young, Jr., "Jonson, Crashaw, and the Development of the English Epigram," *Genre,* 12 (1979), 145, sees the adaptation of Martialian form to "the moral purpose of Christian humanism" as Jonson's major problem. Helgerson, *Self-Crowned Laureates,* p. 31, notes the difference between Martial's exclusion of Cato and Jonson's welcome.

sixteenth century, and that his sense of the genre was shaped by the early writers' experiments with the morally authoritative epigram.

I shall look at those writers in England who published collections of epigrams between 1518 and 1577, sketch out the interactions of rival forms of the genre, and trace some sources of its less conventional manifestations. I shall confine my attention largely to the collections produced by Thomas More, William Lily, John Constable, John Heywood, Robert Crowley, John Parkhurst, and Timothy Kendall, offering some suggestions as to how they may have influenced Jonson.[16] It is particularly important to consider English and neo-Latin poems together, since Latin and vernacular epigrams influenced each other.

Leicester Bradner and Charles Lynch have called the years 1505 to 1520 "the golden age of English humanism," and it is appropriate that the close of this period was marked by the appearance of several collections of what I shall call "Humanist" versions of the epigram.[17] More's epigrams were published (with some by Lily) in 1518, Constable came out with his collection in 1520, and Lily published a small pamphlet of epigrams in 1521.[18] Hoyt Hudson recognizes the relationship of these collections to the school exercises of the time, which involved the composition of epigrams; students were often required to translate Greek epigrams into Latin and Latin epigrams into Greek, or to compose epigrams on set themes.[19] More and Lily dem-

---

16. Whipple and Hudson consider poets like Turberville who include translations of epigrams in collections of other kinds, and neo-Latinists like Haddon who wrote only a few occasional epigrams. During the sixteenth century, however, only those who published collections were usually referred to as epigrammatists. Parkhurst refers to Heywood and Crowley; Kendall mentions Parkhurst; and Meres lists More, Heywood, and Kendall (as well as Drante, whose epigrams are not extant, and Bastard and Davies who wrote in the 1590s).

17. Leicester Bradner and Charles Arthur Lynch, eds., *The Latin Epigrams of Thomas More* (Chicago, 1953), p. xi.

18. William Lily, *Epigrammata* (London, 1521), and "Ioannis Constablii Londinensis et artium professoris epigrammata" (London, 1520).

19. Hudson, *Epigram in the English Renaissance*, pp. 145–155. See also Erasmus' colloquy "The Poetic Feast" for a contemporary description of this practice, in *The Colloquies of Erasmus*, trans. Craig R. Thompson (Chicago, 1965), pp. 158–176.

onstrate just such an exercise in their joint *progymnasmata,* and Constable admits that some of his poems were written when he was still in school. Hudson, however, does not fully explore the importance of these educational epigrams in shaping the English conception of the genre.[20]

The Humanists' desire to combine rhetorical and ethical instruction led them to experiment with different forms of the epigram. The variety of More's collection has often been praised: it includes satiric, epideictic, amatory, and anecdotal epigrams, as well as aphoristic.[21] The *Greek Anthology* offers prototypes for all of these varieties, and, as scholars have recognized, More relies largely on the *Anthology* for his models. But More departs from the *Anthology* and from most of its continental imitators in choosing a higher proportion of gnomic poems for translation and imitation; he has more poems of this kind than any other, except the satiric.[22]

It is easy to see why the Greek admonitory poems would appeal to the early Humanists. In the writings of More and his Humanist friends, the importance of a knowledge of Greek was a continuing theme. More, for example, wrote a letter defending the study of Greek at Oxford.[23] Erasmus declared in his *De ratione studii* that "almost all knowledge of things is to be sought

20. Thomas M. Greene, *The Light in Troy: Imitation and Discovery in Renaissance Poetry* (New Haven, 1982), p. 82, cautions against failure to connect imitation as "pedagogical tool" and imitation as "poetic praxis," and the same holds true for the composition of serious epigrams: "learning to write well is not a distinct activity from writing well; the work of the child's classroom cannot be segregated from the work of the adult's desk."

21. See Bradner and Lynch, *Latin Epigrams,* introduction, for an account of More's sources. They note that he differs from continental epigrammatists in imitating a higher proportion of the satiric epigrams of the *Greek Anthology,* but tend to overlook his high proportion of moral poems. For detailed accounts of the influence of the *Anthology* in Europe, see James Hutton, *The Greek Anthology in France,* Cornell Studies in Classical Philology (Ithaca, 1946); and James Hutton, *The Greek Anthology in Italy* (Ithaca, 1935).

22. Of his 253 poems, about 25 percent are moral or aphoristic, and about 30 percent are satiric. The rest are divided among a number of other kinds.

23. Pearl Hogrefe, *The Sir Thomas More Circle* (Urbana, 1959), p. 166. See letter 60 in Elizabeth Rogers, ed., *The Correspondence of Sir Thomas More* (Princeton, 1947).

in the Greek authors. For in short, whence can one draw a draught so pure, so easy, and so delightful as from the very fountain-head"; some pages later he described the importance for students of composition in Greek and Latin and translation from Greek into Latin.[24] The admonitory epigrams of the *Greek Anthology* combine the authority of the Greek language with ethical precepts acceptable to a Christian, so that their translation or imitation would provide a lesson in *eloquentia* and *sapientia* simultaneously. For More and his friends, then, the Greek gnomic epigram provided a classical precedent for the aphoristic poetry often considered by modern scholars to be a medieval vestige rather than a conscious Humanist innovation.[25] This precedent established the epigram as a genre suited for serious moral themes.

The admonitory epigrams from the *Anthology* generally take the form of abstract statements about the nature of fortune, wealth, friendship, and other such topics. Many of them are distichs expressed in the third person, as is this version by More from the *progymnasmata:* "Multas aedificare domos et pascere multos / Est ad pauperiem semita recta quidem."[26] The speaker in these poems assumes the voice of an experienced man, a moral authority, slightly world-weary perhaps, offering advice to his equals. Occasionally he shifts to direct address, offering advice or judgment in epigrams that seem to bridge the admonitory and satiric categories: "Divitias locupletis habes, inopis tibi mens est, / O miser haeredi dives inopsque tibi."[27]

Whereas More and Lily offer translations of this kind of epigram, others soon learned to imitate them. Constable offers the

24. Craig R. Thompson, ed., *The Literary and Educational Writings 2: De copia and de ratione studii, The Collected Works of Erasmus* (Toronto, 1978), XXIV, 669, 679.

25. See Bradner, *Musae Anglicanae*, p. 18; Whipple, *Martial and the English Epigram*, p. 322, for the idea that moralizing poetry was "medieval."

26. Bradner and Lynch, *Latin Epigrams*, p. 7. "To build many residences and to feed many people is surely the direct road to poverty" (p. 130).

27. More's translation, p. 7. "You have the wealth of a rich man, but yours is a poor man's mind, unhappy man, rich for your heirs and poor for yourself" (p. 129).

epigram "De Fallaci amicitia": "Verus amicitiae modus est sprevisse bilingues: / Syncerum pectus postulat illa magis."[28] And he extends this form of epigram to comment upon specifically Humanist themes, as in his poem "De lingua latina": "Quot steriles viguere priori [in] tempore linguae / Tempore tot nostro docta palata virent."[29] Constable's poem, "Exosa est superis, hominumque superbia turbae: / Fastum ideo a pravo corde re-velle tuo," seems related to the aphoristic poems of the *Greek Anthology* but perhaps resembles more closely another impor-tant model for the moral epigram.[30] The use of the imperative *revelle* as well as the slightly condescending stance of the speaker seem closer to the *Disticha Catonis* than to the admonitory epigrams of the *Anthology.*

Whipple noted that sixteenth-century epigrammatists went "for material, but not of course for models" to "medieval, semi-medieval, and contemporary" collections of adages, including the *Disticha Catonis.*[31] There is evidence, however, that the *Distichs of Cato* were considered epigrams, and that they were respected as a product of antiquity, perhaps, ironically, as the work of that Cato whom Martial considered the antithesis of the epigrammatic spirit. As late as 1659, an editor of the *Distichs* thought it possible that these verses were written by Cato the Censor.[32] Scaliger, who denied authorship of the *Distichs* to Cato the Censor, nevertheless felt that their stylistic purity could only be a product of antiquity: "character et dictionis puritas non patiuntur tam recentem esse, quam volunt quidam. Nos

28. Constable, A3r. "The means of true friendship is to avoid hypocrisy: that [friendship] demands instead a pure heart." (Translations of Constable are my own.) The echo of *syncerum* implies influence of Lily's translation, "De ficto amico," p. 9. Constable was a student of Lily's at St. Paul's School.

29. A2v. "As many sterile tongues as flourished in an earlier age, so many learned palates thrive in our own time."

30. A2r. "Pride is hateful to the gods and to the crowd of men: therefore tear arrogance out of your evil heart."

31. Whipple, *Martial and the English Epigram,* p. 301. Helgerson, *Self-Crowned Laureates,* p. 27, also notes the influence of "Isocrates' *Ad demonicum,* Cato's *Distichs,* and Cicero's *De officiis*" on the Humanist antipoetic ideal of the educated man.

32. Charles Hoole, ed., *Catonis disticha de moribus* (London, 1659), B2.

temporibus Commodi aut Severi recentiorem non credimus."³³
Thus the *Distichs* were not scorned by sixteenth-century Humanists, who considered them an acceptable model of pure,
ancient Latin. In English grammar schools, according to T. W.
Baldwin, they were "almost universally required for construction in the second form, being occasionally required in the first."³⁴
Erasmus' edition was the most frequently used in English schools,
and it contained variously the *Distichs* themselves, Erasmus'
commentary on them, Greek versions by Maximus Planudes
(who compiled the *Greek Anthology*), Apophthegmata of Au-
sonius and learned Greek sages, the "Mimi" of Publilius Syrus,
and versions of the creed and other religious texts translated
into elegiac couplets by Erasmus.³⁵

The *Distichs of Cato* seem to have been considered a kind of
epigram, even though they are in hexameter distichs rather than
the usual epigrammatic meter, and even though they are printed
as continuous verse with individual distichs distinguished by
numbers in the left margin. First of all, they clearly influenced
medieval epigrammatists. Both F. J. E. Raby and Bradner agree
that the *Distichs* were as important as Martial, and perhaps more
so, in providing models for writers such as Godfrey of Cam-
brai.³⁶ Godfrey calls his poems *epigrammata;* they imitate the
form and sometimes echo the poems of Martial, but they preserve the manner and stance of the *Distichs:* "Discendi, Dam-
iane, modum te quaerere dicunt; / Discas, dum nescis, sit modus

33. Christian Koenig, ed., *Historica critica Catoniana* (1759), p. 3, quotes
this passage from Scaliger, which says: "the character and purity of the diction
would not allow this work to be as recent a one as some would have us believe.
We do not believe it to be more recent than the times of the emperors Severus
or Commodus" (my translation). It was Scaliger who mistakenly associated the
name "Dionysius Cato" with the collection. Today most scholars believe that
this collection represents a late (third-century) compilation of earlier materials,
and that the verses were attributed to Cato, as Erasmus believed, because they
were worthy of his moral authority. For a modern scholarly edition, see Marcus
Boas, ed., *Disticha Catonis* (Amsterdam, 1952).

34. T. W. Baldwin, *Shakespere's Small Latine and Lesse Greeke* (Urbana,
1944), I, 595–596.

35. Ibid., 603.

36. F. J. E. Raby, *A History of Secular Latin Poetry*, 2 vols. (1934; rpt.
Oxford, 1957), II, 89; and Leicester Bradner, "The Neo-Latin Epigram in Italy
in the Fifteenth Century," *Medievalia et humanistica*, 8 (1954), 63.

iste tibi."[37] Scholars have also recognized the influence of the *Distichs* on the medieval epigram in France and Germany.[38]

In the Renaissance in England, Puttenham associates the epigram with poets called "Mimistes" who produced "short and sententious meetres, very pithie and of good edification."[39] Puttenham is probably referring to the "Mimi" of Publilius Syrus, which were often published with the *Distichs* proper. Lily's imitation of the *Distichs,* known variously as "Carmen ad discipulos, de moribus" or "Qui mihi discipulos," was included in every edition of Colet's *Aeditio,* and was identified on the title page as "G. Lilii epigramma."[40] This poem appears first in the little pamphlet of *Epigrammata* by Lily that de Worde published in 1521, preceding the eight epigrams in praise of various prominent people. In this edition Lily's poem is printed in the manner of the *Distichs,* as continuous verse with separate distichs (or, occasionally, slightly longer units) marked off in the left margin.[41]

Early sixteenth-century poets often write a single distich, sometimes in the form of an elegiac couplet, which clearly imitates a distich from Cato. We might compare this famous epigram by Erasmus, placed over the portrait of the boy Jesus in Colet's school and published with Erasmus' collected epigrams: "Discite me primum pueri, atque effingite puris / Moribus, inde pias addite literulas," with these verses from the *Distichs:* "Disce

37. Thomas Wright, ed., "Godefridi prioris epigrammata," in *Anglo-Latin Satirical Poets and Epigrammatists of the Twelfth Century* (London, 1872), II, 103. "They say, Damian, that you seek a bound to your learning. Learn while you are ignorant, and let that be your bound" (my translation).

38. Friedrich Fuchs, "Beitrag zur Geschichte des franzoesischen Epigramms," *Das Epigramm,* ed. Gerhard Pfohl (Darmstadt, 1969), p. 237, notes that "In der alt-und mittelfrz Literatur finden sich also epigramaehnliche Gedichte nur als Spruchstrophen, die entweder Uebersetzungen der beruehmten Catonischen Disticha oder von denselben direkt beeinflusst sind" (In old and middle French literature one therefore finds epigramlike poems only as proverb verses, which are either translations of the famous *Distichs of Cato* or are directly influenced by them).

39. Puttenham, *Arte of English Poesie,* p. 26.

40. John Colet, *Aeditio* (Menston, 1971).

41. Hudson, *Epigram in the English Renaissance,* says that Lily's "Carmen ad discipulos" is "not an epigram" (p. 86), but he had not seen Lily's *Epigrammata.*

sed a Doctis, indoctos ipse doceto, / Propaganda etenim rerum doctrina bonarum.''[42]

The *Distichs* thus resemble the admonitory poems of the *Anthology* in their treatment of moralizing themes, but differ somewhat in manner or stance. As noted earlier, the *Distichs* tend to use the second person indicative or imperative instead of the third person, furnishing advice aimed more directly at the reader.[43] The speaker's tone is also somewhat different; he speaks as an older man, a father or teacher, giving advice to his son or to a student and not to someone of equal stature.[44] As Erasmus and Scaliger both note, Cato the Censor, the man whom Martial banned from reading his epigrams, represents just the sort of moral authority assumed by the speaker of the distichs. We can find a number of epigrams in the collections of More and Constable that assume this stance of moral authority, a position greatly at odds with that of Martial's epigrams. More, for example, seems to combine the manner of the *Distichs* and the *Anthology* in this poem: "Tristia qui pateris perfer, sors tristia solvet. / Quod si non faciat sors, tibi mors faciet.''[45] Constable

42. Cornelis Reedijk, ed., *The Poems of Desiderius Erasmus* (Leiden, 1956), no. 86. "Learn from me first, boys, and achieve pure moral habits, then add pious letters" (my translation). I quote the other example from Erasmus' 1523 edition of the *Distichs:* "Learn only from the learned, and you yourself teach the unlearned, for the teaching of good things must be propagated" (my translation).

43. The so-called future imperative (*doceto, dirigito*), usually confined in classical Latin to laws and treaties, is fairly common in the *Distichs* and in imitations of them. David Daube, *Forms of Roman Legislation* (Oxford, 1956; rpt. Westport, Conn., 1979), pp. 93–96, comments on the use of this form in Cato's *De agricultura* and on the possibility that it first appeared in edicts written by Cato. Thus, use of this distinctive form in the *Distichs* may be a sign of a purposefully "Catonian" stance.

44. Rudolph Habenicht, ed., *John Heywood's A Dialogue of Proverbs* (Berkeley, 1963), pp. 3–5, traces this tradition of didactic works in which "an older man counsels a younger man with proverbs" from the Egyptian *Precepts of Ptah-hotep* through the book of Proverbs in the Old Testament and the *Distichs* of Cato.

45. Bradner and Lynch, *Latin Epigrams,* p. 37. "Sufferer, endure; chance will end your sorrow. And what chance does not do for you death will do," p. 160, which combines the direct advice of the *Distichs* with the fatalistic attitude of the *Anthology.* More actually shows less influence of the *Distichs* than does Constable.

offers explicitly Christian advice in this distich: "Christicola o sacram Christi quum tendis ad aedem / Ling[u]am, oculos, pectus, dirigito ad dominum."[46] We might compare Herbert's "The Church-porch" and "Superliminare," in which he assumes a similar stance of moral authority and provides precepts for a young person entering the church.

The early English Humanists, then, found clear models for the didactic epigram in the admonitory poems of the *Greek Anthology* and in the *Disticha Catonis.* More seems to include a higher proportion of moralizing epigrams in his collection than do most continental epigrammatists of the time, and Constable and Lily include only didactic and encomiastic poems in their collections. In England, then, by the year 1520 the epigram was well established as a vehicle for a kind of authoritative advice that would have seemed the antithesis of the witty trifles of Martial. Constable, in the preface to his volume, implies that the publication of a volume of didactic and encomiastic epigrams would demonstrate that one was a serious Humanist writer: "Commune esse video studiosis o[mn]ibus optime lector e memoriae thesauro aliquid in medium proferre / unde honesta possint adiuuari & candida promoueri studia."[47] Such a volume would be virtually a Humanist manifesto, demonstrating that the author possessed a pure Latin style and sincere moral purpose.

Constable, however, provides evidence that the Humanists had not completely established the epigram as a serious genre. He goes on in his preface to express the fear that readers will think that a man of his profession (*artium professor*) should not be occupied "in re frivola et nugaci . . . scilicet in pauculis condendis epigrammatis" (in such a frivolous and trifling thing . . . that is, in writing little epigrams). These remarks constitute what Helgerson has identified as a common "amateur" gesture of self-presentation, a gesture intended to differentiate the poet's

46. A2v. "O Christian, when you move toward the sacred hall of Christ, direct your eyes, your tongue, and your heart to the Lord."
47. A1v. "I see that it is a common practice, worthy reader, among all studious men to bring forth publically something from the storehouse of the memory, whence honest studies might be aided and pure studies promoted."

stance from that of a "Humanist."[48] Constable also asserts that
"seria tamen sunt" (serious things are present here), placing his
collection of epigrams uneasily on the line between amateur and
Humanist. He does not seem entirely comfortable with the concept of the serious epigram, and similar doubts resurface later
in the century.

Surprisingly, scholars have largely ignored the Pasquil tradition as another nonclassical source for the serious epigram in
England.[49] The Pasquinade provided a model for a kind of epigram that would be popular with reformers in the early part of
the century, and later on, with Protestants, as a vehicle for
increasingly serious criticism of the Roman Catholic church.
The early history of the Pasquil or Pasquinade is hazy. At some
point in the late fifteenth or early sixteenth century, a statue in
Rome became a place where people posted anonymous writings—often epigrams—attacking prominent people, especially
high officials in the church.[50] Puttenham mentions the Pasquil
in connection with his description of the epigram as a form of
graffiti, and I would suggest that the theory grew out of his
knowledge of the Roman tradition.[51] Soon, annual collections
of these satires were published, containing prose and verse of
various kinds.[52] The most influential of the collections was edited
by a Protestant living in Switzerland and was published in Basel
in 1544. It was entitled *Pasquillorum tomi duo* and contained
Erasmus' "Julius exclusus" as well as dialogues by the noted
Protestant Ulrich Hutton. Most important for the epigram, however, was a section with the heading "quae sequuntur Epigram-

48. Helgerson, *Self-Crowned Laureates,* pp. 39–58, discusses the pattern of
youthful authorship and mature repentance that was common in the careers of
Elizabethan amateurs.

49. Hudson, *Epigram in the English Renaissance,* p. 98, mentions Parkhurst's
relationship to the Pasquinade very briefly, but does not explore its consequences for the epigram in England.

50. John W. Spaeth, "Martial and the Pasquinade," *Transactions of the
American Philological Association,* 70 (1939), 242–246.

51. Puttenham, *Arte of English Poesie,* pp. 53–56.

52. In England "Pasquil" became a common pseudonym for the author of
ecclesiastical satire in prose; cf. "Pasquil's Apologie" and "Pasquil's Return"
in the Marprelate exchange.

mata diversa ex diversis tam Pasquillicis quam aliis doctorum hominum scriptis collegimus."[53] There follow epigrams by Conrad Celsus, Iannus Pannonius, Marullus, and other influential neo-Latinists. Two of Thomas More's anticlerical satires are included: his "In episcopum illiteratum" and "Eiusdem de quodam male cantate et bene legente" (pp. 75–76, nos. 186 and 188 in Bradner and Lynch, *The Latin Epigrams of Thomas More*).

Many of the epigrams in *Pasquillorum tomi duo* were probably, as John Spaeth argues, influenced by Martial. They are almost all satires on sexual impropriety of various kinds and use some of the rhetorical devices associated with Martialian "point."[54] These poems differ from those of Martial in that they usually include the real names of important people. The purpose of the original Pasquinade was wittily to embarrass a public figure as well as to call attention to the vices rampant in the Roman church. The stance of the Pasquil is that of an anonymous mudslinger who tries to subvert the authority of important people and institutions.

More makes several significant changes in the conventional Pasquil form, thereby creating a more suitable vehicle for an authoritative voice. He does not use real names, thus focusing more attention on the vice than on the individual. He does not stress sexual vices; instead, he satirizes the intellectual qualities that Humanist reformers most disliked in the church. This poem, for example, one of those included in the Swiss collection, criticizes the ignorance of the clergy as well as the tendency to cite scriptural tags out of context to support any position:

> Magne pater, clamas: occidit littera. In ore
> Hoc unum, occidit littera, semper habes.
> Cavisti bene tu ne te ulla occidere possit
> Littera, non ulla est littera nota tibi.

53. Caelius Secundus Curio, ed., *Pasquillorum tomi duo* (Basel, 1544), p. 67.

54. Spaeth, "Martial and the Pasquinade," p. 251, lists *paraprosdokia,* antithesis, paradox, irony, innuendo, repetition, and play on words. He could not find any direct echoes, however.

> Nec frustra metuis ne occidat littera. Scis non
> Vivificet qui te spiritus esse tibi.[55]

More has turned the Pasquil into a vehicle for criticism that, although still witty, conveys a serious intellectual concern. The final sentence of the poem stands out, I think, as an unusually earnest "point." Constable includes several poems on the worldliness of monks and friars, but he excludes sexual satire from his collection. We will see in Parkhurst a similar tendency to use the Pasquil tradition of anticlerical satire to criticize aspects of the church that were of serious concern to the poet. These English epigrammatists use a nonclassical epigrammatic tradition to bend the genre toward furnishing a medium for expressing authoritative moral judgments.

The obverse of the satiric epigram is the encomiastic, and there was a similar movement toward serious moral purpose in the English Humanist version of this subgenre. Of course the epigram of praise was still used to flatter important people; Lily's epigrams of praise are all in this vein, More begins his epigrams proper with several on the king, and Constable includes a typical poem in his collection, praising Henry VIII as "Marte potens Caesar, pace sophos Solomon."[56] However, these poets also tend to praise their friends for embodying the intellectual and moral qualities that, as Humanists and reformers, they most approve. Encomiastic poems of both kinds, unlike the satiric epigrams of More and Constable, include the real names of the recipients of praise; and Constable's epigrams on his friends read like a Humanist pantheon: More, Latimer, Lily, and others are praised for their exemplary learning, piety, and moral virtue. This poem "Ad Thomam Shellium" touches an important humanist theme:

> Docte Thome sophiae praeclara volumina sanctae
> Dicunt te miris voluere nunc studiis

---

55. Bradner and Lynch, *Latin Epigrams,* p. 85. "You, mighty father, exclaim 'The letter kills.' This single phrase 'The letter kills,' you have always in your mouth. You have taken good care so that no letter may kill you; you do not know any letter. And not idle is your fear that the letter may kill; you know that you do not have the spirit which will give you life" (p. 206).

56. C1r. "A powerful Caesar in war, a wise Solomon in peace."

Perge rogo, pius est labor hic, fructusque salubris
Doctrinae acquires nomina summa tuae.[57]

Latimer is praised for "eloquium" (D3r) and More for "artes . . . bonas" (C4r). The most significant difference between poems in praise of a friend's good qualities and poems of flattery is, again, one of stance. The flatterer writes as an inferior hoping to gain attention by praising the greatness of his subject.[58] The Humanist who praises his friend writes as one who speaks as a qualified moral judge, as an authority who is able convincingly to point out and commend those qualities he approves. Often, the Humanists use this second kind of encomiastic epigram as much to approve certain qualities and values as to praise a friend for having them.

In 1550, twenty-three years before the publication of Parkhurst's *Ludicra,* Robert Crowley published his *One and Thyrtye Epigrammes,* a collection of strongly Protestant epigrams. Crowley has been described by John King as a "fledgling Puritan," who, "as a corollary to his radical Protestant zeal . . . wrote as a nativist poet."[59] Thus, although his epigrams resemble those of the Humanists in moral earnestness and authoritative stance, he looked back not to classical models but to the native English tradition rejected by the Humanists, particularly to "prophetic estates satire" on the model of *Piers Plowman.* King rightly identifies Crowley's epigrams with "the vivid anecdotes and tales in medieval handbooks of pulpit *exempla* such as the *Gesta Romanorum* and Robert Mannyng of Brunne's *Handlyng Synne.*"[60] Some critics have wondered whether we should consider these poems epigrams at all.[61]

---

57. A4v. "Learned Thomas, they say that you are pondering the foremost volumes of holy wisdom in your admirable studies. I ask you to proceed; this is a pious undertaking and the product is beneficial, so that you may acquire the highest name for your teaching." I think this probably refers to study of the Bible in the original languages.

58. Helgerson, *Self-Crowned Laureates,* pp. 176–177, discusses the inappropriateness of a flatterer's stance for a poet like Jonson with "laureate" ambitions.

59. John N. King, *English Reformation Literature* (Princeton, 1982), p. 319.

60. Ibid., p. 344.

61. Whipple, *Martial and the English Epigram,* p. 303, though he discusses them on the grounds that Crowley was "blindly feeling after" Martialian wit.

Crowley was an educated man, however, and he decided to
call his poems "epigrammes." Parkhurst, who surely knew an
epigram when he saw one, was able to accept them as such,
referring, in his preface, to the epigrams "Heywodi Crow-
leique." Crowley appears to accept the Humanist conception
of the genre as a vehicle for moral instruction and serious ecclesiastical and social satire while sharply rejecting their use of
classical forms and the Latin language. He arranges his epigrams
according to an alphabetical scheme that King associates with
"moralized Renaissance hornbooks."[62] These hornbooks or
"ABCs" were often printed along with a catechism, and sometimes a catechism alone was called an "ABC."[63] We may recall
Erasmus' inclusion of catechetical epigrams in his collection.
Crowley presents his epigrams as an explicitly didactic work,
and implies, by its organization, that he assumes the stance of
teacher or catechist addressing a young student. We also find a
reference to the *Disticha Catonis* at the beginning of one of his
epigrams: "Emonge wyttye Saiynges, this precept I finde, / To
auoid and fle dice (mi son) have ever in mynde."[64] The poem
goes on to expand on this theme and to relate it to more explicitly Christian teachings. Pasquil-like ecclesiastical satire is
also present in Crowley's collection, including poems castigating
"Obstinate Papistes," "Laye men that take tythes," "Double
beneficed men," and the incomplete dissolution of the abbeys.
Crowley resembles the Humanists in his avoidance of sexual
topics and his attention to theological issues, but looks back to
medieval tradition in the anecdotal nature of his poems and in
stressing the social rather than doctrinal consequences of an
unreformed church.

Crowley, then, through the Humanist collections, the Pasquil

62. King, *English Reformation Literature,* p. 344, although he cautions that
Crowley intends his collection for both "humble and educated readers."

63. Kenneth Charlton, *Education in Renaissance England* (London, 1965),
pp. 100–102. Crowley may also have been imitating alphabetically arranged
collections of aphorisms such as Thomas Elyot's *Bankette of Sapience* (1534),
which contains the wise sayings of Solomon and various classical and patristic
writers grouped under the headings "Abstinence," "Adversitie," "Affection," . . . through "Virginitie" and "Wrathe."

64. Robert Crowley, *Select Works,* ed. J. M. Cowper, Early English Text
Society, e.s. no. 15 (1872), "Of Dicears," p. 25.

tradition, and the *Disticha Catonis,* would have associated the epigram with ecclesiastical satire and with serious moral instruction. Moreover, he found additional models for the Protestant epigram in the Bible, and goes beyond even Erasmus in his use of biblical themes and forms. He initially adopts the stance of a prophet, taking that role as a biblical model for satire: "But as Esaye hath bydden, so muste he nedes crye, / And tell the Lordes people of their iniquitie" ("The Boke to the Reader," ll. 11–14). In the Book of Psalms, the major biblical precedent for lyric genres, most of the psalms were associated with the ode or hymn, but a few were considered short satires or wisdom verses.[65] Crowley uses a passage from Psalm 14 as a theme for one of his poems:

> Holye Dauid, that was boeth propheth and kinge,
> Sawe in hys tyme (as appeareth by hys wrytynge)
> That in those dayes there were men of wycked hert,
> That dyd all godlye wayes utterlye peruerte.
>
> (p. 35)

It is clear that Crowley associates this particular psalm, at least, with satire.

The Bible also provided a model similar to the *Disticha Catonis.* Like the *Distichs,* the Book of Proverbs, as Barbara Lewalski notes, "was said to be addressed in a special way to the young, or to beginners in the religious life, with the author assuming the stance of father or teacher."[66] Melanchthon did a translation of Proverbs partly in the form of epigrams.[67] The other biblical and apocryphal wisdom books, Ecclesiastes, Ecclesiasticus, and Sapience, were associated with a similar didactic stance, though sometimes related more specifically to that of a preacher addressing his congregation. Crowley begins his poem "Of Commune Liars" with a reference to Wisdom: "Solomon the sage, in Sapience doeth saye, / That the mouthe that

65. Barbara K. Lewalski, *Protestant Poetics and the Seventeenth-Century Religious Lyric* (Princeton, 1979), pp. 39–53. See p. 47 on the psalm as satire; and Carole Kessner, "Entering 'The Church-Porch': Herbert and Wisdom Poetry," *George Herbert Journal,* 1 (1977), 10–25, on the wisdom psalm.

66. Lewalski, *Protestant Poetics,* p. 55.

67. Ibid., pp. 56–57.

lyeth doeth the verye soule sleye" (p. 24). As in the case of Psalms, however, this book seems to provide Crowley not so much with a formal model as with a stance, and with a source of themes upon which to write, perhaps in the manner of a school exercise. The related wisdom book Ecclesiasticus is also used by Crowley in this way:

> The sonne of Syrach wryteth playnelye
> Of suche menne as do sweare blasphemouselye.
> "The manne that sweareth muche shall be fylled," sayeth he,
> "Wyth all wicked maners, and iniquitie."

> (p. 18)

We might again remember Herbert's "The Church-Porch," which addresses moral instruction to the young in the manner of bib-lical wisdom literature, and the *Distichs of Cato*.[68] Crowley seems to refer to the wisdom books more often than to any other part of Scripture, a sign that he found their stance particularly ap-propriate to the epigram. He often uses passages of Scripture as epiphonemata or final, clinching statements. He ends "Of Abbayes," "Of Alehouses," "Of Baudes," "Of Laye men that take tythes," "Of Marchauntes," "Of Rente raysars," "Of Un-saciable Purchaysars," and "Of Usurars" with citation of a scrip-tural passage.

John Heywood also departed consciously from the generic precedents set by the Humanists, but he reacted against Crowley as well. He provided not only another vernacular version of the epigram but also a version that sought to subvert aphoristic wisdom and return the genre to a stance of amateur frivolity. In the opening poem of his "fyrste hundred of Epigrammes," probably published in 1550, he refers to his poems as "trifles" (the usual translation of the Latin word *nugae*) and calls atten-tion to the fact that they are written in "rough rude termes of homely honestie."[69] The poems themselves use doggerel verse and colloquial diction, dissociating Heywood from the learned epigrammatic tradition of his friend Thomas More and the school

68. Ibid., pp. 290–291 on Proverbs, Ecclesiastes, and Herbert's "The Church-Porch."

69. Burton A. Milligan, ed., *John Heywood's "Works" and Miscellaneous Short Poems* (Urbana, 1956), p. 104.

exercise. Heywood's pose of frivolity is underscored in this poem
printed with his "fifth hundred":

> Art thou Heywood with the mad mery wit?
> Ye forsooth maister, that same is even hit.
> Art thou Heywood that applieth mirth more than thrift?
> Ye sir, I take mery mirth a golden gift.

(no. 100)

In 1555, five years after Crowley's *One and Thyrtye Epigrammes* appeared, Heywood published "Three hundred Epigrammes upon three hundred prouerbes." Most of these poems
are in the form of distichs, the first line quoting a popular proverb and the second furnishing some comment upon it. There is
evidence that Heywood's proverbial epigrams were associated
with the aphoristic distich in the Renaissance; when John Davies
of Hereford wrote his "Upon English Proverbes" in acknowledged imitation of "Olde Heywood," he arranged his verse
typographically in the unusual manner in which the *Disticha*
were usually printed; the separate poems, usually distichs, are
not separated by indentation, spacing, or titles. Instead, they
are printed as continuous verse, separated only by numbers in
the margins.[70] Hudson associates Heywood's pattern of statement and comment with the school exercise in which students
were asked to write epigrams on proverbial or aphoristic themes.[71]
In the school exercise, however, students were taught to imitate
or assume the voice of authority, which Heywood does not do.
Instead, he offers a conscious parody of this kind of aphoristic
poetry.[72]

Heywood dissociates himself from the stance of moral adviser
in several ways. First of all, he chooses only "homely" native
proverbial wisdom rather than classical *sententiae*. The *Distichs
of Cato,* the aphoristic poems of the *Greek Anthology,* and the
poems encouraged by the school exercise tended to be abstract

---

70. Alexander B. Grosart, ed., *The Complete Works of John Davies of
Hereford* (Edinburgh, 1878), II, 41–50.

71. Hudson, *Epigram in English Renaissance,* p. 149.

72. Burton A. Milligan, "Humor and Satire in Heywood's Epigrams," *Studies
in Honor of T. W. Baldwin,* ed. D. C. Allen (Urbana, 1958), p. 27, sees satire
on proverbial wisdom and those who employ it in Heywood's poems.

and elevated. Heywood, in an impulse comparable to Crowley's nativism, stresses the fact that his maxims are the brief, concrete sayings of everyday life. In his "Epigrammes upon Prouerbes," the proverbial statement is usually given first and is separated by punctuation from Heywood's answer or comment. He often uses personal pronouns in his answer to set himself off from the impersonal voice of authority: "So many heades, so many wittes, nay, nay. / We see many heades, and no wittes some day."[73] Even when he does not directly contradict the voice of authority, his confirmation is flippant or cynical: "The weaker hath the woorse, in wrestlyng alway, / Best for the weake to leave wrestlyng then I say" ("Three hundred," no. 156). Here the "I say" distinguishes his comment. Sometimes he talks back to the proverbial advisor: "I will mend this house, and peyre another. / Ye, but when wylt thou mend thy selfe brother?" ("Three hundred," no. 81). He also champions the proverbial underdog, as in "Three hundred," no. 40. And he puts the proverbial saying into the mouth of traditional objects of satire (such as "wife," in "Three hundred," no. 43). In his imitation of the school exercise in which the student wrote alternative versions on a single theme, Heywood questions authority by giving radically different interpretations of the same saying.[74]

Heywood, then, wrote anti-authoritarian "trifles" in a deliberately rough, vernacular verse form. His epigrams seem too consciously different from the serious Latin poems of the humanists to be unrelated to them, and I would suggest that Heywood offers his poems as a deliberate counterstatement about the ideal form of the genre. We might ask why he would want to return the epigram to a stance of Martialian witty flippancy. The first epigram of the "Three hundred" may provide a partial answer:

> If every man mende one, all shall be mended.
> This meane to amendment, is now intended.

73. Milligan, *John Heywood's "Works,"* "Three hundred Epigrammes," no. 8, p. 148.
74. As in his variations on "Better bow than break," where he contradicts the saying in one poem and confirms it in another.

> For though no man looke to mend him self brother:
> Yet eche man lookth to controll and mend other.

Heywood disparages the relentless moral instruction that the humanist and school exercise epigrams were intended to provide. In addition, unlike his predecessors, Heywood avoids using the epigram to comment on religious issues. His few references to the religious issues of the day are pro-Catholic, but flippant, as in his epigram on the accession of Mary Tudor, which is based on the proverb "Roome was not bylt on one day" ("Three hundred," no. 274).[75] He may take a stab at reformist innovation in the epigram about a rustic who, when forced by his priest to attempt to learn the Pater Noster in English, forgets it in Latin as well. But we might expect more explicit religious commentary from the author of *The Spider and the Fly* and *The Four PP*. The publication of Crowley's seriously moral and strongly Protestant epigrams in 1550 might well have prompted the Roman Catholic Heywood to offer his own version of the genre in 1555, after Mary's accession. Disturbed by Crowley's appropriation of the serious epigram for Protestant purposes, Heywood sought to return this kind of poem to its former "trifling" stance, thus undermining its effectiveness as a vehicle of moral and religious authority. In so doing, he helped to preserve the tradition of the witty epigram in England.

Two epigrammatists whose works were published in the 1570s seem to show signs of confusion over the proper uses of the genre. Both John Parkhurst and his translator (and imitator) Timothy Kendall seem unsure whether the epigram is a serious or "trifling" form. Parkhurst entitles his collection *Ludicra sive epigrammata juvenilia* and offers repeated apologies for the publication of these youthful "trifles" in the three biblical epigraphs on the title page, in his prose preface, and in the poems "Ad lectorem" scattered throughout the volume. His poems are called *ludicra,* he says, because "Ludicra vel potius, quia nil nugalia

75. Milligan, "Humor," pp. 29–31, identifies the subject of a series of poems in "Three hundred Epigrammes" as the religious turncoat, and that of no. 67 in the "Fifth hundred" as religious turncoats during the early years of Elizabeth's reign.

praeter, / Nil praeter nugas ludicra pene dabunt."[76] In a later
poem, Parkhurst warns the "morosum et severum lectorem"
that "haec lusi in adolescentia: / omnes semel stultescimus" (p.
117, with an obvious echo of Horace, "these poems I played
with in my youth, when all of us act foolish"). Hudson notes
that Parkhurst must have written some of his poems when he
was at least forty years old, and attributes his insistence on his
youthful authorship to reluctance on the part of a "grave bishop
of an important diocese" to be associated with frivolous poems.[77]
Helgerson identifies the claim of youthful authorship as an important self-presentational gesture of the amateur poet, and
Parkhurst might seem initially to be identifying his collection as
an amateur effort.[78]

Parkhurst undercuts his claims of youthful frivolity, however,
by the less prominent but still insistent idea that there are serious
things mixed in with the jokes: "Plurima nam cecini ioculari
carmina plectro, / Nec desunt laetis seria mista iocis" ("Now I
have sung many songs with a joking lyre, nor are serious poems,
mixed in with the happy jokes, entirely absent" [p. A. i]). The
prefatory poems by Parkhurst's friends that are attached to the
volume consist almost exclusively of variations on the themes
"miscuit utile dulci" and "seria mista iocis." And if Parkhurst, in the last of three poems "Ad lectorem" that begin the
collection, does not exactly invite Cato to read his poems, he
at least hopes that if he should read them, he would enjoy
them:

> si forte Catones
> Adiicere huc oculos, et legere ista velint:
> Multa hic invenient, quae possint pellere curas,
> Plurima, quae maestos exhilarare queant.
>
> (p. 1)

76. John Parkhurst, *Ludicra sive epigrammata juvenilia* (London, 1573), p.
1. Many of them were probably written while he was in exile in the 1550s.
77. Pages 103, 95.
78. Helgerson, *Self-Crowned Laureates,* pp. 55–59. Of course the serious
epigrams written as a school exercise were often truly written in youth, so that
there is some tension between the serious and amateur signals inherent in this
gesture.

Kendall, similarly, calls his original poems "trifles," and yet
chooses "miscuit utile dulci" as his epigraph and identifies himself as an arbiter who culls the epigram tradition to provide his
readers with the choicest and chastest "flowers."[79] The concern
with "miscuit utile dulci" in these two poets runs deeper than
mere repetition of the Horatian *topos.* They seem genuinely
torn between a sense of the epigram as a youthful trifle and as
a vehicle for moral instruction; that is, between the two approaches to the epigram that were current in England in the
sixteenth century.

The contents of both collections evidence a similarly split view
of the genre. The reader who somehow missed all of the prefatory references to *seria* in Parkhurst's *Ludicra* would be in for
a surprise; the book begins, after three poems "Ad lectorem,"
with an epigram based on Ezekiel 34, followed by seventeen
poems on the "Cursus vitae . . . Iesu Christi." In the collections
of both Parkhurst and Kendall, we find examples of the serious
kinds of epigram that we found in More, Constable, and Crowley. Parkhurst imitates the admonitory poems of the *Anthology*
(p. 55), the *Disticha Catonis* (p. 49, in a striking imitation of
Erasmus' "Boy Jesus" poem), and the Pasquil.[80] Some of his
Pasquils are the most doctrinal we have yet seen, condemning
the sale of indulgences (p. 47), the doctrine of justification by
works (p. 40), and the lack of learning among priests (p. 32),
and supporting the marriage of priests with a biblical citation
(pp. 68–69). Protestant encomia are included in the collection,
praising Henry VIII, Edward VI, and Elizabeth I at the expense

79. Timothy Kendall, "Flowers of Epigrammes," *Spenser Society,* 15 (1874),
9. "I have left the lewde, I have chosen the chaste."

80. Hudson, *Epigram in the English Renaissance,* p. 98, mentions that some
of Parkhurst's poems resemble Pasquils but does not indicate which collection
he used or the extent of his reliance on it. Parkhurst used *Pasquillorum tomi
duo,* and several of his poems are based on poems in that volume: Parkhurst's
"De Innocento Octavo Pontifice Romano" from "De Innocentio VIII" (*Pasquillorum,* p. 78); "De Ioanne eius nominis octavo" (p. 82), from "De Paparum
creandorum ritu immutato" (*Pasquillorum,* p. 70); "In Episcopos Romanenses"
(Parkhurst, p. 83), from "In Alex. VI. Pont. Max." (*Pasquillorum,* p. 78); "In
eandem Lucretiam" (Parkhurst, p. 83), from "Lucretiae Alexandri VI filiae
tumulus" (*Pasquillorum,* p. 79).

of Mary and echoing official Edwardian royalist mythology in
identifying Edward as the "frater et alter ego" of King Josiah.[81]
Also, a series of poems lists, by name, several good Protestants
in England, ending each with a prayer for Christ to defend them
"sancta dextra" (pp. 55–56). In addition, Parkhurst writes a
number of poems on biblical and religious topics, using a
prophetic voice in several of them (pp. 15, 177) and in
the final epigraphs. He also translates Psalm 11 (pp. 87–88)
and uses biblical references throughout. His preface cites Paul
and Christ as providing biblical models for satire and invective.[82]

Kendall includes a poem on education in his "trifles" that
resembles the *Distichs of Cato*. He translates some of Parkhurst's Pasquils, and offers versions of some of them (unac-
knowledged) among his own epigrams ("Pope Alexander VI,"
p. 251). Again, one or two of his original poems deal with
doctrinal differences between Catholics and Protestants (see p.
269, on prayer), and he also bases one of his epigrams on a
psalm text. He was clearly familiar with the range of serious
epigram forms and imitates several of them.

And yet, both Parkhurst and Kendall include many real "trifles" in their collections. Parkhurst offers some of the sexual
Pasquils, for example, as well as a section of love poems. Kendall, as he promises, avoids obscenity but translates some purely
witty poems by a number of writers. Both of them include
anecdotal "jest-book" epigrams of the kind found in More and
Heywood and avoided by Constable and Crowley. Parkhurst's
collection seems exactly what we would expect from a man who
cites Heywood and Crowley as his predecessors in the genre.
He seems to want to use the epigram to express serious moral
and religious concerns, and yet he is constantly distracted by
the strong countertradition of the frivolous epigram. Thus, both
he and Kendall assume the voice of authority in some of their
poems but undermine it in others. Kendall, of course, was primarily a translator, but Parkhurst seems to be struggling to find

81. Parkhurst, *Ludicra*, p. 184. See King, *English Reformation Literature*,
p. 161, on Edwardian propaganda.

82. Parkhurst, *Ludicra*, preface, A4v, says "nec primus hoc, nec sine exemplo
feci," and lists epithets applied to the wicked by Paul and Christ.

the true epigrammatic stance. It is appropriate that he would not welcome Cato yet hoped that he might like what he saw once he entered.

The epigrammatists of the first half of the sixteenth century knew what they wanted to do with the genre. More, Lily, and Constable used several serious and learned models to shape the epigram into an erudite and morally authoritative form. Crowley turned the serious epigram from classical forms to native and biblical models and overtly Protestant themes. Heywood disliked their poetic appropriation of secular moral authority and offered instead a homely, vernacular, secular epigram with a flippant, anti-authoritarian stance. Parkhurst and Kendall, however, seem torn between the serious and nugatory traditions of the epigram, and both currents of the genre run through their collections.

The epigrammatists of the 1590s seem quite certain about the form that the genre should take. As Whipple has noted, they more closely resemble Martial in form and stance than did any of their predecessors.[83] They also look back to "Olde Heywood" as a model, and refer to their poems as ephemeral trifles. Weever, for example, says that "epigramms are much like unto Alma-nacks serving especially for the yeare for the which they are made."[84] Guilpin proclaims, "Ile onely spit my venome, and away," implying that his epigrams are products of the moment, intended only for the moment.[85] These writers associate their epigrams with their harsh and rough verse satires, poems in which the satirist's moral authority is often subverted by his prurient obsession with vice.[86]

Ben Jonson has been described as returning to Martialian epigram in his attempt to revise the genre as it was practiced in the 1590s.[87] Certainly, Jonson's objections to the structure of previous English epigrams indicate that he had a more Mar-

---

83. Whipple, *Martial and the English Epigram,* pp. 364–366.

84. John Weever, *Epigrammes in the Oldest Cut and Newest Fashion,* ed. R. B. McKerrow (London, 1911), p. 13.

85. Everard Guilpin, *Skialetheia,* ed. D. Allen Carroll (Chapel Hill, 1974), p. 39.

86. Kernan, *The Cankered Muse,* p. 102.

87. Clark, "Ben Jonson's Imitation," p. 117; Winner, "Ben Jonson and Conventions," pp. 61, 74.

tialian form in mind, and he imitates that form better than anyone else in English.[88] But he also objects to the content and stance of those satiric epigrams, rejecting their obscenity and "gall" as well as their trivial and ephemeral intent. In Epigram 28 he urges the reader not to judge his poems "so fast" (l. 9) and in another objects to pages posted for the quick perusal of passers-by.[89] Instead of apologizing for his poems as the trivial products of his youth, Jonson calls them "the ripest of my studies," that is, presumably, carefully wrought works by a mature man. In the *Epigrammes,* Jonson sets himself up as a moral arbiter, an authority dispensing advice, praise, and blame for the edification of the reader.[90] This alternation of praise and blame has been seen as the key element in Jonson's greater seriousness as a moralist, and some have attributed his use of this device to the Renaissance theory that Martial, too, praised virtue and chastised vice.[91]

But Martial alone could not provide the model for a "chast" and serious book. Jack Winner has explored Jonson's attitude toward the voice of moral authority at some length, and contrasts Jonson's tone sharply with the "cynical, world-weary air" of Martial, Jonson's seriously ethical praise with Martial's flattery.[92] Jonson experiments with multiple satiric voices in some of his plays, searching for a stance that would be neither too harsh nor too smugly condescending.[93] In the preface to *Volpone*

88. In his "Conversations with Drummond," Jonson objects to the epigrams of John Owen and Sir John Harington because they are "Narrations" and to the conclusion of those by Sir John Davies (Herford and Simpson, *Ben Jonson,* I, 133, 138, 143).

89. In 3.6–7, as noted by Jennifer Brady, "Authority and Judgment in *Epigrammes,*" *Studies in English Literature,* 23 (1983), 107.

90. Jack D. Winner, *Poetic Self: A Study of the Speaker in Ben Jonson's Non-Dramatic Poetry,* Ph.D. diss., Bryn Mawr, 1978.

91. See David Wykes, "Ben Jonson's 'Chast Booke': The *Epigrammes,*" *Renaissance and Modern Studies,* 13 (1969), 77, for the alternation of praise and blame, and Clark, "Ben Jonson's Imitation," p. 114, for the Renaissance theory of Martial as an epideictic poet.

92. Winner, *Poetic Self,* pp. 18–19.

93. Winner, ibid., p. 34, points to *Every Man Out, Cynthia's Revels,* and *Poetaster.* Helgerson, *Self-Crowned Laureates,* pp. 131–144, discusses these plays, concluding that Jonson was unable to "discover a language of self-presentation that would allow him to be both satirist and laureate."

he describes the poet as one who "is said to be able to informe yong-men to all good disciplines . . . that comes forth the interpreter, and arbiter of nature."[94] In the *Epigrammes* themselves, he often comments on the authority of his subjects, praising Camden, the ideal teacher, for having "what weight, and what authority in thy speech." Clearly, Jonson was concerned with the nature of moral authority and the poet's assumption of it, and his collection of epigrams contains a number of experiments in the moral stance appropriate to that genre.

We have just seen, at some length, that the epigram was, prior to the 1590s, the focus of an extended series of experiments in poetic moral authority. In his conception of the epigram as a product of "ripeness" and in his adoption of a pose of moral authority, Jonson was evidently influenced by the struggles of the early epigrammatists with this stance. As a neoclassicist, Jonson would be less likely than the earlier poets to admit the influence of nonclassical works, especially when writing in a classical form. And yet, the practice of Constable and Parkhurst provided a precedent for Jonson's alternation of anonymous satire and attributed praise. Their collections also furnish earlier examples of encomia that offer serious and specific moral judgment instead of flattery. Jonson wrote only a few aphoristic distichs, and we must look to Herrick for the continuation of that tradition in the seventeenth century. But Jonson's concern with authoritative stance and serious judgment link him to the sixteenth-century epigrammatists.

We know that Jonson read Parkhurst. He had also read the *Disticha Catonis,* and he may even have associated them with Cato the Censor. In *Poetaster,* he has Virgil begin the corrective reading list that he offers to Crispinus with:

> Looke, you take
> Each morning, of old CATOES principles
> A good draught, next your heart; that walke upon
> Till it be well digested.

> (5.3.536–539)

In the first of his epigrams, Jonson asks those who take his "booke in hand, / To read it well, that is, to understand." The

---

94. Herford and Simpson, *Ben Jonson,* V, 17.

preface to the first section of the *Disticha Catonis* reads: "Nunc te, fili carissime, docebo quo pacto morem animi tui componas. Igitur praecepta mea ita legito ut intellegas. Legere et non intellegere neglegere est." (Now I will teach you dearest son in what way you can store up morality in your heart. Therefore so read my precepts that you understand them: for to read and not to understand is to be negligent.) In echoing this passage, Jonson signals his assumption of an attitude of moral and intellectual authority that he found in the "epigrams" of Cato and his sixteenth-century imitators, and not in the poems of Martial. In the preface to the *Epigrammes* Jonson welcomes Cato into his theater, a gesture usually interpreted as referring to the absence of obscenity in his collection.[95] But Jonson, like the serious epigrammatists of the sixteenth century, also welcomes Cato as representing, if not explicitly the authorship of moral epigrams, then at least the great exemplar of the kind of moral authority he hoped to assume in some of them. Perhaps Jonson's "old way" is not entirely as old as he would have us believe.

95. Ibid., XI, 1.

# III  Genre, Politics, and Society

BARBARA J. BONO

# Mixed Gender, Mixed Genre
# in Shakespeare's *As You Like It*

Does Shakespeare's preoccupation, especially in the comedies, with strong female characters and an underlying complex of "feminine" concerns—sexuality and familial and domestic life— provide evidence for what Juliet Dusinberre calls a "feminism of Shakespeare's time"?[1] Or does the same evidence indicate male projections of what women must be, what Madelon Gohlke terms a "matriarchal substratum or subtext within the patriarchal text" that "is not feminist," but rather "provide[s] a rationale for the structure of male dominance"?[2] Put more generally,

This essay is a revised and expanded version of a paper delivered at the 1984 Ohio Shakespeare Conference on "Shakespeare and Gender." It was first drafted during my 1982–83 tenure as a Junior Fellow at the Cornell Society for the Humanities. I am grateful to the Society and for the 1983–84 Harvard Mellon Faculty Fellowship that allowed me to continue work on it.

1. Juliet Dusinberre, *Shakespeare and the Nature of Women* (London, 1975), p. 1.

2. Madelon Gohlke, " 'I wooed thee with my sword': Shakespeare's Tragic Paradigms," in *Representing Shakespeare: New Psychoanalytic Essays,* ed. Murray Schwartz and Coppélia Kahn (Baltimore, 1980), p. 180.

189

does the literature and social practice of the early modern period exhibit, as Stephen Greenblatt and Natalie Zemon Davis suggest, a theatricality, a ready embrace of role playing and social inversion, that nonetheless functions most often to test and strengthen traditional authority?[3] And if, with Davis and, more tentatively, Greenblatt, we wish to argue that the subversion occasionally escapes its cultural containment, how does this escape occur, and in what does it, or our latter-day perception of it, consist? In this essay I seek to erect a framework of contemporary feminist theory around a traditional genre-based analysis of the heroic, romantic, and pastoral strains in Shakespeare's *As You Like It* in order to conjure a complex response to these questions.

Recently Nancy Chodorow has offered a powerful and influential new model for psychoanalysis and the sociology of gender that seems very useful for analyzing the representation of gender in literature as well.[4] In an object-relations account of identity formation that stresses the temporal primacy of the mother, Chodorow presses her analysis back beyond the oedipal phase to the preoedipal phase, significantly revising Freud's classic accounts of both masculinity and femininity.

Freud privileges the male sex in his account of gender identity, speaking of the oedipal castration fear of the boy child and the penis envy of the girl child. But by placing the mother as socializer at the heart of her account, Chodorow characterizes gender and sexual differentiation not "as presence or absence of masculinity and the male genital" but as "two different presences."[5] The male child defines himself in a tension-fraught opposition to his potentially engulfing mother, while the female

3. Stephen Greenblatt, "Invisible Bullets: Renaissance Authority and its Subversion," *Glyph,* 8 (1981), 40–61; Natalie Zemon Davis, *Society and Culture in Early Modern France* (Stanford, 1975), esp. "The Reasons of Misrule," pp. 97–123, and "Women on Top," pp. 124–151.

4. Nancy Chodorow, *The Reproduction of Mothering: Psychoanalysis and the Sociology of Gender* (Berkeley and Los Angeles, 1978).

5. Ibid., pp. 141–158, esp. p. 157.

child has the more complex and extended, if less extreme, task of simultaneously affirming a gender identity with the mother and an individual differentiation from her.[6] A girl child's "penis envy" is, then, not a recognition of a primary lack but a secondary, defensive reaction against maternal power and an attempted appropriation of what is seen as greater masculine autonomy from it. Chodorow argues that the events of the oedipal period must be understood against this preoedipal background that is itself more centrally a social than a biological experience: "In fact, what occurs for both sexes during the oedipal period is a product of this knowledge about gender and its social and familial significance, rather than the reverse (as the psychoanalytic accounts have it)."[7]

The strengths of Chodorow's clinically documented and tenaciously argued model seem to me many. Her stress on the early, preconscious psychological formation of these patterns in interaction with a female mother who is primary caretaker explains the seeming universality, rootedness, and strong elements of complicity in those arrangements through which women become the "second sex." Although the responsibility has often been diffused or configured somewhat differently, primary female mothering has been a cultural and historical constant. However, it need not be an inevitability. Chodorow's theory is genuinely anthropological and sociological in denying biological determinism and in noting considerable differences in the social practice of mothering, and it shares with thinkers like Dorothy Dinnerstein a revolutionary feminist belief in the possibility of change in our sexual arrangements based on changing the sexual

6. Ibid., p. 169: "Women's mothering, then, produces asymmetries in the relational experiences of girls and boys as they grow up, which account for crucial differences in feminine and masculine personality, and the relational capacities and modes which these entail . . . From the retention of preoedipal attachments to their mother, growing girls come to define and experience themselves as continuous with others; their experience of self contains more flexible or permeable ego boundaries. Boys come to define themselves as more separate and distinct, with a greater sense of rigid ego boundaries and differentiation. The basic feminine sense of self is connected to the world, the basic masculine sense of self is separate."

7. Ibid., p. 151.

division of labor into shared parenting.[8]

It also contains an embryonic historical dimension, for Chodorow notes that the emphasis on the single female mother has altered over time. She comments especially on the effects of modern capitalism in widening the sexual division of labor by separating home and workplace and institutionalizing within the workplace a division between largely female service occupations and the ideal of a male worker detached from prior community, eager to succeed, and highly malleable to organizational needs.[9] Certain features of this analysis seem relevant to the early modern period in England, during the rise of capitalism—the period when Shakespeare's plays were written. Then men, often no longer owners or caretakers of land in a feudal system, were sent out early for education or apprenticeship and took up entrepreneurial schemes in court and city, while patriarchal values kept women even more closely tied to the work of childbearing and motherhood.[10]

Coppélia Kahn has demonstrated the applicability of Chodorow's theory of gender formation to the representation of male personality in Shakespeare's plays, particularly *King Lear*. Arguing that Lear's unconscious male fear of maternal power is displaced into metaphoric expression, Kahn instances his loathing of his "pelican daughters" and his shame at his own woman's tears and "female" hysteria (the "climbing mother," the disorder of the wandering womb).[11] She might also have added the most inclusive metaphoric expression in the play of this threatening female power, the goddess-Mother Nature whom Edmund invokes to "stand up for bastards," and who proves Lear and his followers not ague-proof. The implication of this sexual metaphorization of landscape is that pastoral and antipastoral—"soft" and "hard" primitivism—may figure the op-

8. Dorothy Dinnerstein, *The Mermaid and the Minotaur: Sexual Arrangements and Human Malaise* (New York, 1977).

9. Chodorow, *Reproduction,* pp. 173–190.

10. See, for example, Lawrence Stone, *The Family, Sex and Marriage in England, 1500–1800* (New York, 1977), pp. 123–218.

11. Coppélia Kahn, "Excavating 'Those Dim Minoan Regions': Maternal Subtexts in Patriarchal Literature," *Diacritics,* 12 (1982), 37–41.

posite sides of the male crisis of individuation from the mother—nurturance or antipathy.

Kahn's methodological tactic supports Louis Montrose's excellent sociological reading of that pastoral play, *As You Like It*.[12] Focusing explicitly on the historically sensitive oedipal situation of brothers' rivalry over a paternal inheritance, Montrose rightly restores balance to the interpretation of the play by dwelling on the very engaging plot of Orlando's rise that frames Rosalind's androgynous disguising. He devotes the penultimate section of his essay on "the complex interrelationship of brothers, fathers, and sons in *As You Like It*" to a suggestive discussion of Rosalind and of the play's strategies for containment of the feminine. In Montrose's shrewd formulation, "The 'feminism' of Shakespearean comedy seems to me more ambivalent in tone and more ironic in form than such critics [those infatuated with Rosalind's exuberance] have wanted to believe."[13] Kahn's work suggests that from a male point of view both Rosalind and Arden are initially threatening but eventually beneficent manifestations of a nonfeminist maternal subtext. It is possible, then, that in Shakespeare's works both the explicitly threatening women of the tragedies and the seemingly benevolent women of the comedies operate within a "universe of masculinist assumptions" about the nature of women.[14]

Yet Chodorow's model would also argue for a positive female identity, although one severely handicapped by the perception of itself as culturally secondary. Kahn and Montrose do not inquire whether Shakespearean drama can plausibly represent this point of view, and if so, whether that drama can provide us with any tool for dislodging "the universe of masculinist assumptions" in which it is embedded. In what follows I would like to sketch both Orlando's and Rosalind's roles in the play on the basis of Chodorow's model for the formation of gender identity. I shall argue that the patriarchal, oedipal crisis of the

12. Louis Montrose, " 'The Place of a Brother' in *As You Like It:* Social Process and Comic Form," *Shakespeare Quarterly,* 32 (1981), 28–54.

13. Ibid., pp. 53, 52n.

14. The phrase is Myra Jehlen's, "Archimedes and the Paradox of Feminist Criticism," *SIGNS,* 6 (1981), 576, as cited by Kahn, "Maternal Subtexts," p. 32.

first act of the play is displaced back onto its preoedipal ground in the nature of the forest of Arden—that place named suggestively after Shakespeare's own mother, Mary Arden, and the forest near his birthplace at Stratford-on-Avon.[15] There the play can represent both the male struggle for identity and a female "double-voiced" discourse—Elaine Showalter's term for one that simultaneously acknowledges its dependence on the male and implies its own unique positive value—within it.[16]

For this Shakespeare employs, of course, not a modern psychoanalytic or sociological vocabulary, but his period's vocabulary of genre, set within the consciously experimental frame of the mixed genre of pastoral.[17] Orlando's masculine heroic quest, couched simultaneously in the language of biblical typology and classical epic, is resolved within Arden's "sweet style." There Rosalind, fully acting out romance's conventions of disguise, transforms the social perception of woman from the Petrarchan conventions that both idealize and degrade them to a new convention of companionate marriage. Unlike Orlando's simpler quest, Rosalind's "double-voiced" discourse, criticizing the subject of which she is a part, can thus offer a method for cultural change. She performs *within* the text the critical task feminists today must perform *toward the text as a whole*. As Madelon Gohlke says, "For a feminist critic to deconstruct this discourse is simultaneously to recognize her own historicity and to engage in the process of dislocation of the unconscious by which she begins to affirm her own reality."[18]

But only begins. Rosalind's deconstructive efforts within her own text are one such beginning—a method, not an ideal end. Ironically, she resubordinates herself through marriage to masculine hierarchy, giving herself to her father to be given to her husband, and thus serves the socially conservative purpose of

15. For the forest of Arden and Mary Arden, see Samuel Schoenbaum, *William Shakespeare: A Compact Documentary Life* (Oxford, 1977), pp. 4, 19–22.

16. Elaine Showalter, "Feminist Criticism in the Wilderness," *Critical Inquiry*, 8 (1981), 201–204.

17. Rosalie Colie, *Shakespeare's Living Art* (Princeton, 1974), pp. 243–261.

18. Gohlke, "Shakespeare's Tragic Paradigms," p. 184.

Shakespearean romantic comedy. And "she," of course, acts out a fiction of femininity on an exclusively male stage, her part played by a boy. The representation of women has, more often than not, functioned this way in literature, as in life—as an accommodating device within the dominant fictions of male identity.

Thus far I have emphasized Rosalind's critical role within the text and her eventual surrender of it. Nonetheless, the interaction in *As You Like It* between masculine heroic discourse and feminine romantic "double-voiced" discourse, which it is the burden of this essay to document, forms the dramatic "inside" to a metadramatic context or "outside" of more pure interpretative possibility. Rosalind's disguise, initially the most striking convention of romance implausibility in this text that is so largely structured like an "old tale" (1.2.120), ultimately functions to create new possibilities for it. Her mutable action most fully demonstrates Touchstone's peacemaking "If" (5.4.97–103); Ganymede—the lovely boy whose rapture connected earth and heaven—predicates Hymen, the god of marriage who will "atone" all the elements of the play. In this play romance sustains the constructive, as well as the critical, aspects of pastoral. Arden and the audience addressed in the "Epilogue" function as the complementary environments of the play. Although, looking ahead to *Lear,* I shall characterize the pastoral environment of Arden as a sometimes harsh, sometimes nurturing "Mother Nature"; it is also, as Amiens hints to the Duke, a theater for literary and social criticism and change. For the culturally belated urban artists of the Renaissance, pastoral, which in theory promised a return to origins and a poetic apprenticeship, in practice often presented itself as a field for heightened reflexivity, itself criticizing the subject—the larger culture—of which it formed a part. The "Epilogue" to *As You Like It* freely acknowledges affect as in part constituting the meaning of a work of art: although we may never know what Shakespeare's audience made of the actor-playing-Rosalind's final address, we are licensed to make of it what pleases. At the close of this essay I shall offer a few tentative speculations on why Shakespeare himself, in his later career, made difficult or surrendered this "poco tempo silvano," this play-space of pastoral. But within *As You Like It*, at least, we and the forest are the final judges.


In Shakespeare's *As You Like It* both Duke Senior and Orlando are victims of parricidal rage. The anger of Orlando's brother Oliver is given biblical and classical archetypal overtones as their old family retainer Adam, a representative of the Golden Age "When service sweat for duty, not for meed" (2.3.58), stands in place of their father to bemoan the loss of original "accord" and to denounce Oliver, that Cain figure, who has made "this house . . . but a butchery" (1.1.64; 2.3.27). Shakespeare heightens the at once fairy-tale and all-too-contemporary figure of the impoverished younger brother into an image of paradise lost, where the rising spirit of one's father threatens to turn into rankling bitterness.[19]

Orlando does not seek the patrimony. He desires only his "poor allottery" of "but poor a thousand crowns" (1.1.73; 2–3) and his due "breeding" in gentility. Ironically, he has only his physical strength, his wrestler's skill, to prove these largely immaterial claims, and even his victory over Charles is immediately frustrated by Duke Frederick's antipathy. As with Chodorow's oedipally fraught male child, these problems in the patriarchy open a greater void in his identity, a potential regression to a threatening maternal subtext. Orlando fears that his growth may prove, as Oliver says, "rank" (cf. 1.1.13 with 1.1.85–86). In the wrestling scene Charles taunts him with being, like Antaeus, "desirous to lie with his mother earth" (1.2.201). Although Orlando at first inverts the allusion by defeating Charles

19. Shakespeare first evokes the ideal image of Arden—where echoes of Eden fuse with Hesiodic hints of "the golden world" and more local, English tales of social inversion (1.1.114–119)—within the socially oppressive opening scene, where Orlando complains that Oliver mars the *imago dei* and "the spirit of my father" within him (1.1.29–34 and 1.1.21–23, 46–51, 70–71). See Montrose, "Place of a Brother," pp. 45–47, for parallels between the biblical story of Cain and Abel and the contemporary problem of the patrimony and unequal inheritance. Throughout my essay I cite the text of *As You Like It* from *The Riverside Shakespeare*, ed. G. Blakemore Evans (Boston, 1974).

as the moral Hercules defeated Antaeus, he then assimilates
some of its force when, in a "modest" displacement of Charles's
incestuous image, he finds himself violently in love with Rosalind.[20] His formerly dignified speech before Rosalind is now
shattered as the deepest dimension of his insecurity, his lack of
good breeding, surfaces (cf. 1.2.165–193 and 245–260), and he
fears exile in an inhospitable nature where he might have to
beg, or, like Tom Jones, fall in with robbers (1.1.75; 2.3.31–
35).[21]

When Orlando flees to the forest, he expects to encounter
savagery. Instead, this young man struggling for gentility—"inland bred" (2.7.96)[22]—meets not brigands but a kindly, paternal, philosophic ruler, the exiled Duke: "Sit down and feed,
and welcome to our table" (2.7.105). Shakespeare compresses
in this brief exchange the ancient ideal of hospitality, those
guest-rites most fully performed in the offering of a meal, the
contemplative counterweight to epic's celebration of martial
deeds and heroic adventure. And as with Odysseus at Alcinous's
house or Aeneas at Dido's banquet, the gesture releases Orlando's pent-up memory and social desire. His deeply moving
litany of the ceremonies of civilization is ritually echoed by the
Duke:

> True is it that we have seen better days,
> And have with holy bell been knoll'd to church,
> And sat at good men's feasts, and wip'd our eyes
> Of drops that sacred pity hath engend'red;

20. See Montrose, "Place of a Brother," pp. 37–38, for a glossing of the
significance of the fight, and Richard Knowles, "Myth and Type in *As You Like
It*," *ELH*, 33 (1966), 1–22, on the allusions to Hercules.

21. *As You Like It* has often been compared with *Lear*. Some of the deepest
filiations connect Orlando's vague misgivings about his breeding with Edmund's
vigorous embrace of his bastardy as cause of his naturalistic villainy, and Orlando's fear of nature with Edgar's painful exposure on the heath as poor Tom.
*As You Like It* avoids painful male confrontation with the threatening maternal
subtext of nature through Orlando's own restraint and the benign paternal
mediation of Duke Senior, but it remains a latent menace.

22. See Madeleine Doran, " 'Yet am I inland bred,' " *Shakespeare Quarterly*,
15 (1964), 99–114, for a discussion of the rich traditions of civility that inform
the play.

> And therefore sit you down in gentleness,
> And take upon command what help we have
> That to your wanting may be minist'red.
>                                 (2.7.120–126)

The text expands momentarily into a calm reflective pool of
noble pity—"sunt lacrimae rerum et mentem mortalia tangunt"
("here, too, there are tears for misfortune and mortal sorrows
touch the heart," *Aeneid,* 1.462). A moment later Orlando visually contradicts Jaques's vivid but reductionistic image of the
"seven ages of man" by entering with the frail old Adam, quite
possibly borne on his shoulders, and thereby evoking that classical image of *pietas,* Aeneas carrying his father Anchises from
burning Troy (2.7.139–168). Then, even while Amiens sings of
man's ingratitude, the Duke discovers that Orlando is his beloved "good Sir Rowland's son" (2.7.191–192) and welcomes
him to his new society.

The Duke's masculine governing identity has not been violently dislocated by exile. Unlike Lear, who feels the "climbing
mother," gives way to women's tears, and, in a sharply discontinuous action marked by disjoint, raving speech, exposes himself to the raging elements, Duke Senior exercises seemingly
benign verbal control over his environment. The balanced blank
verse of his first speech moves to contain the sharp sensuous
apprehension of difference: "the icy fang / And churlish chiding
of the winter's wind, / Which . . . bites and blows upon my body"
is literally bracketed by his declaration that "Here feel we *not*
the penalty of Adam" and his smiling philosophic conclusion
(2.1.5–17, emphasis mine). The Duke tries to surround the
threatening nature that had opened up with the failure of the
patriarchy in the first act, controlling it so that Orlando, and to
a large extent we, now experience it as the playfulness of Rosalind, rather than the threat of the unnurturing and devouring
mother. His "kindly," "sweet" stylization—the words resonate
with the high philosophic seriousness of the *dolce stil nuovo* and
its ideals of gentility—now permits the growth of Orlando's
romantic art.

Chodorow speaks of boys as having to "define themselves as
more separate and distinct [from the mother], with a greater

sense of rigid ego boundaries and differentiation," and thus resolving their oedipal crisis more rapidly, extremely, and definitively than girls. The resolution takes the form of "identification with his father . . . the superiority of masculine identification and prerogatives over feminine" (in Freud's more extreme language, "What we have come to consider the normal male contempt for women"), and the eventual displacement of his primary love for his mother onto an appropriate heterosexual love object.[23] Orlando, after initial conflict with paternal figures—his older brother and Duke Frederick—which nearly culminates in archetypal tragedy, experiences nature as harshly threatening. He is saved from its ravages by a kindly father figure who thus metaphorically restores the archetypal line of paternal descent. With the confidence of that masculine relatedness he is able to play seriously at the civilized game of love without threatening his basic male heroic identity. Then Rosalind-as-Ganymede can work to refine his personality while being herself ultimately contained by an overt masculinist sexual ideology.

Meanwhile, similar social problems unfold differently in an aristocratic women's world. Instead of Orlando's importunate strivings, Rosalind at court displays a more diffuse melancholy, partially relieved by feminine confidences—Chodorow's female "self in relationship."[24] Rosalind's musings about the precarious social position of women in love—"[Fortune] the bountiful blind woman doth most mistake in her gifts to women" (1.2.35–36)—suggest that the Duke's exile, deeply felt though it is, is less important than her problematic femininity, especially without his protection. And the desultory and slightly forced nature of the talk portrays the extreme constraints on women's expression in such a setting. Even Touchstone's flat joke about the pancakes must be triggered by a reminder of their feminine lack of a beard (1.2.60–80)! Against this sense of inferiority and vulnerability the young women here have only ready wit.

Exiled by her tyrannous uncle, Rosalind assumes masculine disguise as a safeguard against female vulnerability in a threat-

---

23. Chodorow, *Reproduction,* pp. 169, 94, 182.
24. Ibid., p. 169; see also n.5 above.

ening male world. Once she is safely installed in her cottage in
Arden, however, there is in theory no need for her to maintain
that role. Indeed, once she hears from Celia that young Orlando, who at court "tripp'd up the wrastler's heels and your
heart, both in an instant" (3.2.212–213), is in the forest poe-
ticizing her praises, she immediately exclaims, "Alas the day,
what shall I do with my doublet and hose?" (3.2.219–220), and
bursts forth with a stereotypically female torrent of questions
and effusions, ending with "Do you not know I am a woman?
when I think, I must speak" (3.2.249–250). She seems on the
verge of throwing off her masculine attire and becoming the
Renaissance total woman: witty, perhaps, but ultimately com-
pliant.

At this moment, however, Orlando and Jaques enter in conversation. They implicitly raise the issue of women's dependence
on men that Rosalind's exile from the court has merely trans-
ferred from the political to the psychological sphere. Orlando's
"pretty answers," the love commonplaces that Touchstone has
already parodied (2.4.46–56; 3.2.100–112) and that Rosalind
herself has criticized as "tedious" and having "more feet than
the verses would bear" (3.2.155, 165–166), are now attacked
by the satiric Jaques, "Monsieur Melancholy." Although Orlando, "Signior Love," holds his own in this comic agon, it is
not at all clear from the women's point of view that his disa-
greement with Jaques is anything more than a battle of wits
masking potentially violent sexual appetite. As Jaques accuses,
Orlando may be tritely copying his "posies" out of the inscrip-
tions inside goldsmiths' rings. More ominously, he may have
"conn'd" the "rings" themselves from the goldsmiths' wives,
where the connotations "con" = "pudendum" and "rings" =
"vagina" suggest seduction. As Celia warns, if you drink in this
type of discourse uncritically, you risk putting a "man in your
belly" (3.2.204). Hearing this affected and subtly threatening
exchange prompts Rosalind to keep her doublet and hose, and
what is more, to use them in exactly the sort of "double-voiced"
discourse that, according to Showalter, has always characterized
the relationship of female to male culture: "I will speak to him
like a saucy lackey, and under that habit play the knave with
him" (3.2.295–297). That is, she will adopt the "habit"—the

clothing and habitual ways—of the dominant male culture, including its view of women, even while skewing it "saucily" toward self-consciousness and criticism, and maintaining a part of herself hidden and inviolate.

Nancy Vickers, in a recent article on Petrarchism, implies the defensive wisdom of this tactic.[25] This tradition imagines a chaste, inaccessible, Dianalike woman as the object of the male speaker's love, engendering in him a narcissistically luxuriant range of contradictory emotions that further objectify her, retributively fragmenting her body. Shakespeare continually documents and criticizes this pathology, from Romeo's bookish love for the chaste Rosaline, to Orsino's self-indulgent laments after the "cloistered" Olivia, to its *reductio ad absurdam* in Troilus' languishing after the parts of Cressida, soon to become nauseating "fragments, scraps, the bits and greasy relics / Of her o'er-eaten faith" (*Tro.*, 5.2.159–160). Within this self-generating fiction the only power that women seem to have is the defensive one of refusal, for then, at least, they may put off being consumed and discarded: as Cressida says: "Therefore this maxim out of love I teach: / Achievement is command; ungain'd beseech" (*Tro.*, 1.2.293–294). Orlando hymns a Dianalike Rosalind in a patently artificial language predicated on the Duke's philosophic sweet style; instead of finding "tongues in trees" (2.1.16), the eager new versifier vandalizes them: "these trees shall be my books, / And in their barks my thoughts I'll character" (3.2.5–6). Rosalind witnesses the hitherto uncultivated Orlando's burgeoning conventional love poetry, and by remaining a boy at first defensively distances herself from it.

But Rosalind ultimately accomplishes something more constructive through her pastoral disguise as Ganymede, that pretty boy beloved by Jove, alternately a figure of sexual degradation or of ecstasy.[26] By self-consciously retaining her superficially

25. Nancy Vickers, "Diana Described: Scattered Woman and Scattered Rhyme," *Critical Inquiry*, 8 (1981), 265–280.

26. For the myth of Ganymede as potentially degrading or exalting, see Erwin Panofsky, *Studies in Iconology: Humanistic Themes in the Art of the Renaissance* (New York, 1962), pp. 212–218. In *As You Like It* Ganymede offers a homoerotic bridge to Orlando's encounter with a "real" female other. Shakespeare's decision to highlight the dramatic fact that boy actors played

plausible disguise as a girlish boy—that is, by seeming to "be" Ganymede offering to "play" Rosalind—Rosalind simultaneously offers Orlando a chance to test "the faith of . . . [his] love" (3.2.428) within the relatively nonthreatening limits of supposed male discourse about women, and attempts to exorcise her own fears about giving herself into such a discourse.

In doing so she illustrates the greater social burden borne by women, in line with Chodorow's contention that the oedipus complex develops "different forms of 'relational potential' in people of different genders" and that "Girls emerge from this period with a basis for 'empathy' built into their primary definition of self in a way that boys do not."[27] Having suffered an oedipal crisis in the first act of the play because of the exile of her father and the opposition of Duke Frederick, Rosalind too is thrown back upon nature. Unlike Orlando, however, she does not experience this preoedipal nature as harshly threatening, nor does she require the immediate assurances of a restored father figure. Instead she arrives "weary" but resourceful; female ennervation in the court here translates into boyish pluck (2.4.1–8). As Chodorow says, "girls do not define themselves in terms of the denial of preoedipal relational modes to the same extent as do boys. Therefore, regression to these modes tends not to feel as much a basic threat to their ego."[28]

Chodorow's careful characterization of "a relational complexity in feminine self-definition and personality which is not

---

women's parts may indicate that we are seeing an essentially male drama of power in which women are even further objectified as mere roles. But I think it also indicates the strain which that convention of representation was coming under, as Shakespeare's portrayal of women shifts from the already powerful girls of the romantic comedies to the explicitly threatening women of the tragedies. In the later plays, although boys still play the woman's part, the extra-dramatic referents of their play have become an imagined woman, not an excluded middle term: we move from the boy actor who plays Portia playing a young male lawyer in *The Merchant of Venice* to the boy actor who plays Cleopatra complaining that a boy actor will misplay her—"Some squeaking Cleopatra boy my greatness / I'th'posture of a whore" (*Antony and Cleopatra* 5.2.220–221)—and to the artifice-shattering resurrection of Hermione in *The Winter's Tale*.

27. Chodorow, *Reproduction*, pp. 166–167.
28. Ibid., p. 167.

characteristic of masculine self-definition or personality"[29] not only highlights the difference between Rosalind's and Orlando's reactions to Arden; it also helps explain why Rosalind/Ganymede behaves the way she/he does there. In Arden Rosalind discovers a female identity that will allow her to complete the difficult, triangulated resolution of a girl's typical oedipal crisis: differentiation from *and* continuity with the mother and transfer of affection from the father onto an appropriate heterosexual love object. She must act out her own involvement with this less threatening "Mother Nature" in a way that does not shatter Orlando's more fragile ego boundaries; having done so she may deliver herself to the restored patriarchy, giving herself to her father to be given by him in marriage to her husband.

Her interaction as Ganymede/Rosalind with Orlando thus functions from the male perspective as a form of accommodation and as a test. In the court Orlando had been tongue-tied before beautiful, young, aristocratic women; freed and newly confident in the forest he understandably blurts out clichés. Talk with an attractive boy about women can work to root and refine his discourse, as encounter with "the real thing" at this point could not. Orlando recovers his quietly dignified desire in conversation with Ganymede: "I am he that is so love-shak'd"; "I would not be cur'd"; "By the faith of my love" (3.2.367, 425, 428). Meanwhile, Rosalind/Ganymede tests "the faith of . . . [his] love" against the tradition of misogyny that the unrealistic idealism of Petrarchism could reinforce. As a young man supposedly educated by a sexually disillusioned and withdrawn "old religious uncle of mine" (3.2.344), she professes scepticism toward Orlando and cynicism toward women (3.2.369–371, 348–350), and in her succeeding therapy, proposing to cure love by counsel, she acts out for his benefit men's stereotypical expectations of women's fickleness and seeming cruelty

in this manner. He was to imagine me his love, his mistress; and I set him every day to woo me. At which time would I, being but a moonish youth, grieve, be effeminate, changeable, longing and liking, proud, fantastical, apish, shallow, inconstant, full of tears, full of smiles . . . that I drave my suitor from his mad humor of love to a living humor of

29. Ibid., p. 93.

madness, which was, to forswear the full stream of the world, and live
in a nook merely monastic.    (3.2.407–412, 417–421)

In response to her trying poses, Orlando remains constant. The
Orlando we see in the final act of the play is now appropriately
sceptical of fanciful love at first sight and has painfully earned
the "real" love he is given.

However, he does not develop a very much more sophisticated understanding of women's ambiguous position in the world.
Throughout Rosalind's disguising, Orlando retains an essentially simple faith grounded in his newly secure identity in the
Duke's service. He has an increasingly melancholy feeling that
this interlude is just a game—that he may be wasting time—
and he breaks off wooing to "attend the Duke at dinner" (4.1.180).
Rosalind's action as Ganymede/Rosalind does not shock or void
his identity in the way nature had earlier threatened to do;
instead she leads him to revise his Petrarchan idealization of
women—"The fair, the chaste, and unexpressive she" (3.2.10)—
toward a desire for a chaste wife, and sets that desire within
the dominant code of his male heroic identity.

Rosalind as Ganymede, however, transforms herself more
thoroughly. As her words imply, she is not a dispassionate ther-
apist: "Love is merely a madness, and I tell you, deserves as
well a dark house and a whip as madmen do; and the reason
why they are not so punish'd and cur'd is, that *the lunacy is so
ordinary that the whippers are in love too*" (3.2.400–404, emphasis mine). Critics have always commented on Rosalind's
control of decorum while in disguise, but in a play written almost
contemporaneously with *Hamlet* her "holiday humor" (4.1.69),
like his "antic disposition," is as much used to exorcise her own
fears about love as it is to criticize or educate her lover. Rosalind's control lies in standing outside of amatory convention,
but it is her action within these conventions that carries her,
almost imperceptibly, into the "magic" of creating a new, and
within the value judgments of this play, more adequate convention of companionate marriage.

This becomes clear in her interaction with Silvius and Phebe.
During a frustrating break in her play with Orlando—he is late
for his appointment with her—she slips from her earlier facile

and uncritical sympathy for Silvius' mooning "shepherd's passion" (2.4.60) to a desire to *do* something, to enter their amusingly static and artificial pastoral "pageant" and "prove a busy actor in their play" (3.4.47–59). What she does there, quite to her surprise, is to become the sexually ambiguous means—a boyish "ripe sister" (4.3.87)—through which their hopelessly stalemated and conventional Petrarchan attitudes are softened toward reciprocal love. Silvius, who has previously been an utter fool in love, running off stage (as Orlando later does for Rosalind, cf. 3.2.9–10) exclaiming "O Phebe, Phebe, Phebe!" (2.4.43), assumes a sober fidelity under Ganymede's rebuke; the disdainful Phebe, having now felt the pang of love for Ganymede, is at least sorry for "gentle" Silvius (3.5.85). When Rosalind dissolves her disguise at the end of the play, they have seen each other through her, and Phebe assures Silvius that "Thy faith my fancy to thee doth combine" (5.4.150).

Rosalind-as-Ganymede's action within Silvius and Phebe's play has double relevance for her action within her own. It makes explicit her androgynous power, even while it implies her own subliminal desire to give herself to Orlando. In her next scene with Orlando she fulfills her earlier plan (4.1), acting as she thinks men expect women to do, alternately Lady Disdain and the threateningly promiscuous dark lady of the sonnets. The vehemence and verve of her acting here argues that she is now doing this as much for her own sake as for Orlando's. It is necessary for her to misuse her sex, to soil her own nest, as Celia half-jokingly puts it (4.1.201–204), in order to hide the "woman's fear" (1.3.119) in her heart. She must act out her ambivalence toward her social inscription as woman in order to participate in male privilege. Yet she has just sharply criticized such behavior in Phebe, urging her to "thank heaven, fasting, for a good man's love" (3.5.58), and in 4.1 she becomes confident enough in Orlando's faithful replies to stage a mock marriage. Temporarily empowered *within* Petrarchan love conventions, she has worked her way through to surrendering them in favor of a provisional trust in her partially tested lover. The imaginative space provided by the forest can take her this far— to an imagined wedding.

It takes an intrusion from outside the forest and a resurgence of male heroic force to turn the imagined wedding into a real one. The Duke's "kindness" and Rosalind-as-Ganymede's "play" have allowed Orlando to become a moral rather than merely a physical Hercules (see the wrestling match and Rosalind's cry at 1.2.210), and thus also a type of Christ.[30] Those inchoate energies which in the court could find expression only through wrestling Charles, in the forest focus on the picture of "A wretched ragged man, o'ergrown with hair" and menaced by a snake and a lioness (4.3.102–132). Suddenly Arden has grown threatening again, its postlapsarian state implied by the snake; its maternal peril implied by the Ovidian "suck'd and hungry lioness"; the masculine fear of return to nature emblematized as the supposed wild man. This threat presents itself to Orlando as a moral dilemma, for he recognizes the endangered man as his brother, his eldest brother, "that same brother . . . the most unnatural / That liv'd amongst men." The "old oak, whose boughs were moss'd with age / And high top bald with dry antiquity" and the "wretched ragged man, o'ergrown with hair" both suggest patriarchal and epic genealogy brought to the verge of savagery and decay by Oliver and Duke Frederick's actions: as Orlando earlier laments, "a rotten tree, / That cannot so much as a blossom yield" (2.3.63–64).[31] The description builds to a climax that Shakespeare will repeat near the end of *The Tempest*. To Rosalind's anxious query, "But to Orlando: did he leave him there, / Food to the suck'd and hungry lioness?" the stranger, like Prospero to Ariel (*Temp.*, 5.1.24–28), replies:

> . . . kindness, nobler ever than revenge,
> And nature, stronger than his just occasion,

30. Knowles, "Myth and Type," pp. 14–18.
31. See Montrose, "Place of a Brother," pp. 50–51, for the female sexual threat of the snake and the lioness, and p. 43 for the genealogical significance of the description of Oliver. The lioness probably descends from the lioness who mauls Thisbe's mantle with her bloody mouth in Ovid's story of Pyramus and Thisbe, *Metamorphoses*, bk. 4, a story that we know from the rude mechanicals' play in *A Midsummer Night's Dream* was much on Shakespeare's mind. I am grateful to B. Cass Clarke for suggesting its relevance here. The genealogical tree is one of the *topoi* of epic, invoked to establish the text's relationship to the past; see, for example, Homer, *Odyssey*, 23.173–204; Vergil, *Aeneid*, 4.437–449; Dante, *Divine Comedy*, "Purgatorio," 31.70–75.

> Made him give battle to the lioness,
> Who quickly fell before him . . .

Orlando redeems Eden, and the story bursts into present reality with all the force of its teller's awaking and sudden conversion to brotherly love: "in which hurtling / From miserable slumber *I* awaked" (emphasis mine).

The stranger is thus revealed as Orlando's eldest brother, Oliver. His conversion is emphasized by the dramatic introduction of the personal pronoun and the succeeding insistent play upon it (4.3.135–137). Oliver declares that his real identity surfaced from disguise through disguise; he states that his former unnaturalness has been "sweetly" transformed in the forest; he undergoes in a flash the experience of male bonding, of kinship, that his brother had found with the exiled Duke, to whose society Orlando now leads him (4.3.142–144).

The bloody napkin Oliver brings to Ganymede/Rosalind emblematizes the male adversarial experience of the world of nature. The sign of Orlando's wounding by the lioness, it intrudes the reality of death into Arden: *et in Arcadia ego*. Because of it Rosalind discovers how empathetically tied she is to Orlando: Oliver reports "he [Orlando] fainted, / And cried in fainting upon Rosalind," (4.3.148–149), and Ganymede also promptly swoons. She can now only lamely maintain her disguise; events have impelled her toward accepting this "reality," even with its implied threat to herself—for the "bloody napkin" will reappear in *Othello* as the strawberried handkerchief, a threatening emblem of the dangers of sexual consummation.

Things happen quickly after this. Orlando, now "estate[d]" with the patrimony by his grateful brother, readily gives consent to Oliver's marriage to Celia (5.2.1–15). The improbability of this marriage is satisfactorily glossed by Rosalind/Ganymede's witty "pair of stairs to marriage" speech (5.2.29–41), which at once raises our objections to the suddenness of it and reminds us that it is her own protracted negotiation with Orlando that predicates our conditional acceptance of this love at first sight. Rosalind is having increasing difficulty maintaining her disguise as Oliver and Orlando's words seem to cut closer and closer to her real identity. Pressured by Orlando's emotional urgency—

"I can live no longer by thinking"—Rosalind/Ganymede declares, "I will weary you then no longer with idle talking" (5.2.50–
52). Persuaded now by Orlando's "gesture" (5.2.62), which I
take to be as much his heroic action in saving his brother as his
fidelity within their love discourse, Ganymede promises to produce Rosalind to marry Orlando in truth tomorrow.

In the final act of *As You Like It* Rosalind seemingly surrenders the play. She gives herself to the Duke her father so that
he may give her to Orlando (5.4.19–20, 116–118). She thus
reminds us that their initial attraction to each other was as much
through their fathers—the old Sir Rowland de Boys whom
Duke Senior loved as his soul (1.2.235–239)—as it was to their
unmediated selves, and gives herself into the patriarchy toward which her defensive behavior all along has been in reference.


Yet in *As You Like It* a tissue of metadramatic discourse has
been woven through and around this penultimate sublimation
of the self-consciously fictive mode of romance to the redeemed
biblical "realism" of its patrilinear plot that may help us suggest
what "kind" of pastoral this play finally is. During the course
of their comic wooing Audrey queries Touchstone, "I do not
know what 'poetical' is. Is it honest in deed and word? Is it a
true thing?" to which Touchstone replies, "No, truly; for the
truest poetry is the most feigning, and lovers are given to poetry;
and what they swear in poetry may be said as lovers they do
feign" (3.3.17–22). Now Touchstone would dearly love to find
Audrey a little more poetical, for then, despite her protesta-
tions, she might feign/fain (pretend/desire) to lie (to tell a false-
hood/to copulate), and either way he might get to have sex
with her. But more seriously, his reply and the play's constant
allusions to the analogous powers of poetry and sexual relations
to make something like, but other than, the previously existing
reality have relevance to the metadramatic question of what its
action produces in us, its audience. Is poetry merely a lie, or
does it work to give apprehensible form to our desires? And
what, we ask as feminist critics, are these desires?

*As You Like It* is the ultimately contextual play. Despite its very firm grounding in contemporary social realities and the conventions of romantic and heroic discourse, the play remains conscious that its pastoral inside reflects a playful outside of continuing interpretation. Thus act 3, scene 2, the initial scene of pastoral negotiation, is prefaced by a debate between Touchstone and Corin on the significance of "this shepherd's life," in which the old shepherd's simple and appropriate tautologies are circumscribed by Touchstone's courtly wit. Touchstone does not decenter the mysterious *esse* of Arden, any more than he discomposes Corin, but he does remind us that as sophisticated, postlapsarian auditors we will never be content to rest here. Structured as a debate in all its details and its major patterns, *As You Like It* also invites us to enter its debates, ourselves "busy actor[s] in their play" (3.4.56).

On the specific issue of the play's treatment of gender identity and sex roles, we need finally to move beyond Rosalind's defensive fears, her complex interaction as Ganymede/Rosalind, and her resubmission of herself to the restored patriarchy of her noble father and tested lover to consider the altered environment of the last movement of the play, including Rosalind's invocation of magic, and the play's metadramatic "Epilogue."

For all its self-conscious artfulness, its impositions and nuances of style, a part of this play remains beyond man's control and is discovered in action. As the play closes, that part, suddenly, and without explanation, turns benign: "the icy fang / And churlish chiding of the winter's wind" (2.1.6–7) turns to "spring time, the only pretty [ring] time" (5.3.19); Rosalind/Ganymede's fictional misogynistic "old religious uncle" (3.2.343–350) becomes an equally fictional but now romantically helpful "magician, most profound in his art, and yet not damnable" (5.2.60–61; see also 5.4.30–34); and from beyond any rational expectations that the text has established, the god Hymen comes to "atone" the play, wedding earth and heaven, country and town. Hymen's own words can serve as an hermeneutic for this final movement of the play: "Feed yourselves with questioning; / That reason wonder may diminish" (5.4.138–139). Rational interpretation and the conversations that the characters conduct beneath Hymen's nuptial lyric can explain in great part how these characters have come together. But though "reason wonder may diminish," it cannot cancel it altogether. The play has worked toward evoking an atmosphere of wonder and a promise of fresh beginnings that Touchstone's realism or Duke Frederick's and Jaques's contemplative withdrawals can anchor but not destroy. *As You Like It* transforms the problem of sexual relations insofar as it suggests a world of possibility for the continued negotiation of these differences.

In the metadramatic "Epilogue" the continued negotiation of sexual difference becomes the tentative metaphor for the most successful art. Here, for once, men bear the greater burden. The Elizabethan boy actor who played Rosalind conjures women to please themselves and men to play with women for mutual pleasure:

My way is to conjure you, and I'll begin with the women. I charge you, O women, for the love you bear to men, to like as much of this play as please you; and I charge you, O men, for the love you bear to women (as I perceive by your simp'ring, none of you hates them), that between you and the women the play may please. ("Epilogue," 11–17)

He thus inverts the sexological situation of the play itself, where Orlando had but to become assured in his male heroic identity, while Rosalind had had, through her disguise, her "double-voiced" discourse, to accommodate herself to him. This final inversion in this consummately playful play suggests that men and women can work together—albeit often awkwardly—to transform a world not deterministically bound by its cultural conventions.

Much of Shakespeare's later career suggests how difficult that is. *As You Like It* itself delicately skirts, with the Duke's sweet style, Orlando's simple heroism, and Rosalind's self-restraint, the excoriating issue of the nonfeminist maternal subtext that will erupt in Shakespeare's tragedies. Although we may use Rosalind's double-voiced discourse and the final metadramatic openness of the play to decenter its patriarchal assumptions,

Shakespeare's later plays gravitate around the threat to these values represented by a woman's projected infidelity, the "nothing" that is the source of her reproductive power.[32] In closing I can only hazard some of the symptoms and causes of this shift from comic playfulness to tragic anxiety about sexuality.

I believe that as Shakespeare perfected his romantic comedies and the movement toward marriage within them, he was compelled to face more directly the threat *within* marriage that coincides with the metaphysical and political crisis uncovered in his history plays. If, as the history plays suggest, there is no clear divine sanction for ruling, nor any untainted or disinterested human succession, you confront your origin in the female body, where no one really knows his father: "there," as Othello cries, "where I have garner'd up my heart, / Where either I must live or bear no life; / The fountain from the which my current runs / Or else dries up" (*Othello,* 4.2.57–60). Literary conventions such as the traditional chaste inaccessibility of the idealized lady and the use of boy actors to play female parts might shield Shakespeare for a time from this threat of the female body, allowing him, in the romantic comedies, to experiment with a dazzling series of sexual permutations that we may now appropriate for our own ends. But Shakespeare also deconstructs these literary conventions in the course of his plays in a way that brings him up against the new social realities of marriage and the family in early modern Europe, where decline of external religious authority, loss of feudal power, urban centralization, and nascent capitalism all function to alienate actual women while making their sexuality the focus of ever more anxious regard. Within Shakespeare's career *As You Like It*

32. This issue has received two recent impressive formulations: "I am reading the development from the comedies through the problem plays and the major tragedies in terms of an explosion of the sexual tensions that threaten without rupturing the surface of the earlier plays" (Gohlke, "Shakespeare's Tragic Paradigms," p. 174); "Possibilities for conflict latent in earlier writings are released in the violent action of tragedy, where boundaries previously provided by separation of genre are broken through, and the drama takes into itself the entire range of family-based conflict in Shakespeare" (Richard Wheeler, *Shakespeare's Development and the Problem Comedies: Turn and Counter-Turn* [Berkeley and Los Angeles, 1981], p. 156).

offers us a brief moment of tremulous poise before we sound those depths.[33]

33. For *As You Like It* as a work of exquisite balance, see the classic essays by Helen Gardner, *"As You Like It,"* in *More Talking of Shakespeare,* ed. John W. P. Garret (London; New York, 1959), pp. 17–32, and Ann Barton, *"As You Like It* and *Twelfth Night:* Shakespeare's Sense of an Ending," in *Shakespearean Comedy,* ed. Malcolm Bradbury and D. J. Palmer, Stratford-upon-Avon Studies 14 (1972), pp. 160–180.

JANEL M. MUELLER

# On Genesis in Genre:
# Milton's Politicizing of the
# Sonnet in "Captain or Colonel"

Approaches to the study of Renaissance poetry by way of genre
have a demonstrated value. They recommend themselves most,
perhaps, in their manifest historical grounding: the opportunity
they offer us of reconstituting in our own minds the categories
and expectations that came into play in that age when poetry
was thought about or taught as poetry. We know that generic
considerations operated at every level of Renaissance literary
culture, from the rudiments dispensed in grammar school, to
the more demanding exercises assigned at university, to the still
more cultivated awareness that poets and other literati could
display in their writings or in coterie discussions. Milton is an
example of an especially acute generic consciousness. Familiar
evidence includes the surveys of the major kinds of poetic composition in the preface to the second book of *The Reason of
Church Government* and in *Of Education,* as well as the explanations of "why the Poem rhymes not" and of "that sort of
Dramatic Poem which is called Tragedy" that respectively in-

troduce *Paradise Lost* and *Samson Agonistes* to the reader,
according to their kinds. So marked, in fact, is this consciousness
in Milton that a generic approach seems the one to take even
with a nonclassical kind like the sonnet, which he employed
without ever explaining his practice.[1]

John S. Smart and F. T. Prince have done influential work
on the genre of Milton's sonnets. It is instructive to review their
concerns and findings briefly, for they furnish an admirable
illustration of what this kind of study at its best can contribute
to our understanding, as well as what, by its nature and mode
of proceeding, it cannot do. Smart's 1921 edition of *The Sonnets
of Milton* first accurately characterized how odd these compositions tended to seem to readers acquainted with other Renaissance English sonnets. Milton, in Smart's view, is much the
most Italianate of English sonnet writers—an anomaly, both at
the time and afterward, in a native tradition heavily predisposed
to three quatrains and a couplet rather than an octave and sestet.
Smart's generic characterization of Milton's sonnets draws some
of its plausibility from contextual considerations, in particular,
Milton's amply attested esteem for Italian literature (and, we
might add, the reciprocal esteem of Italian literati for the verse
Milton showed them as he traveled among them). Nevertheless,
this characterization quickly relegates anything other than formal and stylistic considerations to the sidelines.[2] For Smart's
work with genre achieves its impact through the number and
strength of the correspondences adduced between Milton's sonnets and those of Italian sonneteers in certain poetic features:

1. Milton does, however, reveal his conception of the sonnet by calling it "a
Petrarchian stanza" in his draft letter to an unidentified friend (circa 1633),
preserved in the Trinity College manuscript. For the text, see Don M. Wolfe
et al., eds., *Complete Prose Works of John Milton,* 8 vols. (New Haven, 1953–
1982), I, 319–321. Subsequent references to this edition are abbreviated *CPW*
and incorporated in my text.

2. In representing the controlling concern of Smart's edition as the establishment of Milton's credentials as an Italianate sonneteer, I do not mean by
implication to detract from Smart's vital contributions in historical research—
for example, his identifications of Catharine Thomason and Edward Lawrence
as the respective subjects of the sonnets he numbers 14 and 20. See John S.
Smart, ed., *The Sonnets of Milton* (Glasgow, 1921), pp. 79–82, 110–115.

rhyme patterns, word and phrase ordering, manipulation of line units with respect to caesura and enjambment, and management of the larger bipartite structure that sets off the Italian sonnet from other forms.

Smart's commentary on individual sonnets extends these correspondences into the domains of imagery and diction to establish a network of generic interrelations linking Milton's compositional practice at various points with that of a number of sonneteers: Dante, Petrarch, Bembo, Tasso, and lesser-known poets. Such inventorying of resources, techniques, and practitioners, made as detailed and comprehensive as is relevant to the focal text(s) in question, is a staple of genre study; and Smart's work on Milton's sonnets has proved foundational in this regard. His most significant particular finding identified an especially close link between Milton's compositional practices and those of Giovanni della Casa, whose volume of sonnets Milton had acquired in 1629 while a student at Cambridge, as his signed and dated copy (still in existence) attests.

Prince's two chapters on the sonnet in *The Italian Element in Milton's Verse* (1954) registered a major advance in genre study by enlarging and reinforcing the connection between della Casa and Milton in the areas of poetic theory and technique. From Prince we learn the relevance, to Milton, of the "heroic sonnet"—a subgenre with antecedents tracing to Petrarch and Dante: it was first brought to prominence by Bembo, to facile excess by Tasso, and to eventual mastery by della Casa. The involuted syntax, recondite allusions, and bold rhythmic modulations that mark the heroic sonnet are the express vehicles of an accompanying theory of the "magnificent" style, whose proper subjects were specified as philosophical reflection or contemporary issues and personages of requisite grandeur. Prince, however, does not merely argue that Milton's sonnets anglicize the heroic subgenre, mainly after della Casa's model. He also ascribes to them a key developmental function in Milton's poetic career, invoking in this connection Tasso's precedent in moving from sonnets to epic composition. According to Prince, the chief significance and value of Milton's sonnets lie in the way they prepared, stylistically and technically, for the verse paragraphs of *Paradise Lost*.[3]

Even so brief a review as this will suggest the critical impact of Smart's and Prince's work upon generic approaches to Milton's sonnets. Yet, for all the cogency of their identification of the Italian heroic sonnet as the closest overall prototype for Milton's sonnets, we are left to reckon with certain crucial incapacities of genre study as a mode of understanding. The locus of greatest difficulty lies, in my view, in the very inventorying of the range and variety of techniques, effects, and applications achieved by earlier practitioners of the genre under discussion.[4] No matter how exhaustive such inventorying of "the resources of kind" becomes, it can never help to illuminate the twin aspects of what I here call "genesis in genre." On the one hand, this genesis involves asking why a poet is drawn to write in a particular genre at a particular time (and why one genre may later be abandoned for another). On the other hand, this genesis involves analyzing the often quite sweeping transformations and deformations that a genre may undergo in the course of poetic practice over time. Since concerns with adoption, rejection, and alteration of a genre are historical in their nature, they may blind us to a deep irony in the generic approach. Genre study, for all its historical grounding, in fact sustains itself by a central practice—the inventorying of available options—whose implications are synchronic and static. Only by going outside a master inventory to contextualize a poet's practice of a genre by reference to his own historical situation and consciousness can we hope to cast light on questions of genesis in genre.

Given the descriptive successes scored by genre study, especially with regard to Renaissance poetic practice, we need to be wary of criticism that applies the inertness of generic inven-

3. F. T. Prince, *The Italian Element in Milton's Verse* (Oxford, 1954), pp. 14–33, 89–107.

4. Two influential inventories, the one for the Renaissance period at large, the other for epic prior to *Paradise Lost,* are Rosalie L. Colie's *Resources of Kind: Genre-Theory in the Renaissance,* ed. Barbara K. Lewalski (Berkeley, 1973), and John M. Steadman's *Milton and the Renaissance Hero* (Oxford, 1967), chap. 1.

torying to works that raise questions of choice and change in an acute way. The result of genre study in such cases may well be to blunt these questions, if not to make them seem to disappear altogether. Milton's sonnets are a case in point, for they raise both kinds of questions acutely. While the various partial and overlapping orderings given to us in the Trinity College manuscript and in the 1645 and 1673 editions of Milton's *Poems* must preserve, in general, the chronology of composition, the reader who proposes to treat these sonnets generically as a Renaissance sonnet sequence soon encounters trouble of several kinds.

There is unprecedented thematic and linguistic discontinuity: for a start, six sonnets—the first in English, the next five in Italian—exploit and apparently exhaust a Petrarchan strain that, however, receives a distant, culminating transformation in the last sonnet of all, "Methought I saw my late espoused Saint." Directly after the first six follows the sonnet "How soon hath time the suttle theef of youth," written on the occasion of Milton's twenty-fourth or twenty-third birthday. This sonnet's sober self-examination and its affirmation of a guiding divine purpose for the speaker's life signal a break with the amatory subjects of the preceding sonnets. And indeed, on the evidence of manuscript titles, there is a break with all sonnet writing at this point for ten years. The series resumes in "Captain or Colonel, or Knight in Arms"—another sharp divergence in tone, theme, and outlook that inaugurates the category of the political sonnet, for Milton and for the English tradition. This category itself develops by way of clusters interspersed with apolitical sonnets: tributes to virtuous female subjects and celebrations of male friendships. Nevertheless, the category of the political sonnet bulks largest in Milton's composition in this genre between 1642 and 1655. Beside "Captain or Colonel," examples include the three written in the aftermath of the publication of Milton's divorce tracts ("A Book was writ of late," "I did but prompt the age," and the tailed sonnet, "Because you have thrown of[f] your Prelate Lord") and the three addressed to Fairfax, Cromwell, and Vane. The importance of the political sonnet to Milton shows further in the three major sonnets by which he takes his leave of this subgenre: "Avenge O Lord thy slaughter'd Saints" and the two sonnets on his blindness. These register the onset of a postpolitical perspective.

Such marked shifts in the series of Milton's sonnets inevitably raise critical questions. He begins by writing of private concerns, then ceases to write any sonnets for a decade, then resumes composition with the creation of the political sonnet (which he intersperses with minor and more conventional types), and finally countershifts, by way of the postpolitical sonnets, to return to writing of private concerns in the sonnets of the late 1650s, which conclude his work in the genre.[5] Generically induced expectations have, however, made such talk of breaks or shifts in the series of Milton's sonnets recede from critical view over the past twenty years. It is current orthodoxy that Milton's sonnets comprise some sort of sonnet sequence. E. A. J. Honigmann's edition of *Milton's Sonnets* (1966) exerted a major influence in this regard, although his subtle attention to contiguity relations in groupings of two or three sonnets makes his argument one for purposeful sequentiality rather than for sequence as a comprehensive integrating principle.[6] Gradually attenuating Honigmann's special sense of sequence, later studies have tended to affirm that Milton's sonnets are a sequence in a much stronger sense: that they achieve "continuity" through "ordering patterns of concern," or "take the shape of a self-consistent pattern" through "a consistent dialectical progression," or even exhibit "unity" as a concentrically structured presentation of "the ideal community."[7] Among these recent

5. The potential interpretive burden does not really lighten if one adopts the minority view of E. A. J. Honigmann, ed., *Milton's Sonnets* (London; New York, 1966), pp. 76–81. He, returning to Masson's opinion, holds that the sonnets in Italian were written while Milton was in Italy in 1638–39. Although, on this view, the compositional time span becomes much less discontinuous, the shift from love themes to politics is as stark as ever and as much in need of explanation.

6. Honigmann, *Milton's Sonnets*, pp. 59–75.

7. William McCarthy, "The Continuity of Milton's Sonnets," *PMLA*, 92 (1977), 96–109, quotation from p. 99; Mary Ann Radzinowicz, *Toward Samson Agonistes: The Growth of Milton's Mind* (Princeton, 1978), p. 129; Anna K. Nardo, *Milton's Sonnets and the Ideal Community* (Lincoln, Neb., 1979), p. 18.

studies, though at some sacrifice of her "consistency" principle, Mary Ann Radzinowicz's division in terms of five clusters goes farthest to offset the implication of simple homogeneity that is liable to arise in treating Milton's sonnets as poems of the same kind within a single sequence. Yet even Radzinowicz attests to entrenched habits of thinking as she waves aside the questions of genesis—choice and change—with a gesture at the central inventory, the generic monolith: "Like Tasso, whom he admired, Milton composed love sonnets, heroic sonnets, and moral sonnets."[8]

The truth of a pronouncement like the above is at best a weak one. For nothing in Tasso or any other precursor can prepare the reader for "Captain or Colonel," to say nothing of "I did but prompt the age" or "Avenge O Lord thy slaughter'd Saints." Wordsworth's celebrated lines register a truer sense of Milton's impact in and upon the sonnet tradition than does the recent criticism just surveyed, and they do so precisely because the later poet has absorbed himself in the questions of generic choice and generic transformation that genre study is helpless to address from within its own confines. With Milton, exclaims Wordsworth, "The Thing became a trumpet"—

> Scorn not the Sonnet; Critic, you have frowned,
> Mindless of its just honours; with this key
> Shakespeare unlocked his heart; the melody
> Of this small lute gave ease to Petrarch's wound;
> A thousand times this pipe did Tasso sound;
> With it Camöens soothed an exile's grief;
> The sonnet glittered a gay myrtle leaf
> Amid the cypress with which Dante crowned
> His visionary brow: a glow-worm lamp,
> It cheered mild Spenser, called from Faery-land
> To struggle through dark ways; and, when a damp
> Fell round the path of Milton, in his hand
> The Thing became a trumpet; whence he blew
> Soul-animating strains—alas, too few![9]

8. Radzinowicz, *Toward* Samson Agonistes, p. 134, reechoing Honigmann, *Milton's Sonnets*, p. 45, and Smart, *Sonnets of Milton*, pp. 40–41.

9. Ernest de Selincourt and Helen Darbishire, eds., *Wordsworth's Poetical Works* (Oxford, 1952–1959), III, 20–21.

In undertaking, as I do here, to inquire into Milton's resumption of sonnet writing in 1642 and his politicizing of the genre that begins in "Captain or Colonel," one approach to the questions of choice and change clearly lies by way of known or inferrable connections between sonnet composition and what Milton was writing anyway in 1642—and thereafter, into the mid-1650s, if the whole category of political sonnets is taken into consideration. It is a commonplace to notice that Milton's sonnets in these years are his only original poetry in English of which we have certain knowledge. It is equally commonplace to dismiss as simple contrast the possible relation between Milton's sonnets and the bulk of political and other prose that he was more or less continuously producing. Sonnets are short, so this thinking runs; Milton could take no more away in time or energy from his prose.

Yet an assumed disjunction between the sonnets and the prose goes a good way beyond what Milton himself warrants. He writes famously of having "the use, as I may account it, but of my left hand"[10] in his prose compositions, but not of a right hand that does not know what the left hand is doing. The only event in this period that suggests anything like a disjunction in Milton's own thinking about his prose and his verse is his decision to prepare his *Poems, Both English and Latin* for publication (the date of issue was 2 January 1646). Taking his cues from the volume's Virgilian epigraph and from the prefatory Latin commendations supplied by Milton's Italian friends, Masson has claimed convincingly that the motive for publishing the *Poems* was to counterbalance the ill-repute that had fallen on Milton from his divorce tracts.[11] Yet, whatever disjunction is sensed in such a motive, it does not set poetry and prose as such over against each other at all. Rather, the opposition between writing that brings fame and writing that incurs detraction depends precisely on a connection between Milton as author of the poems as well as of the divorce tracts. Otherwise it would

10. In the autobiographical excursus in *The Reason of Church Government* (*CPW*, I, 808).

11. David Masson, *The Life of John Milton: Narrated in Connexion with the Political, Ecclesiastical, and Literary History of His Time*, 2nd ed., 6 vols. (London and New York, 1896), III, 453–455.

make no sense to attempt to salvage his reputation by this means. Milton's right hand knows so well the doings of his left that the former can be trusted, if need be, to rescue the latter.

More indicative, I think, of Milton's ongoing attitude in this period is the eagerness he shows to assimilate to his poetic credit prose compositions in which he takes a special pride of authorship. When Joseph Hall remarked sardonically on a passage in *Animadversions* (July 1641) that projects a bardic figure as an image of Miltonic aspiration, calling the passage *"an astounding prayer,"* Milton counters: "I thank him for that confession, . . . no marvell, if it were fram'd as the voice of three kingdomes: neither was it a prayer so much as a hymne in prose."[12] In a similar vein, as he draws the *Defensio secunda* (May 1654) to its close, Milton declares his satisfaction at having created in his *Defensio prima* (March 1651) what he likens to a national epic: "Just as the epic poet, if he is scrupulous and disinclined to break the rules, undertakes to extol, not the whole life of the hero whom he proposes to celebrate in his verse, but usually one event of his life . . ., so let it suffice me too . . . to have celebrated at least one heroic achievement of my countrymen"—the allusion being to the trial and execution of Charles I.[13]

In the 1645 *Poems* the only English verse demonstrably more recent than "Lycidas" (1637) is a trio of sonnets, of which the first and presumably the earliest, "Captain or Colonel," dates to mid-November of 1642.[14] Here, after Milton's return from

12. *An Apology against a Pamphlet* (*Apology for Smectymnuus*), in *CPW*, I, 930.

13. Translation by Helen North in *CPW*, IV, 685. Also see William Riley Parker, *Milton's Contemporary Reputation* (Columbus, 1940), pp. 12–41, on the increasing hopes for literary recognition that Milton vested in his prose compositions during the period 1642–1654.

14. Honigmann (*Milton's Sonnets,* pp. 101–103) argues, I think unconvincingly, for reassignment of "Captain or Colonel" to May 1641. Although his date would infuse Milton's translation of a portion of a Petrarch sonnet in *Of Reformation* with much more circumstantial import, it rests on a dual implausibility. (1) It requires a forced reading of the sonnet's manuscript heading, "When the assault was intended to yᵉ Citty," as a reference to an abortive plot by a few royalists to prevent Strafford's execution. This plot was exposed in Parliament before it had any impetus that could be called real "intent"; the opposite is true, of course, of the situation in the autumn of 1642. After the

Italy, is evidence of work by his right hand in a genre last
practiced, apparently, a decade earlier, while in the same stretch
his left hand poured forth five antiprelatical tracts. Is a connection to be found? Circumstantially there is a point of contact:
Milton englished the first five lines of the sestet of one of Petrarch's sonnets, the fiercely antipapal "Fontana di dolore, al-
bergo d'ira," for inclusion in *Of Reformation* (May 1641). This
renewal of direct involvement with the genre is not to be min-
imized, especially since Milton translates Petrarch with painstaking attention to phrasing and lineation. (In Milton's one
departure from his source, the omitted last line, he dispenses
with a reference to suffering in purgatory.) Despite this indication of Petrarch's congeniality to the Milton of the antiprelatical tracts, a year and a half would elapse before he composed
"Captain or Colonel," the interim being occupied with his ad-
vocacy of the Smectymnuans. We are left to infer that a sense
of complementarity between sonnet writing and tract writing
would be necessary for Milton to resume work in the former at
a period dominated by the latter. But is the retrieval of any
such sense possible?

It is possible enough to find some warrant for a general
complementarity between polemical prose and the sonnet in
J. W. Lever's description of the Renaissance sonnet sequence
as a genre:

It was preoccupied with an over-riding, all-important engagement of
the self with an other; hence with the exploration of a polarity. That
"other" might stand in the position of mistress, friend, or even god-
head; in any case a relationship was created which drew into its mag-
netic field the poet's whole personality; his sense of his environment;
his response to nature, time, and mutability; his political, religious or
philosophical beliefs.[15]

---

battle of Edgehill (October 23), the royalist army marched on London and
actually sacked Brentford (November 12) before a hastily assembled force of
defenders at Turnham Green blocked any further advance on the panic-stricken
city (November 13). (2) Honigmann's redating proposal requires assuming that
Milton had become notorious by writing his antiprelatical tracts of 1641–42.
Parker marshals the numerous counterindications (*Milton's Contemporary Reputation*, pp. 12–17).

   15. J. W. Lever, ed., *Sonnets of the English Renaissance* (London, 1974), p. 3.

To rest the question in Lever's generic inventorying, however, is to beg it with regard to the often unprecedented sonnets that Milton began to write from 1642 onward, the sonnets I have been calling political and postpolitical. Fortunately there is more precise evidence of complementarity in the dynamic or design of these Miltonic sonnets and the units of argument that become constitutive in the prose tracts. So far as I know, Wordsworth deserves the credit for identifying the dynamic or design that makes the sonnets complementary to the prose. He had expressed his admiration early: "The Sonnets of Milton which I like best are that to *Cyriack Skinner* [of the two, probably "*Cyriack, this three years day*"]; on his *Blindness; Captain or Colonel; Massacre of Piedmont; Cromwell,* except last two lines, *Fairfax* &."[16] A considerably later discussion of Milton's mastery of the sonnet form becomes the context for Wordsworth's observation, drawn from Miltonic practice, that an effectively integrated handling of a topical subject requires a three-part structure. He also noted that Milton had broken significantly with the tradition of Italian sonneteers in this connection:

It should seem that a Sonnet, like every other legitimate composition, ought to have a beginning, a middle, and an end—in other words, to consist of three parts, like the three propositions of a syllogism, if such an illustration may be used. But the frame of metre adopted by the Italians does not accord with this view, and, as adhered to by them, it seems to be, if not arbitrary, best fitted to a division of the sense into two parts, of eight and six lines each. Milton, however, has not submitted to this.[17]

Although the amount of congruence between this three-part structure and the octave-and-sestet divisions in Milton's sonnets

16. W. W. to Correspondent unknown, 1802, *The Early Letters of William and Dorothy Wordsworth,* ed. Ernest de Selincourt (Oxford, 1935), p. 312. The stricture attached to the Cromwell sonnet reflects Wordsworth's dislike of terminal couplets.

17. W. W. to Alexander Dyce, spring 1833, *The Letters of William and Dorothy Wordsworth: The Later Years,* ed. Ernest de Selincourt (Oxford, 1939), p. 652. For discussion that partially anticipates my own, see Lee M. Johnson, *Wordsworth and the Sonnet,* Anglistica (Copenhagen, 1973), XIX, 42–45. I am grateful to my colleague James K. Chandler for this reference and the one in n. 31, as well as a thoughtful critical reading of a draft of this essay.

varies, Wordsworth's beginning, middle, and end principle does indeed identify the compositional dynamic of the sonnets Milton wrote between 1642 and 1655.[18] We may consider an earlier and a later example from among Wordsworth's favorites. "Captain or Colonel" has a four-line opening:

> Captain or Colonel, or Knight in Arms,
>     Whose chance on these defenceless dores may sease,
>     If deed of honour did thee ever please,
>     Guard them, and him within protect from harms . . .

Here the speaker rehearses the present circumstances, laying some ground for the hearer's consent to the appeal that is lodged immediately. The sonnet's midsection of five full lines takes up this appeal as a proposition requiring some inducement toward its acceptance (although nothing like a proof is offered). The inducement delivered, the speaker renews his appeal, exchanging the milder persuasive terms he used at first for hortatory, dissuasive ones:

> He can requite thee, for he knows the charms
>     That call Fame on such gentle acts as these,
>     And he can spred thy Name o're Lands and Seas,
>     What ever clime the Suns bright circle warms.
> Lift not thy spear against the Muses Bowre.

The five full lines left to the end section likewise treat the second appeal as a proposition to be established, but they make an indirect approach through periphrastic recounting of two notable examples. If even dimly apprehended, the examples will serve their purpose, an argument by (mutually flattering) analogy:

> The great *Emathian* conqueror bid spare
> The house of *Pindarus,* when Temple and Towre

18. For an entirely different line of analysis that takes octave and sestet as primary compositional units (and, accordingly, places another construction on Wordsworth's observations), see Taylor Stoehr, "Syntax and Poetic Form in Milton's Sonnets," *English Studies,* 45 (1964), 289–301.

> Went to the ground: And the repeated air
> Of sad *Electra*'s Poet had the power
> To save th'*Athenian* Walls from ruine bare.[19]

What we find in "Captain or Colonel" is not, *pace* Wordsworth, syllogistic sonneteering, for the Miltonic three-part structure owes much more to formal rhetoric than it does to formal
logic. This earlier sonnet segments its parts cleanly at line end-
ings but does not so sharply separate the three functions—the
recounting of relevant considerations, the making of assertions,
and the adducing of reasons or inferences—that operate within
the three parts. Despite the intermixing, these functions bear
clear resemblance, respectively, to the *narratio, propositio,* and
*confirmatio* of traditional oratory. Perhaps Milton's free-ranging
use of these functions suggested the syllogism to Wordsworth,
for its validity is independent of the ordering of major premise,
minor premise, and conclusion. Likewise, the Miltonic parts are
not restricted to their specified locations in the oration, as stan-
dardly schematized in the rhetorical handbooks. In any case,
the earlier "Captain or Colonel" creates one combination of
discrete verse divisions and multiple rhetorical functions, while
the later "*Cyriack,* this three years day" develops another: a
combination of interfused verse units with much more clearly
specialized rhetorical functions.

This later sonnet's five-and-a-half-line beginning plunges
forthwith into personal history, a *narratio:*

> *Cyriack,* this three years day these eys, though clear
> To outward view, of blemish or of spot;
> Bereft of light thir seeing have forgot,
> Nor to thir idle orbs doth sight appear
> Of Sun or Moon or Starre throughout the year,
> Or man or woman.

The speaker's circumstances having been sufficiently articulated, the midsection of the sonnet begins at the caesura of line
6. It enacts the formulation of a *propositio* by setting up an

19. All citations of Milton's sonnets are from Honigmann's text, an old-
spelling edition whose principles he lays out in *Milton's Sonnets,* pp. 54–58.
Manuscript titles are cited from Harris F. Fletcher, *John Milton's Complete
Poetical Works in Photographic Facsimile* (Urbana, 1943), vol. I.

antithetical disjunction in which possible negative determinations are rejected in favor of a positive one:

> Yet I argue not
> Against heavns hand or will, nor bate a jot
> Of heart or hope; but still bear vp and steer
> Right onward.

Up to this point, the caesura of the ninth line, there has been no reasoning to support the affirmed course of action. The end section picks up here with an acknowledgment that reasons are due. It first elaborates one that is represented as being sufficient—*confirmatio* enough—but proceeds to hint at another, far greater:

> What supports me dost thou ask?
> The conscience, Friend, to have lost them overply'd
> In libertyes defence, my noble task,
> Of which all *Europe* talks from side to side.
> This thought might lead me through the worlds vain mask
> Content though blind, had I no better guide.

What Wordsworth's insight into Miltonic three-part structure provides is a basis for drawing a substantive and, indeed, pervasive connection between rhetorical organization in the sonnets and the prose tracts. The compositional dynamic in both often proves so similar at the local level that we can treat it as one kind of presumptive evidence—a formal kind—that will help to account for Milton's return to sonnet writing in the 1640s and 1650s. I shall illustrate with three examples out of many that might have been chosen from the prose tracts; my selection has in part been determined by chronological scope. In each citation I mark beginning, middle, and end divisions with square brackets and new lineation. The first example is a single sustained period like that comprised by several of Milton's sonnets. It is taken from *The Reason of Church Government* (January–February 1642). Its clear internal structure incorporates a *narratio* serving as antecedent to a central dual *propositio,* its consequent. The *confirmatio,* cast in antithetical form, details the sure effects of the refined awareness actuated in a Christian who values himself truly and walks worthily:

[But when every good Christian throughly acquainted with all those glorious privileges of sanctification and adoption which render him more sacred then any dedicated altar or element, shall be restored to his right in the Church, and not excluded from such place of spirituall government as his Christian abilities and his approved good life in the eye and testimony of the Church shall preferre him to,]

[this and nothing sooner will open his eyes to a wise and true valuation of himselfe, which is so requisite and high a point of Christianity, and will stirre him up to walk worthy the honourable and grave imployment wherewith God and the Church hath dignifi'd him:]

[not fearing lest he should meet with some outward holy thing in religion which his lay touch or presence might profane, but lest something unholy from within his own heart should dishonour and profane in himself that Priestly unction and Clergy-right whereto Christ hath entitled him.]   (*CPW*, I, 844)

The second example, "wov'n close, both matter, form and stile," is from *Tetrachordon* (4 March 1645). The passage opens with the *propositio,* itself introduced by a brief though crucial concessive. The *narratio,* also unusually brief, sketches the position that called forth the concessive; the brevity suggests the baselessness of the position. A disproportionately full *confirmatio* follows and concludes; its tight, stepwise reasoning is offered in proof of the abundant truth of the *propositio:*

[Yet grant the thing heer meant were only adultery, the reason of things will afford more to our assertion, then did the reason of words.]

[For why is divorce unlawfull but only for adultery? because, say they, that crime only breaks the matrimony.]

[But this, I reply, the institution it selfe gainsaies: for that which is most contrary to the words and meaning of the institution, that most breaks the matrimony; but a perpetual unmeetnes and unwillingnesse to all the duties of helpe, of love and tranquillity is most contrary to the words and meaning of the institution; that therefore much more breaks matrimony then the act of adultery though repeated.]   (*CPW*, II, 674)

My third and final example, a passage added to the second edition of *Eikonoklastes* (1650), makes a virtuoso display of the intermixed rhetorical functions that Miltonic three-part struc-

ture can serve, always to a discernible purpose. Milton confronts
a natural question: who could or would write against the *Eikon
Basilike?* To attest his cognizance of how thoroughly what he
is about to argue runs counter to majority opinion in England,
he begins by gathering reasons under two heads. Their substance
could be a *confirmatio* for the decision not to write, but the
explicitly hypothetical frame ("well it might have seem'd")
transforms this first part into a *narratio* of thoughts that had no
weight with Milton. A brief *propositio* follows; it is a characteristic affirmation of resolve in a characteristic middle position.
The end part takes the form of a *narratio* of what can be expected
to befall a truth in the world, but its one vital element, the
lighting upon a "few" readers "of value and substantial worth,"
transforms this *narratio* into a *confirmatio* of Milton's undertaking to oppose "the Kings book." Here is the passage, again
a single elaborated period:

[And though well it might have seem'd in vaine to write at all; considering the envy and almost infinite prejudice likely to be stirr'd up
among the Common sort, against what ever can be writt'n or gainsaid
to the Kings book, so advantageous to a book it is, only to be a Kings,
and though it be an irksom labour to write with industrie and judicious
paines that which neither waigh'd, nor well read, shall be judg'd without
industry or the pains of well judging, by faction and the easy literature
of custom and opinion,]

[it shall be ventured yet, and the truth not smother'd,]

[but sent abroad, in the native confidence of her single self, to earn,
how she can, her entertainment in the world, and to finde out her own
readers; few perhaps, but those few, such of value and substantial
worth, as truth and wisdom, not respecting numbers and bigg names,
have bin ever wont in all ages to be contented with.]   (*CPW*, III, 339–
340)

Having argued that a strong presumptive reason why Milton
would revert to sonneteering in 1642 can be drawn from the
compositional dynamic shared by his sonnets and his prose at
the local level, I now need not merely to acknowledge but to
insist on some basic distinctions that arise from making comparisons across literary genres. The sonnets are proselike in their
rhetorical structure, but the prose passages are always unson-

netlike in their diffuseness of phrasing.[20] They are often unson-netlike, too, in the imprecision or abstractness of certain formulations, for they are not carrying the whole burden of argument or meaning in the discourse of which they themselves are parts. My point may be all too obvious: if it were largely the same thing for Milton in the 1640s and 1650s to be writing prose tracts or sonnets, the sonnets, we may suppose, would not have been written. What difference, then, did the form of the sonnet and the genre of the sonnet make?

As the prose at the local sentence level did not, the sonnet form jointly imposed brevity and completeness as conditions of utterance. Instead of seeking to moderate these conditions—for instance, by composing an Elizabethan-style sonnet sequence—Milton let them operate in full strength on his work. His sonnets, if they are a sequence, are so in the loosest possible sense—compositions succeeding one another in time that neither create nor imply a sustaining narrative. Indeed, by virtue of their discreteness from one another overall, Milton's sonnets from the 1640s and 1650s highlight one of their major characteristics. With few exceptions, each sonnet registers as occasional, circumstantial, and topical, inseparable in its concerns and impact from some experience undergone at a certain date, though not thereby "dated" in the colloquial sense. Because Milton's poetic language is generally more economical, more salient, and more memorable than that of his prose, the issues in the sonnets remain live ones for readers to an extent rarely matched in Milton's tracts.

As for differences made by the sonnet genre, the most vital seems to be that, as lyric, it privileged personal utterance. We find this privilege so eagerly embraced by Milton the sonneteer in the period of his prose writings that his refusal to dichotomize the expression of his public and private selves wrought an internal transformation in the genre. This was the genesis of the

20. Stoehr, "Syntax and Poetic Form in Milton's Sonnets," p. 289, conjectures that compactness of expression posed a challenge to Milton the prose writer and that he therefore "chose the [sonnet] form, one supposes, exactly because it was demanding, suited by its brevity to the expression of occasional thoughts and feelings, by its complexity and sinewy movement to the development of powerful emotion and tough logic."

political sonnet. As a subgenre of discrete lyrics on national issues and national figures, the political sonnet proved an invaluable instrument. With it Milton probed essential concerns regarding power—its manifestations, possession, uses, effects, and limits—seeking to discover and, if possible, align the relation between objective fact or possibility and subjective desire with respect to power. Earlier I designated the core group of Milton's political sonnets: "Captain or Colonel," "A Book was writ of late," "I did but prompt the age," "Because you have thrown of[f] your Prelate Lord," "*Fairfax, whose name in armes*," "*Cromwell, our cheif of men*," and "*Vane, young in yeares*." These sonnets comprise a core group because their concerns with power are political in a definitional sense: they address issues of due governance and, specifically, of human agency in the control and direction of public life and public affairs. On the basis of this core group, where political signification entails that human agency be seen as efficacious and, indeed, as determinative, it is possible to trace the inception of the postpolitical sonnet in its turn. Here agency is reassigned from the political to the theological sphere in a group including "Avenge O Lord thy slaughter'd Saints," "When I consider how my light is spent," and, marginally, "*Cyriack*, this three years day." Although considerations of space will restrict me to discussion of only the first of Milton's political sonnets, "Captain or Colonel," it is fully representative of the whole, varied group both in its animating central concern with power politically conceived and in the vital closeness of its links with issues in the prose.

In the first of Milton's political sonnets, appropriately enough, the scope of human agency invested with political significance prominently features poetry writing and the figure of the poet. As indicated by its first manuscript title, "On his dore when y$^e$ Citty expected an assault," later altered in Milton's hand to "When the assault was intended to y$^e$ Citty," "Captain or Colonel" both presents and represents itself as a text, a paper to be tacked to a door, while the poet's voice and presence derive from this paper whatever power they can wield. This sonnet's representation of poetry and the poet as vital sources of critique and celebration for a political order initiates the Horatian (and, more distantly, Pindaric) affinities in Milton's sonnets—a sub-

ject that John H. Finley has explored at some length.[21] As
suggestive as such affinities are, the political concerns with which
the political (and postpolitical) sonnets engage most deeply are
those peculiar to the conjuncture between Milton's consciousness and the English revolutionary upheaval of the 1640s and
1650s. His was a consciousness true in its type to puritanism,
but ultimately true to itself, above all in the degree to which it
took personally the making of history in its own times. As Allen
Grossman has observed,

Milton is singular in his acknowledgment of history as part of the
self . . . Milton is the poet of a crisis in the intelligibility of experience . . . An abyss has opened up between fact and value . . . Milton
was throughout his career the apologist of the vast shifts in meaning
which are the condition of the coming to pass of new value and which
at the same time imperil all value . . . Milton's sense of history (and
consequently of moral experience) is always in advance of the intelligibility of that experience, and his poetry is an attempt to restore the
sightedness which the ability to understand experience confers.[22]

The discrete topicality and occasionality registered from one to
another of the political sonnets arise out of recurrent moments
of crisis for the Miltonic speaker. These moments are doubly
threatening: as experiences that must be undergone and as ex-

21. John H. Finley, Jr., "Milton and Horace: A Study of Milton's Sonnets,"
*Harvard Studies in Classical Philology,* 48 (1937), 29–73, esp. pp. 32, 39–62,
on the thematic ties between the Miltonic political sonnet and the Horatian
ode.
22. Allen Grossman, "Milton's Sonnet 'On the late massacre in Piemont':
A Note on the Vulnerability of Persons in a Revolutionary Situation," *Tri-
Quarterly,* 23–24 (1972), 283–301, quotations from pp. 296, 292, 290, 294, 284.
Despite major insights, Grossman misses the mark badly, I think, in implying—
without argument—that a unique capacity to confer value and meaning on
individual existence rested with the hierarchical world order that, in Milton's
day, purported to legitimize the absolute sovereign (pp. 283–284). Grossman
is equally in error, I think, to imply that Milton's yearning for value and meaning
forced him to treat with God as he refused to treat with Charles, and to accept
a tyrant's rule on the tyrant's terms. But God is not a tyrant according to the
definition that Milton evolved and regularly invoked—for example, throughout
*Eikonoklastes.* A tyrant, as conceived by Milton, pursues his own will and
welfare by destroying the wills and welfare of his subjects, whom he enslaves
and consumes. (Plato's *Gorgias,* 471b–d, 479a, 492c, may be the ultimate source
of this Miltonic conception.)

periences that must be interpreted. The crisis in these moments is political because it eventuates or is bound up in an exercise of public power and authority that touches the speaker.

For all the singular acuteness of his consciousness, Milton conceived the threat of political power in the early modern sense that the apologetics of sixteenth- and seventeenth-century absolutism had made explicit. According to Perry Anderson, this new sense manifests itself as a "break with the medieval conception of authority as the exercise of traditional justice"—that is, the due enforcement of preexisting laws. "The modern idea of political power," in Anderson's words, is "the sovereign capacity to create new laws, and impose unquestioning obedience to them."[23] But if an origin in the institutions of feudal monarchy is ruled out, whence arose the autonomy and unconditionality, the quotient of absoluteness in absolutism? Anderson reaffirms the direction taken by Marx, Engels, and Weber in pointing to the Renaissance rediscovery of the notion of "Quiritary ownership," the absoluteness of private or individual property, in Roman civil law. The utility of this notion was immediately recognized in the early modern period, when commodity relations had reached new levels of activity and complexity that required its support. Absolute property became both the means of strengthening the hold of private ownership along preestablished lines and the means of strengthening the hand of the king as the final source and guarantor of private ownership. Anderson explains the contradictory implications of the notion of absolute property by tracing them to their origins:

The Roman legal system . . . comprised two distinct—and apparently

23. Perry Anderson, *Lineages of the Absolutist State* (London, 1974), p. 50. A note cites Jean Bodin, *Les Six livres de la République* (Paris, 1578), pp. 103, 114, and translates as follows: "The principal mark of sovereign majesty and absolute power is essentially the right to impose laws on subjects generally without their consent . . . Law is nothing other than the command of the sovereign in the exercise of his power." For other pertinent treatment of the property-sovereignty connection, see C. B. Macpherson, *The Political Theory of Possessive Individualism, Hobbes to Locke* (Oxford, 1962), and J. G. A. Pocock, *The Machiavellian Moment: Florentine Political Thought and the Italian Republican Tradition* (Princeton, 1975).

contrary—sectors: civil law regulating economic transactions between citizens, and public law governing political relations between the State and its subjects . . . The juridically unconditional character of private property consecrated by the one found its contradictory counterpart in the formally absolute nature of the imperial sovereignty exercised by the other . . . It was the theoretical principles of this political *imperium* which exercised a profound influence and attraction on the new monarchies of the Renaissance.[24]

Such contradictory strengthening of subjects' property rights and the rule of their sovereign could obviously put the two on a collision course. This happened in Milton's England, where Humanist revival of the study of Roman law exercised an influence parallel to but much less important than the compelling new interpretations of common law precedent being evolved in and beyond Parliament. These interpretations focused on defining and defending something that also obsessed Milton: what it is to be free. But for freedom no less than for its obverse, absolutism, the catalytic concept was again that of inviolable private and individual property. Christopher Hill clarifies as follows:

The common law was the law of free men. "He that hath no property in his goods," said a member of Parliament in 1624, "is not free" . . . Note this use of the word "free." *Libertas* in medieval Latin conveys the idea of a right to exclude others from your property, your franchise. To be free of something means to enjoy exclusive rights and privileges in relation to it. The freedom of a town is a privilege, to be inherited or bought. So is a freehold estate. The Parliamentary franchise is a privilege attached to particular types of property. The "liberties of the House of Commons" were peculiar privileges enjoyed by members, such as immunity from arrest, the right to uncensored discussion, etc. "Our privileges and liberties," the House told James in 1604, "are our true right and due inheritance, no less than our lands and goods." Similarly, when James wrote *The Trew Law of Free Monarchies* he wished to emphasise that kings, like their propertied subjects, had their rights and privileges. The problem of early seventeenth-century politics was to decide where the king's rights and priv-

24. Anderson, *Lineages of the Absolutist State,* p. 27. For discussion of Quiritary ownership, see pp. 423–426.

ileges ended and those of his free subjects began: the majority of the population did not come into it.[25]

By the late 1630s and early 1640s the claims of Stuart absolutism with regard to ownership in the realm seemed to leave no place whatever for free subjects. At the trial of John Hampden for refusing to pay ship money, a levy not voted by Parliament but imposed directly by the crown, Sir John Finch voiced the new absolutism tellingly when he claimed that Parliament had no power "to bind the King not to command the subjects, their persons and their goods, and I say their money too." These words, spoken in 1638, became notorious as the expression of a power struggle in which Parliament would stand for the preservation of the individual, in his person and his property, against the encroachments of the crown. Hence the confrontational language of the House of Commons' formal declaration (2 October 1642): "That they will oblige themselves by a mutual Assistance of one another, and of the whole Kingdom, for Defense of the Protestant Religion, the Privilege of Parliament, and the Liberty & Property of the Subject."[26]

The crisis that triggered the composition of "Captain or Colonel" was the imminent threat posed to the property and person of Milton, a London householder, by royalist troops who had advanced to within close range of the city in November 1642. The arch tones in which the blandishments of the opening nine lines are delivered suggest a speaker who is startled at finding his doors "defenceless" and himself within "the Muses Bowre" in need of protection "from harms":

> Captain or Colonel, or Knight in Arms,
>> Whose chance on these defenceless dores may sease,
>> If deed of honour did thee ever please,
>> Guard them, and him within protect from harms,
> He can requite thee, for he knows the charms
>> That call Fame on such gentle acts as these,

25. Christopher Hill, *The Century of Revolution, 1603–1714* (London and Edinburgh, 1961), pp. 44–45.

26. Sir John Finch's remark and the *Commons Journals* are cited by Merritt Y. Hughes in a note on a passage in *Eikonoklastes* dealing with the beginning of the civil war (*CPW,* III, 574n18).

> And he can spred thy Name o're Lands and Seas,
> What ever clime the Suns bright circle warms.
> Lift not thy spear against the Muses Bowre.

But the collateral insights afforded by the prose tracts permit a closer analysis of this note of surprise. It is most unlikely that this Miltonic speaker has been startled into verse by an awakened consciousness of being a "free" property holder. For Milton himself had been repeatedly charging in his antiprelatical tracts of 1641–42 that the English bishops had fomented civil war in 1637–38 (later identified as the cause of his return from Italy)[27] and that they had done so by promoting from their pulpits a doctrine intolerable to true English ears. *Of Reformation* puts the matter thus, handling the king's involvement charily:

What more banefull to *Monarchy* then a Popular Commotion, for the dissolution of *Monarchy* slides aptest into a *Democraty;* and what stirs the Englishmen, as our wisest writers have observ'd, sooner to rebellion, then violent, and heavy hands upon their goods and purses? Yet these devout *Prelates,* spight of our great Charter, and the soules of our Progenitors that wrested their liberties out of the *Norman* gripe with their blood and highest prowess, for these many years have not ceas't in their Pulpits wrinching, and spraining the *text,* to set at nought and trample under foot all the most sacred, and Life blood Lawes, Statutes, and Acts of *Parliament* that are the holy Cov'nant of Union, and Marriage between the King and his Realme, by proscribing and confiscating from us all the right we have to our owne bodies, goods and liberties. What is this, but to blow a trumpet, and proclaime a firecrosse to a hereditary, and perpetuall civill warre. Thus much against the Subjects Liberty hath been assaulted by them. (*CPW,* I, 592–593)

The conclusion of *The Reason of Church Government,* however, warns the English in much rougher language against the bishops and any king they might mislead into tyrannical pretensions:

As they have done to your souls, they will sell your bodies, your wives, your children, your liberties, your Parliaments, all these things, . . . to the arbitrary and illegal dispose of any one that may hereafter be call'd a King, whose mind shall serve him to listen to their bargain . . . And

27. See the *Second Defense* (*CPW,* IV, 619).

indeed they stand so opportunely for the disturbing or the destroying of a state, being a knot of creatures . . . only in the Princes favour, . . . that if it should happen that a tyrant (God turn such a scourge from us to our enemies) should come to grasp the Scepter, here were his spare men and his lances, here were his firelocks ready, he should need no other . . . then these, if they could once with their perfidious preachments aw the people.   (*CPW*, I, 851–852)[28]

In a longer view, this connection between liberty, political identity, and property would undergo considerable clarification as Milton's political consciousness radicalized. Hence its most developed formulation occurs in *The Tenure of Kings and Magistrates* (February 1649) where he specifies conditions for "what the people by thir first right may doe in change of government, or of governour." These conditions are met when they find themselves "under tyranny and servitude; as wanting that power, which is the root and sourse of all liberty, to dispose and *oeconomize* in the Land which God hath giv'n them, as Maisters of Family in thir own house and free inheritance" (*CPW*, III, 236–237). In the same year and in the same vein, *Eikonoklastes* (October 1649) reflects spiritedly on the past decade of revolutionary struggle: "It were a folly beyond ridiculous to count our selves a free Nation, if the King not in Parliament, but in his own Person and against them, might appropriate to himself the strength of a whole Nation as his proper goods" (ibid., 451).

Thus, even as early in the prose as 1642, Milton's sense of individual political identity is fully self-conscious—at least in a national framework—regarding its basis in private property, and it is equally alert to the likelihood that a defense against forcible seizure might soon be called for.[29] What appears to have taken the speaker of "Captain or Colonel" by surprise,

28. Milton reiterates these analyses in chaps. 10 and 27 of *Eikonoklastes* (*CPW*, III, 448, 574).

29. Not before the retrospective reflections in the exordium of Milton's *Second Defense* (May 1654) does he represent himself as choosing between fighting and writing to defend his country. In 1654 he can say that he chose to write rather than enlist in the Parliamentary army because he was better suited to the former activity and his efforts in that line would avail more (*CPW*, IV, 552–553).

however, was a turn of local events that gave the lie to any
complacent distinction between living as a retired, studious head
of a household in "a pretty Garden House . . . in *Alders-gate-
Street*"[30] and bearing arms as a militiaman with other London
citizens to hold off the king's troops. Just such a distinction can
be seen to operate in the autobiographical excursus of *The Reason of Church Government,* where the worst Milton envisages
himself as having to undergo in the upcoming fight is to "leave
a calm and pleasing solitarynes fed with cherful and confident
thoughts, to imbark in a troubl'd sea of noises and hoars disputes"—that is, the squalls of pamphlet wars. Hence he retains
the present tense to write of "labour and intent study (which I
take to be my portion in this life)" and of poetic abilities that
"are of power beside the office of a pulpit, to imbreed and
cherish in a great people the seeds of vertu, and publick civility"
(*CPW,* I, 821, 810, 816). We infer that the archness in "Captain
or Colonel" originates in the strains of a recently struck accommodation between Milton's political and poetic identity—strains
that are suddenly compounded by raw physical danger. He had
thrown his energies behind the force of words, thinking by writing political prose to define and delimit his role in the war. But
what is the force of words to the force of arms? Even when the
former is raised to visionary poetry, as in the five concluding
lines of "Captain or Colonel," the present-tense implications
are by no means certain:

> The great *Emathian* Conqueror bid spare
> The house of *Pindarus,* when Temple and Towre
> Went to the ground: And the repeated air
> Of sad *Electra*'s Poet had the power
> To save th'*Athenian* Walls from ruine bare.

30. The phrase is Edward Phillips', in his *Life of Mr. John Milton* (1694),
ed. Helen Darbishire, *The Early Lives of Milton* (London, 1932), p. 62. Given
all the time that Milton's elder nephew spent with him—first as a pupil, later
as an amanuensis and literary assistant—the odd organization of Phillips' narrative according to Milton's succession of addresses may well bear witness to
the constitutive importance of being a property holder for Milton's sense of
identity. Phillips is observably sensitive to Miltonisms in writing of these residences; one sentence, for example, seems to echo "Captain or Colonel": "And
now the House look'd again like a House of the Muses" (p. 67).

On the evidence of the draft letter to an unidentified friend
preserved in the Trinity College manuscript, the strains discernible in "Captain or Colonel" also had nonpolitical antecedents going back almost a decade from 1642. In this letter
(*CPW*, I, 319) Milton addresses the friend's charge "that too
much love of Learning is in fault, & that I have given up myself
to dreame away my Yeares in . . . studious retirement," in the
process making several crucial concessions. He admits in the
abstract what would become actual experience by November
1642, the date set by Mary Powell for her return to Milton after
their short cohabitation and her long visit to her family—namely,
that "ther is a . . . potent inclination inbred w^ch about this tyme
of a mans life sollicits most, the desire of house & family of his
owne to w^ch nothing is . . . more hindering then this affected
solitarinesse." He also acknowledges the dangers in "unprof-
itable . . . curiosity . . . wherby a man cutts himselfe off from
all action & becomes the most helplesse, pusilanimous & un-
weapon'd creature in the word"—the last being a pen slip that,
significantly, puts "word" in place of "world."[31] Has the speaker
of "Captain or Colonel" borne out the deep misgivings of Milton's friend about Milton in 1633?

No, he has not, for two reasons, at least, that are bound up
with the genesis of the Miltonic political sonnet. First, the mo-
tivating desire is no longer, as in the letter just cited and in
other earlier writings, understood simply in terms of "Fame"
and making a "Name" for oneself in the world; "Captain or
Colonel," in fact, represents this as the other's, the military
officer's, desire (ll. 6–7). Instead, the speaker explicitly desires
what the sonnet's two final lines image as "the power / To save"
the state "from ruine"—that is, the capacity of being a politically efficacious poet under crisis conditions where words might
exert a force superior to arms. Second, with the very composition of this sonnet, poetry emerges from the study and faces
out into the street. It stands ready to function as a counterforce
to force, a species of direct political action whose triumph as

31. On slips of this kind, see the theory and analysis offered by Sebastiano
Timpanaro, *The Freudian Slip: Psychoanalysis and Textual Criticism,* trans.
Kate Soper (London, 1976), chaps. 7 and 9.

counterforce is simultaneously narrated and celebrated in the five concluding lines. Probably the most relevant gloss on "Captain or Colonel" as Milton's first political sonnet remains the autobiographical excursus in *The Reason of Church Government*. Even the analogical impetus of the Greek exempla that figure so prominently in the sonnet's last five lines gains clarity in the light of Milton's express intent "to be an interpreter & relater of the best and sagest things among mine own Citizens throughout this iland . . . content with these British ilands as my world, whose fortune hath hitherto bin, that if the Athenians, as some say, made their small deeds great and renowned by their eloquent writers, *England* hath her noble atchievements made small by . . . unskillfull handling" (*CPW*, I, 811–812).

Having found voice in his first political sonnet by readying poetry to be an instrument of public action and a means of power that relieved the weight of longstanding personal anxieties, Milton would be able only two years later in *Areopagitica* (November 1644) to generalize the occasion of "Captain and Colonel" into a celebratory vision of an entire body politic, Parliament and populace, comprised of kindred spirits who are quite specifically characterized:

When a City shall be as it were besieg'd and blockt about, . . . inrodes and incursions round, defiance and battell oft rumor'd to be marching up ev'n to her walls, and suburb trenches, that then the people, or the greater part, more then at other times, wholly tak'n up with the study of highest and most important matters to be reform'd, should be disputing, reasoning, reading, inventing, discoursing . . . things not before discourst or writt'n of, argues first a singular good will, contentednesse and confidence in your prudent foresight and safe government, Lords and Commons; and from thence derives itself to a gallant bravery and well grounded contempt of their enemies, as if there were no small number of . . . great spirits among us.   (*CPW*, II, 556–557)

What is notable about this passage is that, in its retrospective look at a specific political crisis, it multiplies the figure of the speaker of "Captain and Colonel"—the studious discourser— and makes the body politic in his image. This is the type of the normative citizen, says the passage, the true Parliamentarian and the "great spirit" who shows, by being "wholly tak'n up with the study of highest and most important matters to be reform'd," qualities ordinarily associated with feats of arms: "a gallant bravery and well grounded contempt of . . . enemies." The archness of the sonnet's opening has given way to a magisterial assurance that the force of words and ideas is indeed a match for the force of arms in this civil war.

In larger terms than the local ones of this passage, moreover, *Areopagitica* like "Captain or Colonel" takes the guise of a speech in writing—one whose ancient Greek prototype, Isocrates' *Areopagiticus,* Milton characterizes as "that discourse to the Parlament of *Athens*" written by one "from his private house" (*CPW,* II, 489). There are sustained tactical resemblances to the sonnet, too, in the blandishments that crowd the beginning and end of the tract with offers to praise noble public deeds from a speaker who claims—and displays—the power to praise truly. Even more, perhaps, than the similarities in compositional design discussed earlier, the similarities linking "Captain and Colonel" with *Areopagitica* reveal the attraction and utility that the writing of sonnets, newly politicized, would have for Milton as a writer of prose tracts. The prose tracts, overall, are negative proving grounds for the Miltonic consciousness; they identify and argue what should not be. In the political sonnets, however, the poetic consciousness labors to its utmost to make a positive proving ground of crisis. Despite the constant threat of unintelligibility, the center of consciousness holds. The voice purports to integrate private and public meaning through a mode of poetic utterance that is indistinguishably personal and political. Milton's political sonnets provide an outlet for his constructive energies and vision during the period of his own political activity. They cease with the cessation of that activity and with the new, epic direction he gives to his energies and vision.

ANNABEL PATTERSON

# Pastoral versus Georgic:
# The Politics of Virgilian Quotation

This essay tells a short segment of a long story—the story of
the part played by Virgil's *Eclogues* in European culture, from
the moment when Servius, teacher of rhetoric in the fourth
century, offered the first major reading of the text and established the almost unshakable premise that in the first and ninth
eclogues Virgil configured his own situation at the end of the
Roman civil wars and the beginning of Octavian's supremacy.
Especially in the contrast between Tityrus and Meliboeus in the
first eclogue, between the successful protégé and the dispossessed exile, as well as in the contrast between two ways of
reading pastoral, *simpliciter* and *allegorice*, Servius implied that
the *Eclogues* were from the start encoded ideology, a statement
about Roman politics circa 42–35 B.C. and their consequences
for writer-intellectuals. But because of the issue that divides the
shepherds in Eclogue 1 and unites in anxiety those in Eclogue
9—the expropriations of farmland in Mantua for the purpose
of rewarding Octavian's veterans—Virgilian pastoral would have
indicated its liminal status on the borders of georgic, even if the

*Georgics* had never been written. Meliboeus was as much farmer as shepherd; and the question of culture's relationship to agriculture has therefore been strangely intertwined in Western thought and poetry ever since. What the *Eclogues* offered, in effect, was a dialectical poetics, their subjects the proper subjects of poetry, the relationship of writers to rulers, the consequences for a national culture of wartime and peacetime, and the politics of landownership.

This was particularly well understood in England in the seventeenth century, when the relationship between the two genres became, in effect, a sign-system for other sets of relationships and arguments. We can begin by looking in some detail at Sir Francis Bacon, a writer whose work has already been recognized as deeply organized by the idea of georgic as metaphor; but by making that argument more precise, and by relating it directly to its Virgilian sources, we can begin to see the structure of the code that Bacon and his contemporaries took for granted. At the same time we will see in Bacon a kinship between pastoral and georgic as ideological counters that the subsequent history of the seventeenth century would abrogate. In 1605 Bacon recognized a new century and a new English monarch by proposing a program of intellectual husbandry, whose fruits should be great advances in the proximate fields of ethics and politics. In the second book of the *Advancement of Learning*, a text aimed indirectly at both the vanity and the administrative indolence of James I, Bacon suggested classical precedent for the type of advice he was offering his sovereign, remarking that "the poet Virgil . . . got as much glory of eloquence, wit, and learning in the expressing of the observations of husbandry, as of the heroical acts of Aeneas." Here he quoted *Georgics* 3.289, and continued:

Surely, if the purpose be in good earnest, not to write at leisure that which men may read at leisure, but really to instruct and suborn action and active life, these Georgics of the mind, concerning the husbandry and tillage thereof, are no less worthy than the heroical descriptions of Virtue, Duty, and Felicity.[1]

---

1. Francis Bacon, *Works*, ed. J. Spedding, R. L. Ellis, and D. D. Heath, 14 vols. (London, 1857–1874), III, 419. This quotation has had a famous but

In accordance with this program (which explains and governs the many images of agriculture and gardening in the text),[2] Bacon incorporated into the *Advancement* certain central statements from the *Georgics*, subjecting them to highly original application. Into the service of the new science he pressed the famous lines from the second georgic where Virgil distinguished between two kinds of happiness, that of the simple rustic and that of the stoic philosopher who uses knowledge to acquire intellectual repose:

Virgil did excellently and profoundly couple the knowledge of causes and the conquest of all fears together, as *concomitantia:*

> Felix, qui potuit rerum cognoscere causas,
> Quique metus omnes, et inexorabile fatum
> Subjecit pedibus, strepitumque Acherontis avari.
>                                                (2.490-493)

But in Bacon's conceptual system, where "causes" are determinately secondary and material, Stoic recessiveness has been replaced by the language of psychological, even physiological, amelioration. What his Happy Man gains are "the particular remedies which learning doth minister to all the diseases of the mind; sometimes purging the ill-humours, sometimes opening the obstructions, sometimes helping digestion, sometimes increasing appetite, sometimes healing the wounds and exulcerations thereof, and the like" (3.315).

So too in his discussion of invention, Bacon recalls the Hesiodic theogony of the first georgic, that version of the Fall in which the products of hardship and need are human effort and inventiveness. Highly congenial to Bacon as a general proposition, the theogony serves to underline his point that the instrument of invention is not logic but experience:

---

somewhat misleading afterlife in the title of Stanley Fish's essay "Georgics of the Mind: The Experience of Bacon's *Essays*," in *Self-Consuming Artifacts* (Berkeley and Los Angeles, 1972), pp. 78–155. By attaching this passage to the *Essays*, Fish distracts the reader from its structural function in the *Advancement*. For contrast, see James S. Tillman, "Bacon's Georgics of Science," *Papers on Language and Literature*, 11 (1975), 357–377.

2. As recognized by Brian Vickers, *Francis Bacon and Renaissance Prose* (Cambridge, 1968), pp. 187–198.

Neither is the form of invention which Virgil describeth much other:
"Ut varias usus meditando extunderet artes / Paulatim." For if you
observe the words well, it is no other method than that which brute
beasts are capable of, and do put in ure; which is a perpetual intending
or practising some one thing, urged and imposed by an absolute necessity of conservation of being.    (3.386)

The central principle of the *Georgics*, then, "Labor omnia vincit / Improbus, et duris urgens in rebus egestas," is used by
Bacon not as a reproach to pastoral's "Omnia vincit Amor" but
as a rejection of Aristotle.

It was, however, essential to Bacon to enclose the practicalities of georgic within the intellectualism for which the *Eclogues*
had grown to stand. The *Advancement* begins with a reminder
that Cain and Abel, respectively farmer and shepherd, represent
the rival claims of action and contemplation, and that from the
beginning "the favour and election of God went to the shepherd
and not to the tiller of the ground" (3.297). What Bacon needed
was a counterargument capable of restoring to the activist the
enabling innocence of Abel; and he found it in, or constructed
it out of, that other scripture to which the Renaissance had
given canonical status, discovering in Virgil's canon not an antipathy between pastoral and georgic but their interdependence,
their meeting, so to speak, in the head.

For instance: the most political section of the *Georgics*, the
instructions for bee keeping in the fourth book, appears in the
*Advancement of Learning* with its emphasis on statecraft sup-
pressed. Instead, Virgil's instructions for the setting up of the
hives (4.8) are presented by Bacon as a metaphor for the in-
stitutionalization of learning, "foundations and buildings, endowments with revenues, endowments with franchises and
privileges, institutions and ordinances for government; *all tending to quietness and privateness of life*" (3.323; emphasis mine).
And the bees themselves as collectors of honey, *coelestia dona*,
are an image of "how the mind doth gather this excellent dew
of knowledge . . . distilling and contriving it out of particulars
natural and artificial, as the flowers of the field and garden"
(3.387). The almost lyrical language sweetens the reader's perception of what is actually being defined here, inductive method,
the cornerstone of Baconian science. But if quotations from the

*Georgics* are rendered idyllic, echoes from the *Eclogues* appear in oddly scientific contexts. The would-be black magic of the woman in Eclogue 8, who plans to recover her lover by firing both a clay and a wax image of him, appears in the *Advancement* to support a principle in physics. "Fire," wrote Bacon, somewhat comically, "is the cause of induration, but respective to clay; fire is the cause of colliquation, but respective to wax" (3.354). More profoundly, Bacon transformed the theme of echo in the *Eclogues*, Virgil's metaphor for the sympathy between man and nature, into an argument for the authenticity of the new science. If it was true for the shepherd that all the woods responded to his songs ("respondent omnia sylvae" [10.8]), then "the voice of nature will consent, whether the voice of man do or no" (3.363).

What looks at first sight, then, to be merely a chance scattering of memories of Virgil, the misused traces of a type of education that Bacon himself believed obsolete, becomes on closer investigation a principled synthesis of two conceptual structures— a synthesis that is, for all its minor and deliberate distortions, not untrue to either of them. A pastoralized georgic, or vice versa, as a program for the intellectual development of the seventeenth century, could have served his contemporaries extremely well. Had it taken hold, and particularly had it been given royal or institutional support, it might well have protected England from the polarization that followed, with all its political consequences. What happened instead, as the policies of James I and Charles I became increasingly unpopular and hence on the defensive in terms of their cultural expression, was a split on class lines between intellectuals (a group increasingly conceived in aesthetic terms) and those involved in "work," whether commercial or agricultural. It has recently been argued by Anthony Low that georgic became the form either of radical scientific thought or of social protest, while pastoral became the exclusive terrain of an aristocratic and later royalist elite.[3] And

3. Anthony Low, *The Georgic Revolution* (Princeton, 1985). As minor exceptions to Low's thesis, one might note the attempt by Peter Heylyn to appropriate the georgic ethos to Charles I by way of Saint George, his chosen prototype. In 1633 Heylyn's *Historie of that most famous Saint and Souldier of Christ Jesus, George of Cappodoccia* reminded its readers that the etymology

Low's argument is itself a restatement, however differently documented, of the position established by Stephen Orgel and reinforced, though with contrary sympathies, by Marxist criticism.
Orgel's theory, of course, is that Stuart pastoralism, as expressed in the court masque, was one of the major illusions of
power, creating and supporting a myth of peace and prosperity;[4]
its mirror image can be seen in the arguments of Raymond
Williams and James Turner—that the distorted representation
of country life in seventeenth-century poetry, the magical era-
sure of all signs of agricultural labor, was the effect of hegemony
at work, the language of class consciousness in the defense of
landed property.[5]

This essay will try to modify both of these positions, by sharp-
ening the definition of what constituted "pastoral" thinking in
this period and by somewhat blurring the edges of class conflict.
Instead of subsuming under pastoralism any reference to country life or landscape, I shall follow more narrowly the historical
traces of Virgil's *Eclogues* as a text; and because that text arrived

---

of "George" is "ploughman" or "husbandman"; "and thereunto the famous
Spencer thus alludeth" (p. 124). And Joseph Aylett had attempted a georgic
representation of James I, in *Thrift's Equipage* (London, 1622), that blends
biblical georgic (Proverbs 28:19: "He that tilleth his Land shall have plen-
teousnes of bread") with Virgilian allusion ("Happy is he, who never saw that
one / With whom he would exchange his meane estate"), and defends James's
pacificism under "a true Idea of high labour" (p. 38) that includes intellectual
work.

4. Stephen Orgel, *The Illusion of Power* (Berkeley, 1975), esp. pp. 49–52.
5. Raymond Williams, *The Country and the City* (New York, 1973); James
Turner, *The Politics of Landscape: Rural Scenery and Society in English Poetry,
1630–1660* (Cambridge, Mass., 1979). Turner, p. 163, points out that the landscape of literary pastoral bore an actual and, for some, shocking relationship
to the landscape produced when mixed agricultural land was subjected to enclosure: "Nothing remains but a champant wildernesse for sheepe, with a Cote,
a pastorall boy, his dogge, a crooke, and a pipe." The quotation is from Robert
Powell, *Depopulation Arraigned, Convicted, and Condemned* (London, 1636),
another interesting exception to Low's thesis. Powell's attack on enclosure was
presented as praise of Charles I, under the premise that he *wished* to enforce
the antienclosure laws; and he defined the "future reformation" of English
agriculture as the fulfilment of Virgil's credo in *Georgics* 2.458: "O fortunatos
nimium bona si sua norunt Agricolas" (pp. 116–117).

in seventeenth-century England already potent with ideology, and was generally understood to be so, it follows that those traces will constitute a deliberately chosen political vocabulary, rather than the workings of the political unconscious. Second, while I do not intend to challenge in its broad outlines the belief that seventeenth-century pastoral was ideologically the property of the most privileged class, and never more so than during their temporary defeat, the story of the *Eclogues* as political discourse is rather more complicated than either the illusionist or the Marxist models imply. Neither will account, for instance, for Andrew Marvell's use of the *Eclogues* in the service of the Commonwealth, or the enigmatic case of Milton's 1645 *Poems*, whose relationship to Virgilian pastoral defeats all attempts at explanation in terms of class conflict. And there is also a whole range of eccentric responses *within* the hegemonic corpus— intimations of doubt, criticisms of self, or of the monarch, or of the sociopolitical system—that may be generated either by some temporary alienation of the writer from his privileged environment or by some deeper affinity with Virgil's profound open-mindedness. It is well to bear in mind, therefore, the potentially liberating alternative model defined by Bakhtin, in which the principle of heteroglossia, multilanguagedness, is constantly at work throughout cultural history.[6] Whenever, in Bakhtin's terms, "a sealed-off interest group, caste or class . . . becomes riddled with decay or shifted somehow from its state of internal balance and self-sufficiency," it becomes theoretically vulnerable to penetration by the sound of other voices, the recognition of otherness that leads to genuine self-consciousness or "novelization." "It is necessary," wrote Bakhtin (though thinking primarily of what conditions are productive of the novel), "that heteroglossia wash over a culture's awareness of itself and its language, penetrate to its core, relativize the primary language system underlying its ideology and literature and deprive it of its naive absence of conflict" (p. 368). It will be part of my argument here that the seventeenth century in England, with which Bakhtin does not directly concern himself,

6. M. M. Bakhtin, *The Dialogic Imagination*, ed. Michael Holquist, trans. Caryl Emerson and Michael Holquist (Austin, 1981).

but which was in almost every respect a century of novelization,
manifests the force of cultural heteroglossia almost from the
beginning, not merely by the explosive sectarianism of the revolution itself. And because to read one's own culture in terms
of Virgil's was inevitably to expose oneself to another language,
to historicity and difference, even the most conservative of
writers who did so, thinking thereby to align themselves with
"tradition," became participants, willy-nilly, in the dialogic
imagination.

    And third, I shall argue that we have here a particularly useful
test of the concept of what Michel Foucault has called a discursive practice,[7] a concept fashionable to discuss but remarkably difficult to document. We know, to begin with, how widely
this code was disseminated, because it was actually taught in
the schools. When John Brinsley produced his grammarian's
translation of the *Eclogues* "chiefly for the good of Schooles"
in 1620, he justified his choice of a text "as being the most
familiar of all Virgil's workes, and fittest for childrens capacities."[8] It was *already* familiar, part of the culture, and therefore
a suitable exercise on which to practice one's grammar. But at
the same time he hoped, somewhat self-contradictorily, that
"happie experience" of the kind his translation offered would
"in time drive it, and all like it, utterly out of the schooles and
into the minds of all." He was partially right on both counts.
And in fact the Virgilian semiotics was so well and so widely
known, in the same decade that Brinsley's textbook entered the
schools, that it became a kind of public shorthand. Because the
conceptual structure of this language was so well understood,
its units could be used elliptically, without the syntax showing,
as it were. Brief quotations could stand for larger arguments,

7. In *Language and Political Understanding: The Politics of Discursive Practices* (New Haven and London, 1981), p. 131, Michael Shapiro points out that
although Foucault never addressed himself specifically to political discourse or
behavior, he envisioned this extention of his theory. See Michel Foucault, *The
Archeology of Knowledge* (New York, 1972), p. 194.
    8. John Brinsley, *Virgils Eclogues, With His Booke De Apibus, concerning
the government and ordering of Bees . . . Translated Grammatically* (London,
1620), A4v.

or even for an entire ideology; and the text could be splintered into what, borrowing a phrase from Fredric Jameson, we might call *ideologemes*.[9] As writers, statesmen, and even kings grasped the capacity of the original to contribute to their own debates, fragments of the *Eclogues* became nodes of political theory, such as the nature of liberty, or political policy, such as the value of English isolationism from Europe. We have, therefore, a rare instance of a discursive practice that permeates the culture but was nevertheless fully intelligible to those who practiced it at the time.

For instance, in 1612 Sir John Davies published a pamphlet ostensibly in support of James I and his policy for Ireland. Certainly its title leads one to suppose that this was his intention: *A Discoverie of the True Causes why Ireland was never entirely Subdued, nor brought under Obedience of the Crowne of England, untill the Beginning of his Maiesties happy Raigne.* Yet the *Discoverie* consists largely of an account of the stupid and cruel mistakes perpetrated in Ireland by previous administrations; and in a section on taxation of "Mansmeate, Horsemeat, & Money . . . at the will and pleasure of the soldier" (p. 173), something rather extraordinary happened. "This Extortion," wrote Davies, "was originally Irish, for they used to lay *Bonaght* upon their people, and never gave their soldiers any other pay":

But when the English had Learned it, they used it with more insolency, and made it more intollerable . . . This extortion of Coyne and Livery, did produce two notorious effects. First, it made the Land wast; Next, it made the people, ydle. For, when the Husbandman had laboured all the yeare, the soldier in one night, did consume the fruites of all his labour . . . Had hee reason then to manure the Land for the next yeare? Or rather might he not complaine as the Shepherd in Virgil:

> Impius haec tam culta novalia miles habebit?
> Barbarus has segetes? En quo discordia Cives
> Perduxit miseros? En queis consevimus Agros?

9. Fredric Jameson, *The Political Unconscious* (Ithaca, 1981), p. 76: "When . . . the semantic Horizon within which we grasp a cultural object has widened to include the social order . . . our object of study will prove to be the *ideologeme,* that is, the smallest intelligible unit of the essentially antagonistic collective discourses of social classes."

Shall the impious soldier possess these well-tilled grounds? A barbarian possess these crops? See where fighting has brought our miserable countrymen. See for whom we have sown our fields!

Not only does this passage stand out as Davies' *only* classical quotation in this pamphlet, but its emotional force works directly against its supposedly hegemonic function. Was it the Virgilian text, we may ask, or something unspoken in Davies' own experience that moved him to so deep an identification with the social and political Other, the Irish peasantry, who are here dignified by the Roman term *Cives*, "citizens," while it is the English standing army who are registered as barbarous?

Similar ambiguities pervade the next example. In the winter of 1623–24 a group of young troubleshooters appeared in London, under what was obviously a code name. As Walter Yonge wrote in his diary:

The beginning of December, 1623, there was a great number in London, haunting taverns and other debauched places, who swore themselves in a brotherhood, and namd themselves *Tytere tues* . . . There were divers knights, some young noblemen and gentlemen of this brotherhood, and they were to know each other by a black bugle which they wore, and their followers to be known by a blue ribbond. There are discovered of them about 80 or 100 persons, and have been examined by the Privy Council; but nothing discovered of any intent they had. It is said, that the king hath given commandment that they shall be reexamined.[10]

Now the political context of this episode, so badly in need of official interpretation, was the public unrest created in England by the vacillating foreign policy of James, who refused to intervene in Europe on behalf of his ousted son-in-law, Frederick, the Elector Palatine, and pursued instead his myth of becoming, through conciliation of Spain, the great European peacemaker. Other contemporary comments make it clear that the "Tityre tues," those living quotations, were perceived as antagonistic to James's policies, at least at the level of ritual embodiment

10. Walter Yonge, *Diary at Colyton and Axminster, 1604–1628,* Camden Society Publications, vol. 184, no. 8 (London, 1848), p. 70. See also *Calender of State Papers Domestic* for 6 and 19 December 1623, pp. 56, 125.

of an argument. Richard Brathwaite remarked that in the current mood of suspicion and unrest, wearing a blue ribbon, however innocently, could get one arrested as "a Tityre-tu; / An enemy to th' State."[11] And Robert Herrick congratulated himself on the peace of a country Christmas, in contrast to what has been going on in London. In Devon, there is

> No noise of late spawn'd Tittyries:
> No closset plot, or open vent,
> That frights men with a Parliament:[12]

This conservative's response to the threat of a parliament points forward to the defeat of Jacobean pacificism as a political program, when in February 1624 James was forced to recall the recalcitrant Parliament he had dissolved in a rage two years earlier, and to receive their advice in favor of war with Spain.

Why should such a situation have been presented in terms of Virgil's first eclogue? The answer is both obvious in its outlines and elusive in its details. Whether we take the "Tityre tues" as standing for the voice of Meliboeus or as an entry code to the whole eclogue, the issues so addressed, *in the circumstances of 1623–24*, were the advantages of peace versus the ethical weakness of Tityrus' position, at ease in the shade while others suffered expropriation and exile. The relevance of Virgil's dialectic to the German wars was created not only by analogy (the selfish pacificism of England, the expropriation of the Palatinate and exile of James's daughter and her husband) but also by the king's adoption of the ethos of Tityrus, or a version of it, to authen-

11. Richard Brathwaite, *An Age for Apes* (London, 1658), p. 247. Though published late in the Protectorate, Brathwaite's satires were written mostly in 1623–24. "The Age of Observation" is clearly set in the context of the German wars.

12. Robert Herrick, "A New-Yeares gift to Sir Simeon Steward," *Poetical Works*, ed. L. C. Martin (Oxford, 1956), p. 126. The poem can be quite precisely dated by virtue of the fact that the writ recalling Parliament was signed on 28 December 1623. See also Ben Jonson's allusion in *The Fortunate Isles* (1624) to the poet Skelton as the "Tityre-tu" of Henry VIII's court (ll. 306–308); and Richard Brome's later parody of the allusion in *The Weeding of Covent Garden and the Sparagus Garden*, 2.1.61–62, where Clotpoll remarks, "So, now I am a Blade, and of a better row than those of Tytere tu, or Oatmeal Hoe."

ticate his own position. On 26 March 1621 James had opened a new parliament with a defense of his style of government presented as a version of *otium*:

And now I confesse, that when I looked before upon the face of government I thought . . . that the people were never so happy as in my time . . . and for peace, both at home and abrode, I may truely say more setled, and longer lasting than ever before, together with as great plenty as ever: so as it was to be thought, that every man might sit in safety under his own vine, and his owne figge-tree.[13]

The adaptation, as was only to be expected of the British Solomon, was by way of Kings 4:24, 25: "And [Solomon] had . . . peace on all sides round about him: And Judah and Israel dwelt safely, every man under his own vine and his fig-tree." Yet the classical origins of the pacifist shade remained clearly apparent and were often reinforced by other writers as James's speech, which was promptly published, entered the cultural spectrum.[14]

James in the meantime had himself confirmed the Virgilian origins of his language, if not of his thinking, in a contribution to another political controversy arising from his foreign policy. Closely connected to the question of nonintervention in the fate of the Palatinate was his plan to bring about peace in Europe by marrying his son to the Spanish infanta. And in 1623 this

13. *His Majesties Speech in the Upper House of Parliament, on Munday, the 26 of March, 1621* (London, 1621), B3v.

14. See, for example, William Loe, *Vox clamantis* (London, 1622), an appeal for peace addressed to the "Three-Thrice honourable Estates of Parliament," p. 23; Samuel Buggs, *Miles Mediterraneus: The Mid-Land Souldier* (London, 1622), pp. 2–3; Philip Massinger, *The Maid of Honour* (1621–22), in *Plays and Poems*, ed. Philip Edwards and Colin Gibson, 5 vols. (Oxford, 1976), I, 125. The *topos* was subsequently applied to Charles I and his decision, in 1628, to return to the pacificism of his father. See Massinger, *Believe as You List* (1630), *Plays and Poems*, III, 351; William Habington, *The Queene of Aragon* (1640), c4v; Francis Quarles, *The Shepheards Oracles: Delivered in Certain Eglogues* (1646), "To the Reader." And for retrospective applications of the *topos* to both Jacobean and Caroline pacificism, see Richard Brathwaite, "Solomon's Reign," in *The History of Moderation* (London, 1669), p. 112. But the most poignant of all such appearances of the peaceful shade must surely be in Charles's own speech of defense at his trial in 1649; see Charles Petrie, ed., *The Letters, Speeches and Proclamations of King Charles I* (London, 1968), p. 27.

highly unpopular project exploded in a wave of public anxiety
when it was learned that Charles and Buckingham, impatient
at the slow speed of the marriage negotiations being conducted
by the earl of Bristol, had taken matters into their own hands
and left in disguise for Spain to do the royal wooing in person.
James's response to the public dismay at this development, which
put the heir to the throne literally in Spanish hands, was to
write, of all things, a pastoral poem—a poem whose echoes of
Virgil's fifth eclogue, the lament for Daphnis, could scarcely
have been unconscious:

> Whatt: suddayne Chance hath darkt of late
> The glorye of th'Arcadian State
> the ffleecye fflockes, reffuse to feede
> the Lambes to playe the Ewes to breede.
> > The Altars smoak the Offringes Burne
> > that Jacke and Tom, maye safe Returne.
>
> The Springe neglects his Course to keepe
> the ayre contynual stormes doth weepe
> The pretty Byrdes, disdayne to singe
> the Meades to smyle, the Woodes to springe
> > The Mountaynes droppe the ffountaynes mourne
> > tyll Jacke and Tom, doe safe Returne.
>
> Whatt maye they bee that move this woe
> whose want afflicts Arcadia soe
> The hope of Greece the propp of Artes
> was prencely Jacke the joye of hartes,
> > And Tom, was to our Royall Pan
> > his truest Swayne and cheiffest Man.
> . . . . .
> Kinde Sheappeardes, that have lov'd them longe
> bee not soe rashe, in Censuring wronge
> Correct your ffeares, leave off to murne
> the Heavens will favour there returne,
> > Remitt the Care, to Royall Pan
> > of Jacke his Sonne, and Tom, his Man.[15]

However modified by previous Renaissance imitations of the

15. See James Craigie, ed., *The Poems of King James VI of Scotland*, 2 vols.
(Edinburgh, 1958), II, 192–193.

elegy, the Jacobean audience must have noted the parodic traces
of Virgil's text; and they may have wondered whether James
was intelligent enough to argue thereby that the public outcry
over the prince's absence was in excess of its cause. That there
was an audience for this poem is indicated by the fact that copies
of it were quickly handed about and discussed in contemporary
correspondence. On 21 March 1623 John Chamberlain sent a
copy to Dudley Carleton in Paris; and the next day the Reverend
J. Mead wrote from Cambridge to Sir Martin Stateville that he
*would* have sent him a copy did he not assume that he had
already been "prevented by others."[16] In other words, the king's
eclogue was an extremely hot item on at least such circuits. The
meaning of the entire episode was clear, and matched the inferences of the king's message to Parliament: England was Arcadia, and its government could safely be left in the hands of
the ruling deity, "Royall Pan."

Caroline Arcadianism was, if anything, more explicit and more
pervasive as cultural statement, owing in large part to Henrietta
Maria's famous preference for pastoral as the expression of *her*
personal style, and the encouragement she gave to writers to
articulate that style. The result was the suppression, during the
so-called halcyon days, and in court masques, plays, and poems,
of most of the Virgilian dialectic, all interpretations of or responses to the *Eclogues* that might have interrogated the myth
of peace and prosperity. Yet the suppression could not be absolute; and although from a distance Caroline pastoral seems
to be merely Caroline propaganda, a closer inspection often
reveals that the ideological power of the model remained intact,
producing even in writers assumed to be court apologists interesting signs of tension and complexity.

A gentleman poet like Richard Fanshawe, for instance, called
on to support the royal proclamation of 1630 "Commanding the
Gentry to reside upon their Estates in the Country," responded
by writing an ode in praise of both foreign and domestic policy,
connecting England's isolation from the Thirty Years' War to
a program of agricultural reform, which was in turn to produce
cultural benefits:

16. Craigie, *Poems,* II, 266.

> And if the Fields as thankfull prove
> For benefits receiv'd, as seed,
> They will, to quite so great a love,
>     A Virgill breed;
>
> A Tytirus, that shall not cease
> Th'Augustus of our world to praise
> In equall verse, author of peace
>     And Halcyon dayes.[17]

Yet the poem not only begins with eight stanzas of heroic language describing the wars in Europe, and among them the achievements of Gustavus Adolphus of Sweden "Revenging lost Bohemia," but it is also perversely structured along a trail of blood. From the "bloudyer rage" of the German wars, the "Spanish bloud" spilled by Gustavus Adolphus, and the "blouds boyling in the North" among the Poles and Russians, Fanshawe turns to proclaiming that the return of the landed gentry to their lands will be the resurgence of "The sapp and bloud o' th' land" to its heart; and in the last section, ostensibly a defense of the innocent country life, the word "blood" appears four times, in a way that makes the mental act of washing one's hands more difficult to perform than might have been possible *without* the poem:

> Nor Cupid there lesse bloud doth spill,
> But heads his shafts with chaster love,
> Not featherd with a Sparrowes quill
>     But of a Dove.
>
> There shall you heare the Nightingale
> (The harmelesse Syren of the wood)
> How prettily she tells a tale
>     Of rape and blood.
> . . . . .
> The Lillie (Queene), the (Royall) Rose,
> The Gillyflowre (Prince of the bloud),
> The (Courtyer) Tulip (gay in clothes),
>     The (Regall) Budd,

17. Richard Fanshawe, *Il Pastor Fido: The faithfull Shepheard. With an Addition of divers other Poems* (London, 1648), p. 227.

. . . . .
Plant Trees you may, and see them shoote
Up with your Children, to be serv'd
To your cleane boards, and the fair'st Fruite
     To be preserv'd:

And learne to use their severall gummes,
" 'Tis innocence in the sweet blood
"Of Cherryes, Apricocks and Plummes
     "To be imbru'd."
                            (p. 229)

Such wresting of "blood" from its normal connotations might
well remind us of *Macbeth*, a play in which the numerical frequency of its use is underscored by the determination (and hence
the failure) of its two protagonists to erase it from their minds.
As Macbeth himself put it, such imaginative strain merely results
in "making the green one red." Nor can it have been uninten-
tional that Fanshawe's final instructions to the gentry to "Plant
Trees . . . and see them shoote / Up with your Children" recalls
both the injunction of Meliboeus to himself to plant his pear
trees and its echo in the ninth eclogue ("Plant your peartrees,
Daphnis, your offspring will enjoy the fruits" [9.50]). But by
blending the two together, Fanshawe's quotation denies both
the sarcasm of the first and the uncertain status of the second,
one of the half-remembered fragments ("oblita carmina") of
cultural uncertainty.

    Fanshawe's entire construct rests, also, on another partially
hidden quotation from Meliboeus anticipating the pains of exile
in a country as distant to his imagination as England ("penitus
toto divisos orbe Britannos" [1.66]). This had already become
a commonplace of English political discourse. In the debates in
Parliament in 1628, for example, as the grievances caused by
the wars against France and Spain led to unprecedented discussions of the constitution and ultimately to the Petition of
Right, Sir Edward Coke reminded his audience of the unique-
ness of England in her dependence on the common law. "No
other state is like this: we are *divisos ab orbe Britannos*."[18] The

18. Robert Johnson et al., eds., *Commons Debates, 1628,* 3 vols. (New Haven
and London, 1977), II, 555; cited by Conrad Russell, *Parliaments and English
Politics, 1621–1629* (Oxford, 1979), p. 357.

classical definition of Britain as a savage place beyond conceptual reach was thus reversed and turned to a praise of an ancient
national heritage of law. After the wars Fanshawe took this
transvaluation a stage further, and what was in Virgil's text a
sign denoting the very opposite of pastoral security became a
defense of Caroline Arcadianism:

> Onely the Island which wee sowe,
> (A world without the world) so farre
> From present wounds, it cannot showe
> An ancient skarre.
>                                        (p. 226)

Even after the pastoral myth of the halcyon days had been
recognized for precisely what it was, a proposition designed to
ratify the behavior and circumstances of the ruling class, many
of whom after 1640 found themselves in the position of Meliboeus, the public practice of allusion to the *Eclogues* continued.
In 1643, Francis Quarles placed on the title page of his *Loyal
Convert* the same motto that had thirty years earlier focused
the sympathy of Sir John Davies for the Irish: "Improbus haec
tam culta novalia miles habebit? / Barbarus has segetes?" But
now it denoted the plight of the royalist supporters of Charles
who found their estates "sequestered" by the Long Parliament.
In the same year a broadside *Letter from Mercurius Civicus to
Mercurius Rusticus* carried on its title page the epigraph "En
quo discordia Cives? [*sic*] / Perduxit miseros" (1.71–72). In this
reinterpretation of the dialogue between fortunate and unfortunate (now contrasted as countryman and citizen), the positions
are ingeniously rearranged so that Civicus, the Londoner, is
both the victim of civil war and its cause:

I cannot but congratulate your happiness that breathe in so free an
ayre, wherein it is lawfull to heare and speak truth . . . Your sad stories
of the Ruine and devastation of the Country are ecchoed in our Streets,
and though we beare it out in a Vaunting way, as if these things
concerned not us, yet I assure you there are many soules that mourne
in private, (for in publique we must be as mad as the rest . . . ) knowing
how justly we stand charged with all those Calamities, which the sword
of Rebellion hath brought upon you . . . But you may aske, Is there
any evill in the Countrey, and the City hath not done it? You have
made us Rich and Populous, and we in foule Ingratitude have prodigally

powered out both our Wealth and Strength to make you and our selves
miserable.   (pp. 1,3)

The Virgilian "quotations" show an equal freedom of application, built and counting on a profound familiarity with the
original. In a different way a small volume published in 1649
tackled head-on the related questions of interpretation and reception that such a politics of quotation engendered. The anonymous translator of La Mothe le Vayer's *Of Liberty and Servitude*
placed on its title page a crucial question and answer from the
first eclogue:

MELIB.    Et quae tanta fuit Romam tibi causa videndi?
TIT.    Libertas: quae sera, tamen respexit Inertem.

(A2r)

And what gave you so great a reason for going to see Rome?
Liberty:   Who, though late, nevertheless remembered me, the idler.

And he added a long explanatory epistle "To Him that reads,"
which, precisely because it is self-explanatory, deserves quotation at large:

This free subject, coming abroad in these Licentious times may happily
cause the World to mistake both the Author, and the Translator;
neither of whom by LIBERTY do understand that impious *Impostoria
pila*, so frequently of late exhibited, and held forth to the People,
whilst (in the meane time) indeed, it is thrown into the hands of a few
private Persons. By FREEDOME is here intended that which the Philosopher teacheth us: *Nulli rei servire, nulli necessitati, nullis Casibus,
fortunam in aequam deducere*, etc. not that Platonique Chimaera of a
State, no where existant save in UTOPIA . . . And of this truth we have
now had the experience of more than five thousand yeares, during all
which . . . never was there either heard, or read of a more equal &
excelent form of Government than that under which we our selves
have lived, during the Reign of our most gratious Soveraignes Halcion
daies . . . If therefore we were once the most happy of Subjects, why
do we thus attempt to render our selves the most miserable of
Slaves?   (A9–10)

Rejecting a literal *translatio* of Tityrus' term "Libertas" into the
political structure of the 1640s, the anonymous author insists
instead on converting it into a philosophical abstraction. Free-

dom cannot mean the manumission of the slave, far less any general principle of democratic egalitarianism, a principle that has in his recent experience been invoked only in order to mask the transfer of power to an ambitious oligarchy; rather, it must now be understood as the stoic principle of self-knowledge and self-sufficiency, the state of mind of the superior, philosophic "felix qui" of the second georgic.

But such revisionary strategies were not confined to the royalists. In 1657 Andrew Marvell celebrated the marriage of Cromwell's third daughter, Mary, by naming her "Menalcas' daughter" and proposing Cromwell himself, as Menalcas, as a figure of cultural plenitude:

> Fear not, at Menalcas' Hall
> There is Bayes enough for all.
> He when Young as we did graze,
> But when Old he planted Bayes.[19]

These were private compliments and private hopes; but three years earlier Marvell's Latinity had been brought into the service of the Commonwealth. To accompany Cromwell's portrait as a gift to Queen Christina of Sweden, on the conclusion of the treaty of April 1654, he provided a Virgilian message:

> Haec est quae toties Inimicos Umbra fugavit,
> At sub qua Cives Otia lenta terunt.   (1.108)

> This shadow-picture is that which absolutely
> puts enemies to flight, but beneath which cit-
> izens enjoy peaceful leisure.

In one deft reordering of the value-bearing fragments of Eclogue 1, this distich reattributed to Cromwell the protective shade of Caroline idyll, while making it clear that the peace of the Commonwealth was based on military activism; and at the same time, Marvell's *umbra* clearly functions as a sign of signifying, picture making representation.

Most interesting, perhaps, because its status in the politics of quotation is so elusive—a minimalist gesture of class and social

---

19. Andrew Marvell, *Poems and Letters*, ed. H. M. Margoliouth, rev. Pierre Legouis, 2 vols. (Oxford, 1971), I, 128.

consciousness—is Marvell's use of Virgil's second eclogue. In *Damon the Mower* Marvell identified his overheated and clumsy lover, who ends by running his scythe into his own leg, as Virgil's Corydon—a Corydon, however, rendered decorously heterosexual. The connection is made by the reappearance of Corydon's "nec sum adeo informis: nuper me in litore vidi . . . si numquam fallit imago" (l. 25) as Damon's irresistible country narcissism:

> Nor am I so deform'd to sight,
> If in my Sithe I looked right;
> In which I see my Picture done,
> As in a crescent Moon the Sun.

Yet the match between Damon's and Corydon's personalities should not distract us from—indeed, should rather direct us toward—the difference in their occupation, Marvell's pastoral singer being unmistakably a worker, a georgic figure, whose "Sweat" the sun himself "licks off," and who deliberately contrasts himself to the "piping Shepherd" (l. 49). He is therefore both sexually and socially a correction of his Virgilian prototype, whose *otium* is signified by his own mention of "reapers weary in the consuming heat" ("rapido fessis messoribus aestu" [l. 10]). These inferences are more than confirmed in *Upon Appleton House*, where the scene of haymaking in the meadows has long been recognized as a metaphor for the Civil War. There is no doubt of the poet's intentions in the main shape of the analogy:

> The Mower now commands the Field;
> In whose new Traverse seemeth wrought
> A Camp of Battail newly fought:
> Where, as the Meads with Hay, the Plain
> Lyes quilted ore with Bodies slain:
> The Women that with forks it fling,
> Do represent the pillaging.
>                         (1.75; ll. 418–424)

But far more delicate is the location of this scene in a Virgilian context, by means of the reference to Thestylis. In Virgil's poem, Thestylis, who pounds thyme and garlic, pungent herbs, for the exhausted reapers, is part of the reminder that Corydon's complaint is made against a background of real rural labor and physical, not merely psychological, discomfort. In Marvell's poem, not only does Thestylis perform the same ideological function by bringing "the mowing Camp their Cates" (1. 402), she also becomes the spokeswoman of realism, mocking the imaginative excesses of the poet-tutor and breaking his self-enclosure in metaphor. When the scythes of the mowers, whom he has compared to the Israelites "walking on foot through a green Sea," slice through the breast of a young rail, a meadow-bird, Thestylis sees only another source of food:

> Greedy as Kites has trust it up,
> And forthwith means on it to sup:
> . . . . .
> When on another quick She lights,
> And cryes, he call'd us Israelites;
> But now, *to make his saying true,*
> Rails rain for Quails, for Manna Dew.
>                              (ll. 403–408)

By identifying himself with Corydon, by identifying Thestylis with peasant realism, Marvell took elegant cognizance of a double dialectic: that between pastoral leisure and rural labor, as in the Virgilian original; and that between Cavalier contempt for the rustic laborer (as exhaustively documented by Anthony Low) and the voice of genuine social protest, most clearly heard in the programs of the Levellers and Diggers.

Yet in *Upon Appleton House*, as conceived by the tutor to Sir Thomas Fairfax's household, this dialectic takes on a peculiar twist. As Margaret James pointed out, the record of the Long Parliament in agrarian policy was conservative at best, involving the suppression by force of antienclosure riots, the dispersal of the Diggers from Saint George's Hill in Surrey, and, most ironically, the acquisition by leaders of the revolution of large estates that had been confiscated from the royalists.[20] In 1647 Fairfax received by parliamentary ordinance land to the value of five thousand pounds, a very considerable estate;[21] and two years later it was to Fairfax that Winstanley and Everard presented the case of the Diggers. As Winstanley informed Fairfax in a

---

20. Margaret James, *Social Problems and Policy during the Puritan Revolution, 1640–1660* (New York, 1966), pp. 80–96.

21. *Journal of the House of Commons,* V, 162.

published letter, the agrarian policy of the revolution required
him to answer a fundamental question: "whether the earth with
her fruits, was made to be bought and sold from one to another?
and whether one part of mankind was made Lord of the land,
and another part a servant, by the law of Creation before the
fall?" Wielding a biblical rather than classical authority, Winstanley asserted that "Abel shall not alwaies be slain, nor alwaies
lie under the bondage of Cains cursed propriety";[22] which brings
us back full circle to Bacon and those beginning-of-the-century
hopes for a reconciliation between pastoral and georgic as cultural principles. What we can see in Marvell's *Upon Appleton
House* is a special instance of how the intellectual's pastoral—
here represented by the poet-tutor—discovers its sociopolitical
difference from labor, that element which pastoral *otium* had
always to keep in the background but just enough in sight to
be able to recognize itself by that difference. It is characteristic
of Marvell that he presents this perception as an act of self-
parody and self-discomfiture, while at the same time proble-
matizing the social criticism implied. Where does a poet-tutor
stand on the question of land-ownership and rural labor when
he serves a revolutionary leader not only more landed than he
was before the revolution, but one who had now retired from
the struggle and adopted the position of Tityrus? In order to
make his "saying" on this issue "true," if not unequivocal,
Marvell referred his reader to Virgil and the dialogic imagination.

In the politics of quotation that I have here begun to sketch,
the case of Marvell bridges, because of its subtlety, what might
otherwise be seen as gap between public and literary discourse,
between ideologemes and far more complex texts that represented themselves to the public as participating in some way in
the Virgilian dialectic. It becomes possible, therefore, to inter-
rogate such texts and to ask about them the kinds of questions
that appeared to be easily answered in the instances adduced

22. Gerrard Winstanley, *Works . . . with an Appendix of Documents Relating
to the Digger Movement,* ed. G. H. Sabine (Ithaca, 1941), pp. 289–291.

so far. Given the presence of Virgilian keys (as, say, in the form
of epigraphs on title pages), what doors were such keys intended
to open? What cultural stance, or sociopolitical alignments, did
they indicate in the writer and assume in the reader? Or, indeed,
was nothing of the kind indicated or assumed? One of the most
tantalizing of such indications appeared on the title page of the
*Poems of Mr. John Milton*, a double volume of English and
Latin poems published in 1645. The quotation Milton chose as
the governing motif for this first collected edition of his writing
was from Virgil's seventh eclogue: *Baccare frontem / Cingite,
ne vati noceat mala lingua futuro*, the lines spoken by Thyrsis
at the beginning of his contribution to the singing match; and
according to Louis Martz, the function of the quotation was to
draw attention to the "rising poet."[23] It is also, in Martz's view,
a statement about the limitations of the *Eclogues* as a poetic
model; and all the other quotations it contains, its allusion to
Mansus as *fortunate senex*, its close imitation of the tenth eclogue in parts of *Lycidas*, and especially the *Epitaphium Damonis*, the last poem in the collection, invoke the *Eclogues* in
order to say goodbye to them. So Milton's *vos cedite silvae* is,
as Martz points out, "a clear echo of the *concedite silvae* with
which Gallus bids farewell to Arcadian pleasures," while his
threat to leave his pipe dangling on some ancient pine tree, far
away and forgotten—"Tu procul annosa pendebis, fistula, pinu /
Multum oblita mihi"—is explicitly another quotation from the
seventh eclogue, this time from Corydon's boasting: "Si non
possumus omnes, / hic arguta sacra pendebit fistula pinu" (ll.
24–25). In other words, the volume is a retrospective arranged
at the age of thirty-seven with the wisdom of hindsight, and its
function was to formalize Milton's "farewell to the pleasures
and attitudes of youth" (p. 37).

Perhaps. But we may see more in this than a statement of
personal evolution. From the very beginning of his poetic career—in the poem that seems to inaugurate that career by making a statement of self-dedication—Milton had apparently cast
doubts on pastoral's ability to comprehend the most serious

23. Louis L. Martz, *Poet of Exile: A Study of Milton's Poetry* (New Haven
and London, 1980), p. 34.

subjects. In the *Hymn on the Morning of Christ's Nativity*, a
pacificist poem composed, incidentally, as Charles was in the
process of negotiating his peace with Spain, Milton produced,
in effect, his own Christian version of Virgil's "messianic" eclogue; yet for all its reference to "the age of gold," the poem
startlingly denies its pastoral origins:

> The Shepherds on the Lawn,
> Or ere the point of dawn,
>     Sate simply chatting in a rustick row;
> Full little thought they than,
> That the mighty Pan
>     Was kindly come to live with them below;
> Perhaps their loves, or els their sheep,
> Was all that did their silly thoughts so busie keep.[24]

Clearly it was the discrepancy between Christian content and
pastoral metaphor that concerned Milton here, the dispropor-
tion between what was genetically "rustick" and "silly" and the
desire to sing a greater song than generic convention would
allow ("Paulo maiora canamus"). And when his subject was
not Christian history but poetics and his own development, he
felt free, as the 1645 *Poems* testify, to cite the Virgilian eclogues
and their shepherd characters as his own role and technical
models.

Yet the fact remains that to associate oneself with the pastoral
ethos in any way in 1645 was to make a political statement; and
it is one of the oddities of this volume that Milton's portrait
appears on the frontispiece, with a pastoral scene in the background, visually reinforcing the impact of the Virgilian quotation and *apparently* identifying the poet (in Cavalier dress and
hairstyle) as a Caroline idyllicist. The title page also defers os-
tentatiously to "Mr. Henry Lawes Gentleman of the Kings
Chappel, and one of His Majesties Private Musick"; and as
Martz himself pointed out, Moseley's preface to the volume
associated Milton with Edmund Waller, recently exiled for a
royalist plot against the Long Parliament. It is difficult to accommodate these gestures to the John Milton whose stance at

24. Frank Allen Patterson, ed., *The Works of John Milton*, 18 vols. (New
York, 1931–1938), I, pt. 1, pp. 4–5.

the beginning of the revolution had been, if not antimonarchical, unmistakably revolutionary, and whose outrage at least at the policies of Laud was already outspoken in *Lycidas*, written in 1637. It is also plausible that the famous allusion in *Lycidas* to Virgil's first eclogue refers disparagingly to the Caroline pastoral poets,[25] who had in Milton's strenuous view betrayed the Virgilian mandate to make pastoral truly meditative, genuinely the intellectual's genre:

> Alas! What boots it with uncessant care
> To tend the homely slighted Shepherds trade,
> And strictly meditate the thankles Muse?
> Were it not better don as others use,
> To sport with *Amaryllis* in the shade . . . ?
>
> (1.1.79)

And yet here he is, in 1645, following his excited and reformist pamphlets of 1641–42 with a document that both politically and aesthetically seems designed to relocate him in the establishment. The explanation may lie in what intervened between the church reform pamphlets and the *Poems* as a public statement. The intermediate text was, of course, the *Areopagitica*, Milton's defense of books and the freedom of the reader to make his own interpretations, in defiance of the Long Parliament's new printing ordinance. And while the *Areopagitica* had had to be published without license, the *Poems* could jauntily assert on their title page that they were "Printed and publish'd according to ORDER," thereby explaining to the reader the greater efficiency and immunity of encoded discourse.

Milton's insistence, then, on a pastoral frame of reference for the 1645 *Poems* is not only ambiguous but possessed of precisely

25. Compare J. W. Saunders, "Milton, Diomede and Amaryllis," *ELH*, 22 (1955), 254–286. For a similar argument with respect to *Comus*, see Maryann McGuire, *Milton's Puritan Masque* (Athens, Ga., 1983). It is important to remember that *Comus* had also been published in 1637 with its own Virgilian epigraph from the second eclogue (Eheu / quid volui misero mihi! floribus austrum / Perditus"; an identification of the aspiring poet with Corydon, which McGuire correctly reads as peculiar, presenting this first publication with "a sense of foreboding that goes beyond the conventional modesty of a youthful poet" (p. 1). This epigraph disappeared from the 1645 *Poems*, only to be replaced by the equally peculiar emphasis on "mala lingua."

those ambiguities that Virgil's *Eclogues* had made intelligible. On the one hand, the allusion to the seventh eclogue, already frequently interpreted as a poetics, suggests that the volume as a whole can be read as such, a conception that embraces the large claims made for poetry's cultural and spiritual efficacy in *Ad patrem* and *At a solemn music*, the plans for a British epic in *Mansus* and the *Epitaphium Damonis*, and the vocational doubts of *How soon hath Time* and *Lycidas*. In the light of the volume's explicit relationship to the question of censorship under the Long Parliament, the program it articulates is recognizably in the tradition of Marot and Spenser, as the poet in retrospect perceives his work, past and future, to be dependent on the survival of Humanist ideals of the immunity of the intellectual from state control. Yet the paradoxes inherent in the *Eclogues* from the beginning, and prefigured in the predicament of Tityrus, are no less visible here, since to assert the identity of pastoral and intellectual liberty *at this particular moment of the revolution* was inevitably *not* to be independent and reclusive, in the shade. To protect oneself against the "mala lingua" of 1645 was, willy-nilly, to participate in ideological conflict; given the recent history of the *Eclogues* in Caroline culture, it was also to align oneself with political conservatism. This was an alignment from which Milton would, of course, recant, one of the most literary signs of that recantation being his attack in *Eikonoklastes* on the pastoral romances and Caroline cultural Arcadianism.[26] And when the revolution was finally, and from Milton's perspective, futilely over, he built into the great poems his recognition that pastoral speaks continually with a double tongue. While the shepherd origins of Moses, David, and Abel are essential to their prototypical roles as inspired lawgiver, poet-king, and first martyr respectively, the Satan of *Paradise Regained* disguises himself (as had Comus) as a shepherd, his own "mala lingua" disguising itself as "tunable as Silvan Pipe or Song" (3.480). And the visions of biblical history at the end of *Paradise Lost*, offered under the symbol of angelic "eyes,"

26. See my *Censorship and Interpretation* (Madison, 1984), pp. 176–180. We should note, however, that Milton also added to the 1645 volume a defiant headnote to *Lycidas*, to the effect that it "foretells the ruin of our corrupted Clergy then in their height." At least within the conventions of *church* pastoral, therefore, he apparently wished to retain a reformist and iconoclastic posture.

are explicitly more realistic than the lost pastoral of the Garden, "more wakeful than to drowse / Charm'd with Arcadian Pipe, the Pastoral Reed / Of Hermes, or his opiate Rod" (11.131–133).

These, then, are some examples of how the politics of Virgilian quotation worked in the seventeenth century. The system of communication that they reveal is one that (assuming its extension to be much greater than just these surviving traces) we might reasonably envy. For what we can surely see here are the signs of education not gone to waste but alive and working in the public interest, however the individual might define that, and evidence that there is no natural divide between literature and politics, but only the trenches dug by later writer-intellectuals around what they hoped to make their own territory. It will be some time before we get enough distance from the poetics of the twentieth century to see for certain who has been dispossessed by whom.

STEVEN N. ZWICKER

# Politics and Literary Practice
# in the Restoration

I want to begin rather far afield, not with questions of literary
kind, but with a parliamentary debate that took place on 6
February 1689.[1] The debate addressed those crucial events of
the previous months—the departure of James II and the arrival
of his nephew and son-in-law, William, prince of Orange—and
the passages that I am about to quote occur midway through a
lengthy exchange in which members of Parliament are troubling
themselves over two questions: how best to describe James's
absence—whether demise, abdication, desertion, withdrawal,
or vacancy—and, in turn, how to transform a prince of Orange
into the king of England, no small problem in a hereditary
monarchy or among men who had sworn oaths of loyalty and

---

Some material in this essay appears in different form in *Politics and Language
in Dryden's Poetry: the Arts of Disguise* (Princeton, 1984) and is reprinted by
permission of Princeton University Press.

1. The debate can be followed in William Cobbett, *Parliamentary History
of England*, 36 vols. (London, 1806–1820), V, 61–108.

passive obedience to the person of the now absent king.[2] The debate is an important document in the history of the Glorious Revolution because it shows how eager men were to disguise the revolutionary character of their actions.[3] Their scrupling over language also indicates how they thought about words and meaning and how the adjustment of words to meaning might be understood as an important form of political behavior.

It is this last issue that interests me here since such adjustment of words to meaning, the self-conscious manipulation of language for political interest, characterizes the dominant mode of political discourse in the later seventeenth century and suggests that an important change had taken place not only in politics but also in the perception of language.

EARL OF CLARENDON.    That no act of the king's alone can bar or destroy the right of his heir to the crown, which is hereditary, and not elective. And then, if this matter goes no farther than king James 2 in his own person, how comes the Vacancy and Supply to be devolved upon the people? For if he only be set aside, then it is apparent, whither the crown is to go, to the person that hath the next right of succession, and consequently there is no vacancy.

EARL OF NOTTINGHAM.    Gentlemen, I would not protract time, which is now so necessary to be husbanded; nor perplex debates about any affair like that which now lies before us; it is not a question barely about words, but things, which we are now disputing.[4]

Part of the force of Nottingham's rejoinder is urgency, but I want to take the distinction that Nottingham allows, indeed on which he insists, between words and things as the crucial linguistic and political issue. What sort of a distinction could one make between words and things in 1689, and how had men come to the point where they might openly, even casually, acknowledge it? Such an admission would not have come easily at the beginning of this century of revolutions, and some un-

2. See J. P. Kenyon, *The Stuart Constitution, Documents and Commentary* (Cambridge, 1966), pp. 376–378.

3. On the conservative character of the Glorious Revolution see J. R. Jones, *Country and Court* (Cambridge, Mass., 1978), pp. 235, 252–255; and Lucile Pinkham, *William III and the Respectable Revolution* (Cambridge, Mass., 1954).

4. Cobbett, *Parliamentary History*, V, 77.

derstanding of the linguistic issue can be achieved by placing the changing theories of language within a political frame.

At the beginning of this century language theorists, nor were they alone, insisted on the essential and god-given integrity of words and things; by the end of the century language theorists were willing to allow that this relationship was arbitrary, that there was no "divine ordinance and governance of language."[5] Hobbes had so insisted at midcentury, and in 1690 Locke described the connection between words and things as "a perfectly arbitrary imposition."[6] In the *Essay Concerning Human Understanding,* the only one of Locke's major works that bore his name at publication, a book of immense and immediate prestige in its own time, Locke wrote of language and community:

The Comfort, and Advantage of Society, not being to be had without Communication of Thoughts, it was necessary, that Men should find out some external sensible Signs, whereby those Invisible Ideas which his thoughts are made up of, might be made known to others. For this purpose, nothing so fit, either for Plenty or quickness as those articulate Sounds which with so much Ease and Variety he found himself able to make. Thus we may conceive how Words, which were by Nature so well adapted to that purpose, came to be made use of by Men, as Signs of their Ideas; not by any natural connexion, that there is between particular articulate Sounds and certain ideas . . . but by a voluntary imposition, whereby such a word is made arbitrarily the Mark of such an idea.[7]

The revolution in language theory was effected by grammarians and schoolmasters, and its history as it took place in the

5. On Adamic language see Murray Cohen, *Sensible Words, Linguistic Practice in England, 1640–1785* (Baltimore, 1977), chap. 1, and David Katz, "The Language of Adam in Seventeenth-Century England," in *History and Imagination,* ed. Hugh Lloyd-Jones, Valerie Pearl, and Blair Worden (London, 1981), pp. 132–145. On the development of language theory through this century see Hans Aarsleff, *From Locke to Saussure* (Minneapolis, 1982), "Introduction," "Leibniz on Locke on Language," "Thomas Sprat," "John Wilkins," and "An Outline of Language-Origins Theory since the Renaissance"; and Vivian Salmon's introduction to *The Works of Francis Lodwick* (London, 1972).

6. Thomas Hobbes, *English Works,* 10 vols. (London, 1893), I, 13–16; John Locke, *An Essay Concerning Human Understanding,* ed. Peter Nidditch (Oxford, 1975), p. 408.

7. Locke, *An Essay,* p. 408.

work of these theorists has been carefully charted.[8] But the connections between political revolution and language have not been so fully explored. Such a link allows us to see continuities between politics and language as they were understood by contemporaries of Hobbes and Locke. It was such a connection between language and political behavior that king and Parliament acted on in 1660 when they banned "any reproach or term of distinction and all notes of discord, separation, and differences of party."[9] Names, words of reproach, any utterance that might revive the memory of the "late differences" was wholly to be avoided. Politicians must have known that men's hearts could not be changed by suppressing a set of terms; but such action changed the way in which political discourse was conducted, for the law suggested, indeed courted, political deceit. The law gave legitimacy to political fiction, to the name of concord, and to the fragile stability that masked party and disquiet over the whole of the later seventeenth century. Eventually the name of concord became the thing itself, and the fictions of stability turned into a powerful political reality in the early eighteenth century.[10]

But such coincidence of language and behavior was long in the making. Nothing more sharply characterizes political discourse between the return of Charles II and the close of this century than the use and subsequent revelation of deceit. The political literature of this age is filled with deceptions and with acts of disclosure; wherever we turn, the true nature of a politician, a plot, or a principle is being unveiled.[11] Restoration politics was a snake pit of guile and suspicion, but perhaps there is a way of seeing deception as a necessary means of political

8. Vivian Salmon, *The Study of Language in Seventeenth-Century England* (Amsterdam, 1979).

9. Kenyon, *The Stuart Constitution*, p. 366.

10. On this theme see J. H. Plumb, *The Growth of Political Stability in England, 1675–1725* (London, 1967).

11. The range of this political literature in the later seventeenth century can be gauged and followed by examining first-word entries under such words as "true," "faithful," "plain," and "character" in Donald Wing's *Short-Title Catalogue . . . 1641–1700* (New York, 1964); the relations between politics and imaginative literature in early Stuart England have been most recently explored by Annabel Patterson in *Censorship and Interpretation* (Madison, 1984). Pat-

accommodation. A case might even be made for the social and
political beneficence of disguise. It was Charles II's capacity for
lying that helped him avoid armed conflict during the quarter-
century of his rule; and I suspect that James II was driven out
of England not only because he was stupid and belligerent but
also because he was frank about politics and religion in an age
when such authenticity was not much of a virtue. Perhaps deception was a recoil from the hectoring authenticity of puritan
politics, from its visionary frenzy and its moral authoritarianism.

Deception allowed men to approximate civic stability in an
age when tempers and provocations had once driven them to
civil war and might easily do so again. The Exclusion Crisis and
the Glorious Revolution might both have ended in civil war.
But in each crisis an overriding concern of its agents was to
reinterpret events as they took place, to fit them up in a language
that would allow many if not all to accept what was proposed
and what had happened not simply as convenience but as legitimacy. The Exclusion effort failed, but the function of the
Popish Plot in that crisis was to provide a cover for constitutional
change, to marshal support for revolutionary action on the basis
of political hysteria. The function of the Convention Parliament
was to find a vocabulary for the Glorious Revolution that would
allow change to be accepted under the guise of stasis and continuity. The annals of that Parliament record an effort by which
men fixed such words to the revolution as more exactly suited
their political needs than those things which the words represented. It was only by long and ingenious exchange that members of the Parliament were finally able to say how James's
precipitate flight and his hurling of the great seal into the Thames
were in fact an act of abdication, a voluntary withdrawal from
the offices of government. The proceedings of that Parliament
might aptly be called a treatise in the art of political lying. Such
a treatise could not, I think, be so easily produced from parliamentary records before the Civil Wars. It is to overstate the
case to say that Englishmen went to war in 1639 because of the

---

terson's important new work not only explores the conditions of political writing
but also addresses the theoretical issues raised by censorship, coding, and interpretation in this literary and political culture.

intractability of their political language, but such a proposition is a significant part of Clarendon's thesis in *The History of the Rebellion*.[12] One of the clearest themes in the early chapters of this subtle and nearly disinterested analysis of the origins of the Civil War is that sharp words beget sharper actions. Of course, it was not only the imperative of sharp words that had driven men to arms. The frame of sacred history that puritans had so forcefully applied to the conflict between king and Parliament implied holy war.[13] Elect Nation was opposed only by the damned; the inauguration of Christ's thousand-year rule was impeded only by the body and agents of Antichrist.[14] But what was sacred history itself other than a language?

Men came to understand that if language had driven them to arms, then future conflict might be avoided by suppressing language and in turn by changing fundamentally the understanding of its meaning and efficacy. One act is political, the other epistemological; and while the first was encoded as law, the second is no less important though it remains a subtler and more protean event that cannot be fixed precisely in time or place. We can nevertheless hypothesize the philosophical implications of change in political language and even more clearly see how useful and how determined were the linguistic and philosophical inquiries into the origins and nature of language in the later seventeenth century.[15] The steady rift of words from things in this age allowed men to recover from the polarities to which words had earlier driven them; to see polarity itself in a new way; and to conduct a second political revolution without a single battle or the loss of one life. By using the rift between words and things, men brought about change and explained its legitimacy to one another as stasis; they embraced conquest and usurpation as if

12. Edward Hyde, first earl of Clarendon, *History of the Rebellion*, ed. W. D. Macray, 6 vols. (Oxford, 1888), I, 222, 385, 404, 448, 456, 493, 506, 537, 549; II, 26, 56, 84.

13. The background to scriptural politics in the seventeenth century is to be found in William Haller's *Foxe's Book of Martyrs and the Elect Nation* (London, 1963).

14. Best on this theme is Christopher Hill, *Antichrist in Seventeenth-Century England* (London, 1971).

15. See, for example, John Wilkins, *Essay Towards a Real Character and a Philosophical Language* (London, 1668).

they were principles of the ancient constitution; and they brought about such change through language rather than arms. The memory of the Civil Wars remained sufficiently sharp over the whole of the later seventeenth century for men to recognize not just the convenience but the necessity for deceit and simultaneously to understand that no divine and hence fixed relationship existed between words and things. Once language had been freed from the imperatives of divine ordinance, the arbitrary imposition of words on things might allow the most convenient apposition to occur.

My argument has turned thus far on the nature of politics and political language in the Restoration, but what I have suggested about deception in political discourse characterizes far more than Restoration politics. It is true that parliamentary politics dominate this culture to a remarkable and unprecedented extent, but the place of deception in this age does not derive solely from such dominance. There is, I think, something like a deep structure to this deceit, and its effects are visible at every turn. Vocabulary alone bears out my argument, social behavior illustrates the thesis, but more to the point, the preoccupations and anxieties of this culture are revealed in the forms and substance of its literature: in comedy that seems to prize deception in new and exalted ways; in epic whose most characteristic expression is in travesty and translation; in the dominance of satire whose social role is revelation; in the refinement and complication of historical parallel so that it might become an instrument of political commentary in dangerous times; in the emergence of new genres that take deception as their subject and whose function is to act as screen and mask; and finally in the transformation of old genres to accommodate the need for indirection and masquerade.

Perhaps now the distance from Convention Parliament to the problems of genre will begin to close. The essential activity of that Parliament and indeed the dominant characteristic of politics in this age was a cultural condition and preoccupation. Men lied as never before; it was a crucial ploy in the aftermath of the Civil War and interregnum. Men understood the necessity of deceit, they were aware of and at times outraged by its extent and importance, but they were also powerfully and ineluctably in its grip. Words had come loose from things, and this condition had an effect not only on the way in which political discourse was practiced but on discourse in general, on the language of politics, and on the language of high culture. It would be surprising if political and linguistic revolution did not manifest significant change in literary discourse, in literary practice, and in literary kinds. As never before, genre now functioned to make meaning oblique, to disguise identity, and to obscure and complicate motive. In this age the most characteristic and at times the most brilliant play of mind is to be found when genre is used to mask and diffuse meaning, not simply to accommodate but to enhance disguise.

I have pressed my thesis about deceit in Restoration politics in order to argue what I believe to be a crucial and distinguishing feature of the landscape; but it was not the only condition of speech in the age. To argue that all political talk was deceitful or that all those who entered into public exchange could do so only under false colors is of course to simplify the effect of deceit on politics by rendering it a monolithic condition and ignoring the possibility that some men both spoke and believed the ideological and political shibboleths of the age. With politicians we must discriminate between those who believed what they spoke and those who believed that it would be useful to speak common tongues. And such measure can often be taken by observing the distance between language and behavior. When we extend deceit from a precondition of political discourse to a cultural situation, we must exercise even finer discriminations, for the arts of disguise are more subtly practiced in poetry than in politics. And though fictions have long rendered poetry a suspect endeavor for the ideal polity, the arts of and apologias for poetry have just as urgently argued the special role and power of poetry as prophecy.

And what more obvious candidate than John Milton for poet as divine truth teller? Indeed, it is difficult to think about Milton as anything but an accidental feature of the landscape that I have described. But the problem of Milton's Restoration identity cannot be addressed by dismissing him from the age. Here is a poet who outlived his time, whose work in old age is brilliantly retrospective, personally and culturally. Yet to imagine

Milton in the 1660s and 1670s as aloof and indignant, retired from the fray to practice an occult and higher calling, is to simplify both his circumstance and his art. And no text better demonstrates his engagement with Restoration culture than *Samson Agonistes*.[16] Preface and poem display not only Milton's revulsion for this culture but also his traffic with it. These texts record a deep shudder at the moral and political betrayal of a godly society, but they do not register that shudder with the boldness of Milton's political tracts of the 1640s and 1650s. Nor is this a distinction between prose and verse, for the prose preface to *Samson Agonistes* sets the mode and is a striking instance of the measure to which political dislocation moves even a poet of Milton's temperament.

"Tragedy, as it was anciently composed, hath been ever held the gravest, moralest, and most profitable of all other poems . . ."[17] But this tragedy was not anciently composed; it was written and published in the Restoration,[18] a time, according to this poet, when tragedy had fallen to small esteem, indeed to infamy. The argument of this preface is wholly literary, but the tone is not. The voice of the prefatory essay is tense and hectoring: "Heretofore men in highest dignity have laboured not a little to be thought able to compose a tragedy . . . This is mentioned to vindicate tragedy from the small esteem, or rather infamy, which in the account of many it undergoes at this day with other common interludes; happening through the poet's error of intermixing comic stuff with tragic sadness and gravity; or introducing trivial and vulgar persons, which by all judicious hath been counted absurd; and brought in without discretion, corruptly to gratify the people."[19] The aesthetic agenda of this preface is in part a cover for the political argument of the epistle.

16. The politics of *Samson Agonistes* has been examined by Mary Ann Radzinowicz, *Towards Samson Agonistes* (Princeton, 1978), pp. 167–179; Christopher Hill, *Milton and the English Revolution* (New York, 1977), pp. 428–448; and Nicholas Jose, "*Samson Agonistes:* The Play Turned Upside Down," *Essays in Criticism*, 30 (1980), 124–150.

17. John Carey and Alastair Fowler, eds., *The Poems of John Milton* (London, 1968), p. 343.

18. Most Miltonists accept a post-1660 date for the composition of *Samson Agonistes*, but see Carey and Fowler, *The Poems*, pp. 330–332.

19. Carey and Fowler, *The Poems*, p. 344.

Of course the aesthetic terms mattered to Milton—he was after all composing a poem and not a battle plan—but the language of literary criticism does not delimit the subject. The harshness of judgment and vehemence of tone, the careful attention to the interdependence of society and its art, and the steady derogation of modern taste, its slighting juxtaposition with ancient and heroic standards, convey more than aesthetics: they argue social and political urgency. Milton is waging war on Restoration theater, on the mixing of genres, on modern tragedy and its audience; but he would press home a more fundamental argument. His quarrel is not only with taste but with the entire moral and political character of his society, with men who had turned their backs on godliness, who had spurned righteousness for luxury, who had in the person of Charles Stuart chosen themselves a captain back to Egypt.[20] Such a statement could not now and not by this poet be openly made.

And it is Milton's resistance to disguise of any sort that is responsible for the tension that we feel in this preface. Here is no soaring eloquence, a tone and stance we might have expected if the function of the preface were only to celebrate the ancient tragedians. But Milton's argument is burdened by a political subject, and its expression is complicated by the strictures placed on such a subject. So Milton turned to literary apologetics and implied another set of terms. Argument by suggestion and innuendo could not have been easy for Milton, and the preface expresses both the urgency of the political text and the constraints working against its expression. The resolution to this tension came in the poem itself. Milton chose subject and form because Scripture enabled him to address both ancient and contemporary politics, and tragedy expressed both the necessity for and ultimate failure of political revolution.[21] For Milton, the simultaneously historical and prophetic character of Scripture was fundamental; the literal was paradigmatic. Samson's story is enacted with every revolution and with every political failure.

20. The language is, of course, from Milton's *The Ready and Easy Way,* a tract that Milton published on 3 March 1660, almost literally on the eve of the Restoration.

21. On this theme see Barbara K. Lewalski, "*Samson Agonistes* and the 'Tragedy' of the Apocalypse," *PMLA,* 85 (1970), 1050–62.

The very mode of the poem insists on multiple perspectives, nor were they only the general conditions of every warfaring Christian but the quite specific conditions of this warfaring Christian and his society. And the pressure of the exactly contemporary reference, enfolded into the ancient story, can be felt at crucial junctures:

> But what more oft in nations grown corrupt,
> And by their vices brought to servitude,
> Than to love bondage more than liberty,
> Bondage with ease than strenuous liberty;
> And to despise, or envy, or suspect
> Whom God hath of his special favour raised
> As their deliverer; if he aught begin,
> How frequent to desert him, and at last
> To heap ingratitude on worthiest deeds?[22]

What nations might be included in this roll call, what heroes had God of his special favor raised? Israel and England; Samson and Milton. But the imagination is not allegorical; the method is not parallel history; the narrative does not invite us to fit a steady series of mythic against historical particulars. The mode is prophetic, and it is the character of prophecy to allow but not to insist on application.[23] The text is complete in its ancient enactment; and yet because it is prophetic it tells of other times as well. The text inveighs against Philistine luxury; it allows us to hear Stuart corruption:

> an impious crew
> Of men conspiring to uphold their state
> By worse than hostile deeds, violating the ends
> For which our country is a name so dear.[24]

The condemnation is harsh and arresting, the mode invites but does not insist on contemporary application; nor could it have been different.

Milton's *Samson* is a classic case of disguise in the face of

22. Carey and Fowler, *The Poems*, p. 356.
23. On political application in the seventeenth century, see John Wallace, " 'Examples are Best Precepts': Readers and Meanings in Seventeenth-Century Poetry," *Critical Inquiry*, 1 (1974), 273–291.
24. Carey and Fowler, *The Poems*, p. 375.

political danger; it occurs in an unexpected personality, but in familiar circumstance. If, however, political danger alone drove men to cover in this age, we would not be able sharply to distinguish it from other times; think of the Roman satirists; think of Ben Jonson in the 1620s conceiving Roman plots and court politics fitted to one mode. Republicans and other conspirators might find it useful to write philosophical treatises rather than political programs in the late seventeenth century,[25] but, in this age, even court poets, men writing from the center of power, sought and manipulated cover. And their circumstance and art seem an even more telling commentary on this culture than the example of Milton.

What more telling expression of this culture than its central literary figure, its poet laureate? Dryden was *the* Restoration man of letters; he defined cultural standards in criticism, in satire, in drama, and in translation. He created the idiom of Restoration literature, and for much of his life he wrote from the center of power. He was also constantly blackened as a liar and a hypocrite by his contemporaries. Of course, the accusations of disguise and deceit were hardly disinterested opinion; they were epithets hurled by political enemies intent on damaging and discrediting a public voice. But the idea of Dryden as timeserver and cheat was also the more measured opinion of Johnson and Macaulay.[26] It was, as well, the conviction of Eliot and Van Doren, though their critical manners prevented its full expression. But my aim here is not to celebrate the blackening of Dryden's character; it is rather to suggest something about the conditions under which Dryden and his contemporaries practiced their arts. Whatever Dryden's private character was like, the public and literary characters were bril-

25. The most striking example is the translation and annotation of Boethius made by Richard Graham, viscount Preston, *Of the Consolation of Philosophy* (London, 1695); Graham was a Jacobite and a convicted plotter against William III.

26. For Dr. Johnson on Dryden see G. B. Hill, ed., *Lives of the English Poets,* 3 vols. (Oxford, 1905), I, 398–401; Macaulay's essay on Dryden first appeared in the *Edinburgh Review* (1828) and can be consulted in Lord Macaulay, *Critical, Historical, and Miscellaneous Essays,* 6 vols. (New York, 1860), I, 321–375.

liantly elusive, and it is this very elusiveness that is central to the poet's handling of genre.

I suspect that the generic question is the right place to begin puzzling over such a poem as *Heroique Stanza's;* why, if Dryden were intent on mourning and celebrating Cromwell, did he avoid the obvious epideictic forms and gestures? But the tactical uses of genre are even more obviously in play in the poet's defense of court policy in *Annus Mirabilis*. Title, dedication, and preface bristle with instruments of cultural authority, and the celebration of London as perfect model of loyalty and courage is a clever denial of the facts and history of opposition that so marked the city's participation in the Civil Wars. The preface to this poem begins with such a dedication, with insistent praise of the enemy, in order to use generosity and highmindedness to disarm the opposition and to derail their criticism. The posture is crucially reminiscent of one of the central strategies of the king's own Act of Oblivion—a denial of the language and facts of opposition—and it anticipates the portrait of the king in the poem, not a man embattled by sharp criticisms but the crown as beloved servant and redemptive saint.

The technique of denial and misrepresentation is exercised with surprising abandon in this early work, the discussion of literary kind being especially inventive. Dryden insists that the subject of his poem is heroic, and yet he refuses to yield the poem its deserved epic status: "I have taken upon me to describe the motives, the beginning, progress and successes of a most just and necessary War."[27] Perhaps this is the beginning of a new *Iliad* or another *Aeneid;* here is the matter of epic poetry, and yet the poem itself is steadfastly refused the epic genre. It is history, a designation that Dryden claims he needs because singleness of action has not been observed.[28] The literary distinction between epic and history allows the poet the luxury of having his poem simultaneously circumscribed by the "rigorous" laws of history and enhanced by the clear demands of epic, yet the actions themselves, reported in the "broken manner" of the

27. James Kinsley, ed., *The Poems of John Dryden*, 4 vols. (Oxford, 1958), I, 44.
28. Ibid.

poem, are denied epic designation. Epic is "too bold a Title for a few *Stanza's*."[29] The choice of genre and the mixing of designations are determined by the poet's desire to position his poem happily and simultaneously within the bounds of history and heroism.

Nor is it only the opposition of epic and history that Dryden uses to advance his claims as historian of the Dutch wars. The whole discussion of literary theory and literary models turns on the same issue as the initial confrontation with generic questions. This poet, somewhat against his will, has chosen Virgil rather than Ovid as literary model, judgment over imagination. Ovid is the poet of passion; he delights the imagination. Virgil is praised for "accuracy of expression." Ovid excels in wit and suddenness of expression; Virgil speaks most often in his own person. The claims for Virgil seem surprisingly humble. The contrast between the two poets is heightened by their respective handling of Dido and Myrrha. Dido, Dryden admits, is well described, and yet Virgil "must yield in that to the *Myrrha,* the *Biblis,* the *Althaea,* of *Ovid* . . . *Ovid* has touch'd those tender strokes more delicately then *Virgil* could."[30] It is a curious way to prepare a claim for Virgil as your master, by humbling him below Ovid in the faculties of imagination and expression, but the strategy has the same point as the contrast between epic and history. The extended comparison of Virgil and Ovid aims to establish Dryden as judicious and disinterested literary arbiter. Almost against his will, certainly against taste and inclination, Dryden chooses Virgil as his master in *Annus Mirabilis* because Virgil is the poet of accurate representation, and this poem demands exactness, the accuracy of a Virgil. Dryden aims at truth and not at wonder. He is the artless panegyrist, the judicious and guileless historian. "Ti'd too severely to the Laws of History," this poem cannot aspire to epic manners though its subject calls for epic treatment. And Virgil as master certainly heightens the potential claims that might be laid on behalf of *Annus Mirabilis* as epic rendering of England's "just and necessary War"; yet it is Virgil's exactness and judiciousness that

29. Ibid.
30. Ibid., p. 47.

are invoked for this poem. The polemical agenda of the preface
determines every gesture in the refined and elevated discussion
of literary models. Even the discussion of technical language,
Dryden's attempt at mastery over the terms of nautical warfare,
is shaped by the polemical currents of the preface. The poet
makes a small but insistent point out of his search for technical
language because he wants to claim for *Annus Mirabilis,* down
to the smallest detail, the severity of history. Such language has
been mastered because the poet aims, disinterestedly and obe-
diently, not at epic but at annal. The handling of questions of
genre, literary authority, and linguistic detail bears everywhere
the traces of this overriding polemical need for history. Of course,
it is in the nature of the traffic between political argument and
the forms of high culture that such argument be transfigured,
but the need for such transfiguration seems to have been especially pressing after the decades of momentous change in the
middle of the seventeenth century.

We do not have to know very much about the Dutch wars or
about the court's management of finance, supply, and battle to
judge how strained were Dryden's claims on the court's behalf.
Nor can we suppose that those members of Dryden's audience
who had battened on and even participated in the savage attacks
on the court could have been anything but contemptuous of the
poet's efforts to reverse the tide of that criticism through claims
of highmindedness and historical accuracy. But the polemical
aims of preface and poem are not confined to the propaganda
war that had been mounted in dissenting sermons and pamphlets
and swelled by the *Advice* poems and their satiric reversals.
With *Annus Mirabilis* Dryden was also filing a claim for patronage and attention, and the rather elaborate and rarefied
plumage of preface and poem must have been displayed not
only to elevate the poem to aery heights above dissenting broadsides—though its address to the criticisms contained in those
broadsides is thorough and canny[31]—but also to argue the poet

31. The fullest treatment of the relations between *Annus Mirabilis* and the
dissenters' sermons and broadsides is to be found in Michael McKeon, *Politics
and Poetry in Restoration England* (Cambridge, Mass., 1975).

as historian and panegyrist of the Restoration court.[32] To judge by results, Dryden's appointments in 1670 as poet laureate and historiographer royal,[33] the poem was a brilliant polemical success. Of course, *Annus Mirabilis* is not Dryden's most sophisticated essay in the polemics of literary kind, but it is an illustrative example of the pressures that politics exerts on poetics, and part of its interest for us derives from the very visibility of its seams. Had it been a subtler and more plausible case, had the claims for disinterestedness been mounted with the subtlety that Dryden managed for *Absalom and Achitophel,* we would not be able to trace so easily the lineaments of posture and self-presentation. In 1667 we can watch the poet maneuvering behind the scenes that he has assembled for our pleasure and instruction. By the time of Exclusion we are dealing with a master illusionist, one particularly adept in the art of mixing genres and holding aloft the conflicting claims of those generic appeals, as if the arguments of history, prophecy, panegyric, and satire did nothing but reinforce one another or heighten our belief that artistic power and political guile are contradictory events.

I have in mind of course the brilliant little essay on literary kind that prefaces *Absalom and Achitophel.* Indeed, the efforts of this essay to mount overlapping, at points contradictory, and certainly disingenuous claims on behalf of the poem begin in the very title that argues the authority of Scripture in its composition, suggests the mode of political parallel in its structure and hence excites our experience with and anticipation of application, and finally, through its broad and indeterminate subtitle, insists on the primacy and prerogatives of art: *Absalom and Achitophel, A Poem.* The opening paragraph is thoroughly defended against what the poet knows will be the polemicized reception of his work; how could any man, even the most determined and innocent of artists, escape the powerful currents of polemicization in the midst of the present constitutional crisis?

32. See Charles Ward, *The Life of John Dryden* (Chapel Hill, 1961), pp. 71–72.
33. Ibid.

And yet the claim here is for innocence and honesty, and "honesty" seems to imply simplicity almost to the point of simple-mindedness. *Absalom and Achitophel* as *poem* insists on the primacy of design in the formal and not political sense; in the wake of these repeated artistic claims comes a political positioning. Art is made to imply political neutrality; poetry is hoisted above party in an effort to insist that the shrewd political positioning and arguments of this poem—its harsh and at points splenetic condemnation of dissent, its argument for the proscription of the Whig leadership, its attempts to defuse and ridicule the deeply embarrassing and injurious revelation of the duke of York's ties to the court of Louis XIV—have nothing of politics about them at all. The imperatives of this work, Dryden claims, are artistic, and yet as the prefatory paragraphs unroll, we hear of history, politics, satire, epic, and mock heroic. What are the generic and modal determinates of composition? Nor has this seemed a question with so obvious an answer for students of *Absalom and Achitophel*.

The debate over literary kind in *Absalom and Achitophel* is extensive and serious.[34] At one point the poet claims the mantle of historian, at another he is satirist; at the opening he is unwilling partisan, pushed against his own intentions into the unfortunate label of party man; but by the close of the preface we see him ironically allowing party. Genre and mode here are not categories to identify and reveal meaning, but conditions deftly to be invoked and avoided. The poem has an array of satiric, political, quasi-historical, and epic kinds of business to conduct, but it will not do so under limiting conditions. The poet induces a confusion over genre: he plants conflicting signals, for he wants to enhance the multiple effects of the poem, but he also wants to dodge generic determinacy. If this poem is epic, then the

34. The debate over literary kind in the critical literature reflects Dryden's maneuvering in the preface; see, for example, Chester Cable, "*Absalom and Achitophel* as Epic Satire," in *Studies in Honor of John Wilcox*, ed. A. D. Wallace (Detroit, 1958), pp. 51–60; Morris Freedman, "Dryden's Miniature Epic," *Journal of English and Germanic Philology*, 57 (1958), 211–219; and R. G. Peterson, "Larger Manners and Events: Sallust and Virgil in *Absalom and Achitophel*," *PMLA*, 82 (1967), 236–244.

claims of history are compromised; if the poem is satire, then the prophetic calling, the argument of the poem as sacred history, is endangered; if this is history, then epic and panegyric are slighted. The poem is all the various kinds as Dryden well knew, indeed as he makes sure that we understand, by direction, by gesture, by Virgilian and Miltonic echo and allusion, but it is not any one of them. It is a poem, no genre finally at all, not because Dryden was uncertain how to press conflicting claims, but because he knew how delicately balanced they were, often one directly against the other: satire redeeming prophecy, prophecy suggesting a perspective that satire cannot allow; history strengthening the hand of veracity; epic enlarging the dimensions of history. This is a complicated balancing act; here is a set of overlapping, even at points contradictory, agendas best accommodated by generic confusion, by refusing to identify kind, by allowing, even insisting, that the reader entertain the multiple directives about meaning and intention that genre encodes. *Annus Mirabilis* is history; the work is intently and narrowly focused; but Dryden's arts and ambitions are much fuller in 1681 than in that year of wonders, and those arts are in evidence from the moment we examine the title, in every line of the preface, and through the complex maneuvering of the poem that follows.

Of course the most brilliant instance of political poetry may not necessarily serve as representative example, nor is it exactly meant to do so. Deception was a condition that some hands turned to high art; the necessity for disguise spurred the development of a special poetic; it focused and intensified certain literary gifts. And Dryden became the central figure of his age because he adjusted so surely to the conditions of speech set by politics. But Dryden was not alone in those arts. Pamphlets, ballads, and histories were bent to the purpose of political argument; at the same time they often served as screen and mask; in fact whole genres were governed by the principles of illusion. The short history of the advice-to-painter poem is a splendid example of this pressure, for the whole genre, especially in the satiric recoil that followed the first examples of the poem in the 1660s, argues a poetic of illusion and disguise, and it is a literary kind peculiar to these years.[35] The poem itself turns on an act of illusion, the poet giving instructions to a court painter whose task it is to depict the glories of some battle or hero, but it is the poet's painterly descriptions that alone do justice to the pace and character of heroic deeds. Clearly none composing such "instructions" ever intended to instruct in the art of perspective or portraiture; the fiction is a pleasantly transparent machine that allowed a novel form to the inflations of panegyric. The device gains power and interest only when the genre is turned on its head and these instructions, intended for praise, are leveled against their earlier subjects:

> Nay, Painter, if thou dar'st design that fight
> Which Waller only courage had to write,
> If thy bold hand can, without shaking, draw
> What e'en the actors trembl'd when they saw
> (Enough to make thy colors change like theirs
> And all thy pencils bristle like their hairs)
> First, in fit distance of the prospect main,
> Paint Allin tilting at the coast of Spain.[36]

Now the initial premise comes into its own, for the format of the poem allows a brilliant and ironic play of satiric images against the court and court poetics, the satiric instructions strip away pretense and inflation, they expose the court and explode its praise. Men and motives are unmasked, character revealed, ambitions unveiled. One disguise abets another; nor is this quite all, for while the satirist poses as corrective lash, he practices his own disguise, the poet as disinterested patriot, a man who would abuse the court and its ministry only in the name of king and country. Vitriolic satire is presented as virtue and disinterestedness. After the savage attacks have leveled their targets, the poet as patriot emerges to present an envoy to the king that insists on the monarch's innocence of the corruption that surrounds him, a trope which is of course an ancient constitutional

35. See the discussion by George deF. Lord, *Poems on Affairs of State,* ed. George deF. Lord et al., 7 vols. (New Haven, 1963–1975), I, 20–21; a full bibliography is provided by M. T. Osborne, *Advice-to-a-Painter Poems, 1635–1856, An Annotated Finding List* (University of Texas, 1958).

36. Lord, *Poems on Affairs of State,* I, 36.

fiction. Here is Marvell in the *Second Advice,* conducting the envoy in the very language of adulation that he has throughout abused:

> Imperial Prince, King of the seas and isles,
> Dear object of our joys and Heaven's smiles:
> What boots it that thy light does gild our days
> And we lie basking in thy milder rays,
> While swarms of insects, from thy warmth begun,
> Our land devour and intercept our sun?[37]

And the envoy to the *Third Advice* begins, "Great Prince, and so much greater as more wise, / Sweet as our life, and dearer than our eyes . . ."[38] It is difficult to credit this language, but the idea of turning the genre into self-protection, into a legitimation of opposition politics, seems remarkably suitable for the age. If we trace the growth of opposition politics into the party structures of the late seventeenth and early eighteenth centuries, we can observe the development of literary languages and forms as legitimating instruments for politics. The sudden revival of Milton's reputation on the eve of the Glorious Revolution must have been, in part, an effort to yoke the authority of literary form to the cause of revolutionary principles.[39] Bedecked with fictions and strategies, premised on an illusion, the advice-to-painter poem seems a quintessential genre for the opening years of the Restoration.

The closing decades of the century reveal a culture yet more deeply entangled in fictions and disguise; such we have observed in the brief exchange from the debates in the Convention Parliament over the "abdication" of James II, and we can trace this entanglement in two remarkable and related literary developments: the rise of fable and the sudden and quite dramatic increase in literary translation. If uncertainty and volatility had persuaded men to adopt codes and masks in the early years of

37. Ibid., p. 52.
38. Ibid., p. 87.
39. The revival of Milton's reputation after 1688 has not been thoroughly examined, although Bernard Sharratt has a number of interesting suggestions for such a study in "The Appropriation of Milton," *Essays and Studies, 1982,* coll. Suheil Bushrui (London, 1982), pp. 30–44.

the Restoration, to suppress forthright expression and deny party
and faction, nothing in the years following Charles's death would
have done much to invite them into the open. There is a moment
of relative calm in the Tory purge that followed the Exclusion
Crisis,[40] but the stability and hegemony of the crown was quickly
destroyed by James II. He undermined his own power and
credibility and convinced a nation, all too willing to believe such,
that he was intent on invading property and liberty, destroying
the Protestant religion, and enslaving the English people. He
had come to power with a surprisingly wide approval; within
three years he had fled over the channel, no doubt mindful of
his father's fate.

In such a time of shifting power, of political uncertainty and
fear, those who dissented from the government were not alone
in seeking comfort in disguise; such an impulse swept the entire
nation. In the last decade of the century, a time of precipitate
change, of invasion threats and assassination plots, of continued
political debate over the legitimacy of William III, of dramatic
shifts in court policy and ministry, in party identity and alle-
giance, the whole of the literate nation seems to have gone
under cover. This is a decade of remarkably interesting political
change, but it is also a decade of remarkably little literary composition. The great achievement of this decade was in translation.

The years under James and William were an age of fable and
translation, a time of deep political uncertainty and confusion,
and such a political climate was the fundamental cultural condition. Not only did those who plotted the Glorious Revolution
sign their documents in code and cypher, and not only did those
who plotted against the Dutch usurper do so in secret assig-
nation, under codes and through clandestine clubs, but the whole
of the nation was gripped by political uncertainty. The rise of
fable in such an age seems imperative. Moreover, the shelter
of fable and translation was not simply a cover for those who
undertook to attack the court or plot a revolution. Sir Roger
L'Estrange was the most famous Aesopian—a translator as well
of Josephus, Cicero, and Seneca—and he sought fable and parable to attack from the center. Fable became a condition for

40. On these years, see Jones, *Country and Court,* pp. 217–233.

all men; instability was not exclusive to those who would force change. Under James and William instability was a constant political reality. The alarming pace with which James seemed to desire change, to impose his mission on England, to raise a standing army, to staff that army with Catholic officers, and to break the grip of the Anglican church on office and place not only shook the Anglican establishment but frightened his natural allies, even members of his own court.[41] Those who opposed such change attacked the court in a spate of anonymous ballads and satires, but even those who would celebrate and defend that court must have found James's policies difficult to celebrate openly. And there is no more obvious and illustrative example of the interplay between policy and poetry than the literary centerpiece of James's reign, Dryden's endless beast fable, *The Hind and the Panther*. This poem is Dryden's longest original work—by more than a thousand lines. It has three main divisions, subsections within those, fables hidden within fables, talking beasts, satiric portraits, hidden morals, allegories, allusions, and satires. This is the most complicated machine that Dryden had yet invented, and we might calculate the poem's complexity in direct relation to the difficulty of the tasks he undertook in this work.

The clever allegory of *Absalom and Achitophel* suggests a genius of resourcefulness. Here was the game of poetry with a key played to the hilt. Part of the pleasure of the biblical allegory was in its application, fitting the politicians to the portraits, and this was a game that Dryden's audience, whatever their political convictions, played with relish. Early editions of the poem are covered with handwritten names, and keys to the poem were quickly put in circulation. But *The Hind and the Panther* was received rather differently. Instead of keys to the poem, Dryden's contemporaries published imitations that ridiculed his invention. Of course, Dryden's conversion to Rome had made him an even more visible target for such attack,[42] but the imitators of *The Hind and the Panther* took direct literary issue

---

41. Ibid., pp. 236–245.

42. See Hugh Macdonald, "The Attacks on Dryden," *Essays and Studies by Members of the English Association*, 21 (1936), 41–74; and the "Drydeniana" section of Macdonald's *John Dryden: A Bibliography* (Oxford, 1939).

with the invention.[43] They thought the poem vulnerable as poem; they found it long and ridiculous. It violated the proprieties of the beast fable; it was too complicated; it was difficult and preposterous to follow the niceties of theology when it was beasts who discoursed on Arianism and the authority of the oral tradition. *The Hind and the Panther* suggested Aesop, but what exactly was the moral of its fables? Who were the chickens and pigeons? How were they like the Goths and Vandals who demolished Rome? Small wonder that the notes to the *California* Dryden should run to 132 pages. We still have not decided so fundamental a question as the identity of the Buzzard in part 3 of the poem. Is this unattractive bird supposed to represent Bishop Burnet or William, prince of Orange? It is as if we could not decide whether Achitophel were meant to depict Monmouth or Shaftesbury. Such a confusion is unthinkable in *Absalom and Achitophel*, but if my sense of the connection between politics and fable is accurate for *The Hind and the Panther*, the confusion embedded in this fable is calculated, the obscurity deliberate. The choice of genre and mode was determined by political circumstance and political problems; the intricacies of this poem were an effort to complicate issues that for most Englishmen were very clear. By the time this poem was published in 1687, most Englishmen were quite clear about James's identity; rather than the simple-minded chicken farmer of Dryden's fable, James was understood to be the pope's lieutenant in the subjugation of the English nation. He intended by all legal and illegal means to exterminate the Northern heresy; and the Declaration of Indulgence, issued only two months before the poem was published, was but the latest trick to align dissenters and Roman Catholics into a new power base, to defy the law, and to ignore custom and privilege. These were not obscure issues, and there can be little wonder that Dryden chose either to ignore or to imbed them in the most intricate folds of this allegory whose every line the poet knew would be parsed with malice and with care.

43. The most famous of these imitations was by Charles Montagu and Matthew Prior, *The Hind and the Panther Transversed* (London, 1687); see G. M. Crump, ed., *Poems on Affairs of State*, IV, 116–145.

And where the poem takes the offensive through open satire, the poet first argues that he aims only at the refractory few and then denies satiric intention altogether: "There are in it two *Episodes*, or *Fables*, which are interwoven with the main Design; so that they are properly parts of it . . . In both of these I have made use of the Common Places of *Satyr*, whether true or false, which are urg'd by the Members of the one Church against the other. At which I hope no *Reader* of either Party will be scandaliz'd; because they are not of my Invention: but as old, to my knowledge, as the Times of *Boccace* and *Chawcer* on the one side, and as those of the Reformation on the other."[44] The dodge is familiar: "were I the inventor who am only the historian"; as the mantle of historian had once served, so the pose of translator would now become an important determinant in Dryden's literary production in the last decade of the century when he assumed the stance and tropes of Juvenal and Persius, Chaucer and Boccaccio, Ovid and Virgil.

Nor was Dryden alone in the 1690s as he turned to ancient voices. The translation of Roman poetry and history in the closing years of the seventeenth century is a remarkable phenomenon. Throughout the century poets and politicians had turned to Rome for precedent and analogy, but the numbers now argue something more than precedent. There was a dramatic increase in translations and editions of Roman poets and historians, and these works were accompanied by commentary and paraphrase, by citation and allusion, by studies of the Roman law and religion, by collections of Roman biography and antiquities, by engravings and catalogues.[45] What I am suggesting is

44. Kinsley, *The Poems*, II, 469–470.

45. The bibliography on this topic is vast; two primary literary studies are Paul Fussell, *The Rhetorical World of Augustan Humanism* (Oxford, 1965), and J. W. Johnson, *The Formation of English Neo-Classical Thought* (Princeton, 1967); as a historical subject, see Z. S. Fink, *The Classical Republicans* (Evanston, 1945); Caroline Robbins, *The Eighteenth-Century Commonwealthsmen* (Cambridge, Mass., 1959); J. G. A. Pocock, *The Machiavellian Moment* (Princeton, 1975); and Blair Worden, "Classical Republicanism and the Puritan Revolution," in *History and Imagination*, ed. Hugh Lloyd-Jones, Valerie Pearl, and Blair Worden (London, 1981), pp. 182–200; see also Peter Burke, "A Survey of the Popularity of Ancient Historians, 1450–1700," *History and Theory*, 5 (1966), 135–152.

that in the sudden rise of literary translation we have a symptom of an entire culture trying to find cover and new identity through the idioms and metaphors of another age. Eventually such cover took on a character of its own, something we have come to think of as the Augustan age. The creation of that idiom is a very large subject; the more limited point that I would like to suggest is that one of the impulses that drove men to discover the Roman meaning of their own lives and institutions was an effort to hide, to use the screen of the Roman past as distance and mediation and, at points, specifically as camouflage. Not all the English Romanism of the late seventeenth century was sought as cover, but in the stability of that history, in the permanence of Roman institutions, even Roman ruins, there must have been some general comfort for those who had witnessed half a century of revolution and fear and precipitate constitutional change.

I began with an example of poetry and political dislocation in Milton's *Samson Agonistes,* and I want to conclude with another example of the effects of political dislocation, in this instance the most important translation of the later seventeenth century and a text that served as a major constituent of the Roman analogy for those years. The text is Dryden's translation of the *Aeneid,* and the parallel with Milton's *Samson* is worth some notice. Both poets suffered political dislocation in old age, both lived out their lives in fear and in real political danger, and both used ancient texts as vehicles for political commentary. For both Milton and Dryden, the integrity of the ancient text was fundamental, but their renderings are throughout marked by the pressure of their own political experience. Milton chose a freer mode than Dryden, but within the limits of his careful translation of Virgil, Dryden achieved a powerful commentary on society and politics. In their prefaces both poets used poetics as a way of situating their works and of covertly arguing the political urgency of their efforts to translate texts and idioms. That Milton chose Scripture and Dryden turned to Virgil for such a vehicle is a history unto itself, but the parallel between their circumstances and their responses is illuminating, for it tells us something of the ways in which poets think about the dialogue they have with their own culture and the effects of political circumstance on the tone and shape of that dialogue; it tells us something of literary choice and decision.

And the idea of translating Virgil was one such decision. It was a choice that derived from financial need and convenience but as well from the desire for political statement. This translation had been long in contemplation,[46] and that it should have come when it did, despite all the arguments that might be made against such logic, some of which Dryden himself keenly and poignantly observed, suggests that Dryden had conceived his own agenda for Virgil, his own conception of the meaning of epic late in his own life and that of his century.[47] By the time he undertook the project for his publisher, Dryden had been ejected from the laureateship, ridiculed for his conversion, marked as a Jacobite. He was a man precarious in his safety, his health, and his finances, dependent on the leavings of a few minor gentry and loyal patrons who bore him no grudge in what he himself perceived as a rather shabby circumstance. And yet he now chose to make a true and lasting English Virgil, to translate a poem of empire and sublimity. But Dryden took up his translation not simply in defiance of odds and circumstance. He knew that an English Virgil would both honor the Roman poet and enshrine the translator who thought himself Virgil's likeness and heir. Moreover, he was able to see that the central analogy between Rome and England need not compliment revolution and usurpation, that in fact he might maneuver the whole of the epic subtly into an opposition stance that would give him a way of asserting both his literary and civic identity. The analogy with Rome allowed Dryden to see himself as patriot, to celebrate those families that still obliged him as the Roman nobility,

46. Prior to his agreement with Tonson, Dryden had published translations of passages from several books of the *Aeneid* in the 1685 *Sylvae;* on Dryden's long engagement with epic, see H. T. Swedenberg, Jr., "Dryden's Obsessive Concern with the Heroic," *Studies in Philology* (Extra Series, January 1967), 12–26.

47. See Dryden's "Postscript to the Reader," in Kinsley, *The Poems*, III, 1424: "What *Virgil* wrote in the vigour of his Age, in Plenty and at Ease, I have undertaken to *Translate* in my Declining Years: strugling with Wants, oppress'd with Sickness, curb'd in my Genius, lyable to be misconstrued in all I write; and my Judges, if they are not very equitable, already prejudic'd against me, by the *Lying Character* which has been given them of my Morals."

and to scorn the revolution that had displaced the legitimate king and poet laureate with tyranny and the mob.[48] The analogy with Rome provided Dryden with a language and a history for such an assertion.

Not only did Dryden conceive his translation in political terms, but he saw or claimed to see Virgil's poem itself as political commentary: a warning to Augustus Caesar on the dangers of tyranny and elective kingship, and such a political reading of Virgil was the key to his own conception of the epic and to the force of his translation. The political understanding of the Latin poet can be traced through the dedicatory essay and the translation; its presence seems quite overt at moments, but over the brooding and melancholy whole its presence is less sharply argued, its realm cooler and more sustained. What some men must have seen as the celebration of a new order, an England turned more clearly toward European interests than ever before, and a panegyric to a foreign prince and to a king bound by marriage to the throne, Dryden conceived very differently. For he understood Virgil's celebration of empire in more compromised and less heroic ways than such men could have imagined.

I do not want to suggest that Dryden conceived the translation of the *Aeneid* as an occasion for political allegory, something akin to *Absalom and Achitophel,* but rather that he saw a relationship between the conduct of Roman politics in the century of the Caesars and English history in his own time. He read Roman history in terms of English politics; he conceived this poem to have been Virgil's meditation on Roman politics, and he used Virgil for his own political ends. Dryden's subjects in his *Aeneid* were conquest and usurpation, oaths and bonds, the role of providence in the disposition of governments, the complaint of justice against fate. Virgil's poem might have been applied quite differently; indeed in Thomas Fletcher's 1692 translation of book 1 of the *Aeneid,* Jove's prophecy of Aeneas' bloody triumph was intended as an allusion to and celebration of William's victory at Boyne.[49] But the *Aeneid* might also be

48. On the contemporary meaning of the Virgil translation, see Steven N. Zwicker, *Politics and Language in Dryden's Poetry* (Princeton, 1984), chap. 6.

49. Thomas Fletcher, *Poems on Several Occasions, and Translations* (London, 1692), p. 83.

turned against the revolutionary settlement, against the European wars and foreign interests, against the legitimation of invasion and conquest. This was a daring political application, and direct argument would not have been possible for this poet. But translation allowed such play; irony and insinuation were the mode of Dryden's commentary. The poet must have thought the screen sufficient for his needs.

The political reading of Dryden's translation requires long and careful explication, but listen for a moment as Dryden's Juno addresses Venus at the opening of book 10, harshly and ironically rehearsing the causes and the character of the war that is about to unfold between the Trojans and the Latians:

> You think it hard, the *Latians* shou'd destroy
> With Swords your *Trojans,* and with Fires your *Troy:*
> Hard and unjust indeed, for Men to draw
> Their Native Air, nor take a foreign Law:
> That *Turnus* is permitted still to live,
> To whom his Birth a God and Goddess give:
> But yet 'tis just and lawful for your Line,
> To drive their Fields, and Force with Fraud to join.
> Realms, not your own, among your Clans divide,
> And from the Bridegroom tear the promis'd Bride:
> Petition, while you publick Arms prepare;
> Pretend a Peace, and yet provoke a War.[50]

In part the translation is exact, but Dryden seems everywhere intent on shading the political idiom to accommodate his own concerns with the injustice of the Glorious Revolution, with the shame of foreign conquest and fraudulent laws. "Hard and unjust indeed, for Men to draw / Their Native Air, nor take a foreign Law:" the tone here is resentful and xenophobic, and the language has no original in Virgil. Nor does the following line, "Realms, not your own, among your Clans divide"; Dryden is rendering here the Latin phrase *avertere praeda,* "to carry off plunder," with language that makes inescapable the political character of his translation, for the plunder that Dryden had quite specifically in mind was the distribution of English and Irish estates to William's subordinates and friends. And the final

50. Kinsley, *The Poems,* III, 1323.

lines of this passage draw the *Aeneid* close to the charges laid
against the expanding European wars that Dryden and others
claimed were draining the English treasury in an endless European escapade. The topics derive from Virgil but the application, the particular thrust of the language, is Dryden's own.
And so it is at crucial junctures throughout both epic and dedicatory essay:

> We are to consider him as writing his Poem in a time when the Old
> Form of Government was subverted, and a new one just Established
> by *Octavius Caesar:* In effect by force of Arms, but seemingly by the
> Consent of the *Roman* People.[51]

Such language clearly suggests the Jacobite reading of the Glorious Revolution: the subversion of government under the pretense of reform, the use of arms under the guise of public consent, the tyranny consequent on altering fundamental laws and
constitutions. None who spoke the language of late-seventeenth-
century politics could possibly have mistaken the English identity
of this Roman history. And yet of course Dryden's dedicatory
essay is a work of literary criticism; it addresses the nature of
epic, but it wanders into long digressions on Roman history,
and it is through such digression that Dryden establishes the
subtext of his argument. Dryden was engaged in an elaborate
and artful masquerade, a mode of political argument in which
he and his contemporaries had long been schooled. And there
is something quite fitting that the great epic project of these last
years of the seventeenth century should have been a translation,
and moreover a translation that chose not to celebrate empire
and conquest but to see those martial achievements in a compromised light.

   That this century should end on a note of irony is especially
fitting not only to the argument that I have made about the
intersection of political motives and literary enactments but as
well to our sense of the whole of the age and to the perception
of men living through those times. That Virgil's epic should be
rendered in Dryden's brooding political translation, that the
celebration of empire should turn into a lament over the inev-

51. Ibid., p. 1012.

itability of invasion and conquest, and that epic should become elegy argues not only that men were willing to allow literary conventions to mask political statement, but that the very forms and conventions themselves underwent their own translation in the course of this age, that the steady undermining of literary genres had an effect on the stability and function of those genres and on the way in which conventions and idioms allowed men to see the world they addressed. No one understood the effect of deceit on language and politics better than John Wilmot, the earl of Rochester, and his address to that complex interplay returns us to the speculations on language and disguise with which this essay began:

> Is or Is Not, the two great ends of Fate,
> And True or False, the subject of debate,
> That perfect or destroy the vast designs of state—
>
> When they have racked the politician's breast,
> Within thy bosom most securely rest,
> And when reduced to thee, are least unsafe and best.
>
> But Nothing, why does Something still permit
> That sacred monarchs should in council sit
> With persons highly thought at best for nothing fit,
>
> While weighty Something modestly abstains
> From princes' coffers, and from statesmen's brains,
> And Nothing there like stately Nothing reigns?
>
> Nothing! who dwellst with fools in grave disguise,
> For whom they reverend shapes and forms devise,
> Lawn sleeves and furs and gowns, when they like thee look
>      wise:
>
> French truth, Dutch prowess, British policy,
> Hibernian learning, Scotch civility,
> Spaniards' dispatch, Danes' wit are mainly seen in thee;
>
> The great man's gratitude to his best friend,
> Kings' promises, whores' vows—towards thee they bend,
> Flow swiftly into thee, and in thee ever end.[52]

52. "Upon Nothing," *The Complete Poems of John Wilmot, Earl of Rochester*, ed. David M. Vieth (New Haven, 1968), pp. 119–120.

This poem argues that the corruption of politics and morals is consequent on the dislocation of language, a lesson that few of Rochester's contemporaries were able to contemplate with such detachment. It was, I think, a lesson best learned at court, but it must have taken an act of powerful disinterestedness to teach it with such clarity and precision. The satire makes sweeping universal claims; it has as well contemporary application. The apposition of kings' promises and whores' vows is a comment on the ways of this fallen world, but it also conjures with startling explicitness the center of that world in the late seventeenth century.

IV  Genre and Audience

MARJORIE GARBER

# "What's Past Is Prologue": Temporality and Prophecy in Shakespeare's History Plays

> *Will you see the players well bestow'd?*
> *Do you hear, let them be well us'd, for they are*
> *the abstract and brief chronicles of the time.*
>
> —*Hamlet*, 2.2.522–525

> *Transference, far from being a time machine by*
> *which one may travel back to see what one has*
> *been made out of, is a clarification of certain*
> *constituents of one's present psychoanalytic actions.*
> *This clarification is achieved through the circular*
> *and coordinated study of past and present.*
>
> —Roy Schafer, *The Analytic Attitude*

Immediately after the assassination of Julius Caesar, Brutus proposes a macabre ceremony to consecrate the act:

> Stoop, Romans, stoop,
> And let us bathe our hands in Caesar's blood
> Up to the elbows, and besmear our swords;
> Then walk we forth, even to the market-place,
> And waving our red weapons o'er our heads,

> Let's all cry, Peace, freedom, and liberty!
>> (*Julius Caesar,* 3.1.105–110)

Cassius' response to this scenario is significant, for he speaks of it in terms of both theater and history:

CASSIUS Stoop, then, and wash. How many ages hence
  Shall this our lofty scene be acted over
  In states unborn and accents yet unknown!
BRUTUS How many times shall Caesar bleed in sport,
  That now on Pompey's basis lies along
  No worthier than the dust!
CASSIUS             So oft as that shall be,
  So oft shall the knot of us be call'd
  The men that gave their country liberty

>> (3.1.111–119)

For the audience in the theater this is an extraordinary dramatic moment. We are, in fact, watching that "lofty scene . . . acted over" in a state which was then unborn and an accent then unknown, for Shakespeare's *Tragedy of Julius Caesar* is the reenactment of the conspirators' bloody deed. But the audience is hardly disposed to view Caesar's murderers as "the men that gave their country liberty." Instead the disjunction between Cassius' confident prediction and the scene we see before us underscores the irony; the scene is the theatrical equivalent of a double take. We are privy to knowledge that Cassius and Brutus cannot have, and what we see before us is a flat contradiction of their expectations.[1]

In *Antony and Cleopatra,* another play of Roman history, Cleopatra creates a scenario of her own. Since she has been defeated by Octavius Caesar, she imagines that she and Antony will be ridiculed upon the Roman stage:

> The quick comedians
> Extemporally will stage us, and present
> Our Alexandrian revels: Antony

---

1. Herbert Lindenberger, in *Historical Drama* (Chicago, 1975), comments on the "exemplary nature of the action" and the "continuity between Roman greatness and the Elizabethan present" in this scene (p. 8). Lindenberger mentions parenthetically, but does not discuss at length, "the irony with which we read the words 'lofty' and 'acted.' "

> Shall be brought drunken forth, and I shall see
> Some squeaking Cleopatra boy my greatness
> I' th' posture of a whore.
>
> (5.2.216–221)

This is, of course, exactly what the spectators in Shakespeare's theater would have seen—a boy in the part of Cleopatra, Antony portrayed as drunken and doting. Like Cassius and Brutus, Cleopatra anticipates an event—and a play—that is for her as yet unwritten, but that we now see and hear. Yet once again disjunctive ironies are at work. The boy does not detract from Cleopatra's greatness, and Antony's participation in Alexandrian revels adds to his attractiveness as a dramatic character, especially when we compare him to the straight-laced and abstemious Octavius Caesar. Cassius foresaw a play that would ennoble him, and instead he is diminished. Cleopatra foresees a play that will demean her, and instead she is glorified. In both cases the spectator is offered a double vision of history, as chronicle and theater.

A similar prediction of future response is made in *Troilus and Cressida,* but in this case the irony comes not from the disjunction of prediction and outcome but from the conjunction of the two. Learning that Cressida returns his affections and his passions, Troilus declares his faith to her and is answered with similar pledges from Cressida and Pandarus:

TROILUS True swains in love shall in the world to come
   Approve their truth by Troilus. When their rhymes,
   Full of protest, of oath and big compare,
   Wants similes, truth tir'd with iteration,
   As true as steel, as plantage to the moon,
   As sun to day, as turtle to her mate,
   As iron to adamant, as earth to th' centre,
   [Yet] after all comparisons of truth
   (As truth's authentic author to be cited)
   "As true as Troilus" shall crown up the verse,
   And sanctify the numbers.
CRESSIDA        Prophet may you be!
   If I be false, or swerve a hair from truth,
   When time is old [and] hath forgot itself,
   When water-drops have worn the stones of Troy,

And blind oblivion swallow'd cities up,
And mighty states characterless are grated
To dusty nothing, yet let memory,
From false to false among false maids in love,
Upbraid my falsehood! When th' have said as false
As air, as water, wind, or sandy earth,
As fox to lamb, or wolf to heifer's calf,
Pard to the hind, or step-dame to her son,
Yea, let them say, to stick the heart of falsehood,
"As false as Cressid."

PANDARUS  Go to, a bargain made, seal it, seal it. I'll be the witness.
Here I hold your hand, here my cousin's. If ever you prove false to
one another, since I have taken such pain to bring you together, let
all pitiful goers between be call'd to the world's end after my name;
call them all Pandars. Let all constant men be Troiluses, all false
maids Cressids, and all brokers-between Pandars! Say, amen.

(3.2.173–204)

Pandarus' prayer, of course, has already been answered by the
time the members of the audience behold this spectacle upon
the stage. "Prophet may you be!" says Cressida, and prophet
Troilus becomes. But he prophesies something that the audience
already knows to have come true. Troilus and Cressida *are* the
legendary patterns of truth and falsehood in love. By an adroit
manipulation of time, a kind of theatrical sleight of hand, Shakespeare has his characters look forward to an event on which the
audience looks backward.

The subject of prophecy has been raised earlier in *Troilus
and Cressida* by the appearance of Cassandra, who predicts the
fall of Troy. "Cry, Trojans, cry! lend me then thousand eyes, /
and I will fill them with prophetic tears" (2.2.101–102). "Troy
burns, or else let Helen go" (l. 112). Hector rightly understands
these words as "high strains / Of divination" (ll. 113–114) and
urges that they be heeded, but Troilus and the rest of the Trojans
dismiss them as the "brain-sick raptures" of "our mad sister"
(l. 98). Once again, the audience knows the facts of history as
the characters within the play cannot. Cassandra's prediction is
no news to us, and when the Trojans ignore it we are again
placed in an anomalous position. Because of the conventions
of the theater the audience cannot intervene, cannot speak out
to tell the truth.

We are left with an awareness of dramatic irony that is akin to our frustration, in other dramatic genres, at not being able to inform Othello of Iago's plots, or Romeo that Juliet is alive, or Lear of Cordelia's love. Yet what is disconcerting about *Troilus and Cressida* and *Julius Caesar* is not that the audience has understood better or observed more closely than characters on the stage, but rather that it enjoys—or suffers—the benefit of hindsight. We are in fact in a situation very similar to that of Cassandra. Like her, we possess a vision of historical events which we are powerless to communicate in such a way that it could influence the course of dramatic action. And this powerlessness is paradoxically a function of our very belief in the truth of history: dramatic irony not only accompanies but indeed reinforces a sense of historical inevitability.

This mode of dramaturgical manipulation bears a striking resemblance to the doctrine of moral teleology known as providential history. Providential history, which dates back at least as far in Western culture as Augustine's *City of God,* maintains that however muddled or unfortunate events may seem from the clouded vantage point of earth, God has a plan, and historical events—including war, riot, regicide, and deposition—are all preordained to bring about a glorious end. "And God saw that it was good." Works of deterministic national or typological history from Genesis to the *Aeneid* offer such a view to their readers, and in the middle of this century a number of influential literary critics, notably E. M. W. Tillyard, Lily B. Campbell, and Irving Ribner, maintained that providential history in the form of the so-called Tudor myth gave shape to Shakespeare's English history plays.[2] Edward Hall's *Union of the Two Noble and Illustre Families of Lancaster and York* (1543) was the premier (but by no means the only) example among the chronicles to emphasize God's guidance of England during the fifteenth century toward the ineluctable and gratifying dominance of the House of Tudor, the union of the white rose and

2. E. M. W. Tillyard, *Shakespeare's History Plays* (New York, 1946); Lily B. Campbell, *Shakespeare's "Histories": Mirrors of Elizabethan Policy* (San Marino, Calif., 1947); Irving Ribner, *The English History Play in the Age of Shakespeare* (rev. ed. New York, 1965); M. M. Reese, *The Cease of Majesty: A Study of Shakespeare's History Plays* (New York, 1961).

the red. The chaotic events of the Wars of the Roses, which
would be aptly (if inadvertently) characterized by Horatio's be-
wildered account of the plot of *Hamlet* ("carnal, bloody, and
unnatural acts . . . accidental judgments, casual slaughters, /
. . . deaths put on by cunning and forc'd cause, / . . . purposes
mistook / Fall'n on th' inventors' heads" [*Hamlet*, 5.2.381–385])
all conduced with a pleasing inevitability to the accession of
Richmond (Henry VII) and his splendid successors, Henry VIII,
Queen Elizabeth, and King James. Recent revisionist criticism
of the history plays—and indeed of fifteenth-century history—
has challenged the preeminence of this belief in Shakespeare's
mind as in his sources. But where as a naive object of political,
ethical, or theological faith the idea of providential history seems
increasingly questionable, a similar process of interpreting or
reshaping the events of the past in light of their results makes
considerable sense in terms of the dramatic construction of the
plays—not God ordaining births and deaths and the outcome
of battles, but the playwright's hand manipulating the expectations and responses of the audience. Here a reader-response,
or more properly an audience-response, approach to the play
usefully translates a problem in moral teleology into a problem of structural analysis: how do we know that certain developments are likely to follow from certain actions? How
does that prior knowledge affect our observation, interpretation, and evaluation of those actions? And can the ways in
which our knowledge is manipulated by the playwright serve
as a starting point for the definition of the history play as a
genre?

   While the history play is not the only dramatic genre to make
the claim that "it happened this way," it is perhaps alone in
situating the represented events at a definable temporal distance
from, but along the same line as, the audience's present. The
history play seems to say to the audience: "This is your past."
In the experience of the playgoer, however, the past becomes
a future: when the audience enters the theater, the historical
events are yet to come. The history play as such is thus lodged
in the paradoxical temporality of what the French call the *futur
antérieur,* the prior future, the tense of what "will have oc-

curred."[3] Jacques Derrida has analyzed the logic of the anterior future in his discussion of the preface as a genre:

> The preface would announce in the future tense ("this is what you are going to read") the conceptual content or significance . . . of what will *already* have been *written* . . . From the viewpoint of the fore-word, which recreates an intention-to-say after the fact, the text exists as something written—a past—which, under the false appearance of a present, a hidden omnipotent author . . . is presenting to the reader as his future.[4]

A similar logic of retrospective anticipation underlies the "prior past that is still to come"[5] in Shakespeare's histories. And the most condensed form of the temporal paradoxes of the historical *futur antérieur* occurs in the form of the prophecy. A close analysis of the functioning of prophecy in these plays may therefore help to clarify the specificity of the history play as a dramatic genre.

The position of the prophet and diviner was an ambiguous one, historically as well as theatrically. Although widely practiced, the arts of sorcery were viewed by orthodox Christians as contrary to God's law. Thus Dante placed fortunetellers and diviners in the Eighth Circle of Hell, where they are aptly punished by being forced to walk backward in order to see where they are going. They are condemned, that is, to advance relentlessly—and hopelessly—in the wrong direction, as retributive punishment for their presumptuous claims to see into the future.

> mirabilmente apparve esser travolto
> ciascun tra 'l mento e 'l principio del casso,
>     ché da le reni era tornato 'l volto.
> e in dietro venir li convenia,
> perché 'l veder dinanzi era lor tolto.
>
> each, amazingly, appeared contorted
> between the chin and where the chest begins;

---

3. The generic applications of this paradox have been exploited by Jean Giraudoux in the title of his play *La Guerre de Troie n'aura pas lieu*.

4. Jacques Derrida, *Dissemination*, trans. Barbara Johnson (Chicago, 1981), p. 7.

5. Ibid., p. 334.

>they had their faces twisted toward their haunches
>and found it necessary to walk backward,
>because they could not see ahead of them.
>
>                                            (*Inferno*, 20.11–15)[6]

We may take the curious physical deformity of Dante's diviners as an appropriate metaphor for the dramatic function of Shakespearean prophets and their prophecies. In "real" time—the time of the audience, the time of the performance—they are, so to speak, looking backward, at events that have already taken place. In dramatic time—the context of the plays in which they appear—they are looking forward at anticipated events in the future. The result is a remarkable theatrical illusion, hindsight masquerading as foresight.

Political prophecy as a mode of predicting future events not only existed but indeed flourished in England from the twelfth century to the seventeenth. Such prophecies, attributed to authoritative figures like Saint Jerome, the Venerable Bede, Thomas à Becket, Merlin, and the Cumaean Sibyl, had a remarkable persuasive force; as was the case with Shakespeare's particular dramatic use of this device, historical prophecies derived some of their considerable power from the fact that they employed history as a predictive fiction—once again purporting to describe events taking place in the future while actually chronicling developments from the past. As a recent student of these prophecies observes, "the greater part of most of them was actually disguised history; gaining their credibility by this 'foretelling' historical events, the prophecies then went on to present their own partisan messages . . . Filled with veiled topical allusions and disguised references to contemporary figures, these pieces were both lively and compelling—lively because they responded to the political fortunes and misfortunes of the moment, compelling because they predicted the fate of powerful men and women and foretold the future of England."[7]

6. Allen Mandelbaum, trans., *Inferno*, in *The Divine Comedy of Dante Alighieri* (Berkeley, 1980).

7. Sharon L. Jansen Jaech, "Political Prophecy and Macbeth's 'Sweet Bodements,' " *Shakespeare Quarterly*, 34 (1983), 291. See also, on the general topic of political prophecy, Rupert Taylor, *The Political Prophecy in England* (New York, 1911).

This art of retrospective prognostication was often put to use when contemporary events seemed to require—or potentially to benefit from—authoritative validation, preferably supplied by historical (or mythic) figures who were both suitably well known and conveniently deceased, and thus, as Keith Thomas notes, "in no position to deny [the] authenticity" of prophecies attributed to them.[8] Although most worldly-wise observers tended to discount such prophecies as fit only for superstitious old people and children (the impatient and "modern" Hotspur, for example, dismisses them as "skimble-skamble stuff" [*1 Henry IV*, 3.1.152]), they were forced to acknowledge the effect no matter how much they deplored the cause. Thus Francis Bacon writes in his essay *Of Prophecies* that such prognostications "ought all to be despised; and ought to serve but for winter talk by the fire side," but he goes on immediately to point out that "they have done much mischief," and attributes their popular success to three things: "First, that men mark when they hit, and never mark when they miss; as they do generally also of dreams. The second is, that probable conjectures, or obscure traditions, many times turn themselves into prophecies; while the nature of man, which coveteth divination, thinks it no peril to foretell that which indeed they do but collect . . . The third and last (which is the great one) is, that almost all of them, being infinite in number, have been impostures, and by idle and crafty brains merely contrived and feigned after the event past."[9]

The most important source for the language of prophecy in Tudor and Stuart England was *The Whole Prophecies of Scotland, England, France, Ireland, and Denmark,* published at Edinburgh in 1603 and again in 1615. The single most influential prophetic figure was the legendary "Merlin," a conflation of historical and mythic figures sometimes identified with the Welsh bard Myrddin, and sometimes with the "Ambrosius Merlin" mentioned by Geoffrey of Monmouth in the seventh book of his *History of the Kings of Britain.*[10] The association of Wales

8. Keith Thomas, *Religion and the Decline of Magic* (London, 1971), p. 392.

9. James Spedding, Robert Lesle Ellis, and Douglas Denon Heath, eds., *The Works of Francis Bacon* (London, 1861), VI, 465.

10. Thomas, *Religion,* p. 394.

with prophecy in general, and the authoritative figure of Merlin in particular, is several times acknowledged by Shakespeare in such a way as to indicate his audience's general familiarity with these traditions. Thus the Fool in *Lear* footnotes his own riddling prophecy with characteristic temporal handy-dandy, calling attention to its paradoxical structure of belatedness: "This prophecy Merlin shall make, for I live before his time" (3.2.95). Likewise in *1 Henry IV* a disbelieving Hotspur speaks contemptuously of both "the dreamer Merlin and his prophecies" and the Welshman Owen Glendower's faith in a variety of animal prognostications, all identifiable as actual historical prophecies of the time: "a dragon and a finless fish, / A clipwing'd griffin and a moulten raven, / A couching lion and a ramping cat" (3.1.49–51), and, most famous of all, "the moldwarp and the ant" (l. 147).

The celebrated "moldwarp prophecy," which dated from the early fourteenth century, predicted the division of England into three parts after the wicked mole (or moldwarp), the sixth king after John, has been driven from the kingdom by a dragon, a wolf, and a lion. Keith Thomas points out that it "had been used by the Percies in their rising against Henry IV in the early fifteenth century, and, despite obvious difficulties of chronology, was [late] brought into action to combat Henry VIII."[11] Holinshed remarks on the "foolish credit given to [this] vain prophecy" and cites, approvingly, a witticism of his fellow chronicler: "Such is the deviation (saith Hall) and not divination of those blind and fantastical dreams of the Welsh prophesiers."[12] Hotspur's invocation—and summary dismissal—of this hoary forecast indicates at once his impatience with the irrational and imaginative side of human behavior—we may recall his equal disdain for poetry and for Lady Mortimer's enchanting song in Welsh—and his view of this particular prophecy as old-fashioned and especially beneath a modern man's notice—a short-sighted and unwise (though not uncharacteristic) political judgment. Indeed, as Thomas observes, the revival of such

11. Ibid., p. 399.
12. Richard Hosley, ed., *Shakespeare's Holinshed* (New York, 1968), p. 102 (Chronicles, 1587 ed., p. 149).

prophecies was often the result of a deliberate and highly plotted purpose:

at the heart of the belief in prophecies there lay an urge to believe that even the most revolutionary doings of contemporaries had been foreseen by the sages of the past. For what these predictions did was to demonstrate that there was a link between contemporary aspirations and those of remote antiquity. Their function was to persuade men that some proposed change was not so radical that it had not been foreseen by their ancestors. This had the effect of disguising any essentially revolutionary step by concealing it under the sanction of the past approval. Prophecies, therefore, were not simple morale-boosters; they provided a "validating charter" (to adopt the anthropologists' phrase) for new enterprises undertaken in the face of strong contemporary prohibitions. They justified wars or rebellions and they made periods of unprecedented change emotionally acceptable to those who lived in them.[13]

Such prophecies might be conservative or monarchist as well as revolutionary; King James was popularly supposed to be the fulfillment of a "Merlin prophecy" about the restoration of Britain under a new Arthurian king.[14] But whatever their political objectives, prophecies offered the playwright a useful and suggestive model for the "emplotment"[15] of historical drama by

13. Thomas, *Religion,* p. 423.

14. Robert F. Brinkley, *Arthurian Legend in the Seventeenth Century* (New York, 1970), p. 7.

15. "Emplotment" is Hayden White's useful term for the arrangement of historical detail into a story. White distinguishes stories from chronicles, observing that "Chronicles are, strictly speaking, open-ended. In principle they have no *inaugurations;* they simply 'begin' when the chronicler starts recording events. And they have no culminations or resolutions; they can go on indefinitely . . . The historian arranges the events in the chronicle into a hierarchy of significance by assigning events different functions as story elements in such a way as to disclose the formal coherence of a whole set of events considered as a comprehensible process with a discernible beginning, middle, and end" (*Metahistory* [Baltimore, 1973], pp. 6–7). "Unlike the novelist," White explains, "the historian confronts a veritable chaos of events *already constituted,* out of which he must choose the elements of the story he would tell. He makes his story by including some events and excluding others, by stressing some and subordinating others. This process of exclusion, stress, and subordination is carried out in the interest of constituting *a story of a particular kind.* That is to say, he 'emplots' the story" (ibid., p. 6n.).

encoding a foreseeable (and fulfillable) end within the unfolding story line of the play.

Historical prophecies occurred in a wide variety of styles and forms, many of them represented in Shakespeare's plays. Among these were animal symbols like the heraldic beasts favored by Glendower, or the prophecy of the "lion's whelp" in *Cymbeline*—another play with a Welsh setting—that foresees the happy reunion of Posthumus Leonatus with his wife Imogen and the restoration of the King's lost sons: "then shall Posthumus end his miseries, Britain be fortunate and flourish in peace and plenty" (5.4.143–144); astrological prophecies, like those scornfully discounted by Cassius and Edmund; and alphabetic prophecies, like the one that sends Clarence to the Tower in *Richard III*. This last instance is a good example of the characteristic way in which Shakespeare turned current historical practice to his own dramatic purposes. According to the chronicler Edward Hall, "the fame was that the king or the Quene, or bothe [were] sore troubled with a folysh Prophesye, and by reason thereof began to stomacke & grevously to grudge against the duke [of Clarence]. The effect of which was, after king Edward should reigne, one whose first letter of hys name shoulde be a G."[16] In Shakespeare's *Richard III* we hear about this prophecy from the disheartened Clarence himself, who confides his account of the King's displeasure to an apparently sympathetic Richard. Edward, he reports, "hearkens after prophecies and dreams,"

> And from the cross-row plucks the letter G,
> And says a wizard told him that by G
> His issue disinherited should be;
> And, for my name of George begins with G,
> It follows in his thought that I am he.
>                                 (1.1.55–59)

Here Clarence and the chronicle agree, and Richard is quick to reinforce this sense of royal caprice: "Why this it is," he says, "when men are rul'd by women; / 'Tis not the King that sends you to the Tower, / My Lady Grey his wife, Clarence, 'tis she /

16. Edward Hall, *The Union of the Two Noble and Illustre Families of Lancaster and York* (1548), in Geoffrey Bullough, *Narrative and Dramatic Sources of Shakespeare* (London and New York, 1975), III, 249.

That tempers him to this extremity" (ll. 62–65). For this assev-
eration, too, there is authority and corroborative detail in Hall's
chronicle: "the king or the Quene, or bothe" are responsible
for Clarence's plight. But moments before the audience has
privately been vouchsafed a different version of the prophecy
story by Richard himself in his opening soliloquy:

> Plots have I laid, inductions dangerous,
> By drunken prophecies, libels, and dreams,
> To set my brother Clarence and the King,
> In deadly hate the one against the other;
> . . . . .
> This day should Clarence closely be mew'd up
> About a prophecy, which says that G
> Of Edward's heirs the murtherer shall be.
>
> (ll. 32–40)

"Plots" and "inductions" are properly theatrical as well as historical contrivances. Moreover, the prophecy itself has an implicit ambiguity about it, typical of its genre (because capable
of multiple "right" interpretations and fulfillments) but also
highly germane to Shakespeare's own plots and inductions. "G"
is to be the murderer of Edward's heirs. Twice in this scene,
following Hall, "G" has been identified with Clarence's Christian name, and the identification has been underscored by Richard's characteristic gallows humor. Why has the King sent
Clarence to the Tower? "Because my name is George." "Alack,
my lord," rejoins Richard, "that fault is none of yours; / He
should for that commit your godfathers" (ll. 46–48). And again,
a few lines later, Clarence says that "for my name of George
begins with G, / It follows in his thought that I am he" (ll. 58–
59). In the King's thought, perhaps, but not in Richard's—nor
in Shakespeare's. If "G" can stand for George, it can also stand
for Gloucester—and understood in this second way the prophecy indeed comes true. In effect Richard signs his own name—
or, at least, his initials—to the crime. "G" will murder Edward's
heirs. And like Oedipus, or the hapless man who had an appointment with death in Samarra, Edward brings on his own
fate even as he seeks to avoid it.

In this episode Shakespeare takes an extant political prophecy
of the time and turns it to his own purposes, presuming upon

the dramatic convention that prophecies always come true, but adding a twist of his own. Each of the play's competing playwrights—Richard and Shakespeare—uses the prophecy for his own ends, appropriating any foreknowledge the audience might possess about the historical prophecy concerning "G" and building it in to our sense of discrepant awareness or dramatic irony, since the audience's interpretation of the encoded text, the magic letter "G," is sharply different from Clarence's own. That the most evidently true answer to this riddle ("G" signifies Gloucester, not George) is never explicitly developed in the text intensifies the discrepancy between onstage and offstage perception.

A similar Shakespearean twist is given to historical prophecy as it appears in *King John*. In this case we have two prophecies, the first functioning as a kind of norm or control, offering a context of expectation that the second prophecy will violate by fulfilling itself in an unexpected and ironic fashion. In act 3, scene 4, Pandulph, the Pope's legate, predicts young Arthur's death at the hands of his uncle, King John. Pandulph's speech has all the hallmarks of prophetic self-advertisement, signaling to the audience a by-now-familiar inexorability:

> Now hear me speak with a prophetic spirit;
> For even the breath of what I mean to speak
> Shall blow each dust, each straw, each little rub,
> Out of the path which shall directly lead
> Thy foot to England's throne. And therefore mark:
> John hath seiz'd Arthur, and it cannot be
> That whiles warm life plays in that infant's veins,
> The misplac'd John should entertain an hour,
> One minute, nay, one quiet breath of rest.
> A sceptre snatch'd with an unruly hand
> Must be as boisterously maintain'd as gained;
> And he that stands upon a slipp'ry place
> Makes nice of no vild hold to stay him up.
> That John may stand, then Arthur must needs fall:
>                                    (3.4.126–139)

The Dolphin of France at first obtusely refuses to see how this can be to his advantage but is soon instructed in terms that recall Richard II's conscious theatricality: "John lays you plots; the times conspire with you" (l. 146). Any disturbance in the natural order will be perceived by the people as evidence of the King's guilt:

> No natural exhalation in the sky,
> No scope of nature, no distemper'd day,
> No common wind, no customed event,
> But they will pluck away his natural cause
> And call them meteors, prodigies, and signs,
> Abortives, presages, and tongues of heaven,
> Plainly denouncing venegeance upon John.
>
> (ll. 153–159)

Notice that the audience in the theater is, once again, offered a privileged insight that sets it apart. *"They"* will interpret natural events as signs, presages, and tongues of heaven, while those in the know (the Cardinal, the Dolphin, the audience) are warned against any such vulgar error. "Methinks I see this hurly all on foot" (l. 169), Cardinal Pandulph concludes with satisfaction. " 'Tis wonderful / What may be wrought out of their discontent" (ll. 178–179).

The play's second dramatic prophecy occurs in the very next scene and involves Peter of Pomfret, a local hermit whose powers of prophecy are dismissed by Holinshed with unusual vehemence. Peter was, he says,

a man in great reputation with the common people because that, either inspired with some spirit of prophecy as the people believed or else having some notable skill in art magic, he was accustomed to tell what should follow after. And forsomuch as oftentimes his sayings proved true, great credit was given to him as to a very prophet, which was no good consequence that therefore his predictions comprised undoubted events. Nay, rather [continues Holinshed with indignation] sith in this pseudoprophet or false foreteller of afterclaps, these necessary concurrents . . . were wanting . . . necessarily it followeth that he was not as he was taken but rather a deluder of the people and an instrument of Satan.[17]

These are strong words, skeptical both of the "pseudoprophet's" powers and the common people's judgment. When Shakespeare uses the Peter of Pomfret episode in his play, he transfers

___

17. Hosley, *Shakespeare's Holinshed,* p. 48 (*Chronicles,* 1587 ed., p. 180).

this skeptical attitude to King John. Thus, having returned from
among the gullible and "strangely fantasied" people in the countryside, Faulconbridge the Bastard introduces his companion to
the King:

> here's a prophet that I brought with me
> From forth the streets of Pomfret, whom I found
> With many hundreds treading on his heels;
> To whom he sung, in rude harsh-sounding rhymes,
> That, ere the next Ascension-day at noon,
> Your highness should deliver up your crown.
> KING JOHN    Thou idle dreamer, wherefore didst thou so?
> PETER    Foreknowing that the truth will fall out so.
> KING JOHN    Hubert, away with him; imprison him;
> And on that day at noon, whereon he says
> I shall yield up my crown, let him be hang'd.

> > (4.2.147–157)

Peter's prophecy is in fact fulfilled, though in an ironically troped
and diminished form, when John voluntarily agrees to surrender
his crown to Pandulph and receive it back from papal authority.
"Is this Ascension-day?" he asks.

> Did not the prophet
> Say that before Ascension-day at noon
> My crown I should give off? Even so, I have.
> I did suppose it should be on constraint,
> But (heaven be thank'd!) it is but voluntary.

> > (5.1.25–29)

The play tells us no more about the fate of Peter, though Holinshed reports with mild satisfaction that he was hanged, and
that the people blamed the King for this, since "the matter fell
out even as he had prophesied," and the words of the hermit
were "one cause, and that not the least, which moved King John
the sooner to agree with the Pope."[18]

The surprising and even disconcerting way in which this
prophecy comes true (John surrenders his crown only theatrically, in the course of a formal ceremony designed to reinvest

18. Ibid.

him with it) may remind a Shakespearean audience of an incident in a later play, when King Henry IV pledges to die in Jerusalem—a boast that ironically proves accurate when he dies, not in the Holy Land, but instead in the Jerusalem chamber at Westminster:

> It hath been prophesied me many years,
> I should not die but in Jerusalem,
> Which vainly I suppos'd the Holy Land.
> But bear me to that chamber, there I'll lie,
> In that Jerusalem shall Harry die.
>
> (*2 Henry IV*, 4.5.236–240)

Here, as so often, prophecy takes on the witty pointedness of riddle, and works by lowering or diminution. Freud distinguishes riddles from jokes by their "awakening of conscious intellectual interest" in the hearer—something jokes never do.[19] And like the riddle, the specific irony of the unexpectedly fulfilled prophecy functions in a theatrical context in a way parallel to more common kinds of discrepant awareness and so-called dramatic irony onstage.

The best examples of these Shakespearean double takes are probably the "riddles and affairs of death" (3.5.5) in *Macbeth,* the witches' puzzling and paradoxical prophecies: "none of woman born / Shall harm Macbeth" (4.1.80–81); "Macbeth shall never vanquish'd be until / Great Birnan wood to high Dunsinane hill / Shall come against him" (ll. 92–94). Both prophecies are recorded by Holinshed, who ascribes them to "a certain witch whom [Macbeth] had in great trust," and comments that "By this prophecy Macbeth put all fear out of his heart, supposing he might do what he would, without any fear to be punished for the same; for by the one prophecy he believed it was impossible for any man to vanquish him, and by the other impossible to slay him. This vain hope led him to do many outrageous things, to the grevious oppression of his subjects."[20] Once again, from the point of view of the audience, there is a double reversal in the semiotics of theater; even without knowledge of the

---

19. Sigmund Freud, *Jokes and Their Relation to the Unconscious,* trans. James Strachey (New York, 1960), p. 150.

20. Hosley, *Shakespeare's Holinshed,* p. 22 (*Chronicles,* 1587 ed., p. 174).

chronicle account, we are conditioned as spectators and auditors by the dramatic convention of historical prophecy. The audience knows that these "impossible" things will prove true, and it can do nothing with that knowledge but wait for the fulfillment of the future anterior—the future that is already inscribed.

When we speak of the "audience" we are, of course, speaking of two different audiences in temporal terms. Shakespeare's contemporaries might well be expected to know the facts of their own recent history, or at least a version of those facts. For them, anachronistic prophecies set within the plays would be reminders of what they already knew about the ensuing pattern of events, and would therefore reinforce the sense of foreboding fostered by the dramatic action. Yet Coleridge notes that even in periods immediately succeeding Shakespeare's own, the history plays seem to have been for many people the chief source of information about historical events: "Shakespeare's historic dramas produced a very deep effect on the minds of the English people, and in earlier times they were familiar even to the least informed of all ranks . . . Marlborough, we know, was not ashamed to confess that his principal acquaintance with English history was derived from them; and I believe that a large part of the information as to our old names and achievements even now abroad is due, directly or indirectly, to Shakespeare."[21] This is certainly the case for theatergoers today, as will be manifest to anyone who has ever tried to explain to students the genealogical complexities of "Edward's sacred blood." Only a small fraction of those watching Shakespeare's history plays in our time will be familiar with the personages and events they describe. For modern audiences, therefore, the relationship between history and theater is reversed. The act of prophecy becomes by convention its own guarantor of truth, and whenever we hear a prophecy spoken by an English king, noble, or cleric, we know it is destined to come true. Functionally, then, the effect of these anachronistic prophecies is really the same for both audiences, Elizabethan and modern. Whether they derive their authority from history or from theatrical convention, such

21. Terence Hawkes, ed., *Coleridge's Writings on Shakespeare* (New York, 1959), pp. 222–223.

prophecies are harbingers of truth and become a kind of plot against which the plays' protagonists may struggle in vain.

In fact, the plays themselves offer internal proof of this reversal in textual authority; repeatedly in the English history plays pointed reference is made to an authorizing, "emplotting" prophecy or curse, the most memorable and resonant evidence for which is to be found in a previous Shakespearean play, rather than in Hall or Holinshed. Thus, for example, Richard of Gloucester reminds Queen Margaret of "the curse my noble father laid on thee / When thou didst crown his warlike brows with paper" (*Richard III*, 1.3.174–175), at the same time reminding the audience of a visually arresting scene from *3 Henry VI* (1.4); and at Bosworth the ghost of Henry VI identifies himself as "Harry, that prophesied thou shouldst be king" (*Richard III*, 5.3.219), citing his own lines in an earlier play (*3 Henry VI*, 4.6.68–76). *Richard III,* as the concluding play of the first tetralogy, is particularly full of these internal self-quotations and cross references, which underscore the inevitability of prophecy and validate that inevitability with theatrical rather than chronicle precedent.

Prophecies of this kind abound in the English history plays. In *3 Henry VI* the King foresees the succession of Richmond, later to be Henry VII. At the moment when he encounters Richmond for the first time, his own son and heir, Edward, is alive, yet his prediction is instantaneous and unambiguous:

> Come hither, England's hope. *(Lays his hand on his head)*.
> 　　　　　　　　　　　　If secret powers
> Suggest but truth to my divining thoughts,
> This pretty lad will prove our country's bliss.
> His looks are full of peaceful majesty,
> His head by nature fram'd to wear a crown,
> His hand to wield a sceptre, and himself
> Likely in time to bless a regal throne.

> 　　　　　　　　　　　　　　　　(4.6.68–74)

What Somerset describes as "Henry's late presaging prophecy" (92) is of course already a fact of history to Shakespeare's audience, though in dramatic terms Richmond's victory does not take place until the end of *Richard III,* the final play of the tetralogy. Nonetheless, an awareness of that impending victory—and of the King's "divining thought"—pervades both plays. In *Richard III* Richard recalls King Henry's prophecy when he hears that his former friends are deserting his side to join forces with Richmond.

> KING RICHARD  I do remember me, Henry the Sixt
> Did prophesy that Richmond should be king,
> When Richmond was a little peevish boy.
> A king—perhaps—perhaps— . . .
> KING RICHARD  How chance the prophet could not at that time
> Have told me, I being by, that I should kill him? . . .
> KING RICHARD  Richmond! When last I was at Exeter,
> The mayor in courtesy show'd me the castle,
> And called it Rouge-mont, at which name I started,
> Because a bard of Ireland told me once
> I should not live long after I saw Richmond.
>
> (4.2.95–107)

Later, on the battlefield at Bosworth, the ghost of King Henry appears to Richmond and once more reminds us of the prophecy, identifying himself as "Harry, that prophesied thou shouldst be king" (5.3.129). The inexorable teleology of this prophecy assures Richard's defeat even before the battle. Even as the combatants prepare for their encounter on Bosworth Field, the audience knows the outcome, though Richard does not. Our roles as spectators are advanced in time; not only do we see, we foresee. Whatever sympathy we may have for Richard as compared to his faceless opponent, we know that Richmond will prevail, and that nothing succeeds like succession.

Richard ironically remarks that King Henry had not predicted his own death at Richard's hands. In fact he *had* done so, asking pointedly, "Wherefore dost thou come? Is't for my life?" (*3 Henry VI,* 5.6.29). But the King's real anguish was for the murder of his son. And on that occasion he had again looked into the future:

> thus I prophesy, that many a thousand
> Which now mistrust no parcel of my fear,
> And many an old man's sigh and many a widow's,
> And many an orphan's water-standing eye—

> Men for their sons, wives for their husbands,
> Orphans for their parents' timeless death—
> Shall rue the hour that ever thou wast born.
> *(3 Henry VI, 5.6.37–43)*

What he foresaw was, on the one hand, the Wars of the Roses, in historical time now past—but on the other hand, Shakespeare's play of *Richard III,* still to come. His prophecy thus functions in one way as the dramatic equivalent of what in the film industry is called a "trailer"—a brief anticipation of coming attractions upon the stage. From the vantage point of history, the audience knows that what he predicts has already come true. From the vantage point of drama, they must attend upon the playwright's articulation of those historical truths.

*Richard III* itself contains another famous prophecy, Queen Margaret's curse, which accurately predicts the untimely deaths of King Edward IV and the lords Rivers, Dorset, and Hastings, the change in fortunes of Queen Elizabeth, and Richard's own descent into guilt, sleeplessness, and fear. Margaret's curse becomes in effect the true plot of *Richard III,* placed in opposition to, and ultimately defeating, the "plots" and "prophecies" (1.1.32–40) Richard himself invents to gain the throne. Her curse is remembered repeatedly in the course of the play. As Rivers, Grey, and Vaughn are taken off to Pomfret and their deaths, Grey laments, "Now Margaret's curse is fall'n upon our heads" (3.3.15), and Rivers reminds him—and the listening audience—of its particulars: "then curs'd she Richard, then curs'd she Buckingham, / Then curs'd she Hastings" (ll. 18–19). Queen Elizabeth expresses the fear that she will "die the thrall of Margaret's curse" (4.1.45), and Buckingham, as he is led to execution, likewise remembers her words: "Now Margaret's curse falls heavy on my neck: / 'When he,' quoth she, 'shall split thy heart with sorrow, / Remember Margaret was a prophetess' " (5.1.25–27). Margaret's curse is in the hortatory rather than the indicative mood, expressing a wish rather than stating a fact, but it has the same structural effect as Henry VI's prophecies: it foresees what history has already told, and what the playwright—in his play—is about to tell.

The prophecy of the Bishop of Carlisle in *Richard II* anticipates, in a similar way, the events of plays to come—the civil
wars of *1 and 2 Henry IV* that are the direct result of Bulling-
brook's usurpation.

> My Lord of Hereford here, whom you call king,
> Is a foul traitor to proud Hereford's king,
> And if you crown him, let me prophesy,
> The blood of English shall manure the ground,
> And future ages groan for this foul act . . .
> O, if you raise this house against this house,
> It will the woefullest division prove
> That ever fell upon this cursed earth.
>
> (4.1.134–147)

His words—which lead to his arrest for treason—in fact look
further into the future, because the "houses" of which he speaks
are those of Lancaster and York, and his prophecy thus describes not only the political and historical action of the second
tetralogy but also that of the first. His prophecy therefore becomes anachronistic in a double sense. For while Shakespeare's
audience had yet to hear—or the playwright himself to write—
the last three plays of the second tetralogy, the audience in the
theater might well be familiar with the four plays that comprise
the first. Henry VI as an historical personage is not even a gleam
in his ancestors' eyes as *Richard II* begins, but as a dramatic
character he—and his successors—were well known to Elizabethan theatergoers from Shakespeare's early and popular series of history plays, as well as from their direct knowledge of
historical events.

The design and composition of the history plays thus enact
precisely the same pattern the plays describe. The "first tetralogy" was written earlier but chronicles events that occur in time
after the events of the "second." Theatergoers who attended
the *Henry VI* plays would have had the opportunity to learn
from them a version of the story of Henry IV and his son, a
story that would later be actualized on the stage in the *Henry
IV* plays and *Henry V*. The first tetralogy is therefore prior to
the second with respect to the consciousness of the contemporary audience, though the events of the second tetralogy are
historically prior to those of the first. Which time takes priority

here, "historical time" or the time of theatrical history? The fact that the first comes second and the second comes first instructively problematizes the whole question of double time as it relates to the genre of the history play. The first tetralogy predicts the second; the second also predicts the first.

In fact, the chronological reversal of the two tetralogies—the first beginning with the life of Henry VI, the second ending with that of his father, Henry V—suggests yet another use for the device of anachronistic prophecy. In *1 Henry VI* the Duke of Exeter remembers a "fatal prophecy,"

> Which in the time of Henry nam'd the Fift
> Was in the mouth of every sucking babe,
> That Henry born at Monmouth should win all,
> And Henry born at Windsor lose all:
> (3.1.195–198)

Shakespeare could have found this prophecy in Hall, who writes that when Henry V heard that his son had been born at Windsor, "whether he fantasied some old blind prophecy, or had some foreknowledge; or els judged of his sonnes fortune, he sayd to the lord Fitzheugh his trusty Chamberlein these words: 'My lorde, I Henry borne at Monmouth shall small tyme reigne & much get, & Henry borne at Wyndsore shall long reigne and al lese, but as God will so be it.' "[22] Shakespeare and his audience would have no need of old blind prophecies, since they had historical foreknowledge of the famous victories of Henry V and the tragic reign of his son. Like that of the Bishop of Carlisle, Henry V's prophecy as reported by Exeter prefigures not only the rest of the first tetralogy but also the entirety of the second.

Moreover, at the end of *Henry V,* as the King celebrates his triumphs in France and prepares to unify his kingdoms by marrying Princess Katherine, we hear once again of reversals to come. The political marriage is arranged with much pomp, and the King departs the stage on a ringing note: "My Lord of Burgundy, we'll take your oath, / And all the peers', for surety of our leagues. / Then shall I swear to Kate, and you to me, /

22. Hall, *Union* in Bullough, *Sources,* III, 42–43.

And may our oaths well kept and prosp'rous be!" (5.2.371–
374). But the play does not end with this happy pledge. Instead
the Chorus offers an epilogue that undoes all that had been
done and brings us back to the *Henry VI* plays:

> Henry the Sixt, in infant bands crown'd King
> Of France and England, did this King succeed;
> Whose state so many had the managing,
> That they lost France, and made his England bleed;
> Which oft our stage hath shown; and for their sake,
> In your fair minds let this acceptance take.
>                                    (Epilogue. 9–14)

At the beginning of each act of *Henry V* the Chorus had urged
the audience to use its imagination, to "piece out our imper-
fections with your thoughts" (1.prologue.23), to "entertain conjecture of a time / When creeping murmur and the poring dark /
Fills the wide vessel of the universe" (3.prologue.1–3), to "behold, / In the quick forge and working house of thought / How
London doth pour out her citizens!" (5.prologue.22–24). But
in the epilogue the audience is invited, not to imagine, but to
remember—and specifically to remember Shakespeare's *Henry
VI* plays ("Which oft our stage hath shown") as well as the
historical events contained in them. The Chorus' remarks are
at the same time a prediction of the future and a memory of
the past—the future in history, the past in theater.

In the opening lines of the epilogue we are once more reminded of the act of composition: "Thus far, with rough and
all-unable pen, / Our bending author has pursu'd the story, /
In little room confining mighty men, / Managing by starts the
full course of their glory" (ll. 1–4). By reminding us that we
are watching a play, he reminds us of our role as spectators.
Furthermore, he then goes on to quote from Henry V's own
prophecy (which, as we learned from Exeter, in *Henry VI*, "was
in the mouth of every sucking babe" [3.1.196]), "Small time;
but in that small most greatly lived / The star of England" (ll.
5–6). Henry V had predicted, according to Hall, that he would
"small tyme reigne & much get." The circle is complete. The
epilogue of *Henry V*, the last play of the second tetralogy, leads
the audience back to *1 Henry VI*, where many do indeed have

the managing of the state, and England bleeds. Once again the audience is encouraged—and enabled—to look forward by looking backward.

The whole pattern of history come full circle within the double perspective of the history play is nicely encapsulated in Shakespeare's last dramatic work, *Henry VIII,* which itself comes generically full circle by returning to the topic of chronicle and English pageantry with which the dramatist's earliest works were engaged. Where in the last play of the second tetralogy we had a final moment (the epilogue to *Henry V*) that brought us back to the earliest of the history plays from the point of view of composition, we here have a play dated 1613 that predicts the glorious reign of Elizabeth, who ruled from 1558 to 1602, as well as the reign of her successor, the monarch then on the throne, King James. If speculations on the occasion for which *Henry VIII* was written are correct, there would have been yet a further Janus effect in time, linking past figures and events with present ones, for—as Herschel Baker and others have pointed out—there is a probable link between the play and the wedding of James's daughter Elizabeth to the Elector Palatine, a leader of Protestants on the continent, which was celebrated on 14 February 1613. As Baker writes, "whether or not it was the unnamed 'stage play' scheduled for a court performance on February 16 and then abruptly cancelled because 'greater pleasures were preparing,' *Henry VIII* was most likely prompted by, if not commissioned for, the sumptuous wedding celebrations."[23] Thus James would have been envisaged as sitting in the audience, as well as on the throne, to hear the prophecy of his success—the prophecy, that is, of what was taking place at the time. Likewise his daughter, the fortunately named Elizabeth, would have received news of the future that lay ahead for her illustrious namesake and royal ancestor, Elizabeth.

*Henry VIII* concludes with what amounts to a secular epiphany scene, the presentation of the royal child, "the high and mighty Princess of England, Elizabeth" (5.4.3) in her swaddling clothes, and the by-now-customary figure of the oracular church-

---

23. Introduction to *Henry VIII,* in *The Riverside Shakespeare,* ed. G. Blakemore Evans (Boston, 1974), p. 976.

man, in this instance Cranmer, the archbishop of Canterbury. "Let me speak, sir," he entreats in the familiar predictive mode, "For heaven now bids me; and the words I utter / Let none think flattery, for they'll find 'em truth."

> This royal infant—heaven still move about her!—
> Though in her cradle, yet now promises
> Upon this land a thousand blessings,
> Which time shall bring to ripeness. She shall be
> (But few now living can behold that goodness)
> A pattern to all princes living with her,
> And all that shall succeed.
> . . . . .
>                                    Truth shall nurse her,
> Holy and heavenly thoughts still counsel her.
> She shall be lov'd and fear'd;
> . . . . .
> In her days every man shall eat in safety
> Under his own vine what he plants, and sing
> The merry songs of peace to all his neighbors.
> God shall be truly known.
> . . . . .
> Nor shall this peace sleep with her, but as when
> The bird of wonder dies, the maid'n phoenix,
> Her ashes new create another heir
> As great in admiration as herself,
> So shall she leave her blessedness to one.
> Who from the sacred ashes of her honor
> Shall star-like rise as great in fame as she was,
> And so stand fix'd. Peace, plenty, love, truth, terror,
> That were the servants to this chosen infant,
> Shall then be his.      (ll. 14–49)

"His"—that is, "yours, King James." "Thou speakest wonders," comments the King on the stage, Henry VIII, gazing upon *his* daughter Elizabeth, and describing Cranmer's prophecy as "this oracle of comfort" (ll. 55, 66). Two kings, two daughters called Elizabeth, and past history presented as future wonder. Furthermore, Shakespearean audiences then and now might call to mind a very similar anachronistic prophecy of James's reign in all its glory—the *"show of eight Kings, (the eighth) with a glass in his hand"* that predicts the triumph of Banquo's descendants in *Macbeth* (4.1.SD). That play, too, was written for court performance before the King, and James of course traced his ancestry to Banquo. Though what to Henry is an "oracle of comfort" is to Macbeth a "horrible sight" (l. 122), the two stage pictures are functionally similar in the way they conflate onstage and offstage audience, displaying to King James the present, and to the theater audience the past, through an imagined vision of the figure.

In this case the transition between theater and reality (or "stage" and "age") is a benign if not a benignant one, flattering the King with his similitude to a noble precursor. But history plays could come alive as agents of historical action in more polemical and potentially dangerous ways. The most celebrated instance of a performance staged to incite the audience to action in Shakespeare's time is that of his own *Richard II*, which was probably first performed in 1595. The play's revival in 1601 at the time of the Essex rebellion, sponsored and underwritten by the Earl's supporters, was intended as an encouragement by example for the people to depose the reigning monarch. In a spasm of regal irritation Queen Elizabeth is said to have remarked when she heard the news, "I am Richard II. Know ye not that?"[24]

Moreover, it is not only through flattery or incitement but also through seduction and betrayal that Shakespeare makes use of this predictive *hysteron proteron,* this placing of the historical cart before the theatrical or dramaturgical horse. History plays are particularly prone—as we have already seen—to the fostering of an unwilling or unwanted complicity between audience and actor. When the dramatic event the audience witnesses is either overtly or covertly one of persuasion and seduction, and when the audience is aware of the historical result of that seduction, its position is uncomfortably compromised. Under such circumstances, detachment and objectivity are difficult to maintain, especially when—as is often the case—the rhetorical

24. Peter Ure, ed., *Richard II* (London, 1961), pp. lvii–lxii. Lindenberger notes "the influence of our present situation on our interpretation of the work. Like history itself, a history play changes its meaning for us according to the shifting historical winds" (*Historical Drama,* p. 10).

persuasiveness of the dramatic character is considerable, and the pitch is being made to onstage and offstage audiences at once. Three striking Shakespearean instances of this kind of amoral suasion come to mind from the historical plays: the seduction of Lady Anne in *Richard III,* Mark Antony's funeral oration in *Julius Caesar,* and Prince Hal's "I know you all" soliloquy in *1 Henry IV.*

"We fix our eyes upon his graces, and turn them from his deformities, and endure in him what we should in another loathe and despise."[25] This is Doctor Johnson, writing not, as we might expect, of one of Shakespeare's dramatic characters, but rather of the playwright himself. Yet it is remarkable how aptly this observation fits our contemporary perception of Richard III. What really happens in the wooing scene is the seduction of the *audience*—mediated through the onstage seduction of Anne. "I cannot prove a lover," he announces with complacency (1.1.28), and thereupon proposes marriage to the widow of a man he has had killed, in the presence of the corpse of her father-in-law. His power—at once rhetorical, energetic, and erotic—is simply too much for her. And his audacity fascinates his offstage listeners as well as his onstage victim, appalling, titillating, captivating. "I'll slay more gazers than the basilisk," he had predicted in *3 Henry VI,* "I'll play the orator as well as Nestor" (3.2.187–188).

In *Julius Caesar* it is Antony who plays the orator, who sets the murderous Machiavel to school. For the theater audience the problem in the funeral oration scene is in fact one of dissociation and disentanglement, of seeking to distinguish itself from the "common herd" (1.2.264), the hooting "rabblement" (l. 244) with their "chopp'd hands" and "stinking breath" (ll. 245–246) so disparagingly described by Casca as the crown is offered to Caesar. Cassius accurately predicts the devastating effect Antony's rhetoric will have on the Roman citizens, despite Brutus' bland confidence in the power of "reason." "You know not what you do. Do not consent / That Antony speak in his funeral. / Know you how much the people may be mov'd / By

25. Arthur Sherbo, ed., *Johnson on Shakespeare,* in *Works of Samuel Johnson* (New Haven, 1968), VII, 91.

that which he will utter?" (3.1.231–234). Yet despite these warnings members of the audience are often moved by Antony's words, and consequently discomfited when, alone again upon the stage, he dismisses his easy conquest. "Now let it work. Mischief, thou art afoot, / Take thou what course thou wilt!" (ll. 259–260).

Although neither of these episodes takes the straightforward form of prophecy as we have noted it elsewhere in the history plays, both are strikingly similar to a third that does take a more direct prophetic form, and that has proved particularly disturbing to audiences in recent years: the celebrated (or notorious) "I know you all" soliloquy of Prince Hal near the beginning of *1 Henry IV.*

The prophet here is also the subject of his own prophecy. When he pleases, Hal tells us, he will "imitate the sun" (1.3.197), throw off his "loose behavior" (l. 208), "pay the debt he never promised" (l. 209), and "show more goodly and attract more eyes" than if he had never appeared delinquent, "redeeming time when men think least I will" (l. 217). Over the years listeners to this speech have labeled Hal Machiavellian, a cold user of others, one who abuses his intimacy with Bardolph, Nym, and above all, Falstaff. The shocking rejection of the broken Falstaff as an "old man," a "fool and jester," at the end of part 2 is seen as part of this same manipulative attitude, revealing Hal as an ingrate, no true friend of his innocent dupes in the tavern, whom he selfishly exploits and then casts aside (almost as Richard III does his victims).

Thus Alvin Kernan, one of the most perceptive of modern commentators on Shakespeare's history plays, notes that "There is from the beginning something cold, withdrawn, and impersonal, even icily calculating, about Hal. He jokes, drinks, and joins in the fun of the tavern world, holds long conversations with the hostess and her servants, but he seems to be *in*, not *of* this lower world. Though he may enjoy the company of Falstaff and his gang, he is fully aware of a very practical, political reason for being here, and he regards his boon companions with a hard awareness of their worth." Here Kernan quotes the "I know you all" speech in full, and comments that "There is something grim about the phrase, 'I know you all,' and something even grimmer about the adjective 'unyok'd.' "[26]

There is indeed something grim about Hal's phrase "I know you all," especially when uttered to an empty stage. The scene that ends with this famous and disquieting soliloquy has shown us Hal in easy, bantering conversation and comradeship with Falstaff and Ned Poins and has laid the plans for the Gadshill caper involving their confederates. But when Falstaff and then Poins leave the stage, and Hal begins his summary remarks with "I know you all," we in the audience may well ask ourselves how large and diverse a group is, or could be, included in that ambiguous "you." "The unyok'd humor of your idleness" may refer as aptly to the spectators in the theater as it does to the "cowards" and "rogues" in the tavern.

"I know you all." It is a chilling thought. We may recall once more Richard III's dismissive scorn, and Antony's almost anarchic joy in the workings of "mischief." Hal, of course, is no Richard; he does not despise so comprehensively, he listens, he learns, he even learns to love. And Antony, too, weeps real tears over the body of his murdered friend, even as he prepares himself for the public and powerful role of triumvir—a role that requires him, only two short scenes later, to damn his sister's son with a spot from his pen. My purpose here is not to obliterate these necessary distinctions or to adduce all these figures to an inflexible Machiavellian pattern, but merely to point out the ways—the uncomfortable, intimate ways—in which each of these characters seems to be speaking to *us,* seeking us out in our seats as they plan their futures. "I know you all." Once again, an audience may seek to displace the referent, to make "you" mean "them," not "us," to wear our rue with a difference. But the rueful fact remains that there is no difference. The audience in the theater is, despite or because of its own responses, assimilated into the shape of history as it is fashioned by these self-fulfilling prophets. We may not want Prince Hal to pluck out the heart of our mystery. But he does; he will.

Hearing these anachronistic prophecies, we know their truth

26. "The Henriad: Shakespeare's Major History Plays," in *Modern Shakespearean Criticism,* ed. Alvin B. Kernan (New York, 1970), pp. 265–266.

and are powerless to alter the course of a history that has already taken place. Only Shakespeare can do that, and he does, modifying his sources as he sees fit, introducing Queen Margaret into the English court in *Richard III* when she was by that time already in France, a pensioner of Louis XI, or altering chronology to make Hal and Hotspur contemporaries.[27] But in addition, Shakespeare uses the audience's own knowledge to validate his characters' predictions of the future. Whether we have acquired that knowledge from history or from the convention of the incremental prophecy, we become in effect Cassandras, knowing what will happen before it does, witnesses to an instant replay of something that occurs, paradoxically, both in the present and in the past. In a literal and dramaturgical sense these are indeed self-fulfilling prophecies, earnest of success—and succession—commencing in a truth.

27. Samuel Daniel describes Henry Percy as "young Hotespur" (*The First Fowre Bookes of the Ciuile Wars Between the Two Houses of Lancaster and Yorke*," 1595, 3.97.1). The Arden editor, A. R. Humphreys, is thus correct in asserting that "His unhistorical youthfulness is not new . . . it derived from Daniel" (p. xxvi; see also xxviii–xxvix), but the full dramatic effect of generational twinning of Harry Percy and Harry Monmouth is Shakespeare's own achievement.

ROBERT N. WATSON

# The Alchemist and Jonson's
# Conversion of Comedy

Ben Jonson's comedies are acts of theatrical imperialism. Dryden's famous praise of Jonson's adaptations—"He invades Authours like a Monarch; and what would be theft in other Poets is onely victory in him"—aptly describes the strategy of plays such as *The Alchemist*.[1] Jonson's thefts are not furtive: they are tactics in a proud campaign for sovereignty in the drama. He systematically subsumes the more conventional plays of his rivals. The technique is parodic, but not in any simple sense: instead of placing ridiculous versions of those plays on his stage,

1. John Dryden, *Essay of Dramatic Poesie,* in his *Works* (Berkeley, 1971), XVII, 57. For Jonson's views on imitation see his *Discoveries,* in *Ben Jonson,* ed. C. H. Herford and Percy and Evelyn Simpson, 11 vols. (London, 1947), VIII, 638–639, ll. 2466–82. The *Discoveries* also provides ample evidence that Jonson understood his writing as a constant and violent battle for precedence over contemporary rivals, for freedom from ancient authorities, and for space within genres; see, for example, Herford and Simpson, pp. 567 and 627, ll. 129–142, 2095–2100; similar arguments appear in the Induction to *Every Man Out of His Humor,* ll. 226–261.

Jonson places them implicitly in the minds of his foolish characters and shows those characters trying to live out their melodramatic fantasies within the more realistic world of Jacobean city comedy. The project he undertakes in the realm of drama is kindred to the project Cervantes undertook in the realm of fiction during the same period.[2] Jonson establishes his own generic space by creating truly quixotic characters, characters who in various ways suppose themselves central figures in a conventional plot suited to their humors—for example, a prodigal-son story (Wasp, the Knowells, the Penniboys), a sentimental melodrama (Celia, Bonario), a cuckolding fabliau (Kitely, Corvino, Fitzdotterel), a Petrarchan love story (Deliro), a disguised-magistrate plot (Overdo), a legacy-hunting fable (Volpone), a morality play (Pug, Busy), an antimasque (Truewit), a cony-catching tale (Meercraft), a New Comedy (Brainworm, Mosca), even a dumbshow (Morose).

These onstage expectations are then surprised by satire, overridden by a superior playwright-figure who (as Jonson's surrogate) encourages the conventional and egoistical expectations to collide with each other, creating his own mordant and triumphant plot out of their collision. Our own conventional expectations of plot, meanwhile, have been similarly aroused, exploited, and overruled by Jonson himself.[3] He recognized, in the dy-

2. Rosalie Colie, *The Resources of Kind,* ed. Barbara K. Lewalski (Berkeley, 1973), p. 117, describes *Don Quixote* as "a book in which literary myths of reality are faced up against that reality, to show the shallowness of rigid doctrines of *mimesis.*" While there are elements of mock-heroic in Jonson's comic strategy, he uses self-inflated characters (as does Cervantes) primarily to belittle unhealthy literary forms, rather than using the forms (as does mock epic) to belittle the characters.

3. Various critics have noted aspects of this pattern. W. David Kay, "Ben Jonson and Elizabethan Dramatic Convention," *Modern Philology,* 78 (1978), 18–28, discusses Jonson's strategies for positioning himself against the practices of his theatrical rivals; Jonas Barish, "Jonson and the Loathed Stage," in *A Celebration of Ben Jonson,* ed. W. Blissett et al. (Toronto, 1973), pp. 27–53, connects Jonson's mistrust of the popular theater with his satires on self-dramatizing characters. Nancy Leonard, "Shakespeare and Jonson Again: The Comic Forms," *Renaissance Drama,* n.s., 10 (1979), 46, notes that satiric comedy can be distinguished from romantic comedy by its tendency to "disconfirm" its characters' beliefs. Gabriele Bernhard Jackson, "Structural Interplay in Ben Jonson's Drama," in *Two Renaissance Mythmakers,* ed. Alvin Kernan (Balti-

namics of reader-response, an opportunity to ambush, not only
a variety of hackneyed traditions, but also the intellectual complacency that sustained those traditions. His victory is truly a
*coup de théâtre,* a subversive seizure of territory within the
dramatic genre. Metadrama, which serves to blur the distinction
between art and life in so many Renaissance plays, serves in
Jonsonian comedy to dispel that pleasant theatrical enchantment; it becomes a strategy for demonstrating that the audience,
like the characters and the naive playwrights for whom those
characters think they are working, has an unhealthy willingness
to surrender its grip on reality and its intellectual alertness.[4] If
we allow ourselves to be lured into mistaking the characters'
melodramatic self-conceptions for Jonson's signals of his own
generic intentions, we leave ourselves vulnerable to a humiliating reminder that, like the characters on stage, we have been
perceiving only residual images of our previous experiences at
the theater rather than the more immediate reality confronting
us in Jonson's play.

In *The New Organon* Francis Bacon calls one crucial set of
obstacles to scientific progress the "Idols of the Theater." The
theater was his metaphor for the human tendency to subjugate
what we see to what we have read, to perceive according to
received authoritative schemes (such as those of Aristotle) instead of applying our own rational judgment to the information
provided by our own senses. Jonson explicitly praises Bacon's
warning in his critical *Discoveries,*[5] and in his comedies he lit-
eralizes the metaphor in order to warn against an obstacle to
progress in the drama: the gulls in these plays are usually idol-
ators of the theater. Gestalt and genre, as Paul Hernadi has

---

more, 1977), p. 116, similarly sees the destruction of a character's fantasy as a
central action of Jonsonian comedy. Randolph Parker, "A Rite for Scholars:
The Experience of Jonsonian Comedy," Ph.D. diss., Cornell, 1975, p. 17 et
passim, discusses Jonson's exploitation of the audience's expectations.

4. Alan Dessen, *Jonson's Moral Comedy* (Chicago, 1971), p. 106, remarks
on "Jonson's characteristic assumption that his audience must be bullied out of
their complacency and stupidity into a realization of the truths he is about to
offer"; I am suggesting that the complacency is generic as well as moral, and
that the truths include dramatic realism as well as moral insight.

5. Herford and Simpson, *Ben Jonson,* VIII, 627, ll. 2090–2100.

suggested, are profoundly linked,[6] and the correlation allows Jonson to parody other playwrights in the course of satirizing common human follies. He juxtaposes the human tendency to cling to established patterns for interpreting the world with the tendency of his dramatic rivals and their admirers to cling to conventional motifs of plot and character. Only if we cast away the stale melodramatic expectations we brought to the theater and approve instead Jonson's new approach can we identify ourselves with the triumphant wits instead of with the gulls who have paid dearly for an unrealistic and unrewarding fantasy. The subliminal plays-within-the-play are the things wherein Jonson catches our literary consciences.

The confusing multiplicity that critics have often mistrusted in Jonson's plots thus becomes an artful *bricolage:* this is parody by pastiche. All generic innovations involve a reshuffling of elements from established genres, but Jonson's innovation in comedy occurs at what Alastair Fowler calls a tertiary stage, where the generic conventions are exploited as symbols in their own right.[7] The wealth of allusions to earlier forms (Old and New Comedy, Estates Moralities, and so on) that Jonson's critics have listed tirelessly are (as in Milton) less a deferential gesture toward earlier writers than an ironic and didactic subsuming of those writers. What have been enumerated as Jonson's literary sources are in many cases merely the sources from which Jonson's characters have apparently derived their doomed heroic poses and social tactics.

To recognize these allusions is to recognize that Jonson's attacks on his rivals are considerably more extensive and subversive than is commonly acknowledged: beyond the famous *poetomachia* and the explicit parodies in *Bartholomew Fair* and

---

6. Paul Hernadi, *Beyond Genre* (Ithaca, 1972), pp. 5–6.

7. Alastair Fowler, *Kinds of Literature* (Cambridge, Mass., 1982), pp. 156, 162–164. Jurii Tynyanov, "On Literary Evolution," in *Readings in Russian Poetics,* ed. Ladislaw Matejka and Krystyna Pomorska (Cambridge, Mass., 1971), asserts that "Any literary succession is first of all a struggle, a destruction of old values and a reconstruction of old elements"; cited by Heather Dubrow, *Genre* (London, 1982), p. 90. Jonson wages that struggle in a highly conscious, playful, and aggressive manner.

*The Devil is an Ass* are countless moments when the appetites and affectations of Jonson's comic characters take on a derivative literary coloring. Alvin Kernan has observed that great satire tends to exploit characters who "create grand inflated images of themselves and pompously attempt to reconstruct the world";[8] Jonson exploits characters whose grandiose self-images oblige them to reconstruct the Globe. The idea of the *theatrum mundi,* which pervades medieval and Renaissance literature, hovers in Jonson's comedies somewhere between a strategy of allusion and an existential principle: in satirizing other playwrights, Jonson is also satirizing life's tendency to imitate art, the self-dramatizing instinct by which people seek to make sense of their lives. That instinct, as Stephen Greenblatt has shown, wielded remarkable power over Elizabethan minds,[9] and Jonson himself was by no means immune.[10] Jonson's world as well as his plays must have been full of people striking half-conscious poses as unrequited lovers, court intriguers, family revengers, underpromoted malcontents, and underappreciated poetic geniuses. Jonson writes in the *Discoveries,*

I have considered, our whole life is like a Play: wherein every man, forgetfull of himselfe, is in travaile with expression of another. Nay, wee so insist in imitating others, as wee cannot (when it is necessary) returne to our selves; like Children, that imitate the vices of Stam-

8. Alvin Kernan, *The Plot of Satire* (New Haven, 1965), p. 36.

9. Stephen Greenblatt, *Renaissance Self-Fashioning* (Chicago, 1980), passim.

10. Jonson's relentless attacks on this tendency may reflect a lifelong struggle against his own impulses to replace reality with literary poses. Anne Barton, *Ben Jonson, Dramatist* (New York, 1984), p. 2, observes that Jonson's service in the Low Countries "obviously fuelled his innate romanticism—in particular the need to validate the classical literature he loved by making it part of his own, deeply felt experience. The man who told Drummond about how he had dared one of the enemy to single combat, killed him in the sight of both armies, and taken 'opima spoila' from him, clearly did what he did at the time because he was acting out things he had read." Perhaps Jonson needed the literary models to validate his experience, rather than vice versa. Poems such as "My Picture Left in Scotland" portray his frustrated hopes to replace the unromantic realities of his body with his poetic inventions, and in "A Celebration of Charis" (2, ll. 27–32) Jonson blames his conventional romantic yearnings for rendering him vulnerable to mockery as "Cupid's statue with a beard, / Or else one that played his ape / In a Hercules's shape."

merers so long, till at last they become such; and make the habit to another nature, as it is never forgotten.[11]

Characters who understand this susceptibility (as the conspirators and Lovewit do in *The Alchemist*) can both mock and manipulate those who do not, and the playwright who recognizes his fellow-playwrights' naive conventionality can achieve a similar and simultaneous conquest.[12]

Jonson's dramatic structures thus become devices for carrying on the War of the Theaters by other and subtler means, and some Renaissance equivalents of Walter Mitty are his secret agents in that war, eventually immolating themselves behind enemy lines and taking much of the enemy arsenal with them. The peculiar shape of Jonsonian comedy can be explained as the result of what might be termed generic engineering. Mikhail Bakhtin argues that the novel "fights for its own hegemony in literature . . . The novel parodies other genres (precisely in their role as genres); it exposes the conventionality of their forms and their language; it squeezes out some genres and incorporates others into its own peculiar structure, re-formulating and re-accentuating them."[13] Jonsonian comedy undertakes a very similar project. Beneath the surface action of plays such as *The Alchemist* is the ruthless and resourceful struggle of a new kind of drama—satiric city comedy—for a place in the Renaissance constellation of genres.[14]

*     *     *

11. Herford and Simpson, *Ben Jonson*, VIII, 597, ll. 1093–99.

12. Not all of Jonson's rivals, of course, were as naive as he chose to portray them. Plays such as Marston's *The Malcontent* and Beaumont and Fletcher's *Knight of the Burning Pestle* exploit dramatic conventions in similarly sophisticated ways.

13. Mikhail Bakhtin, "Epic and Novel," in his *The Dialogic Imagination,* ed. Michael Holquist, trans. Caryl Emerson and Michael Holquist (Austin, 1981), pp. 4–5. Kernan, *Plot,* p. 24, comments that "satire draws much of its nourishment from . . . false styles, delighting in parodying and inflating them until they burst." Gilbert Highet, *The Anatomy of Satire* (Princeton, 1962), p. 68, remarks that satiric parody, unlike mere playful imitation, "wounds the original." Jonson's allusions clearly damage the credibility of their sources.

14. Here I am combining several familiar terms in an effort to suggest the range, the precedents, and the inward tensions of Jonsonian comedy. Jonson

The gulls in *The Alchemist* surrender their money, their honesty, even their perceptions, in exchange for the conspirators' promise to fulfill their secret melodramatic fantasies. Jonson invites his audience to make the same mistake, and then rebukes them in a way that argues for the superiority of realistic satire. Finally he invites them to drop the role of gull and take up the role of Lovewit, sharing in Lovewit's material and intellectual triumphs by endorsing the schemes of Jonson, their own wily servant. Subtle's promises to make gold from lead are actually a cover for his more realistic project of making gold out of human follies; Jonson's representation of that fraud is similarly a cover for an effort to transform the base drama of his time into something resembling its classical Golden Age.

The play strongly suggests a correspondence between Lovewit's house and the theaters of Elizabethan London.[15] Like those theaters, the house is officially closed when the frequency of deaths from the plague reaches a certain threshold. The play's Argument explains that such an onset of plague has encouraged a group of "Coz'ners at large"—a characterization often applied to actors themselves—to form something like an Elizabethan theater company: "they here contract / Each for a share, and all begin to act. / Much company they draw, and much abuse," until "they, and all in fume are gone."[16] Along with the philosopher's stone, these author-actors melt away into thin air like Prospero's rough theatrical magic. The house of glories is merely a grimy shed once the enchantment of language has ceased to fill it (5.5.38–42).[17] The resemblance between the

himself described some of his early plays as "comicall satyres," and many works by Jonson's contemporaries have been categorized as "city comedies," a genre largely adapted from classical New Comedy and augmented with sharp portrayals of contemporary social follies. See Lee Bliss, *The World's Perspective* (Brighton, Sussex, 1983), pp. 2–10; and Brian Gibbons, *Jacobean City Comedy*, 2nd ed. (London, 1980), p. 45.

15. Herford and Simpson, *Ben Jonson*, II, 87–88, lists some of the parallels.

16. All citations of *The Alchemist* are based on the Yale edition, ed. Alvin Kernan (New Haven, 1974). The correspondence between the evanescence of the gulls' empty hopes and the evanescence of a theatrical production is suggested similarly in *Every Man in His Humor*, 4.6.55, and in *Volpone*, 1.4.159; cf. Shakespeare's *The Tempest*, 4.1.148–158.

17. Barton, *Ben Jonson*, p. 152, discusses this sad transformation.

play's opening scene and the usual backstage frenzy just before a performance is suggestive: these are indeed actors trying to quiet their nervous bickerings (including bickerings over top billing and top salary) and to redirect their predatory attentions from one another to the anticipated paying audience. Even the location of the house, in Blackfriars (4.1.131), suggests a connection with the private theater the King's Men had taken over in 1608, where many of Jonson's and Shakespeare's works were performed.

As Jonson converts that stage into Lovewit's house, Face converts Lovewit's house into an overpopulated Jacobean stage. The character of the profitable little plays Face produces suggests that Jonson is using the gulls' headlong pursuit of their fantasies to educate his audience about his parodic mode; we are invited to read satire, as if in a heavy-handed palimpsest, beneath the melodramas the characters attempt to write for themselves. Although Alexander Leggatt is doubtless correct that "behind the variety of motives the dupes profess is the lowest common denominator of greed," there is another denominator that is virtually as low and as common.[18] The house is full of tales of the sort that packed Elizabethan theaters and bookstalls: not only cony-catching stories but also versions of Marlowe's dramas of supernatural riches and pleasures, Webster's and Middleton's dramas of dynastic marriage, Shakespeare's and Spenser's adult fairy tales, even Deloney's chronicles of triumphant middle-class commercial diligence.

The first visitor to the house is Dapper, and the conspirators easily convince him that he is the star of a fairy tale, embraced by a doting Fairy Queen. Ten years earlier London audiences had laughed at the egotistical Bottom's easy acceptance of his ludicrous match with Titania in Shakespeare's *Midsummer Night's Dream;* now that same literary fantasy makes an ass of Dapper. Subtle "never heard her Highness dote till now," Face assures their eager victim. Muriel Bradbrook reports that "tradesmen wooed by the fairy queen" were one of the common devices by which Elizabethan comedies appealed to "the simple dreams of

18. Alexander Leggatt, *Citizen Comedy in the Age of Shakespeare* (Toronto, 1973), p. 74.

the unlettered audience," and one poetical soul, according to
court records, was actually prepared to pay some Jacobean
tricksters a considerable sum of money to arrange his marriage
to the Queen of Fairy.[19] Dapper is just such a manipulable
audience to Subtle and Face. A compulsive gambler is generally
someone who is perpetually pursuing evanescent hints that he
is favored by Dame Fortune, and once the conspirators have
deduced what Dapper wants to believe about himself, they can
control his perception of reality. Face claims that Subtle has
divined that Dapper was "born with a caul o' your head" (a
conventional predictor of good fortune), and when Dapper swears
this is untrue, Face simply bullies him into believing it:

>                          How!
>     Swear by your fac, and in a thing so known
>     Unto the Doctor? How shall we, sir, trust you
>     I' the other matter?
>                          (1.2.128–133)

Dapper should instead be asking the conspirators how he can
trust them in the other matter when they are wrong about a
thing so known to him as his own nativity. But the standard
fantasy of the "family romance," here sustained by the plot
device of the changeling and the context of a fairy tale, suits
Dapper's childlike mind so well that it supplants his true personal history.

Dapper's imagination is so lacking in creativity, for all its
activity, that Face can make him appreciate the benefits of the
Queen's favor only by couching them in the terms of another
standard sort of play:

>     Her Grace is a lone woman,
>     And very rich, and if she take a fancy
>     She will do strange things. See her, at any hand.
>     'Slid, she may hap to leave you all she has!
>                          (1.2.155–158; cf. 5.4.53–56)

---

19. Muriel Bradbrook, *The Growth and Structure of Elizabethan Comedy*
(1955; rpt. London, 1973), p. 78; on the same incident, see Herford and Simpson, *Ben Jonson*, X, 47–48; Herford and Simpson, X, 98, cites also the story
of John and Alice West, who swindled other dreamy innocents by posing as
"the King and Queene of Fayries."

The young wastrel redeemed by the whimsical affection of a wealthy widow was a favorite subject in the city comedies of Jonson's rivals, such as Middleton, Marston, Dekker, and (later) Fletcher.[20] Face reinforces the credence and appeal of the fairy tale, itself merely a literary convention, by conflating it with another literary convention.

As the gulling continues, Dapper's will to believe induces him to accept a stinking privy as "Fortune's privy lodgings" (3.5.79), a dead mouse as a delicacy from the Fairy Queen's private trencher (3.5.65), pickpockets as punitive fairies, a mugging as a purifying ritual, a whore as the Queen herself, and an instruction to "Kiss her departing part" (5.4.57) as evidence of her favor. Subtle and Dol each shift the play's blank verse briefly into rhyme to lend a properly poetical atmosphere (3.5.5–18, 5.4.30–31), and even the pinching that punishes Dapper for withholding a few coins is kept in line with literary precedents. The conspirators' accompanying cries of "Ti, ti, ti, ti" were evidently conventional noises for theatrical fairies, and the physical battery matches those described in *John a Kent and John a Cumber,* in Shakespeare's *Merry Wives of Windsor,* and in Lyly's *Endimion:*

> Pinch him, pinch him, blacke and blue,
> Sawcie mortalls must not view
> What the Queene of Stars is doing,
> Nor pry into our Fairy woing
>
> . . . . .
> For the trespasse hee hath donne,
> Spots ore all his flesh shall runne.[21]

One thing that makes funny Dapper's pitiful cry near the end of the play—"For God's sake, when will her Grace be at leisure?" (5.3.64)—is our recognition that this pathetic figure,

---

20. Bradbrook, *Elizabethan Comedy,* pp. 45, 154, and 251n19, discusses this motif in the works of Marston and Middleton. Among the characters similarly redeemed in Fletcher's plays are Valentine in *Wit without Money* and Young Loveless in *The Scornful Lady;* see Leggatt, *Citizen Comedy,* p. 47.

21. W. Gifford, ed., *Works of Ben Jonson* (London, 1816), IV, 114n1; Charles Baskervill, *English Elements in Jonson's Early Comedies,* Texas Univ. Studies in English (Austin, 1911), I, 12n2.

whom we and the conspirators have long forgotten, has been clinging to his ridiculous dream all this time amidst the choking stench of the privy, and speaks up only in a mannerly way that seeks not to offend the goddess who offered him this lodging and this provender. Not even Lovewit's return can shatter his fantasy: when Dapper leaves Jonson's stage for the final time, the fairy tale is still running vividly (and expensively) on the stage of his mind (5.4.57–61).

The second gull to appear, Abel Drugger, is virtually the opposite of Dapper. Their names are similar, and their gullibilities similar in extent, but where Dapper is the model of the young wastrel, Drugger is the model of the young worker, diligently striving to improve himself through commerce. So where the conspirators cast Dapper as the dashing young gallant, forever thriving at child's play, winning card games and fairy queens alike, they cast Drugger instead as the model of middle-class success, forever thriving in adult works. He is encouraged to imagine himself the hero of a Dekker play about virtue overcoming social rank, or perhaps more extensively, as the hero of a Deloney novel from the same period, about a hard-working young man propelling himself up through the social classes by his shrewd mercantile enterprises, and by the upward misalliance they permit. Where Dapper is supposedly allied to the Queen of Fairy, Drugger is promised alliance to the "rich young widow" next door (2.6.29–30). Face has evidently anticipated Drugger's dubiety and adapts it into another extension of Drugger's characteristic dream of social climbing:

DRUGGER.        No, sir, she'll never marry
   Under a knight. Her brother has made a vow.
FACE. What, and dost thou despair, my little Nab,
   Knowing what the Doctor has set down for thee,
   And seeing so many o' the city dubbed?
                          (2.6.50–54)

If this is a risky piece of satire on King James's selling of peerages, it is also an effective satire on the wish-fulfillments that lesser authors were selling to the middle class.

From his first appearance, Drugger speaks in the humble,

earnest, determined tones of one of Deloney's Horatio Algers beginning his upward journey:

> I am a young beginner, and am building
> Of a new shop, an't like your worship, just
> At corner of a street. Here's the plot on 't—
> And I would know by art, sir, of your worship,
> Which way I should make my door, by necromancy.
> And where my shelves? And which should be for boxes?
> And which for pots? I would be glad to thrive, sir.
> And I was wished to your worship by a gentleman,
> One Captain Face, that says you know men's planets,
> And their good angels, and their bad.
>
> (1.3.7–16)

The anatactic form of Drugger's speech seems to be a representation of his vision of a steadily building commercial success, and the tasks in which he wants to enlist Subtle's "necromancy" are ridiculously common and simple. Subtle agrees that he does know men's angels, and he is telling the truth, not only in his ability to recognize cozenable coins ("angels"), but also in his ability to recognize and thus manipulate the dominant spirits possessing each of the gulls. What Drugger supposes is the voice of his good angel is actually a reading from the popular literature of the time. Face, who knows exactly what conventional commercial virtues Drugger has been trained to value in himself, gains credibility with his victim by mimicking that voice:

> This is my friend Abel, an honest fellow,
> He lets me have good tobacco, and he does not
> Sophisticate it with sack-lees or oil,
> Nor washes it in muscadel and grains,
> Nor buries it in gravel underground,
> Wrapped up in greasy leather, or pissed clouts,
> But keeps it in fine lily pots that, opened,
> Smell like conserve of roses, or French beans.
> He has his maple block, his silver tongs,
> Winchester pipes, and fires of juniper.
> A neat, spruce, honest fellow, and no goldsmith.
>
> (1.3.22–32)

If this sounds exactly like a commercial advertisement, it is because that is exactly how Drugger enjoys picturing himself, standing with a friendly open face in front of all the finest products and all the latest equipment. The fate Subtle then predicts for him—"This summer / He will be of the clothing of his company, / And next spring called to the scarlet," with some greater fortune thereafter (1.3.35–37)—is precisely the progression through peer and public ranks that characterized the hero's rise in Deloney's novels and in plays such as Dekker's *Shoemaker's Holiday*. Drugger will be "the honestest fellow" and "the goodest soul"—provided he brings Subtle "a new damask suit" and a pound of tobacco (2.6.72–79); the conspirators characteristically arrange things so that Drugger must pay them to confirm his secretly treasured image of himself. Near the end of the play Face sends him off to acquire the costume of a Spanish nobleman and asks if he is well enough acquainted with the players to borrow one. "Yes, sir," Drugger replies, "did you never see me play the Fool?" (4.7.69). Drugger plays the fool here again in Lovewit's house in Blackfriars—and the irony would have been even sharper if Drugger was played by Robert Armin, the leading clown of the King's Men, as has been suggested—precisely because he does not realize he is still playing. His effort to recast himself as a citizen-hero out of Middleton, Heywood, Dekker, or Deloney has only renewed his employment as a fool in Face's and Jonson's plays.[22]

The arrival of Kastril and his sister allows the conspirators to produce profitably some other conventional plays. Though apparently rustic and illiterate, Kastril carries within him a jumble of impulses that look suspiciously like the propelling motives of several late Elizabethan dramas. He aspires to be the "Roaring Boy" of many popular comedies and ballads, and he aggrandizes that role for himself by associating it with the tragic role of

22. F. H. Mares, "The Structure and Verse of *The Alchemist*," in *"Every Man in His Humor" and "The Alchemist*,*" ed. R. V. Holdsworth (London, 1978), p. 179, suggests that "Drugger, almost certainly, was played by Robert Armin." It is interesting to consider the prominence that the role of Drugger gained as the fantasy of success by diligent and honest merchandizing became increasingly essential to England's economic system; see, for example, the brief history of the role provided by Holdsworth in his introduction, pp. 34–35.

avenger, defending his family's honor as well as his own from the seductive wiles and the social slights of more urbane fellows. He has arrived seeking not only a roaring reputation for himself but also a match for his widowed sister that will, he says grandly, "advance the house of the Kastrils" (4.4.88). Dame Pliant seems to envisage herself in such a comedy of dynastic marriage: when Subtle reads in her palm that she will soon marry "a soldier, or a man of art" who "shall have some great honor shortly," she tells her brother, "He's a rare man, believe me," suggesting that Subtle's fortunetelling has indeed matched her own dreams of the future (4.2.48–50).

Sir Epicure Mammon makes a rich study in the psychology and the paradoxes of self-dramatization. Even the role of public benefactor, which he may originally have assumed in order to conceal his selfish purposes from the supposedly pious alchemist, appeals so strongly to Mammon's vanity that he becomes absorbed by it. His visions of great innovations are precisely what prove him to be a disastrously conventional thinker. Subtle introduces Mammon as a man who has recently been talking of the stone

> as he were possessed.
> And now he's dealing pieces on 't away.
> Methinks I see him ent'ring ordinaries,
> Dispensing for the pox; and plaguy houses,
> Reaching his dose; walking the Moorfields for lepers,
> And off'ring citizens' wives pomander-bracelets
> As his preservative, made of the elixir;
> Searching the 'spital, to make old bawds young;
> And the highways for beggars to make rich.
> I see no end of his labors. He will make
> Nature ashamed of her long sleep, when art,
> Who's but a step-dame, shall do more than She
> In Her best love to mankind ever could.
> If his dream last, he'll turn the age to gold.
>                                              (1.4.16–29)

When Subtle says, "Methinks I see him," he is mockingly evoking the ridiculously worshipful way Mammon envisions himself in these holy enterprises. The only thing turned to gold by the endurance of this dream will be Subtle's pockets. But the mental picture Mammon has of his own magnificent deeds is very much a mediated vision, shaped by Renaissance literature. The Elizabethan theater, as Muriel Bradbrook has demonstrated, was obsessed with the idea of restoring the Golden Age.[23] Mammon is indeed "possessed," by a naive misreading of the more grandiose writings of his era.

Mammon at moments seems to perceive himself as the sort of modern savior who appeared frequently in Jacobean poetry, the spiritual, scientific, or sensual creator of a new world for this new age. Mammon's claim that he will have the power to "make an old man of fourscore a child" (2.1.53), already degraded by Subtle's earlier suggestion that Mammon will use the stone to "make old bawds young," clearly resembles the heroine's promise to "make the old man young" in Jonson's "Celebration of Charis" (1, 1. 20), a poetic sequence that satirizes the fatuous claims of Renaissance love lyricists. As Mammon first speaks, he reveals the accuracy of Subtle's parody, describing himself to Surly as the potential embodiment of all Renaissance aspirations, in exploration, wealth, pomp, and pleasure:

> Come on, sir. Now you set your foot on shore
> In Novo Orbe; here's the rich Peru,
> And there within, sir, are the golden mines,
> Great Solomon's Ophir!
> . . . . .
> You shall start up young viceroys,
> And have your punks and punkatees, my Surly.
> And unto thee I speak it first, "Be Rich."
>
> (2.1.1–24)

Mammon echoes the *fiat lux* of Creation here, but he is no better a God than he is a Redeemer.[24] Despite his richly festooned language, he cannot envision a world beyond the extremes of human greed and lust. Mammon, like everyone else, cannot serve both God and Mammon.

23. Bradbrook, *Elizabethan Comedy*, p. 202.
24. Dessen, *Moral Comedy*, p. 113, calls Mammon's declaration "a parody of the *fiat lux*," but it is important to note that the parodist is not Mammon but Jonson, who is using the altered phrase to reveal Mammon's thoughtless and graceless conversion to his own desires of the greatest roles he has encountered in his reading.

Mammon gradually becomes a recognizably Marlovian character, a Tamburlaine in his thirst for universal conquest, a Barabas in his absolute greed, a Faustus in his determination magically to reshape the world according to his desires.[25] The irony is that he plays the parts of these characters too well, especially that of Faustus. He unwittingly sells, if not his eternal jewel, at least his temporal ones, for a conquest of nature that can never quite lift him above mundane physical objects and mundane human appetites. Mammon's true potential, as convincingly mocked by Face, is as limited as that of Faustus, who managed only to perform some slapstick violence and to acquire fresh grapes out of season. Face says that Mammon

> would ha' built
> The city new; and made a ditch about it
> Of silver, should have run with cream from Hogsden;
> That every Sunday in Moorfields the younkers
> And tits and tom-boys should have fed on, gratis.
>                                    (5.5.76–80)

This version of Faustus' plan to erect a brass wall around Germany is absurdly domesticated.[26] Mammon's instincts as a worldly sensualist thus mar not only his performance as a magnificent conjurer but also his performance as a creating deity. At the very least, he envisions himself as one of the London Worthies praised in moralistic chronicle-plays such as Heywood's *Edward IV* and *If You Know Not Me, You Know Nobody*. In advocating his grand projects of urban renewal, Mammon repeatedly mouths "the citizen-hero code of social conduct" that had become a conventional heroic signature in Elizabethan drama.[27] Mammon speaks in texts the way possessed souls speak in tongues. His mind is like an editor's nightmare: the texts are garbled and legible only as a series of overlapping palimpsests. Mammon is approximately six characters in search of a single authentic identity. Surly tells him that, if he can indeed eliminate the plague, "the players shall sing your praises then, / Without their poets"

25. Gibbons, *City Comedy,* p. 18, remarks that "Sir Epicure is partly a parody, partly a comic counterpart of Faustus."

26. Holdsworth, *"Every Man,"* p. 32, comments briefly on this parallel.

27. Leggatt, *Citizen Comedy,* p. 76.

(2.1.71–72), but Mammon is himself a player who has forgotten his author. Those who do not understand the subtler plays of the period, Jonson suggests, are condemned to repeat them.

When Mammon tries to prove to Surly that his grand visions are realistic, he is constantly forced to resort to literary models, under the assumption that they are historical. His carelessness about that distinction reveals not only his determination to believe in the stories that would make him heroic but also the mode of misreading by which that belief primarily sustains itself:

> I'll show you a book where Moses, and his sister,
> And Solomon have written of the art;
> Ay, and a treatise penned by Adam.
> . . . . .
>        I have a piece of Jason's fleece too,
> Which was no other than a book of alchemy,
> Writ in large sheepskin, a good fat ram-vellum.
> Such was Pythagoras' thigh, Pandora's tub;
> And all that fable of Medea's charms
> The manner of our work.
> . . . . .
> Both this, th' Hesperian garden, Cadmus' story,
> Jove's shower, the boon of Midas, Argus' eyes,
> Boccace his Demogorgon, thousands more,
> All abstract riddles of our stone.
>
>                         (2.1.81–104)

The fantasy Mammon has drawn from his readings now shapes all his readings to itself; there is a warning here for critics who heap up instances without examining the validity of their grand unifying theses. He seems to be as much compelled to believe by the glorious heritage his belief provides him, as he is allowed to believe by the existence of such vague precedents.

In the next scene Mammon announces his intention "To have a list of wives and concubines / Equal with Solomon," and to satisfy them by improving his body "With the elixir" until it is "as tough / As Hercules' " (2.2.34–40). Again he is confusing the pursuit of personal physical desires with the pursuit of experiences and identities transmitted by literature.[28] Mammon

28. Myrddin Jones, "Sir Epicure Mammon: A Study in 'Spiritual Fornication,' " *Renaissance Quarterly*, 22 (1969), 233–242, suggests that Mammon

manages to become enthralled by the voluptuous roles he plays
for Surly and Dol, as well as by the contrastingly pietistic role
he plays for Subtle; he deludes himself, as he had thought to
delude others, with the false glamour the allusions lend to his
appetites. The self-alienation of Mammon's self-regard, the fact
that he is admiring himself in poses rather than participating
directly in the experience of desiring, is further emphasized by
his narcissistic plan to have his bedroom mirrors "Cut in more
subtle angles, to disperse / And multiply the figures as I walk /
Naked between my succubae" (2.2.46–48). He lets literature
mediate between himself and the most wanton indulgences of
his senses: the notes in both the Gifford edition and the Herford
and Simpson edition dissect Mammon's visions of pleasure into
a string of allusions to Seneca, Suetonius, Aristophanes, Lam-
pridius, Juvenal, Pliny, and Apicius Caelius.

Mammon recurs several times to the comparison between his
alchemical triumphs and "Jove's shower." That persistent comparison again reveals the confused grandeur of Mammon's self-
conception. His magnificent gilding of the world becomes, through
puns on "Heighten" and "stone" as well as the overall allusion,
a transparent cover for his sexual vanity:

> Now, Epicure,
> Heighten thyself, talk to her all in gold;
> Rain her as many showers as Jove did drops
> Unto his Danaë; show the god a miser
> Compared with Mammon. What! the stone will do't.
> She shall feel gold, taste gold . . .
>
> (4.1.24–29)

A hundred lines later, the same allusion is clearly lurking in his
mind, transforming his promise to fulfill Dol's wishes into a
Rabelaisian display of sexual megalomania:

> Think, therefore, thy first wish now; let me hear it,
> And it shall rain into thy lap, no shower
> But floods of gold, whole cataracts, a deluge,
> To get a nation on thee.
>
> (4.1.125–128)

---

attempts repeatedly to cast himself as King Solomon and is so taken with the
glamour of the role that he overlooks its negative implications.

The role of gold-maker is conflated, by the mythic allusion, with the role of superhuman lover; and that confusion is precisely what the conspirators use to make Mammon actually apologize to them for the disappearance of his own money and hopes in the laboratory "explosion." Mammon strikes the poses of Neo-platonic, Petrarchan, and Metaphysical love-poet, telling Dol that she "sparkles a divinity beyond / An earthly beauty!" and that he desires only "To burn i' this sweet flame: / The phoenix never knew a nobler death." "O, you play the courtier," is her chiding reply (4.1.64–69), but Mammon no longer knows himself and his sentiments from his various ennobling literary roles. He becomes a gathering of seductive clichés. His arguments against the propriety of virginity for a beautiful woman had been literary commonplaces for centuries, and that derivativeness (as with the similar arguments of Milton's Comus) is part of Jonson's point. The hyperbolic sensual inducements with which Mammon bolsters his rational arguments are (like the ones Volpone offers Celia) commonplaces in the Renaissance catalogue of exotic and exalting pleasures (4.1.96–107, 155–169). Their love affair is to be the living fulfillment of countless old love stories—"we but showing our love, / Nero's Poppaea may be lost in story!" (4.1.144–145)—but that ambition risks converting the affair itself into little more than a literary artifact.

The disaster that befalls this courtship, like the disaster that consequently befalls his pursuit of the philosophers' stone, is a poetically just punishment for the narcissistic use of literary allusions. At some point Mammon's bookish promises inadvertently echo a forbidden book, Broughton's *Concent of Scripture,* by promising to erect her "a fifth monarchy" (4.5.34), and Dol spits back at him her own mad concoction of literature, as if she were Spenser's Dragon of Error vomiting theological tracts on a similarly erroneous knight. It is also fitting that Mammon understands this disaster as poetic justice, but of the sort found in the most conventional moral tale rather than in Jonson's satiric comedy. He interprets as a divine judgment against his lust what is actually a fraudulent exploitation of his literary infatuation (4.5.82–86). The same bookishly self-important sensibility that led him into the alchemical fraud now leads him back out of it without the least sense that he has been cheated.

Face finally convinces him to flee empty-handed for fear that to stay "may breed a tragedy" (4.5.91). Even after he learns exactly how he has been gulled, his instinctive reaction is not to renounce all theatricalism, but rather (like Sordido in *Every Man Out of His Humor*) merely to seize a new kind of role on a new kind of stage: "I will go mount a turnip-cart and preach / The end o' the world within these two months" (5.5.81–82).

Mammon's companion Surly is apparently his opposite, as gruff as Mammon is grandiloquent, as skeptical as Mammon is gullible, and (despite his knowledge of bawdy-houses) almost as anhedonic as Mammon is epicurean. The irony is that Surly is nearly as enamored of his own laconic skepticism as Mammon is of his encompassing visions, and that Surly may therefore be gulled through his pride in refusing to be gulled. He resembles Edmund Wilson's image of Jonson in his anal-retentive concern with control, but Jonson's devotion to varied and vivid language contrasts sharply with Surly's monotonous speech, which suggests an overly repressive spirit.[29] Surly resorts again and again to his blunt phrase of resistance to Mammon's sort of letting-go. "I would not willingly be gulled," he says (2.2.78); he tells Subtle that he "would not be gulled" (2.3.27), swears he will not "gull myself" (2.3.124), says he is "loath to be gulled" (2.3.263), and urges Mammon to "Be not gulled" (2.3.246) and not "To gull himself" (2.3.282). This is a provocation to both the conspirators and the audience to gull the poor man, much as the wits in *Bartholomew Fair* are provoked to rob Wasp by his nagging censures of Cokes's carelessness. Subtle afterwards echoes Surly's phrase (and, in performance, probably his voice also) in gleefully speculating on ways to fool this "Monsieur Caution, that will not be gulled" (2.4.15; cf. 2.3.236); the artist in Subtle knows that "to ha' gulled him / Had been a mast'ry" (3.3.7–8).

Surly perceives that Lovewit's house has become a sort of

29. Edmund Wilson, "Morose Ben Jonson," in *The Triple Thinkers* (New York, 1948), pp. 213–232. In the *Discoveries* Jonson argues that "Language most shewes a man"; see Herford and Simpson, *Ben Jonson,* VIII, 625, ll. 2031–35. Jonas Barish, *Ben Jonson and the Language of Prose Comedy* (Cambridge, Mass., 1960), comments extensively on the correlation between speech pattern and personality in Jonson's characters.

exploitative theater, with the conspirators' baseness hidden under
the grandest disguises. He properly identifies Dol as simply a
whore, whereas Mammon had characteristically identified her
as "a Bradamante" (2.3.225), a woman knight from Ariosto's
*Orlando Furioso*. Face comments that Mammon experiences "A
kind of modern happiness, to have / Dol Common for a great
lady" (4.1.23–24). It is also a kind of theatrical happiness—to
have a boy in secondhand garments for Cleopatra, for example—and Surly is deeply unwilling to suspend his disbelief. He
comes to sound less like an incisive critic of this play, however,
than like its moralistic chorus:

> Heart! can it be
> That a grave sir, a rich, that has no need,
> A wise sir, too, at other times, should thus
> With his own oaths and arguments make hard means
> To gull himself?
> . . . . .
> I'll have gold before you,
> And with less danger of the quicksilver,
> Or the hot sulphur.
>
> (2.3.278–288)

The closing suggestion that Mammon's trust in this house exposes him to both alchemical frauds and venereal disease[30] has
been phrased in such a way that it also resembles the warning
of an old-fashioned dramatic chorus, aptly like that of *Dr. Faustus,* about the danger of hellfire.

Surly's response to the false drama he has largely penetrated
is to begin writing a moralistic drama of his own. His observations that "The hay is a-pitching" in Subtle's delaying jargon,
and that Mammon is "bolted" when he assents to the workings
of this "ferret," reveal his fixation on the conventional rabbit-
hunting metaphor of "cony-catching" stories (2.3.71–88). Surly
then begins to speak to the audience in sly asides, like the outcast
protagonists of Elizabethan plays of vengeance. But the fact
that the role of Hieronimo from Kyd's *Spanish Tragedy* is mentioned so dismissively throughout Jonson's play augurs very badly
for Surly's plan to take the role of a Spaniard and overthrow

30. See Kernan's note in his edition of the play, p. 81.

the villains by constructing his own play-within-Face's-play. Surly promises to meet Face, but tells us it will only be

> by attorney, and to a second purpose.
> 'Now I am sure it is a bawdy-house;
> I'll swear it, were the marshal here to thank me:
> The naming this commander doth confirm it.
> Don Face!
> . . . . .
> Him will I prove, by a third person, to find
> The subtleties of this dark labyrinth;
> Which if I do discover, dear Sir Mammon,
> You'll give your poor friend leave, though no philosopher,
> To laugh; for you that are, 't is thought, shall weep.
>
> (2.3.297–312)

He will laugh at how deeply Mammon was enthralled by an aggrandized vision of himself, but the way he envisions that triumph suggests much the same narcissistic error.

Surly returns to Lovewit's house prepared to defeat the conspirators at their own game, to be one level deeper into the dramatic irony than they are. His Spanish costume and language will serve to penetrate their disguises and outflank their alchemical cant. Subtle and Face's usual tactic of plotting their tricks right in front of the gulls in alchemical allegories backfires because the disguised Surly fully understands the English they suppose is foreign to him. But Surly is nonetheless defeated, and he is defeated because he is out of tune with the intentions of his creator. Jonson is certainly using echoes of Plautus here, but he is using them in a more strategic and ironic way than has been suggested. Surly has in effect dutifully memorized a role from the *Poenulus,* the role of Hanno, who rescues a young woman from a thieving procurer after strategically feigning ignorance of his native language and enduring the consequent abuse.[31] But when he tries to recite his lines, he discovers to his humiliation that Jonson has chosen to present a version of a different Plautine comedy, the *Mostellaria,* in which a wily servant (Face's ancestor) escapes with the benefits of his chicanery.

---

31. Herford and Simpson, *Ben Jonson,* X, 103, mentions part of this parallel to the *Poenulus.*

No one, including Jonson, is interested in letting Surly fulfill the role he has so proudly prepared.

In his conference with Dame Pliant, Surly makes the mistake of supposing that, as a sort of morality-play Good Counsel figure to this jeopardized female soul, he can and should simply bring the exploitative play to an end. A Jacobean audience would also have expected such a virtuous reversal at about this point in the play, like the one Wittipol provides at a similar juncture in *The Devil is an Ass,* rescuing the good woman from both gulls and gullers without preying on her himself.[32] Once he is alone with Dame Pliant, Surly is too obsessed with the notion of his triumphant reversal of the plot to act with any spontaneous self-interest, and she is simply not up to her part as his co-star in such a sentimental romance. This captive maiden does not have in herself the character to recognize and repay his witty rescue. Like Dapper earlier, Surly expects the standard reward of a reformed gamester in the period's drama—a wealthy widow—to be bestowed on him in a standard scenario of just deserts:

> I am a gentleman, come here disguised,
> Only to find the knaveries of this citadel,
> And where I might have wronged your honor, and have not,
> I claim some interest in your love. You are,
> They say, a widow, rich; and I am a bachelor,
> Worth nought. Your fortunes may make me a man,
> As mine ha' preserved you a woman. Think upon it,
> And whether I have deserved you or no.
> DAME PLIANT.                    I will sir.
> SURLY. And for these household-rogues, let me alone
> To treat with them.
>
> (4.6.8–17)

---

32. Holdsworth, *"Every Man,"* p. 27, comments that if Jonson had followed straightforwardly the formula of New Comedy, "Surly would be the play's hero and agent of release." William Empson, *"The Alchemist* and the Critics," in Holdsworth, p. 199, takes a similar view of Surly's defeat: "The moral atmosphere beng so firmly like Dickens, one expects this good deed to be rewarded with an ample competence." Peter Fleming, "Harlequinade: *The Alchemist* at the New Theatre," in Holdsworth, p. 222, remarks that "almost any other dramatist would have . . . put down Surly as an Honest Fellow or a Plain Dealer and given him the right to the play's final triumph."

The idea that Surly is finally defeated because (as a gamester) he is not moral enough for Jonson to permit him the victory[33] may in one sense be accurate: the moralistic and sentimental pose he strikes with Dame Pliant is so far removed from his normal self as to suggest the self-exalting, self-dramatizing impulse Jonson usually felt obliged to punish. As Lovewit suggests later, Surly was foolish to play such an elaborate and calculated role in courtship and then not follow it through immediately into a profitable marriage (5.5.50–55). When Surly triumphantly throws off his disguise—"I am the Spanish Don that should be cozened"—he is too enthralled with his listing of the offenses he has discovered to notice the accused Face slipping away under the cover of the melodramatic rhetoric. Surly has made the characteristic error of forgetting that his is not the only plot, not the only play, evolving on this particular stage.

Face is wiser in the ways of combining multiple plots. He allows Surly to cast himself complacently as the hero of the moral comedy Surly has in his head, concentrating instead on casting Surly as the villain of the plays various other characters have in *their* heads. He quickly convinces Kastril that Surly is the enemy for whom his quarreling skills have been developed, an enemy of honor and of Kastril's own family (4.7.1–3). The fact that Kastril then calls Surly "an Amadis de Gaul, or a Don Quixote" (4.7.40) indicates how successful Face has been in making Kastril perceive Surly as merely a representative foreign opponent for a duel of the sort exalted in sixteenth-century romances. Face similarly convinces Drugger that "This cheater would ha' cozened thee o' the widow" (4.7.29), enlisting Drugger's dreams of an elevating marriage to cast Surly again in the role of discovered villain—the more so because Surly now appears to be the sort of well-born wastrel who always opposes Drugger's sort of industrious social climber in Elizabethan popular literature. Then Ananias arrives and (after some confusion of language that parallels the confusion of plots) Subtle convinces Ananias that Kastril's motive is

> Zeal in the young gentleman,
Against his Spanish slops—

33. C. G. Thayer, *Ben Jonson* (Norman, Okla., 1963), p. 93.

ANANIAS.                      They are profane,
  Lewd, superstitious, and idolatrous breeches.
SURLY. New rascals!
KASTRIL.        Will you be gone, sir?
ANANIAS.                  Avoid, Sathan,
  Thou art not of the light. That ruff of pride
  About thy neck betrays thee, and is the same
  With that which the unclean birds, in seventy-seven,
  Were seen to prank it with on divers coasts.
  Thou look'st like Antichrist in that lewd hat.
SURLY. I must give way.

                                    (4.7.47–56)

He must give way, not because they are "new rascals," but
because they are parts of other old plays. His choice of costumes
is unfortunate, because it encourages Drugger to interpret him
as a rival for Dame Pliant, Kastril to interpret him as a quarreling enemy, and Ananias to interpret him as a Catholic and
therefore as the Satanic enemy against whom Puritans directed
their internal melodramas. Surly had planned to call an end to
all their plays by injecting truth and common sense into Lovewit's house, but (like Overdo and Busy in *Bartholomew Fair*)
he finds himself absorbed by their plays instead. Face's satiric
awareness of humanity's self-dramatizing impulses thus triumphs
over Surly's conventional ethical impulse, as a concomitant to
the subjugation of naively moralistic comedy by Jonson's strategic satire.

   What would serve as the conclusion of many more ordinary
didactic plays—Surly's detection of the abuses and his gallant
rescue of the maiden—thus becomes merely an interruption
that serves to emphasize Jonson's greater insight into human
nature.[34] Surly is compelled to the bitter recognition that people
would rather be told grand ridiculous lies about their own splen-
dor than plain moral truths about their own folly, and he may
therefore again represent the surly and pertinacious artist of

   34. Judd Arnold, "Lovewit's Triumph and Jonsonian Morality," *Criticism*,
11 (1969), 160, argues that Jonson is here representing "a conventional sentimental or moralistic solution being overridden in order to clear the way for a
more cavalier solution."

social reform that Jonson felt compelled to abandon in himself.[35] The defeat of Surly may be read as a surrender in Jonson's campaign to scourge the evils of Renaissance society, and as the renewal of his more limited campaign against the follies of Renaissance drama. In a critical preface to the Quarto edition of *The Alchemist* (and in a virtually identical passage in his *Discoveries*), Jonson suggests the kind of literary judo-throw by which he demonstrates not only the flaws in the technique of his rivals but also the flaws in the judgment of spectators who prefer those rivals:

> For they commend writers as they do fencers or wrestlers, who if they come in robustuously and put for it with a great deal of violence, are received for the braver fellows; when many times their own rudeness is the cause of their disgrace, and a little touch of their adversary gives all that boisterous force the foil.[36]

Jonson's characteristic *catastasis,* where the plot pauses near a false resolution, serves as a kind of slow-motion replay of this subtle touch. The moment between Surly's triumphant revelations and his ultimate defeat serves to crystallize our expectations so that Jonson may crush them all the more effectively. He is marking a division that parallels the distinction between conventional comedies and his own.

The false crisis in Jonson's plot has compelled the conspirators to bring all of their plots into collision, instead of keeping them carefully apart as before. The question is what plot will remain running at the end of this literary demolition derby. Drugger, who has had enough theatrical experience to "play the Fool," is dispatched to borrow "Hieronimo's old cloak, ruff, and hat" from the players so that he may properly court Dame Pliant

---

35. Holdsworth, *"Every Man,"* p. 31, speculates that *"The Alchemist* might be said to dramatise the collision between Jonson the pessimistic *censor morum* . . . and Jonson the delighter in contrivance, who once himself dressed up as an astrologer . . . in order to play a joke on a lady." See also J. B. Steane, "Crime and Punishment in *The Alchemist,"* in Holdsworth, pp. 187–189, on the role of Surly in representing this conflict and on the inducements it offers to the audience.

36. "To the Reader," ll. 14–18; for the parallel passage in the *Discoveries,* see Herford and Simpson, *Ben Jonson,* VIII, 583, ll. 634–639.

(4.7.64–71). Face evidently has plans to steal this role (4.7.99–100), and it is probably significant that Jonson himself had been mocked in Dekker's *Satiro-mastix* for having borrowed such a costume when he played Hieronimo.[37] Face and Jonson now seem poised to work together, using popular dramatic conventions against the former's gulls and the latter's literary rivals.

But this last flurry of dramatic artifice is interrupted by the return of the real master to this house-turned-theater and later exploited by him for his own financial and sexual benefit. To meet him, Face must return to an original identity that seems to have become essentially another costumed role: "I'll into mine old shape again, and meet him, / Of Jeremy the butler" (4.7.120–121). There is an intriguing suggestion here of an actor removing part of his mask to deliver an apologetic epilogue to an audience, and the fifth act may indeed be taken as a subversive afterword to the complete moral comedy Surly attempted to conclude. Lovewit is the audience for this afterword, and Jonson invites the gentleman-wits of the Blackfriars audience to identify with Lovewit in order to enlist their support in the overthrow of naive playwrights such as Surly.[38] Face achieves the usual purpose of an epilogue by bestowing his praise and his profits on Lovewit, as a reward for Lovewit's forgiving the cynical plot in which Face usurped his house and humiliatingly plundered the gulls: the audience, to earn an analogous reward, must forgive the analogous usurpation of their playhouse by Jonson's satiric comedy, with its thieving humiliation of conventional playwrights.

The fifth act opens with Lovewit's neighbors playing the parts of dimwitted reviewers, milling around just outside the house with vague and shifting reports of the wild events and personages that had filled it in his absence. Face almost succeeds in ending

37. Herford and Simpson, *Ben Jonson*, X, 108.

38. Wayne A. Rebhorn, "Jonson's 'Jovy Boy': Lovewit and the Dupes in *The Alchemist*," *Journal of English and Germanic Philology*, 79 (1980), 355–375, argues for the identification of Lovewit with the audience—"those urban gentlemen who habitually attended performances" in Blackfriars (p. 373)—rather than with the playwright; my argument suggests that both identifications may be active as part of a strategy to compel the audience's sympathetic participation in the transformation of standard comedy into Jonsonian satire.

the show there and denying any misbehavior, except that Dapper has been left in the middle of his fairy tale, which he now pathetically pleads to finish. Face tries to lure Lovewit into unwittingly reenacting the scene from Plautus' *Mostellaria* in which the wily servant Tranio diverts his suddenly returned master from entering the house that has been converted to immoral purposes in his absence. The echo of earlier literature may again be read as an adaptation by a character rather than by the author. Face's remark about his "guilty conscience" at the end of act 5, scene 2, makes sense only as an excerpt from that role, not as an expression of his own character. His insistence that Surly must have the wrong house is directly out of Plautus, as is his boast that he has diverted Lovewit by warning him that "the house is haunted."[39]

But where Theopropides temporarily accepts Tranio's warning that the house is haunted, Lovewit immediately dismisses Face's typically melodramatic suggestion that Dapper's cry proves the house has been visited by "some spirit o' the air" as well as by the plague. In place of this old tale, Lovewit demands "The truth, the shortest way" (5.3.66–74). To prevent Surly's conventional conclusion from triumphing by revealing the blunt facts to everyone, or the play from ending with none of the plots satisfyingly resolved, Face must ask permission to extend the fiction a short while longer, and to cast Lovewit as yet another performer assigned to the role of the wooing Spanish count (5.3.87).

Lovewit evidently decides that his servant's plot is good enough to merit his playing a part in it. He answers the furious attack on his doors much as Face had answered it three scenes earlier, when Lovewit himself had been the assailant: "Hold, gentlemen, what means this violence?" (5.5.10). Several of the gulls have returned to demand a proper conclusion to the plots that had lured them to this house in Blackfriars. They behave like the spectators at the first performance of Ibsen's *A Doll's House* who reportedly remained seated after the final curtain, insis-

39. Herford and Simpson, *Ben Jonson*, X, 111. Subtle evidently does not penetrate Face's Plautine pose as Lovewit does: he mistakes this wily servant of an ancient wit for "the precious king of present wits" (5.4.13–14).

tently waiting for Nora to fulfill their conventional expectations by returning penitently to her family. Jonson's onstage spectators want an opportunity to hiss the company for its expensive and unsatisfying performance of their preconceived scripts, but they cannot even agree on the cast of characters:

MAMMON.  Where is this collier?
SURLY.                              And my Captain Face?
MAMMON.  These day-owls.
SURLY.                              That are birding in men's purses.
MAMMON.  Madam Suppository.
KASTRIL.                         Doxy, my suster.
ANANIAS.              Locusts
  Of the foul pit.
TRIBULATION.       Profane as Bel and the Dragon.
                                        (5.5.11–14)

Lovewit sees the advantage he can derive from the plots Face has multiplied and driven into collision, and simply asks,

                              Whom do you seek?
MAMMON.  The chemical cozener.
SURLY.                              And the captain pander.
KASTRIL.  The nun my suster.
MAMMON.                     Madam Rabbi.
ANANIAS.                     Scorpions,
  And caterpillars.
                                        (5.5.18–21)

The officers would have to arrest the tiring-house to satisfy these accusations, and even then the evidence would be hard to find, since the costumes are finally provided as much by the desiring imaginations of the gulls as by the shreds of disguise used by the conspirators.

Jonson's audience is left with an easy choice between identifying with these fools in demanding a conventional resolution of the plot, or identifying instead with the aptly named Lovewit and endorsing Jonson's satirical structure that gives innovative wit precedence over standard morality. All the vestigial plots have degenerated into self-parodies, and Lovewit provides Jonson's own sort of conclusion, forgiving the witty for the sake of their wit, and punishing the fools with their own folly. He wraps up the loose ends, not only by playing the courting Spaniard with more alacrity and effect than Drugger or Surly, but also by out-quarreling Kastril, by shamelessly seizing all the wealth that Mammon (now ashamed of his greed) had greedily brought to the house, and by cozening Dol and Subtle out of the profits that cozenage had gathered there. As one critic notes, Lovewit "acts like a roguish parody of a romantic protagonist,"[40] and he triumphs over the others because he is fully aware that he is performing a parody rather than a heroic role. He earns our intimacy and rogue-sentiment largely by keeping his satiric distance from the grandiose temptations of his position up on stage.[41]

Such theatrical self-consciousness gives Lovewit an obvious advantage over the gulls. What is less obvious, but no less crucial, is the advantage it gives him over the conspirators. Subtle, Face, and Dol suffer from a milder form of the self-aggrandizing, self-dramatizing disease that they exploit in their victims, and it leads to their downfall. The disasters that eventually befall the conspiracy at the hands of Surly and Lovewit demonstrate that even expert plotters such as Subtle and Face sometimes overlook the possibility of another, ultimate plot beyond their own: the conspirators, like their victims, are in headlong pursuit of financial profits and sexual pleasures that may disappear in fume with the collapse of the alchemical/theatrical artifice.

For four acts the conspirators are masters of the stage, and their plots evince a Jonsonian talent for subsuming more conventional plots. In the final act they are still busy sorting the pelf they gained by playing to the melodramatic appetites of a seemingly unlimited supply of gulls: a jewel from a waiting-maid who wanted to know "If she should have precedence of her mistress," a whistle from a woman who wanted to know whether her husband was at sea with the great pirate Ward, and so on (5.4.110–116). It is worth noting that at least one melodrama on the subject of Ward's adventures, Daborne's *A Christian turn'd Turke,* had appeared on London's stages shortly before *The Alchemist* was written.[42] Subtle and Dol even try to con-

40. Leonard, "Shakespeare and Jonson Again," p. 68.
41. Arnold, "Lovewit's Triumph," p. 161, suggests that Lovewit triumphs because "He has no dream to sell himself."
42. Herford and Simpson, *Ben Jonson,* X, 113.

vert Lovewit's return into a convenient development in their
plot to cheat the cheater Face. But when the master returns to
his house in Blackfriars, and retrieves it from the realm of
conventional theater, those who converted others into actors
are revealed as merely actors themselves. A number of critics
have suggested that the conspirators must finally be replaced
by Lovewit because their immorality is incompatible with the
moral purpose of Jonsonian drama. My analysis suggests something rather different: Lovewit replaces the conspirators not
because he is more socially ethical but because he is more theatrically self-conscious.

The disguised Surly nearly overthrew them all in the previous
act by enlisting them in his play when they smugly assumed they
had trapped him in theirs; Face's failure in the role of Tranio
is another indication of the problem. The conspirators gloat
over their conventional role as wickedly clever fishers of men:

SUBTLE.   Has he bit? Has he bit?
FACE.                              And swallowed, too, my Subtle.
   I ha' given him line, and now he plays, i' faith.
SUBTLE.   And shall we twitch him?
FACE.                              Through both the gills.
   A wench is a rare bait . . .

                        (2.4.1–4)

Indeed, Face seems to assume some correspondence between
his role and that of his nominal counterpart in Skelton's *Magnyfycence,* who introduces himself in terms that suggest the
shows to which Face gives countenance in Lovewit's house:

> For Counterfet Countenaunce knowen am I.
> This worlde is full of my foly.
>
> . . . . .
>
> A knave wyll counterfet nowe a knyght,
> A lurdayne lyke a lorde to syght,
> A mynstrell lyke a man of myght,
> A tappster lyke a lady bryght:
> Thus make I them wyth thryft to fyght.
>
> . . . . .
>
> To counterfet I can by praty wayes:
> Of nyghtys to occupy counterfet kayes;

> Clenly to counterfet newe arrayes;
> Counterfet eyrnest by way of playes.
>
> . . . . .
>
> I counterfet suger that is but sande;
> Counterfet captaynes by me are mande;
> Of all lewdnesse I kyndell the brande.

In the next few lines this character refers to the "Counterfet kyndnesse," "Counterfet langage," and "counterfet coynes" he uses on his victims.[43] Whether or not Jonson intended any direct allusion to Skelton, it seems clear that Jeremy conceives his role as Captain Face along the lines of a traditional stage Vice. Lois Potter has demonstrated that Vice characters in early English drama often appeared in groups of three, and that the term "Vice" may have referred not to sin but rather to the "vizard" such characters present to the world.[44] This suggests a parallel to the "venter tripartite" of *The Alchemist* and to the pseudonym "Face" chosen by its instigator. Face, as a petty schemer in a low farce, is in constant danger of mistaking himself for the grand diabolical tempter of a morality play. Even the stage action of Face's battle with Dame Pliant for control of Kastril during the Surly crisis would have been "reminiscent of the morality conflict of a vice and a virtue over a fateful decision to be made by mankind."[45]

There are hints from the very first lines of the play that the conspirators confuse drama with reality in self-aggrandizing ways. As John Mebane has suggested, the conflict arises in the opening scene because the conspirators are each willing to remind the others, but not to be reminded themselves, that "By assuming theatrical costumes and adopting an inflated jargon they have undergone illusory transformations to higher states of being."[46] The struggle over who will control the "venter tripartite" is

43. *Magnyfycence*, ll. 410–446, in John Skelton, *Complete English Poems*, ed. John Scattergood (New Haven, 1983), p. 152.

44. Lois Potter, "The Plays and Playwrights," in *The Revels History of Drama in English*, ed. Norman Sanders et al. (London, 1980), II, 151 and 172.

45. Dessen, *Moral Comedy*, p. 129.

46. John S. Mebane, "Renaissance Magic and the Return of the Golden Age," in *Renaissance Drama*, n.s., 10 (1979), 127. Richard Dutton, *"Volpone* and *The Alchemist:* A Comparison in Satiric Techniques," *Renaissance and*

actually a struggle over who will be allowed to assert that his pose is his real identity, and the effort to preserve the alliance is actually an effort to preserve their chief asset, which is a lively awareness of the distinction between role and reality. The conspirators vacillate between playfully ironic role-playing and dangerously proud self-dramatizations. Several editors have observed that the opening exchange of insults between Face and Subtle closely resembles an exchange in the *Plutus* of Aristophanes.[47] Dol mollifies them with a literate allegory that makes her the republic (with a pun on *res publica*) in which they play the roles of Sovereign and General. They will soon reward her, not with a cash bonus, but instead with a noble role from *The Mirror of Knighthood:* they tell her she has "Spoken like Claridiana, and thyself!" (1.1.87–88, 110, 175). A similar transaction occurs halfway through the play, when Dol greets Face by quoting an inquiry from *The Spanish Tragedy,* and he replies by calling her "My Dousabel," a typical name for a romance heroine (3.3.33, 41). The implicit agreement to indulge each other's vain fantasies is necessarily a dangerous one in the context of this play. It holds the conspiracy together, but only by compromising its operating principle of superior realism. The "venter tripartite" is finally hoist with its own petard. Dol aptly asks her partners in crime,

> Ha' you together cozened all this while,
> And all the world, and shall it now be said
> You've made most courteous shift to cozen yourselves?
> (1.1.122–124)

By the end of the play Subtle and Dol will have done very much that: their vision of a triumphant escape is really only a degraded version of Mammon's dreams of unbounded voyages, riches,

---

*Modern Studies,* 18 (1974), 50, perceives "a hint in Subtle's claim that he carries a disproportionate part of the venture (1.1.144–145), that—without actually believing what he says—he is sometimes carried away by his own eloquence, by the artificial dignity of his disguise, which is potentially as much a flaw as the blindness of his dupes."

47. Coburn Gum, *The Aristophanic Comedies of Ben Jonson* (The Hague, 1969), p. 165 and n. 32. In fact, through much of the play, Subtle seems to imagine he can take a standard Aristophanic role as an evil educator who is never punished for his knavery; see Gum, pp. 39–43.

and sensual indulgences (5.4.74–91), and it is easily victimized by the superior plotters. Jeremy is fortunate that his master is Lovewit and that his creator is a lover of classical New Comedy, which provides a successful role for a wily servant. He survives, but only by knowing when to stop playing and resume serving, only by surrendering his proud authority along with his Face.

*The Alchemist* ends with a brief epilogue in which both Lovewit and Face, without moving completely out of character, apologize for any breaches of the conventional rules of drama. It is appropriately unclear, at the end of a play about the confusion of drama and life, whether they are apologizing as actors or as characters, and it would be risky, in a play so carefully positioned against the audience's mindless assertion of dramatic conventions, to accept such apologies at face value. The only loose end left hanging in this play of failed plots is a baited hook dangled in front of the audience by the surviving plotter, Face. He coyly confesses to the audience that

> My part a little fell in this last scene,
> Yet 'twas decorum. And though I am clean
> Got off from Subtle, Surly, Mammon, Dol,
> Hot Ananias, Dapper, Drugger, all
> With whom I traded; yet I put myself
> On you, that are my country; and this pelf
> Which I have got, if you do quit me, rests,
> To feast you often, and invite new guests.
> (5.5.158–165)

It would be a bold audience indeed that dared to criticize Face's creation, having seen the fate of all those who tried to outplot him. He offers to shape any number of new plays from these various old plots, and the audience would be well advised to stand aside as his benevolent patron until he invites them into the action, never letting go of either their wallets or their intellectual alertness, lest they suddenly discover they have become the complacent gulls at whom they had been laughing. The only way to cease being a gullible guest is to make league with the exploitative host. There is still an alchemist at work in the house in Blackfriars, and he mocks the naive Londoners who gather there, even while he transforms the base dramas they bring to him into his own satiric gold.

# V  Genre and Interpretation

JOHN N. KING

# Spenser's *Shepheardes Calender* and Protestant Pastoral Satire

Spenser's *Shepheardes Calender* encompasses native Protestant and biblical elements whose significance has long been over-shadowed by concern for the classical or Italianate origins of the text. His fundamental contribution to pastoral is, however, the infusion of the spirit of classical literary models into forms

This essay was prepared with support from a Huntington Library–NEH Fellowship and an ACLS Grant-in-Aid. It was completed shortly before the appearance of David Norbrook's *Poetry and Politics in the English Renaissance* (1984), hereafter cited as Norbrook. Despite Norbrook's primary concern with politics rather than genre, our arguments complement each other and often arrive at similar conclusions. I am indebted throughout to conversations with James P. Bednarz, Leah S. Marcus, and Susan Snyder, and to the editing of Barbara K. Lewalski. The modern use of i/j, u/v, and vv is followed; contractions are expanded. London is the place of publication unless otherwise noted. Quotations from *The Shepheardes Calender* refer to vol. 7, pt. 1 of *The Works of Edmund Spenser: A Variorum Edition,* ed. Edwin A. Greenlaw, C. G. Osgood, F. M. Padelford, et al., 10 vols. in 11 (Baltimore, 1932–1957), hereafter cited as *Variorum.* Scriptural texts are from *The Geneva Bible,* facsimile of the 1560 edition, intro. Lloyd E. Berry (Madison, 1969).

that are intrinsically English and Protestant.[1] Spenser was a
great amalgamator who modeled himself on "auncient Poetes"
like Chaucer and, probably, Langland.[2] The inclusionist strategy
in the *Calender* relies on the mixing of genres in order to overgo
poetic predecessors. The native conventions and techniques clearly
furnish only one of many overlapping generic layers in the collection, but the mixing of "some Satyrical bitternesse" in the
five moral eclogues counterbalances the ostentatious use of imported elements in the plaintive and recreative eclogues. Spenser's allusion to and transformation of recognizable techniques
and conventions of Reformation satire shows that he is self-
consciously fashioning a new kind of Protestant pastoral satire.[3]

By selecting the pastoral eclogue for his debut as a professional
public poet, Spenser chose a form associated not only with the
apprenticeship of epic poets but also with the cause of religious
reform. Petrarch first adapted pastoral to ecclesiastical satire in
attacks on the corrupt court of the Avignon popes during the
"Babylonian Captivity."[4] When Baptista Spagnuoli (Mantuan)

1. Anthea Hume rightly documents Spenser's Protestantism in *Edmund Spenser: Protestant Poet* (Cambridge, 1984), but her reduction of the satirical eclogues to tractarian arguments ignores genre theory or practice. For a reply to
her view that Spenser adopts a "Puritan" posture in the *Calender,* see John N.
King, "Was Spenser a Puritan?" *Spenser Studies,* 6 (1985). Norbrook concludes
that although Spenser's argument is broadly Protestant rather than narrowly
Puritan, he was read with approval by Puritans (see pp. 61, 64, 66–67, 76, and 89).
2. The few considerations of Spenser's relationship to the native literary
tradition include Edwin A. Greenlaw, "The Shepheards Calender," *PMLA,*
26 (1911), 438–445, and the commentary in W. A. Renwick's edition of *The
Shepherd's Calender* (1930), pp. 200–206, passim. See also Norbrook, pp. 59–
60 et seq.
3. Hallett Smith notes Spenser's use of popular techniques and conventions
of Tudor satire in *Elizabethan Poetry: A Study in Conventions, Meaning, and
Expression* (Cambridge, Mass., 1952), pp. 42–45, 212–214. Norbrook observes
that Spenser "linked himself with the Protestant satiric tradition" (p. 69).
4. *Bucolicum carmen:* "Pastorum pathos" ("The Shepherds' Suffering") and
"Grex infectus et suffectus" ("The Infected and Replenished Flock"). Frances
Yates observes that Petrarch as well as Dante were, for their attacks on the
Bishop of Rome, viewed by Elizabethans as proto-Protestant reformers in *As-
traea: The Imperial Theme in the Sixteenth Century* (1975), pp. 41, 44, and 77n3.

wrote *Adolescentia seu Bucolica* (Mantua, 1498), he expanded upon Petrarch's satirical application of biblical texts in pastoral. It is misleading, however, to identify the harsh Mantuanesque voice of Spenser's satirical eclogues with medieval Catholicism,[5] for Mantuan's anticlericalism aligns him closely with the antipapal stance taken by Tudor Protestants.

Shakespeare's "old Mantuan" (*Love's Labour's Lost,* 4.2.99) was anglicized as a model for Protestant satire even before Spenser's birth. Prior to George Turberville's 1567 translation of the *Bucolica,* John Bale, the Reformation activist who became a bishop under Edward VI, radicalized Mantuan by interpreting him as a crypto-Protestant who "smelled out more abuses in the Romysh churche, then in those daies he durst wele utter." Bale praises the first and ninth eclogues especially for their attack on clerical corruption.[6] Long before the composition of Spenser's *Calender,* Mantuan's bucolics had been drawn anachronistically into the library of Protestant propaganda in a manner similar to prereformist English authors such as the *Piers Plowman* poet, Chaucer, and Skelton.

Underlying pastoral satire on religious topics is the Bible, which loomed as a model for attacking the corrupt papacy and the ecclesiastical abuses it generated. The Scriptures furnished a treasure house of allusions, imagery, and narratives for imitation, and Spenser attaches revolutionary Protestant meanings to many of the biblical *topoi* once used in the reformist appeals of Petrarch and Mantuan. Although Spenser often uses similar gospel imagery, his plain vernacular diction and style renders his verse accessible to popular audiences, in contrast to the readership of clergy and scholars addressed by those continental predecessors.

5. See Norbrook, p. 61 and n. 10, for a reply to Paul McLane's identification of Spenser as a religious conservative with Catholic sympathies in *Spenser's "Shepheardes Calender": A Study in Elizabethan Allegory* (Notre Dame, 1961), pp. 117–118, 126. McLane follows Virgil K. Whitaker, *The Religious Basis of Spenser's Poetry* (Stanford, 1950). On "Mantuanesque" pastoral, see Patrick Cullen, *Spenser, Marvell, and Renaissance Pastoral* (Cambridge, Mass., 1970), pp. 19–26.

6. *A Lamentable complaynte of Baptista Mantuanus . . . wherin he famylyarly commoneth* [communes] *wyth hys owne mynde, that Deathe is not to be feared* (circa 1551), sig. A2r.

The fundamental biblical metaphor for Christian pastoral, which equates the individual believer with a sheep in Christ's flock, may extend to good ministers and priests if they imitate Christ in fulfilling their clerical vocations. The pun implicit in the word "pastor" ("shepherd" and "minister") in the Latin Vulgate translation supports the infusion of religious satire into eclogue. Psalm 23:1–3 ("The Lord is my shepherd, I shal not want") and Christ's parables of the Lost Sheep and the Good Shepherd (Matt. 18:12–14 and John 10:1–16) fuse with the *topoi* of biblical pastoral concerning the dangers to the flock from wolves and thieves. Thus Spenser looks beyond Mantuan's eighth eclogue ("Religio") to scriptural texts such as Matthew 7:15 ("Beware of false prophets, which come to you in shepes clothing, but inwardely they are ravening wolves") for the imagery of "September," and its equation of "Popish prelates" with wolves and foxes (ll. 141–155 et seq.).[7] Similarly, the messianic prophecy of Isaiah 40:1–16 fuses with characters and themes from Mantuan's ninth eclogue ("Falco") as a model for "July," with its critical contrast between "proude and ambitious Pastours" and "good shepeheardes." Related scriptural parables and metaphors concerning the sowing of seed and divine husbandry were readily assimilated into pastoral satire.

Spenser reshapes the eclogue into a form that seems intrinsically English and Protestant. Scripturalism, hostility to the Roman church, and imitation of the British vernacular tradition of religious protest characterize his pastoral satires, where a nativist Protestant manner is most noticeable. Dividing the eclogues into "moral," "plaintive," and "recreative" categories, E.K. claims that the largest group ("February," "May," "July," "September," and "October") is made up of poems in "which for the most part be mixed . . . Satyrical bitternesse." The "rec-

7. See Barbara K. Lewalski, *Protestant Poetics and the Seventeenth-Century Religious Lyric* (Princeton, 1979), pp. 96–97, on pastoral metaphor as a trope for the Christian life. William Nelson comments on Petrarch's identification of pastoral shepherds with priests in *The Poetry of Edmund Spenser: A Study* (New York, 1963), p. 44.

reative" ("March," "April," and "August") and "plaintive" ("January," "June," "November," and "December") groups contain the texts in which foreign precedents are especially important, but the "plaintive" laments also feature the persona, Colin Clout. Spenser modeled this pen name on the native satirical observer fashioned by John Skelton (with an overlapping allusion to Clément Marot's pseudonym, Colin).

Spenser overgoes Mantuan and his continental antecedents by forging an extremely homely voice for pastoral. The satirical eclogues all feature nativist speakers and style and fuse vernacular devices and techniques with foreign models—paradoxically an "innovation" at a time when other poets are abandoning the archaic diction and versification of the Middle English poets. Sidney, by contrast, favors British diction but experiments at the same time with quantitative verse and other techniques based upon avant-garde continental models.

Although the classical assumptions of Sidney and George Puttenham led to their exclusionist denigration of native conventions and techniques, Spenser was an inclusionist. His style looks backward to Edward VI's reign, when, according to Thomas Wilson, the "fine Courtier wil talke nothyng but Chaucer"; Wilson was well acquainted with fellow Cambridge scholars who had gone to the royal court, such as John Cheke and Roger Ascham.[8] Mid-century courtiers seem to have affected archaic mannerisms—what E.K. refers to as "the shewe of such naturall rudenesse"—and Sidney's disdain for such language may reflect the coming of age of a new generation of courtly poets. Chaucer's complete works were first collected at the court of Henry VIII by William Thynne, Clerk of the Kitchen.[9]

E.K. acknowledges the inventiveness of looking to unorthodox native models, but clearly he assumes that the *Calender* will disappoint believers in linguistic augmentation and Latinate au-

---

8. *The Arte of Rhetorique* (1553), sig. Y2v. See Winthrop S. Hudson, *The Cambridge Connection and the Elizabethan Settlement* (Durham, N.C., 1980), p. 54.

9. See Thynne's 1532 edition of *The Works* of Geoffrey Chaucer "newly printed, with dyvers workes whiche were never in print before," facsimile ed. D. S. Brewer (1974), with additions and expansions by Thynne's successors.

reation: "Other some not so wel seene in the English tonge as perhaps in other languages, if them happen to here an olde word albeit very naturall and significant, crye out streight way, that we speak no English, but gibbrish . . ." Implicit in this dispute over language is the contemporary effort to expand British vocabulary in "Renaissance" works modeled on Italian and classical originals. E.K. addresses the divisive question of stylistic decorum when he suggests that Immerito may believe that archaic English diction is "fittest for such rusticall rudenesse of shepheards." Although the writings of the master poet Chaucer were universally admired, and Spenser chose him as the most fit model for the native poet, Sidney in the *Apologie for Poetrie* finds no precedent for such poetic imitation of archaic language, despite his favorable judgment of Spenser's eclogues: "That same framing of his stile to an old rustick language I dare not alowe, sith neyther *Theocritus* in Greeke, *Virgill* in Latine, nor *Sanazar* in Italian did affect it." Puttenham in *The Arte of English Poesie* also censures old-fashioned native diction: "Our maker therfore at these dayes shall not follow *Piers plowman* nor *Gower* nor *Lydgate* nor yet *Chaucer,* for their language is now out of use with us."[10] Spenser was himself eclectic and capable of practicing both new and old poetic modes, but he must have known that his native English models seemed dated.

Sidney evidently exercised little if any influence over the poetic manner of the *Calender.* Although Spenser's service to the earl of Leicester placed him in proximity to Sidney and Dyer at Leicester House by 5 October 1579,[11] E.K.'s completion of his preface on 10 April of the same year supplies a *terminus ad quem* for composition of the eclogues. Spenser probably wrote most if not all of the *Calender* during residence in the household of his previous patron, John Young. Spenser had studied at Pembroke Hall, Cambridge, when Young was master. He entered into Young's service in 1578 soon after the scholar's appointment as bishop of Rochester ("episcopus Roffensis"), whose title Spenser commemorates in the name of the good shepherd

10. G. G. Smith, ed., *Elizabethan Critical Essays,* 2 vols. (Oxford, 1904), I, 196; II, 150.
11. *Variorum,* IX, 12.

Roffy (or Roffyn). [12] Hobbinol's praise of Roffy as "meeke, wise, and merciable" identifies him as Spenser's patron: "Colin clout I wene be his selfe boye" ("September," ll. 174–176). The proliferation of references to Kent throughout the *Calender* may reflect Spenser's familiarity with the vicinity of the bishop's residence at Bromley in Kent. The influence exerted on Spenser's writings by all of his later patrons (Lord Grey, Raleigh, and Queen Elizabeth) suggests that the archaic diction of *The Shepheardes Calender* may reflect academic taste going back to the period of Young's mastership at Pembroke Hall.

Spenser's use of a flat plain style and alliteration and his transformation of the medieval persona of the blunt truth-telling plowman into various shepherd characters allude to the ancient tradition of English estates satire and complaint. Piers's voice is typical in this attack on prideful clergy:

> Some gan to gape for greedie governaunce,
> And match them selfe with mighty potentates,
> Lovers of Lordship and troublers of states:
> ("May," ll. 121–123)

Diggon Davie, the shepherd who most closely resembles Piers's staccato pugnacity, speaks in a similar voice:

> The rampant Lyon hunts he fast,
>     with Dogge of noysome breath,
> Whose balefull barking bringes in hast
>     pyne, plagues, and dreery death.
> ("July," ll. 21–24)

By the end of the sixteenth century the neoclassical standards of formal verse satire eclipsed native satirical conventions, for aspiring satirists like Marston, Donne, and Jonson looked to Juvenal, Horace, and Persius as literary models.

Spenser drew upon a native tradition of "georgic" satire, available in the many fables and dialogues featuring a simple plowman who implicitly or explicitly represents Christian social ideals, such as poverty, hard work, piety, and humility. By

---

12. Israel Gollancz, "Spenseriana," *Proceedings of the British Academy,* 3 (1907–08), 103. See Alexander C. Judson, *The Life of Edmund Spenser,* in *Variorum,* VIII, 52.

conflating devices of language, characterization, and thought
linked to this tradition with the shepherd conventions of pastoral
satire, Spenser achieved a synthesis that stresses not Theocritean
*otium* but the real hardships of recognizably English peasant
workers, who endure the seasons' labors and the conflicts of
youth and age. This harsh, georgic strain has classical sources
also, as far back as Hesiod's *Works and Days*.

Long before the middle of the sixteenth century, the persona
of the plain-speaking plowman or roaming countryman had
evolved into a device for religious and social protest. A distinct
subgenre of Reformation satire emerged in a prolific series of
conventional debates between a bluntly honest Protestant peasant and a Catholic cleric whose ignorant attempts at sophisticated eloquence cannot mask his spiritual ignorance.[13] Typical
of this convention is the humble laborer's stubborn skepticism
about transubstantiation in Luke Shepherd's *John Bon and Mas-
t[er] Person* (1547), because it can be neither tasted nor seen:

> Yea but mast parson thynk ye it were ryght
> That if I desired you to make my blake oxe whight
> And you saye it is done, and styl is blacke in syght
> Ye myght me deme a foole for to beleve so lyght.
>                                                 (Sig. A4r)

Reformation editors such as John Bale and Robert Crowley
reconstructed a library of medieval anticlerical satire complaint,
including many writings by Wyclif and his contemporaries, that
enabled Elizabethan readers to impose a new generic identification on the medieval authors cited in E.K.'s glosses. The
master authors in this company were Chaucer and the *Piers
Plowman* poet (known during the sixteenth century as Robert
or William Langland). Even though these authors styled their
works within the medieval conventions of dream vision, beast
fable, and homiletic discourse, Tudor readers often reinterpreted those works as proto-Protestant satire and complaint.
Those poets held out special appeal as "Protestant" models
because of the association of their rustic figures with the re-

13. See John N. King, *English Reformation Literature: The Tudor Origins
of the Protestant Tradition* (Princeton, 1982), pp. 258–260, 286–287.

lentless search for spiritual truth. Although neither author was a Wyclifite, both were praised during the Reformation for anticipating later attacks on the Roman church establishment.[14] The mute honesty of Chaucer's Plowman (*General Prologue,* ll. 529–541) was seen to represent an extension of the simple gospel ethic of his brother, the Parson, in potent contrast to the unsavory greed of the Monk, Summoner, and Pardoner, who are standard types from medieval anticlerical satire.

*Piers Plowman,* in particular, amalgamated simple colloquial speech and subjective inward piety in a manner that was thought compatible with the Protestant belief in justification by faith alone and everyone a priest. It was the best-known model for the association between heavy alliteration and satirical attack on the Roman church. When the text first appeared in print, the editor Robert Crowley eagerly applied passages like the following as prophecies of the dissolution of the abbeys and the English Reformation:

> And there shal come a king, and confesse you religious
> And beat you as the bible telleth, for breking of your rule
> And amende moniales, monkes, and chanons
> And put hem to her penaunce.[15]

He and other Protestant satirists used the poem as a model in their own appeals for ecclesiastical and social reform. The reformers also drew Lollard additions to the *Piers Plowman* apocrypha, such as *Pierce the Ploughmans Crede* and *The Pilgrim's Tale,* into their expanding canon of radical poetry. The composition of *The Plowman's Tale*—a revision of an early-fifteenth-century original—exemplifies how Tudor Protestants embraced the apocryphal tradition. This expansion of the literary canon immediately preceded the effort led by Sidney and Puttenham to rule such works off limits as models for imitation. The addition of lexical notes and glossaries to the black-letter

14. Ibid., pp. 50–52, 323, 325.
15. Quoted from the third edition, sig. N2r; see Walter W. Skeat, ed., *The Vision of William Concerning Piers the Plowman,* 2 vols. (Oxford, 1886), B.10. 317–320. Norbrook notes that Crowley was still influential in London at the time that Spenser published the *Calender* (p. 59).

editions of *Plowman* works suggests that contemporary readers would have recognized the archaism of the *Calender* and E.K.'s explanatory notes on word meanings as constituent elements in the tradition of native Protestant satire.

Because of Chaucer's reputation both as England's chief model for vernacular poetry and as a proto-Protestant, the canon of his poetry underwent radical expansion during the sixteenth century to include works by Lydgate, Hoccleve, anonymous Lollard reformers, and others. Chaucer was first linked to Langland as a Protestant prophet through the fraudulent publication of the apocryphal *Plowman's Tale* as a gathering out of an edition of *The Canterbury Tales* (circa 1535). Some Tudor scholars like John Leland even tried to credit *Piers Plowman* itself to Chaucer.[16] The frequent republication of Chaucer's complete works from the 1530s onward suggests that he was known universally as a native poetic model. Until the 1557 publication of Tottel's *Miscellany,* these expanded folio editions of Chaucer's works were the major anthologies of English vernacular poetry. They presented *The Plowman's Tale* as a complement to Chaucer's *Parson's Tale,* and by convention the two came to be located as a reformist coda at the end of *The Canterbury Tales. Jack Upland* was brought into the enlarged canon in 1602. Another pseudo-Chaucerian satire against monasticism, *The Pilgrim's Tale,* achieved notoriety when it was circulated in the reformist *Court of Venus* along with the poetry of Sir Thomas Wyatt.[17]

Spenser's homage to Chaucer under the name of Tityrus, as a model for poetic style, craftsmanship, and thought, alludes to this Reformation tradition of the radicalized Chaucer. Such praise anticipates the identification in *The Faerie Queene* of "Dan

16. Anthony Hall, ed., *Commentarii de Scriptoribus Britannicis* (Oxford, 1709), p. 423. Andrew Wawn demonstrates in "The Genesis of *The Plowman's Tale,*" *Yearbook of English Studies,* 2 (1972), 21–40, that the work is a sixteenth-century reformist revision and expansion of an early-fifteenth-century Lollard original.

17. King, *English Reformation Literature,* pp. 50–52, 71, 226–227. The introduction and facsimile texts in Chaucer's *Works,* ed. Brewer, document the inclusion of apocryphal works within the Chaucer canon during the sixteenth century. Spenser could have used either the 1542 or circa 1550 reprints of Thynne's edition, or John Stow's 1561 expansion of Thynne's collection.

*Chaucer,* well of English undefyled" (4.2.32) as a model for versification, uses of language, and moral earnestness. Immerito openly acknowledges his poetic mentor with affected modesty in the Chaucerian envoi to the *Calender:*

> Goe lyttle Calender, thou hast a free passeporte,
> Goe but a lowly gate emongste the meaner sorte.
> Dare not to match thy pype with Tityrus hys style,
>     Nor with the Pilgrim that the Ploughman playde a whyle:
> But followe them farre off, and their high steppes adore,
> The better please, the worse despise, I aske nomore.

Spenser's association of pastoral with a Protestant gospel ethos is apparent in the lines preceding this salutation, which state unequivocally the collection's satirical function in advocating further reform of the church. They refer explicitly to Reformation readings of biblical texts such as the Parable of the Good Shepherd:

> To teach the ruder shepheard how to feede his sheepe,
> And from the falsers fraud his folded flocke to keepe.

Under the guise of Immerito, Spenser clearly defines his place as both the heir and peer of Chaucer. To do so means that he dons the disguise of the Reformation satirist.[18]

When Spenser refers to the pseudo-Chaucerian *Plowman's Tale* as a model for Protestant pastoral satire, he pays homage to a text that E.K. assigns to the Chaucer canon (gloss to "February," l. 149). Two direct quotations and allusions are found in the "moral" eclogues, while both they and a third

18. In "The Visions of *Piers Plowman* and *The Faerie Queene*," included in *Form and Convention in the Poetry of Edmund Spenser,* ed. William Nelson (New York, 1961), A. C. Hamilton observes that Spenser alludes both to Chaucer and to Langland in the epilogue (pp. 2–3). Thomas Warton first cited these references and the general relationship between Spenser and those predecessors in *Observations on the Fairie Queene* (1754), pp. 89–90, and 99–142, passim. See also Warton's treatment of Chaucer and the *Piers Plowman* poet as models for anticlerical satire in *The History of English Poetry,* 3 vols. and vol. 4 unfinished (1774–1781), I, 226–266, 278. Spenser's epilogue refers to *The Plowman's Tale* and *The Pilgrim's Tale* according to Norbrook (p. 59). Judith Anderson, in *The Growth of a Personal Voice: "Piers Plowman" and "The Faerie Queene"* (New Haven, 1976), pp. 1–2 and n. 6, argues that Spenser's allusion excludes "the poet of *The Plowman's Tale.*"

contain alliteration. By way of contrast, the *Calender* contains
neither quotations from nor close textual allusions to *Piers Plowman.* The Briar's "stirring up sterne strife" by appealing to the
Husbandman for aid against the Oak ("February," l. 149) echoes,
for example, the opening line of *The Plowman's Tale* proper,
"A Sterne stryf is stered newe" (l. 53). Thomalin's hostility to
ostentatious Catholic vestments "ygirt with belts of glitterand
gold" ("July," l. 177) accords with the Pelican's attack on corrupt priests in *The Tale:*

> That hye on horse willeth ryde
> In glitterand golde of grete aray,
> I-paynted and portred all in pryde;
> No commun knight may go so gay.
> Chaunge of clothing every day,
> With golden girdles grete and small . . .
>                               (ll. 133–138)

E.K. notes that the participle "glitterand" is "used sometime
in Chaucer." The aside in Colin's lay in praise of Eliza, "Albee
forswonck and forswatt I am" ("April," l. 99), goes without an
attribution to Chaucer, for E.K. only explains that the phrase
means "overlaboured and sunneburnt." This allusion to the
Plowman's description in the *Tale*'s prologue, "He was for-
swonke and all forswat" (l. 14), nevertheless aligns Spenser's
persona with the humble speaker whom the Tudors accepted as
a member of the Canterbury pilgrimage.[19]
   That Renaissance readers recognized a "Chaucerian" tradition of anticlerical satire is suggested by the marginalia of an
edition of *The Plowman's Tale* published in 1606, within a decade of Spenser's death. The anonymous editor expands the
work's title with an explanatory note: "Shewing by the doctrine
and lives of the Romish Clergie, that the Pope is Antichrist and
they his Ministers." The tale proper is presented as a "complaint
against the pride and covetousnesse of the Cleargie: made no

19. Quoted from Walter W. Skeat, ed., *Chaucerian and Other Pieces* (Oxford,
1897). This discussion of *The Plowman's Tale* is indebted to William A. Ringler,
Jr. Norbrook suggests that E.K. refuses to identify the allusion in "April" in
order to avoid possible offense to the queen, who favored a policy of religious
conservatism (p. 87).

doubt by *Chawcer,* with the rest of the Tales." A marginal gloss on avaricious clergy who exploit their flock interprets *The Plowman's Tale* explicitly as a subtext for Spenser's ecclesiastical eclogues by observing that "of such shepheards speakes maister *Spencer* in his Kalender" (sig. A3v). A note on the "making of a Crede" in *The Plowman's Tale* (l. 1066) invokes other apocryphal texts: "Some thinke hee means the questions of *Jackupland,* or perhaps *Pierce Ploughmans* Creede. For *Chaucer* speakes this in the person of the Pellican, not in his owne person" (sig. G1r–v). The Plowman's retelling of the religious debate between the Pelican and Griffin was evidently interpreted in favor of the former, who is aided in victory by an apocalyptic Phoenix symbolic of Christ and the advent of Christ's kingdom during the Reformation.

From the initial publication of the "moral" eclogues, E.K.'s notes led readers to interpret them in terms of the general conflict between "two formes of pastoures or Ministers, or the protestant and the Catholique" (argument of "May"). According to William Webbe's *Discourse of English Poetrie* (1586), the "morall lessons" of the *Calender* include "the commendation of good Pastors, and shame and disprayse of idle and ambitious Goteheardes, in the seaventh: the loose and retchlesse lyving of Popish Prelates, in the ninth . . ."[20] Not until the eve of the English Civil War were these satires reinterpreted as Puritan antiprelatical propaganda, when Milton argued that it is the prelates of the Church of England whom "our admired *Spencer* inveighs against, not without some presage of these reforming times."[21] Milton evidently used the *Calender* as a model for ecclesiastical satire in his own pastoral elegy, *Lycidas* (1638), which "by occasion foretells the ruin of our corrupted Clergy then in their height."[22] Milton's fondness for Spenser's satires suggests that Piers's defense of poetry in "October," ll. 19–20 (*"Cuddie,* the prayse is better, then the price, / The glory eke

20. Smith, *Essays,* I, 264.
21. *Animadversions against Smectymnuus* (1641), in *Complete Prose Works,* ed. Don M. Wolfe et al., 8 vols. in 10 (New Haven, 1953–1982), I, 722–723.
22. See the treatment of the *Calender* as "a general context for *Lycidas*" by Joseph A. Wittreich, Jr., in *Visionary Poetics: Milton's Tradition and His Legacy* (San Marino, Calif., 1979), pp. 105–116.

much greater then the gayne"), is one exemplar for the first
consolation in *Lycidas:*

> "But not the praise,"
> *Phoebus* repli'd, and touch'd my trembling ears;
> *"Fame* is no plant that grows on mortal soil,
> Nor in the glistering foil
> Set off to th'world, nor in broad rumor lies . . ."
>                                                    (ll. 76–80)

During the Restoration Henry More reverted to Webbe's position by interpreting "February" not as a Puritan attack but as
a prophecy of how Puritans would suffer as a result of their
attack on the episcopacy.[23] The variety of such readings is a
tribute to the open-endedness of Spenser's allegories.

Recognition of the pastoral conventions of English Protestant
satire permits better understanding of the themes of the moral
eclogues. Critics who argue that Spenser is a Catholic sympa-
thizer disregard the religious ideas attributed to his satirical
models, as well as E.K.'s commentary and other early interpretations of the *Calender.* Neither the text nor its immediate
literary context supports the longstanding tradition that Spenser
articulates a Puritan attack on the Elizabethan church settlement.[24] This anachronistic view of Spenser cannot be identified
prior to Milton's antiprelatical interpretation. Early readers of
the *Calender,* such as William Webbe and the anonymous editor
of the 1606 edition of *The Plowman's Tale,* agree that the "moral"
eclogues should be placed in an anti-Roman, not an antiepis-
copalian, context.

Repetition in the moral eclogues of a network of Reformation
satirical conventions and techniques makes them a coherent
subsection within the *Calender.* They are woven together further
by the rudimentary narratives concerning the fate of Algrind
and Palinode's pilgrimage to Rome. Formulaic features of these

23. *A Modest Enquiry into the Mystery of Iniquity* (1664), pp. 514–515.
24. Hume's *Protestant Poet* revives a line of critical argument going back to
1863, which is summarized in *Variorum,* VII, pt. 1, 600–609. See King, "Was
Spenser a Puritan?" for a critique of this position.

poems include the juxtaposition of blunt, truth-telling shepherds with pastors exhibiting a variety of clerical failings; the gospel ethos of the plain-speaking pastors; the use of type names from Reformation satirical tradition; the use of the native plain style as well as the flat metrical and stanzaic structures of vernacular verse; and the embedding of "tragic" fables within the debates on clerical topics. The didacticism and the repetition of *de casibus* formulas in the eclogues suggests that we are being told the same kind of monitory tale again and again.

Avoiding traditional classical names for his shepherds, such as Thyrsis, Corydon, and Damoetas, Spenser uses simple English names that establish reformist vernacular works as a generic context. As the type of the Protestant pastor in "May," Piers (or Pierce) invokes the native alliterative tradition of *Piers Plowman* and the apocryphal satires ascribed to both Chaucer and Langland. This character's name and occupation suggest a nature that probes beneath outer surfaces to discern inward truth. Although Diggon Davie (that is, Dickon Davy) is original to Spenser, the name suggests an inheritance from "Dawe the dyker," a poor ditch digger whose prophesied death by starvation is cited in the attack on avaricious clergy and landlords in *Piers Plowman*.[25] This name, like that of Piers, suggests a probing seeker who is on a quest for spiritual understanding. He is a close literary cousin of Chaucer's Plowman, of whom it is said: "He wolde thresshe, and therto dyke and delve" *(General Prologue,* l. 536). The Reformation vogue for *Piers Plowman* spawned a truth-telling character named Davy Diker in Thomas Churchyard's imitation of Langland, a millennial vision of a perfect commonwealth entitled *Davy Dycars Dreame* (circa 1552).[26] Piers as a defender of poetry is linked to Colin Clout, whom he praises in "October" as the embodiment of Du Bartas' Protestant theory of poetry. Even Colin's name furnishes a vestigial link to Protestant satire as a hybrid derived from Skelton's

25. Sig. G1v; see Skeat, *Piers Plowman,* B.5.320.

26. William Waterman's *Westerne Wyll* acknowledges Churchyard's debt to Langland: "This Diker sems a thryving ladde, brought up in pieres scole / The plowman stoute, of whom I thynke ye have often harde." See *The Contention bettwyxte Churchyeard and Camell, upon David Dycers Dreame, Newlye Imprinted* (1560), sigs. A1r-v, C4v, G1r.

*Collyn Clout* (composed 1521–1522) and the homiletic pastorals
of the Huguenot poet Clément Marot. Despite Skelton's hostility to the Lutherans, reformers approved of his verse because
they read his satire on Cardinal Wolsey and abuses in the church
in the Lollard tradition of *The Plowman's Tale*.[27] Marot's pastorals look to the parable of the Good Shepherd as a model for
Protestant reform.[28]

Spenser confers the classical name Tityrus on both Chaucer
and Virgil, as a means of affirming that England possesses a
literature equal to that produced by ancient and modern continental authors. The ambiguity of Tityrus, whose attributes as
Roman Virgil are overlaid with those of English Chaucer, typ-
ifies the double nature of a complicated collection whose dense
layers integrate a simultaneous appeal to creativity and authority. E.K., acknowledging that pastoral is the lowest form
in the neoclassical hierarchy of kinds, implicitly lodges a claim
that Spenser rivals Virgil (and Chaucer) as a composer of eclogues and in the probability that he will ultimately become
England's epic poet. As Colin's master and the ancient model
for British vernacular poetry, the English Tityrus exemplifies
the traits of the rustic truth-teller. Thenot, for example, declares
that in his youth he learned a "tale of truth" from him ("February," ll. 91–93). The overlay of the English Tityrus and "the
Romish *Tityrus*" ("October," l. 55 and gloss) enables Spenser
to lodge an exalted claim both to inherit and to overgo native
and classical exemplars of poetic excellence. Thus Chaucer furnishes Spenser's model for the structures and conventions of
the satirical eclogues, as well as the role of the new English poet
as defined in the envoi and in E.K.'s prefaces. The discipleship
of Colin to the English Tityrus as a singer of songs is acknowledged in "January" and "June," a relationship cited repeatedly
in E.K.'s glosses.

Sidney's censure of Spenser's imitation of "an old rustick
language" in the *Calender* applies most notably to the "Chau-

27. John Bale, *Scriptorum illustrium maioiris Brytanniae . . . catalogus,* 2
vols. (Basel, 1557–1559), I, 651.
28. "Sermon très utile et salutaire du bon pasteur et du mauvais" in *Psalmes
de David* (Anvers, 1541), and *La Complaincte d'un pastoureau chrestien* (Rouen,
1549).

cerian" style of the satirical eclogues. E.K.'s derivation of "aeglogue" from the Greek term for "Goteheards tales" justifies the *Calender*'s vernacular style by analogy to the stock association of "satire" (spelled "satyr" in the sixteenth century) with the rough shagginess of the satyrs and ancient Greek satyr plays.[29] E.K. argues that the "most auncient Poetes . . . devised this kind of wryting, being both so base for the matter, and homely for the manner" as an appropriate medium for the fledgling poet. Accordingly, he glosses archaic "Chaucerian" diction as a lexical aid to the Tudor reader.

Spenser's echoes of Chaucer's rhetorical device of affected modesty flag his use of a plain style within individual eclogues. Thomalin's disclaimer—"How be I am but rude and borrell" ("July," l. 95)—reduplicates, without the irony of Chaucer's original, the Franklin's protest: "I am a burel man" (*Franklin's Prologue*, l. 8). Similarly, Diggon Davie's self-reflexive comment that his "english is flatt" confirms Hobbinal's opinion of the "plaine" speech of "September" (ll. 104–105, 136). Although the "medieval" verse patterns Spenser adopts were in their origins complex and sophisticated, by the sixteenth century they seemed homely and provincial. The nine-syllable accentual verse of all but one of the religious satires reflects Chaucer's lines as the Tudors imperfectly read them, having lost the medieval pronunciation of the accented terminal "-e." The use of fourteeners (a variation of ballad measure) in the remaining poem, "July," recalls the Reformation adaptation of traditional folk song to religious purposes in the Common Measure of Sternhold and Hopkins' Psalter. (Common Measure is also used in the arguments to the cantos of *The Faerie Queene*.) Robert Crowley, the first editor of *Piers Plowman,* was also an early experimenter in the use of ballad measure for Psalm paraphrase. The universal influence of the popular vernacular translations of the Bible provided a counterweight to neoclassical standards and aureation.

The religious satires contain debates between Protestant- and Catholic-type characters, which in turn enclose exemplary fables

---

29. Alvin Kernan, *The Cankered Muse: Satire of the English Renaissance* (New Haven, 1959), pp. 54–63.

or tales. Distinctively Protestant literary texts mediate between the embedded tales of "February" and "September" and the fabular paradigms of Aesop and the medieval Reynard tradition. The embedded tales of the Fox and the Kid, and Roffy and the Wolf emulate not only medieval prototypes such as the Reynard story in *The Nun's Priest's Tale* but also the debate between the Pelican and the Griffin in *The Plowman's Tale* and the polemical beast fables by William Turner and John Bale.[30] Spenser's enclosure of tales exhibits the same format as *The Plowman's Tale,* in which an outer dialogue articulates different religious viewpoints by way of introduction to a fable in which opposed allegorical types—a Pelican and a Griffin—personify the Reformation conflict. This work varies the Chaucerian habit of embedding a tale narrated by a member of the Canterbury pilgrimage, such as the Pardoner or Wife of Bath, within a prologue and an epilogue involving a dramatic exchange between pilgrims in the company. Sidney may well allude to Spenser's innovative inclusion of beast fables within eclogues when he lists animal tales among the variations of pastoral: "Is the poore pype disdained, which . . . sometimes, under the prettie tales of Wolves and Sheepe, can include the whole considerations of wrong dooing and patience."[31] William Baldwin varies the conventional Protestant scenario of the "hunting" down of "Romish" wolves and foxes in *Beware the Cat* (1570; composed 1553), in which cunning cats witness the falsity of their human counterparts.

Spenser embeds within his satires "tragedies" that identify moral and spiritual failures as the effects of individual sin and clerical abuses. E.K. then fuses undeveloped notions of catastrophe and pathos with Spenser's obvious biblical models ("May," glosses to ll. 174, 189). Thomalin's description in "July" of the

30. John Bale's *Yet a Course at the Romyshe Foxe* (Antwerp, 1543) initiated a series of Protestant polemics including William Turner's *The Huntyng and Fyndyng Out of the Romishe Fox* (Bonn, 1543) and *Rescuynge of the Romishe Foxe Other Wyse Called the Examination of the Hunter Devised by Steven Gardiner* (Bonn, 1545). The latter work quotes Gardiner's *Examination of the Hunter,* a counterattack that circulated in an edition now lost or only in manuscript.
31. Smith, *Essays,* I, 175.

dangers of high estate repeats commonplaces concerning the operations of Fortune that were familiar from Chaucer's *Monk's Tale, The Mirror for Magistrates,* and mirror visions by George Cavendish and others:

> Ah God shield, man, that I should clime,
>     and learne to looke alofte,
> This reede is ryfe, that oftentime
>     great clymbers fall unsoft.
>
> (ll. 9–12)

E.K.'s comment on the universality of the Fall makes it clear that individual tragedies recapitulate the primal sin of Adam, who, "by hys follye and disobedience, made all the rest of hys ofspring be debarred and shutte out from thence" (gloss to l. 63). This archetypal cycle is recapitulated in the experience of the Kid, Algrind, and both the Oak and Briar.

The Christian stoic response to misfortune is assimilated to the clerical paradigm of the good pastor through the homiletic counsel of Thenot, who, despite his consciousness of mutability and flux, never "was to Fortune foeman, / But gently tooke, that ungently came":

> Must not the world wend in his commun course
> From good to badd, and from badde to worse,
> From worse unto that is worst of all,
> And then returne to his former fall?
> ("February," ll. 11–14, 21–22)

His acceptance of Fortune and awareness of the inevitability of sin and the Fall counterbalance Cuddie's thoughtless hedonism, as he conflates the counsel of the Old Testament Preacher to "remember now thy Creator in the daies of thy youth" (Eccles. 12:1) with St. Paul's admonition, "for the wages of sinne is death" (Rom. 6:23):

> *Cuddie,* I wote thou kenst little good,
> So vainely tadvaunce thy headlesse hood.
> For Youngth is a bubble blown up with breath,
> Whose witt is weakeness, whose wage is death,
> Whose way is wildernesse, whose ynne Penaunce,
> And stoopegallaunt Age the hoste of Greevaunce.
> ("February," ll. 85–90)

Unlike the Oak, Thenot provides a positive example of age and
the possibilities of penance and spiritual regeneration, in contrast to Cuddie who, along with the Briar and the Kid, conforms
to the Protestant type-figure of unrepentant youth that was familiar from Reformation moral interludes like R. Wever's *Lusty
Juventus* (1550).

The tragic fall of the good pastor, Algrind, in the "July"
eclogue suggests that Spenser differentiates between two different kinds of *de casibus* tragedy along the lines practiced in
Bale's plays or Foxe's *Book of Martyrs*. Those authors counterbalance the eternal suffering of "reprobate" Catholics with
the limited, worldly tragedies of the faithful that will eventually
be absorbed into the overarching "comic" pattern of providential history. Their practice finds an analogue in the apocalyptic
commentary in which Spenser's earliest verse appeared, Jan van
der Noot's *A Theatre wherein be represented as wel the miseries
and calamities that follow the voluptuous Worldlings* (1569).

Thomalin's comment on the dangers of high estate suggest
that Morrell, as a "proude and ambitious" cleric, is positioned
for a fall from fortune:

> Ah God shield, man, that I should clime,
>     and learne to looke alofte,
> This reede is ryfe, that oftentime
>     great clymbers fall unsoft.
>                                   ("July," ll. 9–12)

Despite Algrind's evident virtues, however, it is he who falls.
But prediction that he "shall be bett in time" (l. 230) holds out
the prospect that his suffering and misery will receive their final
fulfillment in a recovery of good fortune and eventual salvation.

E.K. claims that the debate in "February" between Cuddie and
Thenot is "rather morall and generall, then bent to any secrete
or particular purpose." Its ambiguity sets it apart from the other
satirical eclogues and their specific controversial topics. Thenot's allegorical fable recapitulates the outer dialogue between
Age and Youth, in which that "olde Shepheard" debates the

meaning of life with Cuddie, the young and energetic "Heard-mans boye." The attribution to Tityrus of the "Aesopic" fable of the Oak and Briar alludes to the apocryphal Chaucerian tradition, including works such as *The Plowman's Tale* with its debaters skilled in religious topics: the Pelican and Griffin. Thenot, who accepts mutability and the attendant tragic nature of life, chides his companion for a careless devotion to a life of ease, love, and pleasure, and his inset fable functions ostensibly as a moralized *exemplum* concerning the frailty of youth.

The association between the "aged Tree" and the old religion clearly introduces a religious dimension into this universal conflict:

> For it had bene an auncient tree,
> Sacred with many a mysteree,
> And often crost with the priestes crewe,
> And often halowed with holy water dewe.
> But sike fancies weren foolerie,
> And broughten this Oake to this miserye.
>                                         (ll. 207–212)

E.K.'s gloss directs the reader to associate the "finall decay of this auncient Oake" with the past when "the popishe priest used to sprinckle and hallowe the trees from mischaunce. Such blind-nesse was in those times . . ." Nevertheless, an interpretative crux results from the disparity between the presence of some degree of sympathy for the "goodly Oake" and the dissimulation of the manifestly flawed and "proude weede," who uses "painted words" to conceal his "colowred crime with craft" (ll. 103, 160–162). Elsewhere Spenser links this kind of hypocrisy to Catholic type characters such as the false Wolves who devour sheep "under colour of shepeheards" ("May," l. 126).

The double tragedy of the Oak and Briar is the first of several examples of the *de casibus* formula, all of which reduplicate the archetypal tragedy of the sin and fall of Adam and Eve. Although this fable lacks an explicit topical application, and thereby differs from those in the eclogues on ecclesiastical concerns, it nevertheless articulates a double-edged warning against the religious excesses of both radical Protestants and Catholic recusants. Even though the Oak has earned its "miserye" through "foolerie" and false belief (ll. 211–212), its destruction leaves the Briar fatally exposed.

Although a persuasive argument may be mounted against the recusancy of the Oak—after all, Protestantism claimed that it was the ancient "religion of the apostles and Catholicism a latter-day distortion"—Reformation satirists used generational conflict conventionally as a complex allegorical figure that could be directed against either "old" Catholic believers or headstrong Protestant youth.[32] In Wever's *Lusty Juventus,* for example, the youth (Juventus) is torn between the "young" faith of the Protestant and the "old" carnal corruption of the Catholic. Donne similarly uses the transition from one generation to the next as a paradoxical metaphor for religious reform in "Satire III," whose speaker fears that Catholic forebears may be closer to salvation than those living in the present age of religious reform:

> . . . and shall thy fathers spirit
> Meete blinde Philosophers in heaven, whose merit
> Of strict life may be imputed faith, and heare
> Thee, whom he taught so easie wayes and neare
> To follow, damn'd?
>
> (ll. 11–15)

The "generational" nature of tradition and authority was a fundamental question during the Reformation, when Protestants claimed to return to the practices of the primitive church of the New Testament and apostolic age, while Catholics claimed validity for the nonscriptural traditions or "unwritten verities" promulgated by church councils or the papacy after the apostolic age. Most assuredly Spenser issues no defense of the recusants, but he does acknowledge that there is some goodness worthy of preservation in the old religion. "February" takes a qualified stand on reform through its sentiment that it is best to retain whatever goodness inheres in old religious tradition while throwing away abuses. Many Tudor readers assumed that the Protestant movement should preserve valid practices from old tradition.

32. Nelson, *Poetry of Edmund Spenser,* pp. 44–45. See also King, *English Reformation Literature,* pp. 280–281.

"May," "July," and "September" all consider the manner in which shepherd-pastors embody the ministerial ideals of poverty, humility, and dedication to pastoral care. In these poems a set of anagrams and nicknames points to a circle of reform-minded, progressive bishops who supported this evangelical model for the church. The tragic tale of the idealized pastor, Algrind, provides a thin veil for the fall from royal favor of Edmund Grindal, the recently sequestered archbishop of Canterbury. Grindal's protégé John Young, bishop of Rochester, was Spenser's patron during the composition of the *Calender*. This circle may also include Thomas Cooper, bishop of Lincoln, and Richard Davies, bishop of Saint David's.[33]

The chief speaker in "May," Piers, comes from the line of radical visionaries descending from Piers Plowman and the pseudo-Chaucerian Plowman, just as the Catholicism of his interlocutor, Palinode ("countersong"), may be inferred from his fondness for holidays and his devotion to "Sir John" (a Tudor cliché for a Roman priest). The later report in "July" (ll. 181–192) of Palinode's recusancy and pilgrimage to Rome weights this dialogue in favor of Piers. Although E.K.'s comment on "two formes of pastoures or Ministers, or the protestant and Catholique" ("May," argument) reduces the complexity of these characters, his urgent warning that "the protestaunt beware, howe he geveth credit to the unfaythfull Catholique" (gloss to l. 304) leads the reader to interpret the text in terms of the fundamental Reformation division between England and Rome. This is the interpretation assumed by William Webbe in his notes on the *Calender*.

Piers's railing attack on Maying customs and the proliferation of holidays and veneration of the saints raises fundamental Protestant issues concerning clerical ignorance and avarice and the spiritual failures due to hireling shepherds who "playen while their flockes be unfedde":

> Perdie so farre am I from envie,
> That their fondnesse inly I pitie.

---

33. On the Grindal allusions, see Norbrook, pp. 68–69. McLane supplies a detailed context for the identification of topical allusion in *Study of Elizabethan Allegory*, esp. pp. 176–187, 190, 207, 216–234.

> Those faytours little regarden their charge,
> While they letting their sheepe run at large . . .
> (ll. 37–40)

Spenser uses biblical texts to evoke a gospel vision of the primitive church in Piers's invective and exemplary tale. The attack
on both hireling shepherds and those who abandon their flock
by putting them out for hire (that is, nonresident holders of
benefices) compares both to the unworthy servant in Christ's
Parable of the Talents (Matt. 25:14–30):

> I muse, what account both these will make,
> The one for the hire, which he doth take,
> And thother for leaving his Lords taske,
> When great *Pan* account of shepeherdes shall aske.
> (ll. 51–54)

And his attack on the increasing worldliness of false shepherds,
resulting in the destruction of their flock, invokes the Sermon
on the Mount (Matt. 7:15):

> Tho under colour of shepeheards, somewhile
> There crept in Wolves, ful of fraude and guile,
> That often devoured their owne sheepe,
> And often the shepheards, that did hem keepe.
> (ll. 126–129)

Scriptural allusions underlie Spenser's pervasive pastoral imagery of the wolves and the sheep (see Jer. 5:6, Matt. 10:16,
and Luke 10:3). E.K.'s comment on Pan as "Christ, the very
God of all shepheards, which calleth himselfe the greate and
good shepherd" (gloss on l. 54), links "May" to the fundamental
metaphor of biblical pastoral. E.K.'s glosses also explicitly invite
the reader to apply Piers's embedded tale of the Fox and the
Kid—an exemplum illustrating Christ's admonition to beware
of wolves in sheep's clothing (Matt. 7:15)—to questions of Protestant reform by identifying the Kid as "the simple sorte of the
faythfull and true Christians" and the Fox with "the false and
faithlesse Papistes." According to E.K., the Kid's tragic fall
exemplifies the dangers of religious backsliding, warning "the
protestaunt beware, howe he geveth credit to the unfaythfull
Catholique."

The strident scripturalism of "May," E.K.'s biases, and the homage paid by Spenser to the *Piers Plowman* poet, Chaucer, and the apocryphal works associated with them seem to balance this dialogue in favor of Piers. Nevertheless, the poet himself takes no explicit stand. Palinode's call for tolerance is not altogether lacking in sympathy, and his position approaches that of Hobbinal, the friend of Colin Clout who is idealized in "September," and whose stoical counsel of acceptance and contentment is opposed to the unbending rigorism of Diggon Davie, a radical cousin of Piers:

> Ah fon, now by thy losse art taught,
> That seeldome chaunge the better brought.
> Content who lives with tryed state,
> Neede feare no chaunge of frowning fate:
> But who will seeke for unknowne gayne,
> Oft lives by losse, and leaves with payne.
> (ll. 68–73)

Furthermore, Piers's attack on Maying customs is at this time associated with attacks on drama and fiction because they "lie" or exert a morally corrupting influence. Palinode's tolerance for dancing and entertainment, however, mirrors Spenser's evident approval of fictionality and artistry, as it is embodied in the complex interplay of narrative and dramatic structures in the *Calender*. This line of argument becomes explicit in "October," with its reasoned justification of poetry, paralleling in some ways the Protestant activist Sir Philip Sidney's formal defense of fictional art in *An Apologie for Poetrie*. "February" also indicates Spenser's concern to frame a complex dialectic in which both speakers and their arguments contain a mixture of wisdom and folly. His pastoral dialogues are genuine discussions in which speakers disagree and valid arguments may be brought forward on both sides. In "May," despite the weakness of Palinode's position, Piers is neither flawless nor a simple mouthpiece for Spenser's religious opinions.

Algrind's fall from favor provides the kernel of the July eclogue, where Spenser models Thomalin's attack on ecclesiastical corruption on the messianic prophecy that "Everie valleie shalbe exalted, and everie mountaine and hill shalbe made lowe" (Isa.

40:1–5). Tudor Protestants viewed this call for moral and spiritual renewal as the *locus classicus* for satirical attacks on avarice and clerical failure.[34] Spenser's eclogue, E.K.'s argument in "commendation, of good shepeheardes" and "disprayse of proude and ambitious Pastours," and a pointed allusion to *The Plowman's Tale* identify the hill-dwelling Morrell (evidently an anagram for Grindal's opponent, John Aylmer, bishop of London) with Catholic veneration of the saints and retention of clerical vestments. Although the vestiarian movement that began in the 1560s was still alive, here the ostentatious apparel of false shepherds is linked to the vestments of "Popes and Cardinalles" rather than to the surplice and square cap to which the Puritans objected (ll. 171–177 and gloss to l. 173).

Christ's division between the elect sheep and reprobate goats (Matt. 25:32–33) underlies the conflict between the haughty pride of Morrell and the simplicity of Thomalin, who tends his sheep in "the lowly playne." The biblical imagery of the unfaithful goats links "May" and "July" by suggesting that Morrell the goatherd exemplifies the kind of clerical corruption that made the Kid in the earlier eclogue vulnerable to the stratagems of the false Fox. Thomalin's reference to Palinode's pilgrimage to Rome (ll. 181–184) further interlaces the two dialogues by furnishing a narrative postscript to "May"; Protestants identified pilgrimages, shrines, and relics with idolatry and the Catholic doctrine of justification by good works.

This eclogue dramatizes the conflict between the Protestant desire for a return to the simple, evangelical piety of the primitive church and the perceived abuses of Roman Catholic traditions and church hierarchy. The humble shepherd Thomalin accordingly pays homage to "the great God *Pan*":

> O blessed sheepe, O shepeheard great,
>    that bought his flocke so deare,

---

34. Robert Crowley, for example, uses it as an epigraph for the series of reformist appeals to twelve hierarchical estates including priests and clergy in *The Voyce of the Laste Trumpet* (1549). According to the Stationers' register, the *Voyce* was still on sale in London at the time that Spenser wrote the *Calender*. See also n. 15.

And them did save with bloudy sweat
from Wolves, that would them teare.
(ll. 53–56)

His words allude to the dramatization of the gospel parable of
the Good Shepherd begun in "May," where E.K. identified Pan
as "Christ, the very God of all shepheards, which calleth himselfe the greate and good shepherd" (gloss on l. 54). In an
inversion of Christ's parable, sheep are "sold" to false shepherds
by "theyr Pan," identified by E.K. as "the Pope, whom they
count theyr God and greatest shepheard" (l. 179 and gloss).
Thomalin's tale of Algrind emphasizes the clerical ideal of humility exemplified by Christ, the Good Shepherd, and the Old
Testament types for priesthood, Moses and Aaron.

Algrind's fable daringly alludes to current ecclesiastical affairs. The name of that lamented shepherd is a palpable anagram
for Edmund Grindal, whose refusal to execute Queen Elizabeth's order to suppress the prophesyings (gatherings of zealous
clergy for Bible study) led to his disgrace, and Thomalin's tale
unreservedly articulates the yearning of Protestant progressives
of the "Grindalian" era (1575–1577) for a ministry and episcopacy characterized by poverty, humility, simplicity, and a
devotion to pastoral care (ll. 127–136). Despite Algrind's obvious virtues as a clergyman, it is he who suffers the tragic fall
that would seem due instead to Morrell as a "Goteherd prowd."
No hint is given that Algrind is tainted by the pride and ambition
that are so often a feature of *de casibus* tragedy (see ll. 9–12,
101–104). Thomalin applies his tale as a generalized moral *exemplum* that warns against "height":

He is a shepherd great in gree,
but hath bene long ypent.
One daye he sat upon a hyll,
(as now thou wouldest me:
But I am taught by *Algrins* ill,
to love the lowe degree.)
(ll. 215–220)

Although the hazardous analogy between the high-flying Eagle
and Queen Elizabeth is clear enough, neither explanation nor

blame is attached to her decision to brain Algrind with a shellfish
in the manner of the legendary account of Aeschylus' death.
The self-protective praise of "the meane and lowly state" in the
glosses and concluding emblem generalizes the issues by tactfully acknowledging both royal fiat and the conventional danger
of rising high on Fortune's Wheel. Indeed, Protestant politiques
like Leicester and Walsingham who were in sympathy with the
progressive program always tempered their opposition to royal
policy with a prudent awareness of the royal supremacy. At no
point does Spenser criticize the queen over her handling of the
incident, and the attribution of Algrind's destruction to "hap,"
"myshap," and "chaunce" (l. 229 and gloss on l. 213) accords
with the fable's character as a *de casibus* tragedy. Nevertheless,
"July" holds out hope for Algrind's restoration.

"September" offers a variation of the biblical *topoi* of wolves
in sheep's clothing and the lost sheep. The character of Diggon
Davie combines the latter image and that of the returned prodigal who sought to better his fortune in "a farre countrye," only
to be disillusioned by the pride and greed of the false shepherds
he found there. Although there is some evidence for identifying
Wales as this distant land,[35] E.K.'s reference to the "abuses
. . . and loose living of Popish prelates" ("September," argument) suggests Rome as the likely locale. Palinode's pilgrimage
to that city serves as a vehicle for attack on many related clerical
failings. Diggon's tale of "Argus eyed" Roffy (or Roffyn) is a
variation of Piers's emphasis in "May" on the need for watch-
fulness against the skillful dissimulation of the false Fox (a type
for Antichrist according to E.K.). Although the specific details
of the incident remain enigmatic, Diggon's narrative styles Roffy
as a type of the Good Shepherd, Christ. Roffy epitomizes the
vigilance appropriate to the ideal cleric: he discerns the depra-
dations against his flock of "a wicked Wolfe . . . / Ycladde in
clothing of seely sheepe" (ll. 184, 188; see Matt. 7:15), and kills
the predator.

"October," the last of the satirical eclogues, is in a category
by itself, for E.K. defines the object of its attack as "the com-

35. *Study in Elizabethan Allegory*, pp. 126, 216–234.

tempte [*sic*] of Poetrie, and the causes thereof" rather than
religious abuses. This climactic hymn to poetry addresses one
of the problems that occasioned Sidney's *Apologie for Poetrie:*
whether there is suitable matter, audience, and reward for the
poet in this age. Spenser here evolves a Protestant theory of
poetry (that is, fiction) that aligns him with the sacred poetry
movement associated with Guillaume de Saluste Du Bartas and
articulated in *La Muse Chrestiene* (Bordeaux, 1574). Spenser
found it easy to incorporate into Piers's speeches neoplatonic
views of poetry as a divine gift and a poetic rapture, because
of his belief that the Bible is not only the source of spiritual
truth but also a fundamental model for poetic art. Cuddie's
possession by a "Poeticall furie" is not unlike Bartesian inspiration.

This eclogue articulates the *Calender*'s most explicit statement
concerning poetic imitation, because Cuddie ("the perfecte
paterne of a Poete" according to E.K.) epitomizes the self-
conscious concern of a poet like Spenser with overgoing his
predecessors to become *the* English poet. The relation to Virgil,
"the Romish *Tityrus*" (l. 55), is particularly complex, because
his career furnishes the classical paradigm for Piers's exhortation
to Cuddie to abandon the lowly style and matter of pastoral for
the romantic epic. That it should be Piers, the type of the plain-
spoken vernacular shepherd-poet, who argues on behalf of
"pierlesse Poesye" demonstrates Spenser's eclecticism in hon-
oring native and foreign models of poetic achievement, at the
same time that he attempts to overgo them. Cuddie's limited
awareness of his own worth and that of poetry in general is set
off against the moral earnestness and idealism of Colin Clout
(a figure for Spenser as poet), which epitomizes for Piers the
possibility of neoplatonic ascent through love and poetry:

> . . . for love does teach him to climbe so hie,
> And lyftes him up out of the loathsome myre:
> Such immortal mirrhour, as he doth admire,
> Would rayse ones mynd above the starry skie.
> And cause a caytive corage to aspire,
> For lofty love doth loath a lowly eye.
>
> (ll. 91–96)

Spenser carefully avoids introducing his own poetic voice, Colin Clout, into the satirical eclogues,[36] an absence that places these poems as only one of several segments in the *Calender* as a whole. The lofty goals and heroic ideals articulated by Piers for Colin and his career look beyond that collection to final fulfillment in his great national epic, *The Faerie Queene,* which was already under way at the time that Spenser published the *Calender.*[37] Spenser's fondness for manifestly Protestant satire extends into the mature work of *The Faerie Queene,* but, as readers have long recognized, his militant use of Revelation and other biblical texts to attack the papacy and Church of Rome is there identified with romantic epic rather than pastoral habits and conventions.

Spenser displays a self-conscious concern with genre in *The Shepheardes Calender,* one that E.K. mirrors in his glosses. The collection is a virtuoso display of metrical and stylistic sophistication by a writer who follows precedent in donning pastoral disguise to claim the title of England's "new Poete." Although Renaissance poets regarded the Arcadian genre of classical eclogue as the ideal environment for the apprentice poet, Spenser would not abandon the native tradition of reforming poetry. Even though he follows the neo-Latin examples of Petrarch and Mantuan in using the eclogue to discuss religious problems, Spenser's bold vernacular voices are new to the pastoral scene. Spenser's imitation of stylistically unorthodox literary models in order to fashion a plain-spoken English voice was, in an apparent paradox, an innovation at a time when neoclassical critics like Sidney and Puttenham were trying to suppress "inferior" native models. The tribute paid to Tityrus, who encompasses both Roman Virgil and English Chaucer, marks Spenser's generic innovation in constructing a new kind of Protestant pastoral satire.

36. Richard Helgerson, *Self-Crowned Laureates: Spenser, Jonson, Milton, and the Literary System* (Berkeley and Los Angeles, 1983), p. 85n37. See also Norbrook, p. 86.

37. *Variorum,* IX, 17 and 474.

HEATHER DUBROW

# A Mirror for Complaints: Shakespeare's *Lucrece* and Generic Tradition

Scholars typically dismiss both *Venus and Adonis* and *The Rape of Lucrece* as mere literary samplers, works in which an undiscriminating preoccupation with rhetorical display precludes a sustained concern for other issues, be they formal, psychological, or moral. According to such interpretations, Shakespeare's overriding concern is to cram as many tropes as possible into these poems, even at the expense of their overall structure. Thus one critic, lamenting the absence of subtle characterization in either poem, observes, "it is brilliance of the surface which has priority."[1] Rooted in a preconceived notion of what Shakespeare could and could not do early in his career and also, perhaps, in a misconceived distrust of elaborate wordplay, such interpretations have shaped our readings of *The Rape of Lucrece*. In particular, while many scholars have noted that Lucrece's lengthy speeches evidently participate in the tradition of

1. Richard Wilbur, introduction to William Shakespeare, *The Narrative Poems*, 2nd ed. (Harmondsworth, 1974), p. 18.

the complaint,[2] none has examined Shakespeare's approach to
that literary type in any depth; we have assumed he was too
preoccupied with the patterns of his tropes to give much attention to the patterns of his genre.

Yet another reason we have neglected the ways Shakespeare
approaches the complaint is that in many respects that literary
form is quite as slippery as Tarquin's rhetoric. Even *A Mirror
for Magistrates* itself changes as it goes through successive editions; most obviously, the later volumes include women among
their speakers. The subsequent works influenced by the *Mirror*
also differ considerably among themselves; thus, for example,
Drayton retains the structure of the dream vision in his "Robert,
Duke of Normandy" but abandons it in the complaint delivered
by that unlovely lover Peirs Gaveston. And if we include in our
descriptions of the genre pastoral complaints and sonnets, the
complaint comes to seem singularly amorphous even in an age
that delighted in loosely defined genres.

Nonetheless, when we compare *The Rape of Lucrece* to contemporary complaints, we uncover an approach to genre quite
as complex and intriguing as that in, say, *Love's Labour's Lost*.
For Shakespeare is writing not merely within the complaint
tradition but also against it: he is rendering many of its assumptions very prominent and very problematical. If Lucrece
delivers a complaint against Tarquin, in a sense Shakespeare
delivers one against his genre.

To explore Shakespeare's critical approach to the complaint,
we must first define that tradition more precisely than we cus-
tomarily do. In the largest sense, of course, his Roman narrative
does participate in that vast tradition of Tudor complaints that
is rooted in the *Mirror* and ultimately in Ovid's *Heroides*.[3] Hal-

2. See esp. Hallett Smith, *Elizabethan Poetry: A Study in Conventions, Meaning, and Expression* (Cambridge, Mass., 1952), pp. 113–117.
3. On that tradition, see, for example, Lily B. Campbell, ed., introduction
to *The Mirror for Magistrates* (Cambridge, 1938); Willard Farnham, *The Medieval Heritage of Elizabethan Tragedy* (1936; rpt. Oxford, 1956), esp. chap. 7;
E. M. W. Tillyard, *"A Mirror for Magistrates* Revisited," in *Elizabethan and
Jacobean Studies Presented to Frank Percy Wilson* (Oxford, 1959).

lett Smith has attempted to place *The Rape of Lucrece* in a narrower framework: the complaints written about inviolably chaste women in the 1590s.[4] Distinguishing these poems from their counterparts in the *Mirror,* he maintains that they substitute increased sentiment for the moral and political concerns of earlier works in the genre; the primary aim of these later complaints, he argues, is to move their readers, not to instruct them.

I would suggest, however, that both Shakespeare and his Elizabethan readers were more likely to interpret his poem in the context of a different type of complaint, a category including certain of the works that Hallett Smith enumerates and a number of others as well. In some poems of this type, the heroine does retain her chastity, but in others she surrenders it. And, significantly enough, she is threatened by a ruler, a situation that invites speculations on the uses and abuses of power. Rather than neglecting the political questions threaded through the *Mirror,* these complaints simply approach them from a different perspective, that of the women who variously yield to the monarch's power or, alternatively, valiantly preserve their chastity in the face of it. No fewer than seven poems of this type appeared within the brief span of two years: Daniel's "The Complaint of Rosamond" (1592); Churchyard's "The Tragedy of Shore's Wife" (1593), a considerably expanded version of a poem in *A Mirror for Magistrates;* Chute's "Beawtie Dishonoured" (1593); Lodge's "The Complaint of Elstred" (1593); Barnfield's "The Complaint of Chastitie" (1594); Drayton's "Matilda" (1594); and, of course, *The Rape of Lucrece* (1594). Although these poems may deviate from the formula in small particulars (most obviously, Tarquin is not a king but the son of one), they follow it closely enough—and appear in close enough conjunction with each other—for contemporary readers to have sensed themselves in the presence of a subgenre.

In certain regards all the poems in that subgenre, including Shakespeare's, are very similar. To begin with, they repeatedly allude to the perils of praise, condemned in Drayton's "Matilda"

4. Smith, *Elizabethan Poetry,* pp. 102–130.

as a "fond pratling Parrat" (l. 153),[5] and of praise's bastard brother, flattery. Chute's "Beawtie Dishonoured" includes a passage on the subject that could serve as a gloss to Collatine's tragically ill-considered boast about Lucrece's beauty:

> For till thou first with thine vnhappie storie,
> Ecchoing relations of my worth and me:
> Intitul'dst my name to my bewties glorie,
> Vnworthie knowne, of such a worth to be
>   Though not performed in so royall measure
>   Yet then I ioy'd a life of quyet pleasure.
>                                   (ll. 486–491)[6]

And these complaints repeatedly draw attention to the moral ambiguities involved in the process of persuasion, with Daniel actually bodying forth those dangers in his portrait of the woman who tempts Rosamond:

> Shee set vpon me with the smoothest speech,
> That Court and age could cunningly deuise:
> The one autentique made her fit to teach,
> The other learnt her how to subtelise:
> Both were enough to circumuent the wise.
>                                   (ll. 218–222)[7]

Wise, Rosamond is not, and she is easily circumvented by the wiles of rhetoric.

Another similarity between these poems and Shakespeare's narrative is their concern for the political implications of what Lucrece herself terms "private pleasure" (l. 1478).[8] Drayton makes explicit an implication in several other poems: a ruler's sexual aggression is a symptom of his tyranny. In "Matilda" we witness lust distorting the king's relationship not only with the title character but also with his other subjects: he actually ban-

5. *The Works of Michael Drayton,* ed. J. William Hebel, Kathleen Tillotson, and Bernard H. Newdigate, 5 vols. (Oxford, 1931–1961).

6. All citations are to [Anthony Chute], *Beawtie Dishonoured written vnder the title of Shores wife* (London, 1593).

7. Samuel Daniel, *Poems and "A Defence of Ryme,"* ed. Arthur Colby Sprague (London, 1950).

8. All citations from *The Rape of Lucrece* are to *The Poems,* ed. F. T. Prince (London, 1960).

ishes Matilda's father, a loyal follower, on trumped-up charges, lest she be protected by her parent. As I have already suggested, the complaints in this group are very concerned with the nature of power, whether it be the sexual power of a woman or the political power of a monarch. One way Churchyard transforms Jane Shore's complaint in the *Mirror* into the version he published in his *Churchyards Challenge* (1593) is by lengthening the heroine's demonstration that she used her own power judiciously; this passage increases our sympathy for her, but it also draws our attention to larger questions about power and the powerful. Similarly, Lucrece adduces Renaissance commonplaces on these issues when she pleads with Tarquin:

> This deed will make thee only lov'd for fear;
> But happy monarchs still are fear'd for love.
> With foul offenders thou perforce must bear,
> When they in thee the like offences prove.
> If but for fear of this, thy will remove,
>    For princes are the glass, the school, the book,
>    Where subjects' eyes do learn, do read, do look.
>                                                   (ll. 610–616)

The popularity of this subgenre in Elizabethan England may in fact be traced at least in part to its treatment of power. In attempting to seduce their subjects, the monarchs in these poems raise broad questions about the abuses of royal prerogatives, questions that extend far beyond the compass of sexual behavior; hence such works are indeed a mirror for magistrates, including the ruler currently occupying the throne of England. But because Elizabeth could hardly be faulted for the particular abuse on which the poems focus, the betrayal of innocent maidens, any potential criticism of her is tactfully deflected. Matilda's defense of her own virginity even involves a tribute to the Virgin Queen.

Despite the links between *The Rape of Lucrece* and the complaints in question, when we read Shakespeare's poem we are mainly aware of suggestive distinctions: *The Rape of Lucrece* includes the "notes of rufull plaint" that Joseph Hall mockingly ascribes to the complaint tradition (*Virgidemiarum*, 1.5.2),[9] but

---

9. *The Collected Poems of Joseph Hall*, ed. A. Davenport (Liverpool, 1949).

this symphony is in a different key. One of the most obvious distinctions is structural: rather than basing his whole poem on Lucrece's complaints (as Middleton was to do in his version of it, *The Ghost of Lucrece*), Shakespeare incorporates those declamations within a larger narrative. As we shall see, that decision shapes our responses to Lucrece and to the genre we are exploring. But another difference between *The Rape of Lucrece* and the other poems in the subgenre I have defined is even more significant: Shakespeare repeatedly renders the values and assumptions of the complaint problematical, generally by directing our attention to the psychological implications behind issues treated more uncritically and straightforwardly in those other complaints and in *A Mirror for Magistrates* itself. In some cases he simply allows a subterranean idea in the more sophisticated complaints to surface; in other instances we can find no precedent at all for the questions he is raising.

What Chute terms "monster fame" (ll. 31, 493) plays as important a role in the 1590s complaints as in the *Mirror*. On the whole, however, it is a clear-cut role. Fame is dangerous, we are told, because it brings the king reports of his potential victim's beauty. At the same time, fame encompasses a concern for reputation that is presented as at the very least understandable; thus these poems typically begin with their heroines lamenting the fact that their names have been forgotten and begrudging the reputations of women with similar or even less virtuous histories. Matilda implies that she has been mistreated not only by the king who failed to seduce her but also by the poets who failed to celebrate her:

> *Shores* wife is in her wanton humor sooth'd,
> And modern Poets, still applaud her praise,
> Our famous *Elstreds* wrinckled browes are smooth'd,
> Call'd from her grave to see these latter daies,
> And happy's hee, their glory high'st can raise.
>    "Thus looser wantons, still are praised of many,
>    "Vice oft findes friends, but vertue seldome any.
>                                            (ll. 43–49)

But the poem nowhere develops the subterranean implication of this conventional passage: however pure she may be in other ways, Matilda's desire for fame is suspect. Such a criticism does emerge from "The Complaint of Rosamond," as a few recent scholars have pointed out.[10] Because Rosamond is distinguished from other complaint heroines by certain psychological mannerisms, such as a marked predilection for blaming others for her downfall,[11] we are encouraged to scrutinize many aspects of her self-portrayal more closely than would otherwise seem appropriate. When we do so we see some of the dangers of fame: her preoccupation with it helps to generate her fatal vanity, while her tendency to transfer her guilt to others is particularly manifest in her diatribes against fame. But Daniel, like Drayton, does not pursue the question; it remains for Shakespeare to look more deeply into the moral and emotional consequences of too deep an interest in fame.

The characters he evokes in *The Rape of Lucrece,* like their counterparts in the Roman plays, are concerned to the point of obsession with their reputations; they are always in the public eye and yet always also utterly, tragically alone. Shakespeare emphasizes their involvement with public opinion by the way he adapts one detail from his sources:

> They did conclude to bear dead Lucrece thence,
> To show her bleeding body thorough Rome,
> And so to publish Tarquin's foul offence.
>
> (ll. 1850–52)

Foregrounded by their position in the final stanza of the poem, these lines ensure that the narrative that has opened on a reference to publishing—

> Or why is Collatine the publisher
> Of that rich jewel he should keep unknown
> From thievish ears, because it is his own?
>
> (ll. 33–35)

10. See esp. Ronald Primeau, "Daniel and the *Mirror* Tradition: Dramatic Irony in *The Complaint of Rosamond," Studies in English Literature,* 15 (1975), 21–36. Clark Hulse also notes that the concept of fame is problematical in the poem (*Metamorphic Verse: The Elizabethan Minor Epic* [Princeton, 1981], p. 63).

11. Compare Primeau, "Daniel and the *Mirror* Tradition," p. 25.

—also concludes on one. The verb "publish" has several possible meanings in these passages, including (as in *Two Gentlemen of Verona,* 3.1.47) "proclaim," but one of the most salient glosses is "make public."[12]

Indeed, throughout *The Rape of Lucrece,* as throughout *Troilus and Cressida,* the characters' most private actions (or other people's ill-informed speculations about them) are continually made public through a network of surveillance and slander: images of eyes and mouths reflect a world whose citizens are engaged in gazing on and gossiping about each other. Thus within only a few pages (ll. 71–112) Tarquin stares lustfully at Lucrece, she returns his gaze uncomprehendingly, he muses on her husband's boasts about her beauty, and in turn praises Collatine to her. And shortly afterward he threatens her with what she literally considers a fate worse than death: being the object of slander.

This emphasis on performing in public, under scrutiny, helps to establish Lucrece's Rome as what anthropologists have termed a shame culture.[13] According to traditional definitions, the inhabitants of guilt cultures suffer from the failure to fulfill internalized values, while their counterparts in shame cultures primarily fear the disapproval of others. One should not push these parallels too far (not least because anthropologists are themselves questioning and revising the categories), but it is significant for our purposes that shame is connected to exposure, the very fear that dominates so much of Lucrece's behavior. She often seems more concerned with how the rape will affect her fame than with her own judgments about it. And it is significant, too, that shame is associated with precisely that experience that informs and deforms the milieu Shakespeare is evoking: a threat to one's identity.

If one lives one's life before spectators, one may come to feel like an actor performing a part. And in fact the poem does

12. *OED,* s.v. "publish."
13. See Helen Merrell Lynd, *On Shame and the Search for Identity* (New York, 1958), esp. chaps. 1 and 2. Ian Donaldson interprets the negative reactions readers have had to various versions of the Lucrece story in terms of the change from a shame culture to a guilt culture (*The Rapes of Lucretia: A Myth and Its Transformations* [Oxford, 1982], pp. 33–34).

adduce theatrical metaphors at a few key moments. Attempting to justify the rape to himself, Tarquin declares, "My part is youth, and beats these from the stage" (l. 278). An appropriate image for his psychomachia, the allusion to acting hints at Tarquin's awareness that the most private actions are in a sense done on a public stage. (The line also exemplifies the flashes of psychological insight that illuminate the characters of this poem, often occurring just when Shakespeare's portraits seem to be at their most conventional and least acute. If one is an actor, then one is adopting a persona rather than behaving normally: thus this metaphor offers Tarquin a way to distance himself from his crime, while at the same time proleptically hinting to the audience of the real loss of identity that that crime will generate.) Lucrece herself adopts what is in effect a theatrical image for her behavior: ironically, in order to convince Collatine of her honesty, she must play her part like an actress:

> Besides, the life and feeling of her passion
> She hoards, to spend when he is by to hear her,
> When sighs and groans and tears may grace the fashion
> Of her disgrace, the better so to clear her
> From that suspicion which the world might bear her.
>
> (ll. 1317–21)

She fears, in short, that "to be direct and honest is not safe" (*Othello*, 3.3.378).[14]

The author of *The Rape of Lucrece* also deviates from other complaints by rendering the concept of guilt problematical. In the *Mirror* and the 1590s imitations of it, virtuous figures like Matilda experience no guilt. Its presence in former sinners such as Rosamond is an important sign of repentance and an earnest of their future redemption. Lucrece's guilt, in contrast, is yet another pathological symptom, a key to the complexities of her character rather than the state of her soul.

Although many readers have ignored the acuity of the characterization in *The Rape of Lucrece*, it is in evidence throughout the poem, and nowhere more so than in Shakespeare's subtle anatomy of Lucrece's guilt. Despite (and to some extent because

---

14. William Shakespeare, *The Complete Works*, ed. Alfred Harbage (Baltimore, 1969).

of) the horrors to which she is subjected, certain patterns remain
constant in her. The most central—and most relevant to her
guilt—is her proclivity for seeing experience in terms of absolutes, of clear and simple values, and of constant and comforting
pieties.[15] Thus, like her predecessors in *A Mirror for Magistrates,*
she greets every situation with a sententious generalization:

> The aged man that coffers up his gold
> Is plagu'd with cramps and gouts and painful fits,
> And scarce hath eyes his treasure to behold;
>                                        (ll. 855–857)

> O opportunity, thy guilt is great!
>                     (l. 876)

Such generalizations are, of course, common in Renaissance
poetry, but that fact need not preclude their use to characterize
an individual temperament.[16] Shakespeare activates the potential psychological significance of these *sententiae,* encouraging
us to read them as manifestations of Lucrece's sensibility, by
incorporating into her speech patterns many additional dem-
onstrations of her belief in absolute verities. Thus she delights
in antitheses, the ultimate expression of a world of blacks and
whites:

> My honour I'll bequeath unto the knife
> That wounds my body so dishonoured.
> 'Tis honour to deprive dishonour'd life;
> The one will live, the other being dead.
>                                     (ll. 1184–87)

---

15. For an argument different from my own, see Bickford Sylvester, "Natural
Mutability and Human Responsibility: Form in Shakespeare's *Lucrece," College
English,* 26 (1965), 505–511; he claims that absolutes are seen as a positive
value in the poem. Yet another approach to the question of absolutes is offered
by R. Thomas Simone in *Shakespeare and "Lucrece": A Study of the Poem and
Its Relation to the Plays,* Salzburg Studies in English Literature, 38 (Salzburg,
1974), p. 168; he suggests that Lucrece is the victim both of dualism and of
man's vision of an ideal.

16. Paul Cantor observes that Shakespeare's Roman characters typically rely
heavily on proverbs (*Shakespeare's Rome: Republic and Empire* [Ithaca, 1976],
pp. 109–110). His suggestion that this habit reflects a reluctance to think for
oneself is as relevant to Lucrece as to her counterparts in the Roman plays.

> My woes are tedious, though my words are brief.
>                    (l. 1309)

>                         Thou worthy lord
> Of that unworthy wife that greeteth thee.
>                    (ll. 1303–04)

And in fact she repeatedly alludes to blacks and whites in the most literal sense, notably in her apostrophe to night.[17]
Equally significant is her use of predication:[18]

> My husband is thy friend;
>                    (l. 582)

> "Thou art," quoth she, "a sea, a sovereign king,
>                    (l. 652)

> Time's glory is to calm contending kings.
>                    (l. 939)

*Copia* and apposition, both of which are common in her speech, function very like predication, for they too assign qualities to an object:

> O unseen shame, invisible disgrace!
> O unfelt sore, crest-wounding private scar!
>                    (ll. 827–828)

> O night, thou furnace of foul reeking smoke.
>                    (l. 799)

The habits of thought and habits of speech that we have been tracing help to explain Lucrece's guilt. For someone so committed to absolutes and antitheses, there can be no middle ground: if, as she firmly believes, she no longer merits the epithet "Lucrece the chaste" (l. 7), then she must exemplify the other extreme, the corruption represented by Tarquin himself. Thus

17. Robert J. Griffin also notes the allusions to night and day but interprets them differently (" 'These Contraries Such Unity Do Hold': Patterned Imagery in Shakespeare's Narrative Poems," *Studies in English Literature*, 4 [1964], 50–51).

18. Compare Joseph A. Porter's analysis of Richard II's use of predication (*The Drama of Speech Acts: Shakespeare's Lancastrian Trilogy* [Berkeley, 1979], chap. 1).

when she declares, "But when I fear'd I was a loyal wife: / So am I now,—O no, that cannot be!" (ll. 1048–49), she is demonstrating her inability to define loyalty in terms more complex than the absolute ones she had previously used: she cannot recognize that though in one sense she has been unchaste and unfaithful to her husband, those definitions of chastity and fidelity are inadequate to the circumstances of a rape. When she describes herself as "she that was thy Lucrece" (l. 1682), she is not only anticipating her suicide but also manifesting in extreme form the consequences of her habit of predication: when predication breaks down, when she cannot avow "Lucrece is chaste," then in some important sense Lucrece ceases to exist. She becomes merely, as she herself puts it, an empty casket.

But it is also significant that women who have been raped typically suffer from irrational guilt. If the poem charts the patterns of a particular temperament, it also documents the reactions produced by a particular situation and in so doing further intensifies the differences that distinguish it from other complaints in its subgenre. Many modern studies of rape have demonstrated that its victims characteristically blame themselves for the attack and, in particular, for not fighting enough.[19] While one could not uncritically adduce all the findings of twentieth-century scholars to illuminate an Elizabethan evocation of a Roman event, it is not unlikely that certain responses to the trauma of rape would recur in different cultures. And Lucrece does in fact exemplify the guilt often associated with modern rape victims, as well as many of the other reactions that have been observed in them:

> "Poor hand, why quiver'st thou at this decree?
> . . . . .
>
> Since thou could'st not defend thy loyal dame,
> And wast afeard to scratch her wicked foe,

19. Many psychologists and sociologists have analyzed this reaction. See, for example, two studies by Ann Wolbert Burgess and Lynda Lytle Holmstrom, "Rape Trauma Syndrome," *American Journal of Psychiatry,* 131 (1974), 983, and *Rape; Victims of Crisis* (Bowie, Md., 1974), p. 39.

> Kill both thyself and her for yielding so."
> (ll. 1030, 1034–36)

This passage also testifies that even early in his career the author of *Hamlet* and *Macbeth* was acutely sensitive to the tortured and tortuous rationalizations spawned by guilt. Shakespeare is in fact borrowing the convention of speakers addressing their own bodies from the well-established formulas of the Senecan set speech.[20] But he skillfully adapts that convention to the complex patterns of Lucrece's psyche. She is attempting at once to castigate and to defend herself, a paradox for which we ourselves no doubt can find all too many analogues in our own behavior; by blaming her hand she is simultaneously criticizing herself and deflecting that criticism onto only one part of her body, with the implication that the rest may be less guilty. In a poem crammed with instances of synecdoche, she in effect invokes that figure while also rejecting it through the claim that the part is not in fact the whole. If, as we have seen, Tarquin adduces a theatrical metaphor to deny his own responsibility, his victim here attempts to accomplish the same ends through a different trope.

Not only Shakespeare's treatment of fame and guilt but also his exploration of sexuality distinguishes *The Rape of Lucrece* from the other complaints in the subgenre we are scrutinizing. Impelled by lust and unencumbered by scruples, the monarchs in those poems single-mindedly pursue their prey; their motives are not anatomized in any detail. Shakespeare, in contrast, does dissect the motivations behind the rape he portrays, concentrating especially on the interplay between sexual desire and competition:

> Perchance his boast of Lucrece' sov'reignty
> Suggested this proud issue of a king;

20. On the characteristics of the Senecan set speech, see esp. Wolfgang Clemen, *English Tragedy before Shakespeare: The Development of Dramatic Speech*, trans. T. S. Dorsch (London, 1961), pp. 215–252. Other relevant studies include John W. Cunliffe, *The Influence of Seneca on Elizabethan Tragedy* (London, 1893), esp. pp. 14–41; T. S. Eliot, "Seneca in Elizabethan Translation," in *Selected Essays* (New York, 1932), pp. 52–61; G. K. Hunter, "Seneca and the Elizabethans: A Case-Study in 'Influence,' " *Shakespeare Survey*, 20 (1967), 17–26.

For by our ears our hearts oft tainted be.
Perchance that envy of so rich a thing,
Braving compare, disdainfully did sting
    His high-pitch'd thoughts, that meaner men should vaunt
    That golden hap which their superiors want.

                                                    (ll. 36–42)

Shakespeare's treatment of another aspect of sexuality, the concept of chastity, is equally complex. The heroines in other complaints may sinfully abandon or sedulously guard their chastity, but neither they nor their readers experience any doubts as to the definition of that virtue. It remains uncomplicated even in "The Complaint of Rosamond," in many respects the most sophisticated poem of the subgenre, save for *The Rape of Lucrece* itself. We simply recognize, so to speak, that nice girls don't. In scrutinizing Lucrece's guilt and the reactions of other Romans to the rape, Shakespeare, in contrast, renders the idea of chastity very complicated.

On the one hand, on some level Lucrece has indubitably been unfaithful to her husband.[21] This is a particularly grave offense in her society; the poem portrays a culture that glorifies the sanctity of the family with an unthinking fervor worthy of the Moral Majority. Yet even citizens of that culture, the Roman knights to whom she tells her tale, unite in declaring that "Her body's stain her mind untainted clears" (l. 1710). Shakespeare's examination of chastity is further complicated by the curious imagery suggesting that Lucrece is virtually virginal despite her marriage: "Her breasts like ivory globes circled with blue, / A pair of maiden worlds unconquered" (ll. 407–408). While "maiden" could merely signify "that has not been conquered, tried, worked, etc.,"[22] it seems more than likely that discordant connotations of virginity would continue to adhere to the word. Behind these lines, I would suggest, lies an implication that we also find in Shakespeare's Roman plays: Roman matrons are typically so cold and restrained that even sex itself seems cu-

---

21. Saint Augustine goes so far as to raise the possibility that Lucretia actually welcomed the attack. See *The City of God*, trans. George E. McCracken et al., 7 vols. (Cambridge, Mass., and London, 1957–1972), I, 1.19.

22. *OED*, s.v. "maiden." Prince unpersuasively suggests that "maiden" merely signifies "chaste" (p. 87).

riously without passion.[23] Although these troubling hints are never followed up in the course of the poem, they do make Lucrece's view of chastity even more complex, further distinguishing this poem from the other complaints that invoke that concept.

*The Rape of Lucrece* complicates and criticizes not only the ethical values raised by other complaints but also the ethical response they so often adduce, pious *sententiae*. The complaints we are examining are nowhere closer to the *Mirror* than in their straightforward and sententious didacticism.[24] Admittedly, some moral points are made more subtly—the obvious instance is the ironic portrayal of Rosamond[25]—but by and large these poems are unashamedly direct in pointing to ethical lessons. The dying Matilda, for instance, shares with us her "pure thoughts" (l. 918), which include a paean to chastity and a critique of "fond preferments" (l. 932). In contrast, as we have observed, the moral truisms that Lucrece delivers are more significant as symptoms of emotional tendencies in the speaker than as sources of eternal truths. We learn from judging and rejudging—and often misjudging—the events before us, rather than from garnering the judgments of others.

This analysis of Lucrece's *sententiae* points to one of the most important—and most intriguing—ways Shakespeare renders the values of the complaint problematical: associating the genre with Lucrece herself, he suggests that limitations in the complaint mime limitations in her own sensibility, and vice versa. Given the popularity of that genre in the 1590s, we may well assume at first that Lucrece's proclivity for it reveals nothing significant about her own temperament: Shakespeare is merely following a fashion. But by referring so pointedly and so frequently to the act of delivering complaints, the poem foregrounds the use of the form. Thus Lucrece draws attention to her own predilection for the genre:

23. On this issue in the Roman plays, see Cantor, *Shakespeare's Rome*, esp. pp. 22–23.

24. Compare Campbell, *Mirror for Magistrates*, esp. pp. 48–51.

25. On Daniel's mode of didacticism, see Primeau, "Daniel and the *Mirror* Tradition"; his thesis is that the poem's didacticism resides not in direct statement but rather in its ironic presentation of its heroine.

> In vain I rail at opportunity,
> At time, at Tarquin, at uncheerful night;
> In vain I cavil with mine infamy,
> In vain I spurn at my confirm'd despite;
> This helpless smoke of words doth me no right.
>
>                              (ll. 1023–27)

Moreover, because Lucrece's complaints do not constitute the entire poem but rather are embedded within it, we can play them against the other responses to grief that Shakespeare charts in the poem. Comparing them to the declamations delivered by her husband and father and contrasting them with Brutus' espousal of action rather than lamentation, we recognize that the complaint represents only one of many possible ways of responding to experience, a choice that may reflect the sensibility of a particular character rather than the author's indiscriminating adoption of a literary convention.[26]

Hence we begin to see Lucrece's complaints as symptomatic of her temperament. Her belief in absolutes lends itself naturally to the hyperbolic utterances of the declamation: exclamations, not subjunctives, are her natural mode. And the fact that she criticizes her own rhetoric but continues to employ it is yet another symptom of the divisions in her being. We share her impatience at the length of her speeches, recognizing that she is getting too carried away with emotion, as Shakespeare's Venus does under very different circumstances. The conventional length of those speeches, in other words, comes to seem a sign of something individual about Lucrece herself. For Shakespeare is qualifying the common Renaissance belief that language provides a useful purgative for our emotions.[27] When carried to an extreme, he demonstrates, it may exacerbate, not purge the passions: "For sorrow, like a heavy hanging bell / Once set on ringing, with his own weight goes" (ll. 1493–94).

This is not to say, however, that the text supports the cynical appraisal of Lucrece's histrionics proffered by some critics. To

26. On the significance of the temperamental differences between Brutus and Lucrece, compare my article, "The Rape of Clio: Attitudes to History in Shakespeare's *Lucrece*," *English Literary Renaissance,* forthcoming.

27. For an analysis of that belief, see Jane Donawerth, *Shakespeare and the Sixteenth-Century Study of Language* (Urbana, 1984), pp. 57–61.

assert, for example, that Lucrece is "seizing the occasion to enjoy a good rant" or to refer to her "elephantine ego"[28] is to ignore the sympathy for his heroine that Shakespeare builds. His detailed anatomies of both the horrors of Tarquin's behavior and the values of Rome make her emotion seem an understandable reaction to the rape, if not an ideal one. And the poem balances its expositions of Lucrece's melodramatic self-absorption against frequent reminders of her unselfish concern for Collatine. If her complaints suggest that her responses to grief are in some sense unhealthy, we are also reminded that they are very understandable. Like Desdemona—whom she resembles in many other respects as well—Lucrece evokes compassion and respect even as we recognize her limitations.

If, then, other authors in the subgenre here defined hold certain truths to be self-evident, Shakespeare is concerned to challenge those verities; in the course of writing his complaint he calls in question many of the values in which that genre is rooted. In a sense we should not be surprised to find that he—or any writer—does so. We too often forget that parody and the most straightforward literary imitation are simply two ends of a spectrum. Nonetheless, the extent to which Shakespeare questions and even undermines the values of his genre is unusual. Why does he do so?

Part of the answer lies in the habit of mind that Rosalie Colie so perceptively anatomizes in relation to his plays. As she points out, Shakespeare is prone to see in literary "forms" of all types representations of the forms of human behavior.[29] Doing so evidently encourages him to explore the psychological and moral dangers a genre may both present and represent. Indeed, recognizing how frequently and how skillfully Shakespeare adduces

28. Richard A. Lanham, *The Motives of Eloquence: Literary Rhetoric in the Renaissance* (New Haven, 1976), pp. 103, 107. Robert L. Montgomery, Jr., also observes that Lucrece gets carried away with her own passion, but his criticism of her behavior is more temperate ("Shakespeare's Gaudy: The Method of *The Rape of Lucrece,*" in *Studies in Honor of DeWitt T. Starnes,* ed. Thomas P. Harrison et al. [Oxford, Texas, 1967], esp. pp. 32–33).

29. Rosalie Colie, *Shakespeare's Living Art* (Princeton, 1974), esp. chap. 1.

the literary patterns of genre to represent the psychological patterns of human experience should warn us against the simple distinctions between the rhetorical and the mimetic that, as I suggested earlier, have formed and deformed our approach to *The Rape of Lucrece.*

Shakespeare's approach to the complaint is, then, characteristic of the way he reshapes genres in his dramatic oeuvre as well. But the subgenre that we have been exploring was especially likely to provoke in him a response that is critical in the several senses of that adjective. On the one hand, he was probably very attracted to the form, particularly because its preoccupation with the uses and abuses of power echoes the ideas he was exploring in his history plays. On the other hand, the simplistic didacticism that marks—and mars—*A Mirror for Magistrates* and its many heirs and assigns must have troubled the writer who was to guy such habits of thought by creating a Polonius. Writing the type of complaint he did allowed him to criticize the form even as he was writing within it, much as the authors of the formal verse satires of the 1590s both delight in and deplore elaborate rhetoric.

This reflexive type of literary imitation proved singularly appropriate for the work in question. The poem that repeatedly undermines its own genre bodies forth many other types of internalized conflicts; in this regard (as in so many others), form and content are inseparable in *The Rape of Lucrece.* The very plot is based on the notion of an enemy within the city walls: a Roman is attacked not by a barbarian but by a Roman. The society that Shakespeare portrays is an organism attacking its own tissues: the familial and military values on which it is based are responsible for the tragedy, in that Lucrece justifies her suicide by citing obligations to her family, while her rapist excuses his attack by invoking military metaphors. And, of course, the characters themselves are self-destructive: Tarquin is repeatedly described in terms of a civil war, while Lucrece literally takes her own life.

These internalized divisions are mirrored on the rhetorical level as well: one of the most common figures is syneciosis, defined by the Renaissance writer Angel Day as "when one contrary is attributed to another, or when two diverse things are in one put together."[30] Thus we encounter enough oxymora to satisfy even a sonneteer: "niggard prodigal" (1. 79), "naked armour" (1. 188), "living death" (1. 726), and so on. The internal tensions in these figures are intensified in the case of one formulation that recurs several times in the poem, phrases like "lifeless life" (1. 1374), in which opposites have the same etymology. In these cases the expectation of congruity is based not only on the relationship between subject and modifier but also on the visual and etymological similarities between the terms; hence the conflict between them is all the more striking.

Throughout *The Rape of Lucrece,* as we have seen, the complaint itself enacts a pattern very like that of these tropes. Although Shakespeare treats certain characteristics of his subgenre, notably the concern for power, with great respect, he also criticizes the assumptions of that literary type, much as instances of syneciosis undermine the very comparison they establish. For *The Rape of Lucrece* is as didactic as *A Mirror for Magistrates,* but what it teaches us above all is the danger of the simplified values promoted by other works in its own genre. Later in his career Shakespeare was to compose dramas that may be termed "problem comedies" not only in that their values are ambiguous and their conflicts unresolved but also in that they render comedy itself problematical. In *The Rape of Lucrece* he writes what we may justly consider a problem complaint.

30. Angel Day, *The English Secretorie* (London, 1595), p. 95. After completing this essay I heard Joel Fineman's paper, "The Temporality of Rape," at the 1984 Modern Language Association convention. He too notes the presence of syneciosis in the poem but interprets the significance of the figure very differently from the way I do.

JOHN KLAUSE

# The Montaigneity of
# Donne's *Metempsychosis*

The suggestion that Donne's *Metempsychosis,* or *The Progresse of the Soule,* marked "the very nadir of [his] belief in God and man"[1] has met stern and understandable resistance. The incomplete, less than urgent narrative, tracing the peregrinations of the "deathlesse soule" of Eden's apple (l. 1) up the scale of being and, in the process it seems, down the scale of innocence, is itself an unlikely vehicle of defiant or desolate impiety.[2] The

---

1. M. M. Mahood, *Poetry and Humanism* (New Haven, 1950), p. 107. This view has been seconded by Janel Mueller in "Donne's Epic Venture in the *Metempsychosis,*" *Modern Philology,* 70 (1972), 109–137.

2. Quotations from *Metempsychosis* are taken from Wesley Milgate's edition of *John Donne: The Satires, Epigrams and Verse Letters* (Oxford, 1967). Other works by Donne are quoted from the following editions: *Biathanatos,* reproduced from the first edition (1647), with a bibliographical note by J. W. Hebel (New York, 1930); *Devotions upon Emergent Occasions,* ed. Anthony Raspa (Montreal, 1975). *The Divine Poems,* 2nd ed., ed. Helen Gardner (Oxford, 1978); *The Elegies and the Songs and Sonnets,* ed. Helen Gardner (Oxford, 1965); *The Epithalamions, Anniversaries and Epicedes,* ed. W. Milgate (Oxford, 1978); *Essays in Divinity,* ed. Evelyn Simpson (Oxford, 1952); *Letters to*

poem seems too humorous to be the fruit of somber meditations.[3] Where it is daring, it need be considered no more a frank
revelation of a deeply troubled mind than are, some would say,
Donne's libertine and cynical lyrics. The moral relativism proposed in the final lines of *Metempsychosis*—

> Ther's nothing simply good, nor ill alone,
> Of every quality comparison,
> The onely measure is, and judge, opinion

—is not, it has been claimed, in any sense radical.[4] Donne's
firm declaration in "Satyre III," a poem composed in all likelihood not long before *Metempsychosis*,[5] that truth is "one,"
unambiguous (even if difficult to discover), and "elder" (however slightly) than falsehood (ll. 66–75) appears to come much
more directly from the author himself than does the arch commentary in the narrative poem. And yet, knowing how seriously
Donne takes elsewhere some of the issues raised in his Pythagorean saga, we might hesitate before deciding that he treats
them in this work with "high-spirited fun," in a mood of "im-
pudence, not anguish."[6]

Later in his life he considers the poem's major motifs weighty
enough for sermon and devotion:

Aquinas notes . . . that there were Hereticks that held, that the very
soul of Adam was by a long circuit and transmigration come at last
into Paul, and so Paul was the same man (in his principal part, in the

---

*Severall Persons of Honour* (1651), a facsimile reproduction with an introduction by M. Thomas Hester (Delmar, N.Y., 1977); *Paradoxes and Problems,*
ed. Helen Peters (Oxford, 1980); and *The Sermons of John Donne,* ed. George
R. Potter and Evelyn M. Simpson, 10 vols. (Berkeley and Los Angeles, 1953–
1962).

3. See Milgate's "General Introduction" in *John Donne,* pp. xxv–xxxii; Susan
Snyder, "Donne and Du Bartas: *The Progresse of the Soule* as Parody," *Studies
in Philology,* 70 (1973), 407.

4. See Milgate's "Commentary" in *John Donne,* p. 191.

5. Milgate dates "Satyre III" 1594 or 1595; John Shawcross suggests 1597 or
1598 ("All Attest His Writs Canonical: The Texts, Meaning and Evaluation of
Donne's Satires," in *Just So Much Honor,* ed. Peter Amadeus Fiore [University
Park, Penn., 1972], p. 252). See also M. Thomas Hester, *Kinde Pitty and Brave
Scorn: John Donne's Satires* (Durham, N.C., 1982), pp. 138–139n49.

6. Milgate, *John Donne,* p. xxxii; Snyder, "Donne and Du Bartas," p. 402.

soul) as Adam was; and in that sense it was literally true that he said, he was *primus peccatorum* the first of all sinners, because he was the first man Adam: but this is an heretical fancy, and a Pythagorean bubble.  (*Sermons,* 1.316)[7]

The soule of sinne, is disobedience to thee; and when one sinne hath beene dead in mee, that soule hath passed into another sinne . . . This transmigration of sinne, found in my selfe, makes me afraid, O my God, of a Relapse . . .   (*Devotions,* p. 123)

Thoughts about the Fall and original sin sit rather testily in *Metempsychosis,* jostling with the half-humorous notions in the midst of which they are paced:

> Man all at once was there by woman slaine,
> And one by one we'are here slaine o'er againe
> By them. The mother poison'd the well-head,
> The daughters here corrupt us, Rivulets,
> (ll. 91–94)

>                                    Of every man
> For one, will God (and be just) vengeance take?
> (ll. 105–106)

These theological doctrines would hardly seem to a reflective mind less momentous here than in other, more solemn contexts:

> One woman at one blow, then kill'd us all,
> And singly, one by one, they kill us now.
> (*The First Anniversarie,* ll. 106–107)

> Wilt thou forgive that sinne where I begunne,
>     Which is my sin, though it were done before?
> ("A Hymne to God the Father," ll. 1–2)

Donne muses naturalistically in *Metempsychosis* about the sexual "liberty" of animals (ll. 195–200) and, in consequence, about the arbitrariness and relativity of Nature's prescriptions:

> Men, till they tooke laws which made freedome lesse,
> Their daughters, and their sisters did ingresse;
> Till now unlawfull, therefore ill, 'twas not.
> (ll. 201–203)

---

7. Italics when used only for emphasis have been omitted from this prose passage and from all subsequent ones.

A similar naturalism in such poems as "The Relique" (l. 30), "Elegie III" ("Change"), and "Confined Love" seems prompted more by wit than by a libidinous nostalgia for the freedom of a Golden Age, but we need not think that humor evaporates all of Donne's seriousness. There were times when he must have meditated on the words of Saint Paul concerning the deadliness of law:

I had not known sin, but by the law: for I had not known lust, except the law had said, thou shalt not covet. But sin taking occasion by the commandment, wrought in me all manner of concupiscence. For without the law sin was dead.     (Rom. 7:7–8)

Sin lives and kills through the "letter" (2 Cor. 3:6) when the law is *applied*. But God may introduce and retract his precepts as he wills: "nothing is so evill," says the casuist in *Biathanatos,* "but that it becomes good, if God command it" (p. 145). And in the knowledge that the moral law and its application are flexible, Donne can sometimes wonder about the absolute necessity of a sentence unto damnation—as he does in "Holy Sonnet IX," with what would be only petulance were not so much at stake:

> If poysonous mineralls, and if that tree,
> Whose fruit threw death on else immortall us,
> If lecherous goats, if serpents envious
> Cannot be damn'd; Alas, why should I bee?
> Why should intent or reason, borne in mee,
> Make sinnes, else equall, in mee, more heinous?
> And mercie being easie, and glorious
> To God, in his sterne wrath, why threatens hee?
> But who am I, that dare dispute with thee?
>                                         (ll. 1–9)

For a man who often fears conviction by the law, even that it will have him "perish on the shore" ("A Hymne to God the Father," l. 14), the subject of moral obligation is rarely a *mere* occasion for the venting of wit.

Furthermore, a compulsive intellectual whose thirst for learning is "Hydroptique" (*Letters,* p. 51) but who broods questioningly over the validity and worth of his knowledge, professing himself exasperated by the mind's inability to grasp essential truth—"Poore soule, in this thy flesh what do'st thou know?" (*The Second Anniversarie*, l. 254)—would not be likely to find the problems of epistemology trivial. Donne may sound flippant in his skeptical comment about "the measure" and "judge" of "every quality" (*Metempsychosis*, ll. 519–520), but behind his words we can imagine a grave distress.[8]

In short, it may be as unsatisfactory to judge *Metempsychosis* wittily impersonal as to make it represent a truly heartfelt anxiety, cynicism, or disgust; to see it merely as the *jeu d'esprit* of "a clever, 'advanced' young man having fun at the expense of the literary and religious Establishment" as to discover in it the impassioned, "gloomy sublimity of Ezekiel or Aeschylus."[9] Perhaps, indeed, it is the kind of poem that will never lend itself to a "satisfactory" reading (an interpretation that accounts for all major details within a design), so easily does it produce confusion about its character and purpose. The poet's approach to establishing his meaning is casual, free of a dutiful attention to consistency. And this capriciousness is no more evident than in his mingling of genres in a way that raises doubts about their compatibility.

Recent commentary, denying the author's claim that his work is simply a *poema satyricon,* has revealed how exotic a salad *(satura)* it may be. The poem clearly begins in the epic manner, with a Virgilian *cano* ("I sing the progresse of a deathlesse soule" [l. 1]) and a bow to "Fate" (l. 2); an Ariostan boast ("A worke" will follow "t'outweare *Seths* pillars, brick and stone, / And (holy writt excepted) made to yeeld to none" [ll. 9–10]); and an Ovidian promise to survey the entire span of human

8. Two of the more recent discussions of Donne's attitude toward "reason" are to be found in John Carey's *John Donne: Life, Mind and Art* (New York, 1981), pp. 231–260, and in Terry G. Sherwood's *Fulfilling the Circle: A Study of John Donne's Thought* (Toronto, 1984), pp. 21–62. Sherwood seeks to refute the view, reformulated by Carey, that Donne's skepticism was profound and drove him into anxious inconsistencies. While pointing out that some of the more sweeping claims about Donne's distrust of reason should be qualified, Sherwood, in his misreading of some texts and his avoidance of evidence against his claims, fails to establish his central point.

9. Snyder, "Donne and Du Bartas," p. 407; Thomas De Quincey, *Blackwood's Magazine,* 34 (1828), 892–893 (cited in Milgate, *John Donne,* p. xxxi).

history (ll. 3–6). Because of its satiric intent and the patent futility of its project, it has been called an "anti-epic," a "parody of a grand Renaissance design," a parody, even, of a specific epical work, Du Bartas' *Sepmaines*.[10] It has been shown to have affinities with Ovid's *Metamorphoses,* which is an epic of sorts that parodies Virgil's, a *carmen perpetuum* led from the beginning of the world through its several "ages" down to the poet's own time (see *Metamorphoses,* 1.3–4) and infused with the spirit of Pythagoras, who appears in the final book to advance his doctrine of the transmigration of souls.[11] In its theological dimension, *Metempsychosis* has prompted reference to Saint Augustine's *City of God,* a work of exposition, meditation, and apology that is generically an exegesis of history. Donne's incomplete story of the apple's "deathlesse soule" might represent the first steps in what Augustine conceived to be the concomitant evolution of the "two cities," the one heavenly (associated as in Donne's poem with Seth), the other earthly (associated as in Donne's poem with Cain).[12] *Metempsychosis* also borrows from other theological treatises, rabbinical as well as Christian, and occasionally sounds like one itself.[13] Tertullian's *De anima,* which contains an extended discussion of Pythagorean theory, may have provided Donne's poem with its final lines in reporting the principle of Carpocrates that "there is nothing which is accounted evil by nature, but simply as men think of it [*non natura quid malum habeatur, sed opinione*]."[14] And whatever its themes,

10. Milgate, *John Donne,* pp. xxvii–xxviii; Snyder, "Donne and Du Bartas," pp. 392–407.

11. Mueller, "Donne's Epic Venture," pp. 113–122.

12. Richard E. Hughes, *The Progress of the Soul: The Interior Career of John Donne* (New York, 1968), pp. 71–79.

13. See the "Commentary" in the editions of Milgate and of H. J. C. Grierson, *The Poems of John Donne* (Oxford, 1912). Also, Mueller, "Donne's Epic Venture"; Don Cameron Allen, "The Double Journey of John Donne," in *A Tribute to George Coffin Taylor,* ed. Arnold Williams (Chapel Hill, 1952), pp. 83–99; M. Van Wyk Smith, "John Donne's *Metempsychosis,*" *Review of English Studies,* n.s. 24 (1973), 17–25, 141–152.

14. See Mueller, "Donne's Epic Venture," pp. 123–124; *De anima,* 35 (Migne, *Patrologia Latina,* 2.709–712), English version in *The Writings of Quintus Sept. Flor. Tertullianus,* trans. Peter Holmes, in the *Ante-Nicene Christian Library,* ed. Alexander Roberts and James Donaldson, vol. 2 (Edinburgh, 1870), p. 494.

*Metempsychosis* has continued to invite the suspicion that it is an allegory of some kind—historical or Alexandrian—in the guise of a beast fable.[15]

While it is not impossible a priori that all of these elements might combine peaceably into a unified whole (*Paradise Lost* contains all of them in some form or other, proving how capacious epic can be), the odds are against such a union in Donne's heterogeneous fragment, which does not contain enough of any one element in its purity to serve as a unifying factor. The epic strain in *Metempsychosis* is weak indeed. The poem offers no epic task that can become the occasion for heroic exertion. The soul merely wanders from body to body completely at the mercy of events, with nothing to achieve, with no purpose but to "animate." The plot does not even pretend to epic complexity but simply details in chronological sequence the brief adventures of the bodies to which the soul lends its force. We expect of an epic that it will somehow envision in experience or impose upon it a significant shape. One Homeric poem, for example, is an epic of the hero's return (*nostos*) to his proper place, the other a portrayal of the shape of heroic life, as presented in the pictures on Achilles' shield. Virgil's and Milton's poems describe the structures of providential history. In looser, more sprawling epics like Ariosto's or Spenser's, all is not madness and miscellany, for their events are rooted, however tentatively or ironically, in a fated design (for the triumph of Christendom, for the exaltation of the House of D'Este or Tudor) or in an allegorical purpose. And even the swirl of Ovid's *Metamorphoses,* in which the only constant seems to be change itself, has its own principles of patterned coherence and culminates officially, if not convincingly, in a prophetic review of Rome's place in history, anticipating the apotheosis of Augustus.[16]

Donne announces that "Fate" determines the course of the soul's journey that is his epic subject, but to what end it is difficult to see. "Great Destiny" seems more like "Fortune" or

15. See Grierson's "Introduction and Commentary," in *Poems,* pp. xviii–xix; Mahood, *Poetry and Humanism,* p. 106; W. A. Murray, "What Was the Soul of the Apple," *Review of English Studies,* n.s. 10 (1959), 141–155; Smith, "John Donne's *Metempsychosis,*" pp. 141–152.

16. See Brooks Otis, *Ovid as an Epic Poet* (Cambridge, 1966), pp. 278–305.

"Chance" than like "Providence."[17] It creates no shape. The soul moves aimlessly, making "progresse" from a vegetal to a rational existence but finding itself destined to travel through its human history not upward but onward.[18] This is the action that makes the poem (as the epigraph claims) *"Infinitati Sacrum,"* sacred or dear to Infinity.[19] Personified, *Infinitas* is here surely not the positive, rich infinity of God, but what Aquinas calls the "imperfect" infinity of formlessness (*Summa Theologica*, 1.7.1). Just as the will may be called "infinite" because it can always desire something "more" ("The will is infinite . . . and the act a slave to limit," says Shakespeare's Troilus), the "deathlesse soule" would forever seek a new body to vivify were not God at some point to put an end to dying. There is no form where there are no limits (*fines*, in Latin). There is no goal where no end is a culmination. From the epic point of view Donne gained as much—that is, as little—by concluding his "fragment" before the end of a first canto or book as he would have achieved by carrying the story forward to his own day.

It might be thought that the satiric strain in *Metempsychosis* would at least be strong enough to integrate other modes. But in fact the poem, even as it presents the satiric point of view, challenges its validity. When the voice of the satirist is heard condemning the gluttony of a sea bird (1. 294), the motiveless malice of killer fish (ll. 341–350), the murderous envy of a mouse (1. 396), the shrewd and manipulative lust of a wolf (ll. 401–420), the treachery of a mongrel wolf dog (1. 450), and the "through-vaine" lust of an ape (ll. 471–480), its fervor is clearly inappropriate. The actions of animals have no moral dimension, for they do only what comes "naturally," without rational knowledge or choice. Similar acts by human beings would of

17. In calling "Destiny" the "Commissary of God," Donne echoes Dante's description of *"la fortuna,"* who is called God's *"general ministra e duce"* (*Inferno*, 7.78).

18. The *OED* cites instances in which "progress" has no implication of improvement or escalation.

19. Some commentators have translated the Latin phrase as "dedicated to infinity." *Dedicatum* would be the more usual Latin word in this case, but *sacrum* may indeed mean *dedicated*.

course justify the satirist's complaint—except that he makes a point of calling into doubt the absoluteness of moral norms. By demonstrating that "treachery, / Rapine, deceit, and lust" (ll. 507–508) are in a sense natural; by suggesting that law turns "natural" actions into crimes by arbitrary fiat (ll. 201–203); by emphasizing the relativity of value—"Of every quality comparison, / The only measure is, and judge, opinion" (ll. 519–520)—he undermines the legitimacy of an appeal to clear and definite standards of good and evil. He could have done otherwise. He could have presented a traditional view (which had been recently enunciated by Richard Hooker) that "nature" can mean "what ought to be" as well as "what is"; that "natural law" is not arbitrary, but grounded in "the first law eternal," or the law which God is unto himself; that the Fall in some way vitiated created nature, thereby destroying the synonymity of the "natural" (in one of its definitions) with the "good." The satirist, however, chooses to express bafflement rather than certitude. He has, indeed, an instinct about what is right and wrong; but when he begins to think about moral issues, daring, for example, to "aske why" the taint of the Fall should be universal (ll. 102–106), he is led to reasoning ("Reckoning") that faith tells him is hazardous and "vaine" (ll. 98–120). He does not, then, subject "Nature" to any deep metaphysical analysis: the natural as matter is only creation; as manner, only creation's *modus operandi*. The relationship of nature to law he describes only in the elementary way that we have already noted. Reasoning about value ("quality") ends in "opinion," which leaves poet and poem becalmed in an ambiguity fatal to satire.

However disappointed or resentful, perplexity does not in *Metempsychosis* proscribe humor, of which the poem is full. Yet Donne's facetiousness seems to clash with the theological earnestness that would claim its moments in the work. Not every instance of such conflict should be considered irreligious. When Donne boasts that his opus yields in worth only to "holy writt" (l. 10), or refers to Noah's "boate" (rhymed comically with "floate") as "That swimming Colledge" (ll. 21–23), he is no more disrespectful than were, in the Middle Ages, authors of seriocomic mystery plays. His witty reference to the Tree of Knowledge as "the forbidden learned tree" (l. 78) appears somewhat more irreverent, especially in light of his troubled thoughts about the Fall, some of which he presents with sardonic humor in a mock recoil from the heretical:

> So fast in us doth this corruption grow,
> That now wee dare aske why wee should be so.
> Would God (disputes the curious Rebell) make
> A law, and would not have it kept? Or can
> His creatures will, crosse his? Of every man
> For one, will God (and be just) vengeance take?
> Who sinn'd? 'twas not forbidden to the snake
> Nor her, who was not then made; nor is't writ
> That Adam cropt, or knew the apple; yet
>     The worme and she, and he, and wee endure for it.
>
> But snatch mee heavenly Spirit from this vaine
> Reckoning their vanities, lesse is the gaine
> Then hazard still, to meditate on ill,
> Though with good minde; their reasons, like those toyes
> Of glassie bubbles, which the gamesome boyes
> Stretch to so nice a thinnes through a quill
> That they themselves breake, doe themselves spill:
> Arguing is heretiques game, and Exercise
> As wrastlers, perfects them; Not liberties
>     Of speech, but silence; hands, not tongues, end heresies.
>                                         (ll. 101–120)

The poet's dissociation of himself from the "curious Rebell" and from argumentative "heretiques" is (as it is meant to be) amusingly disingenuous. He would hardly advocate the use of inquisitional "hands" to "end" his *own* heresy, metempsychosis; and he has, no doubt, pursued his own perilous arguments on the subject of divine justice as far as he wishes to take them. But now religion turns into wit. To what effect?

If, as some have proposed, the humor is not radically "defiant" and the poem as a whole not deeply serious,[20] no problem of tonal consistency arises. If, however, wit is an expression of or refuge from disillusion and pain, it emerges as a protest against the order of things, uttered by the same voice that throughout the poem spells out conventional moral lessons and

---

20. See Milgate, *John Donne*, p. xxx.

speaks with no mock solemnity devout words and thoughts that
would later be transported into the author's "Divine Poems":

> That Crosse, our joy, and griefe, where nailes did tye
> That All, which alwayes was all, every where;
> Which could not sinne, and yet all sinnes did beare;
> Which could not die, yet could not chuse but die;
> Stood in the selfe same roome in Calvarie,
> Where first grew the forbidden learned tree . . .
>                            (*Metempsychosis*, ll. 73–78)[21]

To deny the poem seriousness makes it without question easier
to read. But such an homogenized reading demands the much
more difficult assumption that Donne did not take theodicy
seriously, or, as an alternative, that he felt free to play irrev-
erently with sacred truths in the cause of parody. A more satisfactory inference would be that Donne writes out of a genuine
sense of scandal, which he can neither fully accept nor renounce,
and thus leaves in their full and disturbing integrity certain
inconsistencies in his text.

Ambivalence is evident also in the poem's "Augustinian"
attempt to explicate history. The project of a "spiritual" history
beginning with the Fall, proceeding into the age of Cain, and
promising to continue through the age of "th'Empire, and late
Rome" (l. 68), beyond the revolutions of "Mahomet" and "Luther" (l. 66), recalls in purpose and scope the *City of God*. We
can easily conceive of Donne's imagination seizing upon, twist-
ing the meaning of, and venturing to "illustrate" with his own
ironic narrative, *The Progresse of the Soule,* words of Saint
Augustine:

Now Cain was the first son born to those two parents of mankind, and
he belonged to the city of man; the later son, Abel, belonged to the
City of God. It is our own experience that in the individual man, to
use the words of the Apostle, "it is not the spiritual element which
comes first, but the animal [*animale*]; and afterwards comes the spiritual," and so it is that everyone, since he takes his origin from a
condemned stock, is inevitably evil and carnal to begin with, by derivation from Adam; but if he is reborn into Christ, and makes progress,

21. Cf. "Hymne to God, my God, in my sicknesse," 21–22; *La corona*, 2.2–4.

he will afterwards be good and spiritual. The same holds true of the whole human race. (*De civitate Dei*, 15.1.596)

The "progress" *(procursus, progressus)* of the individual soul and of the City of God was Augustine's major theme.[22] And even if Donne's *Progresse* depicts what in a Christian soul would be moral regression, he might be seen to have concentrated with the same intentions as his predecessor on the reprobate population. But ultimately, of course, Donne's Augustinianism serves only to tantalize. The great Doctor of the Church does not derive moral corruption, as does the poet of *Metempsychosis*, from a source outside the angelic or human will (in subrational souls of apple, mandrake, and animals). Augustine explicitly condemns the doctrine of the transmigration of souls, which he finds stated, interestingly enough, in Porphyry's *De regressu animae* (*CD*, 10.30). When Donne affirms that God has "made, but doth not controule" Fate (l. 2), he directly contradicts the Augustinian view (see *CD*, 5.1.180).[23] Of greater significance is the dramatic contrast between Augustine's confidence in his knowledge of the truth and Donne's epistemological diffidence: where the one finds design and meaning in history, the other sees lamentable (or amusing? or ridiculous?) facts that seem to lead only "on." Again, it should not be inferred that Donne has failed to take religion seriously. One may mock wittily in dead earnest. What remains uncertain in the poem is whether truth mocks a religious vision or the human intellect that cannot appropriate it. What remains undeniable is that Augustinian vision and form are accorded no more privileges than are any others.

The absence of an authoritative point of view in *Metempsychosis* renders hopeless the quest for allegorical meanings, which in any case fail to emerge with perceptible consistency. In asserting that the soul's journey has a contemporary significance,

22. The translation of *De civitate Dei* used here and throughout is that of Henry Bettenson (Harmondsworth, 1972).

23. Seneca (*De providentia*, 5.8) explained how God might be bound by "Destiny" without a loss of majesty: "Although the great creator and ruler of the universe himself wrote the decrees of Fate, yet he follows them. He obeys forever, he decreed but once" (trans. J. Basore, in *Seneca: Moral Essays* [Cambridge, Mass., 1958]).

Donne clearly invites a search for the *clef* to an historical allegory:

> For this great soule . . . here amongst us now
> Doth dwell, and moves that hand, and tongue, and brow,
> Which, as the Moone the sea, moves us . . .
>
> (ll. 61–63)

The regnant "Moone" would seem to be Queen Elizabeth, Ralegh's Cynthia—from which point of reference one might begin an investigation. Yet Donne announces in his prefatory Epistle that the soul's current body is masculine: "shee [the soul] is hee, whose life you shall finde in the end of this booke"; and Elizabeth could not have shared a soul with Luther (l. 66), who lived on for more than twelve years after her birth.[24] The poet, it appears, has enticed his readers into a labyrinth from which there is no exit. No political reading of *Metempsychosis* has yet, in fact, offered a compelling claim to legitimacy: neither the fall of the Earl of Essex nor the rise of Robert Cecil can adequately account for the particulars of the narrative or the course of the narrator's ironic and ambiguous commentary.[25] Unlike Spenser's *Mother Hubberds Tale,* Donne's poem contains no plausible clues to allegorical meaning but provides a large cast of hastily drawn characters and a string of episodes whose brevity, randomness, and generality diminish the pressure for an allegorical reading. When Donne raises questions of universal moral import, he fails to develop an arch-concept that would inform a moral allegory;[26] when he emphasizes the particular, his work grows profuse with physical details (such as those found in the description of the mandrake, the baby sparrow, or the embryo

24. See Milgate, *John Donne,* p. xxvi.
25. On the "Essex" theory, see Milgate, *John Donne,* p. xxxii; the "Cecil" theory has been advanced by Smith in "John Donne's *Metempsychosis."*
26. W. A. Murray's view that *Metempsychosis* is a commentary on the corruption of the power of moral choice, of which the "soul of the apple" is an allegorical embodiment, is not very plausible. As Milgate points out, "Donne insists over and over again that the soul is completely at the command of Destiny or Fate" (p. xxix). Besides, since Donne's plants and animals are *contrasted* finally with the human beings into which the soul eventually moves, they would not be icons of spiritual and mental states.

of Themech)²⁷ that lead away from public history toward discrete and self-sufficient scientific facts.

In *Metempsychosis*, then, all of these attempts at generic form—epic, satire, theological commentary, metahistory, and allegory—are somehow checked and defeated. The genres are alluded to rather than embodied. They conspire to form a work that requires a unity which none of them singly can provide and which cannot be achieved even by, or especially by, their combination. If we allow a certain appropriateness to Donne's subtitle, *Poêma Satyricon*, we must do so with another *Satyricon* in mind: that of Petronius, whose novelistic fragment has been described as a "hodgepodge of genres . . . relentlessly blending the comic, the mock-heroic and the satirical, the realistic and the poetic," a "farrago" or "mélange" that would be, were such a thing possible, a "genre on its own."²⁸

But is *Metempsychosis* in its idiosyncratic blending of kinds true only to itself? Or does it manifest a larger purpose that might furnish a rationale for its waywardness? We can, indeed, discover such a purpose in relating the poem to a literary genre that had been newly invented when Donne undertook his *Progresse*, and that at first seems quite incompatible with the intentions of a narrative poet: to wit, the essay.

In a letter "to Sir G. M.," written not many years after *Metempsychosis*, Donne reveals that he has read in the *Essais* of "Michel Montaig[n]e" (*Letters*, p. 106).²⁹ Donne's own formal exercise in the genre, his *Essayes in Divinity*, would contain reference to Raymond of Sebond (p. 7) and to "Sextus Empiricus the Pyrrhonian" (p. 28),³⁰ whose notoriety Montaigne had helped to establish. If we can judge by the Frenchman's own

27. See Milgate, *John Donne*, p. xxi; Carey, *John Donne*, pp.149–158.

28. William Arrowsmith, trans., *The Satyricon of Petronius* (Ann Arbor, 1959), pp. vii, xi.

29. The letter is usually dated 1604. See Montaigne's *Essais*, 1.39.116, in the translation of John Florio (1603, etc.) as edited by Henry Morley (London, 1893). The *Essais* are subsequently quoted in English from this edition; in French, from the edition of Maurice Rat, 2 vols. (Paris, 1962). Where modern editors number individual essays differently from Florio, the modern reference is given in brackets.

30. Helen Peters lists the "Essay of Valour," often considered to be Donne's, among the *Dubia*. See *Paradoxes and Problems*, p. xlviii.

blunt words (which vaguely anticipate a famous statement by Dryden), Donne was a poet for whom he would have had little use:

The learned . . . have in these dayes so filled the closets, and possessed the eares of Ladyes, that if they [the ladies] retaine not their [books'] substance, at least they have their countenance: using in all sorts of discourse and subject how base or popular soever, a newe, an affected and learned fashion of speaking and writing . . . and alledge Plato and Saint Thomas for things, which the first man they meete would decide as well . . .  (3.3.418)

But Donne found much in the *Essais* that was of use to him in the years before and after the writing of *Metempsychosis*. The pun in his epigram "A Lame Begger"—

> I am unable, yonder begger cries,
> To stand, or move; if he say true, he *lies*

—may have been suggested by the "Liar Paradox" recorded in "An Apologie of Raymond Sebond": "If you say I lye, and in that you should say true, you lye then" (2.12.268).[31] The woman in Donne's epigram "Phryne" may have taken her name from the celebrated courtesan whom Montaigne mentions tantalizingly in "Of Physiognomy" (3.12.542). Stoical precepts that are sprinkled liberally throughout the *Essais* would have nourished the mood of the poet whose writings often evince a similar concern with Senecan virtue. "Oh, what a vile and abject thing is man . . . unlesse he raise himselfe above humanity!" quotes Montaigne (2.12.310). Donne agrees: "Be more then man, or thour't lesse then an Ant" (*The First Anniversarie*, 190).[32] "Seeke wee then our selves in our selves," Donne advises a friend ("To Mr Rowland Woodward," 19), echoing Montaigne, who quotes Persius (1.5): *nec te quaesiveris extra* ("Seeke [not] youre selfe abrode" [2.16.321]). Montaigne muses often about the extreme precariousness of human life:

How many severall meanes and waies hath death to surprise us! . . . Hast thou not seen [a man] choked with the kernell of a grape? And an

31. See Cicero, *Academica*, 2.29; Diogenes Laertius, *Lives*, 2.108–111.
32. See Seneca, *Naturales quaestiones*, preface to bk. 1.

Emperour die by the scratch of a combe . . . ? [1.19.29 (1.20)]. Dionysius the father . . . obtained the victory over the tragicall poets of Athens, who were much better than he was . . . after which usurped victorie, he presently deceased: and partly through the excessive joy he thereby conceived [2.12.326]. The least pricke of a needle and passion of the mind . . . [1.42.130], a gust of contrarie winds . . . a sodaine voice, a false signe, a mornings mist, an evening fogge, are enough to overthrow [a man] [2.12.239].

In these meditations Donne follows him:

There is scarce any thing, that hath not killed some body; a haire, a feather hath done it . . . Men have dyed of Joy . . . Even that Tiran Dyonisius . . . dyed of so poore a Joy, as to be declard by the people at a Theater that hee was a good Poet . . . [*Devotions*, pp. 35–36]. A pinne, a combe, a haire, pulled, hath gangred, & killd . . . a vapour . . . [ibid., p. 63].

And what else but Montaigne's famous *Que scay-je?* (2.12.588) could Donne have had in mind when stating a major theme of his *Second Anniversarie:* "Poore soule, in this thy flesh what do'st thou know?" (l. 254). Most striking, however, is the enormous debt that *Metempsychosis* owes to the *Essais*—a debt so large, in fact, that this collection of prose pieces must be accounted among Donne's chief sources of inspiration for his poem.

It has long been recognized that in a general way the "naturalism" and "skepticism" of *Metempsychosis* have antecedents in the thought of Montaigne.[33] The "Apologie of Raymond Sebond" is only the most well known of his many assertions that the debility of the human mind and the contradictoriness of human experience reduce all reasoning about law and value to the status of "custom" and "opinion." Indeed, we might

33. See Louis I. Bredvold, "The Naturalism of Donne in Relation to Some Renaissance Traditions," *Journal of English and Germanic Philology*, 22 (1923), 471–502; also, Bredvold's "The Religious Thought of Donne in Relation to Medieval and Later Traditions," in *Studies in Shakespeare, Milton, and Donne*, University of Michigan Publications, Language and Literature (New York and London, 1925), I, 193–232. Robert Ornstein, in "Donne, Montaigne, and Natural Law" (*Journal of English and Germanic Philology*, 55 [1956], 213–229), doubts that Donne owes anything to Montaigne, finding no evidence for debt in the poetry and evidence more apparent than real in *Biathanatos*.

observe that the very words of the relativistic creed proclaimed
at the end of Donne's poem—

> Ther's nothing simply good, nor ill alone,
> Of every quality comparison,
> The onely measure is, and judge, opinion
> (ll. 518–520)

—recall passages in the *Essais:*

We have no other ayme of truth and reason, than the example and
Idea of the opinions and customes of the countrie we live in.   (1.30.94
[1.31])

No qualitie doth embrace us purely and universally.   (1.37.107 [1.38])

Our qualities have no title but in comparison.   (3.9.509)

Although the author of *Metempsychosis* may have been somehow intellectually in league with Montaigne, it has been proposed that the ideas from the passage about "comparison" are
"quite in agreement with [Donne's] mature opinions," and not
in any deep sense unorthodox. Donne may be asserting merely
that no earthly good or evil exists in a pure state, without ad-
mixture of its opposite; and that the human means we have of
discerning and judging value is our limited, but not useless,
human intellect. Donne the preacher will say as much in sermons
nearly twenty-four years later: "Nothing is Essentially good,
but God . . . This Essentiall goodnesse of God is so diffusive,
so spreading, as that there is nothing in the world, that doth
not participate of that goodnesse . . . So that now both these
propositions are true, First, That there is nothing in this world
good, and then this also, That there is nothing ill" (*Sermons,*
6.231). "Opinion" is "a middle station, betweene ignorance,
and knowledge; for knowledge excludes all doubting, all hesitation; opinion does not so; but opinion excludes indifferency,
and equanimity" (ibid., l. 317).[34] In 1601, however, Donne is
not a sober priest engaged with his congregation, but a free-
thinking layman, alone with his own dangerous thoughts and those

34. See John P. Wendell, "Two Cruxes in the Poetry of John Donne,"
*Modern Language Notes,* 63 (1948), 471–478, and Milgate, *John Donne,* pp.
190–191.

of the essayist who encourages them. The notion that "ther's nothing simply good, nor ill alone" first occurs to him as the Montaignean principle (2.20) that "we taste nothing purely," then grows into the equally Montaignean idea that our judgments about the "quality" of each part of the mixture have no claim to objectivity. Had Donne wished to speak as prudently in the poem as he was to do in his sermons (and in August 1601, hardly in a cautious frame of mind, he was on the verge of taking one of the most imprudent steps of his life in eloping with Ann More), he would not have called subjective "comparison" and "opinion" the *only* "measure" and "judge" of value; he would not have done so at the end of a work that had already challenged complacent humanistic and religious pieties; and he would have avoided the company of Montaigne.

But Donne sought out Montaigne assiduously for help with the general themes of his poem and to provide suggestions for many of its details. Not only does metempsychosis appear in the *Essais* as matter for jest (2.12.283) and at the same time part of a more serious general context in which all is perennial and contradictory movement (*branloire;* 3.2.222); the idea of transmigration is introduced, as in Donne's poem, by reference to Ovid (2.11.217), with an eye to "divine justice" (218), and it is followed by the "Apologie of Raymond Sebond," with its conclusions about "custom," "opinion," and the ambiguities of human judgment. Montaigne even refers to the soul's migration from body to body as its "progress" *(son progrès)* (2.12.622). Most of Donne's menagerie can be found either in Montaigne's discussion of metempsychosis: the wolf, the unnamed fish, and the dog (2.11.218); or in the vicinity thereof: the pike, the whale, the elephant (2.12.232), the swan (1. 233), the mouse (1. 277), birds that (like Donne's sparrow) mate with a parent, and "munkies ragingly in love with women" (1. 237).[35] Montaigne's "Apologie," citing Plato's *Timaeus,* suggests one reason why the soul in Donne's cynical *Progresse* eventually reaches the sister-wife

35. In his prefatory epistle, Donne considers "the same soule in an Emperour, in a Post-horse, and in a Mucheron." Montaigne had spoken of transmigration from "a Horse to a King" (2.12.283). Perhaps Shakespeare was also reacting to Montaigne when (circa 1601) he has Hamlet observe that "a king may go a progress through the guts of a beggar" (4.3.30–31) and that "there is nothing

of Cain: "Beholde [the soul's] progresse elsewhere: he that hath
lived well reconjoyneth himself unto that Star or Planet to which
he is assigned: who evill, passeth into a woman . . ." (2.12.283).
In *Metempsychosis,* the narrator observes that "hands, not
tongues, end heresies" (l. 120); in "Of the Lame or Cripple,"
the essayist thanks God that his belief is not controlled by fists
(*ma cr[é]ance ne se manie pas à coups de poing* [3.11.479]). If,
as has been suggested, Tertullian and Saint Augustine have left
their marks on the poem, perhaps it is because Donne was
insistently reminded of them by Montaigne's frequent reference
to the works of Tertullian and to the *City of God.*[36]

These points of contact between *Metempsychosis* and the *Essais,* taken in sum, give the skeptical Montaigne a rather large
share in the poem, and they suggest in Donne a restless intellectual mood appropriately vented in the process of allusion.
The purpose of allusion, however, is not simply to utter a vague
discontent. The use that Donne makes of the essays defines, in
a way, the kind of work he was writing. And out of considerations of genre come indications of theme.

At the very beginning of *Metempsychosis,* in the epigraph and
epistle, there are features that recall attitudes most typical of
Montaigne. Donne makes a special point of affixing a date to
his poem: *16 Augusti 1601.* He offers to the reader his "picture"—not an engraved frontispiece, but a depiction of his
"minde" as it reveals itself in his words and thoughts. Although
his borrowing will be heavy, he claims to "have no purpose to
come into any mans debt." He "would have no such Readers
as [he] can teach." And, as we have noted, he deems his work
"sacred to Infinity." All of these details, apparently uncon-

---

either good or bad, but thinking makes it so" (2.2.249–250). The idea, mentioned by Donne in the epistle, that the soul might inhabit a "melon," might
derive from Tertullian, *De anima,* 32.

36. See the references pointed out by Donald Frame in the index to his
translation of the *Essais* (Stanford, 1958). Also, Montaigne may have been
quoting from Tertullian's *De anima,* 1, when in the apology for Sebond he
recounts an anecdote about Socrates and Xanthippe: "Socrates, his wife, exasperated her grief by this circumstance. 'Good Lord (said she) how unjustly
doe these bad judges put him to death.' 'What! wouldest thou rather they should
execute me justly?' replied he to her" (2.12.298; see Diogenes Laertius, *Lives,*
2.35).

nected, bespeak definite, plausibly related habits of mind that seek their own appropriate mode of literary expression. A date is more properly placed at the head of an ephemeral journal entry than at the beginning of an epic. The epic poet does not (at least, not officially) "launch" out (*Metempsychosis*, l. 57) at a particular moment, uncertain of his stores ("how my stock will hold out I know not"), vague about his plans. Extemporaneousness is the prerogative rather of the diarist or the essayist, who has license to write in the moment, expressing his thoughts in all their tentativeness, inconsistency, and incompleteness, and who with no strict agenda may end where he wishes. Essays may be as dogmatic as pronouncements ex cathedra; but the form itself, that of an "attempt," is the product of diffidence. If his mind were able to take hold of truth, says Montaigne, he would make not essays but decisions (3.2.409). Without a holdfast in the wide field of potential knowledge, the essaying mind stays within its narrow competence, relating its changing perceptions as they pass. Montaigne declares:

I cannot settle my object; it goeth so unquietly and staggering, with a naturall drunkennesse . . . I describe not the essence but the passage; not a passage from age to age, or as the people reckon, from seaven yeares to seaven, but from day to day, from minute to minute. (3.2.409)

A date would then be important as marking a transient mental present, which (as Donne said of "Greatnesse") "a period hath, but hath no station" (*Metempsychosis*, l. 340) and is not to be relied upon to fix belief:

> I could
> Dispute, and conquer, if I would,
> Which I abstaine to doe,
> For by to morrow, I may thinke so too.
> ("Womans Constancy," ll. 14–17)

The passing that Donne portrays in *Metempsychosis* is more than the parade of the soul's adventures; like Montaigne, who had announced at the beginning of his book, "it is my selfe I pourtray" ("The Authour to the Reader"),[37] he presents a "pic-

37. See also Montaigne, *Essais*, 2.6.189; 2.17.335; 2.18.340; 3.5.452.

ture" of himself—that is, of his mind (hardly "plaine" and "flat") as it follows and unsuccessfully tries to make sense of the flux of things. Donne's portrait, then, is not only the preface in which he speaks about himself but the entire poem, which collects the opinions that are the "onely" fruits of his judgment. What does the skeptic "know," and therefore what can he depict, *but* the contents of his own mind?

If he is enclosed in the world of his private judgment, it seems strange that an essayist should "borrow." Montaigne's seventeenth-century translator, John Florio, was struck by the inconsistency in his author's attitudes toward tradition: "He, most writing of himselfe, and the worst rather then the best, disclaimeth all memorie, authorities, or borrowing of the ancient or moderne; whereas in course of his discourse he seemes acquainted not onely with all, but no other but authors . . ."[38] Montaigne once offered a defense of his practice—"I never speak [the minds] of others, but that I may the more speake of my [own]" (1.15.63 [1.16])—but also admitted that he might have been more true to his principles:

> By some [it] might be saide of me, that here I have but gathered a nosegay of strange flowres, and have put nothing of mine unto it but the thred to binde them . . . Certes, I have given unto publike opinion that these borrowed ornaments accompany me, but I meane not they should cover or hide me . . . [I] would make show of nothing that is not mine owne, yea mine owne by nature. And had I believed myselfe, at all adventure I had spoken alone. (3.12.541)

Donne's resolve to avoid "debt" to other writers was, of course, just as unlikely to be kept. Even as he made it, he was probably thinking of Montaigne, to whom, among others, he would resort time and again for inspiration. Never acknowledging any specific indebtedness, however—and he had promised to "pay" what-

38. Florio's preface to his translation, quoted from the Everyman's Library edition of the *Essays*, 3 vols. (London, 1910), I, 10. Although Donne was certainly able to read the *Essais* in French, it is possible that he saw, before or while writing *Metempsychosis*, Florio's translation—which was first published in 1603 but had been entered in the Stationers' Register in 1599. Donne's friend the essayist Sir William Cornwallis had read Florio's work in 1600 (see *Dictionary of National Biography*, 7.337) and may have shared it with his comrade-in-letters.

ever bill he should incur—he maintains in his poem the image of an isolated observer whose only truth is his own, unable to learn and unwilling, he says, to "teach."

When the author of the *Essais* disclaimed the role of teacher, he did so because he believed himself "not sufficiently taught to instruct others"—*"Je n'enseigne poinct, je raconte"* (1.25.63 [1.26]; 3.2.224)—and because in a world of isolated consciousnesses and chimerical truths, useful communication happened *"par accident"* (2.6.414). Donne sounds far less humble in desiring "no such readers" as he can "teach." Into his poem only initiates need inquire. Yet essayist and poet are closer than they may seem; for Montaigne is clearly proud of his knowledge of the humiliating vanity of "knowledge," and the knowledge that Donne would share only with fellow savants turns out to be no great wisdom after all, simply facts that embarrass the critical intellect.

The moment, the monadic self, the incompetent mind: these themes in Montaigne's *Essais,* then, taken up by Donne, help to explain why an "epic" like *Metempsychosis* is doomed to be only an "attempt." We have seen that such an essay is "Infinitati Sacrum" because of the formlessness inherent in its subject. There is as well a Montaignean dimension to the problem of the infinite. The word *infini* and its cognates appear one hundred and twenty times in the *Essais,*[39] often as merely intensifying modifiers (arguments may be "infinitely true"; one may love poetry "infinitely"), but sometimes with serious import. The infinite could terrify Montaigne, as it would his opponent-to-be, Pascal, whose fear of *les espaces infinis* is well known. Montaigne confessed that he could not endure the sight of what seemed like "infinite precipices" without "horror" and "trembling" (2.12.305). He feared even more intensely the kinds of infinity implied by his philosophy. Nervously aware that the infinite might be absolute dissipation ("The minde," he said, "that hath no fixed bound, will easily loose itselfe . . . To be everiewhere is to be nowhere" [1.8.13; see also 2.12.300]), he yet formulated an epistemology and an ethic that atomized truth into an "infinite varietie" of contradictory opinions (1.22.43

---

39. See Roy E. Leake, *Concordance des essais de Montaigne* (Geneva, 1981).

[1.23]; 2.12.246, 275, 278). Where there are no universals, there
are no norms; and discrete empirical facts, which seem of "infinite number," barely add up to empirical truth (2.12.303) and
do not amount to any value. Montaigne acknowledged that
"mans minde"—to be consistent, he should have said his own
mind—could not keep forever "floting up and downe" in an
"infinite deepe" of ideas (2.12.260). To avoid intellectual and
moral giddiness he willfully bound himself, he said, to the faith
of his Church (1.26.82 [1.27]; 1.56.157), to the custom of his
country (1.22.47 [1.23]), and to the promptings of a rather ill-
defined "nature" (2.12.231; 3.12.543).

In *Metempsychosis* Donne does not bring faith (or, for that
matter, the law of expediency) peremptorily to the rescue. Although religious faith lurks about the poem in references to
God, the Church, the Book of Genesis, the cross of Christ, and
a number of theological dilemmas, it is not here a compelling
intellectual force that can check the infinite drift of a skeptical
mind. It leaves questions about the problem of evil to be answered only by the violence of the will and its instruments
("hands"), and *Donne's* will is nowhere seriously brought into
play. The poet's faith participates in rather than dissolves ambiguity, because it reveals good and evil to be linked in a strange
and terrible alliance that leaves him wondering why, for example,

> . . . most of those arts, whence our lives are blest,
> By cursed *Cains* race invented be,
> And blest *Seth* vext us with Astronomie.[40]
>
> (ll. 515–517)

That Christ's cross

> Stood in the selfe same roome in Calvarie,
> Where first grew the forbidden learned tree
> (ll. 77–78)

is in the poem more of a bewildering than a consoling symbolic
fact.

At this point, where Donne appears to surpass the intellec-

40. That is, astrology.

tually adventurous Montaigne in the daring that may court despair, the question should again be posed: does *Metempsychosis* represent "the very nadir of [his] faith in God and man"? We must acknowledge that the poem conveys neither the solemnity nor the contempt of blasphemy. The author tries with some success to make his work "light" (l. 55); and the levity is a mark of caution, a deliberate evasion of candid outrage at divine or human wickedness and of psychic nausea in the face of absurdity. Yet he cannot deny that his "Writ" is also "sullen" (l. 511). Can *Metempsychosis* betoken comic insouciance and anguished rebellion at the same time? Both Tertullian and Montaigne may have suggested to Donne the utility of a *psychological* essay in or attempt at a kind of self-exorcism that would allow unholy thoughts and feelings life without granting them mastery. In Tertullian's *De anima,* the magician Carpocrates is reputed to have proposed that transmigration made possible the full and desirable consummation in a soul of all its possibilities, whether, as "opinion" would have it, they were good or evil. In his *De pudicitia,* Tertullian spoke with ironic contempt of those who professed that "for continence sake . . . incontinence is necessary—[that] 'burning' will be extinguished by 'fires.' "[41] Montaigne, however, taking this passage out of context, removed some of the irony and offered its doctrine (in how much seriousness, it is not clear) as a plausible justification for some kinds of human behavior (3.5.436). The principle at issue for Carpocrates and for Montaigne is that life must be seen as a process in which the "irresponsible" part of the self will have its way in moments that may be unsavory in themselves but salutary in the continuum. We might see Donne as tempted by this view—not that he ever showed signs of subscribing fully to its logic or of living by its counsel; but that he was attracted by the opportunity to harbor in his imagination rambunctious, rebellious notions that he could bring himself to translate into poetry but never, at least not decisively, into conduct or "official" doctrine. He knew the cathartic value of imaginative effort:

41. "On Modesty," in *Ante-Nicene Fathers,* ed. Alexander Roberts and James Donaldson; *Fathers of the Third Century,* vol. 4 (Edinburgh, 1885), p. 74.

> I thought, if I could draw my paines,
> Through Rimes vexation, I should them allay,
> Griefe brought to numbers cannot be so fierce,
> For, he tames it, that fetters it in verse.
>                                ("The Triple Foole," ll. 8–11)

And if Donne could never become in fact a libertine, a misanthrope, or an adversary of deity, he could experience their outlaw passions as a poet whose fancy was allowed "for continence sake . . . incontinence." His casuistical defense of suicide, *Biathanatos,* which was as heterodox in content as *Metempsychosis,* he could neither fully claim nor abjure: "Reserve it for me, if I live," he asked of his friend Sir Robert Ker, "and if I die, I only forbid it the Presse, and the Fire: publish it not, but yet burn it not; and between those, do what you will with it."[42] Just so, he could neither sponsor nor suppress the impious thoughts about "God and man" that prompted his attempt to chronicle the "progresse of a deathlesse soule." He kept them, therefore, safe and harmless, in the limbo of a poetical essay.

If the poet, as Sidney protested, "nothing affirmeth," and if the essayist, like Montaigne, makes essays instead of decisions, Donne was doubly safe from moral reproach. Yet it may not be said that his main concern was security. A restlessness, a sense of aspiration, prevented him from adopting the stance, taken by Montaigne, that he should be content to live a merely "excusable" life (3.9.486). Whereas Montaigne's book of *Essais* implied, even prescribed a way of life, the author of "Satyre III," who had license to doubt "wisely" but not forever, could not allow *Metempsychosis* to serve as a metaphor for a *condition,* in which the human soul aspired to the epic, was limited and mocked by history, and was bound to judge and choose only tentatively in essays. Judgment and choice had finally to become definite, definitive, perhaps heroic; thus the moment that Donne

42. See R. C. Bald, *John Donne: A Life* (Oxford, 1970), p. 342. Also, p. 158: "Donne's motive in writing [*Biathanatos*] was, like that of Burton in composing *The Anatomy of Melancholy,* to overcome a temptation, not by trying to banish it altogether from the mind, but by giving it full place there and at the same time rendering it innocuous by transferring it from the plane of action to that of learned investigation and contemplation."

called 16 August 1601, when ideas combined to produce a stalemate that freed a skeptic from the imperatives of truth, could not be repeated indefinitely as part of a strategy of evasion. Donne read in the *Essais* even late into his life (as his borrowing from them for his *Devotions* indicates). But there was finally a momentous difference, for all their kinship, between Donne's *satura* and what Montaigne had called (3.13.532) his *fricassée*.

JAMES S. BAUMLIN

# Generic Contexts of Elizabethan Satire: Rhetoric, Poetic Theory, and Imitation

In his *De inventione dialectica,* Rudolph Agricola observes that a speaker conveys his emotions to an audience through style, making it "imperative that the language express all the thoughts, vows, regrets, desires, prayers, and disputes in accordance with the nature of each emotion." He continues:

> Language itself recreates tumult and turmoil through mental agitation. Indeed, that force which we sometimes call the "color" of language especially consists of this imitation through the emotions. Thus, even though many say the same thing, whether in exposition or in argumentation, still one will exhibit the color of a man advising merely, another of one angry, another of one complaining, another of one grieving.[1]

That style should reflect a speaker's emotional state is a commonplace from classical rhetoric: as Cicero, Quintilian, and Longinus suggest, one cannot elicit emotions from an audience

1. J. R. McNally, "Rudolph Agricola's *De inventione dialectica libri tres:* A Translation of Selected Chapters," *Speech Monographs,* 34 (1967), 417.

unless one first feels and displays them himself. What makes Agricola's observation significant, however, is his choice of illustration, the three Roman satirists. Agricola suggests that Horace, Persius, and Juvenal each treat "the same subject," and each pursues "the same purpose" in writing satire, which he defines broadly as "the amending of manners and life and the reproval of vice." But each of the Romans chooses to "color" his satire in ways that evince different emotions:

Horace affected the appearance of being amused and strove, as he himself said, by candid portrayal to unmask faults. Persius took on a more severe and almost moralistic character: in teaching he reproved and by reproving taught. Juvenal as a rule presents the appearance of indignation and anger, and so a slightly more direct and flowing poetic style suited him, as also a more pungent wit and greater freedom of expression.[2]

Style thus reflects the emotions and the moral values of each individual satirist, and these together comprise his persona, the character he projects to his reading audience. Similarly, the satirist's emotional state determines his aim or approach to vice: Juvenal's anger and *saeva indignatio* erupt in an equally strong rebuke and bitter indignation; Horace's calmer, more pleasant personality leads to a gentler mockery and ridicule; and Persius' high seriousness, avoiding the extremes of amusement and anger, prefers moral instruction to ridicule and invective. These are, of course, generalized and somewhat idealized descriptions of the classical personae and their styles; one might say oversimplified, given the variety and complexities in each satirist's works. But these and similar descriptions form the basis of Renaissance criticism of the Roman satirists, delineating them as three distinct personae—and thus three distinct models—for imitation

2. Ibid. In a similar vein Julius Caesar Scaliger suggests that "Juvenal burns, he threatens openly, he goes for the throat; Persius scoffs; Horace laughs" (*Poetices libri septem,* facsimile rpt. [Stuttgart, 1964], p. 149.) And François Vavasseur observes that "Horace, quietly and gently stealing into our minds, persuades by laughing; Persius, while he mocks, prefers to philosophize; and Juvenal, as if upset and nauseated, expresses his indignation at all things" (*De ludicra dictione,* p. 241, quoted in Henricius Christianus Henninius, *Decimi Junii Juvenalis Aquinatis satyrae* [Antwerp, 1695]). Translations, unless otherwise noted, are my own.

in the vernacular. Agricola points us, then, to two major concerns of this essay: the rhetorical nature of formal satire, and the Renaissance characterization of each Roman satirist.

Like the orator, the satirist knows that persuasion is impossible unless one moves the will through an appeal to the emotions. Conviction, the intellectual assent to some good or value, may be borne of *logos,* or rational argument, but actual persuasion, the assent of the whole man to some value, affects the will through the emotions as well as the mind. And only the latter provides a basis for real change and action. The classical satirists therefore seek to move the will through *pathos,* and they do so by appealing to a range of emotions. Horace and his imitators appeal to the gentler emotions, laughter and ridicule, while followers of Juvenal elicit more vehement emotions from their audience, anger and scorn. And yet neither pathetic nor logical proof appears as crucial to the effect of satire as the third and final mode of rhetorical proof, *ethos.* Aristotle observes that the rhetor's character "may almost be called the most effective means of persuasion he possesses," for only by projecting an image of good sense, good will, and good moral character can the rhetor gain the trust and confidence of his audience.[3] Similarly, a satirist's success in persuasion depends on his audience's estimation of his particular character.

The character, or ethos, of the Elizabethan satirist is conventional, modeled after the different personae of the classical satirists—and thus dependent upon the ethical authority and weight of their models to effect change. Scholars have recently explored other models of ethos as well: the satyr figure, a licentious and bitterly railing persona; the somber, homilizing figure of Piers the Plowman; and the zealous voices of the biblical prophets. All three are real influences and demonstrate that the Elizabethan satirists inevitably turn to *some* conventionalized persona, some model of ethos, to endow their words with ethical authority. Yet the Elizabethan satirists consistently blend these ancient Greek, biblical, and medieval voices with the conventionalized personae of Roman satire. I would argue

---

3. *Rhetoric,* 1356a, in *The Basic Works of Aristotle,* ed. Richard McKeon (New York, 1941), p. 1329.

that for all the Elizabethan satirists, the classical personae are the primary models—these other personae being accretions, influential but subordinate.[4] And when the Elizabethans imitate the ethos of a Roman satirist, they make an equal use of the structural and stylistic devices characterizing their particular model. Their rhetorically based education (one similar to the rhetorical training the Romans themselves received), would make the Elizabethans sensitive to the features of Horace's sermo, Persius' diatribe, and Juvenal's declamation, as well as the different elements of invention, arrangement, and elocution used by the Romans—and would make them masters of these same arts of language. Rhetoric would also teach the Elizabethans to discover a decorum in each of the Roman satirists, to discover a dynamic unity of purpose and approach, style and structure that would distinguish each Roman as a unique model for imitation.

Imitation of the classical models is thus at the heart of Elizabethan satire, responsible even for the resurgence of the genre during that fruitful literary decade of the 1590s. At the same time the Elizabethans were faced with the challenge of *adapting* this classical genre to changed social conditions and to their Christian religion. Elizabethan satire, as a result, became an ambitious experiment in *revision* as well as imitation, where Donne, Hall, and Marston test and critically evaluate their Roman

4. Alvin B. Kernan first discussed the satyr figure in *The Cankered Muse: Satire of the English Renaissance* (1959; rpt. Hamden, Conn., 1976); other works have challenged and revised his views, most notably Raman Selden, *English Verse Satire, 1590–1765* (London, 1978). John Dermond Peter discusses the influence of Piers in *Complaint and Satire in Early English Literature* (Oxford, 1956); and M. Thomas Hester explores the influence of the biblical prophets in *Kinde Pitty and Brave Scorne: John Donne's Satyres* (Durham, N.C., 1982). Hester's work deserves particular notice. The Christian elements in Donne's *Satyres,* which he has traced sensitively throughout his book, are central to the meaning of these poems; Donne's speaker is, above all, a Christian satirist, spurred on by a homiletic zeal to reform his audience. Yet Hester argues— unnecessarily, I believe—that "Donne replaces the spokesman of Horace, Persius, and Juvenal with a speaker of Christian zeal" (p. 15). I argue instead that Donne, as a Christian satirist, deliberately assumes the different personae of the classical satirists in order to *test their efficacy* in a Christian world. This testing and implicit criticism of models is in fact a primary motive in Donne's englishing of this classical genre.

models as much as follow them, consciously rejecting as many
of their models' values and attitudes as they retain. In addition,
the Elizabethan imitations are mediated by contemporary critical judgments of the Roman models. Continental critics of the
sixteenth century identify the range of classical features that the
Elizabethans will experiment with in their satires—some of which
they will creatively adapt, some of which they will criticize and
ultimately reject. I hope to show that Renaissance criticism
provides a firm basis for the imitative practice of the Elizabethan
satirists, and to illustrate that practice with examples of how
Joseph Hall, John Marston, and especially John Donne imitate
(and test) one particular Roman model, Horace.

In his influential *Poetices libri septem* (1561), Julius Caesar Scaliger initially describes two general styles of formal satire, "one
of which is calmer, like Horace's, and akin to prose; the other
more agitated, which Juvenal and Persius preferred" (p. 20).
Later, Scaliger also identifies two general subjects: satires "are
sometimes grave, at other times even humble, and thus are
either terrifying or humorous. A terrifying subject is poisoning,
a lowly subject the feast of Nasidienus" (p. 149). Themes range,
therefore, from the low and comic to the high tragic—the former
to be identified with Horace, the latter with Juvenal. For Horace, who describes the "feast of Nasidienus" (*Sermo*, 2.8), creates a comic mode of satire whose style is low and subject
laughable; Juvenal, on the other hand, treats the "terrifying
subject" of poisoning—and refers to his work as being tragic
in theme (*Satire*, 6). Francesco Robortello made similar distinctions between tragic and comic modes of satire. His *Para-
phrasis in librum Horatii* (1548) and the essay on satire appended
to it *(Explicatio eorum omnium, quae ad satyram pertinent)*
initially describe a thoroughly Horatian technique: "Satire imitates with joking and laughter. Pitiable things do not arouse
laughter, but rather sorrow; and we do not laugh at wretched
men, but commiserate with them. Hence these things belong
not to satire, but to tragedy; likewise the 'terrifying,' and things
of this sort." It is the laughable, rather, that pertains to satire,
as it does to comedy (*Explicatio*, p. 30). Yet the satirist, as

Robortello goes on to say, must use severer methods when his subjects are the more reprehensible and criminal vices:

While we laugh at those things which have shame in them and the appearance of vice, still shameful things should not be dealt with in only one way. For some are deserving of laughter, others of hate. In laughter there is contempt rather than hatred, and in hate there is no ridicule, but harsh rebuke. The satiric poet treats of both, for he engages in carping at and reprehending the vices of men. (*Explicatio*, p. 30)

Here the tragic, Juvenalian mode takes its place beside the Horatian. Both Robortello and Scaliger suggest that satire is a genre of the *genus mediocre*, or middle style; Scaliger observes, nonetheless, that the style may be "more elevated, or lower, or more licentious, in accordance with one's subject matter" (*Poetices*, p. 149). In this way Horace's "calmer" and Juvenal's "more agitated" styles adapt themselves decorously to the issues these satirists explore.

Throughout the *Poetices* Scaliger distinguishes carefully between Horatian and Juvenalian satire; one of his goals, moreover, is to prove Juvenal's superiority over Horace and Persius— to show he is "unquestionably the chief" among the Roman satirists. The Stoic Persius he describes as an "inept" writer with a "crabbed," deliberately obscure style: "for although [Persius] desired his writings to be read, he did not wish for them to be fully understood" (p. 323). Scaliger adds that "Persius, a parader of his feverish learning, neglected all else," pointing out the dangers of imitating this Roman's erudition in satire (ibid.). Antonio Sebastiano Minturno, perhaps with Persius in mind, also argues that the satirist should leave abstract discussions of virtue to the philosophers.[5] Though unflattering, this characterization of Persius has important consequences for Donne and Marston. When Donne (to use Dryden's phrase) "affects the metaphysics . . . in his satires"—especially in "Satyre III" and "Satyre V"—he does so in imitation of Persius. Similarly, Marston imitates Persius in "Satyre IV" of his *Scourge of Villanie*, book 1, by addressing the philosophical questions of free will

5. *De poeta* (1559), facsimile rpt., ed. Bernhard Fabian (Munich, 1971), pp. 423–424.

and moral sufficiency—both central issues in Persius' Stoic satires. Horace, however, was a more formidable rival to Juvenal:
Scaliger notes the opinion of many sixteenth-century admirers
that Horace "alone knew how to write satire, and that Juvenal
ought not to be considered a satirist, but a declaimer" (*Poetices*,
p. 334). In his stylistic comparison of the two satirists Scaliger
indeed underscores Juvenal's extensive use of declamatory rhetoric, but he also proves, at least to his own satisfaction, that
Juvenal excels Horace even in the most "Horatian" of elements,
such as wit and urbanity.[6]

Scaliger's precepts had considerable influence on subsequent
writers. Juste Lipse praises Scaliger's choice of Juvenal as "his
truest judgment." Juvenal's "ardor, elevation, and liberty" are
unsurpassed; "he takes hold of vices, scolds and rebukes, engages rarely in jests, often in bitter wit—all of which are contrary
to Horace, who is gentle, calm, quiet, and advises more often
than he punishes."[7] If Lipse adds anything to Scaliger's argument, it is that Juvenal excels as a moralist as well as stylist:
"no one," he suggests, "is more capable of correcting morals."[8]
This is also the judgment of the English satirists Hall and Marston. Of course, Hall's and Marston's choice of Juvenal as their
preferred model is in keeping with their own poetic powers and
personalities, for neither succeeds in capturing the lighter touches
of Horatian *sermo*; their imitations of both Persius and Horace
are poetically inferior to their Juvenalian works. Indeed, the
only Elizabethan to imitate Persius successfully—to draw on his
moral seriousness and tendency to philosophize, and make effective use of his structural and stylistic devices—is Donne. As

6. *Poetices*, p. 335. Beyond these Juvenal excels Horace in "variety of arguments" and "wealth of invention," sharpness of language and pungency of
rebuke (ibid., p. 336).

7. *Epistulae*, 2.9, in *Opera omnia* (Antwerp, 1614), I, 240.

8. "Nemo idoneor ad mores corrigendos Juvenali." Phillipo Beroaldo, a
Bolognese scholar of the later fifteenth century, also argues for the moral efficacy
of Juvenal's *saeva indignatio*: " . . . in insectandis vitiis eminentissimus et in
objurgandis moribus vehemens dicendi genus habet elegans atque venustum."
*Oratio in principio lectionis Juvenalis*, in *Reden und Briefe Italienischer Hu-
manisten*, ed. Karl Mullner (Vienna, 1899; rpt. Munich, 1970), p. 63.

I have argued elsewhere, Persius is Donne's preferred model.[9]
Continental criticism, nevertheless, is far from universal in
its elevation of Juvenal. Bartolommeo Ricci, for example, criticizes his moral efficacy as well as his persona, suggesting that
Horace is the better model:

For although there are two ways to amend vices (which is most important in this kind of verse), he [Juvenal], induced either by an un-
sound judgment or by a perverse nature, chose for himself the more
offensive method, which is to attempt to lead sinners back to health
through constant reproaches and placing before them the fear of punishment. In this method of accusation he acts as so fierce a castigator
and so severe an admonitor that he drives offenders to greater delin-
quency and even to despair, when they should grow ashamed of or
repent their sins.[10]

Indeed Ricci calls the opening of Juvenal's first satire *(Semper
ego auditor tantum . . . )* "too haughty, if not insolent."[11] Other
critics show a similar preference for Horace. In *De poeta* (1559)
Minturno outlines a theory of satire that stresses urbanity, friendly
admonition, and good humor as the satirist's most effective
weapons, noting Horace's ability to satirize an individual and
at "the same time win over with jests the person whom he
reprehends" (p. 424). This same concept of sly jesting and insinuation lies at the heart of Sir Philip Sidney's brief discussion
of the satiric poet, who

*"omne vafer vitium ridenti tangit amico";* who sportingly never leaveth
until he make a man laugh at folly, and, at length ashamed, to laugh

9. See James S. Baumlin, "Donne's Christian Diatribes: Persius and the
Rhetorical *Persona* of *Satyre III* and *Satyre V,*" in *The Eagle and the Dove:
Essays Reassessing John Donne* (Columbia, Mo., forthcoming).
10. *De imitatione,* in *Tratatti di poetica,* ed. Bernard Weinberg, 4 vols. (Rome,
1970–1974), IV, 447.
11. Ibid. Donne's critical parody of Juvenal, "Satyre II," begins, suggestively,
with a similar expression of hauteur: "Sir; though (I thanke God for it) I do
hate / Perfectly all this towne . . ." To "thank God" for one's hatred is to turn
Juvenal's *saeva indignatio* into an affectation. Quotations are from *John Donne:
The Satires, Epigrams, and Verse Letters,* ed. Wesley Milgate (Oxford, 1978).

452       James S. Baumlin

at himself, which he cannot avoid, without avoiding the folly; who, while *"circum praecordia ludit,"* giveth us to feel how many headaches a passionate life brings us to.[12]

The techniques Sidney describes are not so much a teaching as an entangling of the audience, an indirection that Horace himself noted: "Why laugh? Change but the name, and the tale is told of you."[13] Minturno, in comparison, finds a simpler though no less important goal for the Horatian *risus:* to gain the good will and assent of the reader, or even of the person criticized. This goal, according to Minturno, accounts for another aspect of Horace's satiric persona, his self-effacement or *deprecatio:* "Doubtless it is a skillful and witty shrewdness to attribute to himself another's vices, so he can carp slyly at others even in his own person."[14]

Minturno may have preferred Horace over the other satirists, and Scaliger, among others, may have preferred Juvenal; but Persius also had his sixteenth-century admirers. In his *De poetica et carminis ratione* (1518) Joachim Vadian admits that Juvenal is the best poet, since he uses "great licence and an abundance of wit . . . is refined and graceful in his versification, serious and candid in his spirit,"[15] but he is not the best teacher of morals. And this, as Isaac Casaubon would argue a century later, is the more important quality for a satirist. According to Vadian, Juvenal's licentiousness and occasional obsceneness, as well as the fierceness of his indignation, overstep the bounds of Christian decency and moderation. Not even Persius is suitable reading for youth, but because Persius is the most modest and most serious or sober among the Roman satirists, he wins Vadian's greatest praise: "This I dare say about Persius: among

12. *An Apology for Poetry,* in *Critical Theory since Plato,* ed. Hazard Adams (New York, 1971), p. 165. Sidney quotes from Persius, who had already recognized this subtle use of friendly insinuation.

13. *Sermo,* 1.1.69–70. Quotations are from H. Rushton Fairclough, *Horace: Satires, Epistles, and Ars Poetica,* The Loeb Classical Library (Cambridge, Mass., 1926).

14. *De poeta,* p. 426. So clearly Horatian are these and other precepts that Minturno's avowed preference for this satirist over Juvenal should cause no surprise.

15. *De poetica,* ed. Peter Schaeffer (Munich, 1973), p. 262.

teachers of morals he is surpassed by no one in gravity and
elegance, and he, most of all, is in accord both with truth and
with our religion."[16]

Persius is also the classical satirist whose teachings and general
manner are most akin to Christianity; his *sanctitas scribendi* is
a central aspect of Persius' Renaissance reputation, attested to
by such sixteenth-century critics as Bartolommeo della Fonte,
Johann Baptista, and, in the following passage, Pietro Crinito:
"He [Persius] is called the most learned satirist by the divine
Jerome, and deservedly so: for he is surpassed by no one in the
holiness of his writing, the gravity of his *sententiae,* the dignity
of his words, or in satiric wit."[17] Since Persius is a pagan author,
some of the terms may initially surprise; but as Crinito's reference to Saint Jerome testifies, these praises have the support
of Church Fathers. Jerome finds in Persius' first satire an echo
of the psalmist David, and Saint Augustine quotes from Persius
many times to exemplify and even explain passages in Scripture.
And if Persius' Stoicism accounts for his moral seriousness, it
also accounts for his emphasis on persuasion over invective.
Persius owes the peculiar form of his moral preaching to the
techniques of the Cynic and Stoic diatribists, such as Diogenes
or the elder Seneca; popular moral subjects, passionate address
and embedded dialogue, hyperbolic and sharply satiric language, and, above all, a desire to teach and persuade. Persius'
satires make use of all these diatribe elements. Fonte writes
particularly of Persius' protreptic or persuasive zeal—as does
Giovanni Britannico, who finds this protreptic tendency to be
specifically Senecan (and thus Stoic) in origin.[18] This tendency
makes Persius a unique model for the Elizabethan satirists: as
an alternative to Horace's laughter and Juvenal's vituperation
one may imitate Persius' moral seriousness and persuasiveness.

Finally, however, no defender of Persius could neglect to

16. Ibid., p. 263. Vadian adds that Persius' moral seriousness more than
compensates for the quality of his verse (p. 264).

17. "De satyrographis," in *A. Persii Flacci satyrae sex, Joanne Murmellio*
(Cologne, 1568), fol. H7r. The same formulation may be found in Baptista's
earlier edition, *Flacci Persii poetae satyrarum opus* (Venice, 1495), p. 311.

18. *Flacci Persii poetae satyrarum opus* (Lyons, 1523), p. 317. Cited in Me-
dine, "Isaac Casaubon's *Prolegomena,*" p. 274.

address the one charge brought time and again against this
Roman, his presumed obscurity. As Vadian observes, "To many
he has appeared deliberately obscure; whether this results from
his nature, or (though I do not believe this) from his own diligence, the pains of so many interpretors bear witness to his
obscurity" (*De poetica*, p. 263). And yet his darkness, Vadian
later suggests, is due to contemporary ignorance of an age and
idiom long past, not to the deliberate obscurity of the writer
(ibid). John Marston agrees:

> *Persius* is crabby, because antient, and his jerkes, (being perticularly
> given to private customes of his time) duskie. Juvenal (upon the like
> occasion) seemes to our judgment, gloomie. Yet both of them goe a
> good seemely pace, not stumbling, shuffling. Chaucer is harde even to
> our understandings: who knows not the reason?

Marston continues, "had we then lived, the understanding of
them had been nothing hard."[19] Actually Marston, like Hall,
writes individual satires in a style deliberately obscure; and among
Elizabethan critics obscurity (as Kernan and Selden both suggest) becomes associated with all the classical satirists, not just
Persius. Nevertheless, darkness of sense is not a necessary feature of the imitation of classical satire, Persian or otherwise:
Marston states as much in the passage above, and Donne demonstrates this in his own re-creations of the form.

I have indicated that the Elizabethan practice of imitation
involves re-creating the decorum of the individual Roman satirists; and such an approach necessarily generalizes features of
the model, searching out the most characteristic effects and
overlooking the nuances. And as we have seen, sixteenth-
century criticism contributes to this by keeping generic and stylistic
bounds among the three classical satirists distinct. Both Renaissance critics and practitioners of satire ignore that Horace
uses elements of Stoic diatribe as well as the sermo, and that
Juvenal modulates his bitter invective to gentler strains of ridicule. With a few exceptions, Renaissance critics and satirists
emphasized and even exaggerated the rhetorical features as-

---

19. Preface to *The Scourge of Villanie*, in *The Poems of John Marston*, ed.
Arnold Davenport (Liverpool, 1961), p. 100.

sociated with the decorum of each Roman satirist. (Many of the exaggerations in the style of Elizabethan satire thus result from an imitation based, as it were, on caricature—and only rarely do the Elizabethans recognize that the products of such imitation tend to become parodies.) At any rate, the Renaissance critics distinguish among the Roman satirists in subject matter, in aim and intended effect, in manner of rebuke, in qualities of style, and in ethos or persona. This kind of critical tradition established a repertoire of rhetorical and, indeed, generic features identified with each model, any combination of which could be foregrounded in imitation. Renaissance writers on imitation do recommend such a broad repertoire. For example, Cardinal Bembo, writing to Pico della Mirandola, suggests that the imitation of models should range through all aspects of invention, arrangement, and style, setting but one requirement for so broad an imitation: "that whatever we have borrowed appears more splendid and illustrious in our own writing than in that from which we have taken it."[20] For Vives too it is the "similar artifice" that the imitator attempts: "Let him copy the same workmanship, but not the same words"—for this alone separates imitation from literary theft.[21] This aspect of imitation emphasizes the similarities in style, structure, and voice between text and model. There is also, however, a second aspect of imitation that emphasizes the differences between text and model and that treats the model as a rival.

Elizabethan satire established a dialectic with its models: in imitating, it extends as well as adapts, criticizes as well as follows. It is also experimental: Hall, Marston, and Donne test, as it were, the resources of each Roman model to enact change in contemporary society. Indeed, the preference that each of

20. *De imitatione ad Picum,* included in Giovanni Pico della Mirandola, *Opera omnia* (Hildesheim), II, 201. Bembo poses the question: "Who does not take from those whom one has read both thoroughly and often either their *sententiae* or their similes, comparisons, and other figures and colors of rhetoric; who does not make use of their descriptions of places or of times or some particular arrangement and logical sequence; and who does not take some image of war or peace, of storms, wanderings, counsels, loves, or of other subjects in general . . . ?"

21. *Vives: On Education, a Translation of the De tradendis disciplinis of Juan Luis Vives,* trans. Foster Watson (1913; rpt. Totowa, N.J., 1971), p. 196.

the Elizabethans shows toward one particular model (Hall and Marston choosing Juvenal, Donne choosing Persius—and Lodge and Jonson choosing Horace) is proof enough that their imitations are critical and ultimately evaluative. Often these writers ask us to see why one or other of the Romans *fails* them as a model—why Horace, who proves so useful to Thomas Lodge, fails Donne, and why Persius, whom Donne uses so effectively, fails Hall and Marston. Three aspects of imitation thus deserve attention: the role *decorum* plays in the recreation of a model and its effects; the rhetorical elements of imitation; and the revision of the model to accord with a new culture and new religious beliefs. These elements can be illustrated by examining the ways Elizabethan satirists imitate one particular model, Horace's *Sermones*. Horace, as I have suggested, is *not* a preferred model for Marston, Hall, or Donne, so their adaptations of this Roman highlight for us the dialectical, evaluative, and often revisionary nature of their imitative practice.

John Marston's *Scourge of Villanie* is most noted for its Juvenalian invective. His second satire, for example, begins with the precipitant rage of its Roman model:

> I Cannot hold, I cannot I indure
> To view a big womb'd foggie clowde immure
> The radiant tresses of the quickning sunne.
> Let Custards quake, my rage must freely runne.[22]

Like the opening line of Juvenal's first satire *(Semper ego auditor tantum? . . . )* Marston's opening—with its thrice-repeated "I," trebling Juvenal's *ego*—draws immediate attention to the satirist's emotional state. In this clearly exaggerated expression of Juvenal's *saeva indignatio,* Marston's satirist can no longer keep silent or keep his rage in check: "My soule is vext, what power will'th desist? / Or dares to stop a sharpe fangd Satyrist? . . ." (1. 7ff.). But while "Satyre II" exemplifies Marston's Juvenalian persona, "Satyre III" begins in a voice and style clearly Horatian:

22. "Satyre II," ll. 1–4. Quotations are from *The Poems of John Marston,* ed. Arnold Davenport (Liverpool, 1961).

It's good be warie whilst the sunne shines cleere
(Quoth that old chuffe that may dispend by yere
Three thousand pound) whilst hee of good pretence
Commits himselfe to Fleet to save expence.
No Countries Christmass: rather tarry heere,
The Fleet is cheap, the Country hall too deere.

(ll. 1–6)

Marston takes the epigraph to "Satyre III" from Horace (*"Redde, age, quae deinceps risisti"* ["Pray, tell us what you laughed at next"], *Sermones,* 2.8.80), and the motto itself should alert us to a change in Marston's satiric voice: at least initially, Marston here chooses to laugh rather than rage. Folly and matters of intemperance are the ostensible subjects, and through the first forty lines the satirist indeed "sports" (24) over the moral demise of Codrus and his profligate son, Luxurio. Marston does not, however, commit himself fully to the Horatian mode: as the satire progresses and examples of incontinence multiply, the anger of his persona mounts. By the end of the poem the satirist is unable to restrain his invective or continue to jest and ironize in the manner of Horace:

Nay, shall a trencher slave extenuate,
Some *Lucrece* rape? and straight magnificate
Lewd *Jovian* lust? Whilst my satyrick vaine
Shall muzled be, not daring out to straine
His tearing paw? No gloomie *Juvenall,*
Though to thy fortunes I disastrous fall.

(ll. 191–196)

Marston's experimentation with Horatian elements is thus short-lived: grave vices demand strong rebuke, of the sort "gloomie Juvenall" used. But the fact that this poem ends by choosing Juvenal does not deny that it begins in the Horatian mode. Indeed, this brings the Horatian elements into sharper focus: for by imitating and in the same poem rejecting the Horatian attitude toward vice, Marston demonstrates his familiarity with the model, points out its inability to deal effectively with the graver vices, and so justifies his ultimate choice of Juvenal. Donne does the same thing in his fourth satire, which begins with Horace's dramatic wit—only to shift, in midcourse, to the more fiery and angry declamation reminiscent of Juvenal. This shift from Horace to Juvenal has the same cause in both poems: both satirists discover that their subject is not human folly but grave vice.

The Horatian persona's direct involvement in dialogue and action—and his involvement in the follies he describes—are part of his technique of self-deprecation. Similarly, the persona in book 3, Satire 3, of Hall's *Virgidemiae* implicates himself in the same hypocrisy that he finds in the "courteous Citizen":

> The courteous Citizen bad me to his feast,
> With hollow words, and overly request:
> Come, will ye dine with me this Holy day?
> I yeelded, tho he hop'd I would say *Nay:*
> For I had mayden'd it, as many use,
> Loath for to grant, but loather to refuse.[23]

Yielding to this "hollow" invitation leads the speaker ultimately to repent his foolishness, especially when he discovers the "meaning" of this lavish feast: "Had'st thou such cheer? wer't thou ever ther before? / Never: I thought so: nor come there no more. / Come there no more, for so ment all that cost: / *Never hence take me for thy second host*" (ll. 27–30). The "feast of Nasidienus" (*Sermones,* 2.8) was the subject Scaliger identified with the low, comic mode of satire, and this Horatian poem was doubtless an inspiration for Hall. And as the subject is low, so is the style, daily conversation being the linguistic norm of this and other satires in book 3. Hall has not fully captured Horace's wit or subtler ironies, but he achieves his model's plain, colloquial style and dramatic structures. He also discovers that Horatian ironies and dramatic situations implicate the satirist himself in the follies he ridicules: he becomes culpable, his satire serving to perpetuate rather than cure vice. Donne, we shall find, carries this implicit criticism of the Horatian persona a step further, by both involving the satirist in the folly of his *adversarius* and redefining this folly as Christian sinfulness.

\*     \*     \*

23. *Virgidemiae,* 3.3.1–6. Quotations are from *The Collected Poems of Joseph Hall,* ed. Arnold Davenport (Liverpool, 1949).

A notable feature of Donne's first satire is its use of the characterization and dramatic situation of Horace's *Sermo* 1.9—in which, "While taking a morning stroll, Horace is joined by a mere acquaintance, who insists upon accompanying him, hoping through closer intimacy to secure an introduction to Maecenas. The poet vainly endeavors to shake him off, and it is only when the man's adversary in a lawsuit appears on the scene—a genuine deus ex machina—that Horace is rescued from his unhappy situation."[24] Horace's satire uses the boor's misunderstanding of Maecenas and his circle to celebrate the virtues of this elite social group, where wealth of talent can be respected more than monetary wealth, where nobility of spirit can be given its place next to nobility of lineage, and, conversely, where fraud, jealousy, and opportunism can have no place whatsoever. Horace's own urbanity and good manners reflect both the cultural and moral values of this circle: within such an ideal society, modest but fine behavior, compliment and polite conversation become refinements of nature, truly elegant expressions of one's true thoughts and feelings. Yet in the world outside this circle, marked by personal discontent, insincerity, and opportunism, "polite" language and behavior quickly become affected, if not vicious. So while the boor's importunity offers Horace the opportunity to praise the social values of the Maecenas circle, Horace's inability to deal with the boor illustrates how frail these social values are, when confronted by their opposites.

In *Sermo* 1.9, the satirist's own sense of social decorum works humorously against him. For even as he lies and gives the broadest hints by his behavior and language that he is anxious to be left alone, his own "good manners" prevent him from dismissing the boor outright; and the boor, an opportunist to begin with,

24. H. Rushton Fairclough, *Horace*, p. 103. The major Horatian elements of Donne's "Satyre I" and "IV"—their structural similarity to *Sermo*, 1.9 and their use of an "Impertinent" or *adversarius*—have been discussed briefly by Raman Selden, *English Verse Satire*, pp. 63–64, and in greater depth by Howard Erskine-Hill, "Courtiers out of Horace: Donne's *Satyre IV*, and Pope's *Fourth Satire of Dr. John Donne, Dean of St Paul's, Versifyed*," pp. 273–293. For an alternative view—one arguing for Persius as Donne's thematic and structural model—see Y. Shikany Eddy and Daniel P. Jaekle, "Donne's 'Satyre I': The Influence of Persius's 'Satire III,' " *Studies in English Literature*, 21 (1981), 111–122.

takes advantage of Horace's good manners by continuing to dog him, even as he senses the poet's consternation. Horace's politeness turns then to irony, and gaps develop between what he says and what he feels or actually means. And while the satirist's words deliberately understate his emotional disturbance, the description of his feelings and behavior greatly exaggerates it:

As he kept dogging me, I break in with, "nothing you want, is there?" But he: "You must get to know me; I'm a scholar." To this I say, "Then I'll esteem you the more." Dreadfully eager to get away I now walk fast, at times stop short, then whisper a word in my slave's ear, while the sweat trickled down to my very ankles.   (1.9.6–11)

A passage like this is designed for humor, but humor at the satirist's own expense. And on its more serious side, the passage reveals Horace playing a game of mutual hypocrisy with his *adversarius*.

This is only an undercurrent in Horace; but in Donne the hypocritical use of polite conversation becomes a thematic focus. In "Satyre IV," trapped into a "polite" conversation at court, Donne's persona uses wit and verbal equivocation as offensive weapons against his own version of Horace's "Impertinent." Neither character can understand the other, because each constantly—and at times deliberately—confuses figurative with literal meanings of the other's words; so what begins in Horace as ironies perceived (though ignored) by the *adversarius* becomes in Donne the breakdown of polite discourse as meaningful communication. And if polite language is a thematic focus in Donne's imitations of Horace, social behavior becomes a dramatic focus. As Horace's *Sermones* demonstrate, when the satirist engages himself dramatically in the world of his satire, his words and actions become as open to scrutiny as those of his *adversarius*. Self-revelation and the expression of individual personality (not to mention the self-deprecation that accompanies these) are hallmarks of the Horatian persona; Donne learned from Horace that the satirist's own characterization, with his likes, dislikes, strengths, and indeed weaknesses, may be part of his poem's subject matter.

A specifically Horatian feature of "Satyre I" is the speaker's manner of rebuke; moral criticism of the *adversarius,* the "motley humorist," is more than implied yet by no means approaches a direct or a bitter invective. Like his Horatian model, Donne's persona is an ironist rather than a railer, allowing the *adversarius* to condemn himself through his flighty words and frantic behavior. In the Horatian manner, then, Donne's satirist strives to "tell the truth with a smile." And on the poem's surface at least, the smile is appropriate, given its themes of vanity in dress and behavior and, on a deeper level, of inconstancy. Such theorists as Robortello and Scaliger see these as mere follies rather than as tragic, criminal vices, suited to the Horatian manner of gentle mockery and ridicule. The persona of "Satyre I" is thus a decorous imitation of the Horatian satirist, "who sportingly never leaveth until he make a man laugh at folly, and at length ashamed, to laugh at himself, which he cannot avoid, without avoiding the folly." Of course for Sidney, the author of this passage, it is the reader who is "at length ashamed" and made "to laugh at himself." For Donne, ironically, the person at length ashamed is the satirist. Since self-deprecation is an attribute of the Horatian persona, we should not be surprised that in "Satyre I" much of the irony and implied criticism redounds upon the satirist himself; yet complications arise in the text's attitude toward its model, when Donne's satirist cannot laugh at his own inconstancy. A Christian deepening of satiric tone thus occurs, which goes far beyond Horace in its spiritual implications and must ultimately be considered a major revision of the classical model.

Structurally, "Satyre I" recalls Horace by its dramatic setting: the satirist, presenting himself as a young scholar-recluse, allows a friend to lure him from his study to experience the sights and pageantry of the city street. The fictional walk that Horace inspired allows Donne to create a world of varied sights and characters, a parade of soldiers, justices, puritans, prostitutes, youths, fools, courtiers. Yet the satirist is hardly objective in his presentation of this world: details are humorous as well as vivid and sensual, while the descriptive terms are as often symbolic as verisimilar. This brings us once again to recognize that the persona of "Satyre I" is a subjective voice, participating in the action of the poem and revealing his own personality as he speaks to others. We can find no better illustration of these features than the poem's opening lines:

> AWAY thou fondling motley humorist,
> Leave me, and in this standing woodden chest,
> Consorted with these few bookes, let me lye
> In prison, and here be coffin'd, when I dye;

Throughout the satirist's address to his friend—and particularly when he makes the humorist swear not to leave him once they get out on the street—we find a witty, conversational speech imitating Horace's *sermo pedestris;* we also find a language highly revelatory of character. The satirist's description of his study as a prison and coffin arrests our attention through its wit and is equally remarkable for what it says about the satirist's mood: if his study is like a prison to him, he should indeed want to escape from it. And even as he remonstrates with his flighty companion, his own mind is far from deeper studies—in fact the speaker's ambivalent description of his reading material hints broadly at his attraction to the city. So the satirist's question—"Shall I leave all this constant company . . . ?"—has already, at least implicitly, been answered.

At this point we can begin to see more clearly the relationship between Donne's text and its model. Donne attempts far more than a rehashed version of the Horatian plot; he strives instead for an exact reversal of the dramatic situation in *Sermo* 1.9. Horace's Impertinent wishes to accompany the satirist, while Donne's persona chooses to accompany the humorist. And while Horace hopes for nothing more than to be rid of his *adversarius,* Donne's persona goes so far as to make his friend swear *not* to abandon him on the street, even if he should meet "some more spruce companion." Finally, we may fault Horace for enduring the boor's importunities, yet we can at least say that their meeting and walk together is inadvertent; Donne's speaker, however, lacks even this excuse for his city stroll. Coupled with the other reversals of role and plot, this makes Donne's satirist all the more culpable.

Donne's speaker, nonetheless, does not yet recognize (or admit) his personal fall into folly and temptation. Indeed he

utters his warnings against three kinds of "spruce compan-
ion(s)," a captain, a courtier, and a justice, with an air of complete self-righteousness. Ironically, these vignettes—which add
both wit and liveliness to the poem and are the satirist's first
attempt at social criticism—serve only to whet his friend's desire
for such affluent companionship. For while the reader recognizes the moral criticism in the speaker's vivid details, the humorist sees only the glitter and pleasure. The satirist's claim
that his words have brought repentance to his friend is, therefore, either naiveté or thinly veiled sarcasm:

> But since thou like a contrite penitent,
> Charitably warn'd of thy sinnes, doth repent
> These vanities, and giddinesses, loe
> I shut my chamber doore, and 'Come, lets goe.'
> But sooner may a cheape whore, that hath beene
> Worne by as many severall men in sinne,
> As are black feathers, or musk-colour hose,
> Name her childs right true father, 'mongst all those:
> . . . . .
> Then thou, when thou depart'st from mee, canst show
> Whither, why, when, or with whom thou wouldst go.
> (1.49–56, 63–64)

The satirist continues to reveal aspects of his personality as
he here plays priest-confessor and "prophet" to the humorist.
He describes the oath of constancy that he demanded from his
friend as an act of penitence; yet even as he "forgives" his
friend's past sins (one may imagine as a stage direction to this
quasi-drama the satirist playfully making the sign of the cross
over his repentant companion), he admits that his friend has no
capacity for repentance, when he prophesies that the humorist
will in fact abandon him. In his flightiness and almost mindless
following of passions the humorist bears about as much responsibility for his actions as a child, whose powers of moral
choice and self-reflection remain undeveloped. The satirist,
though, cannot say the same of himself, nor can he approach
his own inconstancy—his own yielding to the allurement of the
city street—with such tongue-in-cheek expressions of moral
understanding. The sportful and even slightly blasphemous
tone of the section rises suddenly to high seriousness when the

satirist reveals, frankly and poignantly, his own spiritual conflict:

> But how shall I be pardon'd my offence
> That thus have sinn'd against my conscience?
>                                   (1.65–66)

Unlike his *adversarius*, he *has* a conscience, which also demands "Whither, why, when, or with whom thou wouldst go." On the one hand, the satirist makes a mockery of absolution by playing priest to his weak-willed and obviously unpenitent friend; on the other hand, he despairs of his own forgiveness by knowingly yielding to temptation.

In his typically candid and casual manner, Horace's speaker suggests that "I am free from vices which bring disaster, though subject to lesser frailties such as you would excuse" (*Sermo,* 1.4.129–131). Here Horace himself provides a source for the distinction between tragical and comical vices, the former deserving of hate and severe reprehension, the latter of more gentle techniques, laughter and mockery. This statement also exemplifies the kind of witty self-deprecation that Horace practiced—and that Minturno, as we have seen, greatly praised: "how cunningly he ridicules the folly of men when, to inveigh against others without arousing hatred, he does not even spare himself." Minturno's observations have relevance, it seems, to Donne's practice. N. J. C. Andreason suggests that

Part of the irony of the poem derives from the fact that the protagonist, aware of the inconstancy of the young man's friendship, goes off with him anyway . . . He admits that he too sins, he establishes himself as an honest and human man, a man who can be believed and whose charitable warnings should go heeded, all the more because they grow out of his own experience of sin.[25]

I would add that this technique is typically Horatian, and one that Donne could have learned, if not from a critic like Minturno, then from suggestions in Horace himself. I do not mean to imply that Donne's expression of personal guilt is but a pose or mere imitation of his classical model. As a Christian satirist,

25. N. J. C. Andreason, "Theme and Structure in Donne's *Satyres,*" *Studies in English Literature,* 3 (1963), 66.

his introspectiveness and sense of conscience perhaps surpassed that of the pagan and philosophically eclectic Horace. Horace wryly faults himself for his weaknesses, but in Donne's Pauline and Christian milieu such weakness is, simply put, sinfulness; and this recognition of personal sinfulness gives to the persona of "Satyre I" or "IV" a moral complexity that Horace never attains. Donne's formulation of personal guilt is far more serious than Horace's wry admission of fallibility. In perhaps his most significant revision of the Horatian model, Donne turns Horace's *deprecatio* into an expression of conscience too dire for laughter.

In fact, Donne rejects totally the ethical foundation upon which Horace's comic mode of satire is based, as he redefines Horace's "lesser frailties" and folly as Christian sinfulness. The ethical relativism that Isaac Casaubon would find in Horace's satires is inappropriate in a satirist with a Christian conscience, for there can be no ultimate distinction between sinful folly and "tragical vice." Although the words, "how shall I be pardon'd my offence . . . ?" form but two lines in an otherwise light-hearted, comic satire, they change the tone drastically and cast a dark shadow over the poem as a whole. They also establish attitudes toward Horatian satire and its persona that Donne continues to develop in later poems, as in the speaker's literal "confession" of his "sin" in the opening of "Satyre IV," or his outright rejection of laughter in the openings of "Satyre III" and "V."

Immediately after this sobering reflection, though, the scene in "Satyre I" changes from the study to the street; and we follow the satirist through the London streets as he tries, and fails, to keep his friend by his side and away from his several gaudy companions and mistresses. Both the action and thematic movement of "Satyre I" come full circle when a fight forces the humorist's limping return. Donne enacts the final reversal of the Horatian plot, as resolution comes not by the removal of the *adversarius* from the satirist but by their reunion. Equally ironic—and significant—is the satirist's return to the issue of constancy. He chose deliberately to leave the "constant company" of his books when following the humorist; now it is the humorist who must "constantly a while . . . keep his bed." Here the satirist reminds us of his inability to "shepherd" his friend, to deter him from his vice. If there is a lesson here, it has not been learned by the humorist: his constancy will last but "a while." Thomas Hester writes that the poem is in many ways "a comic study in failure, a witty dramatization of the radical and seemingly irremedial gap between the intentions of the satirist and the obduracy of his *adversarius*."[26] I would add that the ineffectiveness of the satirist's intentions is due, by implication, to the limitations of Donne's pagan model. Horace's rhetorical technique has proved, at least in Donne's hands, peculiarly ineffectual as a tool for moral reform, so that his rejection of Horace's civil jesting and definition of folly becomes central to the meaning of the poem. "Satyre I" enacts Donne's search for an effective voice in classical satire and his failure to find such a voice in the *Sermones*.

Donne rejects Horace in "Satyre I," but in the other satires he continues the search for a suitable model. "Satyre II" tests—and rejects—Juvenal: the speaker's "hate" and "just offense" erupt in a bitter invective against the criminal Coscus, and yet his words cannot bring such a man to justice—he has learned that crime demands the retribution of law, in the place of which Juvenalian invection is ineffectual. "Satyre IV" also criticizes its Roman models: there Donne's initially Horatian voice renounces satirical laughter, finding that ridicule does not teach temperance. Even the Juvenalian manner of the poem's second half is repudiated, since the speaker admits that immorality and intemperance demand "Preachers" for reform. Yet "Satyre III" and "Satyre V" find the speaker acting as just such a preacher, persuading and teaching his audience rather than ridiculing or punishing. Persius is the model for these poems, both of which rely heavily on this Roman's moral gravity and protreptic zeal. While Hall and Marston chose Juvenal as their preferred model, Donne found in Persian satire the best vehicle for his own serious Christian insights—but could not have been secure in this choice had not he, like Hall and Marston, tested the resources

26. *Kinde Pitty and Brave Scorn*, p. 17.

of all three Roman models. Much of the significance of Elizabethan satire lies below the referentiality and the social concerns. Elizabethan satire is a conscious exercise in literary judgment as well as creation. It is an attempt to evaluate as well as understand an important classical form. It is imitation, but it is above all a critical interpretation and revision of this form. Central to the meaning of Elizabethan satire is its intertextuality. Certainly our own understanding of this literature is incomplete without an awareness of the ways the Elizabethans read, reshaped, and at times rejected the classical materials upon which their own satire is based.

FRANCIS C. BLESSINGTON

# "That Undisturbed Song of Pure Concent": *Paradise Lost* and the Epic-Hymn

Following the recent rebirth of interest in the Renaissance concept of mixed genres, we can now appreciate more subtly the polygeneric nature of *Paradise Lost.*[1] At the same time, we are learning to be more attentive to the hierarchy of genres within the poem. In one such study Earl Miner has shown that the narrative mode, the chronological ordering of events, reigns

---

1. The basic book is Barbara K. Lewalski, *Paradise Lost and the Rhetoric of Literary Forms* (Princeton, 1985). *Composite Orders,* ed. Richard S. Ide and Joseph Wittreich, *Milton Studies,* 17 (1983), contains essays on Milton's mixed genres in *Paradise Lost* and elsewhere. Of particular interest for my essay are the editors' preface, pp. ix–xiv; Thomas Amorose, "Milton the Apocalyptic Historian: Competing Genres in *Paradise Lost,* Books XI–XII," pp. 141–162; Richard S. Ide, "On the Uses of Elizabethan Drama: The Revaluation of Epic in *Paradise Lost,*" pp. 121–140; O. B. Hardison, Jr., "*In Medias Res* in *Paradise Lost,*" pp. 27–41; Barbara K. Lewalski, "The Genres of *Paradise Lost:* Literary Genre as a Means of Accommodation," pp. 75–103; Earl Miner, "The Reign of Narrative in *Paradise Lost,*" pp. 3–25; Balachandra Rajan, "*Paradise Lost:* The Uncertain Epic," pp. 105–119; and Joseph Wittreich, " 'All Angelic Na-

over the lyric and dramatic modes in *Paradise Lost* because the epic narrator, and we, the readers, live in the fallen world of time and earthly struggle.[2] As Miner and Joseph Summers remind us, the ideal genre in the poem is the hymn.[3] I shall investigate how Milton presents this ideal and antithetical generic alternative to the epic narrative, and how the hymn conflicts with the epic story and represents the perfect literary genre, whose timeless world of eternal bliss is what the epic strives for. My major thesis is twofold: that the dynamic opposition of epic and hymn constitutes a major generic paradigm for the theme of the poem and that Milton sums up and transcends the hymn of traditional epic poetry.

First I shall delineate some relevant subgenres of the hymn, then illustrate the existence of the epic-hymn tradition and how the hymn functions structurally and thematically within the epics that Milton knew, drew upon, and emulated. I shall also glance at Milton's concept of the hymn as the perfect genre and show Milton's fulfilling of the epic-hymn tradition by setting epic and hymn at odds in *Paradise Lost*. In dealing with the epic tradition,

---

tures Joined in One': Epic Convention and Prophetic Interiority in the Council Scenes of *Paradise Lost*," pp. 43–74. For the tension between drama and epic within the poem, see John M. Steadman, *Tragic and Epic Structure in Paradise Lost* (Chicago, 1976); Helen Gardner, *A Reading of Paradise Lost* (Oxford, 1965), pp. 99–120; and Marianna Woodhull, *The Epic of Paradise Lost* (1907; rpt. New York, 1968). On the different genres contained within the poem, see Joan Malory Webber, *Milton and His Epic Tradition* (Seattle, 1979), p. 4; Joseph Wittreich, *Angel of Apocalypse* (Madison, 1975), p. 168; and Rosalie L. Colie, *The Resources of Kind: Genre-Theory in the Renaissance* (Berkeley, 1973), pp. 119–122. On the principle of inclusion as a characteristic of Renaissance poetry in general, read Alastair Fowler, *Kinds of Literature: An Introduction to the Theory of Genres and Modes* (Cambridge, Mass., 1982).

2. Miner, "Reign of Narrative," pp. 3–25.

3. Ibid. Joseph H. Summers, *The Muse's Method* (1962; rpt. New York, 1968), p. 71. On the inclusion of the hymn and other lyric genres in *Paradise Lost*, read Lewalski, *Paradise Lost*. See also Sara Thorne-Thomsen, "Milton's 'advent'rous Song': Lyric Genres in *Paradise Lost*," Ph.D. diss., Brown (1985). Richard M. Bridges unveils the poetic properties of Hebrew poetry in *Paradise Lost*, 7.602–632: "Milton's Original Psalm," *Milton Quarterly*, 14 (1980), 12–16. The movement of *Paradise Lost* toward a perfect poem forms the subject of Michael Fixler's *Milton and the Kingdoms of God* (Chicago, 1964).

I have assumed the wide range of epics that critics have shown that Milton knew and used.[4]

The way in which Milton interacts with the tradition is not quotation nor often allusion but echoing, that resonance of troping earlier texts. These texts are echoed not only, or even primarily, by specific words but also by dramatic situation and especially generic coding. Through such echoing Milton, more than almost any other writer, gains depth, power, and significance.[5]

The hymn, of course, extends back to the Greek hymns, which, by definition, praised the gods, as encomia praised men. Traditionally the Greek hymn is divided into two types: the literary or hexametric hymn, like the Homeric Hymns and the hymns of Callimachus, and the lyric or liturgical hymns, like those of Pindar and Bacchylides. If we add the Old Testament hymns found in the psalms and in the lyrical outbursts of the prophets, we have, at least, three hymn traditions functioning in the Renaissance.[6] It is not my purpose to distinguish among these strains but to discuss the distinctive development of the hymn within the Miltonic epic tradition.

Although I shall not need to delineate many subgenres of the

4. See Francis C. Blessington, *Paradise Lost and the Classical Epic* (London, 1979), and Webber, *Milton*.

5. For a subtle analysis of echoing in Milton and after, see John Hollander, *The Figure of Echo: A Mode of Allusion in Milton and After* (Berkeley, 1981).

6. For a discussion of the definition of the hymn and its sources, see C. M. Bowra, "Aristotle's 'Hymn to Virtue,' " *Classical Quarterly*, 32 (1938), 182–189; also R. Wünsch, "Hymnos," Pauly-Wissona, *Realenzyklopädie der klassischen Altertumswissenschaft*. According to Francis Cairns, the ancients might not have conceived of the hymn as a genre at all: *Generic Composition in Greek and Roman Poetry* (Edinburgh, 1972), p. 92. The Renaissance use of the literary hymn and its tradition are treated by Philip Rollinson, "The Renaissance of the Literary Hymn," *Renaissance Papers 1968*, ed. George Walton Williams, pp. 11–20. Rollinson also analyzes Milton's Nativity Ode from the same perspective: "Milton's Nativity Poem and the Decorum of Genre," *"Eyes Fast Fixed": Current Perspectives in Milton Methodology*, ed. Albert C. Labriola and Michael Lieb, *Milton Studies*, 7 (1975), 165–188. Rollinson has also analyzed Spenser's hymns from this viewpoint: "A Generic View of Spenser's Four Hymns," *Studies in Philology*, 68 (1971), 292–304.

hymn, I shall make some use of the traditional categories of literary hymns, categories that were passed from the Greek grammarian Menander the Rhetorician to Scaliger: invoking the presence of a god (klytic), relating a story about the god (mythic), referring to a god's ancestry (genealogic), praying that something happen (euktic), and praying that something not happen (apeuktic).[7]

Also I shall call a hymn that does not contain a prayer a pure hymn, and a hymn that contains a prayer a mixed hymn. The need for such a distinction will become more obvious as I proceed. By way of preface it must be noted that the traditional structure of the classical hymn is tripartite: the poet recites in turn (1) the god's name, lineage, attributes, cult centers, and so on, in the invocation; (2) deeds accomplished by the god, called by Ausfeld the "epic part"; and (3) a request from the worshipper, the prayer.[8] As a rule, epic poetry separates hymns into hymns of praise and hymns of prayer, both preceded by an invocation. By separating hymns into pure and mixed, the epic gains an ideal poem of praise that is without conflict and a tense request poem that underscores conflict. Prayers are much more common in epic poetry, from the often unanswered pleas of Homeric heroes to the antiprayers of the blasphemies of Mezentius in Virgil and of Capaneus in Statius. I shall not consider the many prayers that appear in epic poetry unless they contain an element of praise. In other words, I shall follow strictly the definition of the hymn accepted by Plato, Aristotle, Menander the Rhetorician, Pollux, Isidorus, Proclus, Saint Augustine, Scaliger, and Patrizzi, among others, that a hymn is a praise of

7. Menander the Rhetorician, in *Rhetores Graeci*, vol. 3, ed. Leonard Spengle (Leipzig, 1856), pp. 329–446. Julius Caesar Scaliger, *Poetices libri septem* (1561; rpt. Stuttgart, 1964), I, xliv–xlv. The other categories are: addressing a parting god (apopemptic), stating a god's physical qualities (physic), fictions based upon the myths (peplasmenic), and any combination of the above (miktic). These categories are treated by Theodore C. Burgess in *Epideictic Literature* (Chicago, 1902), and by O. B. Hardison, Jr., *The Enduring Monument* (1962; rpt. Westport, Conn., 1973), pp. 32, 109–113, 195–198. Cf. Rollinson, "The Renaissance of the Literary Hymn," p. 14.

8. Wünsch, "Hymnos." W. K. C. Guthrie, "Hymns," *Oxford Classical Dictionary*, 2nd ed. C. Ausfeld, "De Graecorum precationibus quaestiones," *Jahrbücher für classische Philologie, Supplementband*, 28 (1903), 505–547.

god.[9] I should also add that the pure epic hymn is usually choric, not monodic.

The shift to a hymn in an epic poem is clear and unmistakable: recognition comes about through simple plot signaling ("Then they sang a hymn") or merely through a shift from narrative to lyric mode, accompanied by invocation, apostrophe, and the vocative case of the god's name, an effect praised by Longinus (26–28). We may find settings such as religious festivals or accoutrements such as the harp or chorus. Also we find the expected key words: for example, in Latin, forms of *adsum;* in English, "O" or "hail." The hymn is not, however, conspicuous metrically: it adopts the meter of its matricular poem, rather than have a meter of its own. The Greek literary hymn was usually in heroic meter, and so the hymn easily blended with the meter of the epic poem. At the same time, the hymn is usually removable, so that it can stand as a separate poem on its own: hence it creates a tension immediately by seeming to be an independent poem and also wishing to be a part of the epic. Only Cowley breaks this tradition by interjecting a metrical psalm into his *Davideis* (after 1.40) but, as if aware of the anomaly, does not count its lines as part of the poem's lineation.

The epic hymn functions throughout the epic tradition as an antithesis to the epic narrative, a pause in the action in order to acknowledge the ideal toward which the epic struggles. The epic hymn is a lyric that celebrates a moment of solemn relief from the inexorable action related in the narrative and dramatic structures, a moment without the movement of narrative time,

9. Plato, *The Laws,* 700B, 801B. Menander, *Rhetores Graeci.* Pollux, *Ononmasticon,* I, 38. Proclus, according to Photius, *Biblioteca,* ed. Immanuel Bekker (Berlin, 1824–25), p. 320. Isidorus of Seville, *Etymologiae,* VI, 19, 17. Saint Augustine, *"Enarratio in Psalmum LXII,"* in *Patrologia Latina,* ed. J. P. Migne, XXXVI, 913–929. Scaliger, *Poetices,* 1.3, 44, 45; 3.111–118. Francesco Patrizzi's thorough treatment of the hymn has been overlooked by many commentators: *Della poetica,* ed. Danielo Aguzzi Barbagli (1586; rpt. Florence, 1969–1971), I, 193–209. In English the tradition is carried on by George Puttenham, *The Arte of English Poesie,* ed. Gladys Willcock and Alice Walker (Cambridge, 1936), pp. 24–36, 152. Cf. Sir Philip Sidney, *An Apology for Poetry,* ed. Geoffrey Shepherd (London, 1965), pp. 101–102.

an escape into an ideal world. The epic hymn in its pure form is praise without struggle, a hymn that cannot be continued through the poem, if only because real conflicts are, in literature, more aesthetically pleasing and interesting, especially in long works, than ideal and undramatic moments of rapturous bliss and also because hymns are far removed from the world of conflict, which they temporarily relieve us from but do not resolve.

The epic hymn enters after Homer, although Homer mentions hymns being sung (*Iliad*, 1.472–474). Homer's passage is precedent that hymns exist in the epic world, and we shall see this passage alluded to by other epic poets. But Homer did not compose hymns in his epics. As if in compensation, rhapsodes recited their so-called Homeric Hymns before they recited passages from the Homeric epics.

Ironically the Roman poets so adverse to the composition of the hymn in other forms began the inclusion of the hymn within the epic. In Roman poetry we start to find that the epic hymn is a clear indication of the theme of the poem. It is a further irony that the first epic hymn is the antihymn of Lucretius' *De rerum natura*. Lucretius opens his epic in an expansive invocation to Venus in the form of a hymn. In the course of this hymn, however, Venus is demoted from goddess to force of nature, the natural force of attraction in the world (1.1.49), a hymn more Heraclitean than Homeric. Lucretius superimposes the klytic hymn upon the invocatory prayer to produce a mixed hymn that almost subverts the tradition before it begins, just as Lucretius' later praise of Epicurus as if he were a god (1.62–79; 3.1–30) secularizes and further reduces the hymn to philosophy, as Lucretius tempers emotion with reason. Yet his opening lines are a hymn in their direct praise of the goddess. Before his retraction, they might be the words of Callimachus translated into Latin. Typically, the epic hymn shows an epiphany of peace away from epic strife:

> te, dea, te fugiunt venti, te nubila caeli
> adventumque tuum, tibi suavis daedala tellus
> summittit flores, tibi rident aequora ponti
> placatumque nitet diffuso lumine caelum.
>
> (1. 6–9)

> The winds flee you, goddess, and cloudy skies
> escape at your coming, and the sweet maker,
> the daedal earth springs up flowers; the seas laugh
> and the satisfied sky sports diffuse light.[10]

Since Lucretius is often infatuated with what he tries to rationalize away, he may be said actually to begin the epic hymn tradition. This epic hymn is not merely a shift to the lyric mode but a detachable poem, the full genre itself, which could stand alone as a poem without its epic context. The fact that the debunking of divinities is Lucretius' purpose in *De rerum natura* and that this occurs within this invocation shows one thematic function of the hymn and introduces the notion of the ironic hymn.

Perhaps the most important figure in the epic tradition of the hymn before Milton is Virgil. Virgil's only true hymn appears at the moment when war explodes with full force in Latium: Turnus has just hoisted the ensign of battle and his allies are mobilizing. In the midst of the chaos, the river spirit, Father Tiber, tells Aeneas to visit Evander's idyllic settlement in Latium, whose name means "hidden land" and suggests the lost rites that will restore ideal order (Evander's name means "good man"). Virgil consciously alludes to the contrast between the pure past and the corrupt present by having Aeneas arrive at a festival to Hercules in Evander's pastoral paradise. Rather than being treated as a threat, as he expects, he being a Trojan and they Greeks, Aeneas is regaled as a distant relation to the Arcadians, another reference to a lost and ideal community. Now the reunification of society begins and almost immediately ends. Aeneas takes part in the festival, while Evander explains that it originated in Hercules' saving his (Evander's) people from the attacks of the monster Cacus. Virgil departs from Homer's precedent by actually composing a hymn, rather than being satisfied with a summary. Virgil may also have had in mind Lucretius, as he does elsewhere. Virgil's hymn has the tripartite structure: it invokes the god, then shifts in a startling way to the present tense, in order to recall the god's victorious deeds

---

10. All the translations are my own. My text here is *De rerum natura,* ed. Cyril Bailey (Oxford, 1947).

and his father, Jove. The hymn is supposedly an anthem, since it is sung by two choruses, one of old and one of young men, but in fact we hear everyone in unison, including bard and by extension the audience:

> "tu nubigenas, inuicte, bimembris
> Hylaeumque Pholumque manu, tu Cresia mactas
> prodigia et uastum Nemeae sub rupe leonem.
> te Stygii tremuere lacus, te ianitor Orci
> ossa super recubans antro semesa cruento;
> nec te ullae facies, non terruit ipse Typhoeus
> arduus arma tenens; non te rationis egentem
> Lernaeus turba capitum circumstetit anguis.
> salue, uera Iouis proles, decus addite diuis,
> et nos et tua dexter adi pede sacra secundo."
> (*Aeneid*, 8.293–302)[11]

> You unconquerable, who kill by hand
> The twin-limbed children of the clouds,
> Hylaeus and Pholus, the Cretan bull,
> And the tall lion under Nemea's cliff.
> At your sight, Styx shivered and hell's porter
> Licking bones in his ruddled cave.
> No shape daunted you, not Typhoeus himself
> Who swung stern arms. Nor were you
> Stunned when Lerna's snake embraced
> With a mob of heads. True Son of Jove,
> Graceful addition to the gods, hail.
> Come to us and your rites with favorable foot.[12]

This poem is almost a pure klytic hymn, a song of praise, not a prayer or petition, except for the general and almost formulaic request at the end.

This extended earthly hymn finds its divine counterpart in the Elysium Fields where Aeneas hears shades "singing a happy poem in chorus" (6.657). The Greek structure of the passage— *laetumque choro paeana canentis*—alludes to Homer's passage

---

11. Virgil, *Opera*, ed. R. A. B. Mynors (Oxford, 1969).
12. In a slightly different form, my translation appeared in *The Classical Bulletin*, 60 (1984), 56.

on the hymn to Apollo: "the young men of Achaia singing a
fine paean" (*Iliad,* 1.473).[13]

At the same time that Virgil's hymn unites Troy and Italy in
a symbolic rite, it advocates the use of force that will destroy
Turnus and mark the history of Rome ever after. No Hercules
will come to save Rome, but the god will have many imitators
at loggerheads. Virgil's hymn, like Lucretius', has its irony.

The persistence of the epic hymn after Virgil is conspicuous,
probably because of Virgilian authority. Even Lucan's *Pharsalia,* which is more history than epic, follows the pattern of the
cautious use of the hymn. This is remarkable in Lucan, since
he hardly followed Virgilian precedent in general. If Lucretius
secularized the hymn in epic poetry, Lucan politicized it, just
as he tried to convert other epic conventions from epic to history. Lucan's method is superrealism, but early in the poem,
written before he joined the conspiracy of Piso, Lucan praises
Nero proleptically as a god in an epic hymn. If Lucretius demoted gods, Lucan elevates Nero to a divinity (1.45–66). As in
Lucretius, the invocation is extended into a klytic hymn. Like
Virgil and Lucretius, Lucan's hymn shows the world at peace
under Nero's auspices who will "seek the stars" *(Astra petes):*

> Tum genus humanum positis sibi consulat armis,
> Inque vicem gens omnis amet; pax missa per orbem
> Ferrea belligeri conpescat limina Iani.
>                                              (1.60–63)[14]

> Then, arms aside, let the human race take care of itself.
> Let nations love each other; let peace everywhere
> shut the iron gates of Janus the Warrior.

Lucan's hymn is more idealistic than Virgil's: Virgil's chorus
prays for a deliverer, as if force could be an answer, but Lucan's
vision of peace is immediately lost in the bloody din that follows.
An ideal has been established through the hymn, but its hopeless
idealism makes its use seem cynical. For Virgil, idealism can be

    13. Homer, *Iliad,* ed. David B. Monro and Thomas W. Allen, 3rd ed., 2
vols. (Oxford, 1911–1920).
    14. Lucan, *The Civil War,* ed. J. D. Duff, Loeb Series (Cambridge, Mass.,
1928).

contemplated in the pastoral otium of Evander's settlement, even if Aeneas himself cannot live up to it.

Lucan resorted to the hymn a second time and again established an ideal of peace. In a klytic hymn that may echo Virgil's (cf. Lucan's *ades* for Virgil's *adi*), the narrator calls upon Harmony, an abstraction raised in this hymn to divine personification:

> Nunc ades, aeterno conplectens omnia nexu,
> O rerum mixtique salus Concordia mundi
> Et sacer orbis amor; magnum nunc saecula nostra
> Venturi discrimen habent.   (4.189–192)

> Be present now, embrace all in one embrace,
> Harmony, the health of the whole mingling world
> And the sacred love of the earth; our earth holds
> the key to the future.

The words burst forth from narrational apostrophe and character exclamation at once when Caesar's army cuts off Pompey's retreating forces in Spain and kinsmen recognize each other. Roman fratricidal civil war seems at an end. It turns out, however, to be only a device of Lucan's to heighten the drama of the scene. It is insufficiently motivated and incredible in the realistic context of the epic. Lucan's temperament hardly allows human kindness to prevail for long. Petreus, Pompey's general, arms his slaves in order to reorient the euphoric and disarming troops. The hymn turns upon a Lucretian irony: there never was a goddess Harmony at all, as the Roman audience knew well. Perhaps the utter incongruity of the scene underscores the hopelessness of lessening Roman bloodshed, since it follows the oversanguine description of the Battle of Massilia. The vision soon fades back to the usual *amorem scelerum*. By bringing the hymn onto the battlefield, Lucan suggests the cynicism that permeates the poem. Virgil's hymn was presented in the pastoral, not the epic, mode. If Virgil's hymn is sung in a pastoral setting, Lucan brings the hymn onto the battlefield, where it disappears in the epic strife along with its vision.

Statius' hymn to Apollo (*Thebaid*, 1.696–720) follows Lucan's technique of putting the hymn in the foreground of the epic action so that the commonplaceness of Adrastus' Argos clashes

with the idealism of its sentiment. But Statius' hymn gains irony
from its closely echoing Virgil's hymn to Hercules. Again epic
events militate against its success as a realizable generic ideal.
In Virgil, the festival of Hercules that Evander was reenacting
was a thanksgiving for deliverance from Cacus. The Arcadians
were living in peace, at least at the moment when Aeneas arrives. But the purpose of Adrastus' festival for Apollo is to
appease the wrath of the god for the killing of one of his Gorgons
who was laying waste Argos. As in the *Iliad* (1.472–474), the
purpose is averting evil, not celebrating the glory of a god. Such
a hymn fits this tragic and heroless epic. In the hymn, Apollo's
places of worship are recounted along with his deeds, his skills,
and his names. But the point is a prayer for help. Statius, who
later summarizes Virgil's hymn (*Thebaid*, 4.157–158), echoes
Virgil's *dextra* and *adi:*

> Adsis, o memor hospitii, Iunoiaque arva
> dexter ames.   (1.716–717)[15]

> Be present, mindful of our need.
> Be favorable and love Juno's fields.

The classical hymn is primarily klytic and pure. It offers an
image of ideal peace by breaking the epic action and engaging
the audience and reader in an act of worship, as the epic narrator
turns away from his audience and prays with his back to us, and
we and the characters pray with him. The generic shift is all the
more effective as it is used with hellenic restraint.

If we should expect the Christian epic to make more use of
the hymn, we should be in generic error. The same restraint
prevails, but the dramatic technique changes. In Virgil, Lucan,
and Statius, the epic hymn shows truly, or ironically, the peace
that could end the epic struggle, but the hymn is not relied upon
solely: we find prophecies throughout Virgil, for instance, that
herald a new era. But in Dante and Vida, the hymn is the
symbolic goal toward which the action tends, and the goal may
be true literally, as heavenly souls were thought to be actually
engaged in continual music making. The hymn gradually finds

15. *Silvae, Thebaid, Achilleid*, ed. J. H. Mozley, Loeb Series, 2 vols. (Cambridge, Mass., 1928).

a voice in *The Divine Comedy* when the narrator-pilgrim hears the "Gloria in excelsis deo," the Greater Doxology of the Liturgy (*Purgatorio,* 20.136), but the true epic hymn is held till the end of the poem, where it is a prologue to Saint Bernard's prayer that Dante be granted the Beatific Vision (*Paradiso,* 33.1–39). Dante's hymn follows the classical structure of invocation, recitation of a god's deeds, reminder of favors granted to former petitioners, and the present request. Dante formally baptized the epic hymn in the Empyrean and addressed the Virgin, image of mildness, in place of a god's usually violent deeds. But Dante does not invoke the pure hymn. His hymn is euktic, a prayer that something happen. The poem of pure praise is as far beyond him as the vision of God, which he is unable to relate in his fallen human state. But if Dante is unable to portray God or his perfect music directly, his hymn is at least a promise.

A purer hymn ends Vida's *Christiad,* which is structured like Dante's epic toward a concluding hymn, as if one has reached eternal bliss. Vida's hymn celebrates the deeds of the paternal deity, *opifex rerum* (6.753–800), and though it ends with a short prayer, it is one of the longest epic songs of divine praise outside *Paradise Lost.* If it echoes Dante's structure, it echoes Virgil's recitation of the deeds of Hercules and the rhythmic repetition of *tu* (and *te*) of Lucretius. Vida returns the power of the natural universe from Lucretius' naturalized Venus to a personalized god. Note the Lucretian patterning:

> . . . Tu cuncta moues. tibi maximus aether,
> Quique super latices concrescunt aethere, parent.
> Nubila te, uentique timent. te uesper.
>
> (6.753–755)[16]

> You move all. The highest heaven obeys you
> and whatever waters condense above those heavens.
> Clouds fear you and the winds. The evening [obeys] you.

This hymn is sung by the apostles upon seeing Christ risen. They do not sing spontaneously but imitate the celestial music they

16. *The Christiad,* ed. Gertrude Drake and Clarence A. Forbes (Carbondale, Ill., 1978).

hear in heaven. The hymn in Vida is a divine imitation or direct inspiration. Like Dante, Vida has reclaimed part of the epic for Christianity. His hymn shows the world about to be made over to the peace of God through the coming work of the disciples and *their* disciples. The hymn parallels Virgil's hymn of the descent and ascent of Hercules by emphasizing the harrowing of hell and the ascension just witnessed.

After Vida the epic hymn almost disappears. In all of Harington's Ariosto we find only one religious poem, a lament, and that was added by Sir John Harington in his translation (15.75). Ariosto displaces the epic hymn to the song in praise of his Este patrons, as Spenser displaced his to praise of Queen Elizabeth and followed the Homeric tradition of composing hymns separate from the epic. In *La Gerusalemme liberata* Tasso uses no hymn but feels the need to apologize to the heavenly muse for the omission:

> Tu rischiara il mio canto e tu perdona
> S'intesso fregi al ver, s'adorno in parte
> d'altri diletti, che de' tuoi, le carte.
> $(1.2.6-8)$[17]

> Illuminate my song and please forgive
> If I weave art with truth, if I enhance,
> With other joys than yours, my verse.

No hymn appears in Camoens' *Lusiad* or in Davenant's *Gondibert*. In Sylvester's version of the *Divine Weeks,* Du Bartas praises God only indirectly through His creation. As noted above, Cowley in his biblical epic, *Davideis,* includes only a metrical version of a psalm (114), sung by David, though the narrator describes a College of Prophets who spend their days composing songs in praise of God's works and though Cowley had elsewhere, like Spenser, composed a hymn ("Hymn. To Light"). Part of this dearth of the epic hymn in England might be ascribed to the general Anglican neglect of the hymn as a composition outside of biblical psalms and their metrical renditions. Calvin's

17. *La Gerusalemme liberata,* ed. Lodovico Magugliani (Milan, 1950).

influence in England limited the liturgical hymn to psalmody.[18] A more religiously independent poet would restore the epic hymn and use it to transpose the epic form at the same time that he summed up its tradition.

It is a commonplace of Milton criticism that musical harmony was one of Milton's central symbols of perfection. This perfection is generically expressed in terms of the hymn. In "At a Solemn Music" Milton writes how human song jars after the Fall since sin has broken

> . . . the fair music that all creatures made
> To their great Lord, whose love their motions sway'd
> In perfect Diapason, whilst they stood
> In first obedience, and their state of good.
>
> (ll. 21–24)[19]

This overstated poem seems, like Lucan's passage above, to ask for a harmony that "Voice and Verse" have lost and may regain momentarily and only with difficulty:

> And to our high-rais'd fantasy present
> That undisturbed Song of pure concent
>
> (ll. 5–6)

in "Hymns devout and holy Psalms." In Milton's Sonnet 13, Henry Lawes wins Dante's praise because he is "the Priest of *Phoebus'* Choir / That tun'st their happiest lines in Hymn, or Story" (ll. 10–11). Such music was heard when Christ was born, an event as worthy of hymn as the Creation:

> The helmed Cherubim
> And sworded Seraphim

18. H. Leigh Bennett, "English Hymnody, Early," in *A Hymn Dictionary,* ed. John Julian (London, 1915), rev. ed., pp. 343–350. Also Rollinson, "Milton's Nativity Poem," p. 175. The liturgy and the effect of the Reformation are discussed by Peter Le Hurray, *Music and the Reformation in England* (Cambridge, 1967).

19. All quotations from Milton's poems are from *John Milton: Complete Poems and Major Prose,* ed. Merritt Y. Hughes (New York, 1957).

> Are seen in glittering ranks with wings display'd,
> Harping in loud and solemn choir,
> With unexpressive notes to Heav'n's new-born Heir.
> ("On the Morning of Christ's Nativity," (ll. 112–116)

In *Paradise Regained,* the Son, echoing the position of the Church of England in the Renaissance, tells Satan that the Hebrew hymns and psalms are superior to all other "Music" and "Poem":

> Or if I would delight my private hours
> With Music or with Poem, where so soon
> As in our native Language can I find
> That solace? All our Law and Story strew'd
> With Hymns, our Psalms with artful terms inscrib'd
> Our Hebrew Songs and Harps in *Babylon,*
> That pleas'd so well our Victor's ear, declare
> That rather *Greece* from us these Arts deriv'd;
> Ill-imitated, while they loudest sing
> The vices of their Deities, and thir own
> In Fable, Hymn, or Song, so personating
> Thir Gods ridiculous, and themselves past shame.
> Remove their swelling Epithets thick laid
> As varnish on a Harlot's cheek, the rest,
> Thin sown with aught of profit or delight,
> Will far be found unworthy to compare
> With *Sion's* songs, to all true tastes excelling,
> Where God is praised aright, and Godlike men,
> The Holies of Holies, and his Saints;
> Such are from God inspir'd.    (4.331–350)

The generic awareness implicit in this passage is borne out more clearly in Milton's prose. In *Animadversions* Milton distinguished between hymn and prayer, "lest the Arians, and Pelagians in particular should infect the people by their hymns, and formes of Praier" (1.685).[20] And in *An Apology against a Pamphlet* he defends a passage from *Animadversions* with "neither was it a prayer so much as a hymne in prose frequent both

---

20. All quotations from Milton's prose are from *Complete Prose Works of John Milton,* ed. Don M. Wolfe et al., 8 vols. (New Haven, 1953–1982).

in the Prophets and humane authors; therefore the stile was greater then for an ordinary prayer" (1.930).

From the above we can understand Milton's sense of the hymn as a pagan genre extended and corrected by Christian revelation. In *The Reason of Church Government* we can perhaps see also Milton's awareness of the subgenres of the hymn as he makes distinctions among the lyric hymns of Pindar, the hexametric literary hymns of Callimachus, and the Old Testament lyric hymns:

> Or if occasion shall lead to imitat those magnifick Odes and Hymns wherein *Pindarus* and *Callimachus* are in most things worthy, some others in their frame judicious, in their matter most an end faulty: But those frequent songs throughout the law and prophets beyond all these, not in their divine argument alone, but in the very critical art of composition may be easily made appear over all the kinds of Lyrick poesy, to be incomparable. (*Prose*, 1.815–816)

Given Milton's synthetic historical imagination, we would expect his own hymns to revaluate the epic hymn, through imitation, inclusion, and correction. The epic hymn was lent authority by Virgil, whose precedent in the matter may have been decisive with Milton, who states that the models to be followed in an epic poem were Homer, Virgil, and Tasso: "that Epick form whereof the two poems of *Homer*, and those other two of *Virgil* and *Tasso* are a diffuse, and the book of *Job* a brief model" (*Prose*, 1.813). We should note in passing that Job contains hymns that served Milton well generically in *Paradise Regained* and that neither Homer nor Tasso made any use of the epic hymn. Yet Milton's use of the epic hymn reverberates throughout the epic tradition.

No doubt, as Thomas B. Stroup has pointed out, Milton's independence from the liturgy helped him to create original hymns.[21] It is thought that only about a dozen hymns existed in Milton's

---

21. In *Religious Rite and Ceremony in Milton's Poetry* (Lexington, Ky., 1968). At the same time, he discusses the roots of Milton's hymns in psalm and liturgy. Cf. Lewalski, *Paradise Lost.*

day—that is, hymns available to churchgoers—other than those from the Bible and metrical versions of the psalms.[22] None of the epic poets came under Luther's campaign not "to give the devil all the good tunes." When Milton revived the tradition of the epic hymn, it must have been felt an anomaly, if not a breach of religious etiquette. Only those few who had scrutinized the classical epic would recognize it at all. Songs of man and songs of God had parted into epic or literary hymn. It was for Milton to bring the two types of poetry back into deep conflict and artistic resolution. At the same time Milton answers and develops the epic-hymn tradition. He placed the epic hymn at the generic center of the poem, the ideal for which the other genres strive. The epic hymn, as we have seen, was established in the tradition, but in no other epic would its absence be as inconceivable.

We have seen that the hymn was used ironically by Lucretius, Lucan, and, to some extent, Virgil. Milton too uses the hymn ironically. Like Lucan, Milton has the parodic hymn, which gives significance to even the diabolic aspects of *Paradise Lost:*

> O Parent, these are thy magnific deeds,
> Thy Trophies, which thou view'st as not thine own,
> Thou art thir Author and prime Architect.
>
> (10.354–356)

So Sin parodies the "Gloria Patri" or Menander's mythic hymn, as her parent does in hymning the Tree of the Knowledge of Good and Evil, beginning "O Sacred, Wise, and Wisdom-giving Plant" (9.679–683). Such apostrophes would be only that in another poem, but Milton's extensive use of the hymn and his sacred context make these blasphemies more apparent than those of a Mezentius or a Capaneus. But when Satan and Eve worship the tree in this poem, we feel that Milton may be correcting Lucretius as well as indirectly chastizing his characters.

In another parody the innocent singing of heroic ballads by and about Achilles in the *Iliad* (9.185–191) is turned by Milton into a diabolical hymn of self-praise when the angels

22. Bennett, "English Hymnody," pp. 343–350, and Rollinson, "Milton's Nativity Poem," p. 175.

sing
With notes Angelical to many a Harp
Thir own Heroic deeds.
(2.547–549)

A consequence of being damned in *Paradise Lost* is generic muddling.

Satan and his followers are well aware of the implications of genre and its central place in the poem. Showing their preference for epic battle, they express constant contempt toward the hymn. Mammon argues that if the Father reinstates the fallen angels, they will be compelled "to celebrate his Throne / With warbl'd Hymns" and "Forc't Halleluiahs" (2.241–243). In Eden, Satan mocks Gabriel and the other angelic guards for a Sunday-school attraction to hymning: "Whose easier business were to serve thir Lord / High up in Heav'n, with songs to hymn his Throne, / And practis'd distances to cringe, not fight" (4.943–945). In the war in heaven Satan greets Abdiel with "I see that most through sloth had rather serve, / Minist'ring Spirits, train'd up in Feast and Song; / Such hast thou arm'd, the Minstrelsy of Heav'n" (6.166–168).

Besides the antihymn and the overt mockery of hymning, we find the reluctant hymn, or the dramatically ironic hymn, in which God's deeds are sung unwittingly by Satan and his followers, which proves what Adam learns later: that God turns evil to good (12.471). Satan comes very close to the pure hymn when he first reaches the world. Disguised as a cherub, he hints to Uriel that he wishes to hymn God's new creation so "The Universal Maker we may praise; / Who justly hath driv'n out his Rebel Foes" (3.676–677), as the angels did who were present at the Creation (cf. 7.252–259). It is a further irony that the driving out of the rebel angels forms the subject of a pure hymn later in the poem. Satan comes close to pure hymning when he sees and praises the sun in a Franciscan mood, the sun being an explicit displacement for the Father:

O thou that with surpassing Glory crown'd,
Look'st from thy sole Dominion like the God
Of this new World; at whose sight all the Stars
Hide thir diminisht heads, to thee I call.
(4.32–35)

Satan's hymn has the clear classical structure: the invocation
("to thee I call"(l. 35); the recitation of deeds including again
ironically his own defeat, for example, "Pride and worse Ambition threw me down / Warring in Heav'n against Heav'ns
matchless King" (ll. 40–41); and instead of a concluding prayer,
which Satan can never utter, a confession of his need and guilt,
for example,

> Nay, curs'd be thou; since against his thy will
> Chose freely what now it so justly rues.
> Me miserable! which way I fly
> Infinite wrath, and infinite despair?
>
> (ll. 71–74)

Satan summons a god and recites his deeds only by confessing
his guilt. To fall here is to hymn without knowing it: Satan is
free of the real hymn but a singer of the perverted one. In
sarcastic contrast to the continual hymning in heaven, Raphael
tells Adam that from hell comes "Noise, other than the sound
of Dance or Song" (8.243).

If Satan hymns indirectly without knowing it and deplores
hymnody, the narrator follows Lucretius and Lucan in transforming the invocation into the hymn—not a pure hymn, for
prayer remains the generic mirror of the narrator's need. At
first the narrator, like a Homeric warrior, buries praise in prayer:
in his first invocation his only praise of the divinity is a short
reference to God's works:

> Sing Heav'nly Muse, that on the secret top
> Of *Oreb,* or of *Sinai,* didst inspire
> That Shepherd, who first taught the chosen Seed,
> In the Beginning how the Heav'ns and Earth
> Rose out of *Chaos.*   (1.6–10)

This passage is extended and purified in a sense by the hymn
sung later by the angels, when Raphael relates the story of
Creation to Adam, but the praise element remains relatively
neglected till the next invocation, the hymn to light.

The narrator's second hymn is more closely related to the
epic action than any previous epic hymn, with the exception of
Dante's. Like Satan later in the poem, the narrator journeys in
his imagination from hell to heaven and is struck by the light

of heaven, perceived more truly by the blind bard than by Satan in his indirect hymn. The narrator's hymn is more genuine because he hymns not light but God, who is light, as in the famous hymn of early Greek Christians (Keble's "Hail gladdening light, of his pure glory poured"), or Cowley's "Hymn. To Light." The hymn has the tripartite classical structure of invocation, recitation of divine deeds, and prayer. Like the other hymns in *Paradise Lost* and in other epic poems, it is a generic inset, readily detachable as an independent hymn:

> Hail holy Light, offspring of Heav'n first-born,
> Or of th'Eternal Coeternal beam
> May I express thee unblam'd? since God is Light,
> And never but in unapproached Light
> Dwelt from Eternity, dwelt then in thee,
> Bright effluence of bright essence increate.     (3.1–6)

The hymn continues to relate the creative actions of the deity till it shades into the night of the narrator, whose prayer and mixed hymn dramatize the inability of fallen mankind to rise to pure hymnody.

As in the *Aeneid*, we are gradually led to the pure hymn. Passing through hell, as through Virgil's Latium, we arrive at the pure song of praise but remote from the reader's experience and from the foreground of the epic action. In Virgil the hymn was the rite of the Arcadians living in the pastoral seclusion of the primitive Palatine. In *Paradise Lost* the pure hymn exists only in heaven and to a lesser extent in georgic, prelapsarian Eden. Milton's hymns, as is well known, derive from the psalms or other songs of the Bible. But more than any other epic poet, Milton emphasized the hymn as the ideal toward which epic poetry should evolve. Adam hears the hymn at first from afar, as Dante did in the *Purgatorio* and the apostles in the *Christiad,* but Adam hears both monody and antiphon. Adam and Eve's hymns are an "echo of affirmation" of the songs they hear in heaven:[23]

> how often from the steep
> Of echoing Hill or Thicket have we heard

---

23. The term is Hollander's.

> Celestial voices to the midnight air,
> Sole, or responsive each to other's note
> Singing thir great Creator: oft in bands
> While they keep watch, or nightly rounding walk,
> With Heav'nly touch of instrumental sounds
> In full harmonic numbers join'd, thir songs
> Divide the night, and lift our thoughts to Heav'n.
>                                            (4.680–688)

(Cf. 5.544–548.) Adam and Eve hear the prototype of Matins (Lauds), celebrating the vigils of the early Church.

But Adam and Eve are not moved just by angelic imitation: song rhythms are implicit in the very order of paradisiacal nature:

> The Birds thir choir apply; airs, vernal airs,
> Breathing the smell of field and grove, attune
> The trembling leaves, while Universal *Pan*
> Knit with *Graces* and the *Hours* in dance
> Led on th' Eternal Spring.   (4.264–268)

Such "airs" bring Satan delight upon his arrival in Eden (4.153–159). But the musical task of Milton's human characters in both their fallen and unfallen state is to hymn God's works, while, as we shall see, the task of God's angels is to hymn His actions at which they were present: man's hymns are inspired by the result of God's actions, which are all man can see, while angelic hymns are inspired by memory. Man, caught in time, hymns its passing, indicated by his partial use of the refrain,[24] but angels need no refrain, since they celebrate not passing time but an eternal act that transcends whatever came after. Edenic hymns derive, like Jubal's later (11.558–563), from the order and harmony of God's creation, nature, and the music of the spheres. Adam and Eve in their morning hymn praise "yee five other wand'ring Fires that move / In mystic Dance not without Song, resound / His praise" (5.177–179). In their hymns man—and angels—imitate what seem to be the spontaneous rhythms of creation. As a result, Milton's Edenic hymn celebrates and imitates in the rhythm of poetry those aspects of creation that are in

---

24. Hollander, *Figure of Echo,* p. 37, sees in this hymn (5.153–208) the invention of the refrain.

motion through time: stars, planets, sun, the growing tree, the battle in heaven, the process of creation—in short, whatever moves and develops, a most fitting image for this epic of work and development.[25] That the rhythms of nature are the rhythms of praise is evident to Adam and Eve, who hymn about the hymns already inherent in nature, so that their hymns praise God through ever-shifting nature:

> His praise ye Winds, that from four Quarters blow,
> Breathe soft or loud; and wave your tops, ye Pines,
> With every Plant, in sign of Worship wave.
> Fountains and yee, that warble, as ye flow,
> Melodious murmurs, warbling tune his praise.
> Join voices all ye living Souls; ye Birds,
> That singing up to Heaven Gate ascend.
>
> (5.192–198)

Adam and Eve sing two extensive hymns, one morning and one evening hymn (5.153–208 and 4.724–735). The narrator, perhaps ironically, calls their songs "Orisons" and "prayers," but they are closer to the pure hymn than his invocation is, since their praise exceeds his request. Even their request is without the narrator's anxiety: they ask for the continuance of God's blessing and the fulfillment of His promise to send a race of helpers to aid them in trimming the garden. The hymn to morning is in part a hymn to light, another juxtaposition to the hymns of Satan and the narrator: Satan is moved by light because of its loss in hell, while the blind narrator has experienced an analogous loss of light, though he receives the guidance of the celestial muse back to it at moments of inspiration. But Adam and Eve rejoice at the light naturally out of inborn gratitude. Milton's characters feel the need to celebrate the gift of light and pray for its help:

> and if the night
> have gather'd aught of evil or conceal'd,

25. For this aspect of the poem, see Barbara K. Lewalski, "Innocence and Experience in Milton's Eden," *New Essays on Paradise Lost,* ed. Thomas Kranidas (Berkeley, 1971), pp. 86–117.

> Disperse it, as now light dispels the dark.
> (5.206–208)[26]

The hymns of Adam and Eve are even more closely related
to God's creation than is Vida's hymn, since they are musical
preludes and postludes to their own work in the garden. In this
way they participate in the development of God's creation and
further refine their own gifts through song. The two hymns may
also be taken as the prototypes of Matins and Vespers, the two
hymns the early Christians borrowed from the morning and
evening worship, respectively, in the synagogue[27] and hence are
the source of the whole hymn tradition on earth, both biblical
and classical. Like Dante and Vida, Milton is returning the epic
hymn to its source.

Such "adoration pure" decays after the Fall into the antihymn: Eve follows Satan in his worship of the tree as a god and
moves the hymn towards its Lucretian form, reversing the hymning of God through His creation by reducing Him or replacing
Him with His handiwork. Eve even promises the tree her Matins: "henceforth my early care, / Not without Song, each Morning, and due praise" (9.799–800).

After they repent, Adam and Eve's hymns become prayers,
like the narrator's and like the many prayers found in the epic
poems of Tasso and other epic poets, where the characters suffer
too much deprivation to praise the deity they are praying to.
On one level, Milton is finding generic equivalents for the action
of the poem; on another, he points to the origins of the split
between pure hymn and prayer common in the later—fallen—
epic tradition. After their fall, Adam and Eve still perform
Matins, and not to woody plants, but their hymn has changed
from mythic to euktic, a prayer that something happen. Before
the Fall, their prayers were apeuktic, prayers that something
not happen: that no evil appear in the night or that God not
revoke His promise. They begin the precative hymn or prayer

26. Summers' analysis stresses the way context functions in the meaning of
this hymn, in *Muse's Method*, pp. 71–86. He also shows how a strophic hymn
poetic structure lies under the iambic pentameter of the epic narrative mode.

27. On this relationship between the Jewish and Christian hymns, see F. J.
E. Raby, *A History of Christian Latin Poetry*, 2nd ed. (Oxford, 1957), pp. 28–
30.

common to all epic poems and show the reason for them: the loss of innocence. Such loss is dramatized during Michael's vision of the future when Adam, learning of the future Redeemer, tries to hymn but falls into a struggle with remorse:

> O goodness infinite, goodness immense!
> That all this good of evil shall produce,
> And evil turn to good; more wonderful
> Than that which by creation first brought forth
> Light out of darkness! full of doubt I stand,
> Whether I should repent me now of sin
> By mee done and occasion'd, or rejoice
> Much more, that much more good thereof shall spring,
> To God more glory, more good will to Men
> From God, and over wrath grace shall abound.
>
> (12.469–478)

To repent or to rejoice: this is the dilemma and the origin of the split between prayer and pure hymn in the tradition: the song of praise must also be, because of man's fallen condition, a prayer for grace. Just as the epic begins after the fall, so does the mixed hymn, although in priority of time and virtue, the earlier state is to be preferred, a state where epic is unknown to heavenly and georgic hymn. But the pure hymn is interrupted by man's "O Felix Culpa," perhaps the human prototype of that outcry and the thematic echo of "Mea Culpa" that now almost drowns it out.

The pure hymn is not interrupted in Milton's heaven, where the songs are almost continuous, as they are in fact in *Revelation,* where four angels day and night never cease to sing, "Holy, holy, holy, Lord God Almighty, which was, and is, and is to come" (4.8). Milton's angels are more musically exhaustible but likewise hymn without prayer. Milton's pure hymns do not appear at moments of crises in the poem, as in Virgil, Lucan, and Statius, but at moments of release of tension, as in Dante and Vida. In contrast to Adam and Eve, the angels hymn about God's actions, sometimes proleptically, as after the prophetic promise of the Son to die for man, in contrast to Adam and Eve's use of the present tense, refrains, and imperatives to the natural world.

The angels hymn at conspicuous places in the poem and all

are associated, like the hymns of Adam and Eve, with extension in time, the source of rhythm: after the Son's offer of Self-sacrifice on the cross for man, which they hymn proleptically; after the war in heaven; and after the Creation, the last two hymns following and immortalizing those events immediately after the action is completed. Another hymn follows after the Father's diatribe against Sin and Death's progress toward the world in book 10. Milton's determination to include the hymn at these points is deliberate; for instance, the Bible does not include an account of hymning after the Creation, nor does Sylvester's Du Bartas.

Within the poem, hymns begin by fulfilling the prophecy of the Word: after the Father's promise of grace to man, the Son adds, "Heav'n and Earth shall high extol / Thy praises, with th' innumerable sound / Of Hymns and sacred Songs" (3.146–148). Pure hymns, then, are an echo of God's divine actions, in this instance given divine sanction by the Son. Milton then clearly points to the function of the pure hymn: an image, not of longing like the hymns of other epics, but an image of real perfection within a poem where perfection is conceivable. The first actual hymn we hear is the Father's response to the Son's offer to die for man. Beginning with "O thou in Heav'n and Earth the only peace," it forms one of the most elaborate hymns in the poem (3.274–343), which, because of its proleptic meaning, is part prophecy. The Father concludes this euktic hymn on the Son's sacrifice by starting the heavenly chorus:

> But all ye Gods,
> Adore him, who to compass all this dies,
> Adore the Son, and honor him as mee.
> (3.341–343)

The narrator blends with the chorus as Virgil's voice did in the hymn to Hercules. Indeed, we may compare the use of the hymn to Virgil's, which it approaches in purpose and style. There may be direct influence here, since Virgil's authority counted heavily with Milton for epic precedent, and that is Virgil's only hymn. Both hymns are praises establishing the rights of a son to participate in a father's divinity (Menander's genealogic hymn):

> Thee next they sang of all Creation first,
> Begotten Son, Divine Similitude,
> In whose conspicuous count'nance, without cloud
> Made visible, th' Almighty Father shines,
> Whom else no Creature can behold; on thee
> Impresst th' effulgence of his Glory abides,
> Transfus'd on thee his ample Spirit rests.
> Hee Heav'n of Heavens and all the Powers therein
> By thee created, and by thee threw down
> Th' aspiring Dominations: thou that day
> Thy Father's dreadful Thunder didst not spare,
> Nor stop thy flaming Chariot wheels, that shook
> Heav'ns everlasting Frame, while o're the necks
> Thou drov'st of warring Angels disarray'd.
> Back from pursuit thy Powers with loud acclaim
> Thee only extoll'd Son of thy Father's might,
> To execute fierce vengeance on his foes:
> Not so on Man; him through their malice fall'n,
> Father of Mercy and Grace, thou didst not doom
> So strictly, but much more to pity incline:
> No sooner did thy dear and only Son
> Perceive thee purpos'd not to doom frail Man
> So strictly, but much more to pity inclin'd,
> Hee to appease thy wrath and end the strife
> Of Mercy and Justice in thy face discern'd,
> Regardless of the Bliss wherein hee sat
> Second to thee, offer'd himself to die
> For man's offense. O unexampl'd love,
> Love nowhere to be found less than Divine!
> Hail Son of God, Saviour of Men, thy Name
> Shall be the copious matter of my Song
> Henceforth, and never shall my Harp thy praise
> Forget, nor from thy Father's praise disjoin.
>                                   (3.383–415)

As Earl Miner notes, narrative elements form part of this hymn,[28] but, I should like to add, do not rule. Since the hymn repeats what has just transpired in the dialogue of the Father and Son, even its narrative elements point as close as a hymn can to pure

---

28. Miner, "Reign of Narrative," p. 8.

celebration and elation. This hymn, like Virgil's, comes after the prophecies have been made and a happy future predicted or, in the *Aeneid,* an end to Trojan wandering, at least. In both poems the release of tension opens an epiphany of perfection, though Milton corrects Virgil by adding the triumph of mercy as well as the triumph of force.

But in their view of perfection the two poets are similar. Virgil ends his hymn with the words "Come to us and your rites," emphasizing the I-Thou relationship, as Milton does with:

> never shall my Harp thy praise
> Forget, nor from thy Father's praise disjoin.

Here the literary, liturgical, and psalmic hymns blend. Virgil's choir had two parts, but they blended as do both bards and audience. Both poets knew such ecstatic states are rare in epic, but Milton could see from Virgil that it was possible to incorporate them into epic poetry and that his use of the hymn would and could exceed Virgil's. Virgil's pessimism alone would have limited his use of the hymn as it did Lucretius', Lucan's, and Statius'. But Virgil and Milton stand almost alone as poets of the ideal, bards who could turn for a true lyric moment away from their audiences and speak with it and for it to God. It is especially Virgil's and Milton's embodiment of the hymn within the epic that gives the impetus for us to understand the hymn in its deepest and most significant sense. In it, epic struggles and epic glory are kept in perspective and imaginatively transcended into an active and unconstrained musical felicity.

Before Milton, the inclusion of the epic hymn did not change the maternal genre. The hymn as inset became a feature with Roman epic, available in the repertoire, seldom but carefully used as an image of perfection, a genre not a mode, that kept its independence. But Milton, thinking and revising more generically, challenged the epic form itself for priority as the greatest genre. Hymn is the musical goal of all creatures, the expression of social harmony and celestial peace. Only Milton inserted the pure hymn and subordinated the epic to it on the ideal level. The epic and epic struggles remain, but the goal of epic heroism is not heroic song but pure hymn. If man and angels had not sinned, the only song would be canticle. Milton then changed the history of epic hymnody. What was a rationalist invocation in Lucretius; an unrealizable ideal in Virgil; a cynical reflection of harmony in Lucan; an expression of fear in Statius; a prayer in Dante; a single, mixed hymn in Vida; a lament in Harington's Ariosto; political flattery in Ariosto and Spenser; and a metrical psalm in Cowley became for Milton, seizing upon the potential in the tradition, the true generic purpose of literature, the pure song in praise of God. The irony found in the classical epic hymn is given to the devil. And behind both narrative and lyric voice is the human singer. His voice sustains the tragic and epic parts of the poem, but the hymn in which he joins is a temporary answer to his prayer at the beginning of the poem that the heavenly Spirit sing his poem. In the foreground, the narrator sings man's first disobedience, but in the distance, the sacred muse sings the cantus firmus of the blissful seat regained. On the ideal level, *Paradise Lost* is the hymn-epic.

# Contributors

JAMES S. BAUMLIN
Texas Christian University

FRANCIS C. BLESSINGTON
Northeastern University

MORTON W. BLOOMFIELD
Harvard University

BARBARA J. BONO
State University of New York, Buffalo

MARY THOMAS CRANE
Harvard University

HEATHER DUBROW
Carleton College

ALASTAIR FOWLER
University of Edinburgh

MARJORIE GARBER
Harvard University

CLAUDIO GUILLÉN
Harvard University

ANN E. IMBRIE
Vassar College

JOHN N. KING
Bates College

JOHN KLAUSE
Harvard University

HARRY LEVIN
Harvard University

BARBARA K. LEWALSKI
Harvard University

EARL MINER
Princeton University

JANEL M. MUELLER
University of Chicago

**ANNABEL PATTERSON**
University of Maryland

**ROBERT N. WATSON**
Harvard University

**STEVEN N. ZWICKER**
Washington University